Lecture Notes of the Institute for Computer Sciences, Social Informatics and Telecommunications Engineering 399

Joaquin Garcia-Alfaro · Shujun Li ·
Radha Poovendran · Hervé Debar ·
Moti Yung (Eds.)

Security and Privacy in Communication Networks

17th EAI International Conference, SecureComm 2021
Virtual Event, September 6–9, 2021
Proceedings, Part II

Springer

Editors
Joaquin Garcia-Alfaro (iD)
Télécom SudParis,
Institut Polytechnique de Paris
Palaiseau, France

Radha Poovendran (iD)
University of Washington
Seattle, WA, USA

Moti Yung (iD)
Google Inc.
New York, NY, USA

Shujun Li (iD)
University of Kent Canterbury
Canterbury, Kent, UK

Hervé Debar (iD)
Télécom SudParis,
Institut Polytechnique de Paris
Palaiseau, France

ISSN 1867-8211 ISSN 1867-822X (electronic)
Lecture Notes of the Institute for Computer Sciences, Social Informatics
and Telecommunications Engineering
ISBN 978-3-030-90021-2 ISBN 978-3-030-90022-9 (eBook)
https://doi.org/10.1007/978-3-030-90022-9

This Springer imprint is published by the registered company Springer Nature Switzerland AG
The registered company address is: Gewerbestrasse 11, 6330 Cham, Switzerland

Preface

We are delighted to introduce the proceedings of the 17th EAI International Conference on Security and Privacy in Communication Networks (SecureComm 2021). This conference brought together cybersecurity scholars from all around the world, advancing the state of the art and knowledge of cybersecurity and privacy by proposing new methods and tools to address the major cybersecurity challenges faced by our digital systems.

These proceedings contain 43 papers from the main conference, which were selected out of 126 submissions (with an acceptance rate around 34%) from authors in universities, national laboratories, and the private sector from the Americas, Europe, Asia, Australasia, and Africa. All submissions went through an extensive review process undertaken by 82 internationally-recognized experts in cybersecurity. The accepted papers are authored by researchers from 16 countries, with the USA and China being the top two countries with the most papers (18 and 12, respectively).

These proceedings also contain the following papers from two co-located workshops and two other tracks of the conference: five papers accepted to the International Workshop on Post-quantum Cryptography for Secure Communications (PQC-SC), two papers accepted to the International Workshop on Cyber-Physical Systems Strategic and Technical Security (CPS-STS), and four papers to the PhD and Poster Tracks. Submissions to these workshops and tracks were organized by the separate (co-)chairs: Kalpana Singh, Elisa Lorenzo Garcia, Rajeev Anand Sahu, Gaurav Sharma, and T. Chithralekha who co-chaired PQC-SC, Ali Ismail Awad, Charalambos Konstantinou, and Mohammed M. Alani who co-chaired CPS-STS, and Roger A. Hallman who chaired the PhD and Poster Tracks. The accepted papers in these workshops and tracks are authored by researchers from seven different countries (USA, China, Brazil, Italy, South Korea, UAE, and UK).

Any successful conference relies on the contribution of multiple stakeholders, who have volunteered their time and energy in disseminating and publicizing the call for papers, submitting original research results, participating in the reviewing process, and in the end contributing altogether to a great program. First and foremost, we would like to offer our gratitude to the entire Organizing Committee for guiding the entire process of the conference, keeping everything organized and in check. We are also deeply grateful to all the Technical Program Committee (TPC) members for their time and effort in reading, commenting, debating, and finally selecting the papers. We also thank the (co-)chairs, TPC members, and external reviewers of the co-located workshops and the PhD/Poster Tracks for their contributions to the conference. Last but not least, we also thank all the authors who submitted papers to the conference and all participants who attended the conference to support the conference and make it a successful event. Support from the Steering Committee and EAI staff members was also crucial in ensuring the success of the conference. It was a great privilege to work with such a large group of dedicated and talented individuals.

We had hoped for a physical event, and it is unfortunate that we once more had to revert to an online one. We nevertheless hope that you found the discussions and interactions at SecureComm 2021 enjoyable and that the proceedings will simulate further research.

August 2021

Shujun Li
Radha Poovendran
Hervé Debar
Moti Yung

Conference Organization

Steering Committee

Imrich Chlamtac	University of Trento, Italy
Guofei Gu	Texas A&M University, USA
Peng Liu	Pennsylvania State University, USA
Sencun Zhu	Pennsylvania State University, USA

Organizing Committee

General Chair

Shujun Li — University of Kent, UK

General Co-chair

Radha Poovendran — University of Washington, USA

Technical Program Committee Chair and Co-chair

| Hervé Debar | Télécom SudParis/Institut Polytechnique de Paris, France |
| Moti Yung | Google Inc./Columbia University, USA |

Sponsorship and Exhibit Chair

Theodosios Dimitrakos — Munich Research Centre, Huawei Technologies Ltd, Germany

Local Chairs

| Budi Arief | University of Kent, UK |
| Gareth Howells | University of Kent, UK |

Workshops Chair

David Arroyo Guardeño — CSIC, Spain

Publicity and Social Media Chairs

| Jason Nurse | University of Kent, UK |
| Kaitai Liang | TU Delft, The Netherlands |

Publications Chair

Joaquin Garcia-Alfaro   Télécom SudParis/Institut Polytechnique de Paris,
                                   France

Web Chair

Christophe Kiennert   Télécom SudParis/Institut Polytechnique de Paris,
                                   France

Posters and PhD Track Chair

Roger A. Hallman   Naval Information Warfare Center
                                   Pacific/Dartmouth College, USA

Panels Chairs

Julio Hernandez-Castro   University of Kent, UK
Sanjay Bhattacherjee   University of Kent, UK

Tutorials Chair

Anyi Liu   Oakland University, USA

Technical Program Committee

Magnus Almgren   Chalmers University of Technology, Sweden
Elias Athanasopoulos   University of Cyprus, Cyprus
Gregory Blanc   Télécom SudParis/Institut Polytechnique de Paris,
                                   France
Sébastien Bardin   CEA LIST, France
Lorenzo Cavallaro   Kings College London, UK
Lucas Davi   University of Duisburg-Essen, Germany
Gabi Dreo   Bundeswehr University Munich, Germany
Sven Dietrich   City University of New York, USA
Daniel Gruss   Graz University of Technology, Austria
Christophe Hauser   University of Southern California, USA
Vasileios Kemerlis   Brown University, USA
Andrea Lanzi   University of Milan, Italy
Fabio Martinelli   CNR, Italy
Michael Meier   University of Bonn/Fraunhofer FKIE, Germany
Marius Muench   Vrije Universiteit Amsterdam, The Netherlands
William Robertson   Northeastern University, USA
Thomas Schreck   Munich University of Applied Sciences, Germany
Seungwon Shin   KAIST, South Korea
Angelos Stavrou   George Mason University, USA

Gianluca Stringhini	Boston University, USA
Giovanni Apruzzese	University of Liechtenstein, Liechtenstein
Urko Zurutuza	Mondragon University, Spain
Fabio Di Franco	ENISA, Greece
Platon Kotzias	NortonLifeLock Research Group, Greece
Sokratis Katsikas	NTNU, Norway
Razvan Beuran	JAIST, Japan
Youki Kadobayashi	NAIST, Japan
Franco Chiaraluce	UNIVPM, Italy
Igor Kotenko	St. Petersburg Federal Research Center of the Russian Academy of Sciences, Russia
Evangelos Markatos	FORTH, Greece
Silvia Bonomi	Sapienza University of Rome, Italy
Apostolis Zarras	TU Delft, The Netherlands
Jan Hajný	Brno University of Technology, Czech Republic
Gabriele Restuccia	CNIT, Italy
Jacques Traore	Orange, France
Jouni Viinikka	6Cure, France
Pavel Laskov	University of Lichtenstein, Lichtenstein
Michal Choras	ITTI, Poland
Olivier Thonnard	Amadeus, France
Roland Rieke	Fraunhofer SIT, Germany
Ali Abbasi	Ruhr University Bochum, Germany
Claudio Canella	TU Graz, Austria
Jun Xu	Stevens Institute of Technology, USA
Cristian-Alexander Staicu	CISPA, Germany
Guillaume Hiet	CentraleSupelec, France
Sharif Abuadbba	Data61, CSIRO, Australia
Mohiuddin Ahmed	Edith Cowan University, Australia
Nadeem Ahmed	Cyber Security Cooperative Research Centre, Australia
Ehab Al-Shaer	Carnegie Mellon University, USA
Budi Arief	University of Kent, UK
Anirban Basu	Hitachi, Ltd, Japan/University of Sussex, UK
Sanjay Bhattacherjee	University of Kent, UK
Liquan Chen	Southeastern University, China
Jinguang Han	Nanjing University of Finance and Economics, China
Debiao He	Wuhan University, China
Julio Hernandez-Castro	University of Kent, UK
Darren Hurley-Smith	Royal Holloway University of London, UK
Zahid Islam	Charles Sturt University, Australia

Helge Janicke	Cyber Security Cooperative Research Centre, Australia
Shancang Li	University of the West of England, UK
Yingjiu Li	University of Oregon, USA
Kaitai Liang	TU Delft, The Netherlands
Anyi Liu	Oakland University, USA
Zhe Liu	Nanjing University of Aeronautics and Astronautics, China
George Loukas	University of Greenwich, UK
Xiapu Luo	Hong Kong Polytechnic University, Hong Kong
Leandros Maglaras	De Montfort University, UK
Kalikinkar Mandal	University of New Brunswick, Canada
Mark Manulis	University of Surrey, UK
Carsten Maple	University of Warwick, UK
Wojciech Mazurczyk	Warsaw University of Technology, Poland
Weizhi Meng	Technical University of Denmark, Denmark
Nour Moustafa	UNSW Canberra, Australia
Toni Perković	University of Split, Croatia
Siraj Ahmed Shaikh	University of Coventry, UK
Chunhua Su	University of Aizu, Japan
Zhiyuan Tan	Edinburgh Napier University, UK
Ding Wang	Nankai University, China
Wei Wang	Beijing Jiaotong University, China
Yongdong Wu	Jinan University, China
Xiaosong Zhang	University of Electronic Science and Technology of China, China
Deqing Zou	Huazhong University of Science and Technology, China
Sushmita Ruj	Data61, CSIRO, Australia/ISI, Kolkata, India
Guomin Yang	University of Wollongong, Australia
Louis Rilling	Inria Rennes - Bretagne Atlantique, France

Contents – Part II

PQC-SC Workshop

CPS-STS Workshop

Contents – Part I

AI and Security/Privacy

Applied Cryptography

Network Security

Digital Forensics

Web/OSN Security and Privacy

Analyzing Security Risks of Ad-Based URL Shortening Services Caused by Users' Behaviors

Naoki Fukushi[✉], Takashi Koide, Daiki Chiba, Hiroki Nakano, and Mitsuaki Akiyama

NTT, Tokyo, Japan
{naoki.fukushi.kz,takashi.koide.fk,hiroki.nakano.ma}@hco.ntt.co.jp,
{daiki.chiba,akiyama}@ieee.org

Abstract. URL shortening services make URLs shorter and simpler. Ad-based URL shortening services display advertisements to users who access short URLs and reward short URL creators. However, ad-based URL shortening services have specific security risks that URL shortening services without ads do not, such as displaying malicious advertisements to users. In this study, we reveal previously unknown security risks of these services caused by users' behaviors. We conducted a comprehensive measurement of ad-based URL shortening services. First, we accessed short URLs of these services, clicked buttons on the web pages, and reached the final destinations of the short URLs. Then, we reveal the security risks posed to users by monitoring and analyzing traffic logs when such short URLs are accessed. We found that all services generated an average of 86.5 web requests to malicious domain names per short URL. We then showed the security risk of unintentionally communicating malicious domain names even when users click only on buttons that correctly move users to their desired destinations. Finally, we discuss countermeasures to mitigate these risks from the perspective of each stakeholder in ad-based URL shortening services.

Keywords: Url shortening service · Online advertising

1 Introduction

URL shortening services are widely used on the Internet to make URLs shorter and simpler, which enables users to bypass character limits when posting to social media or improve the appearance of URLs themselves. URL shortening services that generate income by displaying advertisements to users who access short URLs are called ad-based URL shortening services. When accessing short URLs, users reach web pages where advertisements are displayed, and by clicking on buttons on the web pages, the users can reach their desired destinations. To

J. Garcia-Alfaro et al. (Eds.): SecureComm 2021, LNICST 399, pp. 3–22, 2021.
https://doi.org/10.1007/978-3-030-90022-9_1

draw users' attention to the advertisements, these buttons may become clickable after a few seconds. Ad-based URL shortening services can receive advertising revenue from advertising providers, and short URL creators can be rewarded in accordance with the number of users' accesses to their short URLs. In this way, ad-based URL shortening services can financially benefit services and short URL creators. A previous study reported security and privacy risks of users of ad-based URL shortening services [20]. That revealed that ad-based URL shortening services display malicious advertisements that automatically forward users to phishing sites or perform drive-by downloads attacks on users. In addition, we found these services have a new strategy for receiving more advertising revenue which is not mentioned in the previous study. For example, these services display many buttons that confuse users as to which to click or require users to go through multiple web pages. Most of these buttons are ad banners. These complex structures unnecessarily increase the number of users' clicks to reach the destinations of the short URLs. To the best of our knowledge, no study has revealed the security risks of ad-based URL shortening services caused by users' browsing behaviors.

In this study, we thus conduct a measurement of these latest ad-based URL shortening services. We consider two types of users' behaviors to reveal the security risks comprehensively: one is when users click on only buttons that correctly move them to the destinations, and the other is when users mistakenly click on ad banners that look like these buttons. It is difficult for users and security analysts to distinguish these ad banners and buttons on the basis of visual information since these ad banners often change their appearance each time they access short URLs. Therefore, we propose a method that automatically detects buttons on the web pages and supports security analysts when accessing short URLs and implemented it as a Chrome extension. Moreover, to analyze malicious web requests, we add a function to the above extension to monitor traffic logs when accessing short URLs. We first comprehensively select ad-based URL shortening services that are heavily accessed by users. Next, we generate short URLs using a benign URL for each selected ad-based URL shortening service. Then, we conduct experiments to access the short URLs and reach their final destinations using the extension described above. The results of our experiment showed that all services generated web requests to malicious domain names even though the final destination of the short URLs was benign. The average number of web requests to malicious domain names generated from each service was 86.5. These malicious domain names mainly included registration pages for scam services and web pages that ask users to allow malicious web push notifications. We also found that there is a risk of communicating malicious domain names even if users click on only buttons on the web pages. Furthermore, we revealed that users' risks of communicating malicious domain names increase when they mistakenly click on ad banners that look like buttons on the web pages. Finally, we discuss countermeasures to mitigate these risks from the perspective of each stakeholder in ad-based URL shortening services.

Our main contributions are as follows.

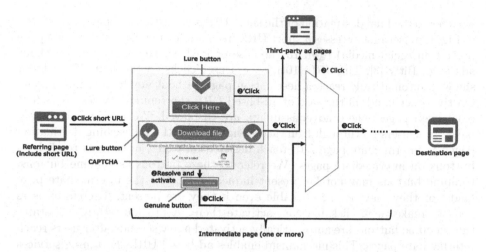

Fig. 1. Overview of structure of ad-based URL shortening services. This figure shows a screenshot of an intermediate page of an ad-based URL shortening service. A user clicks on a short URL included in a referring page and reaches the intermediate page (❶). For this service, the user needs to resolve CAPTCHA to activate the genuine button (❷). If the user mistakenly clicks on the lure buttons, third-party ad pages will be opened (❷'). The number of intermediate pages is one or more and varies with each service. The user clicks on the genuine button and reaches the next intermediate page or destination page (❸).

- We comprehensively investigated the latest ad-based URL shortening services. We are the first to reveal the security risks caused by users' behaviors to reach the final destination of the short URLs.
- We proposed a method that uses a common feature among ad-based URL shortening services to automatically detect buttons that correctly move users to destinations and support security analysts.
- We make recommendations to each stakeholder of ad-based URL shortening services on how users use these services, what kind of advertisements should not be displayed, and how these services should be designed.

2   Background

Ad-based URL shortening services have two characteristics: 1) They require users to go through one or more web pages where advertisements are displayed before reaching the final destinations, and 2) they reward short URL creators in accordance with the number of users' accesses to their short URLs. In the following sections, we describe each characteristic in detail.

2.1   Structure

First, we describe the structure of ad-based URL shortening services. Figure 1 is an overview of the structure of ad-based URL shortening services. In this paper, we refer to the final destination of the short URLs as destination pages. As shown in Fig. 1, a user first accesses a short URL from a referring page (e.g., a web page posted on social media) (❶). In the case of URL shortening services without ads (e.g., Bitly [3], TinyURL [10]), once a user clicks on the short URL, he or she will automatically reach a destination page without any further interaction. On the other hand, in the case of ad-based URL shortening services, users first reach web pages where advertisements are displayed. We refer to these web pages that users go through from accessing short URLs to reaching destination pages as intermediate pages. To reach destination pages, users need to click on buttons on intermediate pages. We refer to these buttons as genuine buttons. Genuine buttons may not be present immediately after the intermediate page loads, or they may not be clickable even if they are present. Therefore, users need to make them clickable, i.e., activate them. A previous study [20] states that genuine buttons are automatically activated a few seconds after users reach intermediate pages. This mechanism enables ad-based URL shortening services to show advertisements for at least a few seconds to users.

Ad-based URL shortening services with new strategies to increase advertising revenue have appeared and are being heavily accessed by users. These services have complex page structures in addition to the above mechanism and have not been reported in previous studies. For example, there are ad-based URL shortening services that require CAPTCHA to be resolved to activate genuine buttons. A CAPTCHA is a type of challenge-response test that is widely used on the web to verify whether a responder is a real human. In the case of the ad-based URL shortening service shown in Fig. 1, the user can activate the genuine button by resolving the CAPTCHA (❷). They are both bordered in red. Also, several ad-based URL shortening services display ad banners that look like genuine buttons on intermediate pages. In this paper, we refer to these buttons as lure buttons. In the case of the ad-based URL shortening service shown in Fig. 1, the lure buttons are bordered in blue. These lure buttons are ad banners that are displayed by advertising providers in the <iframe> or generated as images on intermediate pages. Users cannot reach destination pages by clicking on these buttons, but third-party ad pages will be opened (❷'). Note that these ad banners are not unique to ad-based URL shortening services. A previous study [14] reported that popular file-sharing sites display such ad banners as well. Moreover, users may need to go through multiple intermediate pages before reaching destination pages. Therefore, when the user clicks on the genuine button that has been activated, he or she will reach the next intermediate page or destination page (❸). Moreover, users may have to click on the same genuine button several times to reach the next web pages. The actual security risks caused by users' behaviors in such a complex page structure of ad-based URL shortening services have not been revealed so far.

2.2   Reward

Ad-based URL shortening services reward short URL creators in accordance with the number of accesses to their short URLs. To describe this mechanism,

Fig. 2. Stakeholders of ad-based URL shortening services.

we show the stakeholders of ad-based URL shortening services in Fig. 2. There are five types of stakeholders: ad-based URL shortening services, short URL creators, users (who access short URLs), advertising providers, and advertisers. Advertising providers display advertisements created by advertisers on intermediate pages, and users go through these web pages before reaching destination pages. When users click on these advertisements on the intermediate pages, ad-based URL shortening services can receive advertisement revenue. Short URL creators can be rewarded with a portion of this advertising revenue.

3 Method

3.1 Design and Technical Points of Proposed Method

Our goal is to understand the security risks caused by users' behaviors when they reach the destination pages from ad-based URL shortening services. We consider two types of users' behaviors. One is when users click on only genuine buttons on the intermediate pages. The other is when users mistakenly recognize and click on lure buttons that resemble genuine buttons. By considering two types of users' behaviors, we can comprehensively reveal the security risks caused by user's behaviors. To shed light on such risks, we analyze web requests that occur on the intermediate pages when we access the short URLs. In this experiment, we need to distinguish between the genuine button and misleading lure buttons on the intermediate page. However, the lure buttons are not visually identifiable because they change their appearance every time we visit the intermediate page.

In this paper, we propose a method to support the analysis of ad-based URL shortening services by detecting genuine buttons without visual information. We implemented this method as a Chrome extension to detect a genuine button when we visit the intermediate page of an ad-based short URL. The key point of this method is to take advantage of the common feature among ad-based URL shortening services that the HTML source code changes when the genuine button is activated. Our method is very different from the method proposed in the previous study [14], which uses visual information to identify trick banners that mislead users. To clarify the security risks in detail, we need to monitor

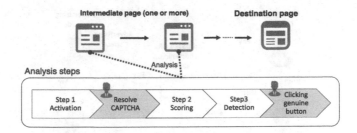

Fig. 3. Overview of steps of detecting genuine buttons and manual operations.

and analyze the traffic logs, such as URL redirections and URLs loaded in the <iframe>. We also added a function to the extension to automatically monitor and save web requests. In the following sections, we explain two functions: detecting genuine buttons and monitoring web requests.

3.2 Detecting Genuine Buttons and Manual Operations

In this section, we describe the function of detecting genuine buttons. This function detects genuine bebuttons on intermediate pages and shows us their locations. This eliminates the need for security analysts to select the next element to click. Figure 3 shows the three steps of this function: activating a genuine button, scoring web elements, and detecting a genuine button. Figure 3 also shows the manual operations required to proceed with the steps in gray with a human icon. We perform two types of manual operation, resolving a CAPTCHA and clicking on a genuine button. We repeat each step and manual operation until we reach a destination page.

Step 1: Activating Genuine Buttons. In step 1, this function activates a genuine button, which is not clickable or visible after an intermediate page is loaded. There are two conditions for activating genuine buttons: users wait for a few seconds and resolve CAPTCHA. In the former condition, ad-based URL shortening services aim to make users pay attention to online advertisements for a certain period of time [20]. The purposes of the latter are to avoid crawling by bots or bypassing the services by adblockers. First, this function checks the current HTML source code for the presence of a CAPTCHA. For example, Google reCAPTCHA is determined if there is an element whose HTML tag is `iframe` and its `src` attribute starts with https://www.google.com/recaptcha/api2. Second, if CAPTCHA is present, our extension changes its Cascading Style Sheet (CSS) style to highlight it and we manually resolve it. If it is not present, our extension waits for up to 30 s before proceeding to step 2, because the genuine button is activated a few seconds after the intermediate page is loaded. Our extension saves HTML source codes after loading intermediate pages, as they are used in step 3 to detect genuine buttons.

Step 2: Scoring Web Elements. In step 2, this function selects candidates of genuine buttons from HTML source codes. To do this, we designed a scoring

Table 1. List of terms for scoring.

Category	Terms
button	"button", "btn"
click	"click", "continue", "get", "go", "here", "next", "skip", "start", "submit"

algorithm to evaluate web elements by focusing on two features of genuine buttons. The first feature is that genuine buttons often contain "btn" or "button" in the `class` and `id` attributes. The second feature is that many genuine buttons contain the terms such as "click" and "continue" in the `value` attribute and their text content to encourage users to click. Thus, we calculated the score as the number of terms shown in Table 1 included in each of the above attributes. The elements to be scored are those with the `a`, `button`, `img`, and `input` tags. We explain the selection criteria for terms shown in Table 1. We pre-analyzed the HTML source code of ad-based URL shortening services and collected samples of genuine buttons. Then, using the previous study [16] as a reference, we collected terms that indicate buttons and that encourage users to click. Only elements with scores greater than 2 will be further analyzed in the next step. The reason the score threshold was set to 2 is that an element with a score of 2 or higher may possess both the aforementioned features. Since this scoring is only used to select candidates for genuine buttons, it is sufficient to use a simple process that focuses on not missing the candidates rather than on accuracy.

Step 3: Detecting Genuine Buttons. In step 3, this function detects genuine buttons from candidates selected in step 2 by using differences in HTML source codes. When a non-existent or non-clickable genuine button becomes active, there should be a difference in the source code of the intermediate page. For example, a genuine button that is not clickable due to the presence of the `disable` attribute becomes active when this attribute is removed. First, this function compares two source codes (one after loading the intermediate page and the other after activating genuine buttons) and extracts the changed or newly created elements. Next, this function finds the union of these elements and the candidate elements selected in step 2. The element with the highest score, i.e., the genuine button, is highlighted by changing its CSS style. Finally, we click on the genuine button. These steps can be repeated until the browser reaches the destination page.

3.3   Monitoring Web Requests

The second function automatically records web requests from a web browser for the time between accessing short URLs and reaching the destination pages. Specifically, we used the chrome.webRequest API [4] to monitor every web request, e.g., a web page is newly loaded in a browser tab, an `iframe` is generated on the web page, a JavaScript file is loaded, and a URL redirection occurs. The types of web requests can be identified from the `ResourceType`. For example, if the `ResourceType` is `main_frame`, the web request is used to load the main content of a web page, and its URL is displayed in the browser's URL bar. If the ResourceType is sub_frame, the traffic is requested from an iframe element. Also, this function obtains a screenshot of the web page after all resources on the web page are loaded.

3.4 Operations We Perform Manually

We use Google Chrome with the extension that implements the proposed method to analyze ad-based URL shortening services. We organize the operations we perform manually to reach the destination pages of short URLs. What we need to do is to resolve CAPTCHA and click on a genuine button that our extension detected on the intermediate page. At that time, we must repeatedly click the detected genuine button until the transition of web pages or content rewrite occurs. This is because, as explained in Sect. 2, many ad-based URL shortening services require multiple clicks on the same genuine button to go to the next web page. Exceptionally, if an advertisement covers the entire intermediate page and the genuine button is not clickable, we click a close button of the advertisement to dismiss it, because such an advertisement is obviously an obstacle to reaching the destination page.

4   Experimental Setup

We conduct a measurement study of ad-based URL shortening services. The purpose of our measurement is to reveal the security risks caused by users' behaviors. In this section, we describe the experimental setup of our measurement. We first explain the selection criteria for the ad-based URL shortening services to investigate. Next, we conduct a preliminary experiment to evaluate our proposed method described in Sect. 3.2. Finally, we explain the environment and procedure of our measurement.

4.1   Selecting Ad-Based URL Shortening Services to Investigate

In this section, we describe the criteria for selecting the ad-based URL shortening services to investigate. We decided to select ad-based URL shortening services that are online as of January 2021 and accessed by a large number of users. We first used a search engine to search for terms related to ad-based URL shortening services, such as "high paying URL shortener" and "best URL shortening service." We then selected a total of 35 online ad-based shortening URL services from the web pages indexed as search results. To select services accessed by many users, we used the Tranco List [22] obtained in January 2021, which is a list of one million domain names ranked by popularity. Finally, we selected a total of 30 services that use domain names listed in the Tranco List for our measurement, out of 35 ad-based URL shortening services. In the *Tranco rank* column of Table 2, we show the Tranco List ranks for the domain names used by each selected ad-based URL shortening service. We then generated one short

Table 2. Summary of measurement results of ad-based URL shortening services. We abbreviate CAPTCHA as C and Adblock Plus as ABP in the column names.

Service	Sect. 4.1		Intermediate pages		Sect. 5.1 Malicious domain names					Sect. 5.2		Sect. 5.3	
	Tranco rank	Novel		C	main_frame	sub_frame	script	Others	Total (unique)	Lure buttons	Malicious domains	Ad-block	
#1	< 2k	✓	1		0	4	17	20	31	0	0		
#2	< 3k	[20]	1		1	8	18	20	32	0	0		
#3	< 6k	✓	3	✓	18	5	56	74	116	0	0	✓	✓
#4	< 9k	✓	3	✓	16	19	60	109	152	0	0	✓	✓
#5	< 13k	[20]	1		0	0	5	2	6	0	0		
#6	< 27k	✓	1	✓	6	7	27	32	53	0	0		
#7	< 33k	✓	3	✓	0	7	33	59	78	0	0	✓	✓
#8	< 38k	✓	2	✓	7	67	75	104	190	0	0	✓	✓
#9	< 39k	✓	2	✓	7	62	70	126	200	0	0	✓	✓
#10	< 43k	✓	2	✓	11	10	50	92	131	2	5		✓
#11	< 46k	[20]	2		6	2	26	39	58	1	6		
#12	< 48k	✓	2	✓	6	19	37	66	106	2	7	✓	✓
#13	< 73k	✓	4	✓	9	7	55	76	112	2	4	✓	✓
#14	< 80k	✓	2	✓	7	11	52	72	113	2	5	✓	✓
#15	< 89k	✓	2	✓	7	10	53	75	112	2	4	✓	✓
#16	< 100k	✓	2	✓	13	14	45	63	104	2	2	✓	✓
#17	< 113k	✓	2	✓	0	1	7	8	12	0	0		
#18	< 133k	✓	2	✓	9	11	35	52	84	0	0	✓	✓
#19	< 182k	✓	2	✓	0	4	12	20	26	8	4		
#20	< 189k	✓	2	✓	6	4	25	28	46	2	2	✓	✓
#21	< 217k	✓	2	✓	5	19	56	81	125	1	7	✓	✓
#22	< 224k	✓	2	✓	6	16	65	111	149	0	0	✓	✓
#23	< 257k	✓	2	✓	0	1	9	12	18	2	1	✓	✓
#24	< 292k	✓	2		7	7	32	34	62	0	0		
#25	< 326k	✓	2	✓	24	10	56	69	109	5	2	✓	✓
#26	< 368k	✓	2	✓	5	1	25	20	37	4	4		
#27	< 426k	✓	3	✓	14	11	49	74	117	6	6	✓	
#28	< 430k	✓	1	✓	5	6	30	32	56	0	0	✓	
#29	< 527k	✓	2		6	5	31	34	61	0	0		
#30	< 865k	✓	3	✓	13	13	47	63	98	3	4	✓	✓

URL for each of these 30 ad-based URL shortening services using a URL of a certain benign web page and investigated them in the following experiments. This means that the destination page is always a single URL that we prepared. In the *Novel* column of Table 2, we put "✓" for the services that we investigated for the first time and "[20]" for the services that were investigated in the previous study [20]. Of the 30 ad-based URL shortening services we selected for this study, only 3 were investigated in the previous study [20]. Moreover, of the 10 services investigated in the previous study, the remaining 7 were offline as of January 2021.

4.2 Evaluating Our Proposed Method

In this section, we describe the preliminary experiment we conducted to evaluate our proposed method of detecting the genuine button described in Sect. 3.2 and its result. We evaluate whether the button detected by the proposed method is the correct genuine button or not. In ad-based URL shortening services, when we click on lure buttons other than the genuine button, we cannot reach the destination page. If we can reach the destination page by clicking on only the button detected by the proposed method, it means that all the detected buttons are the correct genuine buttons. We accessed a total of 30 short URLs of the ad-based URL shortening services we selected in Sect. 4.1. We then investigated whether we could reach the destination page by clicking on only the buttons detected by the proposed method. Here, these short URLs are created by us, so we can find out for ourselves whether we have reached the destination page or not. In the experiment, we reached the destination page from all short URLs, which means that our method correctly detected all genuine buttons. Our proposed method takes advantage of a common feature among ad-based URL shortening services: the source code change when the genuine button is activated. Therefore, our proposed method will work with versatility even when new ad-based URL shortening services are created in the future.

4.3   Environment and Procedure of Our Measurement

We consider two types of users' behaviors to reveal the security risks comprehensively: one is when users click on only genuine buttons, and the other is when users mistakenly recognize and click on lure buttons that look like genuine buttons. First, we investigate the security risks when users click on only genuine buttons. We prepare Google Chrome with our original Chrome extension enabled, which detects genuine buttons and monitors traffic, as described in Sect. 3. We access a total of 30 short URLs with this Google Chrome. Then, we reach the destination page by clicking on only the genuine buttons detected by the proposed method. Also, we analyzed the differences in displayed advertisements caused by users' regional information. We changed our source IP addresses using a virtual private network (VPN) service. We chose six regions that can be selected by the VPN service: United States (US), Brazil (BR), Japan (JP), Germany (GE), Hong Kong (HK), and United Kingdom (UK). We selected these regions as geographically distant regions with a large number of Internet users. For our selection above, we used Statista's survey [6] of the number of Internet users by region in 2020.

Next, we investigate the security risks when users click on lure buttons. We manually distinguished such lure buttons from ad banners displayed on the intermediate pages. Lure buttons contain terms that encourages users to click, such as "DOWNLOAD" or "CLICK HERE." These buttons also contain video play buttons or downward arrows that remind users to download. We conduct an experiment to click on all the lure buttons on the intermediate page and then click on the genuine button to reach the destination page. We experimented with one short URL for each service using multiple environments, instead of experimenting with multiple URLs using the same environment. This is because the previous study [20] has shown that the advertisements displayed on the intermediate pages depend on the environment and behavioral history of users who accessed short URLs, not the destination pages. We also found that the structures from the intermediate page to the destination page of each ad-based URL shortening service such as the number of intermediate pages were always the same regardless of the destination pages.

5 Measurement Results

In this section, we describe the results of our measurement of the ad-based URL shortening services. In Sect. 5.1, we first describe the results of our experiment to reach the destination pages by clicking on only the genuine buttons. In Sect. 5.2, we next describe the results of our experiment to reach the destination pages when we clicked on the lure buttons in addition to the genuine buttons. In Sect. 5.3, we finally describe the results of our experiment to access the short URLs with Adblocker enabled.

5.1 Clicking on Only Genuine Buttons

In this section, we describe the results of our experiment to access the short URLs and reach the destination pages by clicking on only genuine buttons. We conducted our experiment a total of 180 times (the number of combinations of 30 ad-based URL shortening services and 6 source IP addresses varying regional information by using the VPN service described in Sect. 4.3). We fixed our browser language settings to en-US and conduct each experiment at the same time in January, 2021. With this experiment, we reveal the structures to the destination pages of the ad-based URL shortening services, the security risks caused by users' clicks on the genuine buttons, and its regional characteristics.

Structure of Services. In this section, we reveal the latest structures to the destination pages of the ad-based URL shortening services. We investigate these structures in terms of the number of intermediate pages users need to go through before reaching the destination pages. We examined this number for each ad-based URL shortening service. We show the results in the *Intermediate pages* column of Table 2. As shown in Table 2, our measurement of 30 ad-based URL shortening services showed that 5 services had 1 intermediate page, 19 services had 2 intermediate pages, 5 services had 3 intermediate pages, and 1 service had 4 intermediate pages. The number of intermediate pages is equal to the number of genuine buttons we clicked. Therefore, this result indicates that users need to select and click on the genuine buttons at least twice in more than 80% of the ad-based URL shortening services we investigated. This is a mechanism to increase the time spent on intermediate pages of users and increase their advertisements click rate. Such a structure of ad-based URL shortening services requiring users to go through multiple intermediate pages have not been mentioned in previous studies.

Moreover, of the 62 genuine buttons (the total value of the *Intermediate pages* column) we clicked in the 30 ad-based URL shortening services, only 7 were active immediately after the intermediate pages loaded, and the remaining 55 required users to wait for some time or resolve CAPTCHA to activate. For each ad-based URL shortening service, we indicate "✓" in the C column of Table 2 when CAPTCHA resolution was required to activate the genuine button. The number of ad-based URL shortening services that required CAPTCHA resolution was 24 out of 30, and the number of CAPTCHA resolutions required to reach the destination pages was 1 for all of these services. Also, ad-based URL shortening services investigated in the previous study [20], indicated by "[20]" in the *Novel* column of Table 2, did not require CAPTCHA resolution to activate the genuine buttons. These results indicate that the structure to the destination pages of the latest ad-based URL shortening services has changed compared with those investigated in previous studies.

Security Risks Posed to Users. In this section, we reveal the security risks when users click on only genuine buttons. We extracted a total of 2,003 unique domain names from the web requests monitored during our experiments. The above 2,003 domain names exclude the domain names of both the short URLs and the destination page. To determine if these domain names were malicious, we used VirusTotal [11]. By scanning domain names with VirusTotal, we can retrieve URLs containing domain names identified as malicious in the past, along with the number of vendors that identified the URLs as malicious. We decided to consider domain names with at least one URL that have been identified as malicious by at least one vendor in the past to be malicious domain names. Using VirusTotal API to scan 2,003 domain names, we found a total of 688 malicious domain names. As explained in Sect. 3.3, web requests can be classified by the `ResourceType`, such as `main_frame` (loaded in the main content), `sub_frame` (loaded in <iframe>), and `script` (loaded in <script>). Table 2 shows the number of malicious domain names communicated by each ad-based URL shortening service, categorized by the `ResourceType`. The *Total (unique)* column shows the number of unique malicious domain names including all `ResourceType`. The sum of each `ResourceType` column does not match the value in the *Total (unique)* column because some malicious domain names use multiple request types. We found that all services generated an average of 86.5 ($\approx 2594 \div 30$) web requests to malicious domain names. Table 2 shows that 24 ad-based URL shortening services had malicious domain names loaded in the `main_frame`, i.e., included in the main content displayed in the browser tab. The average number of those domain names was 8.9 for these 24 ad-based URL shortening services, and the maximum number was 24 for Service #25.

Here, we divide the malicious domain names loaded in the `main_frame` into two types. One was loaded during URL redirection, and the other was loaded after the redirection. We checked the screenshots of web pages that contain the latter domain names identified as malicious by VirusTotal, i.e., finally reached malicious web pages. As described in Sect. 3.3, these screenshots were taken after all web requests were completed. The total number of unique malicious domain names of the finally reached web pages was 48. The web pages containing these malicious domain names included registration pages for scam services that attempted to steal personal and credit card information by tricking users into creating accounts and adult advertising pages. These web pages also included web pages asking users for permission for web push notifications, which was shown to deliver many malicious advertisements via web push notifications in

Table 3. Number of malicious domain names detected in each region.

Region	# of malicious domain names
BR	442
HK	419
US	415
GE	407
UK	402
JP	378

Table 4. Number of regions in which each malicious domain name was detected.

# of regions	# of malicious domain names
1 region	225
2 regions	74
3 regions	50
4 regions	32
5 regions	30
6 regions	277
Total	688

Table 5. Breakdown of malicious domain names detected in one region and results of analysis using SimilarWeb's data.

Region	(1) # of malicious domain names	(2) # of included in top 5 regions	(3) # of missing data	Percentage $(2) \div \{(1) - (3)\}$
BR	81	30	4	39%
US	38	29	4	85%
UK	33	18	1	56%
HK	31	3	6	12%
GE	30	13	7	57%
JP	12	2	1	18%
Total	225	95	23	47%

the previous study [23]. We investigated why these malicious web pages were loaded as main contents loaded in the browser tab. We found that transparent advertisements covered genuine buttons and CAPTCHA and that the `onclick` attributes of the genuine buttons were set to `window.open`, which is used to display third-party ad pages. In other words, even if users click on genuine buttons or resolve CAPTCHA, which are the minimum required operations to reach the destination page, the users will reach malicious web pages. Users will be then at risk of having their personal information stolen by registering scam services or receiving malicious web push notifications. When users are directed to multiple intermediate pages, the number of their clicks on the genuine buttons increases. Consequently, the risk of reaching malicious web pages also increase.

Region Characteristics. We conducted our experiments from IP addresses in six regions by using a VPN service. By doing this, we could consider that displayed advertisements vary by regions of users accessing short URLs. In this section, we conduct a region-by-region analysis of the 688 unique malicious domain names found in the section above. Table 3 shows the number of unique malicious domain names detected in a total of 30 ad-based URL shortening services per region. We found that an average of 410.5 malicious domain names were detected per region. The highest number was 442 in Brazil, and the lowest was 378 in Japan. For a total of 688 of these unique malicious domain names, we investigated the number of regions in which each domain name was detected. Table 4 shows the results of this investigation. The largest number of regions in which each domain name was detected was 6 and the second largest was 1, accounting for about 73% ($\approx (277 + 225) \div 688$) of the total. This result shows that there are malicious domain names that are specific to users' regions and independent of users' regions. We focused on the 225 malicious domain names that were detected in 1 region. Table 5 shows the number of malicious domain names detected in each region only. The regions with the highest and lowest numbers of malicious domain names detected only in those regions were Brazil, with 81, and Japan, with 12. Also, we investigated the region-by-region access status of these malicious domain names. We used SimilarWeb [9], which passively observes traffic of hundreds of millions of global devices and covers over 220 regions. We extracted the top 5 regions sending web requests to the 225 malicious domain names. The *(2) # of included in top 5 regions* column of Table 5 shows the number of domain names whose regions were included in the top 5 regions. The *(3) # of missing data* column shows the number of domain names for which we could not acquire SimilarWeb's data. As shown in the *(2) # of included in top 5 regions* column, for a total of 95 malicious domain names, the regions where we detected them were included in the top 5 regions. This percentage is 47% $\{\approx 95 \div (225 - 23)\}$ for a total of 6 regions, indicating that about half of the malicious domain names were accessed by many users in the regions in which we detected these malicious domain names. Moreover, we found that in some cases, the regions where these 225 malicious domain names were detected coincided with the regions of the ccTLD of these malicious domain names. For example, 9 of the 30 malicious domain names detected in GE only were acquired under `.de`. In summary, malicious domain names of web requests generated by users' clicks on intermediate pages may depend on the users' regions.

5.2 Clicking on Genuine Buttons and Lure Buttons

In Sect. 5.1, we revealed the security risks when clicking on only the genuine buttons. In this section, we reveal the security risks when clicking the lure buttons. We manually selected ad banners as lure buttons that users might misidentify as genuine buttons. As explained in Sect. 4.3, lure buttons are ad banners that contain terms that encourage users to click, such as "DOWNLOAD" or "CLICK HERE," video play buttons, or downward arrows that remind users to download. Also, lure buttons exclude advertisements of products or services. In February 2021, we conducted an experiment to access 30 short URLs generated one-by-one from all the 30 ad-based URL shortening services. We accessed these short URLs from IP addresses in the US and reach the destination pages. In this experiment, when the lure buttons were displayed on the intermediate pages, we clicked all of them before clicking on the genuine buttons. The third-party ad pages we reached by clicking lure buttons were basically loaded in a new browser window. Exceptionally, when one lure button was clicked for one of the 30 services, a third-party ad page was loaded in the current browser tab as well as in a new browser tab. In this case, we accessed the short URL of the service again, and the second time we reached the destination page without clicking on the lure button above. Also, if we went through multiple intermediate pages before reaching the destination pages, we checked if the lure buttons were displayed on each intermediate page. We analyzed web requests that occurred when clicking on the lure buttons and web requests that occurred when clicking on the genuine buttons.

The *Lure buttons* column of Table 2 shows the number of lure buttons displayed in each ad-based URL shortening service, and the *Malicious domains* column shows the number of malicious domain names included in the URLs loaded in the `main_frame` when clicking on the lure buttons. As explained in Sect. 3.3, URLs loaded in the `main_frame` are URLs of the main contents loaded in the browser tab. In Table 2, the number of lure buttons does not necessarily correspond to the number of malicious domain names communicated. This is because clicking on different lure buttons caused web requests to the same domain names, while clicking on a lure button several times caused web requests to different domain names. As shown in the lure column of Table 2, 15 of the 30 ad-based URL shortening services displayed lure buttons, and the average number of the lure buttons displayed by these 15 services was 2.9, with the largest number being 8 for Service #19. Moreover, the *Malicious domains* column of Table 2 shows the number of malicious domain names included in the URLs loaded in the `main_frame` when we clicked the lure buttons. The average number of these malicious domain names was 4.2 in 15 services, and the largest number of these malicious domain names was 7 in Services #12 and #21. As shown in Sect. 5.1, even if users click only genuine buttons, communications to malicious domain names may occur. Moreover, advertisers display lure buttons to encourage users to click them and receive advertising revenue. When users mistakenly click these lure buttons believing that they are genuine buttons, the risk of users communicating with malicious domain names will increase more than when users only click genuine buttons.

5.3   Anti-Adblocking

Our experiments above have shown that there is the risk of visiting malicious domain names due to user clicks intended to reach the destination pages. For users to reduce such risks, they may install adblockers on their browsers to filter out communications to advertising domain names. On the other hand, anti-adblocking [25] is a common tactic for site owners against adblockers. If this is used by ad-based URL shortening services, adblockers are not very useful in reducing the security risk for the user. In this section, we analyze whether adblockers effectively prevent users from reaching malicious domain names. We accessed short URLs of the 30 ad-based URL shortening services using a web browser with adblockers and investigated whether we can reach the destination pages. We chose two of the leading adblockers (AdBlock [1] and Adblock Plus [2]) and used them with the default filtering list. Table 2 shows the ad-based URL shortening services for which the anti-adblocking feature worked when the two adblockers were enabled. We were unable to reach the destination pages in 19 services with AdBlock and 18 cases with Adblock Plus. These services with anti-adblocking features showed warning messages asking to disable adblockers. Then, the genuine button was hidden on the intermediate page. This result shows that it is difficult to use ad-based URL shortening services and adblockers at the same time to reduce security risks related to malicious advertisements.

6   Discussion

In this section, we first describe the limitation of the proposed method and our implementation. Then, we make recommendations for each stakeholder of ad-based URL shortening services. Finally, we explain the ethical considerations of this study.

6.1   Limitations

The following sections explain the limitations regarding using the proposed method to detect genuine buttons and implementing the proposed method to analyze ad-based URL shortening services.

Detecting Genuine Buttons. First, we describe the limitation of the proposed method's function for detecting genuine buttons. This function detects genuine buttons that have both characteristics inherent to the button elements and characteristics that encourage users to click on them. To evade detection by our method, ad-based URL shortening services can change genuine buttons to elements that do not have such characteristics or add many dummy elements with such characteristics. However, creating such an element would make it difficult for users to identify the correct genuine button, thus lowering the reputations of the services. Also, our method detects genuine buttons on the basis of the difference in the HTML source code when the buttons become active on the intermediate pages. If ad-based URL shortening services disable the activation mechanism of genuine buttons, i.e., activating genuine buttons by resolving CAPTCHA or making users wait for a few seconds, our method cannot detect the buttons effectively. In this case, the services cannot keep users on the intermediate pages to show the advertisements. In addition, they cannot prevent crawling by bots or bypassing by browser extensions. As mentioned above, although there are techniques to evade our method, none is effective and realistic. Therefore, even if new ad-based URL shortening services are created in the future, our method will be able to detect genuine buttons with versatility.

Implementation. We explain two limitations in terms of our implementation to reach the destination pages from short URLs. The first limitation is that our method requires analysts to perform manual operations, such as clicking detected genuine buttons and resolving CAPTCHA. By using common browser automation tools (e.g., Selenium [8], Puppeteer [7]) and human-powered CAPTCHA solving services [18], the proposed method can automate analysis of ad-based URL shortening services containing CAPTCHA. However, due to the previous study [18] showing that CAPTCHA solving services are involved in low-wage work, we conducted a manual analysis in this paper. The second limitation is that we analyzed ad-based URL shortening services using Google Chrome for desktop computers but not mobile phones. Accessing the services from a mobile environment may change advertisements displayed on the intermediate pages and domain names reached from them. We should analyze these services from mobile environments to comprehensively understand the security risks in the future.

6.2 Recommendations

We make recommendations to each stakeholder of ad-based URL shortening services on the basis of the findings in Sect. 5.

Users of Ad-Based URL Shortening Services. The measurement result of Sect. 5.1 showed that if a user only clicks on genuine buttons to reach the destination page without clicking on any of the displayed advertisements or lure buttons, he or she may reach malicious domain names. Also, Sect. 5.3 revealed that about 60% of the ad-based URL shortening services implemented the anti-adblocking function, indicating that it is difficult for users to use the adblockers and these services at the same time. Even if users are guided to short URLs of ad-based URL shortening services by attractive content, they should be aware of the above-mentioned risks and not access them carelessly.

Ad-Based URL Shortening Services. Section 5.1 revealed the increasingly complex of ad-based URL shortening services' structure. These services enhance the chances of user clicks by preparing multiple intermediate pages and placing many lure buttons, which in turn increases the risk of reaching malicious domain names. We argue these services should not create such web pages that trick users into making mistakes. For example, these services should have only one intermediate page. In that case, the number of genuine buttons that users need to click on will be one. Reducing the number of opportunities for users to select and click genuine buttons could reduce the risk of communicating malicious domain names that result in social engineering attacks described in Sect. 5.1.

Advertising Providers. Section 5.2 revealed that half of the 30 ad-based URL shortening services we analyzed displayed at least one lure button. Advertising providers should not display misleading ad banners to users. Users should be able to easily distinguish between ad banners and genuine buttons. The advertising policy published by Google [5] states that buttons that are difficult for users to recognize as advertisements should not be displayed.

6.3   Ethical Considerations

In our experiment, we created accounts for ad-based URL shortening services and generate short URLs. We never received any compensation from any ad-based URL shortening services. We also tried to minimize clicks to avoid ad fraud when we click on ad banners displayed on intermediate pages. To avoid contributing to the spread of malware due to accessing malicious domain names, our experiments were conducted in a virtual environment, and the environment was refreshed frequently.

7   Related Work

We summarize previous studies that identified the risks of URL shortening services and analyzed web-based attacks caused by the browsing behaviors of users.

URL Shortening Services. URL shortening services are often used in social media such as Twitter because of the character limit for posts. Unfortunately, attackers have taken advantage of the ability to hide destinations to share many malicious URLs. Nepali and Wang [19] proposed an approach to detect malicious short URLs using the content of tweets and properties of accounts. Cao et al. [13] proposed an approach to distinguish organized and organic users on Twitter and found that URL shortening services were used to launch spam campaigns from strategically organized accounts. In addition to the abuse of URL shortening services on social media, Yousaf et al. [24] reported that short URLs are used in the redirection chain generated by traffic exchanges, making it difficult to detect malicious sites. Also, previous studies revealed the users' perspective on security threats of URL shortening services [12,17,21]. Most studies mentioned above analyzed the risk of reaching the malicious destination pages from short URLs but not the risk of being forwarded to malicious sites other than the destination pages. Nikiforakis et al. [20] found that ad-based URL shortening services can cause drive-by download attacks or redirect users to phishing sites when they access intermediate pages from short URLs. However, this study did not consider the security risks resulting from the browser operations of users who reached intermediate pages. We revealed the risks involved in proceeding to the next web page and discovered a new psychological strategy with a complex page structure to guide users' behavior.

Social Engineering Attacks. Previous studies proposed approaches to analyze web-based social engineering attacks caused by users' browsing behaviors. Duman et al. [14] implemented TrueClick, a tool to detect fake ad banners that potentially lead to malicious web pages and malware. Although this tool finds buttons that do not link users' intended pages, ours locates the correct buttons for the users to proceed to the next pages. Also, systems have been proposed to collect malicious web pages by automatically manipulating web browsers [15,16]. These studies and ours share a common focus on deceptive buttons on web pages. On the other hand, our study is different in that we focus on ad-based URL shortening services and analyze the communications caused by lure buttons that users may misidentify and click, and we reveal the risk of communication with unintended malicious domain names.

8 Conclusion

In this study, we revealed the security risks of ad-based URL shortening services caused by users' behaviors. We found that even if a user clicks only the genuine button to reach the destination page, there is a risk of reaching malicious domain names that include registration pages for scam services or web pages that ask users to allow malicious web push notifications. We hope that our findings will become a foothold for considering how ad-based URL shortening services should be designed and used.

References

1. AdBlock (2021). https://getadblock.com/
2. AdblockPlus (2021). https://adblockplus.org/
3. Bitly (2021). https://bitly.com/
4. chrome.webRequest (2021). https://developer.chrome.com/docs/extensions/reference/webRequest/#type-ResourceType
5. Misrepresentation (2021). https://support.google.com/adspolicy/answer/6020955?hl=en
6. Number of internet users in selected countries in 2020 (2021). https://www.statista.com/statistics/271411/number-of-internet-users-in-selected-countries/
7. Puppeteer (2021). https://pptr.dev/
8. Selenium (2021). https://www.selenium.dev/
9. SimilarWeb (2021). https://www.similarweb.com/
10. TinyURL (2021). https://tinyurl.com/app
11. VirusTotal (2021). https://www.virustotal.com/
12. Albakry, S., Vaniea, K., Wolters, M.K.: What is this url's destination? empirical evaluation of users' URL reading. In: Bernhaupt, R., et al. (eds.) CHI 2020: CHI Conference on Human Factors in Computing Systems, Honolulu, HI, USA, 25–30 April, 2020, pp. 1–12. ACM (2020)
13. Cao, C., Caverlee, J., Lee, K., Ge, H., Chung, J.: Organic or organized? exploring URL sharing behavior. In: Bailey, J., et al. (eds.) Proceedings of the 24th ACM International Conference on Information and Knowledge Management, CIKM 2015, Melbourne, VIC, Australia, 19–23 October, 2015, pp. 513–522. ACM (2015)
14. Duman, S., Onarlioglu, K., Ulusoy, A.O., Robertson, W.K., Kirda, E.: Trueclick: automatically distinguishing trick banners from genuine download links. In: Jr., C.N.P., Hahn, A., Butler, K.R.B., Sherr, M. (eds.) Proceedings of the 30th Annual Computer Security Applications Conference, ACSAC 2014, New Orleans, LA, USA, 8–12 December, 2014, pp. 456–465. ACM (2014)
15. Kharraz, A., Robertson, W.K., Kirda, E.: Surveylance: automatically detecting online survey scams. In: 2018 IEEE Symposium on Security and Privacy, SP 2018, Proceedings, 21–23 May 2018, San Francisco, California, USA, pp. 70–86. IEEE Computer Society (2018)

16. Koide, T., Chiba, D., Akiyama, M.: To get lost is to learn the way: Automatically collecting multi-step social engineering attacks on the web. In: Sun, H., Shieh, S., Gu, G., Ateniese, G. (eds.) ASIA CCS 2020: The 15th ACM Asia Conference on Computer and Communications Security, Taipei, Taiwan, 5–9 October 2020, pp. 394–408. ACM (2020)
17. Le-Khac, N.A., Kechadi, T.: Security threats of url shortening: a users perspective. J. Adv. Comput. Networks **3**, 213–219 (2015)
18. Motoyama, M., Levchenko, K., Kanich, C., McCoy, D., Voelker, G.M., Savage, S.: Re: Captchas-understanding captcha-solving services in an economic context. In: 19th USENIX Security Symposium, Washington, DC, USA, 11–13 August, 2010, Proceedings. pp. 435–462. USENIX Association (2010)
19. Nepali, R.K., Wang, Y.: You look suspicious!!: leveraging visible attributes to classify malicious short urls on twitter. In: Bui, T.X., Jr., R.H.S. (eds.) 49th Hawaii International Conference on System Sciences, HICSS 2016, Koloa, HI, USA, 5–8 January, 2016, pp. 2648–2655. IEEE Computer Society (2016)
20. Nikiforakis, N., et al.: Stranger danger: exploring the ecosystem of ad-based URL shortening services. In: Chung, C., Broder, A.Z., Shim, K., Suel, T. (eds.) 23rd International World Wide Web Conference, WWW 2014, Seoul, Republic of Korea, 7–11 April, 2014, pp. 51–62. ACM (2014)
21. Onarlioglu, K., Yilmaz, U.O., Kirda, E., Balzarotti, D.: Insights into user behavior in dealing with internet attacks. In: 19th Annual Network and Distributed System Security Symposium, NDSS 2012, San Diego, California, USA, 5–8 February, 2012. The Internet Society (2012)
22. Pochat, V.L., van Goethem, T., Tajalizadehkhoob, S., Korczynski, M., Joosen, W.: Tranco: a research-oriented top sites ranking hardened against manipulation. In: 26th Annual Network and Distributed System Security Symposium, NDSS 2019, San Diego, California, USA, 24–27 February, 2019. The Internet Society (2019)
23. Subramani, K., Yuan, X., Setayeshfar, O., Vadrevu, P., Lee, K.H., Perdisci, R.: When push comes to ads: measuring the rise of (malicious) push advertising. In: IMC '20: ACM Internet Measurement Conference, Virtual Event, USA, October 27–29, 2020, pp. 724–737. ACM (2020)
24. Yousaf, S., Iqbal, U., Farooqi, S., Ahmad, R., Shafiq, M.Z., Zaffar, F.: Malware slums: measurement and analysis of malware on traffic exchanges. In: 46th Annual IEEE/IFIP International Conference on Dependable Systems and Networks, DSN 2016, Toulouse, France, 28 June–1 July, 2016, pp. 572–582. IEEE Computer Society (2016)
25. Zhu, S., Hu, X., Qian, Z., Shafiq, Z., Yin, H.: Measuring and disrupting anti-adblockers using differential execution analysis. In: 25th Annual Network and Distributed System Security Symposium, NDSS 2018, San Diego, California, USA, 18–21 February, 2018. The Internet Society (2018)

XHunter: Understanding XXE Vulnerability via Automatic Analysis

Zhenhua Wang⬤, Wei Xie(✉), Jing Tao, Yong Tang, and Enze Wang

College of Computer, National University of Defense Technology,
Changsha 410073, China
{wzh15,xiewei,ytang,wangenze18}@nudt.edu.cn,
ellen5702@aliyun.com

Abstract. XXE vulnerability is a severe cybersecurity threat. OWASP listed the 10 most serious web application security risks, and XXE ranked fourth. This vulnerability can lead to sensitive information leakage, DoS attacks, and intranet asset discovery. Little attention has been given to this problem, and manual work is still needed to detect these vulnerabilities. Here, we design a penetration test framework, XHunter, to discover and exploit XXE vulnerabilities automatically. XHunter can find the call chain that triggers a vulnerability and determine the vulnerability's influence scope. Specifically, our work addresses many challenges in the analysis of modern web applications, such as object-oriented structures. In addition to detecting vulnerable sinks, we find the exploit path automatically. We give each vulnerability a risk rating based on the potential impact of the exploits. In this paper, we analyze 22 real-world web frameworks and find 8 unreported vulnerabilities, 2 of which have obtained CVE IDs.

Keywords: Static analysis · Web security · XML external entity · Vulnerability ranking

1 Introduction

Extensible Markup Language (XML) plays a significant role in web applications. It is very useful for developers who want to process a document's contents without tag limitations. Its self-defined architecture allows XML to provide highly readable context information and to support data assessment and aggregation. These characteristics have led to the wide use of XML, and many projects have adopted XML. It is used for configuration files, document formats (such as OOXML, ODF, PDF, and RSS), image headers (SVG, EXIF), and network protocols (WebDAV, XMLRPC, SOAP, SAML). Its application is so common that any problems with it could lead to catastrophic results.

The flexible nature of XML also poses security risks. We first need to understand the structure of XML. XML consists of three parts: an XML declaration,

J. Garcia-Alfaro et al. (Eds.): SecureComm 2021, LNICST 399, pp. 23–42, 2021.
https://doi.org/10.1007/978-3-030-90022-9_2

a document type definition (DTD) and document elements. The DTD defines the attributes of the elements and entities in XML documents. It is worth noting that entities can be declared in XML documents or introduced from outside. An external entity is designed for creating shared public references between multiple documents. However, this means that the entity will obtain content from external sources. Attackers could leverage this feature to access internal sensitive data.

The external XML entity (XXE) attack was first put forward by Steuck [27]. Later, researchers proposed more advanced attack methods, such as out-of-bound (OOB) attacks [29], SchemaEntity attacks [26] and billion laugh attacks [1]. These attacks can lead to denial of service (DoS), the leakage of sensitive information, and forged server-side requests. With the generalized use of XML in web applications, XXE attacks have also become widespread. Many famous applications have been found to have XXE vulnerabilities, such as Google [4], Facebook [9], WebSphere [8] and WeChat Pay [10]. Therefore, the Open Web Application Security Project (OWASP) indicated XXE as one of the top 10 application security risks [6].

There have been many studies on web vulnerabilities, such as SQLI, XSS [11,12], SSRF [23] and file upload [20]. With static analysis [16,19,22] and dynamic analysis [7,30], researchers could find these bugs automatically with higher accuracy. However, little research focused on XXE vulnerabilities, and none of the existing techniques can be adapted directly. Therefore, we need to design a new technique to discover XXE vulnerabilities automatically.

Our research aims to find XXE vulnerabilities in the latest popular web applications. The accuracy of detection depends on finding the chain of function calls, which includes two challenges: (1) We need to find the call chain through a complex program that involves multiple files and classes. (2) A successful XXE attack can only be launched when users trigger the vulnerable program segment. We therefore need to verify the reachability of vulnerable sinks.

To address these challenges, we propose a novel static code analysis algorithm. We first leverage program slicing to locate XXE sinks quickly and reduce the search space in our analysis. Then, we trace vulnerable functions circularly and build the call chain with demand-driven backward data-flow analysis. Finally, we give each vulnerability a risk rank based on the possibility of exploitation.

We implement our techniques in a framework called XHunter, a prototype that analyses XXE vulnerabilities. We use XHunter on 22 popular open-source applications, including 55.8K PHP files and 9.2M single lines of code (SLOCs). We locate 193 vulnerable function nodes, and 257 XXE vulnerability sinks are found, among which users can directly access 15 high-risk sinks. Fifty-eight medium-level sinks are located in general parse functions that may be triggered in subsequent programming. The remaining 85 sinks are rated as low-risk; they are concerned with parsing network data, and additional work is needed to trigger them. It is worth mentioning that XHunter is the first reported work that builds exploits and ranks for XXE vulnerabilities.

Contributions. We propose XHunter, a flow-based penetration test framework, to detect XXE vulnerabilities. The three main contributions of our work are listed below:

- We design an efficient and effective XXE detection prototype for complex modern web applications.
- We propose an automatic evaluation mechanism for XXE vulnerability risk ranking.
- We analyse 22 real-world web applications and find 8 high-risk XXE vulnerabilities.

This paper is organized as follows: Sect. 2 introduces the background of XML and XXE attacks. More details about the challenges are discussed in Sect. 3. Section 4 describes the design of XHunter in detail. Section 5 proves the effectiveness of XHunter with experimental results and some typical case studies. In Sect. 6, we review the related work on web vulnerability detection and XXE attacks. Finally, Sect. 7 contains the conclusions.

2   Background

In this section, we introduce the basic XML structure, in particular, the definitions of four different entities. Then, we show common vulnerable code in web applications, taking PHP as an example. Finally, we show the possible damage caused by XXE vulnerabilities.

2.1   XML Structure

As mentioned previously, XML consists of an XML declaration, document type definition (DTD) and document elements. The self-defined structure makes it human readable.

A DTD is a set of markup declarations used to define the document type. Specifically, DTD *entities* are variables used to define shortcuts that refer to ordinary text or special characters. These *entities* are divided into four types: *internal general entities*, *internal parameter entities*, *external general entities* and *external parameter entities*.

Listing 1.1 shows an example of *entities*. In the document below, "&bar;" is defined as "World", so the content of *data* will be "Hello World".

```
<!DOCTYPE data [
<!ENTITY bar "World"> ]>
<data>Hello &bar;</data>
```

Listing 1.1. Internal General Entity Example

Internal parameter entities cannot be referred to directly but can define another entity. As shown in Listing 1.2, "%msg;" defines the entity "&bar;". When dealing with the XML parser, "&bar;" is also replaced with "World".

```
<!DOCTYPE data [
<!ENTITY % msg "<!ENTITY bar 'World'>">
%msg; ]>
<data>Hello &bar;</data>
```

Listing 1.2. Internal Parameter Entity Example

However, putting all entity definitions in the XML head makes documents bulky and is not conducive to code reuse. XML solves this problem by invoking external DTD files. A definition of *external general entities* is shown in Listing 1.3.

```
<!DOCTYPE ext SYSTEM "data.dtd">
<data>Hello &bar;</data>
```

Listing 1.3. External General Entity Example

The value of "&bar;" is defined in "data.dtd", which is shown in Listing 1.4.

```
<!ENTITY bar "World">
```

Listing 1.4. External DTD 1

External parameter entities can also invoke DTD files to obtain entity definitions (see Listing 1.5).

```
<!DOCTYPE data [
<!ENTITY % ext SYSTEM "data.dtd">
%ext;
%msg; ]>
<data>Hello &bar;</data>
```

Listing 1.5. External Parameter Entity Example

The external DTD file "data.dtd" is shown in Listing 1.6.

```
<!ENTITY % msg "<!ENTITY bar 'World'>">
```

Listing 1.6. External DTD 2

2.2 Vulnerable Code

XXE vulnerabilities are caused by the parsing of *XML eXternal Entities*. In web applications, XML is widely used. The most popular programming language in web applications is PHP, powering more than 80% of the top ten million websites. Therefore, we take PHP as the target language in our analysis. Here, we give examples of the XXE vulnerability, in which the program parses XML data without proper sanitation.

The first example is parsing user input directly with the function *simplexml_load_string*. The structured parse result is sent back to the user. This is the most common XXE vulnerability scenario.

```php
<?php
$post = file_get_contents("php://input");
$data = simplexml_load_string($post);
echo "The parse result of xml data is: ".$data;
```

Listing 1.7. Vulnerable Code Example

In addition to the *simplexml_load_string* function, the *loadXML* method of the *DOMDocument* class is widely used in XML parsing. Without disabling external entity, it can also lead to XXE vulnerabilities.

```php
<?php
public static function convertFromXMLString($root_element, $xml)
{
$doc = new DOMDocument('1.0', 'utf-8');
$doc->loadXML($xml);

return self::convertFromDOMDocument($root_element, $doc);
}
```

Listing 1.8. Vulnerable Code Example

2.3   Attack Methods

XXE vulnerabilities can be used to launch different attacks in web applications. Common attack methods are local file disclosure, out-of-bond, SSRF, and DoS attacks. All these attacks will affect the availability or confidentiality of web applications.

Local File Disclosure. Listing 1.9 below shows how *external entities* obtain the content of an internal file. In DTD, "&bar;" is defined as the content of "/etc./ passwd". When the web server returns the parse result, attackers can access the local sensitive file.

```xml
<!DOCTYPE data [
<!ENTITY bar SYSTEM "file:///etc/passwd"> ]>
<data>Hello &bar;</data>
```

Listing 1.9. Local File Disclosure Example

OOB Attack. Sometimes, the web server does not give a response after XML parsing. In this case, we need to get the message out with OOB XXE payloads [29].

As shown in Listing 1.10, the entity "%file;" is defined as the content of "/etc./passwd" (encoded in base64). Then, DTD invokes a remote file, where the entity "&send;" is defined to send a request.

```
<!DOCTYPE roottag [
<!ENTITY % file SYSTEM "php://filter/read=convert.base64-encode
/resource=/etc/passwd">
<!ENTITY % dtd SYSTEM "http://remote_ip/remote.dtd">
%dtd;
]>
<roottag>&send;</roottag>
```

Listing 1.10. OOB XXE Example

The content of "remote.dtd" is shown in Listing 1.11. The parameter entity "%all;" defines the external parameter entity "&send;". This triggers a network request to send the data out.

```
<!ENTITY % all "<!ENTITY send SYSTEM 'http://remote_ip/?x=%file;'>">
%all;
```

Listing 1.11. Remote DTD Example

SSRF Attack.

As *external entities* can send network requests, attackers can also perform a server-side request forgery (SSRF). For example, there is a Redis server at host "192.168.0.2" that cannot be accessed from the Internet. However, when the parser operates on the XML document below (Listing 1.12), attackers can send a request to the Redis server and execute commands.

```
<!DOCTYPE data [
<!ENTITY bar SYSTEM "gopher://192.168.0.2:6379"> ]>
<data>Hello &bar;</data>
```

Listing 1.12. SSRF Attack Example

Furthermore, attackers can perform a port scan or even obtain a bounce shell through the SSRF.

DoS Attack. The most famous DoS attack aimed at the XML parser is the *billion laugh attack* (Listing 1.13). With multiple rounds of entity definitions, this small block of XML can cause heavy load consumption. In this case, "&lol9;" contains ten "&lol8;" strings, and this is also a defined entity that expands to ten entities. After all the entities expand, the "lolz" node contains $10^9 = $ a billion "lol" strings, and 3G of memory will be occupied.

```
<!DOCTYPE lolz [
<!ENTITY lol "lol">
<!ENTITY lol1 "&lol;&lol;&lol;&lol;&lol;&lol;&lol;&lol;&lol;&lol
    ;">
<!ENTITY lol2 "&lol1;&lol1;&lol1;&lol1;&lol1;&lol1;&lol1;&lol1
    ;">
...
<!ENTITY lol9 "&lol8;&lol8;&lol8;&lol8;&lol8;&lol8;&lol8;&lol8
    ;">
]>
<lolz>&lol9;</lolz>
```

Listing 1.13. DoS Attack Example

2.4 Vulnerability Popularity

The number of XXE vulnerabilities reported on Common Vulnerabilities and Exposures (CVE) varies in different years. In general, the number has increased gradually in recent years. Although libxml, after version 2.9.0, disabled external entities in default, OWASP still lists XXE in the top ten security risks. This shows that XXE still exists widely in practical applications.

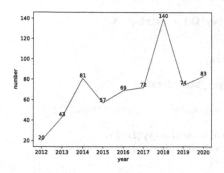

Fig. 1. Number of CVEs related to XXE

3   Challenges

In this section, we first introduce a real-world example that is vulnerable to XXE. Then, we highlight the challenges in vulnerability detection with the example.

3.1   Real-World Example

Lists 1.14–1.16 show the code from chanzhieps [2], a popular content management system (CMS) in China. These code implement WeChat payment order processing, which is used to illustrate our approach in this paper.

As shown in Listing 1.14, the *get_back_data* and *xml2array* method are defined in *"system/lib/wechatpay/wechat.class.php"*. The XXE sink is found in the *xml2array* method, which parses the method parameter $xml without entity prohibition.

However, to determine whether this sink can be accessed, we need to backtrack the call chain of this method. In particular, *xml2array* is a private method that can only be called inside the class. Fortunately, it is called in the *get_back_data* method, and the parameter is controllable. Therefore, we need to find the call of *get_back_data* in the next search round.

```php
private function xml2array($xml)
{
        $array = array();
        $tmp  = null;
        ...
        $tmp = (array) simplexml_load_string($xml);
        ...
        if($tmp && is_array($tmp))
        {
        foreach($tmp as $k => $v)
        {
                $array[$k] = (string) $v;
        }
        }
        return $array;
}
public function get_back_data()
{
        $xml = file_get_contents('php://input');
        /* convert xml to array */
        $data = $this->xml2array($xml);
        if($this->validate($data)) return $data;
        return null;
}
```

Listing 1.14. Class: wechatPay; Method:xml2array, get_back_data

In the file *"system/module/order/model.php"*, the *wechatpay* class is instanced in the *getOrderFromWechatpay* method of the *orderModel* class. Then, the *get_back_data* method is called in an assignment node. Therefore, the *getOrderFromWechatpay* method is marked as a vulnerable function in this round.

```php
public function getOrderFromWechatpay($mode)
{
        $this->app->loadClass('wechatpay', true);
        $wechatpay = new wechatpay($this->getWechatpayConfig());
        $data     = $wechatpay->get_back_data();
...
}
```

Listing 1.15. Class: orderModel; Method: getOrderFromWechatpay

In the file *"system/module/order/control.php"*, the *Order* class processes online order information. The *processWechatpayOrder* method invokes the previously marked *getOrderFromWechatpay* method. The *processOrder* method calls *processWechatpayOrder* when the variable $type equals "wechat".

```
public function processWechatpayOrder($mode = 'return')
{
        /* Get the orderID from the wechatpay. */
        $order = $this->order->getOrderFromWechatpay($mode);
        if(!$order) die('STOP!');
...
}

public function processOrder($type = 'alipay', $mode = 'return')
{
        if($type == 'alipay')
        {
                $this->processAlipayOrder($mode);
        }
        else if($type == 'wechat')
        {
                $this->processWechatpayOrder($mode);
        }
        $this->display('order', zget($this->config->order->processViews
        ,
        $this->view->order->type, 'processorder'));
}
```

Listing 1.16. Class: Order; Method: processWechatpayOrder,processOrder

Then, we need to analyse the CMS routing rules manually. After analysis, we find that the vulnerable function can be accessed by URI (**www/admin.php? m=order&f=processOrder&type=wechat**). Therefore, the attacker could launch an XXE attack remotely.

The process of exploiting this vulnerability involves three files, three classes, and five methods. Dealing with the complicated method call and the object-oriented features is the challenges we need to address below.

3.2   Technical Challenges

As shown in the example, modern CMS frameworks, such as chanzhieps, Joomla [5] and Drupal [3], have very complex call relationships. Therefore, it is non-trivial to build an automatic framework for the XXE exploit path. Specifically, we identify the following challenges:

Complex Structure. Modern web applications have thousands or even millions of lines of code (as shown in Table 1) and contain a number of functional modules. It is challenging to draw call graphs for all the code, as the time and space consumption will be unacceptable. Moreover, model, view and controller (MVC) is a popular design pattern in web applications that separates the data processing (model) and business logic (control) from the presentation (view). This design facilitates the modular development of applications but also brings great difficulty for code analysis.

Complex Logic. Most functions are implemented based on classes and methods. This feature makes a program modular but also brings great complexity to the logic. The calling relationship between methods is very complicated. A method may be called by other methods in the same or different classes, with multiple files between them.

The inheritance of classes and the rewriting of methods make the analysis more complicated. This means part of the code is implicitly included in methods. Moreover, implicit inclusion relationships are also common in complex PHP programs. For example, the *namespace* is used to clarify the use scope of classes and functions. Therefore, we need to analyse the *namespace* to determine the function currently called.

Sink Reachability. After discovering a sink, we need to know whether the sink can be accessed. The method and possibility of exploitation vary for different sinks. Some sinks are located in a general parse function, which may be invoked in follow-up development. In some scenarios, local configuration files are parsed in XML format, which can be exploited with file upload vulnerabilities. Some applications parse API response data for processing orders, obtaining weather or map information. If the response data contain malicious elements, attackers could compromise the web system. Sometimes, the parsed content is pieced together, which makes it difficult to launch attacks. Therefore, we need to judge the reachability of a sink and give a risk level for it.

4   Architecture and Algorithms

In this section, we first present an overview of XHunter. Then, we introduce the design process of XHunter in detail. XHunter is composed of three main parts, and each part is non-trivial.

4.1   Approach Overview

Our goal is to build a precise and efficient framework for XXE vulnerability detection and ranking. We need to consider the structural complexity of modern web applications, which stem from object-oriented and MVC design.

Our approach is implemented in a prototype called XHunter, as shown in Fig. 2. To tackle the challenges mentioned above, we divide our approach into three parts: (1) vulnerabilities verification; (2) call chain analysis and (3) vulnerability ranking.

First, we find vulnerable sinks. As the files related to XML operations account for a minority of the total, we adopt program slicing to find the related files. Then, we build abstract syntax trees (AST) for the target files. In the XXE vulnerability, security-critical functions are *simplexml_load_string* and *load-XML*, which is a method of class *DOMDocument*. We locate the sensitive function(method) call in AST node. Starting from these sinks, we build control flow graph (CFG) to identify the source of critical variables.

In the interprocedural pointer analysis, we build the call chain through multiple rounds of vulnerable function updates. Starting from the sink, we look for the caller of the current function or method. Once it is found, a new node is

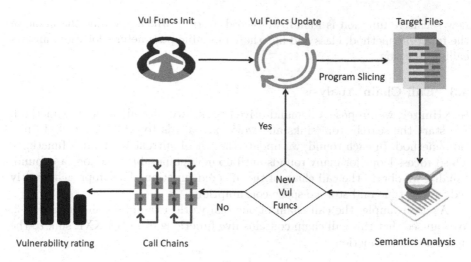

Fig. 2. Overview of XHunter.

added to the call chain, and XHunter updates the current vulnerable functions. This loop will end when no new caller can be found.

We can rank sinks according their call chain. We set four levels, corresponding to different code scenarios. If the last node is accessible to the user, a high-level vulnerability is found. Moreover, lower-level vulnerabilities are also worthy of attention. The level judgment mainly focuses on the source of the parsed data and the application scenario of the vulnerable function.

4.2 Vulnerabilities Verification

We mainly use the two following steps to verify vulnerabilities more quickly and accurately: (1) sinks discovery and (2) interprocedural analysis.

Sinks Discovery. As a small percentage of files are involved in XML data processing, we filter out the files with vulnerable functions. This method sharply reduces the analysis complexity. To discover sinks, we build an abstract syntax tree for the target files. Through this, we can determine the properties of each statement. Starting from the first statement, we recursively scan each node and find the function call node of security-critical functions.

Interprocedural Analysis. After finding sinks, we do taint analysis for sensitive variables of vulnerable functions. If the sensitive variable points to user input or function parameters, its enclosed function will be marked. For the call graph, we do not build it for all functions, but only for the identified sink node. If a new sensitive function is found, we record a node, which contains the name of the function/method, class and file, the vulnerable parameter's location, and its calling function.

4.3 Call Chain Analysis

In XHunter, we propose a demand-driven backward data-flow analysis method. We start the search from sinks and work backwards to find the affected function/method. In each round, we update the list of current vulnerable functions. This process loops for many rounds until no new vulnerable functions are found. Finally, we obtain the call chain of the affected function. This approach greatly reduce the time and storage space consumption.

As an example, the call chain of our real-world example is shown in Fig. 3. We can see that this call chain contains five functions from the XXE sink to the user-reachable function.

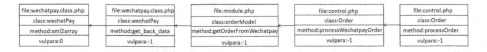

Fig. 3. The call chain of our running example.

4.4 Vulnerability Ranking

The reachability of different sinks varies. To determine the damage of a vulnerability, we design an evaluation standard for risk level judgment. With this standard, we can rate vulnerabilities automatically.

High Risk. The user can trigger the sink directly, which could lead to severe XXE vulnerabilities. It is worth noting that some functions can be accessed from the outside under the routing control of the CMS, which is also accessible. In call chain analysis, if the last node is user accessible, this vulnerability is considered high risk.

Medium Risk. In this case, the sinks are found in general parser functions. The developer may use them in the secondary development process, which could trigger an XXE vulnerability. The call chain may contain only one node, but the function is general-purpose.

Low Risk. These functions parse response XML data from APIs, such as pay, map, and weather information. These data are difficult to control unless the official site is compromised and modified. Attackers could also launch domain name system (DNS) attacks, which direct requests to the attacker's site and control the XML content. The last node of the call chain can be triggered by the attacker, but the data are from the network.

Minimal Risk. These functions deal with local XML files or concatenated strings, which are difficult to exploit. Only with other vulnerabilities (such as unrestricted file upload or database injection) could this lead to an XML injection attack, but it still deserves our attention. After all, the security of the system depends on its weakest part.

5   Evaluation

We implemented a prototype framework of our approach and chose popular web applications to evaluate its effectiveness. All the applications were selected carefully according to the criteria listed in Sect. 5.1. Then, we show the evaluation results from the program analysis, call chain analysis, and vulnerability ranking in detail. Finally, we present case studies to show how XHunter found vulnerabilities in Sect. 5.3.

5.1   Evaluation Set

We evaluated XHunter on 22 real-world PHP applications, as shown in Table 1. Our target applications were gathered from highly rated CMS projects on GitHub and popular CMS applications listed by W3Techs, such as Joomla, Drupal, and Shopware. We selected web applications on the basis of three criteria:

- The application is open source, and the latest version can be downloaded.
- The software are popular and influential (e.g., has more than 1k stars on GitHub or more than 10k downloads).
- They are modern multi-tier web applications with complex logic.

Setup. XHunter was deployed on Ubuntu 20.04 LTS VM with 8 2.3 GHz cores and 16 GB memory. We first downloaded the program code and deployed the vulnerable applications. This process included installing the applications with database initialization and creating an administrator account. Then, we found the exploit paths through XHunter. Finally, we leveraged basic XXE payloads to confirm the existence of the vulnerabilities. After manual confirmation, we responsibly reported the vulnerabilities to the vendors.

5.2   Evaluation Results

Summary of the Results. XHunter constructed a total of 307 sinks and 193 nodes. On the evaluation set, XHunter could find call chains that contained six nodes at most. We gave different security ranks for the sinks, among which 15 were high-level, 58 were medium-level, 85 were low-level, and 99 were minimal-level. At last, we discuss the false positive situation and report bugs.

Table 1. Information on our target applications

App (Version)	Files	SLOC	Popularity
dotplant2	1255	255224	1k stars
drupal (9.0.5)	8911	1246609	3.5k stars
mediawiki (1.35.0)	3869	865591	2.2k stars
microweber (1.0.7)	938	130998	1.8k stars
opencart (3.0.3.6)	1561	197122	5.7k stars
revolution (2.7.3)	3262	397163	1.2k stars
shopware (5.6.8)	3915	632870	1.2k stars
shopware (6.3.1.0)	4205	434047	1.1k stars
silverstripe (4.6.1)	572	131051	1.2k stars
TYPO3.CMS (10.4.7)	2736	486952	1k stars
concrete5 (8.5.4)	4033	351258	1.2k stars
moodle (3.9.1)	10992	2605146	3.3k stars
phpshev7	149	26967	950k downloads
Metinfo (6.0.0)	998	17473	500k downloads
php168 (x1.0)	1014	158625	600k downloads
CmsEasy (7.6.9.3)	2098	341677	670k downloads
chanzhieps (8.6.1)	2033	295011	400k downloads
CatfishCMS (5.4.0)	431	96943	18.8k downloads
XYHCMS (3.6.1012)	447	98927	1M downloads
laiketui (3.5.0)	606	69863	4.2k stars
tjkcms (2.0.9)	1416	307984	18k downloads
youdiancms (9.0)	401	120244	40k downloads

Program Slicing. In preprocessing, we selected files containing vulnerable functions to reduce the complexity of analysis. In the first round, we examined calls to "simplexml_load_string" and "loadXML" as sinks for XXE vulnerability. If new vulnerable functions were found, they were used to check the files in the next round. After program slicing, we sharply reduced the number of files to be analyzed. Table 2 shows the results of program slicing. Each CMS corresponds to a set of numbers. The numbers in parentheses are the number of all files, and the numbers outside the parentheses are the number of files selected after slicing. On average, only 2.79% of the files are needed to be analyzed.

XXE Exploits. Table 3 shows the analysis information of each CMS. Sink1 refers to the calls of function *simplexml_load_string*. Sink2 refers to the calls of function *loadXML*, which is a method of class *DOMDocument*. In each round, we identified vulnerable functions and recorded their information in a node, which contains the name of the function/method, class and file, vulnerable parameter

Table 2. Number of files after slicing

dotplant2 17 (1255)	drupal 3 (8911)	mediawiki 569 (3869)	microweber 5 (938)	opencart 66 (1561)	revolution 10(3262)
silverstripe 2 (572)	TYPO.CMS 16 (2736)	concrete 4 (4033)	moodle 298 (10992)	tjkcms 106 (1416)	youdiancms 92 (401)
php168 137 (1014)	CmsEasy 94 (2098)	chanzhieps 5 (2033)	CatfishCMS 15 (431)	XYHCMS 2 (447)	laiketui 10 (606)
shopware5 12 (3915)	shopware6 3 (4205)	phpshe 3 (149)	Metinfo 8 (998)		

Table 3. Program analysis

App	Sink1	Sink2	FP	Nodes	Time
dotplant2	2	0	0	3	0.71 s
drupal	2	0	1	3	3.51 s
mediawiki	1	8	1	6	9.07 s
microweber	1	2	0	3	1.17 s
opencart	59	3	0	21	8.47 s
revolution	22	1	0	6	2.98 s
shopware5	8	4	0	4	2.62 s
shopware6	4	0	0	2	1.30 s
silverstripe	2	0	0	3	0.26 s
TYPO3	6	0	5	10	4.83 s
concrete5	1	2	0	10	5.25 s
moodle	53	16	39	10	36.76 s
phpshev7	3	0	1	4	0.46 s
Metinfo	2	0	1	4	1.15 s
php168	7	0	1	6	3.39 s
CmsEasy	64	0	2	23	11.41 s
chanzhieps	1	0	0	5	2.17 s
CatfishCMS	1	0	0	3	0.84 s
XYHCMS	2	0	0	2	0.25s
laiketui	6	0	1	10	1.97 s
tjkcms	49	0	33	22	10.99 s
youdiancms	11	4	2	33	13.62 s
Total	**307**	**40**	**87**	**193**	

Table 4. Vulnerability ranking

Application	High	Medium	Low	Minimal
dotplant	1	0	0	1
drupal	0	1	0	0
Mediawiki	2	4	1	1
microweber	0	1	0	0
opencart	1	0	38	23
revolution	1	2	1	19
shopware5	0	6	1	5
shopware6	0	1	3	0
silverstripe	0	1	0	1
TYPO3	0	0	1	0
concrete5	0	3	0	0
moodle	0	5	21	4
Metinfo	1	0	0	0
phpshe	1	0	0	0
php168	1	2	3	0
CmsEasy	0	17	11	34
chanzhieps	1	0	0	0
CatfishCMS	0	1	0	0
XYHCMS	0	0	0	2
laiketui	0	4	0	1
tjkcms	4	5	4	3
youdiancms	2	5	1	5
Total	**15**	**58**	**85**	**99**

location, and calling function. We recorded the number of nodes generated during the analysis of each application.

False Positive and Bug Detection. Table 3 also shows the number of false positive reported by XHunter. The false positives are mainly caused by two reasons and could be pruned in our future research.

1) Prohibiting loading entities. When setting the parameter of function *libxml_ disable_entity_loader* to true, the ability to load external entities is disabled. In this case, the XXE vulnerability can not be triggered. 2) Filtering

user inputs. In some scene, the XML parser need to load external entities. The developer filters some key word, such as *<!DOCTYPE*, *<!ENTITY*, to stop attackers.

Among the vulnerabilities, 5.8% are high level, which allows attackers to trigger the XXE vulnerability directly. 22.6% are medium level, and they can lead to security events only when dealing with malicious XML files. For example, in module "PHPExcel", XML files are parsed without sanitation before version 1.8.0. 33.1% are low level, as only with extra vulnerabilities could we launch the next attack. At last, 38.5% are minimal level, whose trigger conditions are very harsh.

We responsibly reported the details of the vulnerabilities to vendors. Some security groups replied quickly, while others did not consider the reports seriously. Table 5 shows the results of our reports, some of which have received a CVE ID. However, some vendors rejected or ignored our issues due to insufficient security concern. As shown above, XXE vulnerabilities give the attacker opportunities to control the site. We strongly recommend that security vendors fix the reported security issues. However, some vendors do not provide ways to push issues. Not all high-risk vulnerabilities are listed below.

Table 5. Results of XHunter

Application	Issue	Response	Archive
dotplant2	1	Accept	CVE-2020-25750
Drupal	1	Accept	Not Yet
MediaWiki	3	Accept	Not Yet
microweber	1	Ignore	–
revolution	1	Accept	Not Yet
shopware6	1	Accept	Not Yet
TYPO3.CMS	1	Accept	CVE-2020-26229
symphony	1	Nonce	–
phpshe V7	1	Found	CVE-2019-9761

These vulnerabilities pose a significant threat to web application security and may lead to several attacks. Disabling entity resolution is an easy way to patch them. However, for situations that need to resolve entities, we need to establish more fine-grained security protection strategies.

5.3   Case Studies

Drupal. There is a function *parseResourceXml* in the Drupal application that directly processes XML data. This function is widely used in processing network resources. If there are attack vectors in the network resource, an XXE vulnerability will be triggered. The Drupal team accepted this suggestion and fixed it in the latest version. As the vulnerable function can only cause damage when it is called, we evaluate it as a medium-risk vulnerability.

```php
protected function parseResourceXml($data, $url) {
    ....
    $content = simplexml_load_string($data, 'SimpleXMLElement',
        LIBXML_NOCDATA);
    ....
    $data = Json::encode($content);
    return Json::decode($data);
}
```

Listing 1.17. Method: parseResourceXml

phpshe. For phpshe v7, XHunter found a complex call chain for the XXE sink. This vulnerability has been found by other researcher, so we just describe the call chain here. Listing 1.18 shows the vulnerable sink (*simplexml_load_string*) where user input (php://input) is passed in. The function *pe_getxml* parses user input as XML data directly in the file *global.func.php*. Therefore, in the first round, the function *pe_getxml* was added to the vulnerable function list.

```php
function pe_getxml() {
    $xml = file_get_contents("php://input");
    return $xml = json_decode(json_encode(simplexml_load_string(
        $xml, 'SimpleXMLElement', LIBXML_NOCDATA)), true);
}
```

Listing 1.18. File: global.func.php; Function:pe_getxml

As Listing 1.19 shows, the function *pe_getxml* is then called by *wechat_getxml* in *wechat.hook.php*. Although the call point is in the return statement, it does not affect the vulnerable function's trigger.

```php
function wechat_getxml() {
    return pe_getxml();
}
```

Listing 1.19. File: wechat.hook.php; Function: wechat_getxml

Finally, in *notify_url.php*, the vulnerable function can be accessed directly, which means that we found an exploited XXE vulnerability. Therefore, attackers could launch an attack remotely, and we marked this as a high-risk vulnerability.

```php
include('../../../../common.php');
pe_lead('hook/order.hook.php');
pe_lead('hook/wechat.hook.php');
...
$xml = wechat_getxml();
```

Listing 1.20. File: notify_url.php

6   Related Work

In this section, we review security analysis technologies for web applications and related work on XXE attacks. Through this, we evaluate previous studies in identifying control and data flow vulnerabilities. Moreover, we summarize the existing research on XML attacks.

6.1   Vulnerability Detection

Researchers have proposed many methods of finding web vulnerabilities, such as static analysis [13,16,19], dynamic fuzzing [17,18,21] and symbolic execution [11,12,24].

Pixy [19] and RIPS [16] were the first static analysis frameworks. They leverage flow-sensitive, interprocedural and context-sensitive data flow analysis to find web vulnerabilities. Other research [14,15,31] specifically handles the features of dynamic script languages to explore multi-step attacks. We dealt with the details in the large PHP framework carefully so that XHunter could find multi-step vulnerabilities with higher efficiency.

In the fuzzing process, the fuzzer crawls the web application and generates payloads based on rules or mutations. Through fuzzing, novel payloads can be found to trigger unexpected vulnerabilities [30] or bypass security sanitation [18]. However, many web interfaces are not exposed by default, and we still need the assistance of program analysis.

Based on program analysis, Chainsaw [11] and NAVEX [12] can also generate exploits. However, they both take files as a basic block, which is not suitable for modern web applications. Searching the function call graph is more effective for vulnerability detection. This technique can help find exploitable vulnerabilities in modern applications. Meanwhile, through chain call analysis, we can also obtain exploitations directly.

6.2   XML Attacks

As XML is widely used in web applications, related attacks have been proposed and studied by many researchers. The main types of attacks are XML injection attacks, XML signature wrapping (XSW) attacks, and XXE attacks.

Among these attacks, XXE has a wide range of effects, low utilization conditions, and significant damage. Morgan et al. [28] described XXE attack vectors in detail. Spath et al. [25] expanded previous research and conducted research on 30 XML parsers in 6 languages and the Android platform. In real web applications, XML is leveraged in different places, such as configured data, Excel, and data translation. Therefore, it is very important to discover vulnerabilities in real applications. XHunter fills this gap and provides guidance for different levels of vulnerabilities.

7   Conclusion

In this paper, we proposed XHunter, a novel automatic framework that targets and ranks XXE vulnerabilities. This framework implements interprocedural, object-oriented call analysis for modern complex web applications. We tested 22 popular CMSs and found 257 XXE sinks, 15 of which were high risk. The evaluation demonstrates the efficiency and effectiveness of our work.

Acknowledgements. We would like to thank the anonymous reviewers for their valuable comments and helpful suggestions.

References

1. Billion laughs attack. https://en.wikipedia.org/wiki/Billion_laughs_attack
2. Chanzhi eps. https://github.com/goodrain-apps/chanzhieps
3. Drupal. https://www.drupal.org/
4. How we got read access on Google's production servers. https://blog.detectify. com/2014/04/11/how-we-got-read-access-on-googles-production-servers/
5. Joomla. https://www.joomla.org/
6. OWASP top 10 application security risks - 2017. https://owasp.org/ wwwprojecttopten/OWASP_Top_Ten_2017/Top_10-2017_Top_10.html
7. PHP runtime vulnearbility detect. https://github.com/ExploreZone/prvd
8. Security bulletin: Websphere application server is vulnerable to an information exposure vulnerability. https://www.ibm.com/support/pages/node/6334311. Accessed 24 Sept 2020
9. XXE in OpenID of Facebook. https://www.ubercomp.com/posts/2014-01-16_ facebook_remote_code_execution
10. XXE in WeChat pay SDK. https://seclists.org/fulldisclosure/2018/Jul/3
11. Alhuzali, A., Eshete, B., Gjomemo, R., Venkatakrishnan, V.: Chainsaw: chained automated workflow-based exploit generation. In: Proceedings of the 2016 ACM SIGSAC Conference on Computer and Communications Security, pp. 641–652 (2016)
12. Alhuzali, A., Gjomemo, R., Eshete, B., Venkatakrishnan, V.: {NAVEX}: precise and scalable exploit generation for dynamic web applications. In: 27th {USENIX} Security Symposium ({USENIX} Security 18), pp. 377–392 (2018)
13. Balzarotti, D., et al.: Saner: composing static and dynamic analysis to validate sanitization in web applications. In: 2008 IEEE Symposium on Security and Privacy (SP 2008), pp. 387–401. IEEE (2008)
14. Balzarotti, D., Cova, M., Felmetsger, V.V., Vigna, G.: Multi-module vulnerability analysis of web-based applications. In: Proceedings of the 14th ACM Conference on Computer and Communications Security, pp. 25–35 (2007)
15. Cova, M., Balzarotti, D., Felmetsger, V., Vigna, G.: Swaddler: an approach for the anomaly-based detection of state violations in web applications. In: Kruegel, C., Lippmann, R., Clark, A. (eds.) RAID 2007. LNCS, vol. 4637, pp. 63–86. Springer, Heidelberg (2007). https://doi.org/10.1007/978-3-540-74320-0_4
16. Dahse, J., Schwenk, J.: RIPS-A static source code analyser for vulnerabilities in PHP scripts. In: Seminar Work (Seminer Çalismasi). Horst Görtz Institute Ruhr-University Bochum (2010)

17. Duchene, F., Groz, R., Rawat, S., Richier, J.L.: XSS vulnerability detection using model inference assisted evolutionary fuzzing. In: 2012 IEEE 5th International Conference on Software Testing, Verification and Validation, pp. 815–817. IEEE (2012)
18. Duchene, F., Rawat, S., Richier, J.L., Groz, R.: Kameleonfuzz: evolutionary fuzzing for black-box XSS detection. In: Proceedings of the 4th ACM conference on Data and Application Security and Privacy, pp. 37–48 (2014)
19. Jovanovic, N., Kruegel, C., Kirda, E.: Pixy: a static analysis tool for detecting web application vulnerabilities. In: 2006 IEEE Symposium on Security and Privacy, SP 2006, pp. 258–263 (2006)
20. Lee, T., Wi, S., Lee, S., Son, S.: Fuse: finding file upload bugs via penetration testing. In: 2020 Network and Distributed System Security Symposium. Network & Distributed System Security Symposium (2020)
21. Li, L., Dong, Q., Liu, D., Zhu, L.: The application of fuzzing in web software security vulnerabilities test. In: 2013 International Conference on Information Technology and Applications, pp. 130–133. IEEE (2013)
22. Luo, Z., Wang, B., Tang, Y., Xie, W.: Semantic-based representation binary clone detection for cross-architectures in the internet of things. Appl. Sci. 9(16), 3283 (2019)
23. Pellegrino, G., Johns, M., Koch, S., Backes, M., Rossow, C.: Deemon: detecting CSRF with dynamic analysis and property graphs. In: Proceedings of the 2017 ACM SIGSAC Conference on Computer and Communications Security, pp. 1757–1771 (2017)
24. Son, S., Shmatikov, V.: Saferphp: finding semantic vulnerabilities in PHP applications. In: Proceedings of the ACM SIGPLAN 6th Workshop on Programming Languages and Analysis for Security, pp. 1–13 (2011)
25. Späth, C., Mainka, C., Mladenov, V., Schwenk, J.: Sok:{XML} parser vulnerabilities. In: 10th {USENIX} Workshop on Offensive Technologies ({WOOT} 16) (2016)
26. Späth, C., Schwenk, J.: Security implications of DTD attacks against a wide range of XML parsers. Master, Ruhr-University Bochum (2015)
27. Steuck, G.: XXE (XML external entity) attack. OWASP (October 2002)
28. Morgan, T.D., Ibrahim, O.A.: XML schema, DTD, and entity attacks. http://vsecurity.com/download/papers/XMLDTDEntityAttacks.pdf. Accessed 19 May 2014
29. Yunusov, T., Osipov, A.: XML out-of-band data retrieval. In: BlackHat EU 2013 (2013)
30. Wang, E., Wang, B., Xie, W., Wang, Z., Luo, Z., Yue, T.: EWVHunter: grey-box fuzzing with knowledge guide on embedded web front-ends. Appl. Sci. 10(11), 4015 (2020)
31. Xie, Y., Aiken, A.: Static detection of security vulnerabilities in scripting languages. In: USENIX Security Symposium, vol. 15, pp. 179–192 (2006)

Anonymous Short Communications over Social Networks

Francesco Buccafurri$^{(\boxtimes)}$, Vincenzo De Angelis, Maria Francesca Idone,
and Cecilia Labrini

University of Reggio Calabria, Via Graziella, Loc. Feo di Vito, Reggio Calabria, Italy
{bucca,vincenzo.deangelis,mariafrancesca.idone,cecilia.labrini}@unirc.it

Abstract. Social networks nowadays attract a huge number of people
and are an extraordinary platform for applications going beyond the
basic mission of connecting people. In this context, anonymity of senders
and recipients of messages could play an important role to protect privacy in specific cases such as proximity-based services, surveys, crowdfunding, and e-democracy, in which only short communications should
be protected. As the social network provider could be semi-trusted (i.e.,
honest-but-curious), it could play as global passive adversary, monitoring the flow of all the messages exchanged in the social network. In this
paper, we propose a new anonymous communication protocol tailored to
our application context. We show that our proposal offers a good solution to the trade-off between traffic overhead and communication latency,
better than the application of existing anonymous overlay routing protocols.

Keywords: Privacy · Anonymous communication · Social networks

1 Introduction and Motivations

Social networks probably represent the most disrupting digital innovation of the
last twenty years. Different kinds of applications are nowadays implemented on
top social networks. However, their power could be better exploited in some
application contexts, such as e-democracy and e-participation, provided that
communication anonymity is supported against a potentially honest-but-curious
social network provider. Consider for example the domain of market surveys
that a given company wants to submit to a given population for marketing purposes. Implementing this through an existing social network could dramatically
increase the effectiveness and efficiency of the campaign, by easily reaching a
large population and by allowing more sophisticated sample selections than traditional methods. A similar application context is that of innovative participatory models of crowdfunding, in which a company might leverage existing social
networks to enable the anonymous participation of crowdfunders in voting or
opinion evaluation related to the governance of the company.

© ICST Institute for Computer Sciences, Social Informatics and Telecommunications Engineering 2021
Published by Springer Nature Switzerland AG 2021. All Rights Reserved
J. Garcia-Alfaro et al. (Eds.): SecureComm 2021, LNICST 399, pp. 43–63, 2021.
https://doi.org/10.1007/978-3-030-90022-9_3

In the cases above, the communication should happen between anonymous users and explicit entities. However, interactions requiring anonymity among users might occur in other cases, such as anonymous opinion exchange [10], or proximity-based services, delivered on the basis of the proximity of two users who detect this condition by mutually exchanging some messages.

An important point is that the above applications are characterized by the common denominator that only a few asynchronous messages have to be exchanged in anonymous form. Therefore, we do not need the full communication power usually aimed in the domain of anonymous communication networks [22], supporting low-latency and connection-oriented communication.

The problem is not trivial. Indeed, the social network provider should be seen, in a realistic threat model, as a global (at least) passive adversary, able to monitor the whole flow of messages among users. Moreover, privacy is achieved if not only the content of messages is protected against the adversary, but also the communication itself.

A few proposals concerning anonymous communication in social networks are available [10,16] (to the best of our knowledge). However, [16] only deals with anonymous group communication (therefore it does not cover the application targets described earlier), and [10] does not provide sender anonymity against the global passive adversary.

The goal of this paper is to achieve communication anonymity against the global passive adversary in social-network applications (like those described earlier) in which only a few asynchronous messages should be exchanged. If we refer to existing centralized social networks, the only way to follow is of course to require the collaboration of social-network users to implement an overlay network over the application layer provided by the social network itself. Indeed, an alternate approach based on a centralized party playing as anonymizer has very limited effectiveness in our threat model, as shown in [24].

Thus, to not to masquerade the core of the problem under the chosen application context (i.e., social networks), we have to refer to any P2P overlay anonymous routing approach resistant to the global passive adversary.

It is well known that, to have anonymity against the global passive adversary we need to include cover traffic (i.e., dummy traffic to hide the actual messages) [6], which, in our context, results in bandwidth and CPU overhead (thus also battery consumption) for social-network users. Therefore, we have to reduce cover traffic as much as possible.

Existing P2P overlay network routing techniques resisting to the global passive adversary are based either on *mixnets* [2,8,11], or on *buses* [1,9,27].

As shown in the paper, state-of-the-art mixnet-based approaches, require a high amount of cover traffic. On the other hand, mixnets support low-latency applications and bursting-traffic services, as well as the notion of connection. As observed earlier, these are not features required in our application setting.

In the approach based on buses, anonymity is achieved by implementing routes (either deterministic [1,9] or non-deterministic [27]) independent of the intended communication, which senders and receivers can opportunistically exploit. With this approach, cover traffic is drastically reduced with respect to mixnets (at the price of higher latency). Indeed, here, no mixing is adopted and the incoming (cover) traffic, for each node, has exactly one 1-hop source, and each node can indifferently play the role of sender, recipient, or relay node. However, both deterministic (in which the fixed route is an Eulerian path passing through all the nodes) and non-deterministic approaches (in which the latency highly increases with the number of nodes) are unrealistic in scenarios with a huge number of nodes like social networks.

In this paper, we propose a new approach, tailored to the chosen application context (i.e., social networks), that uses the concept of fixed deterministic routes of buses to minimize cover traffic. Differently from buses, deterministic routes are not used to hide inside both senders and receivers, but to obtain separately anonymity of senders and recipients, thus allowing small predetermined cyclic routes (one route in which the sender is anonymized and one route in which the recipient is anonymized) and, then, acceptable latency.

The proposed technique is analytically compared with buses and mixnets, showing that buses produce much higher latency and mixnets require much more cover traffic. Moreover, through experiments, our technique is tested to be feasible in terms of latency, for the chosen applications. The proposed protocol, besides anonymity, also includes a certain degree of redundancy to take into account the possibility that some users are not collaborating.

The structure of the paper is the following. The related literature is analyzed in Sect. 2. We provide some basic notions needed to understand the proposed protocol in Sect. 3. The protocol is presented in Sect. 4 and it is compared with the state-of-the-art approaches in Sect. 5. In Sect. 6, we report the results of an experimental validation of our approach. The security of the protocol is analyzed in Sect. 7. Finally, in Sect. 8, we draw our conclusions.

2   Related Work

As mentioned in the introduction, our paper can be related to anonymous P2P overlay networks, in which participants act as both end users and relay nodes that route the data packets of others. A survey on anonymous communication systems is reported in [22]. Anonymous routing protocols existing in the literature might include full cover traffic. The class of techniques requiring cover traffic (also partially partial) suffers from the drawback that they are not resistant against the global passive adversary. Therefore, they do not reach the objective aimed in this paper, in which the social network provider plays as a global passive adversary. The famous Onion [19], Crowds [20], AP3 [15], and Octopus [25], fall within this class of protocols.

To resists against the global passive adversary, the inclusion of cover traffic is needed. As stated in the introduction, two main different approaches are possible: *buses* or *mixnets*. Our paper mainly relates to buses [1,9,27], by introducing a way to modulate anonymity (by passing from full anonymity to k-anonymity) with an advantage in terms of message latency.

There is a huge literature on mixnets, originally proposed in [4]. The combination of mixnets with cover traffic is a very common approach [8,11,12,26]. In general, by mixing cover with data traffic, one can add noise to the underlying traffic patterns to defeat traffic analysis. A typical approach is to insert cover traffic to maintain a constant transmission rate on any link, so that the traffic patterns observed by the adversary stay unchanged and leak no identifying information. [5] is a very recent mixnet-based approach resistant to the global adversary, but it is designed at network layer (thus it is not easy to understand how to implement network *Autonomous Systems* in a P2P fashion). Despite its age, Tarzan [8] still keeps a relevant position in the landscape of P2P anonymous overlay networks, as provides an effective way to implement the concept of mixnet combined with cover traffic even though some aspects (e.g., the adoption of a gossip protocol) might limit its scalability. Due to space limitations, we cannot analyze the huge literature regarding mixnets. However, in Sect. 5, we provide an analytical comparison of mixnet-based approaches with our proposal, based on a simplified model of mixnets extracted from [8].

Another important class of approaches is based on DC-Nets [22], which uses secure multi-party cryptographic protocols among the participant in the communication. One the most recent proposals falling into this class is [16]. It proposes an approach based on DC-net that allows users to anonymously publish their messages in a group of users. However, it does not provide point-to-point anonymous communication between two users. Moreover, users cannot communicate externally to the group. In general, this class of approaches is not applicable in our context. Indeed, they expect all participants to be involved in every run of the protocol and require pairwise shared keys between the participants. This is impractical in the social network domain. Moreover, as a matter of fact, they are more effective for anonymous group communication.

3   Background

In this section, we provide some basic notions useful for the comprehension of the protocol. They are *Identity-based Encryption (IBE)* and *Anonymity*.

Identity-Based Encryption. Identity-based encryption (IBE) is a type of public-key encryption in which the public key of a user is represented by some unique information associated with the user's identity. In our setting, the public key is the social network ID of the user. The advantage of IBE is that each user may encrypt a message for another user without requiring the public key to any external party. Formally, an IBE scheme consists of four algorithms:

Setup(k): it takes as input a security parameter k and outputs a master secret key MSK and master public key MPK.

Extract(MPK, MSK, ID): it takes as input the master public key MPK, the master secret key MSK and a parameter ID representing the identity of a user. It outputs a private key d associated with the user's identity ID.

Encrypt(MPK, ID, M): it takes as input the master public key MPK, a parameter ID representing the identity of a user and a message M. It outputs a ciphertext C intended for the user with identity ID.

Decrypt(MPK, C, d): it takes as input the master public key MPK, a ciphertext C, and a private key d. It outputs the decryption C of a message M.

IBE requires the presence of a trusted third party called Private Key Generator (PKG). In a setup phase, PKG invokes Setup (k) to obtain MPK and MSK. MPK is provided to all the users and MSK is kept secret by PKG. When a user u with identity ID_u wants to obtain a secret key associated with such an identity ID_u, she/he contacts PKG that invokes Extract (MPK, MSK, ID_u) to obtain d_u and sends it to u. Obviously, PKG sends d_u after making sure about the identity of u, for example through the help of an Identity Provider [18]. If another user y wants to send a message M to u (whose identity ID_u is known to y), then y invokes Encrypt (MPK, ID_u, M) to obtain the ciphertext C and sends C to u. Finally, u invokes Decrypt (MPK, C, d_u) and retrieves the message M. Observe that y does not interact with any party during the encryption process and, as will be clear in Sect. 4, this goes in favour of anonymity. Furthermore, we require that the adopted IBE scheme used is probabilistic and anonymous. Probabilistic means that the same message encrypted more times results in different ciphertexts. Anonymous means that the identity of the recipient of a ciphertext is hidden. The schemes [3,7], for example, satisfy our requirements.

Anonymity. The notion of *anonymity* may have different meanings, depending on context. Anyway, a comprehensive characterization of this concept is given in [17], which this section is inspired to. To enable anonymity of a given item, we have always to refer to an appropriate set of items with, potentially, the same attributes. This leads to the following general definition: "Anonymity of a subject means that the subject is not identifiable within a set of subjects, the anonymity set." The content of the anonymity set depends on the kind of item we are considering. For example, if we want to protect the privacy of who is performing a certain action, the anonymity set is composed of the subjects that are possible actors. In the context of message communication, we have the following specific definitions.

Sender Anonymity: the condition in which the adversary cannot *sufficiently* identify the sender in a set of potential senders.

Recipient Anonymity: the condition in which the adversary cannot *sufficiently* identify the recipient in a set of potential recipients.

Relationship Anonymity: the condition in which the adversary cannot *sufficiently* identify that a sender (in a set of potential senders) and a recipient (in a set of potential recipients) are communicating.

Observe that in the above definitions, with the use of the term sufficiently, we mean that "there is a possibility to quantify anonymity" with a proper threshold.

In our paper, the notion of *communication k-anonymity* defined in [23] is adopted. k-anonymity guarantees that in a network with n honest participants, the adversary is notable to guess the sender or recipient of a particular message with probability non-negligibly greater than $1/k$, where k is a configurable constant possibly smaller than n.

4   The Anonymity Protocol

We denote by SN the social network provider (we refer to a classical centralized social network model). Every user is associated with a numeric *SN identity* SI which is the ID used by SN to address the user (e.g., the ID_user of Facebook).

An anonymous IBE (identity-based encryption) system exists, relying on a PKG independent of SN and referring to the domain of SN identities. Obviously, the price in terms of confidentiality threat that the adoption of IBE in general entails, if the PKG misbehaves, is mitigated by the fact that the encrypted messages are privately exchanged within the social network, thus they are not publicly accessible. In the setup phase, the user demonstrates to the PKG the ownership of a given SI through the SN profile to obtain the private key.

Anonymity is obtained through a cooperative approach, involving the users of SN. The collaboration is thought as a special feature of certain application domains, each forming a *collaboration community*. The users of each community require anonymity when a certain type of service is delivered. In a real-life setting, we can imagine that the presence of a user in an application domain, besides the voluntary adhesion, could be conditioned to other features, such as the verification of the profile (to exclude fake profiles). Consider, for example, an application domain devoted to the submission of anonymous surveys. Besides anonymity (and the other typical requirements of e-voting systems), Sybil attacks (based on the proliferation of dummy identities) must be prevented.

An important feature required for the domains is that, if for the specific application the geographical location (e.g., the IP zone) can be a quasi-identifier with respect to the action that we want to anonymize, then the domain has to be restricted to the geographical area. For example, for national surveys not requiring more specific geographical information, the domain can include only profiles belonging to the national territory. In general, depending on the application, privacy guarantees taking into account also l-diversity [14] and t-closeness [13] should be provided, possibly by a suitable TTP. For space reasons, it was not possible to address this aspect in this paper, even though classical approaches can be applied.

4.1   The Ring Schema

In this section, we describe the structural elements of the model which the solution relies on. We start with the definition of *application domain*.

Definition 1. *An application domain A is a tuple $\langle ID_A, N_A, k_A, r_A \rangle$, where $ID_A \subseteq \mathbb{N}$ is a finite set of the SN identities of the involved users, N_A represents the cardinality of ID_A, $k_A \in \mathbb{N}^+$ is said privacy level, and $r_A \in \mathbb{N}^+ \setminus \{1\}$ is said redundancy level.*

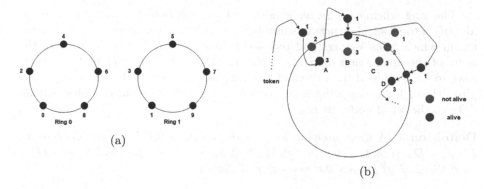

Fig. 1. (a) Ring schema for $\alpha = 2$ and $k_A = 5$; (b) Example of fragment of the route of a token in a ring.

The meaning of the privacy level regards the objective of our protocol, which is anonymity. Anonymity regards sender and recipient of a message (thus relationship) and is reached by requiring a sufficient degree of uncertainty. Given an application domain A, the privacy level k_A represents just the obtained degree of uncertainty, in the sense that the adversary can identify an item (sender or recipient) with probability not greater than $\frac{1}{k_A}$.

As it will be clearer below, the redundancy level indicates the average number of users mapped to a node of a virtual circuit we build for message communication. Virtual circuits are circular circuits, called *rings*. These are the elements of the *ring schema*, defined as follows.

Definition 2. *Given an application domain* $A = \langle ID_A, N_A, k_A, r_A \rangle$, *a number* n_A *such that* $n_A = \alpha \cdot k_A$ *(for any* $\alpha \in \mathbb{N}^+$*) and* $\frac{N_A}{n_A} \geq r_A$, *the set* $D_A = \{0, \ldots, n_A - 1\}$, *and the function* $f_A : D_A \to D_A$ *such that* $f_A(x) = x + \alpha \bmod n_A$, *the* $(\alpha\text{-})$*ring schema (of* A*) is the set of the equivalence classes induced by* f_A *each containing all the elements of* D_A *congruent modulo* α. *Each class is called* $(\alpha\text{-})$*ring (of* A*). A ring is identified by the canonical representative of the equivalence class. Given an element* $x \in D_A$, *we denoted by* $ring(x)$ *(with* $ring(x) \in D_A$*) the canonical representative of the ring which* x *belongs to. The elements of a ring are called nodes.*

It is easy to see that the cardinality of an α-ring schema is α and that the identifiers of the classes are $0, 1, \ldots, \alpha - 1$. Moreover, all the classes are of cardinality k_A. Observe that the ring schema is completely defined by the parameters N_A, k_A, r_A, and α. The parameters of the adopted ring schema are notified to all the users of the application domain.

An example of ring schema for $\alpha = 2$ and $k_A = 5$ (then $n_A = 10$) is reported in Fig. 1a. Therein, being $\alpha = 2$, we have 2 rings (i.e., ring 0 and ring 1) each including $k_A = 5$ nodes. Moreover, for example, $ring(2) = 0$ and $ring(9) = 1$.

From now on, throughout the paper, assume given an application domain $A = \langle ID_A, N_A, k_A, r_A \rangle$ and an α-ring schema, for a given α.

The ring schema is the basic notion of our solution, because allows us to identify a topological structure suitable to support a cover-message-based mechanism which *hides* senders and recipients through mutual collaboration of the users of the application domain. To do this, the so far abstract nodes of rings have to be associated with users of the domain. This is done by uniformly mapping (through a classical hash function h) the set of SN identities of a domain ID_A to the set of nodes in D_A.

Definition 3. *A user mapping on an α-ring schema of A is any function h : $ID_A \rightarrow D_A$ such that the probability that $h(x) = h(y)$ (for each $x, y \in ID_A$, such that $x \neq y$) follows the uniform distribution.*

From now on, we consider, as a user mapping, the hash function h such that $h(x) = x \bmod n_A$, for each SI $x \in ID_A$. It is well-known that this function allows us to fulfil the condition required by Definition 3. However, a different user mapping could be adopted, also by taking into account possible specific characteristics of the set ID_A. Observe that, since $\frac{|ID_A|}{|D_A|} = \frac{N_A}{n_A} \geq r_A$, we obtain an average number of collisions bounded by r_A. Also the user mapping is notified to the users.

The intuition behind the user mapping is to intentionally build (on the basis of the function f_A), virtual cyclic circuits of groups of users. In other words, if the ring v_0 is $\{v_0, \ldots v_{k_A-1}\}$, where $v_i < v_j$ for $0 \leq i < j \leq k_A - 1$, then $f_A(v_i) = v_{i+1}$, for each $0 \leq i < k_A - 1$ and $f_A(v_{k_A-1}) = v_0$. Moreover, with each v_i ($0 \leq i \leq k_A - 1$), a set of at least r_A users (in the average), identifiable by reversing the function h, is associated. The multiplicity of users associated with nodes has the scope to give redundancy to these virtual cyclic circuits (as we better explain in the next subsection). Observe that, through the user mapping, each user belongs to exactly one node in a ring of a given domain.

The user mapping is not materialized by the users. As we will see later, they just could need to compute some of its values. Instead, SN stores a hash table H (based on h) materializing the user mapping in such a way that if a user requires to know the group of SN identities mapped to a given node v of a ring, SN can efficiently provide the correct answer just by accessing the hash table at the index v. Therefore, a user, starting from the knowledge of a given SI, say x, can determine which is the node associated with this SI just by computing $h(x)$, then can calculate all the sequence of nodes of the ring (for example, the node at distance j from x is obtained as $f_A^j(h(x))$), and can retrieve from SN the list of (at least) r_A SIs (in the average) associated with any node of the ring. We can assume that each user knows always the SIs associated with each node of the ring which the user belongs to. This information is called *configuration of the ring*. Any change of the configuration of the ring is communicated by SN, as we will see in Sect. 4.3. For each SI, say y, thanks to the IBE scheme, x can send an encrypted message to y such that only y can decrypt it without relying on a PKI. In contrast, if SN plays the role of PKI or the PKI is internal, the request of a public key results in a leakage of privacy. Anyway, IBE is not strictly necessary. We chose to adopt IBE because it is the most suitable scheme from a theoretic point of view. If, for real-life implementation of our solution, we want to avoid IBE, an external PKI or even an internal PKI with proper measures to prevent privacy leakage (based on timing decoupling between PKI requests and message communication) might be adopted. This is another subject of interest as a future work.

4.2 Redundancy

In this section, we better discuss the role of the redundancy level. Our protocol is collaborative and requires that users, maybe through a delegated app, perform some actions. Regarding this aspect, we introduce the following. First, we fix a (suitably high) probability threshold τ, and say that an event is *sufficiently guaranteed* if it occurs with probability not below τ.

Liveness Assumption. We assume that, if we pick a user, the probability she/he is alive is p. Then, we set an integer value r such that it is sufficiently guaranteed that among r users at least one is alive. r is any value such that $1 - (1-p)^r \geq \tau$. It is worth noting that, as it will be clear in the sequel of the section, our system does not require any kind of registry of the active social network users available to many parties (and, thus, potentially critical from the privacy point of view).

k_A-*Anonymity Threshold.* For reasons that will be clear later, according to the liveness assumption, to sufficiently guarantee k_A-anonymity, the redundancy level r_A must be set in such a way that the minimum number of users associated with a ring is no smaller than $k_A \cdot r$ because it is sufficiently guaranteed that in a ring at least k_A users are alive. The value $k_A \cdot r$ is called k_A-*anonymity threshold*.

4.3 System Update

The previous definitions do not take into account possible updates regarding an application domain. These are joins and leaves of users, managed as follows.

User Join. When a new user U joins the application domain A, once an SI is assigned to this user, say SI_U, it suffices for SN to include the new user in the hash table H at the index $h(SI_U)$. As this addition cannot threaten the number of expected users alive in the affected ring (i.e., the ring which the node $h(SI_U)$ belongs to), the join does not impact the ring schema. The users of the affected ring are notified about the changes occurred in the ring, in such a way that the local information about the configuration of the ring is made coherent. No further action is required.

User Leave. When a user U with SN identifier SI_U leaves the application domain A, SN has to remove the user from the hash table H, at the index $h(SI_U)$. The number of users is obviously updated as $N'_A = N_A - 1$. Similarly to the case of join, the users of the affected ring are notified about the changes occurred in the ring, in such a way the local information about the configuration of the ring is made coherent. However, the event might impact the ring schema if the minimum number of the users of the affected ring goes below the k_A-anonymity threshold (i.e., $k_A \cdot r$) that sufficiently guarantees k_A-anonymity, according to the liveness assumption. If this is the case, n_A has to be decreased. Therefore, SN finds $\alpha' < \alpha$ for which the above threshold is exceeded. Then, SN has to redistribute the users in the new hash table (of size $n'_A = \alpha' \cdot k_A$), with a computational cost of $O(N'_A)$. SN has to notify to all the users of the domain the updated parameters of the ring schema (i.e., N'_A and α') and the new ring configurations. No computation overhead is required user-side.

Even though the worst case for leaves triggers a server-side (albeit linear, in the number of users) computational overhead, we can argue that, in real-life cases, communities tend to grow, or, at worst, joins and leaves balance. Therefore, with proper "safety margins" applied to the set value of α, the above worst case happens very rarely. Observe that, also the growth of the number of users might trigger the resizing of the hash table even though this is not necessary for the correctness of the ring schema. Indeed, it could be opportune not to have rings with an actual privacy level much higher than the required value. Also these aspects will be deepened as a future work, but do not seem to represent an actual drawback of the solution.

Finally, concerning system updates, one could think that drastic changes of the system not corresponding to changes of the communication characteristics can enable classical intersection attacks, thus breaking anonymity. However, this is not the case, because we only consider short communications, whose lifetime is certainly much less than the lifetime of the substantial ring structure.

4.4 Cover-Message Mechanism

At this point, we introduce the cover-message mechanism mentioned earlier which is at the basis of the anonymity service provided by our solution.

Consider a ring $\{v_0, \ldots v_{k_A-1}\}$. With a certain rationale, we choose r users belonging to the nodes of the rings responsible for maintaining the circulation of dummy messages called *tokens*. r is the value that determines the k_A-anonymity threshold (i.e., $k_A \cdot r$). Therefore, it is sufficiently guaranteed that at least one responsible user is alive. Now, we define how the token is built. It is a fixed-length message with three fields: $\langle C_M, C_D, B \rangle$, where C_M is a ciphertext (including either a dummy message or the intended message), and C_D is a ciphertext too, (including either SN or a destination user/node). B is a bit indicating if the token is empty ($B = 0$) or filled ($B = 1$). The exact meaning of the above fields will be clarified with the description of the communication primitives below. Every token turns in the ring in which it was born hop by hop by crossing, for each node, any alive user associated with this node. This is done according to the increasing value of the corresponding SIs. To formally describe the above mechanism, we need the following definition, introducing the notion of *next* alive user for a given user in a ring.

Definition 4. *Given a node v of a ring with at least an alive user, we denote by $first(v)$ the lowest SI associated with v and by $last(v)$ the highest SI associated with v. The closeness between two alive users with SIs x and y belonging to a ring (denoted by $closeness_A(x, y)$), is recursively defined as follows:*

- $closeness_A(x, y) = 0$, if $x = y$;
- $closeness_A(x, y) = |\{z \in ID_A \mid z \neq x \text{ is alive}, h(z) = h(x), x \leq z \leq y\}|$, if $h(x) = h(y)$ and $x < y$;
- $closeness_A(x, y) = closeness_A(x, last(h(x))) + closeness_A(first(h(y)), y) + j \cdot (N_A - 1)$ for the least $j > 0$ such that $f_A^j(h(x)) = h(y)$, otherwise.

We define the function $next_A : ID_A \rightarrow ID_A$ as follows. For any x alive, $next_A(x)$ is the user (alive) with SI $y \neq x$ of the ring such that the closeness between x and y is minimum.

In words, the next user of a user with SI x is the first alive user that is encountered by moving first in the node of the ring $h(x)$ in the direction of increasing SIs, and then (if there is no alive user in $h(x)$ with SI higher than x) to the closest node according to the function f_A with alive users and, therein, by taking the user with lowest SI.

According to Definition 4, the token is sent by an alive user x that received it to the user $next_A(x)$, and proceeds in the ring with the same rule. Therefore, it is not said that the token moves from the node v_i to the next node $f_A(v_i)$, because a jump is possible (in the case no alive user is present in the node $f_A(v_i)$).

At each hop, the token is encrypted with IBE under the identity of the next node so that an external eavesdropper cannot distinguish an empty token from a filled token. For efficiency reasons, the token is encrypted with a symmetric on-the-fly key which is, in turn, encrypted with IBE and sent along with the token. When a node receives the token, first it decrypts (by using IBE) the symmetric key and then the token. For the sake of presentation, when we refer to IBE encryption, we mean the above procedure.

In Fig. 1b, an example of fragment of a route followed by a token is depicted. In the figure, we highlight only 4 nodes of a ring, each composed of 3 users (in general, this number could vary among nodes). Green circles represent alive users, while red circles denote non-alive users. The token turns in the ring according to the function $next$ of Definition 4.

SN publishes a cross-domain random $R \in \mathbb{N}^+$, with a certain rounding protocol obtained as PRNG verifiable by the users. R, implicitly identifies a user per ring, called $bridge\ user$, as follows. To identify the bridge user of her/his ring, a user with SI x has to find the alive user with the lowest SI belonging to the node $f_A^j(y)$, such that $j \geq 0$ is the least value such that at least an alive user is in $f_A^j(y)$ and $y = ring(h(x)) + R \cdot \alpha \bmod n_A$. Observe that all the nodes of a ring identify the same bridge user. The bridge node is responsible for sending the messages outside the ring (playing the role of $exit\ user$) or to inject into the ring the messages coming from outside (playing the role of $entry\ user$).

4.5   Communication Primitives

In this section, we define the communication primitives supporting anonymity against the adversary (as we will see in Sect. 7, it is SN) and utilizable to build privacy-preserving applications. We have three primitives, defined as follows.

P1: Anonymous Sending to Explicit Recipient. It consists in a communication of a message M starting from an SN user U towards a given destination D (possibly SN) requiring that the sender U is anonymous and the recipient is explicit.

U belongs to the node $h(U)$ of a ring. U knows the current bridge user X. In this case, X plays the role of exit user. Then, U waits for the earliest empty token of the ring (recall that any user, when receives a token, to decide if forwarding or processing it, has to decrypt it because the token is encrypted with its identity) and fills it by setting its fields $\langle C_M, C_D, B \rangle$ as follows: C_M=Encrypt(MPK, D, M) (i.e., the IBE encryption with the identity D of the message M), C_D=Encrypt(MPK, X, D) (i.e., the IBE encryption with the identity X of the destination D), $B = 1$ (that represents the fact that the token is filled). Recall that MPK is the master public key of the IBE scheme. We denote by T the so obtained token. Now, U encrypts the filled token T with the identity of the user $Z = next_A(U)$. Then the token is sent to Z. The token turns in the ring until the node X which is the only user able to decrypt C_D, thus obtaining D. If D is a node, then X identifies (with the collaboration of SN to know the alive SIs) the bridge user Y of the ring of D and sends C_M to Y. Otherwise (i.e., D is either a user or SN), X sends C_M to D. Then, it sets B to 0 and forwards the token in the ring to $next_A(X)$.

P2: Anonymous Response by Explicit Recipient. It consists in a communication from an explicit entity belonging to SN (possibly SN itself) to a user U in response to an anonymous sending initiated by U. This primitive requires that the recipient U remains anonymous.

Since this primitive works in response to an anonymous sending, we can refer to the bridge user from which such a communication directly arrived, say X. The explicit entity starting this primitive just has to send the message to X. This response is actually directed to a user of the ring which X belongs and could be encrypted with an on-the-fly key contained in the original message. Anyway, X injects the response in the ring just by waiting for the earliest empty token and filling it with the response. In this case, C_M contains the response, $B = 1$, and C_D remains undefined. Then, the filled token turns in the ring until a user U is able to decrypt C_M. This is the actual recipient of the response. It does not empty the token and just forwards it. This operation is done by X when the token reaches it again by setting B to 0 and by further forwarding it in the ring.

P3: Anonymous Sending to Anonymous Recipient. It consists in a communication of a message M starting from an SN user with SI U towards a given destination user with SI D requiring that both U and D are anonymous.

The primitive invokes first Primitive **P1** with message M'= Encrypt (MPK, D, M), directed as explicit recipient to $Z = f_A^j$ ($h(D)$) for some random j between 0 and $k_A - 1$. Observe that U can encrypt to D without prior asking SN for any information thanks to IBE. Then, when the bridge user of the ring of Z receives this message, it injects the message in the ring as in Primitive **P2**, thus eventually reaching the actual destination D. Observe that a possible reply of D to the message M sent by U can be done by using the same primitive.

5   Comparison with the Existing Approaches

As mentioned in the introduction, there are two possible approaches in the literature that can be used to obtain communication anonymity against the global passive adversary: buses and mixnets.

Buses obtain anonymity by implementing routes (either deterministically [1, 9] or non-deterministically [27]) independent of the intended communication, which senders and receivers can opportunistically exploit.

In deterministic buses [1,9], the route is an Eulerian path, thus a path involving all the nodes of the network. This leads to huge latency times in case of social networks, as the number of nodes of an application domain is potentially huge. It is worth noting that, for a given application domain, for those cases in which primitive **P3** (i.e., anonymous sender to anonymous receiver) is enabled, deterministic buses require to include in the route all possible senders and receivers, therefore all the users of the domain. Consider that, given an application domain $\langle ID_A, N_A, k_A, r_A \rangle$, for our method, the latency time is $\Omega(k_A)$, while for deterministic buses it is $\Omega(N_A)$. In real-life applications, we expect that $N_A \gg k_A$. Coherently with the experiments shown in Sect. 6, any P2P emulation over social networks requires that each anonymous hop between two users is implemented by locally encrypting the message, sending it to the central social network, and then sending it again to the next user. It is easy to see that one hop takes a time of magnitude of 10^{-1} seconds. Therefore, for a realistic domain of 10^4 users, the latency time for a given message communication is 10^3 seconds, which is not suitable for the considered applications (e.g., proximity testing). However, we obtain a very high privacy level, that is 10^4 (in the sense that the adversary identifies the sender or the recipient with probability 10^{-4}. In contrast, with our technique, we can modulate the privacy protection to the still reasonable value of 10^3 to obtain a communication latency of magnitude 10^2 seconds. For a privacy level of order 10^2, we have latency times of magnitude 10^1 (which corresponds to the results obtained in Sect. 6).

Consider now non-deterministic buses [27]. This technique leads to very high latency times, as analytically highlighted in the paper itself. Indeed, the delivery time follows an equation of the form $\frac{K_1}{\left(1 - \left(\frac{n-2}{n-1}\right)^{K_2}\right)}$, where K_1 and K_2 are suitable constants and n is the number of nodes of the network, meaning that, for large values of n, we have huge latency time. Indeed, the simulation conducted in [27], which does not take into account the emulation over social networks, in a network with only 2048 nodes (and thus a maximum privacy level of magnitude 10^3) produces average latency time of 20 min. If we overlay the protocol over the social network layer, then this time (roughly) doubles because, as observed earlier a 1-hop P2P message exchange corresponds to 2 point-to-point message exchange (i.e., from sender to server and from server to recipient).

Consider now mixnets. For mixnets, we adopt a simplified yet general model extracted from [8], in which bi-directional cover traffic over any link of the overlay network is enabled (this is necessary to hide communications against the global passive adversary). The idea is to obtain the anonymity set by mixing the traffic

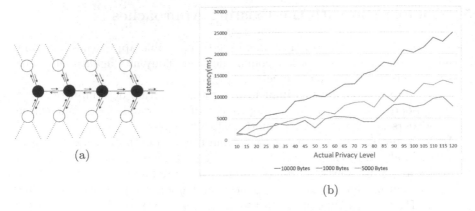

Fig. 2. (a) Mixnet with $n = 4$ and $m = 2$; (b) Latency of Onion-ring vs actual privacy level.

at each hop of the communication and by hiding the real traffic inside cover traffic. This fan-out mechanism allows us to obtain that the cardinality of the anonymity set increases exponentially with the length of the communication path. In Fig. 2a, we represent a simple mixnet with a degree mixing 2 (i.e., the messages of 2 senders are mixed into a receiver at each step). This way, for a communication path of length l, the anonymity set resulting from the knowledge of a given receiver, has cardinality 2^l. However, to obtain this level of uncertainty, as clearly stated in [8], bi-directional cover traffic should be injected, over all the links of the network. For simplicity, we assume that cover traffic is injected at constant rate so that the amount of traffic can be represented just by the number of links in which it is injected. Let denote by m the mixing degree and by n the number of nodes participating in the mixnet. Note that, to achieve the exponential grow of anonymity degree with the number of hops mentioned before, we require that the mixing involves always new nodes, as depicted in Fig. 2a.

Hence, the number of links allowing us to protect the communication among n nodes is $(m + 1) \cdot n$ as the degree of each node is $m + 1$ and the last node (for example, in Fig. 2a, the total number of links is $12 = 4 \cdot 3$, where $n = 4$ and $m = 2$ and the degree of each node is 3). As cover traffic is bi-directional, the estimation of the total amount of cover traffic is $2 \cdot (m + 1) \cdot n$. This means that the minimum required cover traffic is $6 \cdot n$, as, to enable the fan-out mechanism, $m \geq 2$ should hold.

Consider now our technique. Suppose we have n alive nodes. They are partitioned, in average, among $\frac{n}{k}$ rings each of size k. In other words, k represents the average number of alive users in each ring. Accordingly to the Liveness Assumption, $k \geq k_A$. We refer to k as the *actual privacy level*.

In our approach, cover traffic corresponds just to tokens 1-directionally turning in the rings. Therefore, the number of links is just n which also represents the total amount of cover traffic. Moreover, at least (when m is fixed to the minimum value) we reduce cover traffic of a multiplicative factor equal to 6.

Consider that, about communication latency, we can say that, to achieve the same actual privacy level k in the mixnet, we have to set $l = log_m k$. So, the mixnet technique used should adopt fixed-length tunnels like in [8,21]. Therefore, for equal actual privacy level k, we have a communication path of length k in our case and length $log_m k$ if the mixnet model is adopted. Thus, the advantage we obtain in terms of reduction of cover traffic results in a price in terms of communication latency. However, as mentioned before, this is not critical for our application domains as well highlighted in Sect. 6, in which communication times are evaluated.

6   Experiments

Through this section, we conduct an experimental validation of our approach regarding communication latency, by using the popular social network Twitter. In our analysis, we measured the time elapsed between the sending of message by a user and the reception by another user. To do this, we developed a JAVA application that receives the tokens from the users, decrypts, re-encrypts, and sends them to another user. Therefore, our measurements take into account all the aspects involved in our protocol (including IBE and Symmetric encryption). We implemented the exchange of tokens between users through the exchange of *Direct Messages* on Twitter. Each user receives a Direct Message that contains the token (encoded in Base64), decrypts, and re-encrypts it. Then, the token is sent (encoded in Base64) to another user. To send Direct Messages, we used the library Twitter4j. We applied the IBE scheme [7] and AES-128 for symmetric encryption. To automatically trigger the decrypt/re-encrypt/sending process, we rely on the Twitter Account Activity APIs. These webhook-based APIs send a notification message, each time an event occurs, to a web application we have developed. In our setting, the event is the reception of a Direct Message. To receive webhook events, we need to register a public URL of our web application. As suggested by the Twitter Documentation, to test locally our application, we can use *ngrok* that allows us to create a https tunnel (required by the Twitter Account Activity) and redirects every request to the local port where our web application is running. This inter-mediation would be not necessary in a real-life implementation of our protocol. Therefore, we measured the delay introduced by ngrok and subtract it by the total time. The results of our experiment are reported in Figs. 2b, and 3a.

In Fig. 2b the communication latency vs the actual privacy level is reported. The relationship is almost linear and this confirms the results of Sect. 5. We show three plots for different sizes of the token. We can see that, for actual privacy level $k = 100$, the delays are of 8 seconds for tokens of 1000 bytes and of 20 seconds for tokens of 10000 bytes. These communication-latency times appear compliant with the envisaged applications.

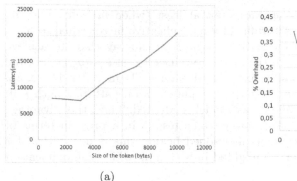
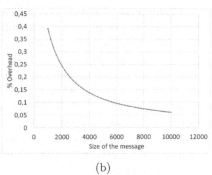

(a)   (b)

Fig. 3. (a) Latency vs Token Size with actual privacy level equals to 100; (b) Overhead percentage vs size of the message.

The plot in Fig. 3a shows as the latency varies as the size of the token varies with an actual privacy level $k = 100$. After an initial plateau caused by a threshold effect, the grow is nearly linear. Finally, the last analysis we conducted regards the overhead introduced by the encryption schemes adopted. We denote by m the size in bytes of the message to be sent. We recall that the structure of the token is $\langle C_M, C_D, B \rangle$. C_M is obtained first by applying AES128 on m by using a random on-the-fly key of 16 bytes. As well-know, the overhead introduced by AES128 is the padding of the last block, therefore, in the worst case, it is 16 bytes. Finally, the on-the-fly key is encrypted by using the anonymous IBE scheme. To encrypt a 16 bytes key, the adopted IBE scheme produces a ciphertext of 192 bytes. Therefore, the total size of C_M is $m + 16 + 192$ bytes. With a similar reasoning, we can realize that the size of C_D is $d + 16 + 192$, where d is the size of the destination address. We assume $d = 16$ bytes (it is enough to represent 2^{128} addresses). Finally, the token has to be further encrypted for the next node. The total size will be $m + 640$ bytes. In Fig. 3b, we report the overhead percentage vs the size of the message.

7   Security Analysis

In this section, we sketch a security analysis of our solution. We start by defining the threat model **TM**. We introduce the following three assumptions:

A1: Application domains are formed in such a way that the background knowledge does not allow the adversary to have more information than sender/recipient uniform distribution.

A2: The token has a fixed length so that, thanks to the IBE scheme, only on the basis of the content, it is not possible to distinguish an empty from a filled token.

A3: We assume that in each ring there are at least k_A users alive.

Observe that Assumption **A1** is intrinsically coherent with the concept of application domain itself, in the sense that users of the domain are someway homogeneous with respect to the interest in the delivered services.

Note that **A3** is sufficiently guaranteed if the liveness assumption holds and the number of users in any ring is not below the k_A-anonymity threshold (see Sect. 4.2).

Adversary Model. We consider the case of a global passive adversary able to monitor the flow of all the messages exchanged in the social network. Realistically, the adversary can be only SN itself.

According to the adversary model above, in which the users are not possible adversaries, we can observe that the anonymity of the adopted IBE has not a role, since any message encrypted by IBE is further encrypted hop-by-hop, so that the identity of the recipient cannot be accessed by the adversary even in case of a non-anonymous IBE. However, the adoption of an anonymous IBE just avoids the unnecessary leakage of information against the users of the social networks collaborating in a given communication. Concerning the significance of the adversary model, we stress the fact that, in real-life, the most serious threat is not the curiosity of some buddies, but the possible massive surveillance and misuse of personal sensitive information from the side of the social network provider.

Security Properties. We study the security properties *sender anonymity (SA)* and *recipient anonymity (RA)*, as defined in Sect. 3. Observe that if one of them is satisfied, then also *relationship anonymity* holds. The above security properties are guaranteed if the adversary is able to identify the protected item (sender or recipient) with probability not higher than $\frac{1}{k_A}$.

Theorem 1. *The security properties **SA** and **RA** hold in the threat model **TM**.*

Proof. The only point of the ring from which the adversary can draw some information more than the random guess to identify senders or recipients, is the bridge user, say it X. Indeed, this is the only point of the ring in which the possible transition empty/filled or filled/empty of a token could be in principle related to the observable incoming or outcoming traffic in/from the bridge. Transitions occurring in other points are not identifiable, due to the Assumptions, with probability higher than $\frac{1}{k_A}$. Therefore, we have to consider the following two cases (they are the only cases potentially helpful for the adversary). Either (1) the adversary observes incoming traffic in X (i.e., X could play the role of entry user), or (2) the adversary observes outcoming traffic from X (i.e., X plays the role of exit user). In case (1), two alternatives are possible. Either (1).a is the case in which X actually injects a token in the ring inserting the message coming from outside, or (1).b X empties a token circulating in the ring as a final step of Primitive **P2** or **P3**, and then X cannot process the incoming traffic. In the case (1).a, the adversary can infer that a recipient exists for this token. The only way to draw more information about this recipient is to follow the token and to observe it when it reaches the bridge. At this point, the adversary can detect a transition filled/empty in X, but this does not give any additional information about where the message has been received. Therefore, due to the Assumptions, the adversary cannot identify the recipient with probability higher than $\frac{1}{k_A}$. Consider now case (1).b. The adversary knows that the token injected by X is empty. Two cases may hold. Either (1).b.1 the token, after a turn, reaches X still empty, or (1).b.2 the token, after a turn, reaches X filled. The adversary may detect which of the above cases ((1).b.1 or (1).b.2) holds, just by observing if outcoming traffic arises from the arrival of the token (i.e., X, after the turn, plays the role of exit user). In the positive case, we are in case (1).b.2, otherwise we are in case (1).b.1. In the latter case, neither senders nor recipients have been involved in this turn. In case (1).b.2, a sender filled the token somewhere in the turn. But, due to the Assumptions, the adversary cannot identify the sender with probability higher than $\frac{1}{k_A}$.

In case (2) (i.e., X plays the role of exit user), the adversary can infer that the token injected by X into the ring is empty. Two cases may hold. Either (2).a the token, after a turn, reaches X still empty, or (2).b the token, after a turn, reaches X filled. The adversary may detect which of the above cases ((2).a or (2).b) holds, just by observing if outcoming traffic arises from the arrival of the token (i.e., X, after the turn, plays again the role of exit user). In the positive case, we are in case (2).b, otherwise we are in case (2).a. In the latter case, neither senders nor recipients have been involved in this turn. In case (2).b, a sender filled the token somewhere in the turn. But, due to the Assumptions, the adversary cannot identify the sender with probability higher than $\frac{1}{k_A}$. The proof is then concluded.

8   Discussion and Conclusions

The main conclusion we can draw from this paper is that when considering the problem of anonymous communication in the social network setting in a specific yet meaningful application domain (i.e., short-communication applications), it is possible to obtain a better result than simply miming any existing anonymous P2P overlay routing protocol. To avoid possible misunderstanding, it is worth noting that the choice of the social-network setting is not opportunistic or orthogonal to our study. It is done because social networks collect all the conditions that are the basis for our protocol (therefore, our protocol can be applied to any setting with similar features). Specifically:

(1) Social networks can be the domain in which the considered applications requiring short-communication anonymity are implemented. It is not evident that this kind of applications might occur in other contexts as they require that users are pre-registered in the system and that fake identities are prevented. Indeed, the social network provider or the party providing the service (if different) can require a secure initial digital identity verification. In other words, the membership of users to a social network could be an effective way to control the subscription to an application domain to avoid fake profiles and Sybil attacks.

(2) The global-passive-adversary threat model is realistic because of the power of the social network provider in existing centralized social networks; this is not the case for generic networks or P2P systems.

(3) Our protocol requires some central management functions, which can be executed by the social network provider. A realistic business model could exist because the users participate in the protocol to obtain privacy and the social network could become a provider of *anonymity as a service* with privacy guarantees and other correlated features, thus attracting larger market segments. Note that the participation of a user in the system has a price in terms of bandwidth and CPU. But this happens also in every P2P or collaborative approach, thus it is not per se a drawback of our solution.

As a future work, we plan to better address the construction of application domains. This is indeed a non-trivial task that we could not treat together with the definition of the anonymous communication protocol (which is the aim of this paper). Indeed, a deep analysis of this aspect, requires the exact definition of the considered use cases, and for each of them, the strategy we have to follow to guarantee that Assumption **A1** stated in Sect. 7 is verified. Another direction of our future research is the full implementation of the system in a "homemade" social network to give a proof-of-concept.

Acknowledgement. This paper is partially supported by Project POR FESR/FSE 14/20 Line A (Action 10.5.6) and Line B (Action 10.5.12).

References

1. Beimel, A., Dolev, S.: Buses for anonymous message delivery. J. Cryptology **16**(1), 25–39 (2003)
2. Bennett, K., Grothoff, C.: GAP – practical anonymous networking. In: Dingledine, R. (ed.) PET 2003. LNCS, vol. 2760, pp. 141–160. Springer, Heidelberg (2003). https://doi.org/10.1007/978-3-540-40956-4_10
3. Brakerski, Z., Lombardi, A., Segev, G., Vaikuntanathan, V.: Anonymous IBE, leakage resilience and circular security from new assumptions. In: Nielsen, J.B., Rijmen, V. (eds.) EUROCRYPT 2018. LNCS, vol. 10820, pp. 535–564. Springer, Cham (2018). https://doi.org/10.1007/978-3-319-78381-9_20
4. Chaum, D.L.: Untraceable electronic mail, return addresses, and digital pseudonyms. Commun. ACM **24**(2), 84–90 (1981)
5. Chen, C., Asoni, D.E., Perrig, A., Barrera, D., Danezis, G., Troncoso, C.: Taranet: traffic-analysis resistant anonymity at the network layer. In: 2018 IEEE European Symposium on Security and Privacy (EuroS&P), pp. 137–152. IEEE (2018)
6. Danezis, G., Diaz, C.: A survey of anonymous communication channels. Tech. rep., Technical Report MSR-TR-2008-35, Microsoft Research (2008)
7. De Caro, A., Iovino, V., Persiano, G.: Fully secure anonymous HIBE and secret-key anonymous IBE with short ciphertexts. In: Joye, M., Miyaji, A., Otsuka, A. (eds.) Pairing 2010. LNCS, vol. 6487, pp. 347–366. Springer, Heidelberg (2010). https://doi.org/10.1007/978-3-642-17455-1_22

8. Freedman, M.J., Morris, R.: Tarzan: a peer-to-peer anonymizing network layer. In: Proceedings of the 9th ACM Conference on Computer and Communications Security, pp. 193–206 (2002)

9. Hirt, A., Jacobson, M., Williamson, C.: Taxis: scalable strong anonymous communication. In: 2008 IEEE International Symposium on Modeling, Analysis and Simulation of Computers and Telecommunication Systems, pp. 1–10. IEEE (2008)

10. Kacimi, M., Ortolani, S., Crispo, B.: Anonymous opinion exchange over untrusted social networks. In: Proceedings of the Second ACM EuroSys Workshop on Social Network Systems, pp. 26–32 (2009)

11. Kotzanikolaou, P., Chatzisofroniou, G., Burmester, M.: Broadcast anonymous routing (bar): scalable real-time anonymous communication. Int. J. Inf. Secur. 16(3), 313–326 (2017)

12. Le Blond, S., Choffnes, D., Zhou, W., Druschel, P., Ballani, H., Francis, P.: Towards efficient traffic-analysis resistant anonymity networks. ACM SIGCOMM Comput. Commun. Rev. 43(4), 303–314 (2013)

13. Li, N., Li, T., Venkatasubramanian, S.: t-closeness: privacy beyond k-anonymity and l-diversity. In: 2007 IEEE 23rd International Conference on Data Engineering, pp. 106–115. IEEE (2007)

14. Machanavajjhala, A., Kifer, D., Gehrke, J., Venkitasubramaniam, M.: l-diversity: privacy beyond k-anonymity. ACM Trans. Knowl. Discovery Data (TKDD) 1(1), 3-es (2007)

15. Mislove, A., Oberoi, G., Post, A., Reis, C., Druschel, P., Wallach, D.S.: Ap3: cooperative, decentralized anonymous communication. In: Proceedings of the 11th Workshop on ACM SIGOPS European Workshop, pp. 30-es (2004)

16. Nosouhi, M.R., Yu, S., Sood, K., Grobler, M.: Hsdc-net: secure anonymous messaging in online social networks. In: 2019 18th IEEE International Conference On Trust, Security And Privacy In Computing and Communications/13th IEEE International Conference On Big Data Science And Engineering (TrustCom/BigDataSE), pp. 350–357. IEEE (2019)

17. Pfitzmann, A., Hansen, M.: A terminology for talking about privacy by data minimization: anonymity, unlinkability, undetectability, unobservability, pseudonymity, and identity management (2010)

18. Recordon, D., Reed, D.: Openid 2.0: a platform for user-centric identity management. In: Proceedings of the Second ACM Workshop on Digital Identity Management, pp. 11–16 (2006)

19. Reed, M.G., Syverson, P.F., Goldschlag, D.M.: Anonymous connections and onion routing. IEEE J. Sel. Areas Commun. 16(4), 482–494 (1998)

20. Reiter, M.K., Rubin, A.D.: Crowds: anonymity for web transactions. ACM Trans. Inf. Syst. Secur. (TISSEC) 1(1), 66–92 (1998)

21. Rennhard, M., Plattner, B.: Practical anonymity for the masses with MorphMix. In: Juels, A. (ed.) FC 2004. LNCS, vol. 3110, pp. 233–250. Springer, Heidelberg (2004). https://doi.org/10.1007/978-3-540-27809-2_24

22. Shirazi, F., Simeonovski, M., Asghar, M.R., Backes, M., Diaz, C.: A survey on routing in anonymous communication protocols. ACM Comput. Surv. (CSUR) 51(3), 1–39 (2018)

23. Von Ahn, L., Bortz, A., Hopper, N.J.: K-anonymous message transmission. In: Proceedings of the 10th ACM Conference on Computer and Communications Security, pp. 122–130 (2003)

24. Wang, G., Wang, B., Wang, T., Nika, A., Zheng, H., Zhao, B.Y.: Whispers in the dark: analysis of an anonymous social network. In: Proceedings of the 2014 Conference on Internet Measurement Conference, pp. 137–150 (2014)

25. Wang, Q., Borisov, N.: Octopus: a secure and anonymous dht lookup. In: 2012 IEEE 32nd International Conference on Distributed Computing Systems, pp. 325–334 (2012)

26. Wang, W., Motani, M., Srinivasan, V.: Dependent link padding algorithms for low latency anonymity systems. In: Proceedings of the 15th ACM Conference on Computer and Communications Security, pp. 323–332 (2008)

27. Young, A.L., Yung, M.: The drunk motorcyclist protocol for anonymous communication. In: 2014 IEEE Conference on Communications and Network Security, pp. 157–165. IEEE (2014)

A Sybil Detection Method in OSN Based on DistilBERT and Double-SN-LSTM for Text Analysis

Xiaojie Xu[1], Jian Dong[2], Zhengyu Liu[1], Jin Yang[1(✉)], Bin Wang[3], and Zhaoyuan Wang[3]

[1] School of Cyber Science and Engineering, Sichuan University, Chengdu 610065, China
yangjin66@scu.edu.cn
[2] Third Research Institute of Ministry of Public Security, Shanghai 200031, China
[3] School of Information Science and Technology, Southwest Jiaotong University,
Chengdu, China

Abstract. Sybil attacks are increasingly rampant in online social networks (OSNs); thus, Sybil detection is one of the key issues in OSN security research. Sybils in OSNs are often used by attackers for public opinion intervention, topic flow filling, and dissemination of false and malicious messages. Therefore, if the credibility of the Sybil can be analyzed, then the harm of Sybil attacks can be prevented to a certain extent. Based on the analysis of existing Sybil detection research, this paper proposes an end-to-end Sybil detection model based on the Bidirectional Encoder Representations from Transformers (BERT) model that analyzes tweet text content. Considering the problems of the existing datasets, we built a dataset for text content analysis of tweets based on the hot political topic of the 2020 US presidential election. Accordingly, this study used a distilled version of BERT, DistilBERT, as the sentence embedding model, and the double self-normalizing long short-term memory (Double-SN-LSTM) recurrent neural network model as the classification detection model. The final experimental effect was greatly improved compared with the existing analysis methods, and it had a better detection effect for the more concealed Sybils.

Keywords: Sybil Attack · DistilBERT · Double-SN-LSTM

1 Introduction

A Sybil attack was originally used to describe a form of attack that acts on a peer-to-peer network (P2P), for example, when an attacker uses a single node in a P2P network to forge multiple identities, weaken network redundancy, reduce network robustness, and interfere with normal activities. Over time, Sybil attacks have also been targeted to the Tor network, Internet of Things (IoT), and Online Social Network (OSN). This paper focuses on Sybil attacks in OSNs, which specifically refers to the attacker using a few nodes in the social network to control multiple false identities, thereby using these identities to control or affect many normal nodes.

© ICST Institute for Computer Sciences, Social Informatics and Telecommunications Engineering 2021
Published by Springer Nature Switzerland AG 2021. All Rights Reserved
J. Garcia-Alfaro et al. (Eds.): SecureComm 2021, LNICST 399, pp. 64–76, 2021.
https://doi.org/10.1007/978-3-030-90022-9_4

We use the method of detecting Sybils in the OSN to reduce the harm of Sybil attacks. The research object is the current popular online social media network, Twitter. Among the existing content-based Sybil detection methods, the most popular is the classification method of machine learning (ML), and its research focuses on feature engineering. The purpose of feature engineering is to construct effective features, that is, to collect and optimize multi-dimensional features from user profiles and user social graph structures to characterize each user. To improve the performance of the classifier, feature extraction requires not only professional experience to extract high-quality features but also manual determination of the contribution of the selected features. Moreover, attackers have proposed a series of bypass strategies based on existing feature engineering perspectives so that such Sybils often have personal information that is very similar to real accounts, such as avatars, a self-introduction, location, and established social network relationships. Overall, the existing content-based methods largely rely on manual intervention, and it is difficult for them to deal with highly disguised Sybils, which results in increased classification errors and high manual consumption.

In response to the above problems, this paper proposes an end-to-end classification model based on the analysis of user-published content for Sybil detection in OSNs. The proposed model can automatically extract features and learn directly from the original input. In other words, the proposed model greatly saves the workload of manual design, selection, and verification of features. Furthermore, judgments are only made based on the contents posted by users, and it achieves or even exceeds the classification accuracy of existing related research with less input, which allows it to better avoid the elaborate disguises of attackers.

The main contributions can be summarized as follows:

(1) We propose an end-to-end classification and detection model based on the content posted by users. This method avoids the highly user-friendly features of carefully forged Sybils, which not only improves the classification accuracy but also reduces unnecessary expenses.

(2) The proposed analysis model uses the Bidirectional Encoder Representations from Transformers (BERT) model that has outstanding performance in natural language processing (NLP) tasks for text analysis. At the same time, it considers the timeliness of BERT and compares and chooses its optimized distilled version of BERT, called the DistilBERT pre-training model. Moreover, to fully consider time features, the time-series association between each text content is extracted through the two-layer long short-term memory (LSTM) recurrent neural network (RNN) model, which was proven to be effective.

(3) Based on tweets regarding the 2020 US presidential election, we constructed a dataset with real accounts and Sybil tags. This dataset contains 222,802 tweets related to Biden or Trump during the election of the US president from October 15, 2020, to November 3, 2020, in which there are 949 real accounts and 987 Sybils. The dataset has now been published in the GitHub open-source warehouse, and it can be used by relevant researchers for further analysis and research.

The remainder of this paper is organized as follows: Section 2 introduces the related work, Section 3 describes the proposed system, Section 4 provides the experimental results, and finally, Section 5 gives a conclusion.

2 Related Work

The detection of Sybils is dynamic and iteratively updated. In this section, we will introduce structure-based methods and content-based detection methods.

2.1 Structure-based Inspection Method

Structure-based detection methods mainly refer to the structure based on the social network graph. These methods distinguish Sybil from human accounts by analyzing the edges and nodes of the social network graph. Yu et al. [1] proposed a decentralized protocol, SybilGuard, to use random routing to identify Sybil nodes and limit the impact of Sybil attacks. Based on SybilGuard, Yu et al. [2] proposed a decentralized protocol SybilLimit with the same idea as SybilGuard, but they applied a different random walk-based method. Danezis and Mittal [3] proposed a centralized Sybil detection algorithm, which calculates the probability of a Sybil by using a Bayesian algorithm. A new method that relies on the basic properties of social network graphs and ranks nodes according to the possibility of Sybil attacks perceived by users was proposed by Cao et al. [4]. Another study [5] mentioned that Sybils can be further detected by removing the edges of the Sybil attacks that have been perceived by the users. Compared with Cao et al.'s method [4], it achieves better detection accuracy. Wei et al. proposed a mechanism based on network topology and random walk to defend against Sybil attacks in large OSNs.

Yang et al. [6] proposed a system that further utilizes user interaction information. They use a trust-based voting distribution and global voting aggregation to evaluate whether a user is a Sybil. It is worth mentioning that the system performs better than many existing ranking systems in the actual OSN environment. To reduce the complexity of running time and reduce the dependence on known trusted nodes, Misra et al. [7] proposed a Sybil community detection algorithm based on the obvious possibility of a Sybil account community.

Bansal et al. [9] modified the previous structure-based methods by using the trust value between each user. Its false positive rate was 14% less than the results in the studies by Yu et al. [1] and other researchers [8]. Wang et al. [10] used some of the advantages of confidence-based propagation and random walk-based methods to make them orders of magnitude more scalable than semi-supervised learning methods [11]. Zhang et al. [12] used a combination of three RW-based algorithms to utilize user activities and detect Sybils.

2.2 Content-Based Inspection Method

Content-based detection methods mainly use ML methods. Many researchers have focused on studying how to make better use of the multi-dimensional features of users in OSNs and then use ML classifiers for classification. Wang et al. [13] proposed a server-side clickstream model, which groups users whose clickstreams are close to each other into behavior clusters. However, when using an unbalanced training dataset, the experimental data shows that the false-positive rate (FPR) increases. Alsaleh et al. [14] established some classification models based on Twitter's user characteristics. They used four different ML algorithms: decision tree (C4.5), decision tree (random forest), support vector machine, and multilayer neural network. Kang et al. [15] combined the characteristics of different users and the reliability of the network structure and constructed a user discriminant formula to identify Sybils in OSNs, and the FPR fluctuated between 3.74% and 14.96%. Xia et al. [16] proposed a Sybil detection method based on the credibility of attribute information. They calculated the credibility of the user by using the Euclidean distance between the center of the Sybil attribute and users' attribute, and the degree is used as a key parameter to classify Sybils. Mulamba et al. [17] chose the ML models AdaBoost and KNN as the classifiers. Al-Qurishi [18] and others further used the user's characteristic information and deep neural network to establish a predictive model. This was the first time that deep learning methods were applied to the field of Sybil detection. Due to the rapid growth of OSNs, the traditional methods lack robustness, and Sybils can imitate human users to bypass detection. In this article, we try to build a hierarchical deep learning network structure to make better use of the user's text feature information and minimize Sybil detection error.

3   Methodology and System Design

The Sybil detection method proposed in this paper includes experimental data preprocessing, and end-to-end detection model classification. The detection model mainly includes two parts, as shown in Fig. 1. The first part is the sentence embedding module, which uses the pre-training model DistilBERT to extract the semantic features of each tweet text posted by the user. The second part is an RNN module, which uses LSTM to extract the inter-related features of multiple tweets posted by a single user to better capture the time period of the state of the user. Finally, it is input into the neuron whose activation function is sigmoid to give the correct judgment. This section will elaborate on each part of the process in detail.

3.1   Data Preprocessing

The number of tweets posted by each user in a period is unpredictable, and thus data preprocessing first needs to determine the maximum number of tweets of each user to build a text matrix. Then, the maximum length of each tweet must be determined. Due to Twitter's limitation on tweet length, the maximum length of the tweet was required to be 256 characters, and the part that exceeded the maximum number of characters was truncated. Furthermore, it was very important to normalize each tweet, that is, to replace all links in the tweets with a unified form of http://u, which helped the model ignore invalid content and optimize the classification effect of the model.

Then, the processing result was input into the tokenizer of DistilBERT for word segmentation and indexing. The tokenizer we chose was WordPiece, which uses Byte-Pair Encoding (BPE) to achieve more fine-grained segmentation. Specifically, in the

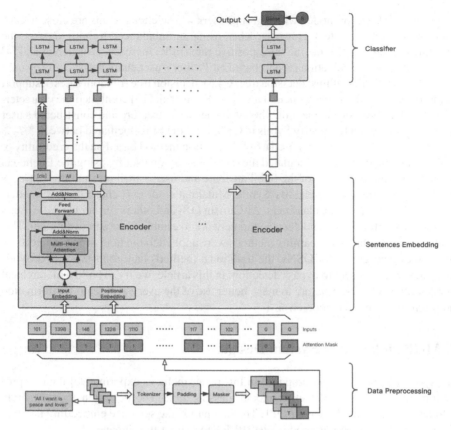

Fig. 1. Architecture of the proposed detection model.

processing of words with different suffixes only, this method divides words with different suffixes only into a collection of the word itself and different suffixes. This reduces the number of words in the vocabulary, thereby increasing the speed of subsequent processing. Indexing refers to replacing the word segmentation of the original sentence with the vocabulary index according to the input vocabulary. The sentence after word segmentation and indexing needs to be filled up to the maximum sentence length and the method used in this article fills in 0 at the end, and thus it is necessary to use Mask to distinguish between the filled part and the data part.

After data preprocessing, each user corresponded to a text matrix and a mask matrix with uniform dimensions. The dimensions of the matrix were the maximum number of tweets and the maximum length of each tweet. The matrix after data preprocessing was further used as the input of the next module for sentence embedding.

3.2 Sentence Embedding

Sentence embedding refers to the conversion of a fixed-length sentence expressed in the form of a word index value into a vector form with a fixed dimension. The embedded vector must well understand and extract the semantic features of the text, as the input of the classifier model helps the classifier model achieve better classification results.

This study used DistilBERT [21] as the sentence embedding model. The DistilBERT model uses **Knowledge Distillation** based on the BERT model to achieve a faster, lighter, and very similar model to the original model. Knowledge distillation can be understood as a method that enables a more lightweight and compact student model to learn a more massive and excellent teacher model. When BERT and DistilBERT are trained in the teacher-student structure, the DistilBERT model simulates the output distribution of BERT, and DistilBERT can learn most of the experience of the BERT model. The objective function of this process is as follows:

$$L = \alpha L_{\text{soft}} + \beta L_{\text{hard}} \tag{1}$$

Here, L_{soft} represents the cross-entropy of the SoftMax output of the student model and the teacher model at the same temperature. The formula is as follows:

$$L_{\text{soft}} = -\sum_{j}^{N} p_j^T \log q_j^T \tag{2}$$

Here, p_j^T and q_j^T respectively represent the output probability values of the teacher model and the student model to the i label at the temperature T.

$$p_j^T = \frac{\exp\left(\frac{v_i}{T}\right)}{\sum_k^N \exp\left(\frac{v_k}{T}\right)} \tag{3}$$

$$q_j^T = \frac{\exp\left(\frac{z_i}{T}\right)}{\sum_k^N \exp\left(\frac{z_k}{T}\right)} \tag{4}$$

Here, L_{hard} Indicates the cross-entropy between the SoftMax output of the Student model and the ground truth when the $T = 1$, and the formula is as follows:

$$L_{\text{hard}} = -\sum_{j}^{N} c_j \log q_j^1 \tag{5}$$

Experiments showed that the number of parameters of DistilBERT was 40% less than that of the BERT model, but it still retained 97% of the performance.

The preprocessed text and mask are used as the input of DistilBERT. After the forward propagation of DistilBERT, the first participle "[CLS]" output by the model is taken as the input of the classification layer. This is because "[CLS]" as the starting tag of the text does not correspond to any word in the text. In the encoder structure of the transformer, it performs self-attention with other words of the input text. In other words, the vector of the "[CLS]" position can be represented as a vector of global text. After the sentence embedding part, the input text matrix is transformed into a vector matrix and the dimensions of the matrix are the maximum number of texts and the sentence embedding dimension.

3.3 Double-Layer LSTM Recurrent Network

The LSTM model structure is shown in Fig. 2. Long short-term memory is carefully designed to solve the long-term dependency problem of an RNN. Its main improvement method based on RNN is to add gate control, including a forget gate, input gate, and output gate.

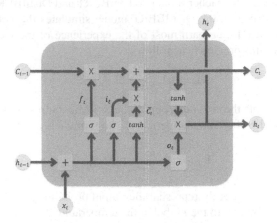

Fig. 2. Architecture of LSTM.

As shown in Fig. 2, the hidden state h_{t-1} at the last moment and the current input data x_t are activated by a sigmoid function to obtain an output f_t, which is the output of the forget gate. The output is a number between 0 and 1, where 1 represents complete retention, and 0 represents complete deletion, that is, the forget gate determines how much of the cell state C_{t-1} of the previous sequence is retained in the cell state C_t of the current sequence. The formula for the forget gate is given below.

$$f_t = \sigma\big(W_f * [h_{t-1}, x_t] + b_f\big) \qquad (6)$$

The input gate determines how much of the input data x_t of the current sequence is stored in the cell state C_t. It consists of two parts. The first part uses the sigmoid activation function to determine the retained value, and the output is i_t. The second part uses the tanh activation function, and the output is $\tilde{C}_t$. The formula for the input gate is given below.

$$i_t = \sigma\big(W_i * [h_{t-1}, x_t] + b_i\big) \qquad (7)$$

$$\tilde{C}_t = \tanh\big(W_C * [h_{t-1}, x_t] + b_C\big) \qquad (8)$$

Displayed equations are centered and set on a separate line. At this point, the state value C_t can be updated, and C_t is composed of the previous state C_{t-1} multiplied by f_t to indicate the forgotten part, and i_t is multiplied by $\tilde{C}_t$ to indicate the new state value.

The formula is given below.

$$C_t = C_{t-1} * f_t + i_t * \tilde{C}_t \tag{9}$$

Displayed equations are centered and set on a separate line. Finally, the output is obtained by multiplying the new state C_t after being activated by tanh with the output o_t of the sigmoid activation function. Here, the sigmoid activation function still determines the retained value, and the product indicates how much of the unit state of the current sequence affects the output value of the current sequence.

$$o_t = \sigma\left(W_o * \left[h_{t-1}, x_t\right] + b_o\right) \tag{10}$$

$$h_t = o_t * \tanh(C_t) \tag{11}$$

The double-layer LSTM RNN used in this model is shown in Fig. 1. The output of the last LSTM neuron in the network is sequentially input to the dropout layer, the fully connected layer, and a neuron whose activation function is sigmoid to output the classification result.

4 Experimental Result

In this section, we will elaborate and analyze the dataset construction, experimental preparation, evaluation indicators, and comparative experimental results.

4.1 Dataset Construction

The baseline dataset in this article was derived from Kaggle's public dataset ① **US Election 2020 Tweets dataset** [19] and ② **Political Tweets from Twitter Bots dataset** [20]. The public dataset ① provides a total of 1,727,003 tweets with Donald Trump and Joe Biden as relevant hashtags during the US general election from October 15, 2020, to November 3, 2020. The public dataset ② provides a total of 198,550 political-related tweets issued by robots during the US general election from October 19, 2020 to 2020.11.3.

To construct a positive sample, we manually selected 987 Sybils from public dataset ②. To construct a negative sample, considering that public dataset ① must include robots and Sybils, we first delete all the data of the users whose username matched the username of the robot and then deleted all the data of users who mentioned robots in the published tweets. Furthermore, the number of tweets published in this time period needed to exceed ten to meet experiment requirements. Finally, a total of 949 negative samples were obtained by manual screening.

It should also be noted that the text content in the positive sample and the negative sample was related to the political election, and the proportion of supporting or opposing a certain party in the positive sample and the negative sample was equal so that interference of the topic content can be excluded.

4.2 Experimental Preparation

In this experiment, we determined that the maximum number of texts per user was 50, and the maximum length of each tweet was 256 characters. For users with insufficient text number and text length, the number 0 was used to fill and mask. The number of neurons in the recurrent neural network was set to 256, the loss function was set to binary cross-entropy, and the optimizer was stochastic gradient descent (SGD). The batch size used during training was 32. The evaluation indicators of the model included confuse matrix, FPR, precision, recall, accuracy, and receiver operating characteristic curve (ROC_AUC). The version of the deep learning framework we chose was Tensor-Flow 2.4.0. The GPU used in the experiment is GeForce RTX2080Ti, the video memory size was 12 G, the CPU model selected is Intel(R) Core (TM) i3-9100F CPU @ 3.60 GHz, and the number of cores was 4.

4.3 Comparative Experimental Results

For the selection of classifiers, we chose common RNN models for comparative experiments, including SimpleRNN, Gated Recurrent Unit (GRU), LSTM, bi-directional long short-term memory (BiLSTM), double long short-term memory (Double-LSTM), and double self-normalizing long short-term memory (Double-SN-LSTM). The inputs of the above models were all the vectors after sentence embedding by DistilBERT. The evaluation indicators of the classifier included confusion matrix, false alarm rate, precision, recall rate, accuracy rate, and ROC_AUC. Through these indicators, the classification performance of the classifier on the problem can be comprehensively evaluated. After 70 epochs, the indicators of each classifier stabilized. The value of each evaluation index on the test set is shown in Table 1.

Table 1. Comparison of the results of the experiment.

Evaluating indicators	RNN	GRU	LSTM	Double-LSTM	BiLSTM	Double-SN-LSTM
FPR	0.0000	0.0000	0.0432	0.0000	0.0000	**0.0000**
Precision	1.0000	1.0000	0.9620	1.0000	1.0000	**1.0000**
Recall	0.9900	0.9901	1.0000	0.9753	0.9950	**0.9950**
Accuracy	0.9783	0.9951	0.9807	0.9711	0.9783	**0.9975**
ROC_AUC	0.9999	1.0000	1.0000	0.9999	0.9999	**1.0000**
Time(s)	**106**	308	438	690	895	681

From the experimental results, after sentence embedding through DistilBERT, the above recurrent neural network models learned the semantic features and mutual relations of sentences very well, and they gave correct judgments. Except for LSTM, each classifier performed extremely well in terms of accuracy and FPR, indicating that the classifier did not classify normal real users as malicious Sybils, which can provide an excellent experience in practical applications. After comparison, the SimpleRNN model had a great advantage in time efficiency due to its simple structure. However, in a comprehensive comparison, Double-SN-LSTM had better performance in various performance indicators.

The loss curve of each classifier on the training set and validation set is shown in Fig. 3. From the observation and analysis in Fig. 3 above, the loss curve of the Double-SN-LSTM model is smoother, and the loss value was lower after reaching the same epoch.

Considering the evaluation index curves of each classifier on the training set and validation set, the Double-SN-LSTM model had better stability in each evaluation index dimension, and the curves are shown in Fig. 4 and Fig. 5. Furthermore, it should be noted

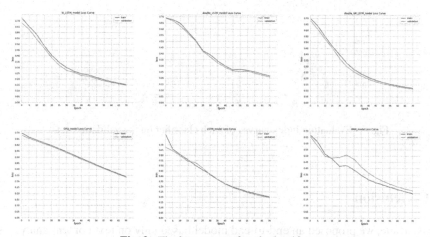

Fig. 3. The loss curve of each classifier.

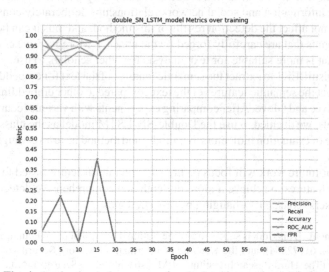

Fig. 4. Evaluation index curves of each classifier on the training set.

that the experiment used a 5-fold cross-validation method to divide the dataset, and it took the average of the five results obtained in a round as the output result of the epoch.

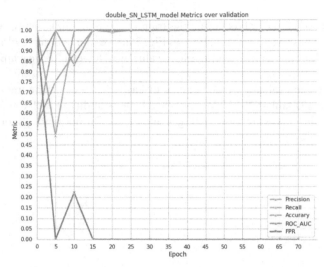

Fig. 5. Evaluation index curves of each classifier on the validation set.

5   Conclusion

In this article, we proposed an end-to-end model based only on text content analysis to detect Sybils in OSNs, that is, to detect such accounts only from the behavioral level. Static account information and social network relationships deliberately constructed by an attacker do not affect the detection results of this method, and thus it can better detect the Sybil accounts that are carefully forged by the attacker. Moreover, we constructed a new dataset that is more suitable for text analysis for other scholars to use.

We used DistilBERT to extract the semantic features of the text for embedding, which can better reflect the semantic features of the text compared to other embedding methods, such as Word2vec and Glove. After comparing experiments with various recurrent neural network models, we decided to use the Double-SN-LSTM model as the classifier. From the perspective of evaluation indicators, our model and method have a very high detection rate for Sybils.

Finally, our future work will focus on how to integrate structure-based features with content-based features to achieve a more in-depth and comprehensive detection to deal with the attackers' constantly changing bypass strategies.

Acknowledgement. This work is supported by the National Natural Science Foundation of China under Grant (No. 61872254), and the Key Lab of Information Network Security of Ministry of Public Security (The Third Research Institute of Ministry of Public Security) (No.C20606), and the Sichuan Science and Technology Program (2021JDRC0004). Xiaojie Xu and Jian Dong contribute equally to this work. We want to convey our grateful appreciation to the corresponding author of this paper, Jin Yang. He has offered advice with huge values in all stages when writing this essay to us.

References

1. Haifeng, Y., Kaminsky, M., Gibbons, P.B., Flaxman, A.D.: SybilGuard: defending against Sybil attacks via social networks. IEEE/ACM Trans. Netw. **16**(3), 576–589 (2008)
2. Haifeng, Y., Gibbons, P.B., Kaminsky, M., Xiao, F.: SybilLimit: a near-optimal social network defense against Sybil attacks. IEEE/ACM Trans. Netw. **18**(3), 885–898 (2010)
3. Danezis, G., Mittal, P.: Sybilinfer: detecting Sybil nodes using social networks. In: Proceedings of NDSS, pp. 1–15 (2009)
4. Cao, Q., et al.: Aiding the detection of fake accounts in large scale social online services. In: 9th USENIX Symposium on Networked Systems Design and Implementation (NSDI), pp. 197–210 (2012)
5. Cao, Q., Yang, X.: SybilFence: Improving social-graph-based Sybil defenses with user negative feedback (2013). arXiv:1304.3819. http://arxiv.org/abs/1304.3819
6. Yang, Z., Xue, J., Yang, X., Wang, X., Dai, Y.: VoteTrust: Leveraging friend invitation graph to defend against social network sybils. In: Proceedings of IEEE INFOCOM, pp. 2400–2408 (April 2016)
7. Misra, S., Tayeen, A.S.M., Xu, W.: SybilExposer: an effective scheme to detect sybil communities in Online social networks. In: Proceedings of IEEE International Conference Communications (ICC), pp. 1–6 (May 2016)
8. Shi, L., Yu, S., Lou, W., Hou, Y.T.: SybilShield: an agent-aided social network-based sybil defense among multiple communities. In: Proceedings of IEEE INFOCOM, pp. 1034–1042 (April 2013)
9. Bansal, H., Misra, M.: Sybil detection in Online social networks (OSNs). In: Proceedings of IEEE 6th International Conference on Advanced Computing (IACC), pp. 569–576 (February 2016)
10. Wang, B., Zhang, L., Gong, N.Z.: SybilSCAR: sybil detection in online social networks via local rule based propagation. In: Proceedings of IEEE Conference Computing Communications, pp. 1–9 (May 2017)
11. Gong, N.Z., Frank, M., Mittal, P.: SybilBelief: a semi-supervised learning approach for structure-based sybil detection. IEEE Trans. Inf. Forensics Secur. **9**(6), 976–987 (2014)
12. Zhang, X., Xie, H., Lui, J.C.S.: Sybil detection in social-activity networks: Modeling, algorithms and evaluations. In: Proceedings of IEEE 26th International Conference Network Protocols (ICNP), pp. 44–54 (September 2018)
13. Wang, G.: You are how you click: clickstream analysis for sybil detection. In: Proceedings of 22nd USENIX Security Symposium, pp. 241–256 (2013)
14. Alsaleh, M., Alarifi, A., Al-Salman, A.M., Alfayez, M., Almuhaysin, A.: TSD: Detecting sybil accounts in Twitter. In: Proc. 13th International Conference on Machine Learning and Applications, pp. 463–469 (December 2014)
15. Kang, K.: Compound approach for sybil users detection in social networks. Comput. Sci. **43**(1), 172–177 (2016)
16. Xia, Y., Pan, L., Shi, L., Zou, F.: Attribute credibility based sybil goup detection in Online social networks. In: Proc. IEEE 1st International Conference on Data Science Cyberspace (DSC), pp. 358–363 (June 2016)

17. D. Mulamba, I. Ray, and I. Ray.: On sybil classification in Online social networks using only structural features. In: Proceedings of 16th Annual Conference on Privacy, Security and Trust (PST), pp. 1–10 (August 2018)
18. Al-Qurishi, M., Alrubaian, M., Mizanur, S.M., Rahman, A.A., Hassan, M.M.: A prediction system of sybil attack in social network using deep-regression model. Future Gener. Comput. Syst. **87**, 743–753 (2018)
19. https://www.kaggle.com/manchunhui/us-election-2020-tweets
20. https://www.kaggle.com/khanradcoder/political-tweets-from-twitter-bots
21. Sanh, V., Debut, L., Chaumond, J., et al.: DistilBERT, a distilled version of BERT: smaller, faster, cheaper and lighter. arXiv preprint arXiv:1910.01108 (2019)

ePayment Security

An Empirical Study on Mobile Payment Credential Leaks and Their Exploits

Shangcheng Shi[1]($\boxtimes$), Xianbo Wang[1], Kyle Zeng[1,2], Ronghai Yang[1,3], and Wing Cheong Lau[1]

[1] The Chinese University of Hong Kong, Hong Kong, China
{ss016,xianbo,wclau}@ie.cuhk.edu.hk
[2] Arizona State University, Tempe, USA
zengyhkyle@asu.edu
[3] Sangfor Technology Inc, Shenzhen, China
yangronghai@sangfor.com.cn

Abstract. Recently, mobile apps increasingly integrate with payment services, enabling the user to pay orders with a third-party payment service provider, namely Cashier. During the payment process, both the app and Cashier rely on some credentials to secure the service. Despite the importance, many developers tend to overlook the protection of payment credentials and inadvertently expose them to the wild. Such leaks severely affect the security of end-users and the merchants associated with the apps, resulting in privacy violations and actual financial loss. In this paper, we study the payment credential leaks for four top-tiered Cashiers that serve over one billion users and tens of millions of merchants globally. Through studying practical mobile payment systems, we identify new leaking sources of payment credentials and find 4 types of exploits with severe consequences, which are caused by the credential leaks and additional implementation flaws. Besides, we design an automatic tool, PayKeyMiner, and use it to discover around 20,000 leaked payment credentials, affecting thousands of apps. We have reported our findings to the Cashiers. All of them have confirmed the issue and pledged to notify the affected merchant apps, while some of these apps have updated the leaked payment credentials afterward.

Keywords: Mobile payment · Payment credentials · Security testing

1 Introduction

In the past decade, mobile payment service has become worldwide popular with total transaction value exceeding \$1.15 trillion in 2019 [16]. Through the mobile apps of third-party Cashiers, end-users can perform the payment within smartphones readily instead of using cash or another physical token, *e.g.*, credit card.

J. Garcia-Alfaro et al. (Eds.): SecureComm 2021, LNICST 399, pp. 79–98, 2021.
https://doi.org/10.1007/978-3-030-90022-9_5

Given its prevalence, a wide range of mobile apps have integrated the service from the Cashiers. The Cashiers also release their SDKs and documents online to ease the deployment of mobile payment.

The mobile payment process involves sophisticated multi-party authentication and authorization. For security purposes, the Cashiers and the apps need to set up various payment credentials beforehand and make use of them in each session. The payment credentials include a collection of unique data (*e.g.*, RSA keys) and confidential files (*e.g.*, PKCS#12 files). With the credentials, either the Cashier or the app can authenticate itself to the other party and conduct privileged operations such as money transferring or refunding.

Given the significance of payment credentials, app developers *must* keep them private. Otherwise, an attacker can exploit the leaked credential to perform privileged transactions by impersonating the benign app. Despite the critical nature, prior research mainly focuses on the discovery of *general* credentials leaked from specific sources, *e.g.*, mobile apps [22] or public GitHub repositories [11]. In contrast, relatively few efforts have been spent to understand to what extent the *payment credentials* are being disclosed in the wild.

Towards this end, in this paper, we perform the first in-depth empirical study of payment credential leaks for four top-tiered Cashiers. These Cashiers serve over 1 billion end-users and tens of thousands of mobile apps. In particular, we aim to address the following three research questions: (1) *Where can the payment credentials be leaked?* (2) *What damage can the leaked credentials cause?* (3) *How to investigate the prevalence of payment credential leaks on a large scale?*

To solve the first two questions, we study the mobile payment services from the four Cashiers and their actual implementations by various merchant apps. Consequently, we find new leaking sources (to be discussed in Sect. 3), besides the known ones studied by previous works. For example, we find that even the backend servers of (merchant) apps, due to the insecure designs of SDKs by the Cashiers, can leak payment credentials unintentionally (Sect. 3.3). Moreover, we find four types of exploits based on leaked credentials that have severe consequences, ranging from privacy violations to financial loss. Notably, two of these exploits leverage extra implementation flaws, enabling the attacker to harm *other innocent apps or another third-party service, i.e., Single Sign-On (SSO)*.

As for the third question, we design and implement PayKeyMiner to automatically identify the leaked payment credentials from all potential sources. Using this tool, we have conducted large-scale testing and discovered around 20,000 valid payment credentials, affecting thousands of apps. We summarize our contributions as follows:

- We have found new leaking sources of payment credentials.
- We have discovered 4 types of exploits with the leaked payment credentials.
- We have proposed an automatic tool, PayKeyMiner, to detect payment credential leaks in the wild.
- Using PayKeyMiner, we have uncovered around 20,000 payment credentials.

The rest of the paper is organized as follows. Section 2 introduces the mobile payment services and related credentials of four mainstream Cashiers. Section 3

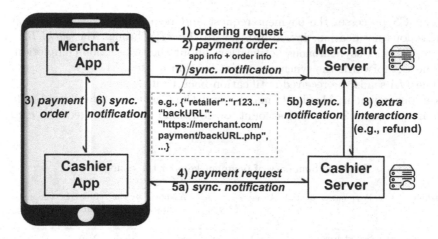

Fig. 1. General workflow of mobile payment service

discusses the leaking sources of payment credentials. Section 4 elaborates on how to exploit payment credential leaks. Section 5 describes the design and implementation of PayKeyMiner, while Sect. 6 presents the empirical testing. We review related work in Sect. 7 and conclude the paper in Sect. 8.

2 Background

A traditional e-payment service involves three parties, namely, the User (User-Agent), the Cashier, and the Merchant. In the context of mobile payment, the Cashier and Merchant map to their backend servers, *i.e.*, Cashier Server (*CS*) and Merchant Server (*MS*), while the User-Agent becomes their frontend mobile apps, *i.e.*, Cashier App (*CA*) and Merchant App (*MA*). For ease of presentation, we will use the notations in the parentheses in this section if not specified.

2.1 Workflow of Mobile Payment Service

The mobile payment service enables the Cashier to acknowledge to the Merchant that the user has paid the order in its app, *i.e.*, *MA*. Since there exists no standard for mobile payment, we review the technical documents from the Cashiers and get its general protocol flow (in Fig. 1), which works as follows:

1. After shopping in an *MA*, a user selects a third-party Cashier to check out. Then, the app sends a request containing the ordering details to its server.
2. The *MS* generates a payment order and feeds it back to its app.
3. The *MA* passes the payment order to the *CA*, which then displays the details, *e.g.*, *trade_amount* and *payee*, to the user for payment authorization.
4. Once the user confirms the payment, the *CA* sends a request to its server.

5. The *CS* processes the payment request and responds to the *CA*, *i.e.*, synchronous notification. It will also notify the *MS* through the *backURL* (in Step 2), *i.e.*, asynchronous notification, about the transaction completion.
6. The *CA* forwards the synchronous notification to the *MA*.
7. The *MA* sends the received notification back to its server.
8. Besides payment, Merchants may request the Cashier to refund paid orders, transfer money into a user account, or download transaction records, *etc.*.

Table 1. Summary of payment keys or the equivalent

Cashier	Payment credential	Usage	Assigned by the cashier?	Shared Cashier's public key among Merchants?
Cashier1 (a)[a]	Secret Key	HMAC	✓	N/A
	RSA (Private) Key	Digital signature	×	✓
Cashier1 (b)[a]	RSA (Private) Key	Digital signature	×	✓
	RSA′ (Private) Key	Digital signature	×	×
Cashier2	Secret Key	HMAC	×	N/A
Cashier3	PFX Cert	Digital signature	✓	✓
	Secret Key	HMAC	✓	N/A
Cashier4	Secret Key	HMAC	✓	N/A

[a] *Cashier1* provides two sets of mobile payment services.

2.2 Payment Credentials

Payment Key. Most of the messages in Fig. 1, in italic, are secured by either the digital signature or hash-based message authentication code (HMAC). Table 1 summarizes the related two types of payment keys and their security settings.

HMAC Secret Key. The Secret Keys in Table 1 belong to the category. When adopted, both the Merchant and Cashier will use the same Secret Key as the salt of a hash function, *e.g.*, MD5, to get the HMAC of payment-related messages. Apart from *Cashier2*, this type of key is generated by the Cashiers.

Signing Key. The other items in Table 1 are used to generate the digital signature. Then, both the Cashier and Merchant need to hold a pair of asymmetric keys and share their public keys. During mobile payment, either party will sign the request with its own private key and verify the response with the other party's public key. In this paper, we focus on the Merchant's private key.

As *Cashier1* supports two digital signing methods, it defines two types of payment keys, *i.e.*, RSA key and RSA′ key. Another crucial difference between these two keys is that *Cashier1 uses the same public key across the Merchants in RSA key, which is instead app-specific in RSA′ key*.

Besides, the Merchant's private key in *Cashier3* is included in a PFX certificate, which is a PKCS#12 file and password-protected. As such, the Merchant needs to unlock its certificate to extract the private key inside to sign the messages in each payment session. Similar to the RSA key in *Cashier1*, *the public key of Cashier3 is shared among its Merchants*, enabling the exploit in Sect. 4.4.

Other Credentials. Some Cashiers define other credentials for better security.

Android Signing Key. When receiving the payment order, *i.e.*, Step 3 in Fig. 1, *Cashier2* and *Cashier4* will validate the *MA* by checking its package signature. Thus, the Merchants should keep their Android signing keys private.

Client Certificate [23]. *Cashier2* issues per-app based certificates to its Merchants. The file is in the format of PKCS#12 and password-protected, which is required in the requests to the Cashier, *i.e.*, Step 8 in Fig. 1, for authentication.

2.3   Threat Model

In our threat model, the attacker aims to steal the payment credentials from publicly available sources (in Sect. 3). Then, he can exploit these credentials to cause financial loss and privacy violations to victim Merchants and their users.

To be specific, the attacker may use the leaked payment credentials to forge messages, *e.g.*, a refunding request, to cheat either the Cashier or Merchant. Meanwhile, the attacker can behave like a normal user in the Merchant App and modify the messages that visible to his smartphone. The attacker can also package a malicious Merchant App and trick the victim users into using it.

3   Leaking Sources of Payment Credentials

We introduce the leaking sources of payment credentials here, among which public GitLab repositories and Merchant Servers have not been studied before.

3.1   Public Git Repositories

Meli *et al.* [11] find some developers push the production code to GitHub without removing their credentials. We further notice that such leaks are still prevalent nowadays, even for payment credentials. Moreover, previous works overlook the leaks that only appear in old commits, while we will bridge this gap (in Table 6).

Meanwhile, we find some companies establish GitLab services on public IPs and make their repositories public, which may contain payment credentials. As such, the attacker can download these repositories and get the credentials inside.

3.2   Mobile Apps

Many developers embed credentials in their mobile apps. The existing works, *e.g.*, [25], study the leaks in the latest version of apps, while such leaks may happen in obsolete app versions only. To address this limitation, we set up a full-scale

Android APK dataset (in Table 4) for our testing. As we will see in the empirical testing result (in Table 6), 31.9% of the leaked payment credentials only appear in old versions of mobile apps, which is beyond the scope of previous works. Since the iOS ecosystem is proprietary, its app packages are encrypted and unsuitable for large-scale testing, so we mainly focus on Android apps. Nevertheless, we still consider the leaks within the iOS projects from public git repositories.

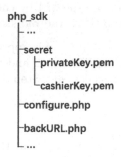

Fig. 2. Structure of an official SDK for Merchant Servers

3.3   Merchant Servers

We discover that the servers of Merchants can be another leaking source of payment credentials. The root causes are the insecure backend SDKs from Cashiers and the lack of access control on the related credential files by Merchant Servers.

The Cashiers provide SDKs to facilitate the deployment of mobile payment. Figure 2 shows the structure of an official SDK for illustration. For this SDK, "backURL.php" processes the asynchronous notifications, *i.e.*, Step 5b in Fig. 1. Besides, the "configure.php" file specifies the location of the Merchant's private key (Sect. 2.2) to a static file, namely "secret/privateKey.pem", while the document also requires the developer to store his private key in the same file. Consequently, this insecure practice enables the attacker to steal the private key file from Merchant Servers.

Specifically, the attacker can get the location of "backURL.php" from the payment order, namely, Step 2 in Fig. 1, *e.g.*, "https://x.com/pay/backURL. php". Based on the SDK structure in Fig. 2, he can then infer the location of the Merchant's private key, *i.e.*, "https://x.com/pay/secret/privateKey.pem". Once the Merchant Server does not block access to this file, the attacker can steal it.

As indicated in Table 2, some SDKs include payment credentials in scripts or other inaccessible files such that the attacker cannot steal them in most cases, while the other SDKs fail to follow this practice. According to our testing, 7.11% of the servers use these vulnerable SDKs and leak their credentials (in Table 6).

Table 2. Summary of backend SDKs from Cashiers

Inaccessible Credentials?	Cashier1 (a)	Cashier1 (b)	Cashier2	Cashier3	Cashier4
PHP	×	✓	×	×	×
Java	✓	✓	✓	✓	✓
C#	✓	✓	×	✓	✓

4 Exploiting Leaked Payment Credentials

The section presents four types of exploits caused by the leaked credentials. Leveraging extra implementation flaws, two of them enable the attacker to harm the other Merchant Apps without leaks and even another third-party service, *i.e.*, SSO. Due to ethical considerations, we cannot fully quantify the impacts of all these exploits, but we have tried to reproduce them in real payment systems.

4.1 Merchant Impersonation Exploit

Previous work [25] finds the attacker can use the leaked payment keys from mobile apps (Sect. 3.2) to get the transaction records of leaking apps illegally. Despite this known exploit, the attacker can also use leaked payment credentials to impersonate benign Merchants for more critical operations, *i.e.*, refunding and money transfer, **causing actual financial loss**. Although *Cashier2* requires the client certificate in these requests (Sect. 2.2), PayKeyMiner detects over 3,000 leaked certificates, which can be uncovered by the attacker (in Table 5).

Remark: The exploit of refund applies to all the leaking apps. As not all the Merchants activate the money transfer function, we cannot quantify the affected apps ethically. However, we have performed Proof of Concept (PoC) tests with demo Merchant accounts (from the Cashiers) under the production environment.

4.2 Android Package Signature Forgery

Although *Cashier2* and *Cashier4* validate the Merchant App (Sect. 2.2), many Android signing keys are leaked in public git repositories as the developers push the whole frontend project online. Thus, the attacker can modify several lines of code and package malicious Merchant Apps with valid signatures. Then, these malicious apps can **trick victim users into paying for the attacker's order** by replacing a payment order with the same amount, *i.e.*, Step 3 in Fig. 1.

Remark: We have performed PoC experiments with the leaked Android signing keys. Overall, PayKeyMiner detects 493 such leaks (in Table 5), where *10 of the related apps have more than one million downloads.*

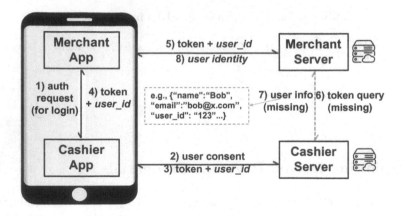

Fig. 3. Workflow of profile exploit

4.3   Backward SSO Attack

Some Cashiers, *i.e.*, *Cashier1* and *Cashier2*, provide SSO service, meaning the user can both login and pay the Merchant App through the Cashier. However, these Cashiers fail to isolate these two services, enabling the attacker to exploit leaked payment credentials to compromise the SSO service of Merchant Apps.

As depicted in Fig. 3, some Merchant Servers trust the *user_ids* from their frontend apps to authenticate the user without querying the Cashier in Step 6. Such flawed implementations enable the so-called Profile Exploit [17,24], where **the attacker may inject the *user_ids* of victim users into his sessions to hijack their accounts in the Merchant Apps**. Although both *Cashier1* and *Cashier2* set the *user_ids* to *private*, their payment and SSO services share the same set of *user_ids*, which appear in transaction records. Thus, the attacker may use leaked credentials to get the *user_ids* of all paying users and launch the exploit above. *We have performed the PoC for this exploit on real Merchant Apps with our own testing accounts.*

Meanwhile, the payment keys in *Cashier2* are generated by the Merchants (in Table 1), while its credentials for SSO, *i.e.*, *SSO_Secret*, are assigned by the Cashier instead. However, some Merchants reuse the values of *SSO_Secret* to be their payment keys, extending the impact of the leak issue in payment to SSO.

Remark: The *user_ids* in *Cashier1* are shared across Merchant Apps. Among the collected APKs (in Sect. 6.1), 26,413 apps (11.3%) include its SSO service and may be affected. Nevertheless, the *user_ids* in *Cashier2* are app-specific, so the exploit above only affects 497 leaking apps. Besides, we test 3,000 randomly-chosen leaked keys in *Cashier2*, and 43 of them (1.4%) act as the *SSO_Secret*.

4.4   Cross-App Payment Notification Forgery

Yang *et al.* [25] show the leaked HMAC secret key enables the attacker to forge notifications and cheat the leaking Merchant App. Even if the digital signature is used, we find the attacker can still deceive the other innocent Merchant Apps with fake notifications, as Cashier's public key tends to be shared (in Table 1).

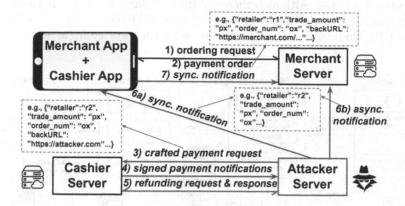

Fig. 4. Workflow of cross-app payment notification forgery

Figure 4 gives the workflow of this exploit. Specifically, the attacker may use a leaked signing key to create an order with the same *trade_amount* and *order_num* (in Step 3) as the target order in the victim Merchant App (from Step 2). After paying for this crafted order, the attacker can get signed notifications by specifying *backURL*, while he may refund the order later. Then, the attacker can send these notifications to the victim Merchant Server, which are cryptographically correct due to the Cashier's shared public key among the Merchants. Once overlooking the app identifier, *e.g.*, *retailer* in Fig. 4, in the notifications, **this victim Merchant will be cheated and let the attacker shop for free**.

Remark: As we cannot examine Merchant Servers without real attack, it is hard to quantify the impact of this exploit ethically. Nevertheless, we have set up a Merchant Server using the server code in a leaking GitHub repository, which is likely for production. Besides, we configure our own credentials (under Cashiers' sandbox environment) in the server and complete the PoC for this exploit.

5 System Architecture of PayKeyMiner

To investigate the prevalence of payment credential leaks, we build an automatic tool called PayKeyMiner. We give its system design and implementation here.

5.1 System Overview

Figure 5 presents the system architecture of PayKeyMiner, which consists of three modules. Crawler (Sect. 5.2) first identifies the git repositories and Android APKs that are likely to support mobile payment. Then, Scanner (Sect. 5.3) analyzes the filtered input and recognizes all potential credentials. Finally, Detector (Sect. 5.4) processes and validates these suspected credentials.

5.2   Crawler

PayKeyMiner crawls public git repositories and Android APKs and detects the payment-related ones. Although there are three leaking sources of payment credentials (in Sect. 3), we cannot directly locate the Merchant Servers. Thus, we use the URL Enumerator in Scanner to detect such leaks later (in Sect. 5.3).

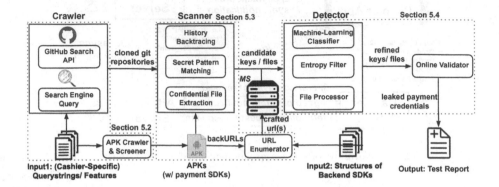

Fig. 5. System architecture of PayKeyMiner

Table 3. Examples of the constructed query strings

Type	Cashier	Sample	Illustration
Data	*Cashier1*	CUXwL**	Segment of Cashier's public key
Code	*Cashier2*	**PayConfigure	Classes in backend SDK
File	*Cashier3*	**PayPlugin.a	Files in iOS SDK

Git Repository Crawling. We count on GitHub Search API [8] and search engines like Google to find public git repositories. To get payment-related input, we study practical payment systems and summarize some *invariant* patterns that app developers cannot circumvent in integrating the mobile payment service. Table 3 shows some examples for better illustration, which can be categorized into three types, namely, data, code, and file. For instance, the RSA public key of *Cashier1* is shared among the Merchants (in Table 1), so the developers have to include it in their servers to validate the incoming messages from the Cashier. Thus, we construct query strings based on these invariants to filter out the git repositories irrelevant to the payment service.

On the other hand, GitHub only returns 1,000 search results, which cannot be tackled by previous works, *e.g.*, [11]. Fortunately, we find the *file_size* metric to partition the search results into continuous ranges and bypass the query quota, enabling PayKeyMiner to cover almost all the related public GitHub repositories. However, similar functionality does not exist in search engines like Google. As a workaround, our tool merges the search results from several sources and identifies related GitLab repositories from them.

APK Database Setup and Screening. As many Merchant Apps work in certain countries only, where Google service is unavailable, most of them do not appear in Google Play. Thus, we take three third-party app markets as data sources, namely, Apkpure [2], Anzhi [1], and Wandoujia [20], while PayKeyMiner crawls all the available APKs from them, including older versions.

Moreover, we identify the APKs with payment services based on some fingerprints of the frontend SDKs from Cashiers that can survive the obfuscations. Specifically, these Cashiers explicitly require the developers not to obfuscate some classes within their frontend SDKs. These classes serve as entry points for inter-app communications, e.g., Step 3 in Fig. 1, and renaming them will make these SDKs out of work. For the same reason, most frontend SDKs require the Merchant App to declare certain Activity entry points in AndroidManifest.xml, which is another fingerprint that can even survive bytecode packing. Although our tool cannot handle stronger packers that encrypt the original AndroidManifest.xml, less than 10% of Android apps adopt this kind of packer [6].

5.3 Scanner

This module scans the filtered input from Crawler to get suspected credentials. Given the target difference, it works in either a whitebox or blackbox manner.

Whitebox Scanning. This type of scanning applies to git repositories or APKs, whose code is available. The Scanner first traces back the history of the input, as the developers may remove the leaked credential in its latest version. Specifically, our tool uses *git-log* to get the previous modifications in the given git repository. As to APKs, the Scanner groups all its old versions and decompiles them for subsequent processing.

To identify candidate payment keys, we manually learn their patterns from the official technical documents from the Cashiers and formulate the corresponding regular expressions. For example, the Secret Key in *Cashier2* is an alphanumeric string with a length of 32. Then, we apply text-based pattern matching algorithms to the input. We take this language-agnostic method because the input git repositories can be written in various programming languages.

The Scanner also searches for credential files, *i.e.*, PKC#12 files and Android signing keys (in Sect. 2.2). Since these files are for specific purposes, they use constant file extensions, *e.g.*, .jks, so that our tool can easily identify them.

Blackbox Scanning. URL Enumerator (in Fig. 5) scans the Merchant Servers to get the exposed credential files caused by flawed backend SDKs (Sect. 3.3).

To examine the Merchant Servers, we need to identify their *backURLs*, which only appear in runtime, *i.e.*, Step 2 in Fig. 1. Besides, it is hard to extract these *backURLs* by simulating user behaviors in each Merchant App, as it involves the complex processes of authentication and shopping. Fortunately, some developers embed the *backURLs* in APKs, making them available after the decompilation.

Meanwhile, we study the structures of backend SDKs, *e.g.*, Fig. 2, for the relative paths from their *backURL* handler scripts to credential files, *i.e.*, Input2 in Fig. 5. With collected *backURLs*, the URL Enumerator then crafts and probes the URLs that may point to the exposed credential files in Merchant Servers. For ethical considerations, we use the HTTP HEAD method to get the metadata of these credential files to check their existence without downloading them locally.

5.4 Detector

For better efficiency, the Detector pre-processes the input from Scanner first with three sub-modules, namely Machine-Learning Classifier, Entropy Filter, and File Processor, to remove the false positives or reduce their impact. Finally, Online Validator validates suspected payment credentials.

Machine-Learning Classifier. The output from the Scanner contains the false positives caused by data files, *e.g.*, system logs, as many developers back up their servers in public git repositories. To distinguish configuration files from data files, we develop a machine-learning-based classifier. Specifically, we use file content, file name, and file path as the features, which are encoded and fed to a model based on XGBoost [4]. Then, we train this model with a dataset of 18,663 files from the initial test output, which have been manually tagged. The resultant model gives 97.47% accuracy with a 2.45% false-positive rate and a 5.63% false-negative rate. In runtime, the sub-module prioritizes the candidates from configuration files to reduce the overhead by false positives.

Entropy Filter. Some payment keys are generated by the Cashier (in Table 1), which may have similar Shannon Entropy [11]. Thus, we run the prototype of our tool to collect enough valid keys as ground truth. Consequently, we deploy Entropy Filter based on their entropy distribution. In runtime, this filter screens out the outliers that are 2 standard deviations away from the mean, as they have little chance to be the true positives ($< 5\%$). We randomly select and retest 500 input screened out by the filter, and none of them turns to be the false negative.

File Processor. As credential files, namely, PKCS#12 files and Android signing keys (in Sect. 2.2), are password-protected, the tool needs to crack them. Meanwhile, it validates Android signing keys by identifying associated apps here.

Notably, it is the Cashiers that assign these PKCS#12 files and guide their settings. For example, *Cashier3* suggests the password be a 6-digit. With the domain knowledge, our tool cracks over 90% of files using John the Ripper [13].

However, the passwords of Android signing keys are user-defined without guidelines. Thus, our tool tries with all available strings from the original git repositories and succeeds in unlocking 61.3% of the files. Based on the Android package names related to these cracked files, the File Processor then identifies the associated Merchant Apps and downloads their APKs. By comparing the hash values of an Android signing key and the corresponding APK, the tool manages to check the activeness of the former. Overall, PayKeyMiner has detected 493 valid Android signing keys (in Table 5).

Online Validator. This sub-module uses the suspected credentials to prepare an order query request with invalid parameters to the Cashier, *i.e.*, Step 8 in Fig. 1. This request is expected to be cryptographically correct but logically incorrect, so the Cashier will return an error message. For example, "Trade_NOT_EXIST" in Fig. 6 means that the given payment credential is valid, while "ILLEGAL_SIGN" indicates the false positive. Thus, we use this heuristic to validate the payment credentials without violating privacy. Note that the tool accesses the Cashier Servers in production mode but not sandbox mode, so the detected payment credentials are owned by the real Merchant Apps. Besides, to avoid affecting the normal production of the Cashiers, we set a timeout of 30 min for each test and control the interval between requests to 1 s. On average, it takes PayKeyMiner around 250 s to test each input.

```
<?xml version="1.0" encoding="utf-8"?>
<Cashier><is_success>F</is_success><error>ILLEGAL_SIGN</error></Cashier>
```
```
<?xml version="1.0" encoding="utf-8"?>
<Cashier><is_success>F</is_success><error>TRADE_NOT_EXIST</error></Cashier>
```

Fig. 6. Sample of error messages from the Cashier

Table 4. Statistics of payment SDK integration in APKs

	#Total	Cashier1	Cashier2	Cashier3	Cashier4
#Android App	233550	29269 (12.5%)	46408 (19.9%)	7234 (3.1%)	466 (0.2%)
#App Version	1240961	182124 (14.7%)	233262 (18.8%)	53516 (4.3%)	3596 (0.3%)

Table 5. Summary of the leaked payment credentials

Cashier	Cashier1 (a)		Cashier1 (b)		Cashier2			Cashier3		Cashier4	
Source\Credential	Secret Key	RSA Key	RSA Key	RSA' Key	Secret Key	Client Cert	Android Key	PFX Cert	Secret Key	Secret Key	Android Key
GitHub Repo	900	944	574	1737	6651	3131	491	188	0	25	1
GitLab Repo	9	12	8	20	57	31	1	1	0	0	0
Android APK	75	1766	184	354	2567	3	N/A	0	2	10	N/A
Merchant Server	0	44	N/A	N/A	0	11	N/A	2	0	0	N/A
Overall[†]	975	2578	754	2085	9093	3170	492	189	2	34	1

[*] Each row has deleted duplicate items.   [†] The overlap among different sources is removed.

6 Empirical Testing

This section presents our empirical testing and the test results from PayKeyMiner.

6.1 Dataset

Our dataset includes 139,206 GitHub repositories related to the payment services. Meanwhile, we collect 943 GitLab repositories from four search engines, *i.e.*, Google, Yahoo, Bing, and Baidu. On the other side, we crawl 233,550 Android apps, with overall 1,240,961 versions (*i.e.*, APKs), in September 2019. As discussed in Sect. 5.2, we preprocess these APKs, and Table 4 gives the result.

6.2 Test Results

Table 5 shows the test results, where PayKeyMiner has detected around 20,000 unique and valid credentials. Specifically, 10.34% of public git repositories, 3.21% of APKs, and 7.11% of Merchant Servers leak payment credentials (in Table 6).

Git Repositories. Through the online validation (in Sect. 5.4), our tool detects 23,011 valid payment credentials from 14,493 public git repositories, including the duplicate credentials (in Table 6). Among these results, 1,792 credentials (7.79%) only appear in old git commits, indicating that *some developers have noticed the leak issue and fixed it wrongly by pushing new commits without revoking their credentials*. On average, it takes the developers around 51 days to make this wrong fix. On the other hand, the other leaked credentials exist in the latest version of code and are available from GitHub search results [8].

Meanwhile, the four search engines perform differently in detecting public GitLab repositories, where Google contributes most of the results (in Table 6). Besides, we find that most of these repositories are owned by some *outsourcing companies*. These companies are responsible for the deployment of payment service but not its maintenance, so that they may not care about security.

Table 6. Statistics of the empirical testing

Source	GitHub	GitLab				Android APK	Merchant Server
		Google	Baidu	Yahoo	Bing		
#Input	139206	410	288	223	51	233550	802
		Overall: 943					
#Detection	14419 (10.36%)	62	9	2	1	7492 (3.21%)	57 (7.11%)
		Overall: 74 (7.85%)					
#Credential Leak	22830	181				9011	67
#Leak in History	1765 (7.7%)	27 (15.0%)				2878 (31.9%)	N/A

* The table shows the result before removing duplicate credentials.

Table 7. Statistics of Android apps with credential leaks

#Download	$(0,10^4)$	$[10^4,10^5)$	$[10^5,10^6)$	$[10^6,10^7)$	$[10^7,10^8)$	$[10^8,\infty)$	#Total
#Leaking App	2606	4698	132	35	17	4	7492

As mentioned in Sect. 3.2, we also search for payment credential leaks in iOS-related git repositories. From the collected input, PayKeyMiner has identified 365 and 347 unique payment keys in *Cashier1* and *Cashier2* separately.

Android APKs. PayKeyMiner detects 9,011 payment credentials, including 4,961 unique ones, from 7,603 APKs that are associated with 7,492 apps. Surprisingly, we find 3 client certificates in *Cashier2* are leaked with payment keys, where the developers implement the server-side operations, *e.g.*, refunding, in their apps. Notably, 31.9% of these credentials only exist in old app versions.

The affected apps range from an official tax-payment app to a financial app with over 5 million downloads, and we will discuss them in Sect. 6.5. As indicated in Table 7, most of these leaking apps have less than 1 million downloads, while 4 of these Merchant Apps have over 100 million downloads.

We also measure the occurrence frequency of the leaked payment keys in APKs. The result indicates that two of these keys appear in 1,446 and 419 APKs separately, which are owned by two *payment syndicators* [5]. The *payment syndicator* helps Merchant Apps to integrate the payment services from multiple Cashiers. Then, Merchant Apps can use the *payment syndicator*'s Cashier account for their payment services. However, these two *payment syndicators* embed payment keys in their frontend SDKs to Merchants, affecting all the related apps.

Besides, we analyze the leaking locations of payment keys in APKs. From the result, over 1,800 keys are leaked from three particular files, *which belong to the official demo project from* one of the Cashiers under our study. Although the code claims that it is for demo use and gives a serious warning on the credential leak issue, many developers still reuse it for ease of implementation.

Merchant Servers. Our tool detects 57 exposed credential files from 802 Merchant Servers. As many Merchant Apps do not embed *backURLs*, we cannot obtain their values directly. However, the attacker may dynamically execute the app and get its *backURL* from the payment order, *i.e.*, Step 2 in Fig. 1. Notably, iOS apps can also leak payment credentials from their servers due to the insecure backend SDKs (Sect. 3.3). From the collected GitHub repositories, we have manually found such cases in the server code of some iOS projects.

6.3   Resolving the Merchant Apps

Some payment credentials are leaked from the server code in git repositories so that we cannot identify the associated Merchant Apps directly. To bridge the gap, we develop the following two approaches.

Crafting Payment Request. Many payment credentials work for both mobile apps and websites. Therefore, we can use the leaked credential to craft a payment request for the latter and send it to the Cashier, whose response contains the name of the related Merchant App used for user consent. Although *Cashier4* validates the Merchant App in mobile payment (Sect. 2.2), all its credentials work for websites, enabling the approach above. We automate this approach and recognize 1,590 apps, while the other credentials in *Cashier1* and *Cashier3* support mobile payment only and require manual efforts to find their owners.

Parsing Client Certificates. Since *Cashier2* checks the origin of payment requests, the first approach does not work for it. Fortunately, over 40% of the payment keys in *Cashier2* are leaked along with the associated client certificates (Sect. 2.2) in git repositories, which contain the information of related Merchant Apps. By parsing the client certificates, we have identified 2,812 apps.

6.4   Longitudinal Study

After our initial testing, we reported the result to the related Cashiers. Specifically, we submitted 624 and 2,728 unique payment keys to *Cashier1* and *Cashier2* separately (in Table 8), which were got from 4,380 payment keys within 3,662 GitHub repositories after removing the duplicate keys. According to the Cashiers, they would notify all the affected Merchants and urge them to update the keys. Meanwhile, we regularly monitor and validate the submitted keys with the online validator (Sect. 5.4) to study the reactions from the leaking Merchants. Surprisingly, less than 20% of these keys have been updated 12 months after our report. Table 8 summarizes the responses from these Merchants as follows.

- **Updating the Leaked Key.** These Merchants updated the leaked keys.
- **Hiding the GitHub Repository.** These Merchants set their GitHub repositories private without updating their keys.
- **Deleting Related Git Commits.** These Merchants removed the git commits that contain the leaked keys instead of revoking their keys.

Table 8. Responses from leaking Merchant Apps after our report

Cashier	Cashier1		Cashier2	
Fixing Methods\Retesting Time	3 months later	12 months later	3 months later	12 months later
#Updating the Leaked Key	2 (0.3%)	255 (35.5%)	337 (9.2%)	443 (12.1%)
#Hiding the GitHub Repo	127 (17.7%)	146 (20.3%)	377 (10.3%)	651 (17.8%)
#Deleting Related Git Commits	117 (16.3%)	65 (9.1%)	218 (6.0%)	198 (5.4%)
#Pushing New Git Commits	8 (1.1%)	3 (0.4%)	29 (0.8%)	24 (0.7%)
#No Response	464 (64.6%)	249 (34.7%)	2701 (73.8%)	2346 (64.1%)
#Detected Key (#Unique Key)	718 (624)		3662 (2728)	

- **Pushing New Git Commits.** These Merchants deleted their keys from the code and pushed new commits online. However, the leaked keys still existed in git history and were valid.
- **No Response.** These Merchants made no response.

As we can see, around 60% of the leaking apps took no reactions after being notified, while the others used four different fixing approaches. Among them, only updating the leaked key is correct because the data leak issue is by nature irreversible, and the keys are still valid and available in the other cases. For example, public GitHub repositories are archived by Google BigQuery [9] such that the attacker can still recover the desired payment credentials from them. Thus, neither deleting git commits nor hiding the repository will work.

This finding shows that *many leaking Merchants have not noticed the severity of the leak issue or take the wrong approaches to fix it.* Given the severe circumstance, we give the Cashiers the following suggestions.

- The Cashiers should explicitly alarm their Merchants about the serious consequences of payment credential leaks (mentioned in Sect. 4).
- The Cashiers should review their services and timely fix the insecure implementations, *e.g.*, flawed backend SDKs (in Sect. 3.3), shared *user_ids* across services (in Sect. 4.3), and misleading demo (in Sect. 6.2).
- The Cashiers should proactively detect and revoke the leaked credentials.

6.5   Case Study

We give two representative samples of leaking Merchant Apps here.

A Tax App. This app belongs to an official tax bureau of a certain region, *with over 80 million population*, which integrates both SSO and payment services from one of the Cashiers under our study. End-users can thus pay the tax through this app. Unfortunately, we find that the app maintains its frontend project in a public GitHub repository. Even worse, the app hard-codes its credentials in the SSO module, which can also be used for the payment service. Thus, the attacker can uncover the leaked key and steal all the tax payment records from the Cashier by impersonating the real Merchant (Sect. 4.1).

A Financial App. This app is from one studied Cashier and has over 5 million downloads, which also uses its own payment service to enable the purchase of financial products by end-users. Beyond our expectations, this app leaks its payment key in APK. As the app also enables the money transferring function, the attacker may launch a notification forgery attack [25] or even steal the money from the app directly by forging a request to the Cashier (Sect. 4.1).

7   Related Work

Online Payment Vulnerabilities. As an increasing number of third-party web and mobile applications have integrated the online payment service, the security of online third-party payment has become a popular research topic in recent years. Wang *et al.* [21] are the first to systematically study logic flaws within the third-party payment services adopted by web applications. Sun *et al.* [18] take a step forward by proposing an automatic approach to detect payment logic vulnerabilities in web applications based on symbolic execution. Mulliner *et al.* [12] study the vulnerability of local signature verification in Android apps and manage to crack the in-app billing service in 60% of apps. [10,14] assess the security of digital wallet services in developing countries and find several vulnerabilities in their protocols and mobile apps. Using some NLP techniques, Chen *et al.* [5] identify several logic vulnerabilities by analyzing the documents from payment syndicators. However, [5] assumes the implementations or designs from Cashiers to be secure, which has been proven incorrect.

[25] is a closely related work in which the authors perform the analysis on third-party payment services integrated by mobile applications and discover several types of common flaws, including the payment credential leak in Android packages. They claim the leak enables the attacker to query transaction information illegally. Compared to [25], we perform a deeper analysis of practical mobile payment systems and uncover more novel attack scenarios based on the leaked credentials and additional implementation flaws by Cashiers or Merchants. Two of these exploits enable the attacker to cheat the other Merchant Apps without credential leaks to shop for free or even compromise their SSO services.

Existing Works on Credential Leaks. Viennot *et al.* [19] perform a market scale measurement study on Google Play apps with their framework PlayDrone and find a significant number of apps leaking Amazon Web Service tokens and OAuth tokens with simple pattern matching. CredMinder [26] also targets credential leak detection in Android apps, but it employs code analysis rather than string matching and can effectively find credentials even when they are obfuscated. LeakScope [27] applies a similar static analysis method to detect misuse of keys for cloud services and uncovers 15,098 vulnerable apps. Wen *et al.* [22] build iCredFinder to fill the gap of credential leak detection for iOS apps. All the existing works, including [25], only analyze one particular version of app packages. In contrast, our framework can detect credential leaks in old app versions, even if the issue has been fixed in the latest version. PayKeyMiner can also detect the leaked credentials from Merchant Servers (Sect. 3.3), which has not been studied before.

Meanwhile, Meli et al. [11], by collecting secrets with GitHub Search API and BigQuery snapshot, show that secret leak in GitHub repositories is also pervasive. Although we also study the leak issue from GitHub, PayKeyMiner performs a thorough analysis of the suspected repositories and considers the leaks in history (in Table 6), while [11] only assesses the files in GitHub search results. Besides, PayKeyMiner circumvents the query quota from GitHub [8] and thus covers almost all searchable repositories, which is beyond the scope of [11]. Moreover, this work manually validates the leaked credentials and fails to resolve related apps, while our tool automates these processes. Compared to [11], we also introduce new exploits with credential leaks and evaluate their impacts.

There are other open-source tools for leak detection in git repositories. For example, truffleHog [3] and Gitleaks [15] can detect credentials in a given git repository, while shhgit [7] monitors the real-time leaks based on GitHub public events API. These tools assume strong patterns or randomness in secret strings and have no validation phase, which will lead to an unacceptably high false-positive rate in our case as some payment credentials are generated by the developers and do not follow strict patterns (in Table 1). Thus, we combine coarse file searching, fine credential digging, and zero-impact online verification to ensure the broad coverage as well as high accuracy of our result.

8   Conclusion

In this paper, we perform an empirical study for mobile payment credential leaks. By studying the mobile payment services from four top-tiered Cashiers, we identify new leaking sources of payment credentials and discover four types of exploits caused by the credential leaks with severe consequences. Besides, we propose an automated tool, PayKeyMiner, to conduct large-scale testing for the leaked payment credentials in the wild. We implement the tool and use it to detect around 20,000 payment credentials that affect thousands of apps. Our study shows that the overall security quality of payment credentials seems worrisome. We hope that the Cashiers review their payment services, conduct pro-active scanning, and revoke the leaked payment credentials timely to protect their Merchants and the end-users behind.

Responsible Disclosure

We have reported all our findings to the Cashiers under our study and got their confirmation and acknowledgements. Many of the affected Merchants have changed their leaked payment credentials upon notifications by the Cashiers.

Acknowledgements. This research is supported in part by the CUHK Project Impact Enhancement Fund (Project# 3133292), the CUHK Direct Grant #4055155, and the CUHK MobiTeC R&D Fund.

References

1. Anzhi: Anzhi App Market (2021). http://www.anzhi.com
2. Apkpure: Apkpure App Market (2021). https://apkpure.com
3. Ayrey, D.: trufflehog (2021). https://github.com/dxa4481/truffleHog
4. Chen, T., Guestrin, C.: Xgboost: a scalable tree boosting system. In: ACM SIGKDD 2016 (2016)
5. Chen, Y., et al.: Devils in the guidance: predicting logic vulnerabilities in payment syndication services through automated documentation analysis. In: USENIX Security 2019 (2019)
6. Dong, S., et al.: Understanding android obfuscation techniques: a large-scale investigation in the wild. In: EAI SecureComm 2018 (2018)
7. eth0izzle: shhgit: find github secrets in real time (2021). https://github.com/eth0izzle/shhgit
8. GitHub: Github Search API (2021). https://developer.github.com/v3/search
9. Google: Google BigQuery (2021). https://cloud.google.com/bigquery
10. Kumar, R., Kishore, S., Lu, H., Prakash, A.: Security analysis of unified payments interface and payment apps in India. In: USENIX Security 2020 (2020)
11. Meli, M., McNiece, M.R., Reaves, B.: How bad can it git? characterizing secret leakage in public github repositories. In: NDSS 2019 (2019)
12. Mulliner, C., Robertson, W., Kirda, E.: Virtualswindle: an automated attack against in-app billing on android. In: ACM ASIACCS 2014 (2014)
13. Openwall: John the Ripper (2021). https://www.openwall.com/john
14. Reaves, B., Scaife, N., Bates, A., Traynor, P., Butler, K.R.: Mo(bile) money, mo(bile) problems: analysis of branchless banking applications in the developing world. In: USENIX Security 2015 (2015)
15. Rice, Z.: Gitleaks: Audit git repos for secrets (2021). https://github.com/zricethezav/gitleaks
16. Savvy, M.: Amazing stats demonstrating the unstoppable rise of mobile payments globally (2020). https://www.merchantsavvy.co.uk/mobile-payment-stats-trends
17. Shi, S., Wang, X., Lau, W.C.: MoSSOT: an automated blackbox tester for single sign-on vulnerabilities in mobile applications. In: ACM ASIACCS 2019 (2019)
18. Sun, F., Xu, L., Su, Z.: Detecting logic vulnerabilities in e-commerce applications. In: NDSS 2014 (2014)
19. Viennot, N., Garcia, E., Nieh, J.: A measurement study of google play categories and subject descriptors. In: ACM SIGMETRICS 2014 (2014)
20. Wandoujia: Wandoujia App Market (2021). https://www.wandoujia.com
21. Wang, R., Chen, S., Wang, X.F., Qadeer, S.: How to shop for free online security analysis of cashier-as-a-service based web stores. In: IEEE S&P 2011 (2011)
22. Wen, H., Li, J., Zhang, Y., Gu, D.: An empirical study of SDK credential misuse in iOS apps. In: APSEC 2018 (2018)
23. Wikipedia: Client Certificate (2021). https://en.wikipedia.org/wiki/client_certificate
24. Yang, R., Lau, W.C., Shi, S.: Breaking and fixing mobile app authentication with OAuth2.0-based protocols. In: ACNS 2017 (2017)
25. Yang, W., et al.: Show me the money! finding flawed implementations of third-party in-app payment in android apps. In: NDSS 2017 (2017)
26. Zhou, Y., Wu, L., Wang, Z., Jiang, X.: Harvesting developer credentials in android apps. In: ACM WiSec 2015 (2015)
27. Zuo, C., Lin, Z., Zhang, Y.: Why does your data leak? uncovering the data leakage in cloud from mobile apps. In: IEEE S&P 2018 (2018)

System-Wide Security for Offline Payment Terminals

Nikolay Ivanov and Qiben Yan$^{(\boxtimes)}$

Michigan State University, East Lansing, MI 48824, USA
{ivanovn1,qyan}@msu.edu

Abstract. Most self-service payment terminals require network connectivity for processing electronic payments. The necessity to maintain network connectivity increases costs, introduces cybersecurity risks, and significantly limits the number of places where the terminals can be installed. Leading payment service providers have proposed offline payment solutions that rely on algorithmically generated payment tokens. Existing payment token solutions, however, require complex mechanisms for authentication, transaction management, and most importantly, security risk management. In this paper, we present VOLGAPAY, a blockchain-based system that allows merchants to deploy secure offline payment terminal infrastructure that does not require collection and storage of any sensitive data. We design a novel payment protocol which mitigates security threats for all the participants of VOLGAPAY, such that the maximum loss from gaining full access to any component by an adversary incurs only a limited scope of harm. We achieve significant enhancements in security, operation efficiency, and cost reduction via a combination of polynomial multi-hash chain micropayment channels and blockchain grafting for off-chain channel state transition. We implement the VOLGAPAY payment system, and with thorough evaluation and security analysis, we demonstrate that VOLGAPAY is capable of delivering a fast, secure, and cost-efficient solution for offline payment terminals.

Keywords: Blockchain · Off-chain interaction · Smart contract · Offline payment

1 Introduction

The popularity of electronic payments has grown significantly over the past decade due to increasing number of online users. Consumers got used to online shopping and payments, however, a number of security incidents have undermined their trust in electronic commerce [19,29,32].

Most electronic payment terminals have to stay online in order to process payments. The online requirement, however, is associated with cybersecurity threats, increased costs, dependency upon third-party infrastructure, and limited locations where the terminals can be installed. Offline payment designs

© ICST Institute for Computer Sciences, Social Informatics and Telecommunications Engineering 2021
Published by Springer Nature Switzerland AG 2021. All Rights Reserved
J. Garcia-Alfaro et al. (Eds.): SecureComm 2021, LNICST 399, pp. 99–119, 2021.
https://doi.org/10.1007/978-3-030-90022-9_6

deliver solutions to these problems [7,14,18,26,28,30], which generally require a payment token to be transmitted between the payer and payee through Near-Field Communication (NFC), Bluetooth, electromagnetic field [20], QR code [22] or even audio signal [2].

Figure 1 illustrates the payment transaction workflows in payment systems with online and offline terminals. An online terminal gathers client's payment credentials, and uses them for authentication and payment validation at the merchants' server. By comparison, a payment transaction with an offline terminal allows the client to request the payment token from merchant servers directly and use it for payment verification on the offline terminal.

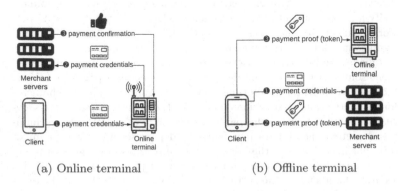

(a) Online terminal   (b) Offline terminal

Fig. 1. Payment transaction workflows with online and offline terminals.

However, one major challenge of designing offline payment infrastructure is to securely manage user balance, including over-spending and double-spending prevention. In traditional payment channels, an offline terminal cannot be timely updated on changes of a user balance, and thus it is subject to token lifting and spending attacks [4]. One way to address this challenge is to use cryptographic payment tokens (i.e., cryptographic proofs of payment) that a user delivers to the payment terminal. Yet, the token-based payment systems face four major concerns: security, privacy, trust, and cost-inefficiency.

First, in the classic payment token designs, the user balances and transactions are stored in a centralized database, which is a single point of failure. The resilience of a payment token infrastructure can be enhanced at the expense of storing multiple copies of encryption and signature keys on different nodes. Second, the sensitive client information, such as credit card number, often has to be stored in the merchant infrastructure, which is notorious for being a target of massive cyberattacks [19]. Third, the classic payment token designs further assume the trustworthiness of the merchants, while the necessity to protect clients from potentially malicious or fake merchants is largely ignored. Fourth, it requires a significant effort and investment to ensure the security and resilience of a classic solution. As a result, the cost and complexity of the payment token infrastructure may outweigh the benefits of using offline terminals.

In this paper, we design a novel payment system, VOLGAPAY, for token-based offline terminals. The design of our system relies on the following two insights:

1. We use blockchain and cryptocurrency, which provide an effective solution for eliminating otherwise unnecessary reliance of client upon merchant's trustworthiness. We supplement the blockchain technology with a multi-hash chain-based micropayment channel and polynomial price representation in order to achieve a balance of security and efficiency for payment transactions between merchant and client.
2. To achieve high efficiency, enhanced security, and operation cost reduction, we propose the *blockchain grafting* technique to conjoin a fast, zero-fee auxiliary smart contract in a private blockchain with a decentralized smart contract on a public blockchain.

VOLGAPAY operates offline points of sale (OPOS) and uses multi-hash chain micropayment channels and *blockchain grafting* to enhance the security and efficiency of offline payment transactions. Each merchant-client association is represented by a novel combination of smart contracts: one smart contract deployed on the public blockchain (public smart contract), and another one deployed on the private blockchain (private smart contract). The public smart contract provides protection of client's deposit and merchant's payoff without any pre-existing trust, while the private smart contract provides secure interface and accounting to the off-chain micropayment infrastructure of the merchant with minimum delays and zero fees.

We implement a VOLGAPAY prototype system using Raspberry Pi-based terminals, Android clients, Ethereum-based public and private blockchains, and a cohort of independent token signer servers scattered across the globe. **A video demonstration of VolgaPay operations is available at** https://youtu.be/rjIhDD2yi5I.

In summary, our contributions are as follows:

- We propose a blockchain-based transaction network, VOLGAPAY, to address the elevated security risks, inefficiency, and high cost of existing payment systems with offline terminals;
- We implement VOLGAPAY, which we thoroughly evaluate to determine its low cost, high speed, and impressive scalability: the token request delay normally does not exceed 12 s, the one-time blockchain fee of establishing a smart contract is less than $1, the communication overhead is light enough to serve 3G-connected clients, and the number of simultaneous token requests can reach 10,000.
- We analyze the security of VOLGAPAY, and prove that: if any component of the system is compromised, the harm will be localized, and the system at large remains secure.

2   Related Work

Off-Chain Payment Channels. The Bitcoin Lightning Network protocol [24] uses Bitcoin smart contract functionality for securing off-chain micropayment channels. To perform off-chain operation, Bitcoin Lightning uses two-way multi-signature channels based on digital signature schemes, supported by a network of multiple dedicated servers. Currently, there are a few test implementations of the Lightning network, including Lightning Labs [17], Casa Node [5], ACINQ [27], Blockstream [12], and MIT lit [16]. Other cryptocurrency micropayment projects include Perun [8], Revive [15], Sprites [21], Bolt [11], SpeedyMurmurs [25], Stellar [1], and a duplex micropayment channel [6]. Blockumulus [13] uses a cloud-based smart contract, called *FastMoney*, for off-chain payments. The functionality and security of all the solutions above largely depend on the setup and performance characteristics of centralized or crowd-sourced servers that serve the off-chain network. To avoid security risks and synchronization complexity associated with centralized micropayment management, VOLGAPAY uses *blockchain grafting* for transaction management. Moreover, the aforementioned solutions are not designed to support payments with offline terminals.

Offline Electronic Payments. There are a few solutions proposed for offline electronic payments. The most popular schemes involve delivering a cryptographically verifiable token from client to terminal using a local offline channel, e.g., electromagnetic or radio transmission [14]. Other solutions propose the use of trusted hardware [9,18], which relies on the assumption of hardware integrity. While trusted hardware is useful in a deeply regulated and controlled environment, such as Apple Pay, it could not support anonymous payments in a low-trust environment, e.g., a self-service station.

3   System Design

We elaborate on the design of VOLGAPAY by describing its fundamental definitions and principles, as well as three classes of elements constituting its topology: *participants, communication channels*, and *protocols*. Figure 2 shows the overall system architecture, in which each transaction between client and merchant is supported by a public smart contract supplemented by a linked (grafted) private smart contract. The public smart contract protects client's deposit and refund, while guaranteeing payoff for the merchant. The private smart contract provides secure interfacing endpoint for the client and secure accounting and ledger-keeping for the merchants' micropayment channels. The client pays the merchant with a set of hashes, and receives a payment token (i.e., verifiable payment receipt), which is a tuple of signatures from several independent signers that respond to the token request blockchain event. Table 1 summarizes all notations used in the design of VOLGAPAY.

Polynomial Multi-Hash Chain Micropayment. Traditional blockchain-based micropayment channels rely on digital signature schemes, which require the protection of private keys and prevention of double-spending complicated by transaction reversals, whereas hash chain-based micropayment channels eliminate the use and storage of private keys and avoid transaction reversals. In this

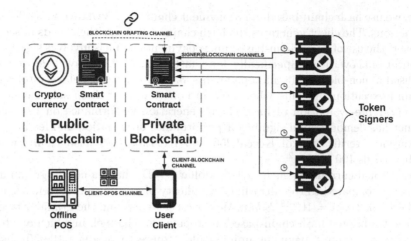

Fig. 2. VOLGAPAY system architecture. The ⊕ label symbolizes an event-listening channel. VOLGAPAY includes seven types of participants and four types of channels. OPOS first delivers the information needed for payment and token request to the client through the client-OPOS channel. The client then provides payment and requests payment token from the private blockchain through the client-blockchain channel. Signers subscribe to the token request event via the signer-blockchain channels. Private smart contract extends the public smart contract through a virtual blockchain-grafting channel. Finally, the client delivers a payment token to OPOS using the client-OPOS channel.

Table 1. Notation table for VOLGAPAY.

Symbol	Meaning
η	Transaction ID randomly generated by OPOS
δ	Item's listed price or single payment amount
D	Human-readable item description
N	Total number of token signers
M	Number of signatures in a token
$\Gamma_i(m)$	Digital signature of message m signed by token signer i
$K(m)$	Digital signature of message m signed by an OPOS
$E(p)$	Private blockchain event with parameter p
τ	Price base—the sum of previous payments.
ϕ	τ-adjusted price (*cumulative payment*): $\phi = \tau + \delta$
Θ	Hash chain polynomial base (max. number of hashes in each hash chain)
Υ	Ordered sequence of payment hash chains $\Upsilon = (\Upsilon_1, \Upsilon_2, ..., \Upsilon_\xi)$
ξ	Number of hash chains in Υ
Υ_i	i-th hash chain in Υ
R_i	The number of hashes released by the client to the merchant from Υ_i
g	Price granularity measured in number of atomic units

paper, we use hash chain-based micropayment channel for VOLGAPAY's off-chain transactions. The client generates the hash chains and keeps their seeds in secret. However, the use of hash chain-based micropayment channels involves significant computational overhead. Specifically, long hash chains, which have been success-fully used in non-blockchain micropayments [3,23], incur large delays, intolerable fees, and execution timeouts when used in non-view blockchain smart contract calls[1]. Our pre-evaluation of hash chain generation performance on Ethereum Mainnet has demonstrated significant performance degradation and fee increase for non-view verification of Keccak256 and RIPEMD-160 hash chains whose length exceeds 100 hashes[2].

Traditional currencies, such as U.S. dollar (USD), have a coarse granularity (i.e., *cent*) compared to the ultra-fine granularity of most cryptocurrencies, e.g., in Ethereum, 1 *wei* $= 10^{-18}$ *Ether*. Moreover, if we assume the granularity of 1 *cent*, the traditional hash chain-based micropayment channel, in which one hash represents one atomic payment unit, would require to produce 10,000 hashes for the verification of a 1,000-*dollar* payment, which is practically infeasible on blockchain due to its significant computational overhead.

To address this problem, we propose a *polynomial multi-hash chain micro-payment scheme* which utilizes several hash chains to process arbitrary micro-payments. Instead of using a very long single hash chain, in which each hash represents a minimal payment unit, such as Ethereum's *wei*, we use a ξ-tuple of short hash chains, each responsible for a single digit with radix Θ. For example, to account for USD prices between 1¢ and \$10,000 (or 10^6¢), we need 7 decimal digits, i.e., $\xi = 7$, $\Theta = 10$, with 7 hash chains and 10 hashes in each chain. Each digit from 0 to 9 can be represented by one of the 10 hashes, totalling 70 hashes for any price in the given range. In comparison, 10^6 hashes are required in the classic single hash chain representation. Therefore, any single payment amount δ can be represented as the following polynomial:

$$\delta = \sum_{i=1}^{\xi} R_i \times \Theta^{i-1}, \tag{1}$$

where R_i is the number of hashes released from hash chain Υ_i. For instance, suppose the client pays \$25.31 (or 2,531¢), the micropayment will be executed by releasing 1 hash from Υ_1 ($R_1 = 1$), 3 hashes from Υ_2 ($R_2 = 3$), 5 hashes from Υ_3 ($R_3 = 5$), and 2 hashes from Υ_4 ($R_4 = 2$), while $R_5 = R_6 = R_7 = 0$.

If *wei* is used as the payment unit, we need 19 hash chains to represent prices up to 9 *Ether*, as 1 *Ether* $= 10^{18}$ *wei*. The number of hash chains can be reduced by increasing the granularity g and capping the maximum cumulative off-chain balance. To process multiple payments, we submit the τ-adjusted price

---

[1] In smart contracts, a "view" function is a read-only function of smart contract that does not modify the state of blockchain. The "view" functions can be executed by the blockchain API layer rather than miners. Thus, the execution is generally fast.

[2] On Mainnet, the fee for 100-hash verification exceeds 80¢ with recommended gas price. The attempt to verify 270 hashes fails with "out of gas" error.

(or cumulative payment) ϕ instead of the single payment δ, and we use the price base τ to track the previous payments corresponding to already released hashes. Thus, we adapt Eq. (1) to include g and τ. For each payment, the client determines a sequence of *hash chain depths* $(R_1, \ldots, R_\xi)$, to express ϕ as:

$$\phi = \tau + \delta = g \times \sum_{i=1}^{\xi} R_i \times \Theta^{i-1}. \tag{2}$$

Increasing granularity g reduces the number of hash chains in the set, and thus reduces the public blockchain fees. In our prototype, we use $g = 10^{13}$, which can represent a range of prices between 0.00001 and 99.99999 *Ether* using just 7 hash chains with 10 hashes for each chain.

Example: Although VOLGAPAY uses *Ether*, we focus on USD in our examples for ease of illustration. Suppose we want to represent USD prices up to \$999,999, with granularity $g = 10^2$, i.e., we round the cost to the nearest dollar. Thus, the granularity-adjusted number of hash chains ξ is 6 rather than 8.

Suppose the client makes three consecutive payments: \$1,720, \$56, and \$56. Assume there are no previous payments in the channel (i.e., $\tau = 0$), then for the first payment, $(R_1, R_2, ..., R_7)$ is $(0, 2, 7, 1, 0, 0, 0)$. For the second payment ($\delta = 56$, $\tau = 1,720$, $\phi = 1,776$), the 7-tuple hash chain depth sequence will become: $(6, 7, 7, 1, 0, 0, 0)$. Comparing the two sequences of sets, we can see that in the second payment, the client reveals 6 hashes from Υ_1 and 5 more hashes from Υ_2. For the third payment ($\delta = 56, \tau = 1,776, \phi = 1,832$), the 7-tuple hash chain depth sequence is $(2, 3, 8, 1, 0, 0, 0)$. Compared to the previous payment, the client releases 1 more hash from Υ_3. It is worth noting that after three payments, the number of hashes known by the merchant for each hash chain is $(6, 7, 8, 1, 0, 0, 0)$, worth \$1,876. A malicious merchant can try to get payoff of \$1,876 (rather than \$1,832), which will be rejected by payoff verification as illustrated in Sect. 3.3.

3.1 VOLGAPAY Participants

VOLGAPAY system includes seven classes of participants described below.

Public Blockchain. Public blockchain is used for storage, access, execution, and integrity assurance of the public smart contract. VOLGAPAY design requires the public blockchain to be universally available, trusted by all parties, capable of executing Turing-complete smart contracts with integrated cryptocurrency.

Public Smart Contract Public smart contract is used in VOLGAPAY to establish an unambiguous and non-repudiable agreement between the merchant and the client. Unlike the deposits in classic electronic payment systems, smart contract allows the client to retain full control over deposited funds irrespective of the merchant's trustworthiness. Each merchant-client pair requires a deployment of at least one separate public smart contract.

Table 2 describes a minimal set of routines that the public smart contract should have. The *set heads* routine, which saves all hash chain heads at once, can only be called by the merchant. The *payoff* routine exchanges the hashes released by the client into the cryptocurrency funds deposited by the client earlier. The *refund* routine allows the client to request unclaimed funds after a certain time period. The *deposit* routine allows the client to fund the smart contract.

Table 2. Minimal set of routines in VOLGAPAY public smart contract.

Routine	Description	Access
Set heads	Store hash chain heads provided by client	merchant
Payoff	Transfer funds to merchant based on cryptographic proof	merchant
Refund	Request refund after a payoff or timeout	client
Deposit	Deposit funds on the smart contract	client

Private Blockchain. Unlike its public counterpart, the private blockchain provides security only for the merchant infrastructure, and is not intended to be trusted by the client. Managed by the merchant and executed under a proof-of-authority (PoA) consensus, the private blockchain achieves high levels of security and redundancy for the merchant payment infrastructure at very little cost. Unlike proof-of-work (PoW) consensus, in which the voting power is restricted by computational limits, the PoA consensus limits the voting power by hard-coding the public keys of the sealers in the genesis block. PoA substitutes mining with sealing, and therefore achieves a better performance and full control over consensus. As an option, several merchants can share one private blockchain based on mutual trust. Alternatively, a merchant can use a third-party PoA blockchain as a service delivered by a trusted provider[3].

Private Smart Contract. For each public smart contract, the merchant deploys a mirroring smart contract on its private blockchain. The public smart contract contains an address of the mirroring smart contract in the private blockchain. We call this technique *blockchain grafting*[4].

Blockchain grafting supplements the public smart contract with the private one, the benefits of which include: first, private smart contract can perform secure execution without paying any blockchain fees; second, private smart contract executes and confirms transactions much faster than its public counterpart; third, private smart contract provides locally-trusted execution and storage within multiple nodes of the merchant infrastructure, such that if one or even several nodes

---

[3] Our VOLGAPAY prototype uses Kovan Testnet as a service.

[4] Grafting is an agricultural technique, in which a part of one plant is conjoined with another plant in order to combine the benefits of both. Similarly, we join public and private blockchains to utilize the properties and strengths of the two.

are compromised, the integrity of the ledger remains intact; fourth, private smart contract can achieve secure and flexible redundancy management at low cost: nodes can be added, removed, replaced or updated without service disruption.

Table 3 describes the minimal set of routines provided by the private smart contract. The *set heads* routine mirrors its public blockchain counterpart: it sets the hash chain heads to exactly the same values as they are in the public smart contract. The *token request* routine verifies the legitimacy of the OPOS and client, checks the hashes and payment amount provided by the client, processes the payment, updates the list of revealed hashes, and finally triggers a blockchain event that activates the token signers. The *one-time deposit* routine funds a smart contract only once (using a control variable); the additional deposits are prohibited to avoid tampering with the private smart contract balance. The *set Γ_i* routines are used by the signers to store their signatures in the blockchain.

Table 3. Minimal set of routines for VOLGAPAY private smart contract.

Routine	Description	Access
Set heads	Store hash chain heads provided by client	merchant
Token request	Process micropayment transaction and generate signatures	client
One-time deposit	Deposit pseudo-cryptocurrency equal to off-chain balance	merchant
Set Γ_i	Save signature $\Gamma_i(\eta, \delta)$ in the smart contract	signer i

Token Signers. To achieve security redundancy, we define the *payment token* as a set of M public-key signatures $\{\Gamma_1(\eta, \delta), ..., \Gamma_M(\eta, \delta)\}$ produced by M out of N signers. The set of signers' public keys is pre-determined by the merchant and stored in all offline terminals. Each token signer is a process running on a physically-separated hardware. All signers are listening to a smart-contract event triggered by the *token request function* of the private smart contract. This configuration allows the signers to communicate with the blockchain using a pull-only protocol, without listening on any ports.

Offline Point of Sale. The offline point of sale (OPOS) stays offline during the normal operation. Each OPOS stores its own private key and the full list of signers' public keys. Each OPOS has its own list of merchandise and pricing policy. If the list of signers' keys is modified in the system, e.g., a new signer is added to the system for extra redundancy, this information must be manually updated on each OPOS. No other change in the merchant infrastructure requires updating OPOS. If OPOS is compromised, i.e., its private key is stolen, the corresponding public key should be removed from or blacklisted in the private smart contract.

Client. VOLGAPAY client is a mobile device, which can establish a client-OPOS channel with an OPOS in proximity. The client also has access to the merchant's private blockchain through a client-blockchain channel. For purchases, the clients do not access the public blockchain.

3.2　Communication Channels

VOLGAPAY has four classes of communication channels: blockchain grafting channel, client-OPOS channel, client-blockchain channel, and signer-blockchain channels, as shown in Fig. 2.

Blockchain Grafting Channel. The blockchain grafting channel virtually links the address spaces of two independent blockchains. Specifically, it connects the public and private blockchains by storing the address of the private smart contract in the public smart contract.

Client-OPOS Channel. VOLGAPAY client establishes a local bi-directional simplex channel with an OPOS in proximity. We assume the channel has limited capacity, possible low bandwidth, and is not persistent. For our prototype, as described in Sect. 4, we use two-way QR-code scanning as client-OPOS channel. However, alternative channels can be established, including electromagnetic, Bluetooth, etc.

Client-Blockchain Channel. The client-blockchain channel allows the OPOS to get necessary updates on the state of the micropayment channel. While OPOS remains offline, the client plays the role of a proxy to the merchant infrastructure, through which the OPOS receives a receipt of successful payment in the form of a verifiable token. For the most common use cases of VOLGAPAY, e.g., vending machine purchase, it is necessary for the client to have access to the merchant infrastructure while interacting with OPOS.

Set of Signer-Blockchain Channels. Each signer is an independent network node subscribed to the token request events of all the private smart contracts through a signer-blockchain channel. This arrangement allows the signers not to listen to any ports and remain anonymous, and therefore significantly limit the exposure to potential cybersecurity threats. In order to serve multiple clients simultaneously, the signer-blockchain channels must maintain sufficient available bandwidth, which is discussed in Sect. 5.4.

3.3　VOLGAPAY Protocols

VOLGAPAY protocols define communication procedures between the participants of the system. VOLGAPAY includes four major protocols: 1) *contract initiation and deposit*, which establishes relationship between client and merchant; 2) *transaction protocol*, which describes the procedure of making transactions; 3) *payoff and refund*, which defines the conversion of the micropayment channel state into a fiat cryptocurrency; and 4) *payoff verification*, which verifies the correctness of the payoff amount. None of the four protocols require the client to share any sensitive or personal information; thus, data privacy and identify anonymization are inherently guaranteed by our blockchain-based design.

Contract Initiation and Deposit. This protocol includes the following sequence of steps:

1. The client requests a contract from the merchant, e.g., through the merchant's website or using a mobile app, and sends to the merchant the heads of hash chains in the set Υ;
2. The merchant prepares a pair of smart contracts for the client—public and private, and sends the client the address of the public contract;
3. The client verifies the code of the public smart contract, extracts the address of the private smart contract, and deposits funds on the public smart contract.

Transaction Protocol. The purchase protocol includes the following steps:

1. A client approaches an OPOS and initiates a purchase, e.g., by selecting an item with description D and price δ from the list of merchandise, as exemplified in Fig. 3;
2. The OPOS generates a random unique transaction ID η, and delivers the tuple $(\eta, \delta, D, K(\eta, \delta))$ to the client;
3. The client converts the item price δ into the τ-adjusted price ϕ, using the variable τ stored in the private smart contract;
4. The client calls the *token request function* of the private smart contract, providing $(R_1, R_2, ..., R_\xi), \eta, \delta$, and $K((\eta, \delta))$ as arguments;
5. The merchant's private smart contract first verifies price, payment, balance, and the authenticity of the signature of the OPOS, and then stores the tuple of payment hashes in the smart contract. It updates the smart contract balance, and adds current payment amount to the sum of previous payments τ, which is stored in the private smart contract. Finally, it triggers the event $E(\eta, \delta)$;
6. Each token signer responds to the event $E(\eta, \delta)$ by storing the signature $\Gamma_i(\eta, \delta)$ in the private smart contract;
7. The client waits until the private smart contract accumulates a minimum required number of signatures, and then it serializes these signatures into a tuple (which is the payment token), and delivers this tuple to the OPOS;
8. The OPOS verifies whether the signatures are distinct, valid, and produced by legitimate token signers, and then delivers the purchased item to the client.

Payoff and Refund. The merchant first verifies the payment hashes in the private smart contract released by the client, and then calls a payoff function of the public smart contract with the inputs of payment hashes, payment amount, and optional client's payoff verification signature (as described below). The unused funds deposited in the smart contract can be delivered to the client as a refund. The implementation specifics of payment and refund are determined by the merchants' policies.

Payoff Verification. VOLGAPAY's polynomial multi-hash chain price representation creates a potential caveat for the merchant to learn more hashes from the hash chains than the desirable number of hashes determined by the value of ϕ, as described in Sect. 3. VOLGAPAY enforces the correctness of the payoff amount by adding a payoff verification signature, $sig(\phi)$, generated and signed by the client to authorize an exact transaction payment amount. The signature will be stored as an additional variable in the private smart contract and updated after each successful token request. The signature and corresponding ϕ will be verified by the public smart contract during the payoff process: if the merchant's requested payment deviates from the correct payment on the blockchain, the payoff will be subsequently rejected. We leave the implementation of this feature as future work.

4   System Implementation

We have implemented the VOLGAPAY payment system. VOLGAPAY prototype includes two independent OPOS emulators and two Android clients. The total size of implementation includes 6,100+ lines of code. The details of different parts of the prototype are discussed below.

Fig. 3. OPOS interface transition.

Fig. 4. VOLGAPAY Android client.

Offline Point of Sale (OPOS). We simulate two OPOS using two sets of Raspberry Pi 3B+ as computing modules, mini-touchscreen for user interaction, and Raspberry Pi camera for reading QR-codes. We use Python 3.6, TkInter, and Web3.py to implement the OPOS software. Both the terminals are offline.

Figure 3 shows a three-step user interface transition of a purchase. The first step is the selection of the item: when the user pushes the touchscreen button, the terminal generates a unique transaction ID, and produces a QR-code. The QR-code contains the transaction ID η, item price δ in *wei*, item description D, and signature of the tuple (η, δ). During the second step, the client scans the QR-code with the Android app, requests a token, produces QR-code for the token, and pushes the "Scan Token" touch button on the screen of OPOS, which activates the QR-code reader. Finally, when the QR-code is scanned, the OPOS verifies the signatures, and delivers the item to the client.

Android Client. We implement a VOLGAPAY Android client using Android SDK and Web3j. Figure 4 shows the screen of the Android client right after obtaining a payment token from the private blockchain. Curious readers please refer to our demo video https://youtu.be/rjIhDD2yi5I for more information.

Mainnet Smart Contract. The public smart contract, which we test on both Ropsten and Mainnet networks, uses preset hash chain heads for executing payoff to the merchant and refund to the client. For our prototype, we use the following parameters: base currency–Ether, $\Theta = 10$, $g = 10^{13}$, $\xi = 7$, which means that we use 7 10-hash-deep chains, with minimal price unit equal to 10 *Szabo*, and maximum supported contract balance of 99.99999 *Ether*.

Kovan Smart Contract. We use Kovan Testnet for VOLGAPAY prototype to simulate the private blockchain. **The code of the private smart contract, written in Solidity, is available through this link:** https://github.com/seitlab/volgapay/blob/main/smartcontract.sol. The requestToken() function performs the validation of client identity, the authenticity of the OPOS, the validity of the payment, and available balance. If all the parameters are verified, the private smart contract decreases the balance of the smart contract, updates the base price τ, updates the payment hashes, and emits a signer-activation event.

The Signers. In our evaluation, we use a network of 10 signers. To demonstrate that the signers are not sensitive to latency and performance, we deploy them on low-tier basic servers (1 CPU/ 1 GB RAM/25 GB HDD/Ubuntu 18.04.2 × 64), located all across the world. Our prototype requires 5 valid signatures to form a payment token, i.e., $M = 5$. The event listeners are written in JavaScript using Web3.js library. When the token request event is issued by the smart contracts, all the ten signers respond by signing the serialized tuple of transaction ID and item price, and write the signatures in the smart contract.

5 Evaluation

Using the prototype, we perform evaluation of VOLGAPAY based on three criteria—delays, communication overhead, and cost of fees. Our prototype is not optimized for production use. Further improvement is possible through software optimization, choice of hardware, data compression techniques, network configuration, and selection of cryptographic routines. In the evaluation, each OPOS is implemented on a separate Raspberry Pi Model 3B+ [10]; each signer has the following configuration: 1 CPU, 1 GB RAM, 25 GB HDD, Ubuntu 18.04.2. As clients, we use Huawei Mate 9 and Motorola Moto G5 Plus, both with Android Nougat.

5.1 Delays

Here, we measure two types of delays, which determine the feasibility of VOL-GAPAY: token request time and payment request delay on public blockchain.

Transaction Latency of Traditional Payment Methods. We conduct a field experiment to measure a payment transaction latency of different types of traditional self-service terminals using Chase VISA debit card and CapitalOne MasterCard credit card, using both magnetic stripe and RFID technologies. We made 2 purchases at 2 different self-service gas stations, 4 purchases at 3 vending machines, 2 purchases at two parking meters, 2 balance checks, 2 cash withdrawals, and 1 PIN verification at 2 ATMs belonging to 2 different banks. We measure the transaction delay between applying the payment and receiving a payment acknowledgement using a handheld stopwatch. In order to adjust for human response delay, we subtract 1 s from each reading rounded to the closest second. The results, shown in Table 4, exhibit a significant variance, with the transaction times ranging from 5 to 21 s, with standard deviation of 5.3, and mean average of 11.7 s.

Token Request Time. We evaluate the token request time by measuring the time delay in milliseconds between pushing the "Get Token" button in the client Android App and the appearance of the token QR-code on the screen of the client. We measure the delay under three different types of Internet connection of the client: fast WiFi, LTE, and 3G. For each of the three connection types, we perform 20 probes, and record the mean average, standard deviation, and the speed profile of each connection[5] in Table 4. The experiment shows the average token request time, ranges between 9 and 12 s.

Table 4. Token request delays with different client connections. The transaction latency of VOLGAPAY is comparable to the credit card transaction delays with traditional payments (ranging from 5 to 21 s in our field experiment).

Client connection	Avg. link bandwidth			Delay (ms)	σ
	Down	Up	Ping		
WiFi	39.67	18.02	10.5	9,399	1,837
LTE	13.57	12.99	26	10,026	1,769
3G	2.54	0.90	80.5	11,618	1,716
Traditional self-service with credit cards	—	—	—	11,700	5,300

---

[5] For speed profile, we measure the speeds using Ookla Speed Test and M-Lab Speed Test, and get their average.

Public Smart Contract Calls. We measure the delays of public smart contract calls on Ropsten Testnet and Etheretum Mainnet networks. Each measurement is repeated 10 times, and the average results recorded in Table 5. The results show that the Ropsten network, despite its similarity with the Mainnet, does not always produce similar execution delays. The measurements also show that all the smart contract calls complete within 30 s on average. The results prove that the VOLGAPAY transactions introduce reasonable delays.

Table 5. Average public smart contract delays on Ropsten and Mainnet networks using Infura API, based on 10 measurements, with gas price 2.2 Gwei.

PHCS operation	Ropsten testnet		Ethereum mainnet	
	Delay (ms)	σ	Delay (ms)	σ
Bytecode check	756	371	10,920	698
Balance check	79	28	700	12
Deposit	28,168	13,874	22,555	20,823
Set 7 hash chain heads	26,467	11,547	26,491	25,222
Retrieve hash chain heads	489	41	554	65
Retrieve stored public key	175	46	236	205
Payoff	23,333	28,338	21,413	16,019
Refund	20,031	15,400	27,898	25,529
Contract deployment	24,481	10,913	20,231	9,623

5.2   Communication Overhead

Token Request. In our prototype, we use Infura API for communication with Kovan network. The summary of the communication overhead through the client-blockchain channel over 30 measurements is summarized in the left half of Fig. 5a. The result shows that the overall communication overhead does not exceed 50 Kbytes, and the incoming traffic volume is slightly larger than the outgoing one. The right half of the graph delivers the summary of communication overhead over signer-blockchain channels, which shows the total overhead per signature rarely exceeds 20 Kbytes, and the incoming traffic volume is also much larger than the outgoing one.

QR-Codes. The ASCII-based QR-code produced by the OPOS in our prototype includes the following fields: transaction ID, price in *wei*, description, and signature. The total length of the sequence encoded in the OPOS QR-code ranges between 175 and 222 bytes. The length of the second QR-code (i.e., payment token) is determined by the parameter M (i.e., the number of required signatures) of the system. For VOLGAPAY prototype, we use $M = 5$ with 0x-prefixes and 1-byte delimiters (for error checking), allotting to 664 bytes per token.

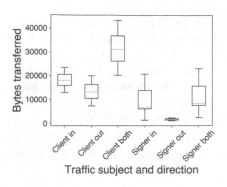

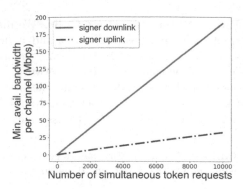

(a) Avg. token request communication overhead over 30 measurements.

(b) Min. avail. bandwidth requirement per signer-blockchain channel.

Fig. 5. VolgaPay communication overhead and associated throughput.

5.3 Fees

Table 6 shows the gas fees of VOLGAPAY prototype's public smart contract implementation over 10 measurements on Ropsten and 10 measurements on Mainnet network. As shown in the table, the operations are cheap, and the most gas-consuming one is contract deployment. Note that smart contract deployment is a one-time cost, which is less than $1.

Table 6. Gas fees, based on 20 measurements.

Smart contract operation	Average gas used	σ	Approximate USD cost[a]
Set addresses	21,040	0	$0.012
Set heads	72,263	65	$0.040
Payoff	55,212	53	$0.030
Refund	30,001	0	$0.017
Contract deployment	922,915	60,545	$0.508

[a]With the gas price 2.2 Gwei.

5.4 Scalability

Number of Simultaneous Token Requests. Let us assume that the available bandwidth of all signer-blockchain links is approximately the same, and the maximum time allotted for one signature response equals the average time T_b (in seconds) of sealing one block in the private blockchain. Then, the minimum available bandwidth B_{min} for one signer (in bps) is $B_{min} = \frac{N_R \cdot L}{T_b}$, where L is communication overhead per request in bits, and N_R is the number of simultaneous token requests. Using this formula and the communication overhead measurements gathered from the VOLGAPAY prototype (see Fig. 5a), we can demonstrate (see Fig. 5b) that a channel with 100 Mbps (200 Mbps) bandwidth is able to support more than 5,000 (10,000) simultaneous token requests.

Number of Clients. The number of clients in VOLGAPAY is not limited by any practical parameter of the system. However, it is important to note that as the number of clients increases, the probability of exceeding the bandwidth capacity of the signer-blockchain channel grows.

Number of OPOS Terminals. The number of OPOS terminals affects two parameters in the private smart contract: the set of OPOS public keys, and the amount of computation required to verify the identity of a terminal. We modify the smart contract by adding 10^3 random OPOS keys, which increases the number of OPOS identity checks from 2 to 1,000 in the token request routine. Then, we re-evaluate the token request delay by running 20 more token requests simulating the worst-case scenario. The results indicate similar delays, which do not exceed 10 s on average. Therefore, for each merchant, VOLGAPAY can support at least 1,000 OPOS terminals without degrading performance.

6   Security Analysis

Here, we account for the possible reasonable scenarios in which important components (participants or channels) are compromised by an adversary. If several types of attacks exist for achieving the same malicious outcome, we elaborate on the outcome, e.g. "gaining full access".

Malicious Merchant. Malicious merchants try to steal funds from the clients. Note that the clients' funds in public smart contract are guarded by the public blockchain and their respective private keys. The only feasible malicious activity would be to receive payment without providing a valid token, in which case the client will lose payment for a single purchase. Given the cost of infrastructure setup, the merchants are unlikely to pursue such attacks.

Full Access to OPOS. Each OPOS stores its own private key, which is used for confirming its belonging to a certain merchant. If the key is stolen, it can be temporarily used for the deployment of a fake OPOS, but it does not allow the attacker to steal any funds since OPOS does not process payments. Therefore, the incentives to steal the private key of an OPOS is limited only to retaliation and vandalism. In order to protect the private key from theft, it is recommended to store the key only in the address space of RAM of the legitimate VOLGAPAY process. Additionally, if an attacker gains full physical access to an OPOS, all the merchandise of the terminal can be stolen bypassing the token verification procedure. This, however, can be prevented by enforcing physical security, which goes beyond the scope of this work.

Full Access to the Client App. The client app can be designed not to store the private key used in public smart contract, or to store it securely encrypted, with mandatory passphrase solicitation before each use. As a result, we exclude the possibility of stealing the private key used for public smart contract even when the adversary gains access to the client software. Thus, the only valuable asset that can be stolen from the client is the set of hash chain heads, and the authentication private key for the private smart contract: the combination thereof can be used to make purchases on behalf of the client, but does not allow to steal funds because fund management is performed via the private key of the public smart contract.

Full Access to One of the Private Chain Sealers. If one of the sealers of the private blockchain is compromised, there is no immediate threat to the system. Moreover, depending on the specifics of the private blockchain's consensus protocol and the size of the clique or quorum, the blockchain remains intact even if several sealers are compromised. In most cases, it requires to compromise 50% of the sealers to attack the private blockchain. However, a compromised sealer likely means one of the private keys used for the consensus is stolen. Although there is no immediate danger, the sealer must eventually be replaced, which will require creating a new genesis block, restarting blockchain, re-deployment of private smart contracts, and changing the grafting links in corresponding public smart contracts, which can be done automatically during a scheduled maintenance.

One way to mitigate the threat associated with compromised private blockchain sealers is to use reputable outsourced PoA blockchain services, or to share blockchain between several mutually trusted merchants. Another solution is to add additional IP authentication to the boot nodes, which grants access to the blockchain's P2P network only to peers from certain IP addresses; this solution, however, requires to run a sufficient number of boot nodes in order to prevent an eclipse attack [31].

Denial of Service Attacks. Although denial-of-service attacks do not yield any immediate fund gain for an attacker, they can be used as a means of retaliation or vandalism. Private blockchain sealers and VOLGAPAY signers are possible targets to this type of attack. The design of VOLGAPAY allows to keep the IP addresses of both signers and sealers in secret; and if this information still gets revealed, to seamlessly replace the IP addresses without changing blockchain-level identities (keys). This is possible because sealers in blockchain are identified by their keys, not by their IP addresses.

Local Channel Sniffing and Spoofing. Among many ways of maintaining the client-OPOS channel, the QR-code exchange is the most feasible and popular approach. The visual channel is subject to eavesdropping attacks, and its payload limitations make it infeasible to secure, e.g., through a Diffie-Hellmann key exchange. Thus, we can assume that the information in the channel can be read (sniffing) and substituted (spoofing). Because of the physical presence of the client at the OPOS for the entire duration of transaction, the sniffing or spoofing of any of the two QR-codes does not yield any gain to the attacker other than creating a minor annoyance to the client.

Man-in-the-Middle-Attacks. The resistance to man-in-the-middle (MITM) attacks in all the VOLGAPAY channels, except the client-OPOS channel described above, can be achieved by establishing encrypted communications. Since most of the channels, such as secure socket or RPC-calls to blockchain, are secure by default, the possibility of such an attack is very low. However, even if an MITM attack is successfully conducted, the potential harm can only be experienced by the client, whose payment token could be blocked by an attacker. There is little incentive for an attacker to do so, as the token validity is limited by the current transaction session.

7 Conclusion

In this paper, we presented a new blockchain-based tokenized payment system, VOLGAPAY, to address the numerous practical challenges towards the deployment and use of offline payment terminals, such as security, privacy, trust in merchant, and significant infrastructure cost. VOLGAPAY incorporates multi-hash chain-based micropayment channels and blockchain grafting to strike a balance in security and efficiency, by leveraging the security and trustworthiness of public blockchain, as well as the speed and cost-efficiency of private blockchain. We implemented the VOLGAPAY payment system and evaluated all the parameters affecting its practical feasibility. Our evaluation shows that the system is fast, cost-efficient, and scalable. Most importantly, through a comprehensive security analysis, we demonstrated that VOLGAPAY is resistant to a variety of cyber-attacks: if any component of the system is compromised, the scope of harm will be minimized, and the threat will not propagate to other components.

Acknowledgement. We would like to thank the anonymous reviewers for providing valuable feedback on our work. This work was supported in part by National Science Foundation grants CNS1950171 and CNS1949753.

References

1. Stellar (2019). https://www.stellar.org/. Accessed 23 May 2019
2. Alipay: Qr code payment (2017). https://docs.open.alipay.com/140/104622/. Accessed 25 July 2019
3. Anderson, L., Cushley, S.: System and method of providing tokenization as a service (Nov 28 2017), US Patent 9,830,595
4. Bai, X., et al.: Picking up my tab: Understanding and mitigating synchronized token lifting and spending in mobile payment. In: 26th USENIX Security Symposium (USENIX Security 2017) (2017)
5. Casa: Casa node (2019). https://keys.casa/lightning-bitcoin-node. Accessed: 23 May 2019

6. Decker, C., Wattenhofer, R.: A fast and scalable payment network with bitcoin duplex micropayment channels. In: Pelc, A., Schwarzmann, A.A. (eds.) SSS 2015. LNCS, vol. 9212, pp. 3–18. Springer, Cham (2015). https://doi.org/10.1007/978-3-319-21741-3_1

7. Dmitrienko, A., Noack, D., Yung, M.: Secure wallet-assisted offline bitcoin payments with double-spender revocation. In: Proceedings of the 2017 ACM on Asia Conference on Computer and Communications Security, pp. 520–531 (2017)

8. Dziembowski, S., Eckey, L., Faust, S., Malinowski, D.: Perun: virtual payment hubs over cryptocurrencies. In: 2019 IEEE Symposium on Security and Privacy (SP), pp. 327–344 (2019)

9. Dziembowski, S., Faust, S., Hostáková, K.: General state channel networks. In: Proceedings of the 2018 ACM SIGSAC Conference on Computer and Communications Security. pp. 949–966 (2018)

10. Foundation, R.P.: Raspberry pi 3 model b+ (2019). https://www.raspberrypi.org/products/raspberry-pi-3-model-b-plus/. Accessed 26 July 2019

11. Green, M., Miers, I.: Bolt: anonymous payment channels for decentralized currencies. In: Proceedings of the 2017 ACM SIGSAC Conference on Computer and Communications Security, pp. 473–489 (2017)

12. Inc., B.C.: Blockstream lightning network (2019). https://blockstream.com/lightning. Accessed 23 May 2019

13. Ivanov, N., Yan, Q., Wang, Q.: Blockumulus: a scalable framework for smart contracts on the cloud. In: 2021 IEEE 41st International Conference on Distributed Computing Systems (ICDCS). IEEE (2021)

14. Jiang, F., Okonkwo, A.P., Aitenbichler, E.: Secure offline payment system (Oct 1 2015), US Patent App. 14/226,785

15. Khalil, R., Gervais, A.: revive: Rebalancing off-blockchain payment networks. In: Proceedings of the 2017 ACM SIGSAC Conference on Computer and Communications Security, pp. 439–453 (2017)

16. Lab, M.M.: layer 2 — the lightning network (2019). https://dci.mit.edu/lightning-network. Accessed 23 May 2019

17. Lightning Labs, I.: Lightning labs (2019). https://lightning.engineering. Accessed 23 May 2019

18. Lind, J., Naor, O., Eyal, I., Kelbert, F., Pietzuch, P., Sirer, E.G.: Teechain: reducing storage costs on the blockchain with offline payment channels. In: Proceedings of the 11th ACM International Systems and Storage Conference (2018)

19. Manworren, N., Letwat, J., Daily, O.: Why you should care about the target data breach. Bus. Horiz. **59**(3), 257–266 (2016)

20. Mendoza, S.: Samsung pay: tokenized numbers, flaws and issues. In: Proceedings of Black Hat USA, pp. 1–11 (2016)

21. Miller, A., Bentov, I., Kumaresan, R., McCorry, P.: Sprites: Payment channels that go faster than lightning. arXiv preprint arXiv:1702.05812 (2017)

22. Nseir, S., Hirzallah, N., Aqel, M.: A secure mobile payment system using qr code. In: 2013 5th International Conference on Computer Science and Information Technology, pp. 111–114. IEEE (2013)

23. Pedersen, T.P.: Electronic payments of small amounts. In: Lomas, M. (ed.) Security Protocols 1996. LNCS, vol. 1189, pp. 59–68. Springer, Heidelberg (1997). https://doi.org/10.1007/3-540-62494-5_5

24. Poon, J., Dryja, T.: The bitcoin lightning network: Scalable off-chain instant payments (2016)

25. Roos, S., Moreno-Sanchez, P., Kate, A., Goldberg, I.: Settling payments fast and private: Efficient decentralized routing for path-based transactions. arXiv preprint arXiv:1709.05748 (2017)
26. Sabba, Y., Scheinfield, J.: Token check offline, 4 August 2016. US Patent App. 15/011,366
27. SAS, A.: Acinq (2019). https://acinq.co. Accessed 23 May 2019
28. Tebbe, H.: Offline mobile payment process (2015), US Patent App. 13/966,053
29. Trautman, L.J., Ormerod, P.C.: Corporate directors' and officers' cybersecurity standard of care: the yahoo data breach. Am. Univ. Law Rev. **66**, 1231 (2016)
30. Van Damme, G., Wouters, K.M., Karahan, H., Preneel, B.: Offline nfc payments with electronic vouchers. In: Proceedings of the 1st ACM Workshop on Networking, Systems, and Applications for Mobile Handhelds, pp. 25–30 (2009)
31. Wüst, K., Gervais, A.: Ethereum eclipse attacks. Technical report ETH Zurich (2016)
32. Xu, W., Grant, G., Nguyen, H., Dai, X.: Security breach: the case of tjx companies, inc. Commun. Assoc. Inf. Syst. **23**(1), 31 (2008)

Horus: A Security Assessment Framework for Android Crypto Wallets

Md Shahab Uddin, Mohammad Mannan, and Amr Youssef$^{(\boxtimes)}$

Concordia University, Montreal, QC, Canada
md_din@encs.concordia.ca, m.mannan@concordia.ca, youssef@cisse.concordia.ca

Abstract. Crypto wallet apps help cryptocurrency users to create, store, and manage keys, sign transactions and keep track of funds. However, if these apps are not adequately protected, attackers can exploit security vulnerabilities in them to steal the private keys and gain ownership of the users' wallets. We develop a semi-automated security assessment framework, Horus, specifically designed to analyze crypto wallet Android apps. We perform semi-automated analysis on 310 crypto wallet apps, and manually inspect the top 17 most popular wallet apps from the Google Play Store. Our analysis includes capturing runtime behavior, reverse-engineering the apps, and checking for security standards crucial for wallet apps (e.g., random number generation and private key confidentiality). We reveal several severe vulnerabilities, including, for example, storing plaintext key revealing information in 111 apps which can lead to losing wallet ownership, and storing past transaction information in 11 apps which may lead to user deanonymization.

Keywords: Crypto wallets · Cryptocurrency · HD wallets · Android apps

1 Introduction

Bitcoin is the world's most popular cryptocurrency, its value has recently surpassed US$60,000 [35] and is getting wider adoption in businesses. Other cryptocurrencies like Ethereum, and Litecoin have established their footprints and going strong among cryptocurrency users. The combined market cap of more than 6000 cryptocurrencies has reached a new high of US$1.24 trillion in 2021 [36]. Unfortunately, this massive growth of cryptocurrencies is also attracting malicious actors to find and exploit vulnerabilities in cryptocurrency-related technologies. The cryptocurrency community has witnessed no less than 34 attacks, breaches, and scams in 2020 alone [16,37], and attackers have stolen approximately US$4 billion [34] worth of assets from users.

Crypto wallets, being an ingrained part of cryptocurrency ecosystem, also encounter attacks ranging from deanonymization to password cracking [15,40, 43]. Due to their importance, past work analyzed several crypto wallet apps. For

© ICST Institute for Computer Sciences, Social Informatics and Telecommunications Engineering 2021
Published by Springer Nature Switzerland AG 2021. All Rights Reserved
J. Garcia-Alfaro et al. (Eds.): SecureComm 2021, LNICST 399, pp. 120–139, 2021.
https://doi.org/10.1007/978-3-030-90022-9_7

example, He et al. [26] analyzed critical attack surfaces in two wallet apps and demonstrated proof-of-concept attacks. Haigh et al. [25] analyzed the forensic artifacts of seven wallet apps, and designed a Trojan attack by repackaging a wallet app to steal user credentials; they chose to analyze non-HD (Hierarchical Deterministic [49]) wallets, although HD-wallets are gaining adoption in recent years and preferred over non-HD wallets in terms of security and portability.

To perform a comprehensive and scalable analysis of current and popular wallet apps (the number of which is growing, currently in the range of hundreds), we developed a semi-automated test framework, Horus[1]. Our framework combines both static and dynamic analysis of crypto wallet apps and can assess whether industry best practices are being followed in the app implementation. Horus has three major components: (1) *scraper module*, which can collect a large dataset of specific categories of apps from the Google Play Store; (2) *static analysis module*, which looks for API pattern to determine if proper security standards are followed in the app implementation; and (3) *dynamic analysis module*, which searches for key revealing information stored in the app's artifact on the device.

Using these components, we collect 310 wallet apps and analyze them for security risks. We conduct a manual inspection of the top 17 crypto wallet apps in the Google Play Store to understand the apps' security practices and evaluate the security risk associated with them. We use popular open-source vulnerability analysis tools, such as Androbugs[2] and Qark.[3] Syntax-based static analysis tools often fall short to determine vulnerabilities accurately [42]. We have noticed two issues with this approach, (1) a significant number of false-positive vulnerabilities and (2) discovered vulnerabilities are generic and do not represent issues specifically applicable to wallet apps. To complement static analysis tools, we also conduct a dynamic analysis to better understand the apps' workflow, and explore a broader set of vulnerabilities, including plaintext key storage, and exported components. In the final step, we inspect the decompiled apps' code to verify our findings and understand the app's operational mechanism in a greater detail. The main observation that follows from our analysis is that critical security standards applicable for wallet apps are missing in the app's binary, which indicates those standards are not implemented or have not been considered in the apps' development process. Additionally, the apps' key revealing information is handled insecurely (e.g., saved as plaintext or encrypted using poorly chosen encryption configuration). Our framework can accurately identify critical issues in wallet apps, and our automated analysis results are consistent with the manual inspection results.

Several design components of our semi-automated framework take into consideration the implicit and varying nature of the wallet apps. Firstly, a wallet-import step varies significantly from one app to another due to the heterogeneous user interface, and the effort requires to make it a generalized automated step is non-trivial. To overcome this problem, we develop a semi-automated framework

---

[1] Horus is one of the ancient Egyptian deities. The Eye of Horus is an ancient Egyptian symbol of protection.

[2] https://github.com/AndroBugs/AndroBugs_Framework.

[3] https://github.com/linkedin/qark/.

with a reduced-effort manual step (see Sect. 4.2). Secondly, most apps are still non-HD wallets and do not support wallet portability features. We developed a separate workflow to analyze non-HD wallet apps (see Sect. 4.2). Lastly, some wallet apps are heavily obfuscated which hinders our reverse engineering phase. To circumvent this problem, we focus on artifacts analysis instead of the obfuscated code. This technique also enables us to be compatible with mobile apps developed using hybrid and cross-platform frameworks (e.g., PhoneGap, Flutter) along with native apps developed for Android and iOS. For the purpose of this work, we keep our focus limited to analyzing Android apps.

Contributions. Our contribution can be summarized as follows:

1. We develop a semi-automated framework, Horus, to statically analyze wallet apps (fully automated), and perform dynamic analysis (with limited manual interactions).
2. We conduct automated analysis of 310 crypto wallet apps on the Android platform. Additionally, we inspect the top 17 most popular crypto wallet apps, with combined downloads of 46M+ and in total 84M+ of 310 apps, in Google Play Store to understand the apps' security practices and evaluate the security risk associated with them.
3. We reveal that 111/310 of the apps store key revealing information in plaintext and 18 HD wallet apps store the encryption key without additional protections, i.e., without Android Keystore or Android Hardware Security Module (HSM). Moreover, 11/310 apps store transaction information that can lead to deanonymization. Only 3/310 apps use HSM the best in class secure storage solution to protect key revealing information.
4. We find that the Android user dictionary can be leveraged to derive the mnemonic phrase used to generate the private key. Only 20/310 apps implement custom keyboard to safeguard against this attack.

2   Background and Threat Model

In this section, we provide brief descriptions of some wallet-related terminologies and our threat model.

Crypto wallet apps generally generate new addresses, store private keys securely, and help automate transactions. Some wallets can handle only one type of cryptocurrency (e.g., Bitcoin), and others can handle multiple types of cryptocurrencies. Furthermore, there are two types of wallets: Hierarchical Deterministic (HD) wallet [49], and non-HD wallet. HD wallets organize user accounts from one or more seed values and utilize open-source community-driven protocols to perform each operation, such as generating seed and creating private keys. On the other hand, a non-HD wallet randomly generates keys (i.e., no connection or hierarchy between the keys); such unrelated keys are also known as JBOK (Just-a-Bunch-of-Keys).

Bitcoin Improvement Proposals (BIPs). Several open-source community-driven protocols known as BIP [12] facilitate various crypto wallet functions.

Each proposal is responsible for a specific goal, and the Bitcoin community can propose, rectify, establish, approve or reject proposals by consensus. As of March 13, 2021, there are 140 BIPs [12], but 3 BIPs are primarily relevant for HD-wallet apps. (1) *BIP 32* which defines a tree structure to populate public-private key pairs from a seed. The seed allows the wallet to be interchangeable with different implementations/devices, and implies the wallet does not need to be backed up often; just saving the seed is enough to recreate the tree structure of keys [49]. (2) *BIP 39* which defines both generating a mnemonic phrase and how to create a seed from the phrase, as compared to a hexadecimal random seed, a phrase is easier to remember and store for users. This proposal also defines a list of 2048 common English words to be selected for mnemonic phrases. The chosen words for a mnemonic phrase and their order are needed to regenerate the same seed afterward. The word list is also available in multiple languages [39]. (3) *BIP 44* which defines a syntax to enable a multi-account hierarchy of keys based on BIP 32. The syntax expresses purpose, coin type, account, address index to generate proper keys [38]. The proposal defines how to generate any number of cryptocurrency-specific child keys.

HD Wallet Generation. A mnemonic phrase is generated using the standardized process defined in BIP 39. The most common phrase length is 12 and 24 words. In Android wallets, the 12-word length phrase is prevalent. First, a random sequence of 12/24 words is selected, providing 128–256 bits of entropy [9]. Then, the PBKDF2 (Password-Based Key Derivation Function 2) key derivation function is used to derive a 512-bit seed from the word sequence. This seed can be used to deterministically generate an HD wallet [49]. An HD wallet root consists of a pair of a master private key and a master chain code. Next, a master public key is generated from the master private key. Both the master private key and the master chain code are used to generate child keys using BIP 44 [38]. Note that there is no way to verify the words and their order in a phrase. If the user adds/removes/scrambles the phrase's words, a new seed is generated, leading to some other wallet keys. The phrase, seed, master private/public keys, and master chain code are all key revealing information and should be protected with equal importance.

Threat Model. We assume the attacker can install a malicious app on the victim's device with the following capabilities (or a subset of those). The app can have virtual keyboard permission, or it is a keyboard app itself, which is set default by the user. The malicious app can take a screenshot of the device. We assume the device is not rooted by the user; however, a malicious app can successfully root the device. Attackers can have physical access to the unlocked device for a few minutes. Note that all these capabilities are not required for all our attacks.

3   Dataset Collection

Google Play Store search displays only the popular apps based on its search algorithm, but does not provide a comprehensive list of all the apps matched with a search term [10,41]. Conversely, a web search engine provides an exhaustive list of apps matched with the provided search term. We develop a specialized search engine scraper module based on a generic scraper tool, Search Engine Scraper,[4] for collecting a large set of apps. Our scraper module can search, parse results, remove duplicate app IDs, and download the APK (Android Application Package) files from Google Play Store automatically. We have used search term site : play.google.com " bitcoin " " wallet ".

We use the search engine bing.com due to API restrictions in google.com (up to 100 pages, but multiple test runs from the same IP address may result in the IP being blocked before this limit is reached). We use a user agent value to appear as a desktop browser to the search engine, and introduce a random delay before scraping each new search result page to emulate normal usage and avoid any API restrictions.

We scraped 24,800 search results and found a total of 636 APK links, with 442 unique app IDs. We use PlaystoreDownloader[5] to download the latest version of the app from the play store. We encountered some exceptions during app download, including: some apps are unavailable in our location (Canada), some apps are available only via the early access program, and some apps are incompatible with our device. Eventually, we downloaded 392 apps and found 82 apps were not wallet apps although the term "wallet" appears in their description; such apps include Bitcoin key generator, currency exchange service, etc. We filtered out non-wallet apps and obtained a collection of 310 wallet apps. We shortlisted all the apps with at least 1M+ downloads in Google Play Store (total 17 apps, accessed: 2021-02-03) for further manual inspection due to their high user base, see Table 1.

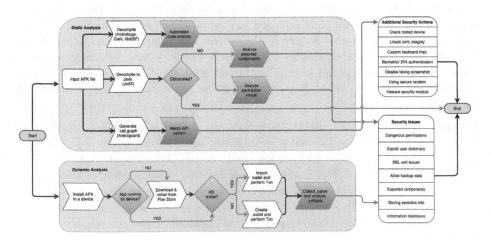

Fig. 1. Overview of proposed framework

---

[4] https://github.com/tasos-py/Search-Engines-Scraper.
[5] https://github.com/ClaudiuGeorgiu/PlaystoreDownloader.

Table 1. Top 17 most downloaded wallet apps in Google Play Store (accessed: 2021-02-03). ✗ indicates non-HD wallet app and ✔ indicates HD wallet app.

Application ID	Version	Downloads	HD?	Supported coins
asia.coins.mobile	3.5.22	5M+	✗	BTC, XRP, ETH, BCH
co.bitx.android.wallet	7.6.0	5M+	✗	BTC, ETH, XRP, USDC
co.mona.android	3.84.0	1M+	✔	80+ coins
com.binance.dev	1.36.3	5M+	✗	200+ coins
com.bitcoin.mwallet	6.9.10	1M+	✔	BTC, BCH
com.breadwallet	4.7.0	1M+	✔	BTC, XBT, BCH, ETH
com.coinomi.wallet	1.20.0	1M+	✔	125+ coins
com.mycelium.wallet	3.8.6.1	1M+	✔	BTC, ETH, ERC-20
com.paxful.wallet	1.7.1.534	1M+	✗	BTC, USDT
com.polehin.android	3.4.9	1M+	✗	100+ coins
com.unocoin.unocoinwallet	3.4.7	1M+	✗	BTC, ETH, XRP, LTC
com.wallet.crypto.trustapp	1.26.5	5M+	✔	50+ coins
com.xapo	5.3	1M+	✗	BTC
de.schildbach.wallet	8.08	5M+	✗	BTC
org.toshi	23.3.357	1M+	✔	100+ coins
piuk.blockchain.android	8.4.7	10M+	✔	BTC, ETH, BCH, XLM
zebpay.Application	3.12.02	1M+	✗	BTC, ETH, XRP, EOS

4 Horus: Our Analysis Framework

The purpose of developing Horus is to automate the analysis process of wallet apps and discover issues in the apps' implementation. The idea and rationale behind building this framework and design decisions for different wallets are explained in this section. An overview of our evaluation methodology is presented in Fig. 1. There are two modules for app analysis in Horus: *static analysis module* and *dynamic analysis module*.

4.1 Static Analysis Module

The static analysis module of Horus looks for API patterns to determine if a particular functionality or security feature is implemented in the app. For instance, a wallet app must implement a custom keyboard; otherwise, it is vulnerable to user dictionary attacks; see Sect. 5. We verify if the APIs required to implement a custom keyboard in Android are called in the app. If the API calls are found, the functionality is assumed to be implemented in the app.

To determine the API calls in an app, Horus takes an apk file as input and constructs a call graph of the app using Androguard.[6] A call graph contains the class name, method name, descriptors, and access flags. Each node in the

---

[6] https://github.com/androguard/androguard.

call graph is a method, and the actual calls with arguments are denoted using edges. For root detection, the app checks the execution of su command [29], or the existence of a list of root enabler apps [19] on the device. The call, Runtime.exec() is used to check the existence of su binary and PackageManager.getPackageInfo() is used to check the existence of a root enabler app. The API calls in the app's

Table 2. API signatures to check for feature existence.; the *Type* column denotes the security standard type, the *API Signature* column points to the API calls and individual class names required to implement the security standard, and the *Usage* column indicates the use case of each API call.

Type	API signature	Usage
Root Detection	Runtime.exec()	Execute runtime command, e.g. su
	PackageManager.getPackageInfo()	Get installed app's information
	Os.stat()	System call for runtime command execution
	Os.access()	System call to query installed app
Integrity Check	PackageManager.getPackageInfo()	Get installed app's information
	Context.getPackageCodePath()	App installer file path
	ZipFile.init()	Execute operation on installer file
	RandomAccessFile.init()	Read, write in system file
Custom Keyboard	KeyboardView.setKeyboard()	Replaces default keyboard app
	OnKeyboardActionListener.onKey()	Listeners for input key
	InputMethodService.onCreateInputView()	Callback when the keyboard view is created
	InputConnection.commitText()	Commit the user input to app
	InputMethod	Handles keyboard type depending on input field
Biometric Authentication	BiometricManager	Provides biometric utilities
	BiometricPrompt	Handles biometric authentication
	FingerprintManager	Defines types of authentication (Deprecated)
	BiometricService	Updates system server for fingerprint
	FingerprintService	Updates system server for fingerprint (Deprecated)
Screenshots Disabled	Windows.setFlags()	Uses for full screen access
	View.setDrawingCacheEnabled()	Access to the current view displayed
Hardware Security Module	KeyStore.getInstance()	Returns a keystore object of specified type
	KeyGenParameterSpec.Builder.isStrongBoxBacked()	Requesting Android to use hardware module
	StrongBoxUnavailableException	Exception if the hardware module is absence
Random Generator	SecureRandom	Cryptographically strong random number generator

call graph indicate the app is checking whether the device is rooted. Table 2 depicts the API signatures we use to determine the existence of the security standard in an app. Below, we discuss several security standards that we verify using our static module.

Secure Random: A secure random number generator is crucial for crypto wallet apps. According to BIP 39 [39], to create a mnemonic phrase, the client must use an entropy of length 128–256 bits. A seed is generated from the mnemonic phrase and used to create the master private/public keys. If the random number generator is predictable, it affects the key generation objective. In Android, /dev/urandom [47] is used to generate seed for SecureRandom [7], which is the recommended API to generate a cryptographically strong random number.

Custom Keyboard: Once a wallet app generates a mnemonic phrase, it asks the user to enter the mnemonic phrase for verification. To import an existing wallet into a new app, the user also needs to enter the mnemonic phrase via keyboard. If the user uses a third-party keyboard app, it can capture all user inputs [5], including the mnemonic phrase. Additionally, the app is vulnerable to user dictionary attack. A wallet app should have a custom keyboard triggered while taking any key revealing input and possibly randomize the keyboard's key location [32].

Disabling Screenshot-Taking: This is another critical risk avoidance feature for wallet apps. Any malicious app with the capability of taking a screenshot can capture the screen content during the wallet import phase. Also, a user may take a screenshot of the mnemonic phrase to save it as a backup. This image is saved in the gallery, and any app with reading storage permission can access the file. Crypto wallet apps must call Android API to disable the screenshot-taking feature for sensitive screens.

Two Factor Authentication (2FA): 2FA or biometric authentication should be implemented before performing any sensitive operation. We observe a significant number of wallet apps do not require user registration. An unauthorized user can perform a transaction with a few minutes of physical access to the device, assuming it is unlocked. Some apps require the user to set a PIN code and ask for the PIN code when confirming a transaction. However, a PIN code can be as short as a 4-digits number which can be brute-forced or seen by shoulder surfing. A 2FA should be incorporated in each wallet app as second-layer protection.

Integrity Check: App's signature verification to check integrity ensure that the app has not been tampered with and installed from a legit source (e.g., Google Play Store). Integrity can also be ensured by calculating a hash of the installed APK file and comparing it with the hash of authenticated APK file. The solution is not foolproof and can be bypassed in a repackaged app. However, integrity checking is a widely adopted practice in financial apps and is considered a self-defense mechanism. The wallet app must perform integrity checks as another layer of security before starting to operate.

Root Detection: An app can be made more secure by implementing 2FA or strong encryption; however, no security on the app end works if the device itself is compromised. Malware apps can have root providers included in the binary and may gain root privilege without the user's consent [50]. This privilege can be exploited in many ways, from monitoring activities of other apps to sending key revealing information to a malicious back-end.

Hardware Security Module: Recent Android smartphones have a separate processor, which provides additional security to keep key revealing information safe, called hardware security module [4]. The key revealing information is stored in a secure enclave that is also protected in a rooted device and safe against brute force attack by utilizing rate limiting. The solution is not foolproof; there is still room for information disclosure if the device contains a malicious keyboard app or a clipboard listener. Nevertheless, the hardware security module provides substantial improvements over any other storage solutions and should be used by wallet apps to secure key revealing information.

Manual Inspection. For in-depth inspection of the top 17 wallet apps, we use three state-of-the-art analysis tools, AndroBugs, Qark, and MobSF.[7] The tools look for generic vulnerabilities by following a defined set of rules and patterns and do not require the app to run. All these tools start with decompiling the app code and looking for several vulnerabilities, including: runtime command execution, SSL certificate verification, and webview vulnerabilities. The tools mark the found vulnerabilities with different severity labels (e.g., Critical, Warning, Info). We consider only the critical vulnerabilities.

We use reverse engineering to discover vulnerabilities in the app code by decompiling the APK file. Reverse engineering reveals permissions usage in the app for malicious purposes, logic bombs, Trojan code, etc. Sometimes the app code is obfuscated, by renaming code components, such as folders, classes, variables, into a shorter, unintelligible name [8]. It is difficult to get out any meaningful information from the obfuscated code; we skip the app in such cases. We use APKTool[8] and JD-GUI[9] for our reverse engineering step. Apktool can decode resources from the Android APK file, and JD-GUI is a Java decompiler and code browser.

4.2   Dynamic Analysis Module

In the dynamic analysis module, we look for key revealing information in apps' internal file structures. If the device is rooted or the target app allows backup, malicious apps or actors can capture the target app's internal files. If the internal files contain key revealing information (e.g., plaintext private key), a malicious actor can easily access such information. In general, the master private key is the most critical information that needs to be protected by wallet apps. Other such

---

[7] https://github.com/MobSF/Mobile-Security-Framework-MobSF.
[8] https://ibotpeaches.github.io/Apktool/.
[9] https://github.com/skylot/jadx.

critical items include the mnemonic phrase, seed, and master chain code—all of which should be protected with equal importance as of the master private key. Note that a mnemonic phrase is used to generate a seed value, which is used to generate its corresponding private key. Similarly, the master public key and any of the child's private key is enough to recreate the master private key [24]. So it is imperative to secure all of the key revealing items along with the master private key. Our goal is to seek answers to the following questions: Are wallet apps storing the above-mentioned key revealing information in plaintext on the device? If encrypted, which encryption algorithm is used? Can we identify the encryption key used to perform the encryption, and if yes, where is the encryption key stored?

HD Wallet Workflow. A HD wallet can recreate the hierarchical tree of keys from a mnemonic phrase. In our HD wallet workflow, we maintain four lists as follows. (1) *Key revealing information:* A list of secret information that can be used to regenerate the master private key. In addition to the master private key itself, this list includes mnemonic phrase, seed, seed hex value, BIP 32 private key, and master chain code. (2) *Candidate encryption key:* Key revealing information should be encrypted before storing on the device. *Candidate encryption key* is a list of all possible encryption keys that wallet apps can use to encrypt key revealing information. We find traces that encryption keys are stored in the app's internal files. Using Horus, we can verify how widespread the practice is to store encryption keys locally. (3) *Cipher key revealing information:* Each item of the *key revealing information* list is encrypted and the resulting ciphertext is encoded using Base64 and then appended to this list. (4) *Search term:* A combined list of *key revealing information* and *cipher key revealing information*. We use this list of items as a search term and look for each item of this list in the wallet's artifact.

To start the dynamic analysis, we install the target app on a rooted device. We generate a mnemonic phrase and import the same phrase in all HD wallet apps. We use a fixed email, username, PIN, password, and phone number in all the apps for account creation, and verification as needed by the app. We append this fixed information in the *candidate encryption key* list as potential encryption keys.

From a mnemonic phrase, Horus gets *key revealing information* list, and by parsing internal files, Horus get *candidate encryption key* list. Horus iterates through the *key revealing information* list and applies encryption algorithms available in the Android platform to encrypt each of the items in *key revealing information* by using items from *candidate encryption key* list as the encryption key. One such operation is as follows, we take the first element of *key revealing information*, encrypt it with AES using the first element of *candidate encryption key*, and add the resulting ciphertext in *search term*. We then repeat the same operation with the next element of *candidate encryption key*, and so on. When done, we use a different encryption algorithm (e.g., Blowfish) and go through the same list of *candidate encryption key* and repeat the process. All the *key revealing information* is also appended as-is to *search term* list because the *key revealing information* can also be found in internal files without any encryption. Horus reads all the app's internal files to find traces of the elements in *search term*. If any of the *search term* element is found, then the wallet app is exploitable if the internal files are exposed.

Horus generates a mnemonic phrase used for all HD wallet apps throughout the analysis. Horus starts a tcpdump[10] session to capture all network requests and clear the logcat buffer for capturing a new session. At this stage, we import the mnemonic phrase in the app. Then, Horus takes the app ID as input and pulls all internal files, tcpdump generated network dump files, from the connected emulator/device, and reads the files sequentially.

Horus identifies common file extensions (e.g., xml, db, pcap) and uses an appropriate parser to extract the file content. In case of an XML file, Horus parses the XML file and reads the content and appends all the string values in *candidate encryption key*. For the SQLite database file, we develop a parser that lists all the tables in the database and reads all the values in the tables and appends them in the same list. We get a pcap file from tcpdump containing network request logs, and we use a Python library Scapy[11] to parse the pcap file and extract the content. Horus can also parse log files and take fixed email, username, PIN, and password used as input. All the parsed content and input are considered potential encryption keys and listed in *candidate encryption key* list.

Horus reads all the internal artifacts again and runs a fuzzy search, using fuzzywuzzy,[12] for the items listed in *search term*. We record the search result whether *search term* items are found and whether in plaintext or encrypted form. Note that all *candidate encryption key* items cannot be used directly as encryption keys. AES requires blocks of 16 bytes key, whereas a PIN is a four-digit number. Thus, a PIN cannot be used as a key. We use four common hashing algorithms (MD5, SHA1, SHA256, and SHA512) to generate a digest for each *candidate encryption key* and use the digest instead as an encryption key. Throughout our reverse engineering step, we observed that the hashing technique to convert a non-suitable key into a proper encryption key is followed in many wallet apps.

Non-HD Wallet Workflow. A non-HD wallet generates a list of public-private key pairs, and there is no relationship among the keys. Non-HD wallets manage many keys; each public-private key pairs are used for only one transaction. The downside of this approach is that the user needs to take backup regularly, ideally after each transaction. This approach is not convenient and error-prone. Additionally, there is a risk of key-exposure if the backup is not handled with caution. In Horus, non-HD wallet workflow is different from HD wallet workflow because, in an HD wallet, keys can be generated predictably with a known mnemonic phrase, but there is no relation among the generated keys in non-HD wallet. So, we look for key patterns in the internal files in the non-HD wallet workflow. For

---

[10] https://www.tcpdump.org/.
[11] https://scapy.net/.
[12] https://github.com/seatgeek/fuzzywuzzy.

instance, Bitcoin public addresses start with the character 1 or 3 [44], are 34 characters long, and formatted as Base58; Ethereum public addresses start with 0x and are 42 characters long. We consider different key formats as well. For example, Bitcoin private keys can be in standard 256-bit hex format (64 bytes long), or WIF format [33] (51 bytes long) and start with 5. The pre-requisite steps of performing dynamic analysis on HD wallets are applicable for non-HD wallets except importing the wallet. Instead of importing the wallet, the keys are generated using the app itself. Different apps of course generate different keys; however, the key format is identical. We incorporate a pattern matching regex to look for Bitcoin public/private addresses and their various derivatives [21] in the app's internal files.

Transactions Workflow. For both HD and non-HD wallets, we make a small transaction [13] of a fixed amount to a pre-defined address. Horus looks for the pre-defined receiver's address and the fixed amount value in the wallet app's internal files. After a transaction is completed, the transaction history should not be saved in the device. If the receiver's address and the transaction value are present in the app's internal files, it stores past transactions and can be abused for deanonymization if the app's internal files are exposed.

To emulate wallet transactions, we use Bitcoin testnet [45]. Since not all wallet apps support testnet transactions, we make transactions only testnet compatible wallet apps. To collect testnet coins, we use coinfaucet[13] and mempool,[14] two freely available services to distribute testnet coins.

Manual Inspection. For in-depth analysis of the top 17 wallet apps, we monitor the apps' workflow and response based on the app's interaction. Our goal is to understand the app's workflow and its process to generate and store key revealing information. We observe changes in the app's internal files (e.g., Shared Preferences, Databases, File IO) based on the activity we perform using the app.

An Android app consists of 4 components: Activity, Service, Broadcast Receiver, and Content Provider. Android enforces a sandbox mechanism to protect the components, where no app gains access to other app's components by default. However, an app can export its components and let other apps access the components. If a component, such as a service, is exported and not protected with permissions, then any app can start and bind to the service. Any app on the device can invoke all the exported components in the target app. We manually verify if it is possible to send crafted intent from any other app to activate the exported components in the target app and make it perform the malicious task.

We use two state-of-the-art tools, Drozer[15] and Frida.[16] We use Drozer to list all exported components, universally accessible URIs using which any other app can ask for key revealing information from the target app and SQL Injection attack surface in the app. We use Frida to monitor critical operations in the app,

---

[13] https://coinfaucet.eu/en/btc-testnet/.
[14] https://testnet-faucet.mempool.co/.
[15] https://github.com/fsecurelabs/drozer/.
[16] https://frida.re/.

e.g., database operations, file IO, and method trace to find out passing arguments and the return value of a method. We also use Frida to trace app logs, bypass SSL pinning, and bypass root detection. We use an additional wrapper tool, House[17] over Frida for ease of use. Both Drozer and Frida are used for monitoring and intercepting app workflow.

5   Experimental Results

We use the LDPlayer[18] emulator, running Android 7.1.2 for all automated analysis, and Alcatel 5041C, running Android 8.1.0 for manual experiments. We use LDPlayer for its faster execution. The two different Android versions we use to cover a large part of contemporary Android phone users. Dynamic analysis requires a rooted device and we root the device using Magisk.[19] We analyze 310 wallet apps using Horus and manually inspect the top 17 most popular apps. In this section, we present some of our main findings and corresponding security risks.

Storing Key Revealing Information: Our dynamic analysis identifies 239 apps (77%) as non-HD wallets, 71 apps (23%) as HD wallets. In total, 111 apps (87 non-HD wallets and 24 HD wallets) store key revealing information in plaintext. In 47/71 HD wallet apps use encryption to store key revealing information; however, 18 of those apps store the encryption key without additional protections. In most cases, where we found an encryption key, the key is located in the Shared-Preference file. In other cases, the key is located in a readable internal file, or it is a user-provided PIN (e.g., 4–6 digits). Among the top 17 apps, 3 apps store key revealing information in plaintext, and 4 apps store key revealing information encrypted with a known encryption key from our list of *candidate encryption key*. The best-in-class storage solution in Android is HSM, but only 3/310 apps are using HSM. If HSM is not available, then Android Keystore should be used, which provides the best available solution provided the Android OS itself is not compromised. The user-provided PIN should not be used as the encryption key because it is brute-forceable. 11 of 310 apps store transaction information on the device, leading to deanonymization if the internal files are exposed.

User Dictionary: On all Android devices, the keyboard app uses a user dictionary (database of words, locale, and frequency count) for predictive text inputs. In wallet apps, the mnemonic phrase contains common English words, and most wallet apps take mnemonic phrase input from the user using the default keyboard. The information regarding the words in mnemonic phrase is saved in user dictionary [18]. This dictionary can be abused to predict the mnemonic phrase [28] by extracting frequency information of typed words. Note that the attacker app requires virtual keyboard permission to access the dictionary, and in general, input editor and spellchecker apps ask for this permission. Multiple

---

[17] https://github.com/nccgroup/house.
[18] https://www.ldplayer.net/.
[19] https://github.com/topjohnwu/Magisk.

apps can have virtual keyboard permission on a device. Only 20 apps out of 310 apps (6%) implement custom keyboards to defend against this attack.

Allow Backup: This is an attribute declared in the AndroidManifest.xml file, and it is true by default. It denotes the app data is backed up upon the app's uninstallation and is restored upon re-install [2]. When enabled, the app data can be backed up using the ADB (Android Debug Bridge) command. It enables an attacker to extract an app's internal files in a non-rooted device within few minutes of physical access. Open-source tools such as Android-Backup-Toolkit[20] can be used to extract the backup and gain access to internal files.

Dangerous Permissions: In the Android ecosystem, some permissions are considered dangerous [3] and require the user's explicit consent before being authorized. Most wallet apps require some common permissions for their functionality (e.g., WRITE_EXTERNAL_STORAGE, READ_EXTERNAL_STORAGE, GET_ACCOUNTS, CAMERA). However, some apps ask for certain privacy-sensitive permissions, such as contact list and record audio, which appear to be non-essential for the app; see Table 3 for such permissions. Each permission has a constant value associated with it, such as android.permission.RECORD_AUDIO for audio recording, which is used to check, request and verify permission from the Android SDK. The constant values of the permissions are stored as a static variable in Manifest.permission class [3]. The presence of the static variable or the associated constant value of a particular permission in the app's codebase conforms the usage of the permission.

Table 3. Unnecessary dangerous permissions usage. Last row provides the total number for all 310 apps. ✗ indicates the app declares the permission requirement in the AndroidManifest file; *Read Profile* allows an app to read the user's personal profile data; *Read Phone State* allows an app to access the device's phone features; *Get Tasks* allows the app to retrieve information about currently and recently running tasks; and *Request Install Packages* allows app to install additional packages on the device.

Application ID	Read contacts	Access coarse location	Access fine location	Read profile	Read phone state	Get tasks	Request install packages	Record audio
asia.coins.mobile	✗	✗	✗					
co.bity.android.wallet	✗			✗				✗
co.mona.android	✗		✗					
com.binance.dev		✗	✗					
com.bitcoin.mwallet	✗	✗	✗					
com.breadwallet		✗	✗					
com.coinomi.wallet								
com.paxful.wallet					✗	✗		
com.polehin.android								
com.unocoin.unocoinwallet	✗	✗	✗					
com.wallet.crypto.trustapp							✗	
com.xapo	✗	✗	✗	✗	✗	✗		
de.schildbach.wallet								
com.mycelium.wallet		✗						
org.toshi								
piuk.blockchain.android								✗
zebpay.Application						✗		
Total	47	75	81	8	84	36	28	40

---

[20] https://sourceforge.net/projects/android-backup-toolkit/.

Root Exploitation: In the Android ecosystem, root exploitation is well-known [46]. There are legitimate Android apps available in the Google Play Store that facilitate rooting of phones, referred to as root providers or one-click root apps. In 2016, 85 million devices downloaded such root provider apps, and the devices are soft-rootable [22]. In wallet apps, we find 70 apps out of 310 are checking if the device is rooted before starting its operation; see Table 4. However, none of the apps terminates upon root detection; instead, the app displays a non-blocking alert and lets the user continue using the app.

Table 4. Static module analysis summary. Here, ✓ indicates the existence of security standard implementation in the app and a blank cell indicates the absence of it. Last row provides the total number for all 310 apps.

Application ID	Root detection	Integrity verify	Screenshot disabled	Bio-metric	Custom keyboard	Secure random	Hardware security module
asia.coins.mobile	✓		✓			✓	
co.bitx.android.wallet	✓			✓		✓	
co.mona.android			✓			✓	
com.binance.dev	✓		✓		✓	✓	
com.bitcoin.mwallet	✓	✓	✓		✓	✓	
com.breadwallet		✓			✓	✓	
com.coinomi.wallet	✓	✓				✓	✓
com.mycelium.wallet			✓		✓	✓	
com.paxful.wallet				✓		✓	
com.polehin.android			✓	✓		✓	
com.unocoin.unocoinwallet		✓				✓	
com.wallet.crypto.trustapp	✓		✓		✓	✓	
com.xapo	✓			✓	✓	✓	✓
de.schildbach.wallet						✓	
org.toshi			✓			✓	
piuk.blockchain.android	✓		✓		✓	✓	
zebpay.Application						✓	✓
Total	70	33	44	46	20	292	10

Strandhogg Attack: This attack [17] is applicable when a malicious app that targets a wallet app opens up before the wallet app. When the user taps on the wallet app, the malicious app opens up instead. The malicious app can mimic the wallet app's UI and ask for its PIN, mnemonic phrase, etc. No permission is required for the malicious app, and Android versions 8.0–9.0 are vulnerable to this attack.

Exported Components: Depending on the responsibilities of a component, it may leak information or perform unauthorized tasks. For example, if a content provider is exported, it can reveal sensitive database information to any other app on the device. We find each one of the top wallet apps exports from 3 to 25 components, expanding the attack surface on wallet apps.

6 Discussions

In this section, we discuss Horus's current capabilities and limitations. Horus's static module is based on the app call graph, enabling the framework to survive the code obfuscation. Android obfuscation techniques work on the app code and not on the SDK APIs. We note that Android API calls remain unobfuscated in the call graph. Our dynamic module is based on the app's artifacts and network trace. The dynamic module does not have any dependency on the app platform and source code. The artifacts analysis technique is equally effective in apps developed using hybrid and cross-platform technologies. Overall, Horus can quickly assess the security standards followed by a crypto wallet app using the static module, and provide a deeper understanding of the app's sensitive data handling process using the dynamic module. However, static analysis tools suffer from obvious limitations. They can only determine whether specific APIs or syntax patterns are present in the source code but cannot indicate whether the implementation is error-free. Depending on the syntax pattern, Horus may indicate that an app has implemented a security feature, but in reality, the implementation may be flawed and may still contain serious bugs.

To make Horus fully automated, we evaluate tools like Monkey[21] and Droidbot[22] to perform signup, import wallet, and complete a transaction. However, in our evaluation, we find that the pseudo-random events that Monkey generates cannot accomplish a set of pre-defined tasks. It is possible to accomplish specific tasks using Droidbot, but it is not well-suited for a generalized workflow. We have to write a customized script for each app. Considering apps' versatility, writing a script for each app beats the purpose of an automated framework, and we settled for a semi-automated solution.

We identify some wallet apps that encrypt key revealing information, use salt with the encryption key. We find hard-coded salt value in the source code and also salt value printed in logs. In Horus we are not automating when salt is used in the encryption key.

Starting with Android 7.0 (API level 24), system-wide private certificates are not accepted in Android. Optionally, an app can explicitly choose to rely on a private certificate [14]. Also, as of Android 9.0 (API level 28), plaintext traffic is not allowed and cannot be configured as well [6]. To overcome this, we use mitmproxy[23] to monitor network traffic and place the mitmproxy certificate in the system certificate folder. Also, we use tcpdump to capture network requests in a pcap file to look for key revealing information in network communication.

7   Related Work

Several wallet app analyses have been carried out in recent years, which expose vulnerabilities and propose new defenses. Volety et al. [48] perform offline brute force dictionary attacks on the mnemonic phrase to gain access to two wallet apps. Guri et al. [23] infect a cold wallet with malicious code during the installation phase and get hold of the private keys. Further, Koerhuis et al. [30] conduct forensic analysis on two popular cryptocurrencies, Monero and Verge, in the

---

[21] https://developer.android.com/studio/test/monkey.

[22] https://github.com/honeynet/droidbot.

[23] https://mitmproxy.org/.

desktop environment. They analyze the host machine's volatile memory, network traffic, hard disks and find critical artifacts like seed and plaintext passphrase. A similar study is carried out on Bitcoin by Zollner et al. [51].

Several studies also look into the security of Android wallet apps. He et al. [26] demonstrate two attack scenarios by capturing sensitive information from device display using accessibility permissions and obtaining user input via USB debugging. This analysis is conducted on only two wallet apps (not among the top 50 wallets in the Google Play Store). Hu et al. [27] devise 3 proof-of-concept attacks targeting deanonymization, spamming, and violating P2P (peer-to-peer) protocol requirements of Bitcoin. Capturing clipboard values [31] also presents a significant risk to crypto wallet apps, e.g., when importing non-HD wallet keys from another app/device, or when copying mnemonic phrases. Haigh et al. [25] analyze the forensic artifacts of seven wallet apps, and develop a Trojan POC by repackaging a wallet app that can steal the users' passwords. Gangwal et al. [1] use machine learning to identify a wallet app by tracing a user's network activity.

UI deception attacks that include clickjacking, phishing, and activity hijacking [20] in Android, are generally applicable for any wallet app. Bergandano et al. [11] develop a hybrid analysis tool by following OWASP guidelines that analyzes vulnerabilities in varying categories of apps (e.g., wallet, food, social). The work lacks manual inspection; thus, the tool's conclusion is unverifiable and focuses on generic vulnerabilities instead of taking into account any specific nature of the apps.

Contrary to prior studies, we explicitly focused on crypto wallet apps and discovered several new attack surfaces specifically applicable to Android wallets.

8   Conclusion

With the massive growth of cryptocurrencies, the number of threat vectors against crypto wallet apps is also increasing. This puts millions of users at risk if security concerns are not adequately addressed in leading wallet apps. We introduced Horus, a semi-automated framework to analyze and detect security issues in crypto wallet apps. We analyzed 310 apps on the Android platform and discover a unique set of vulnerabilities. Our analysis indicates that security standards are not followed when developing apps, and there are vulnerabilities in the protection of key revealing information. Serious security gaps appear in popular wallet apps, including asking for dangerous permissions without a proper need. Based on our analysis, there is a lack of checks and balances in our understanding of wallet apps' security and their actual implementation. Users should be more vigilant and proactive in evaluating apps before relying on them. Additionally, developers should be better informed about the industry's security standards and strictly adhere to the best practices and recommendations.

References

1. Aiolli, F., Conti, M., Gangwal, A., Polato, M.: Mind your wallet's privacy: identifying Bitcoin wallet apps and user's actions through network traffic analysis. In: 34th ACM/SIGAPP Symposium on Applied Computing, pp. 1484–1491 (2019)
2. Android Developers: Auto backup data. https://developer.android.com/guide/topics/data/autobackup
3. Android Developers: Dangerous permissions. https://developer.android.com/reference/android/Manifest.permission
4. Android Developers: HSM. https://developer.android.com/training/articles/keystore
5. Android Developers: Input. https://developer.android.com/guide/topics/text/creating-input-method.html
6. Android Developers: Network security. https://developer.android.com/training/articles/security-config
7. Android Developers: SecureRandom. https://developer.android.com/reference/java/security/SecureRandom
8. Android Developers: Shrink, obfuscate, and optimize your app. https://developer.android.com/studio/build/shrink-code#obfuscate
9. Antonopoulos, A.M.: Mastering Bitcoin. O'Reilly Media, Inc., March 2021
10. Bankhead, P.: Android developers blog: Improving discovery of apps and games on the Play Store. https://android-developers.googleblog.com/2018/06/improving-discovery-of-quality-apps-and.html
11. Bergadano, F., Boetti, M., Cogno, F., Costamagna, V., Leone, M., Evangelisti, M.: A modular framework for mobile security analysis. Inf. Secur. J. **29**(5), 220–243 (2020)
12. Bitcoin: BIPS: Bitcoin Improvement Proposals. https://github.com/bitcoin/bips
13. Bitcoin: Transactions. https://www.bitcoin.com/get-started/how-bitcoin-transactions-work
14. Brubaker, C.: Android developers blog: Changes to trusted certificate authorities in Android Nougat. https://android-developers.googleblog.com/2016/07/changes-to-trusted-certificate.html
15. Cimpanu, C.: Bitcoin wallet update trick has netted criminals more than $22m — ZDNet. https://www.zdnet.com/article/bitcoin-wallet-trick-has-netted-criminals-more-than-22-million/
16. Cimpanu, C.: Hacker group has stolen more than $200m. https://www.zdnet.com/article/cryptocore-hacker-group-has-stolen-more-than-200m-from-cryptocurrency-exchanges/
17. NVD - CVE-2020-0096. https://nvd.nist.gov/vuln/detail/CVE-2020-0096
18. Diao, W., Liu, X., Zhou, Z., Zhang, K., Li, Z.: Mind-reading: Privacy attacks exploiting cross-app keyevent injections. In: European Symposium on Research in Computer Security, pp. 20–39. Springer (2015)
19. Druffel, A., Heid, K.: Davinci: Android app analysis beyond Frida via dynamic system call instrumentation. In: International Conference on Applied Cryptography and Network Security, pp. 473–489. Springer (2020)
20. Fernandes, E., et al.: Android UI deception revisited: Attacks and defenses. In: International Conference on Financial Cryptography and Data Security. pp. 41–59. Springer (2016)
21. ForensicFocus.com: Forensics and Bitcoin. https://www.forensicfocus.com/articles/forensics-bitcoin/

22. Gasparis, I., Qian, Z., Song, C., Krishnamurthy, S.V.: Detecting Android root exploits by learning from root providers. In: 26th USENIX Security Symposium (USENIX Security 2017), pp. 1129–1144 (2017)
23. Guri, M.: Beatcoin: leaking private keys from air-gapped cryptocurrency wallets. In: 2018 IEEE International Conference on Internet of Things (iThings) and IEEE Green Computing and Communications (GreenCom) and IEEE Cyber, Physical and Social Computing (CPSCom) and IEEE Smart Data (SmartData), pp. 1308–1316. IEEE (2018)
24. Gutoski, G., Stebila, D.: Hierarchical deterministic Bitcoin wallets that tolerate key leakage. In: International Conference on Financial Cryptography and Data Security. pp. 497–504. Springer (2015)
25. Haigh, T., Breitinger, F., Baggili, I.: If I had a million cryptos: Cryptowallet application analysis and a trojan proof-of-concept. In: International Conference on Digital Forensics and Cyber Crime. pp. 45–65. Springer (2018)
26. He, D., Li, S., Li, C., Zhu, S., Chan, S., Min, W., Guizani, N.: Security analysis of cryptocurrency wallets in Android-based applications. IEEE Network **34**(6), 114–119 (2020)
27. Hu, Y., et al.: Security threats from Bitcoin wallet smartphone applications: Vulnerabilities, attacks, and countermeasures. In: Eleventh ACM Conference on Data and Application Security and Privacy (CODASPY 2021), pp. 89–100 (2021)
28. Kachakil, D.: Discovering and exploiting a vulnerability in Android's personal dictionary. https://ioactive.com/discovering-and-exploiting-a-vulnerability-in-androids-personal-dictionary/
29. Kim, T., Ha, H., Choi, S., Jung, J., Chun, B.G.: Breaking ad-hoc runtime integrity protection mechanisms in Android financial apps. In: 2017 ACM on Asia Conference on Computer and Communications Security. pp. 179–192 (2017)
30. Koerhuis, W., Kechadi, T., Le-Khac, N.A.: Forensic analysis of privacy-oriented cryptocurrencies. Forensic Science International: Digital Investigation **33**, 200891 (2020)
31. Li, C., He, D., Li, S., Zhu, S., Chan, S., Cheng, Y.: Android-based cryptocurrency wallets: Attacks and countermeasures. In: 2020 IEEE International Conference on Blockchain (Blockchain). pp. 9–16. IEEE (2020)
32. Ling, Z., et al.: Privacy enhancing keyboard: Design, implementation, and usability testing. Wireless Communications and Mobile Computing 2017 (2017)
33. Maksim, B.: What is wallet import format (wif)? https://allprivatekeys.com/what-is-wif
34. Neal, W.: Cryptocurrency hackers steal $3.8B in 2020. https://www.occrp.org/en/daily/13627-cryptocurrency-hackers-steal-3-8-billion-in-2020
35. Newburger, E.: Bitcoin surpasses $60,000 in record high as rally accelerates. https://www.cnbc.com/2021/03/13/bitcoin-surpasses-60000-in-record-high-as-rally-accelerates-.html
36. Online, FE: Market Cap $1.24T, February 2021. https://www.financialexpress.com/market/bitcoin-rally-takes-market-cap-of-over-6000-cryptocurrencies-to-whopping-new-high-of-1-24-trillion/2189730/
37. Osborne, C.: AT&T dragged to court, over SIM hijacking and cryptocurrency theft — ZDNet. https://www.zdnet.com/article/at-t-dragged-to-court-again-over-sim-hijacking-and-cryptocurrency-theft/
38. Palatinus, M., Rusnak, P.: Official specification of BIP-0044, March 2019. https://github.com/bitcoin/bips/blob/master/bip-0044.mediawiki
39. Palatinus, M., Rusnak, P., Voisine, A., Bowe, S.: Official specification of BIP-0039, February 2021. https://github.com/bitcoin/bips/blob/master/bip-0039.mediawiki

40. Powers, B.: This elusive malware has targeted crypto wallets for a year, January 2021. https://www.coindesk.com/elusive-malware-electrorat-targets-crypto-wallets

41. Rahman, M.: Developers are facing huge drop in new installs after Play Store algorithm changes. https://www.xda-developers.com/developers-huge-drop-new-installs-play-store-algorithm-changes/

42. Ranganath, V.-P., Mitra, J.: Are free Android app security analysis tools effective in detecting known vulnerabilities? Empir. Softw. Eng. **25**(1), 178–219 (2019). https://doi.org/10.1007/s10664-019-09749-y

43. Redman, J.: The $700m wallet crack. https://news.bitcoin.com/the-700-million-wallet-crack-bitcoins-7th-largest-address-is-under-constant-attack/

44. Sedgwick, K.: Bitcoin address formats - Wallets Bitcoin News. https://news.bitcoin.com/everything-you-should-know-about-bitcoin-address-formats/

45. Testnet - Bitcoin Wiki. https://en.bitcoin.it/wiki/Testnet

46. Unuchek, R.: Android: To root or not to root — Kaspersky official blog. https://www.kaspersky.com/blog/android-root-faq/17135/

47. /dev/random - Wikipedia. https://en.wikipedia.org/wiki//dev/random

48. Volety, T., Saini, S., McGhin, T., Liu, C.Z., Choo, K.K.R.: Cracking bitcoin wallets: I want what you have in the wallets. Futur. Gener. Comput. Syst. **91**, 136–143 (2019)

49. Wuille, P.: Official specification of BIP-0032, August 2020. https://github.com/bitcoin/bips/blob/master/bip-0032.mediawiki

50. Zhang, H., She, D., Qian, Z.: Android root and its providers: a double-edged sword. In: 22nd ACM SIGSAC Conference on Computer and Communications Security, pp. 1093–1104 (2015)

51. Zollner, S., Choo, K.K.R., Le-Khac, N.A.: An automated live forensic and postmortem analysis tool for Bitcoin on Windows systems. IEEE Access **7**, 158250–158263 (2019)

Systems Security

Leakuidator: Leaky Resource Attacks and Countermeasures

Mojtaba Zaheri$^{(\boxtimes)}$ and Reza Curtmola

New Jersey Institute of Technology, Newark, NJ 07102, USA
{mojtaba.zaheri,reza.curtmola}@njit.edu

Abstract. Leaky resource attacks leverage the popularity of resource-sharing services to conduct targeted deanonymization on the web. They are simple to execute because many resource-sharing services are inherently vulnerable due to the trade-offs made between security and functionality. Even though previous work has shown that such attacks can lead to serious privacy threats, defending against this threat is an area that has remained largely unaddressed.

In this work, we advance the state of the art on leaky resource attacks on both attack effectiveness and attack mitigation fronts. We first show that leaky resource attacks have a larger attack surface than what was previously believed, by showing reliable attack implementations that work across a broader range of browsers and by identifying new variants of the attack. We then propose Leakuidator, the first client-side defense that can be deployed right away, without buy-in from browser vendors and website owners. At a high level, Leakuidator identifies potentially suspicious requests made when a webpage is rendered and for each such request: (1) renders the request by first removing cookies from it, and (2) initiates a second request that is identical with the original request (i.e., contains the cookies that were removed), but does not render its response. This additional request maintains compatibility with existing web functionality, such as analytics and tracking services. We have implemented Leakuidator as a browser extension for three Chromium-based browsers. Experimental results show that Leakuidator introduces a small overhead and thus the impact on user experience is minimal. The extension also includes usability knobs, allowing users to reuse past choices and to adjust how strict is the criteria for identifying potentially suspicious requests.

1 Introduction

The ability to privately share digital media resources, such as image, video, and audio files, provides a convenient mechanism to socialize and interact online, as shown by the popularity of websites that provide resource sharing services among their users [2,5,6]. Unfortunately, resource-sharing services were also shown to introduce avenues to conduct serious privacy violation attacks [28,30]: Information leaked by these services allows an attacker to infer the identity of a victim that visits an attacker-controlled website, which would not be possible otherwise.

© ICST Institute for Computer Sciences, Social Informatics and Telecommunications Engineering 2021
Published by Springer Nature Switzerland AG 2021. All Rights Reserved
J. Garcia-Alfaro et al. (Eds.): SecureComm 2021, LNICST 399, pp. 143–163, 2021.
https://doi.org/10.1007/978-3-030-90022-9_8

The first instantiation of the attack was the *leaky image attack*, introduced in a seminal work by Staicu and Pradel [28], using an image as the shared resource. The attacker first shares privately an image with the target victim using an image sharing service. The attacker then embeds a link to the shared image on a webpage she controls. When a visitor loads that webpage, the image will be successfully retrieved only if the visitor is the targeted victim, since only the victim is allowed to retrieve the image (assuming the victim's browser is logged into the image sharing service). By observing the success of loading the image, the attacker will know if the intended victim has visited the attacker's website.

Even though previous work introduced the attack using images (*i.e.*, leaky images [28]), we found that the attack works with any resource that can be privately shared with the victim and can be rendered on a webpage. In particular, the attack also works with other media files, such as video and audio files. Thus, we generically refer to the attack as a *leaky resource attack*.

The leaky resource attack is a targeted privacy attack, in which an individual browsing an attacker-controlled webpage can be uniquely identified. This is in contrast with other known de-anonymization techniques, such as third-party tracking [15] (*e.g.*, tracking pixels or tracking IPs) or social media fingerprinting, that do not provide this level of accuracy. As such, leaky resources can be abused in a variety of privacy-sensitive scenarios [28], including law enforcement gathering evidence regarding the online activity of individuals, oppressive governments tracking political dissidents, de-anonymizing reviewers for a conference paper, blackmailing individuals based on their online activity, or health insurance companies discriminating individuals based on their online activity.

Although the most natural way to implement a leaky resource attack is to rely on JavaScript, in this work we focus on the scriptless version which uses only HTML. A scriptless attack is more challenging to execute successfully, but will affect even privacy-aware users who limit or disable scripts in their browser [4,26].

In this paper, we advance the state of the art in leaky resource attacks for both attack effectiveness and attack mitigation. We first show that the attack surface is larger than was previously believed, by identifying three new variants of the attack. In the first variant, we show that scriptless leaky resource attacks based on `video` and `audio` HTML tags provide increased reliability compared to the previously known `object` HTML tag: The attack now works against all the vulnerable services we identified and across all browsers we tested with (Firefox, Edge, Chrome). By testing the attack on different categories of sharing services, we reveal a concerning reality: 17 popular resource sharing services are still vulnerable despite the attack being known for more than a year (12 of these services are newly found to be vulnerable by our work).

The other two attack variants work for websites that integrate with a file hosting website and offer access to the hosted resources. When a resource is shared on the file hosting website, this sharing is inherited on the integrator website. Even if the file hosting website fixes a leaky resource vulnerability, the attack may still be possible by accessing the shared resource through the integrator website (attack variant two). Finally, we show a de-anonymization attack that can be performed non-interactively, *i.e.*, without even involving the victim (attack variant three).

On the attack mitigation front, we propose Leakuidator, the first client-side defense that can be deployed right away, without buy-in from browser vendors and website owners. As part of the defense, the browser renders each webpage by removing cookies from potentially suspicions requests made by that webpage before sending those requests. To maintain compatibility with analytics and tracking services, Leakuidator initiates for each original request that was deemed potentially suspicious a second request that is identical with the original request (i.e., it contains the cookies that were removed). However, the response to this second request is not rendered. After loading the webpage, if any observable differences are detected between the two responses, the original request is deemed dangerous and the user gets a small notification on the browser toolbar; if the user deems the webpage trustworthy, she can reload it with the defense disabled. Leakuidator also includes usability knobs, allowing the user to reuse past choices and to adjust the criteria for identifying potentially suspicious requests.

To realize this seemingly simple, yet elegant solution, several challenges need to be overcome (Sect. 5.1). We have implemented Leakuidator as a browser extension for three Chromium-based browsers (Chrome, Edge, and Brave). Our experimental results show that Leakuidator introduces a small overhead, thus minimally impacting user experience. For example, the majority of websites tested experience less than 200 ms in additional load time when Leakuidator is active.

1.1 Motivating Examples

We now describe deanonymization scenarios that leverage leaky resource attacks.

Law Enforcement. Given a target suspect, law enforcement agencies can use this attack to learn if the suspect is visiting specific websites. Also, they can use this attack to link an anonymous account in one resource sharing service to a known user account in another resource sharing service, hence deanonymizing the suspect. For example, FBI employed *Network Investigative Techniques* with similar deanonymization goals since at least 2002 [7].

Sensitive Websites. Discreet or extramarital affairs, users of pornography websites, and sextortion are targets for this attack, as users tend to keep their identities anonymous in these situations. For example, FBI booby-trapped a video to catch a suspected Tor child sextortionist via Dropbox [3].

Blind Peer Review. Academic conferences and journals rely on a blind peer review process, in which the identity of the reviewers is hidden from the authors. Using this attack and starting with the list of program committee members (or editorial board), the authors of an article can mount a series of attacks that leads to learning the identity of the article reviewers [30].

Journalism and Critics. Leaky resource attacks can reveal the identities of anonymous government critics by targeting their social media accounts. For example, when a targeted critic visits an attack webpage with links to leaky resources for a list of candidate accounts, a successful request to one of the links may reveal the critic's identity. Another way to deanonymize such critics is to use the account linking strategy, trying to link the target anonymous account to a known account. As an example, the U.S. government demanded that Twitter release information to identify an account holder whose tweets have been critical of the Trump administration's immigration policies [10].

Insurance Coverage. Insurance companies can use information about the websites visited by users to find their concerns about specific disease, thus affecting the companies' decisions about the coverage and premiums.

2   Background on Leaky Resource Attacks

This section overviews previous work on leaky resource attacks. The leaky resource attack was introduced in the context of a leaky image [28]. At a high-level, the attack consists of the following three steps:

1. Setting up the Attack: The attacker uploads an image to an image sharing service. The attacker then privately shares the image with the victim. The image sharing service uses cookies for user authentication and allows access to the shared image via a state-dependent URL (SD-URL). An SD-URL is a URL for which the response to a user request for the URL is different depending on the user's state with respect to the sharing service. For example, if the user is the targeted victim, the resource will be loaded, otherwise it will not be loaded.

   To determine if the victim is visiting an attack webpage P, the attacker embeds in P an SD-URL for the shared image. P is controlled by the attacker (or, the attacker is able to embed in P a request for the SD-URL of the shared image).

2. Luring the Victim: The attacker lures the victim to visit the attack page P.

3. Communicating the Attack Results: When the victim loads the attack page P, the victim's browser makes a cross-origin request for the shared image at the SD-URL. The Same-Origin Policy would normally prevent the attacker from reading the contents of the cross-origin response. However, the attacker can bypass this policy using an XS-leak [30] to learn information about the response: If the image is successfully retrieved, the attacker is certain that the targeted victim is visiting the attack page.

Scriptless Attack. Previous work has shown a JavaScript-based version of the attack [28] (included in Appendix A for reference). However, privacy-aware users may disable JavaScript or use a protection mechanism that prevents JavaScript-based XS-leaks. Even under such an environment, the attack can still be implemented using only HTML, without relying on JavaScript or CSS. The attacker uses an HTML tag that allows to load fallback content in case the primary content fails to load. This fallback-based mechanism can be used to simulate a *if-then-else* control flow instruction in pure HTML. Previous work identifies the object HTML tag to achieve this functionality [28], as shown in Fig. 1.

```
1  <object data="State-Dependent-URL" type="image/png">
2    <object data="Fallback-URL" type="image/png"></object>
3  </object>
```

Fig. 1. Communication method using the object HTML tag. If the outer object element (State-Dependent-URL) fails to load, then the fallback is to load the inner object element (Fallback-URL, controlled by the attacker).

Other Attack Scenarios. Previous work has shown how to extend this attack from identifying a single user to identifying any specific user in a group of users [28]. This can be done efficiently for a group of n users by embedding $log(n)$ SD-URLs in the attack page and by sharing specific groups of the $log(n)$ resources with each targeted user in the group.

Another attack scenario seeks to link multiple identities a single individual has in different sharing services. For example, an attacker wants to know whether two user accounts in two different sharing services belong to same individual. The attacker shares a resource in each sharing service with the victim and then embeds the SD-URLs of these two resources in an attacker-controlled webpage. Successful response to both requests confirms that the two accounts belong to the same person, potentially linking a known account to an anonymous account.

3   Threat Model and Security Objectives

We consider attackers that can bring together the following necessary ingredients for a successful leaky resource attack:

1. The attacker and the victim are users of the same resource sharing service.
2. The resource sharing service allows its users to share resources privately with each other and authenticates users through cookies.
3. The attacker convinces the victim to visit the attack page (which is controlled by the attacker) while the victim is logged into her account with the resource sharing service (which is not controlled by the attacker).
4. The attacker can determine if the victim loaded the resources successfully.

The attack is effective because these requirements can be achieved in multiple ways and are within easy reach of the attacker. For requirement #1, resource sharing services are very popular, so the victim may have an account; also, many such services have free membership and the attacker can just create an account with a service used by the victim. For requirement #2, these are the de facto mechanisms for many resource sharing services. Some popular services, such as Google Drive, even offer the option to not notify the target users when a file is shared with them. Requirement #3 can be achieved in multiple ways, including via phishing emails, or via a watering-hole approach [30]. It is common for many users to be logged into popular services while surfing the Internet.

Requirement #4 is crucial for the attack and can be achieved as follows. The attack page contains a state-dependent URL (SD-URL) [30] that points to content on the target website (*i.e.*, the resource sharing service). When a user makes a request for the SD-URL, the response is different depending on the user's state with respect to the target website: If the user is the targeted victim, the content will be loaded, otherwise it will not be loaded. The attacker can learn information about this response based on a *XS-leak* [30] that bypasses the Same-Origin Policy which normally prevents the attacker from reading a cross-origin response.

Security Objectives. To properly mitigate leaky resource attacks, we envision that the following security objectives need to be achieved:

SO1: Prevent Leaky Resource Attacks. Suspicious third party requests that may lead to leaky resource attacks should be accurately detected and prevented.
SO2: Allow End Users to Control their Privacy Level. Users should have the ability to decide whether a suspicious request is dangerous and violates their privacy or not, and therefore have control on their privacy.
SO3: Limited Impact on Existing Web Functionality. A defense should not interfere with existing web functionality, including third party authentication, personalized advertisement, tracking, and analytics.

4   Attacks

We present three new variants of the leaky resource attack.

4.1   Variant 1 Attacks: State Dependent URLs (SD-URLs)

Variant 1 introduces two new HTML-only XS-leaks to communicate the attack outcome to the attacker, using the `audio` and `video` HTML tags. Our testing results described in Sect. 4.4 show that these are more reliable than previously known XS-leaks that rely on the `object` HTML tag [28]. Unlike the `object` tag, the new XS-leaks work reliably across different browsers, and they work for some resource sharing websites for which the `object` tag does not seem to be effective.

Another drawback of using the `object` tag as an XS-leak mechanism is that websites can use the X-Frame-Options HTTP response header to prevent a browser from rendering an image in an `object` tag. The new XS-leaks we introduce are not subject to this limitation.

Communication Method: Video Tag. Multiple source elements can be used inside a `video` HTML tag to cover browsers that support different video types. Normally, this is used by website authors to specify multiple alternative media resources for media elements. However, Fig. 2 shows that alternatives can be used to trigger a fallback behavior that mimics an *if-then-else* control flow. Both resources we used have the type webm, but other video file types can be used as well. The attacker can ensure the specific file type is supported by the browser by checking the HTTP Request Headers and preparing an appropriate webpage.

Communication Method: Audio Tag. Similar to the `video` tag, multiple source elements can be put inside an `audio` tag to cover browsers that support different audio types. Figure 3 shows how it is used to trigger a fallback behavior. Both resources used have the type ogg, but other audio file types can be used.

```
1  <video>
2     <source src="State-Dependent-URL" type="video/webm">
3     <source src="Fallback-URL" type="video/webm">
4  </video>
```

Fig. 2. Communication Method: Video HTML Tag. If the first source (State-Dependent-URL) cannot be loaded, then the fallback is to load the second source (Fallback-URL, controlled by the attacker).

```
1  <audio>
2     <source src="State-Dependent-URL" type="audio/ogg">
3     <source src="Fallback-URL" type="audio/ogg">
4  </audio>
```

Fig. 3. Communication method: audio HTML tag.

4.2 Variant 2 Attacks: Mediated SD-URLs

Integrators of sharing services can add extra features that are not available in the sharing service itself. For example, a website can manage resources from multiple cloud accounts in one place by integrating with multiple cloud services. As another example, an automated software testing or delivery service can integrate with source code hosting services. A common property of integrator services is that they often offer access to the resources shared in the sharing service through different URLs on the integrator's domain. If such URLs exhibit the state dependent property, we refer to them as mediated SD-URLs.

For example, the attacker shares *resource* with the victim on a sharing service *sharingX.com*, and the URL to access *resource* is *sharingX.com/resource*. If the victim has an account with a website *integrator.com* that integrates the *sharingX* service and offers access to *resource* through a mediated SD-URL on the integrator's site (e.g., *integrator.com/sharingX/resource*), then the mediated SD-URL can be used to conduct leaky resource attacks. We identified mediated SD-URLs in Buddy, a CI/CD system integrating with GitHub, GitLab, and Bitbucket.

The relevance of this attack variant is that even if the sharing service deploys a fix for leaky resource attacks on its own domain, the problem may persist through its integrators, which are not necessarily following the same security practices. For example, the sharing service may start using a more restrictive policy using the *SameSite* cookie attribute, but this does not guarantee that its integrators will follow similar policies.

4.3   Variant 3 Attacks: No Victim Interaction

We found that it is possible to link user identities without the need for the victim to actually interact or load any webpage. This attack variant also involves an integrator that integrates with a sharing service.

We present a working example using the Slack integration of Google Drive. The attacker's goal is to link two account IDs, one for Google Drive and one for Slack. If the attacker knows the real identity behind one of these IDs, she can then deanonymize the other account ID. The attacker shares a resource privately with the victim in Google Drive. The attacker then uses the Google Drive integration in Slack to send this shared resource to a set of target Slack users, e.g., by attaching the resource to a message to the targeted users. The Google Drive bot in the attacker's Slack message box will prompt to give permission to all the target Slack users except for one. That one user already has permission to access the resource, and the attacker will be able to successfully link the victim's Google Drive and Slack account IDs without even interacting with the victim.

4.4   Attack Test Results

Overall, we found 17 popular sharing services that are vulnerable to the leaky resource attack, as shown in Table 1. Among these, we informed 6 services through the HackerOne and BugCrowd programs and we anonymized them as SharingService1 through SharingService6 in order to comply with their disclosure policies. We found that 5 out of 8 sharing services reported to be vulnerable by Staicu and Pradel [28] remain vulnerable to the leaky resource attack, namely Google Drive, SharingService4, One Drive, Skype, and SharingService6. Interestingly, we found that the scriptless attack based on the `object` tag does not work reliably: for SharingService4 it did not work at all, and for two other services (One Drive, Google Drive) it only worked in one out of three browsers we tested with. However, using the `video` and `audio` tags, the attack works unilaterally for these services in all three browsers. Among the remaining 3 services, Facebook made an ad hoc fix to the vulnerable API, Twitter changed the sharing mechanism, and GitHub restricted the cookies using the *SameSite* attribute.

We then examined major sharing services listed on wikipedia for social networking, image sharing, video sharing, file hosting, source code hosting, blog hosting, and instant messaging, after excluding services that do not have an English language interface, do not have free membership, or do not have the private sharing feature. As a result, we found additional vulnerable services: 4 cloud storage services (SharingService3, CloudMe, IDrive, Koofr) and 6 source code hosting services (SharingService1, SharingService2, Launchpad, Assembla, Buddy, Gitea). Finally, we surveyed several popular photo sharing services, which revealed two additional vulnerable services (SharingService5, Google Photos).

Discussion. We found that the `object` tag XS-leak can be affected by many factors and is unreliable. Although we found SD-URLs in 16 services, using the `object` tag the attack is successful in only 9 services with Firefox, and in only 4 services with Chrome/Edge. In contrast, the new tags we found are more reliable. Out of 16 services tested, the `video` tag led to a successful attack in all

Table 1. Test results for the leaky resource attacks. We denote the browser as follows: E for Microsoft Edge 87.0, F for Mozilla Firefox 83.0, and C for Google Chrome 87.0. The services are grouped into source code hosting (rows 1–6), cloud storage (rows 7–13), photo sharing (rows 15, 16), and others (rows 14, 17). For all services, we used variant 1 of the attack (SD-URL), except for Buddy which is vulnerable to variant 2 (mediated SD-URL). "Not Supported" denotes the service did not support the respective media type. "Not Successful" denotes that the attack was not successful in any of the tested browsers.

#	Service	object tag [28]	video tag	audio tag
1	SharingService1	Not Successful	F	F
2	SharingService2	Not Successful	E, F, C	E, F, C
3	Launchpad	F	F	F
4	Assembla	F	F	F
5	Buddy	F	F	F
6	Gitea	Not Successful	F	F
7	SharingService3	F	F	Not Supported
8	Google Drive	F	E, F, C	E, F, C
9	One Drive	F	E, F, C	E, F, C
10	SharingService4	Not Successful	E, F, C	E, F, C
11	CloudMe	E, C	E, F, C	E, F, C
12	IDrive	Not Successful	E, F, C	E, F, C
13	Koofr	E, C	E, F, C	E, F, C
14	Skype	E, F, C	E, F, C	E, F, C
15	SharingService5	SD-URL Not Found	F	Not Supported
16	Google Photos	F	Not Supported	Not Supported
17	SharingService6	E, F, C	E, F, C	E, F, C

16 services with Firefox, and in 9 services with Chrome/Edge. Out of 14 services tested, the `audio` tag led to a successful attack in all 14 services with Firefox, and in 9 services with Chrome/Edge.

The reason why XS-leaks based on `video` and `audio` tags were not successful in some services when using Chrome/Edge browsers is that different browsers behave inconsistently when the *SameSite* attribute is not set at all. Chromium-based browsers versions 80 and above treat cookies as if a *lax* SameSite attribute is set, whereas Firefox (tested up to version 83) treats them as if SameSite is set to *none*. We also note that version 80 of Chromium-based browsers was rolled out on August 11, 2020, meaning more services are vulnerable when using these browsers with version prior to 80 (*e.g.*., all 16 services tested using video tags and all 14 services tested using audio tags are vulnerable).

4.5 Responsible Disclosure and Feedback from Affected Services

We summarize the responses received after performing responsible disclosures.

Google confirmed the issue for its Drive and Photos products, placing it in a larger context of XS-Search attacks. In response, Google is considering several larger scale changes to their products: a) Auditing which search endpoints exist in their web services that need to be protected against, b) Experimenting with different defenses that do not break existing user functionality but also are effective, c) Working with web browsers to find defenses.

SharingService3 is a top e-commerce and media sharing service. They acknowledged the vulnerability and issued a bug bounty.

Microsoft's response suggests this is as an acceptable risk for its OneDrive and Skype products, as their main focus is to ensure the integrity, availability, and confidentiality of these services. They seem to discard the privacy implications of the attack, without providing any clear justification.

SharingService2 is a major source code hosting service and acknowledged this as a known issue. They considered the SameSite cookie attribute as a defense, but decided against it because it would break one of the integrated services.

SharingService1 is a major source code hosting service and acknowledged the issue, but considers it an acceptable risk. **SharingService4** is a top cloud hosting service who acknowledged the issue and is working on a feasible solution.

SharingService5 is a top media hosting service and confirmed that their internal team is already aware of this issue.

SharingService6 questioned the effectiveness of the attack because it may be non-trivial to convince a victim to accept an invitation from the attacker. In addition, they acknowledged evaluating the SameSite cookie attribute as a defense is a work in progress because some product features would be affected.

Koofr acknowledged the issue and set the cookie SameSite attribute to *lax* as a fix. **Slack** were informed about the attack variant 3, but did not respond.

Among the six anonymized vulnerable services, it is notable that some have either deployed a fix or are actively working on identifying a practical fix. Hereby we also note the duplicitous response from some of the vulnerable services: On one hand, they downplay these privacy issues, with no plan for deploying a fix. On the other hand, they asked us specifically not to publicly disclose the vulnerabilities. Such an attitude may suggest that these services may not value the privacy of their users; it may also pinpoint to limitations in the disclosure policies of bug bounty programs.

5   Leakuidator: A Defense Against Leaky Resource Attacks

5.1   A Solution Suggested by Prior Work

The following suggestion was made in prior work to prevent the leaky image attack [28]. The browser should render authenticated image requests only if there are no observable differences between an authenticated request and non-authenticated one. For this, the browser should perform one request with third-party cookies and one without, and only render the image if the responses are equivalent. Although this idea is inspirational, no details are given on how to take this idea from the suggestion stage to that of an actual defense. In fact, significant challenges need to be overcome.

Algorithm 1. Proposed defense against leaky resource attacks

Input: Req, the request to be evaluated

 1: **if** Req contains cookies **and** $Req.source$ is not equal to $Req.target$ **then**
 2:     Remove cookies from Req and send the request Req
 3:     Deliver to the browser the response Res received for Req
 4:     Send another request Req' identical to Req (i.e., with cookies)
 5:     Let Res' be the response received for Req'
 6:     **if** Res is not equal to Res' **then** classify the request as dangerous

---

First, the browser should wait for both responses to arrive in order to evaluate if they are equivalent. This will delay the rendering of the webpage and has detrimental effects to the user experience, not to mention it is not clear what to do if one of the requests gets delayed or lost. Second, blocking the rendering of the webpage until both responses are received requires modifying the browser. Solutions that do not require buy-in from browser vendors are preferable, as that is a challenging and time-consuming process. Finally, blocking the rendering of the requested image when an observable difference is detected will still cause information leakage, because blocking or not blocking of a request is a binary condition that can be used for information leakage attacks.

5.2   Leakuidator: A Defense Against Leaky Resource Attacks

We propose Leakuidator, a defense that applies the steps described in Algorithm 1 to each request made by the browser when loading a webpage. First, the defense identifies a request as potentially suspicious if the request contains cookies and is cross-origin, i.e., the source and target origins are different (Line 1). The source origin is the origin of the webpage making the request (*i.e.*, the URI shown in the browser's address bar), whereas the target origin is the origin indicated by the request. The next step is to remove the cookies from the request and send the modified request (Line 2). The response to this request will be rendered by the browser in the webpage (Line 3). The defense then makes a second request, identical to the original request, *i.e.*, the request includes the cookies that were removed (Line 4). The responses to the original request and this second request are compared and if any observable differences are detected, the request is deemed dangerous (Line 6).

The proposed approach addresses the aforementioned challenges. The response to the modified request is rendered by the browser as soon as it is received and before being compared to the second response, thus no delays are imposed. Leakuidator can be implemented as a browser extension and does not require buy-in from browser vendors and website owners. Finally, the response to the modified request does not rely on cookies and will be the same even if the user is the targeted victim or not, hence preventing additional information leakage.

Impact on Existing Web Functionality. We now analyze the impact of the proposed defense on existing web functionality.

Third Party Authentication. To keep third party authentication unaffected (e.g., single sign-on services), potentially suspicious requests that are followed by a top-level navigation are excluded from the defense. Since such requests are followed by a top-level navigation to another webpage, the communication methods used in a leaky resource attack are deemed impractical, as the attacker webpage will not get the chance to communicate the result of a dangerous request back to attacker after leaving the attack webpage.

Analytics. The second request, which contains cookies, ensures that tracking and analytics services remain unaffected. However, since the first request is sent without a cookie, the tracking server will normally respond with a *set-cookie* header, which may override any existing cookie and user id and history. Thus, we remove the *set-cookie* header from the response to the first request. If observable, this modified response can help an attacker to at most learn if the user has previously visited or logged in to a third party service or not. However, this is not enough to reveal the identity of the target user.

Personalized Advertisement. An advertisement service may send a personalized ad based on the cookies in the second request. This personalized ad will not be rendered in the browser, instead the user may get a generic ad in response to the modified original request. However, the user will be notified by Leakuidator and has the option to exclude the ad service from the protection. The user will then receive personalized ads for subsequent visits to the webpage. Therefore, assuming the user consents, the impact on personalized ads is minimal.

5.3 Leakuidator Implementation Details

We have implemented Leakuidator as a browser extension for three Chromium-based browsers, Chrome, Edge, and Brave. The extension consists of 1,674 lines of JavaScript and HTML code, amounting to 362 KB, including 36.6 KB for the *punycode* and *publicsuffixlist* libraries, 231 KB for the list of public suffixes, and 22.8 KB for the extension icon. To decide if there are observable differences between the two responses (Line 6 of Algorithm 1), Leakuidator considers the *Status, Content-Encoding, Content-Range, Content-Length*, and *Etag* response headers.

The second request initiated by Leakuidator (line 4 in Algorithm 1) can be implemented as a HEAD request which is identical to a GET request except that the server only returns the headers in the response. Leakuidator can use a HEAD request instead of a GET because the extension only uses information from the response headers to detect potentially dangerous requests. The fact that the message body is not returned reduces Leakuidator's communication overhead.

If the responses to a potentially suspicious request are identical, then Leakuidator does not affect the webpage rendering. Otherwise, after the webpage is loaded, the user gets a small notification in the extension icon on the browser toolbar regarding the existence of dangerous requests; if the webpage is deemed trustworthy, the user has the option to reload it with the defense disabled (i.e., cookies will not be removed from the original request).

This notification on the browser toolbar has minimal impact on the user experience. If the user clicks on the extension icon, a popup window presents a list of potentially dangerous requests attempted by the webpage. For each such request, the source and target origins are shown.

To minimize the impact on the user experience, Leakuidator includes usability knobs. First, when presented with a list of potentially dangerous requests, users can record their choices for future use (*i.e.*, users will not be notified again for such future occurrences). Specifically, for each potentially dangerous request, the user is given four options:

1. Exclude Pair: Exclude the ordered pair of source and target from the protection and allow the suspicious requests with this pair without modification.
2. Exclude Target: It is similar to *Exclude Pair*, but excludes from the protection all requests to the target origin, regardless of the source.
3. Protect Pair: Always provide protection for requests with this ordered pair of source and target.
4. Protect Target: Similar to *Protect Pair*, but provides protection for all requests to the target origin, regardless of the source.

Second, Leakuidator can operate in two modes, allowing users to adjust how strict is the criteria for identifying potentially suspicious requests. In the

Exact mode, the decision if the source and target origins are different (Line 1 of Algorithm 1) is based on comparing the entire URI (*i.e.*, combination of domain, protocol and port altogether). In the *Relaxed* mode, this decision is based only on the registrable part of the URI's domain, as identified by public suffixes maintained at publicsuffix.org. We introduced the *Relaxed* mode after noticing that most popular websites make legitimate requests to their subdomains or sibling subdomains. For example, a request from *outlook.live.com* to *onedrive.live.com* is not flagged as suspicious under the *Relaxed* mode, as the registrable parts of these domains is the same, *live.com*.

Additional Implementation Details. The Leakuidator browser extension has an options page, allowing the user to change the operating mode and prior decisions. For the mode, the user has two options: *Relaxed* and *Exact*. For prior decisions, users have access to the Exclude and Protect lists, and can edit their prior decisions stored in these lists. The lists are maintained separately for the *Relaxed* and *Exact* modes to avoid any conflicts or confusion by the user.

The requests that trigger a top-level navigation are exempt from mitigation. To identify such requests, Leakuidator evaluates *fetch metadata* request headers, by checking that *Sec-Fetch-Mode* and *Sec-Fetch-Dest* request headers are set to *navigate* and *document* respectively.

6 Security Analysis

Even though Leakuidator has the potential to provide immediate protection against leaky resource attacks, users may be skeptical to install a new browser extension. To address this, we will make the extension's source code publicly available and leverage public scrutiny to build confidence in it. We will also publish the extension on the Chrome Web Store, whose vetting process and the user review-based rating will provide additional evidence about its trustworthiness.

We now show that Leakuidator meets the security objectives presented in Sect. 3.

SO1: Prevent Leaky Resource Attacks. The root cause of a leaky resource attack is the ability of a webpage to infer information about the response to a cross-origin request that contains cookies. Leakuidator determines potentially suspicious requests and ensure they are rendered only after removing the cookies from them. This eliminates the root cause of the attack, thus preventing variants 1 and 2 of the attack. We note that variant 3 of the attack cannot be prevented using a pure client-side defense, since it does not involve interaction with the victim. To mitigate attack variant 3, fixes are needed on the server side (*i.e.*, the sharing service and the integrator).

SO2: Allow End Users to Control their Privacy Level. Security-conscientious users may want the ability to maintain control over their privacy level, especially with regard to avoiding leaky resource attacks, regardless of the various policies and implementations deployed by websites. Leakuidator notifies the user whenever it detects a dangerous request, allowing the user to decide if the request is benign or not. Leakuidator also allows users to reuse past choices and to control how strict is the criterion for identifying potentially suspicious requests.

SO3: Limited Impact on Existing Web Functionality. As analyzed in Sect. 5.2, we expect Leakuidator to have minimal impact on existing web functionality.

7 Experimental Evaluation

Experimental Setup. This section evaluates the overhead introduced by the Leakuidator defense. We compared three cases: a *Baseline* case with no extension installed, and *Relaxed* and *Exact* cases with the Leakuidator extension installed and set to the *Relaxed* and *Exact* modes, respectively.

We wanted to test popular websites that have a large user base. Thus, we chose the Alexa top 15 English websites at paper submission time. Data points in this section's graphs are averages over 20 independent runs. The graphs also show the standard deviation. In each run, we used the Puppeteer automation framework [8] to launch a new browser instance, load the website, extract the measurement information, and then close the browser instance. A separate browser instance is used each time to make sure the test is not affected by browser caching. Measurements are extracted from the Chrome Developer Tools UI.

We ran experiments using Puppeteer Core 5.4.1 and Chrome 87.0 on a system with Intel Core i7-7820HQ CPU with 8 cores (each running at 2.90 GHz), 16 GB RAM, and Intel HD Graphics 630 (kBL GT2) card, running Ubuntu 18.04.5 LTS, kernel v.5.4.0-59-generic.

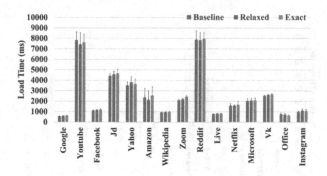

Fig. 4. Load Time for the Baseline, Relaxed, and Exact cases (in milliseconds).

Load Time. Figure 4 shows measurements for the *load time*, defined as the time between when the browser makes the first request to the target website, and when the website is loaded in the browser. The extension's effect on the load time is limited to the modifications made on the original request, *i.e.*, cookie removal for potentially suspicious requests. The second request initiated by Leakuidator does not influence the load time because all responses to requests initiated by the web page are immediately delivered to the webpage without delay. Each website has its own implementation and behaves differently when receiving cookie-less requests. Some websites have identical responses regardless of the presence of cookies. Other websites issue different responses when cookies are removed. The changes in response may increase the load time (*e.g.*, YouTube, Yahoo, Reddit) or decrease it (*e.g.*, Facebook). The majority of websites have slightly faster load time when the extension is not installed. Still, the difference between the three modes is at most 646 ms, with the majority of websites experiencing a difference less than 200 ms. This suggests the impact on user experience is minimal.

Network Traffic. Making two requests instead of one will affect the network traffic. Figures 5 and 6 show the two metrics we used for the network traffic: the number of requests and the amount of data transferred. These are measured for the interval between when the first request is made to the website and when the website finishes loading. When the extension is installed, we add the network traffic caused by the extension during this time interval. Figures 5 and 6 show these measurements. Intuitively, one expects that network traffic should be doubled by having this extension installed, but this is not seen in our measurements. One reason is that third party requests represent a small portion of the requests made by websites. Another reason is that removal of cookies from third party requests will influence the response. For example, the lack of authentication cookies may result in no additional subsequent requests, which are normally sent if cookies were present. Without cookies, some websites return an HTTP error response which is smaller in size than the target resource, whereas other websites may respond with an error webpage that can have larger size than the target resource.

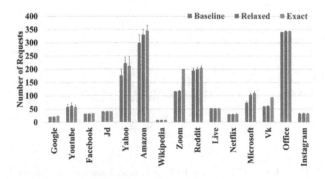

Fig. 5. Number of Requests for the baseline, relaxed, and exact cases.

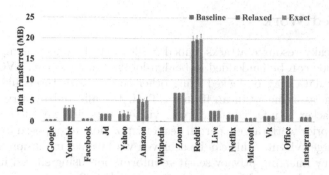

Fig. 6. Data transferred for the baseline, relaxed, and exact cases (in MBs).

Figure 5 reveals that some websites show an increased number of requests due to heavy integration of third party services with requests containing cookies for advertisement and tracking (*e.g.*, Yahoo, Amazon, and Microsoft). However, for the majority of websites, the presence of the extension has minimal impact, adding less than 6% additional requests. Looking at the amount of data transferred, Fig. 6 shows that `Leakuidator` impacts websites differently: the amount increases for Yahoo, but not for Amazon and Microsoft. This shows that `Leakuidator`'s impact depends on the specifics of the third party requests.

When comparing the performance of `Leakuidator`'s *Relaxed* and *Exact* modes, we see that the difference is made by the type of third-party requests. For a website such as Microsoft's, these modes exhibit a similar number of requests, suggesting that third party requests are mostly for domains other than "microsoft.com". On the other hand, for websites such as Yahoo and Zoom, we see a larger amount of data transferred under *Exact* mode, suggesting that third party requests are mostly for sub-domains of the registrable part of the domain.

User Experience Analysis. During the measurement study on these 15 websites, we did not notice any broken functionality. However, more extensive testing would be required to fully assess the impact.

In addition, we measured the number of notifications made to the user by `Leakuidator`. These are measured for the interval between when the first request is made to the website and when the website finishes loading. We performed 10 independent runs for each of the 15 websites, and calculated the average number of notifications made by `Leakuidator` for each website. The results indicate that for the majority of websites the number of notifications is 0 or 1. For three websites (Yahoo, Amazon, and Microsoft), we observe 5.9 to 7.9 and 7.1 to 10 notifications in the *Relaxed* and *Exact* modes respectively. However, the majority of these notifications are for tracking requests, do not affect web functionality and user experience, and so the user can continue without making any decision.

8   Related Work

Attacks. Leaky resource attacks embed XS-leaks in benign-looking webpages. Similarly, code can be emdedded in benign-looking images, *e.g.*, SVG files [18]. Private user data may be leaked using other scriptless methods like CSS [17]. Load time measurements in an iframe HTML tag affected by service workers allow an attacker to infer whether a user visited a specific website [19].

A line of prior work targets partial deanonymization, as opposed to accurately identify a target victim. This can be achieved via browser extension fingerprinting [20,27], by inferring privacy sensitive information using shared images [13], or by leveraging browser history stealing attacks [29,32].

There are techniques for inferring whether a given user has visited a webpage controlled by an advertiser [31], but these cannot be used to track users on third-party websites. Other relevant work includes cross-site script inclusion attacks, which focuses on privacy leaks resulting from dynamically generated JavaScript [21]. Sudhodanan *et al.* [30] generalize and classify cross origin state inference attacks. We continue this line of work by improving effectiveness and reliability of HTML-only XS-leaks and by providing practical client-side defenses.

Server-Side Defenses. In Appendix B, we discuss the drawbacks of using the *SameSite* cookie attribute as a defense. Websites can share secret links with users, instead of using cookies. However, the secrecy of these links may be compromised, *e.g.* if insecure channels are used, through side-channels in browsers, or simply if users handle the links in an insecure way. An alternative is to share resources with users via user-specific secret links. This can result in website performance slow-down and may be challenging due to the mapping needed with content delivery networks for access control. In addition, users can only rely on the website UI for sharing and cannot directly share URLs.

A possible defense is to not respond to requests coming from origins that are not trusted, using the *origin* HTTP request header [11]. Another approach is using the Cross-Origin-Resource-Policy header to limit the websites that can include a specific resource [1]. However, these techniques are problematic as they do not allow cross-origin integration of authenticated resources.

Client-Side Defenses. Browsers can use information flow control techniques to ensure that no information about the outcome of a third-party request is leaked outside of the browser. For example, *tainted canvas* prevents pixel reads after a third-party image is painted on the *canvas* [9]. However, implementing information flow control in the browser can be challenging as there are a multitude of identified and unidentified leak methods in browsers, and may drastically affect the performance [12,14,16,22,23].

A possible partial solution is to separate user sessions in the browser, using the Multi-Account Containers add-on in Firefox, the Add Profile feature in Edge, or the Multiple People feature in Chrome. While not a bullet-proof solution, these can reduce the attack surface. Users can disable third-party cookies altogether. However, the current state of the web is not ready for that, and web functionality will be broken, *e.g.*, advertisement. *ShareMeNot* can be used as a defense against tracking rooted at third party social widgets [24,25]. In contrast, `Leakuidator` is compatible with third-party tracking.

9   Conclusion

In this work, we study leaky resource attacks and show they are a serious privacy concern, even after one year since they were first revealed. We propose `Leakuidator`, a client-side defense that can be deployed right away without buy-in from browser vendors and website owners. We leave as future work conducting a user study to further assess the usability of the proposed defense.

Acknowledgments. This research was supported by the US National Science Foundation under Grants No. CNS 1801430 and DGE 1565478.

A   JavaScript-Based Leaky Resource Attack

Script-Based Attack. The attack page can embed the JavaScript code shown in Fig. 7 in order to disclose information about the outcome of the SD-URL request [28]. The response to the SD-URL request is different depending on the user's state with respect to the target website. In one state, the user is able retrieve the image successfully, triggering the *onload* callback which informs the attacker that the intended victim has visited the attack page. In the other state, the user is unable to retrieve the image, trigerring the *onerror* callback.

```
1  <script>
2    window.onload = function() {
3      var img = document.getElementById("myPic");
4      img.src = "State-Dependent-URL";
5      img.onload = function() {
6        httpReq("Attacker-controlled-URL", "target");
7      }
8      img.onerror = function() {
9        httpReq("Attacker-controlled-URL", "not target");
10     }
11   }
12 </script>
13 <img id="myPic">
```

Fig. 7. Communication method using JavaScript.

B   Drawbacks of Existing Defenses

The SameSite cookie attribute can be used to impose restrictions when cookies associated with a website (i.e., target website) can actually be sent to the target website. When set, this attribute can be assigned three values: *strict*, *lax*, and *none*. If it is set to *strict*, cookies are sent only when the target website matches the website currently shown in the browser's URL bar. If it set to *lax*, cookies will be sent when the condition for the *strict* value is met, but also when the website in the browser's URL bar matches the target website after a top-level navigation. This allows, for example, authentication cookies to be sent to an external website when using a single sign-on service. When the SameSite attribute is set to *none*, the browser will always send cookies along with requests to the target website.

Although setting this cookie attribute to *strict* or *lax* could limit the attack surface in theory, our findings (Sect. 4.4) show that many popular sharing services are still vulnerable, because the attribute is either set to *none*, or not enabled at all. A major reason for this is that the SameSite cookie attribute interferes with services provided by websites, because third party requests require authentication cookies being sent along when embedding the service in another website (*e.g.*, a *watch later* button on an embedded YouTube video, or personalized service such as favorite locations when embedding GoogleMaps).

References

1. Cross-Origin Resource Policy (CORP). https://developer.mozilla.org/en-US/docs/Web/HTTP/Cross-Origin_Resource_Policy_(CORP)
2. Dropbox. https://www.dropbox.com/
3. The fbi booby-trapped a video to catch a suspected tor sextortionist. https://www.vice.com/en_us/article/gyyxb3/the-fbi-booby-trapped-a-video-to-catch-a-suspected-tor-sextortionist
4. Giorgio maone. noscript. https://noscript.net/
5. Google Drive. https://www.google.com/drive/
6. Microsoft One Drive. https://www.microsoft.com/en-us/microsoft-365/onedrive/online-cloud-storage
7. Network investigative technique. https://en.wikipedia.org/wiki/Network_Investigative_Technique
8. Puppeteer. https://github.com/puppeteer/puppeteer
9. Security and tainted canvases. https://developer.mozilla.org/en-US/docs/Web/HTML/CORS_enabled_image#security_and_tainted_canvases
10. The u.s. government has withdrawn its request ordering twitter to identify a trump critic. https://www.washingtonpost.com/news/the-switch/wp/2017/04/07/the-u-s-government-has-withdrawn-its-request-ordering-twitter-to-identify-a-trump-critic
11. Verifying origin with standard headers. https://cheatsheetseries.owasp.org/cheatsheets/Cross-Site_Request_Forgery_Prevention_Cheat_Sheet.html#verifying-origin-with-standard-headers
12. Bauer, L., Cai, S., Jia, L., Passaro, T., Stroucken, M., Tian, Y.: Run-time monitoring and formal analysis of information flows in chromium. In: 22nd Annual Network and Distributed System Security Symposium (NDSS). The Internet Society (2015)

13. Cheung, M., She, J.: Evaluating the privacy risk of user-shared images. ACM Trans. Multimedia Comput. Commun. Appl. **12**(4s) (Sep 2016)
14. Chudnov, A., Naumann, D.A.: Information flow monitor inlining. In: 23rd IEEE Computer Security Foundations Symposium, pp. 200–214. IEEE (2010)
15. Englehardt, S., Narayanan, A.: Online tracking: a 1-million-site measurement and analysis. In: Proceedings of ACM CCS 2016, CCS 2016, pp. 1388–1401. ACM (2016)
16. Groef, W.D., Devriese, D., Nikiforakis, N., Piessens, F.: Flowfox: a web browser with flexible and precise information flow control. In: Proceedings of the ACM Conference on Computer and Communications Security, pp. 748–759. ACM (2012)
17. Heiderich, M., Niemietz, M., Schuster, F., Holz, T., Schwenk, J.: Scriptless attacks: stealing more pie without touching the sill. J. Comput. Secur. **22**(4), July 2014
18. Heiderich, M., Frosch, T., Jensen, M., Holz, T.: Crouching tiger-hidden payload: security risks of scalable vectors graphics. In: Proceedings of the 18th ACM Conference on Computer and Communications Security, pp. 239–250. ACM (2011)
19. 0 Karami, S., Ilia, P., Polakis, J.: Awakening the web's sleeper agents: misusing service workers for privacy leakage. In: Proceedings of NDSS 221 (2021)
20. Karami, S., Ilia, P., Solomos, K., Polakis, J.: Carnus: exploring the privacy threats of browser extension fingerprinting. In: Proceedings of NDSS 2020 (2020)
21. Lekies, S., Stock, B., Wentzel, M., Johns, M.: The unexpected dangers of dynamic Javascript. In: Proceedings of the 24th USENIX Security Symposium, pp. 723–735 (2015)
22. Magazinius, J., Russo, A., Sabelfeld, A.: On-the-fly inlining of dynamic security monitors. In: IFIP International Information Security Conference, pp. 173–186 (2010)
23. Rajani, V., Bichhawat, A., Garg, D., Hammer, C.: Information flow control for event handling and the dom in web browsers. In: 2015 IEEE 28th Computer Security Foundations Symposium, pp. 366–379. IEEE (2015)
24. Roesner, F., Kohno, T., Wetherall, D.: Detecting and defending against third-party tracking on the web. In: Proceedings of USENIX NSDI 2012, pp. 155–168 (2012)
25. Roesner, F., Rovillos, C., Kohno, T., Wetherall, D.: Sharemenot: balancing privacy and functionality of third-party social widgets. In: Usenix; login (2012)
26. Schwarz, M., Lipp, M., Gruss, D.: Javascript zero: real Javascript and zero side-channel attacks. In: Proceedings of NDSS 2018 (2018)
27. Sjösten, A., Acker, S.V., Sabelfeld, A.: Discovering browser extensions via web accessible resources. In: Proceedings of the ACM CODASPY 2017, pp. 329–336 (2017)
28. Staicu, C.A., Pradel, M.: Leaky images: targeted privacy attacks in the web. In: Proceedings of the 28th USENIX Security Symposium, pp. 923–939 (2019)
29. Su, J., Shukla, A., Goel, S., Narayanan, A.: De-anonymizing web browsing data with social networks. In: Proceedings of the 26th International Conference on World Wide Web (2017)
30. Sudhodanan, A., Khodayari, S., Caballero, J.: Cross-origin state inference (COSI) attacks: leaking web site states through XS-Leaks. In: Proceedings of NDSS 2020 (2020)
31. Venkatadri, G., et al.: Privacy risks with Facebook's PII-based targeting: auditing a data broker's advertising interface. In: Proceedings of IEEE S&P 2018, pp. 89–107. IEEE (2018)
32. Wondracek, G., Holz, T., Kirda, E., Kruegel, C.: A practical attack to de-anonymize social network users. In: Proceedings of IEEE S&P 2010, pp. 223–238 (2010)

JABBIC Lookups: A Backend Telemetry-Based System for Malware Triage

Octavian Ciprian Bordeanu[1]([✉]), Gianluca Stringhini[2], Yun Shen[3], and Toby Davies[1]

[1] University College London, London WC1E 6DH, UK
{octavian.bordeanu.16,toby.davies}@ucl.ac.uk
[2] Boston University, Boston, MA 02215, USA
gian@bu.edu
[3] NortonLifeLock Research Group, Arizona, USA
yun.shen@nortonlifelock.com

Abstract. In this paper, we propose JABBIC lookups, a telemetry-based system for malware triage at the interface between proprietary reputation score systems and malware analysts. JABBIC uses file download telemetry collected from client protection solutions installed on end-hosts to determine the threat level of an unknown file based on telemetry data associated with files already known to be malign. We apply word embeddings, and semantic and relational similarities to triage potentially malign files following the intuition that, while single elements in a malware download might change over time, their context, defined as the semantic and relational properties between the different elements in a malware delivery system (*e.g.*, servers, autonomous systems, files) does not change as fast. To this end, we show that JABBIC can leverage file download telemetry to allow security vendors to manage the collection and analysis of unknown files from remote end-hosts for timely processing by more sophisticated malware analysis systems. We test and evaluate JABBIC lookups with 33M download events collected during October 2015. We show that 85.83% of the files triaged with JABBIC lookups are part of the same malware family as their past counterpart files. We also show that, if used with proprietary reputation score systems, JABBIC can triage as malicious 55.1% of files before they are detected by VirusTotal, preceding this detection by over 20 days.

Keywords: Malware triage · Word embeddings

1 Introduction

The anti-malware industry is confronted by the challenge of identifying malware in large amounts of telemetry data from files downloaded by end-hosts using their client protection solutions [20,31]. Typically, antivirus software collect and

J. Garcia-Alfaro et al. (Eds.): SecureComm 2021, LNICST 399, pp. 164–184, 2021.
https://doi.org/10.1007/978-3-030-90022-9_9

transmit telemetry data from a large number of client machines when users download files that are potentially malicious and unknown to the proprietary security vendor. Since security vendors do not possess unknown downloaded binaries but only telemetry reports, they rely on file reputation score systems to prioritize and collect those binaries that require utmost attention. At this stage, however, malware analysts need to make decisions as to which files should be prioritized for collection and analysis based only on telemetry data since state-of-the-art triage systems require the downloaded binaries [11,18,19,37].

A widely used solution is built upon file reputation score systems. Generally, antivirus (AV) engines rely on a backend system which assign reputation scores to unknown files. Hash values of unknown files that are found in the backend system are assigned reputation scores accordingly. When a hash value is not found in the backend system, the AV engine sends back on-device activity data. The backend system verifies if the data matches any predefined behavioral rules and returns a reputation score. Lastly, if the backend system is uncertain then a negative reputation score is arbitrarily assigned. To this end, we develop the JABBIC (judge a book by its cover) triage system which uses download contextual information when looking up a file. This way, the backend reputation score system is provided with additional clues about the extent to which an unknown file can be deemed as malicious.

JABBIC runs at the interface between file reputation score systems and malware analysts, and leverages download telemetry data to match unknown files to known malicious files such that the semantic and relational similarities between their associated telemetry data is maximized. The match itself is accompanied by a confidence score which, if above a set threshold, indicates whether an unknown file and the known malicious file it has been matched with are likely to belong to the same malware family or be siblings by parent files, file naming patterns, signers, or a combination of these. Malware analysts are thus able to better guide their decisions as to which unknown files with negative reputation scores, potentially in the order of millions, to collect and analyze first.

JABBIC uses word embeddings which are an approach developed within natural language processing (NLP) to capture semantic and relational properties between words [24]. Words are projected to a latent space - an n-dimensional vector space - in such a way that vectors that are close in latent space have corresponding data points that have some degree of relatedness [23]. Word2Vec [24], a word embedding algorithm, takes as input a corpus of natural text and, given a window size relative to each sentence, outputs a vector representation for each unique word which reflects its meaning. We adapt this idea by applying the approach to abstract 'sentences' which describe file download events, the 'words' of which refer to characteristics of the download telemetry data (such as ASes, network and host IDs, domain names, and URL paths).

2   Related Work

Researchers have developed state-of-the-art systems that show great promise on detecting malware using word embeddings. The authors in [11] proposed a methodology that used Word2Vec and TF-IDF algorithms to embed API *syscalls* functions from malware binaries. These embeddings captured the infection behavior of malicious files and were used to cluster the malware samples into families. In [37], authors presented an Android malware detection system, called ANDRE, which utilized the raw labels from antivirus vendors, meta-info of binaries, and insights from source code analysis to learn latent representations of labeled malware samples. Clustering and deep learning were then used to assign malware families to weakly labeled samples based on how similar they were to strongly labeled samples. Scalable triage malware triage systems that have also shown promising results include BITSHRED [18], MAST [8], and SIGMAL [19], all of which rely on binary analysis. Nevertheless, these state-of-the-art methods require the binary files and rely on a sequence of static and/or dynamic analysis stages. Such detection systems are thus not suitable for the telemetry-based detection of malware, particularly when it is uncommon for client protection solutions installed on end-hosts to send a copy of the downloaded binary to antivirus vendors.

3   Background and Motivation

JABBIC is positioned at the interface between a proprietary reputation score system – widely used by security companies to flag potentially malicious files using telemetry data – and malware analysts who decide whether files should be submitted for further analysis (Fig. 1). When a file is downloaded, the antivirus software sends telemetry data to a reputation score system that is proprietary to the vendor. The telemetry data of unknown files with negative reputation scores are forwarded to JABBIC which then searches for known malicious files whose telemetry data are similar both semantically and relationally to that of the unknown files. The unknown and known malicious files, their reputation scores, and the confidence score with which JABBIC matched them, are sent to the malware analyst who then decides whether to initiate a file collection request to the end-host. As shown later in this paper, the confidence score quantifies the likelihood that an unknown file and a known malicious file found by JABBIC share the same malware family.

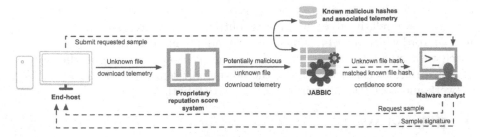

Fig. 1. Improved triage of unknown files using JABBIC at the interface between proprietary reputation score systems and malware analysts.

Table 1. JABBIC triage report sample based on telemetry data.

Row index	Query file (unknown)			Match file (known)			JABBIC confidence score
	Hash	Malware family	Risk given reputation score	Hash	Malware family	Risk given reputation score	
1	AF4EF...	Convertad	Low	01A28..	Convertad	High	0.85
2	F3841...	Installcore	Medium	DF20D...	Installcore	High	0.76
3	1C233...	Yakes	Low	90CDC...	Yakes	High	1
4	D6483...	Opencandy	Low	1B487...	Downloadadmin	Low	0.56
5	38F6E...	Swisyn	High	27A50...	Ardamax	Low	0.49

Prior to the application of JABBIC, the reputation score provides the only means to rank the risk (and therefore priority) of unknown files (see Table 1). However, the matching of these files with known malicious files (with high confidence) suggests that this implied ranking is misleading. The low-risk query files, Table 1 at row indices 1, 3 and 4, are not only matched by JABBIC with known files having high risk levels but also the same malware families. These files would thus be incorrectly given the lowest priority which can lead to significant detection delays. Furthermore, file risk levels based on reputation scores are not necessarily representative of how malicious they are. For example, the unknown and known files in Table 1 with the same malware family have a very large discrepancy in their risk levels despite performing similar malicious activities. Therefore, we propose that the triage process is based on the JABBIC scores once files are flagged as suspicious by the reputation score system. JABBIC scores are also meaningful when compared to reputation scores. For instance, scores of at least 0.6, a threshold which we set in Sect. 6, indicate that two matched files are likely to belong to the same malware family or have some form of sibling relationship, as shown in Table 1.

4   Data

We leverage a dataset from NortonLifeLock's data sharing platform. The telemetry used in this study does not contain any personal identifiable information. The dataset contains information on 33,188,789 download events for the entire month of October 2015, and include the SHA2 string of the downloaded file, the SHA2 string of the parent file that initiated the download, the IP of the file host, the URL of the file host, and the time and date the file was first observed by NortonLifeLock. The data also include file reputation scores denoting low, medium, and high-risk levels. We augmented this dataset with autonomous system (AS) information. The AS number for each download IP was identified using IP to AS mappings published on University of Oregon Route Views Archive [2].

4.1   Ground Truth Labels

We identified 115,705 query file hashes that were downloaded solely on 31 October 2015 to ensure that neither JABBIC nor the baseline methods, which we discuss in Subsect. 8.4, had any prior information about these files. For each query file, we used JABBIC to search its match file in every previous day of the same month; thus each query file has 30 matches, one for each previous day, resulting in 515,571 unique matches across all days. This allows us to evaluate the performance decay of JABBIC over time. Query files can have the same matches across multiple days and two or more query files can have the same matches for one or more days. Similarly, we used the baseline methods to search matches for query files among known files downloaded on 1 October 2015. We limit the search to one day for the baseline methods because we want to compare their performance to that of JABBIC when identifying matches among known files downloaded 30 days prior to when the query files were downloaded. The query file hashes and the returned match hashes were then searched on VirusTotal [3].

Table 2. Query hashes and corresponding match hashes that were identified by Jabbic and variant baselines, found on VirusTotal and labeled by AVClass with a malware family.

Matching method	# hashes	% found on VT	% labelled by AVClass
Query files	115,705	6.71	3.73
Jabbic* matches	515,571	15.34	7.4
Skip-gram** matches	3,012	27.08	12.71
CBOW** matches	4,454	29.88	14.51
fastText** matches	11,618	17.79	9.96
TF-IDF** matches	15,586	22.22	12.38
Bloom filters** matches	25,026	18.57	10.12
LSH** matches	25,099	18.18	9.98
Dropper files	45,567	66.83	63.82

* Unique match and dropper hashes were searched for all 30 days.
** Variant baselines whose performance was evaluated based on their ability to identify match files downloaded on 1 October 2015. For this reason, the numbers for unique match and dropper hashes are much smaller when compared to those reported for JABBIC.

A breakdown of how many queries and unique matches were found as malicious on VirusTotal and labeled with a malware family is shown in Table 2. We used the AVClass labeler [30] with the VirusTotal scanning reports to retrieve their malware families. We also searched the dropper hashes of queries and their matches whose malware families were different but had JABBIC scores within the threshold set in Sect. 7. This allowed us to determine whether a query file and its match were dropped by files with the same malware family despite the query and the match having different malware families.

5 Methods

5.1 Embedding Download Events

Word2Vec is an approach which can be applied to data which is structured as a sequence of 'words'; typically formed into sentences. Unlike natural language, in which words are linked by semantics and sentences arise naturally, in order to apply it in the present context we need to artificially formulate a sentence-like representation of the file download information. We conceptualized a download event as a structured fragment of information of the form *an **AS** that owned an **IP address** facilitated the download of a **file** from a **domain** at a particular location given by the **URL path***. Each download event is therefore represented as the sentence *(AS, network ID, host ID, file SHA2, domain, URL path)* before being fed to a Word2Vec model. The structure of the sentence also preserves the hierarchical structure of the malware delivery infrastructure: (**1**) the domains and URL paths form the full file host URLs, (**2**) ASes own the file host IPs and hence the latent relationships among host IPs are better captured during the training; and (**3**) the position of the file hashes in the sentence ensures that the latent relationships between host IPs and domains are also indirectly preserved due to the chosen window size.

Choice of Word2Vec Model. There are two main types of Word2Vec model – Skip-gram and CBOW – each with different properties. We choose Skip-gram for training word embeddings because (**1**) the aim is to predict the context of a given word rather than predict the word given a context (*e.g.*, predict context given a downloaded file, IP, URL, or AS as input rather than vice versa), (**2**) Skip-gram performs better with infrequent words [26], which is advantageous considering the high cardinality of file hashes (*e.g.*, there are 968,174 unique file hashes for the 1 October 2015 dataset with 1,129,239 file hashes, meaning that each file appears in the dataset 1.17 times on average), and (**3**) Skip-gram does not require large amounts of data to produce high quality embeddings when compared to CBOW [26]. The weights in Word2Vec models are adjusted using negative sampling [25]. The recommended negative samples is between 5 and 20 for small training datasets, and 2 to 5 for large datasets [25]. We chose negative sampling with 5 negative samples to update the model weights. Subsampling of frequent words and discarding of rare words are omitted to avoid both removing valuable file hashes, IP addresses, domain names, and URL paths from the dataset and reducing the vector space within which the search for the local match is carried out.

Temporal Granularity. NortonLifeLock collected and aggregated the download events telemetry on a daily basis. We choose to retain this temporal slicing and train a separate Word2Vec model for each day. JABBIC lookups can be carried out sequentially or concurrently on multiple days. A daily granularity allows us to limit the search space to most recent download events and thus increase training and lookup speeds; for instance, we find that the strongest matches were identified a day prior to that of query files and hence there is no need to increase the search space to an entire month. Lastly, in real-world settings, training a separate Word2Vec based model on a daily basis minimizes the update delay of the search space.

Training Hyperparameters. We set the starting learning rate (α) at its default value of 0.025 and the number of epochs at 10. How to choose a suitable embedding size for Word2Vec (*i.e.*, the dimensionality of the latent space) is the subject of much debate [35]: values between 100 and 300 are usually recommended in the literature, while a guideline introduced by Google is the fourth root of the number of categories (*e.g.*, unique words in vocabulary) [4]. Here we adopt the latter approach: the average vocabulary size across all 30 days of October 2015 is 1,111,775.29, and the average fourth root is 32.44, and so we chose an embedding size of 32. A further choice is the window size to use. Relative to the size of each sentence, larger windows capture topic-specific information about words, while smaller windows capture more functional (*i.e.*, syntactical relationships) information [22]. We set the window size to 2 since we are interested in learning syntactical relationships between words.

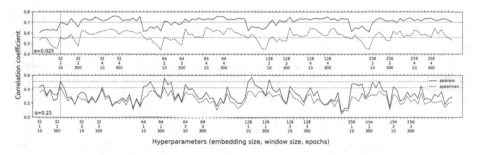

Fig. 2. Correlation values between calculated relatedness scores and cosine similarities, across all pairs of file hashes, for a range of hyperparameter values.

We tested the sensitivity of word embeddings to these choices by training a Word2Vec model for 1 October 2015 data, containing 1,129,239 download events, for all combinations of the following hyperparameter values: *embedding size*: 32, 64, 128, 256; α: 0.025, 0.25; *window size*: 1, 2, 3, 4, 5; and *epochs*: 10, 20, 30, 100, 200, 300. We built a dataset that contained file hash pairs together with an assigned similarity that measured the relatedness between them. The relatedness score was calculated using the R/O score, described in Subsect. 5.2, such that two file hashes that shared similar contexts had higher scores and vice versa. We calculated these scores for 1000 observations that contained the top 200 most downloaded files. We then calculated the Pearson and Spearman [14] correlation coefficients and associated two-tailed p-values between the relatedness scores and the cosine similarities across all pairs of file hashes. A similar approach was used in [28] and [12] with datasets containing 999 [15] and 200 word pairs, respectively.

The accuracy of word embeddings using $\alpha = 0.025$, *embedding size = 32, window size = 2*, and *epochs = 10* was fairly high as indicated by the Pearson and Spearman correlation coefficients of 0.703 and 0.558, respectively, both with two-tailed p-values lower than 0.001 (Fig. 2). The highest correlation coefficients were obtained using $\alpha = 0.025$, *embedding size = 128, window size = 3* and *epochs = 10* ($r = 0.751$, $rho = 0.654$, $p < 0.001$) and $\alpha = 0.025$, *embedding size = 32, window size = 4* and *epochs = 200* ($r = 0.762$, $rho = 0.622$, $p < 0.001$). However, these correlation coefficients were only marginally higher than those obtained with the hyperparameters we initially proposed. We chose to trade off this small difference in embedding quality for highest training speeds; smaller embedding, window size, and number of epochs meant faster training speeds.

5.2   Local Matching

To identify matches for a given input file, we adapt the search method developed by Zhang *et al.* [36] that finds terms in previous time slices that are semantically closest to a given input term in the present time slice. The method of Zhang *et al.* [36] was designed for querying archives and collections of past documents.

Consider a base vector space, which is the set of vectors trained on the data containing query files (*e.g.*, Word2Vec model trained on 31 October 2015 data), and a target vector space, which is the set of vectors trained on the data where the local match searching is carried out (*e.g.*, Word2Vec model trained on 1 October 2015 data). Given a query file q (unknown file represented by its hash) in base vector space, the aim is to find its best representative file hash m in target vector space (known malicious file represented by its hash). We formulate this problem as follows.

Let $S_{sim}(q, m) = cos(M \cdot q, m)$ be the across-time *semantic similarity* between a query file q in base vector space and a local match file m in target vector space, where M is the transformation matrix which projects the base vector space to the target vector space. Let $F_q = (V, \prod)$ be a download event associated with query file q, defined by a set of download event elements V such that $V = q \cup C$, where $C = \{c_1, c_2, c_3, ..., c_u\}$ is a set of u context words (*e.g.*, ASes, network and host IDs, domains, and URL paths) – and a set of associations $\prod = \{\pi | \text{association between } q \text{ and each context word in } C\}$. Similarly, let $F_m = (V', \prod')$ be a download event associated with file m in target vector space, with download event elements V' and associations $\prod'$ defined equivalently. The objective is to find the file m^* such that F_{m^*} in target vector space is most similar to F_q in base vector space. *Relational similarity* is then defined as $R_{sim} = cos(M \cdot (q - c_i), (m - c_i'))$, where $q - c_i$ is the subtraction between the vector of query file q and the vector of its context word c_i, and $m - c_i'$ is the subtraction between the vector of file m and the vector of its context word c_i'.

The local similarity LS between F_q and F_m is calculated as per Eq. 1, where v_0 and v_0' denote the vector representations of query file hash q in base space and its counterpart file hash m in target space, respectively; v_i and v_i' denote the vector representations of all i and i' delivery infrastructure elements (*e.g.*, file hash, AS, network ID, host ID, second-level domain, and host URL) of q and m, respectively; and u is the number of context words. LS is a weighted combination of semantic and relational similarity, with higher λ values corresponding to higher weighting for semantic similarity.

$$LS = \lambda \cdot \frac{\sum_{i=0}^{u} S_{sim}(v_i, v_i')}{u} + (1 - \lambda)\frac{\sum_{i=1}^{u} R_{sim}((v_0, v_i), (v_0', v_i'))}{u} \quad (1)$$

The best local match of query file hash q is given by $argmax_m(LS(q, m))$, which returns the file hash m^* in target space that is most representative of the query file hash q semantically, relationally, and by delivery infrastructure.

Offline training, whereby words are grouped into time bins and then a Word2Vec model is separately trained for each slice, is useful for capturing the semantic content of words at discrete intervals. However, each embedding is specific to its corresponding time bin, which means that embeddings of a particular word across different time bins cannot be meaningfully compared. Vector alignment is required in order to compare vector representations of words in different vector spaces. For vector space alignment, we use orthogonal Procrustes, an assumption-free method [34], to project the base vector space onto the target vector space.

The Ratcliff/Obershelp (R/O) pattern matching algorithm compares two strings and outputs a value between 0 and 1, where 1 denotes a complete match between the two strings and 0 indicates no substrings in common. The iterative process by which the R/O algorithm works is described in [16]. In our context, we use the R/O score to quantify the overlap between the contextual information of pairs of query and match files in a string-like sense. Put simply, this measures the similarity between the contexts of the two files. As shown below, this can be used as a confidence measure that allows us to quantify the certainty with which JABBIC can associate a local match file with a given query file.

6   JABBIC Lookups Architecture

The system architecture is illustrated in Fig. 3. ❶ Determine the temporal granularity by which telemetry data from known malicious files is to be split (*e.g.*, by day). ❷ Train separate target vector-based models for each day, and then store them into a lookup database. This allows for the selection of a specific past timeframe within which searching for a local match is carried out. ❸ Train a base vector space for the day which contains the query files; that is, those files that have not been downloaded in any previous timeframes. ❹ Select a target vector space within which local matches are to be searched given the query files from the base vector-based model (*e.g.*, find local match files downloaded on 1 October 2015 given query files downloaded on 31 October 2015). ❺ Align base and target vector spaces to a common vector space in which cosine similarities can be computed. ❻ Identify query files as those files that have not been seen before. ❼ For each query file in the base vector space, find its most representative match file in target vector space from a previous timeframe and then assess the confidence with which these files are matched using the R/O score. After lookups are completed, the current base vector space can then be added to the lookup database, which can then be queried when local matches are searched for queries downloaded the next day.

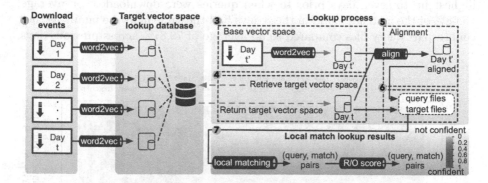

Fig. 3. JABBIC lookups architecture.

7   JABBIC Confidence Score Threshold

In this section, we assess the triage performance of JABBIC on download events from October 2015 for which malware family labels, parent files, and file names are available from both the VirusTotal scan reports and our datasets. First, we identify 115,705 unique hashes of files downloaded solely on 31 October 2015 to ensure that no prior information about these files is known to JABBIC in the lookup process. For each of these files, JABBIC lookups are used to search their match file hashes in every previous day. This allows us to assess the triage accuracy when lookups are performed on data up to thirty days prior to when query files were downloaded. Lastly, we relate triage accuracy to the corresponding R/O scores and then set an optimal confidence score threshold. Unknown query files matched with malicious known files to a confidence R/O score above the set threshold are very likely to be related by malware family.

7.1   Matched Files and Malware Families

On average, across all days of October 2015, 81.18% of unique and labeled *(query, match)* pairs have the same malware family irrespective of the R/O score. The percentage of *(query, match)* pairs with the same malware family increased as the daily proportion of *(query, match)* pairs with R/O scores in ranges $[0.6, 0.8)$ and $[0.8, 1]$ also increased while peaks in R/O scores in range $[0, 0.6)$ led to a percentage decrease (Fig. 4). The highest density of *(query, match)* pairs with the same malware family was associated with R/O scores in range [0.6, 1]; 89.43% and 87.43% of *(query, match)* pairs with R/O scores in ranges [0.8, 1] and [0.6, 0.8), respectively, had the same malware family, while the percentage is much lower for scores in the range [0, 0.6). Thus, for any given *(query, match)* pair, a higher R/O score increases the probability that the malware family of the query file is the same as that of its match. The certainty with which JABBIC found matches with the same malware family as that of their corresponding query files was highest up to seven days prior to when queries were downloaded; on average, 85.68% of the matches found in these days had the same malware family as their counterpart query files compared to an average of 79.81% across previous days.

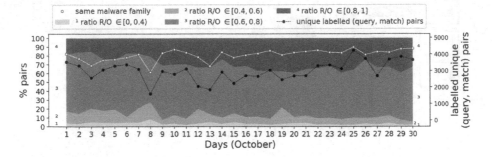

Fig. 4. Percentage of query file hashes and their match file hashes from each previous day of October 2015 with the same malware families. The plot also shows the proportion of pairs falling into each R/O band.

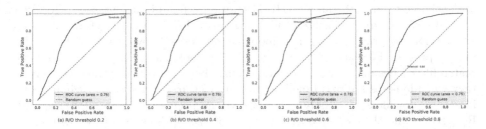

Fig. 5. ROC curves for the R/O score metric ($R/0 \in [0, 1]$ and thresholds 0.2, 0.4, 0.6, 0.8).

Next, we evaluate the reliability of setting the confidence score threshold at 0.6 when deciding whether a query file (unknown) and a match file (known as malicious) are likely to belong to the same malware family. This is particularly useful when, despite missing malware family labels, analysts can rely on the assumption that a query file and a match file, which are paired by JABBIC with a confidence score of at least 0.6, are also likely to have the same malware family. Thus, the query file can be prefiltered for collection and analysis by more than just its reputation score which, as we show in the next section, is not a reliable risk indicator. First, we calculated the weighted precision, recall, and F1 scores across all classes (*i.e.*, malware families) to evaluate the average performance of JABBIC when matching query and known files by malware families. Second, we assessed how the certainty with which JABBIC assigned malware families to previously unseen files changed based on different R/O score thresholds using the receiver operating characteristic (ROC) curve and area under the ROC curve (AUC) metrics. The matching process is framed as a binary classification problem, with each (query, match) pair being assigned label 1 if their families are the same, and 0 otherwise.

Table 3. JABBIC performance at matching unknown and known malicious files by malware families for different R/O confidence score ranges.

R/O range	Weighted precision	Weighted recall	Weighted F1 score	Labeled pairs
$R/O \in [0, 1]$	0.87	0.82	0.84	89,158
$R/O \in [0, 0.6)$	0.5	0.36	0.40	11,355
$R/O \in [0.6, 1]$	0.92	0.89	0.89	77,803

For a second stage triage, we aim for the highest true positive rate – identify as many queries as possible that have the same malware families as their matches – while accepting a higher false positive rate since the cost of collecting and analyzing mismatched unknown files has no significant practical implications. The initial triage of files as either benign or potentially malign has already been done by the reputation score system. Thus, the only implication of JABBIC matching a small proportion of unknown files to malicious known files with different malware families, is that the unknown files are collected and analyzed earlier than they otherwise would. For this reason, we accept a confidence R/O score threshold of 0.6 as optimal, which not only correctly matches the highest proportion of unknown query files to known malicious files by malware families but also achieves the lowest false positive rate (Fig. 5). Most importantly, however, is that 89% of matched files with confidence scores in range [0.6, 1] had the same malware families (F1 score of 0.89 in Table 3). Therefore, malware analysts can rely on the assumption that if a query file is matched to a malicious known file with a confidence score of at least 0.6, then the query file is most likely to be related to the malicious known file by malware family.

7.2 Lambda Parameter

The λ parameter value was set to 0.5, meaning that semantic and relational similarities were given equal weights in the match lookup process. In Table 4 we also show the percentage of (query, match) pairs with R/O confidence scores falling in different ranges had 0.2 and 0.8 been used instead. We find that the confidence scores of (query, match) pairs were not sensitive to the three λ values;

that is, the proportion of *(query, match)* pairs with confidence scores in ranges $[0.6, 8)$ and $[0.8, 1]$ did not differ significantly as the λ parameter value was changed. One reason for this could be that there was a relatively high number of files that were good candidates as local matches for a each query file. Despite the lack of sensitivity of local match lookups to the three λ parameter values, it appeared that setting λ to 0.5 achieved the highest proportion of R/O scores in ranges $[0.6, 0.8)$ and $[0.8, 1]$, although just marginally.

Table 4. Matching R/O scores for different λ parameter values.

λ	$R/O \in [0, 0.2)$	$R/O \in [0.2, 0.4)$	$R/O \in [0.4, 0.6)$	$R/O \in [0.6, 0.8)$	$R/O \in [0.8, 1]$
0.2	1.19%	9.78%	18.90%	41.84%	28.29%
0.5	1.15%	8.89%	18.85%	41.91%	29.20%
0.8	1.02%	8.68%	19.47%	41.83%	29.00%

8   Evaluation

Here we begin by evaluating how the confidence with which JABBIC assigns a match to a query file changes across time. This allows us to determine the optimal search timeframe prior to when query files were downloaded. We then evaluate the extent to which JABBIC can improve the prioritization for collection and analysis of unknown files already prefiltered by reputation scores. We then compare the detection times by VirusTotal with those expected from JABBIC if used as a second stage triage system. Lastly, we compare the triage performance of JABBIC with n-gram, co-occurrence, and set-based matching baselines.

8.1   Longitudinal Decay of Triage Performance

The R/O scores of local matching provide a measure of the confidence associated with the triage of a given query file. On this basis, the 115,705 query files, downloaded solely on 31 October 2015, can be triaged with very high confidence based on files downloaded up to 7 days before; 35.17% and 41.53% of R/O scores are in ranges $[0.6, 0.8)$ and $[0.8, 1]$, respectively (Fig. 6). We recommend that the confidence with which a query and match file are paired by malware family is evaluated based on the following confidence levels: high ($R/O \in [0.6, 1]$) and cannot tell for $R/O \in [0, 0.6)$. We justify this recommendation based on the results from Subsect. 7.1.

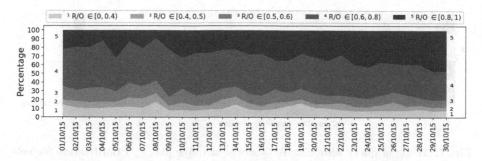

Fig. 6. Confidence decay when query files downloaded on 31 October 2015 are triaged based on matches from every previous day.

8.2   Reliability of File Reputation Scores

File reputation scores are not consistent across files belonging to the same malware families. For example, 616 files with malware family *zusy* had reputation scores denoting low, medium, and high levels of risk. To understand the scale of this observation, we look at the reputation scores of files associated with each malware family. We use 87,532 labeled unique file hashes and their reputation scores, including files that are neither queries nor matches, which span across 2,460 malware families. For each malware family, we count the number of files that fall within it and calculate the standard deviation of their reputation scores. The higher the standard deviation of reputation scores of files belonging to a malware family, the lower the triage reliability of those scores since these files are expected to pose similar threat levels and thus have reputation scores as close as possible. We find that for 42.13% of labeled files, belonging to 21.22% of malware families, the standard deviation of reputation scores is 30. For 84.28% of labeled files, belonging to 29.63% of malware families, the standard deviation of reputation scores is 20. Files with low-risk levels are thus not necessarily less suspicious than those with higher risk levels.

Next, we exemplify how JABBIC can prefilter unknown files with negative reputation scores. Consider that the current date is 31 October for which a large volume of telemetry is received by malware analysts who then identify 115,705 unknown files flagged as suspicious by the reputation score system. We also hold telemetry data of files which were downloaded the previous day and known to be malicious. For each unknown file, JABBIC lookups are then carried out to identify their local matches from the previous day. JABBIC results show that 80.44% of *(query, match)* pairs have R/O scores of at least 0.6, meaning that they are most likely to have the same malware family.

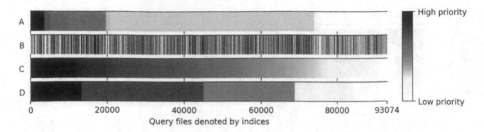

Fig. 7. Triage of query files with R/O scores in range [0.6, 1]. Prioritization for collection and analysis of query files. **A:** Reputation scores of query files from highest to lowest priority); **B:** Confidence R/O scores of query files ordered by reputation scores; **C:** Query files ordered by confidence R/O scores (1 for highest priority and 0.6 for lowest priority) at low granularity; **D:** Query files ordered by confidence R/O scores at high granularity ([0.9, 1], [0.8, 0.9), [0.7, 0.8)], and [0.6, 0.7))

In Fig. 7 we illustrate the prioritization of files using the reputation score system and JABBIC. Query files, sorted in ascending order by their reputation scores, are matched with known malicious files whose reputation scores do not reflect similar levels of maliciousness despite being very likely to have the same malware family (heatmaps A and B). Most notably, query files with lowest priority would have been prioritized for collection and analysis much earlier judging by the risk levels of their match files. Similarly, most of query files with highest priority for collection and analysis are matched with known files having much lower priority. Heatmaps A and B indicate what we have already shown: *(query, match)* pairs have significantly different levels of risk despite belonging to the same malware families. Therefore, file reputation scores are at most reliable for an initial triage of unknown files as either potentially malign or benign but not for further prioritization of malign files. In heatmaps C and D from Fig. 7, query files are sorted in descending order by the confidence R/O scores with which JABBIC paired them with known malicious files.

8.3   JABBIC Triage vs. VirusTotal

VirusTotal reports both the date when a file was submitted for analysis and the date it was detected as malign. We show the number of days elapsed since query files were submitted to VirusTotal until they were detected as malicious. Out of 113,642 unique query files which had at least one match in any previous day with an R/O score in range [0.6, 1], 7,320 (6.44%) were submitted for scanning on VirusTotal by third parties and found malicious (include singletons which are malignware not belonging to a malware family). The detection times of these files by VirusTotal are shown in Table 5. More than half of the query files found as malicious on VirusTotal were detected over 20 days after they were submitted for scanning. We also include the detection times for all hashes that we scanned and found on VirusTotal to show that similar detection times are relevant beyond the sample of query files (Table 5). JABBIC could have triaged and flagged as suspicious over half the query files in less than a day if not hours, depending on the search space size, when compared to over 20 days as per VirusTotal.

Table 5. Number of days until detection by VirusTotal.

	0 days	1–9 days	10–19 days	>= 20 days
Detected query hashes ($N = 7,320$)	33.10%	8.31%	3.13%	55.10%
All detected hashes ($N = 216,582$)	31.53%	7.41%	3.62%	57.12%

8.4 Variant Baselines

State-of-the-art triage systems require binary-level analysis for which reason we are not able to compare their performance against that of JABBIC which is a telemetry-based triage approach. Instead, we compare the performance of JABBIC with Skip-gram and CBOW, fastText [7], TF-IDF [29], Bloom filters [21], and LSH [9] which are commonly used in malware detection systems based on string-level similarity of opcodes, network packet payloads, application programming interface (API) method calls, instruction sequences, and binary strings [5,6,17,32,33]. We used fastText with 3 to 6 g, meaning that the embedding of each download event component was represented by a bag of 3 to 6 n-grams. For LSH and Bloom filters we converted each download event into 5-shingle sets. For example, download event, identified by its file hash `CA756...`, 'China169

Table 6. Triaging performance of Jabbic compared with n-gram, co-occurrence, and set-based matching models.

Matching method	(a) Individual performance based on all labeled (query,match) pairs		(b) Performance comparison based on (query, match) pairs with queries for which both Jabbic and the baseline found a labeled match				Searching time ($\approx$ hours)
	% same malware family	N	% same malware family (Jabbic)	N	% same malware family (baseline)	N	
Jabbic	82.4	3,517	–	–	–	–	5
Skip-gram	23.95	1,027	68.10	840	28.04	731	1
CBOW	7.56	1,680	88.41	2,260	11.37	888	1
fastText (3–6 g)	68.60	1,258	72.38	1,086	73.18	548	1
TF-IDF	74.74	1,437	72.41	1,131	80.56	607	12
Bloom filters (5 g)	81.26	1,446	83.58	1,657	89.18	647	124
LSH (5 g)	80.85	1,504	84.14	1,766	89.57	671	310

JABBIC and variant baselines are compared on query files and their matches downloaded on 31 and 1 October 2015, respectively, irrespective of their R/O scores. (a) The individual performance results are reported based on how many (query, match) pairs, out of all labeled pairs, were found to have the same malware family; (b) Results are reported based on those query files for which both JABBIC and each baseline method have found a match in order to determine their relative performance on the same query files. For example, 348 query files were found in 840 and 731 labeled (query, match) pairs identified by JABBIC and Skip-gram, respectively.

Backbone 218.58.225.7 dxdown.rilibiao.com.cn/cx/2015092118/' is shingled into 5-character substrings 'China', 'hina1', 'ina16', and so forth. Given the small number of 5-character shingles (*e.g.*, not exceeding 50 shingles) per download event, the size of each Bloom filter was set to 1000 with 7 hash functions to ensure a false positive rate not higher than 0.001, as confirmed by this online Bloom filter calculator [1]. As per Table 6, the overall performance of JABBIC not only surpassed that of all baseline methods but was also much faster than those whose performance was relatively close, particularly set-based matching with LSH and Bloom filters.

9   System Performance

Training Word2Vec models for each day was carried out on a home machine using 5 CPU cores with 2 worker threads per core. The lookup process was carried out in batches of 1,500 query file hashes, required 1 CPU core and approximately 140GB of RAM. The average training and search times are shown in Table 7. The lookup time ought to scale approximately linearly with the number of unique files in the search space. The search time of 115,705 query files in a sample of 1,070,606 download events (daily average) took close to 5 h, so even an order-of-magnitude increase should still produce results on useful timescales (and could be mitigated further by the use of multiple machines/cores).

Table 7. System performance assuming an average training/search space size of 1,070,606 download events.

	Machine specifications	Running time
Training	6-core CPU at 2.2 GHz, 32 GB RAM	$\approx 1.3\,\mathrm{min/model}$
Lookups	32-core CPU at 2.4 GHz, 256 GB RAM	$\approx 5\,\mathrm{h}/115{,}705$ queries

9.1   JABBIC Limitations

JABBIC lookups rely on the alignment of one vector space to the other, which requires that some file hashes are found in both vector spaces (*i.e.*, downloaded in both days). If no file hashes are common to both vector spaces, then the alignment of one vector space to another is not possible. However, we found that a sufficiently high number of file hashes were downloaded not only from one day to another but also across multiple days, thereby the alignment of vector spaces should not pose any issues in similar analyses, particularly in the case of malware or potentially unwanted programs (PUP) ecosystems. It is also necessary to know whether file hashes from all previous timeframes are either benign or malicious, otherwise they cannot be used to infer the threat level of a query file.

9.2 Data Limitations

The malware ecosystem has changed since the period between 2015 and 2016 for which the results in our analysis are reported. NortonLifeLock [10] reported an 8,500% and 46% increase in file-based coinminer and ransomware infections on endpoint computers in 2017 alone, respectively, when compared to previous years when these types of attacks were not as common. Nevertheless, the means of propagation continue to rely on droppers or a combination of multiple vectors among which droppers are still present. For instance, file-based cryptojacking spreads in a similar fashion as traditional malware and continues to be prevalent [27]. As such, despite the malware ecosystem increasingly shifting towards ransomware and cryptojacking attacks, it is still common that their distribution vectors rely on users downloading the payloads from malicious hosts. For this reason, malware contextual information – such as payload domains, URLs, IPs, and ASes – is as relevant to newer types of attacks that rely on dropper vectors. We thus argue that JABBIC is a useful triage tool as long as file-based malware – where their distribution is leveraged by drive-by downloads and other social engineering techniques – continue to be part of the malware ecosystem landscape.

9.3 Evasion

JABBIC lookups work under the assumption that the context of malicious file download for a given malware campaign presents similarity over time. JABBIC does not make any assumptions about the number of times a file SHA2 has been downloaded. Indeed, it makes no difference whether or not all files hashes are unique as long as some or all delivery infrastructures are being reused. This makes JABBIC less prone to evasion when compared to signature-based or heuristic detection. One way JABBIC could thus be evaded is if malware writers would avoid reusing, either fully or partially, the same delivery infrastructures over periods longer than 7 days. Another way to evade JABBIC is to drop a higher number of benign files using the same delivery infrastructures that they use to distribute malware and PUPs. This would increase the chance that the returned local match is benign, tricking the system into assessing the level of threat of its corresponding query file as inconclusive. However, these evasion techniques are both atypical for the pay-per-install ecosystem and financially infeasible given the scalability of the required pay-per-install services and delivery infrastructures.

10 Conclusion

We proposed a back-end file triage system that operates on top of file reputation score systems used by security vendors to prioritize the collection and analysis of unknown files downloaded by their clients. When compared to state-of-the-art malware triage systems that use binary-analysis, JABBIC can function along client protection solutions installed on end-hosts and using only download telemetry data. We showed that JABBIC is more reliable for the second stage triage of files flagged as potentially malign by the reputation score systems, which allows for better prioritization of files for collection and analysis. Lastly, we showed that the files triaged by JABBIC could have been flagged as suspicious much earlier than online scanning services such as VirusTotal.

Acknowledgements. This research was funded by the Dawes Centre for Future Crime at UCL.

References

1. Bloom filter calculator. https://hur.st/bloomfilter/?n=50&p=&m=1000&k=7
2. University of oregon route views archive project. http://routeviews.org/
3. Virustotal. https://www.virustotal.com/
4. Introducing tensorflow feature columns, November 2017. https://developers. googleblog.com/2017/11/introducing-tensorflow-feature-columns.htm
5. Awad, Y., Nassar, M., Safa, H.: Modeling malware as a language, pp. 1–6, May 2018
6. Yousefi-Azar, M., Hamey, L., Varadharajan, V., Chen, S.: Learning latent byte-level feature representation for malware detection. In: Cheng, L., Leung, A.C.S., Ozawa, S. (eds.) ICONIP 2018. LNCS, vol. 11304, pp. 568–578. Springer, Cham (2018). https://doi.org/10.1007/978-3-030-04212-7_50
7. Bojanowski, P., Grave, E., Joulin, A., Mikolov, T.: Enriching word vectors with subword information. Trans. Assoc. Comput. Linguistics **5**, 135–146 (2017)
8. Chakradeo, S., Reaves, B., Traynor, P., Enck, W.: Mast: triage for market-scale mobile malware analysis. In: Proceedings of the Sixth ACM Conference on Security and Privacy in Wireless and Mobile Networks, pp. 13–24 (2013)
9. Chauhan, S.S., Batra, S.: Finding similar items using lsh and bloom filter. In: 2014 IEEE International Conference on Advanced Communications, Control and Computing Technologies, pp. 1662–1666. IEEE (2014)
10. Cleary, G., et al.: Symantec internet security threat report (2018). https://docs. broadcom.com/doc/istr-23-2018-en
11. Duarte-Garcia, H.L., et al.: A semi-supervised learning methodology for malware categorization using weighted word embeddings. In: 2019 IEEE European Symposium on Security and Privacy Workshops (EuroS&PW), pp. 238–246. IEEE (2019)
12. Finkelstein, L., et al.: Placing search in context: The concept revisited **20**, 406–414 (2001)
13. Schönemann, P.H.: A generalized solution of the orthogonal procrustes problem. Psychometrika **31**, 1–10 (1966)
14. Hauke, J., Kossowski, T.: Comparison of values of pearson's and spearman's correlation coefficients on the same sets of data. Quaestiones Geographicae **30**(2), 87–93 (2011)
15. Hill, F., Reichart, R., Korhonen, A.: Simlex-999: evaluating semantic models with (genuine) similarity estimation. Comput. Linguist. **41**, 08 (2014)
16. Ilyankou, I.: Comparison of jaro-winkler and ratcliff/obershelp algorithms in spell check. IB Extended Essay Computer Science, 2014

17. Jang, J., Agrawal, A., Brumley, D.: Redebug: finding unpatched code clones in entire os distributions. In: 2012 IEEE Symposium on Security and Privacy, pp. 48–62. IEEE (2012)
18. Jang, J., Brumley, D., Venkataraman, S.: Bitshred: feature hashing malware for scalable triage and semantic analysis. In: Proceedings of the 18th ACM Conference on Computer and Communications Security, pp. 309–320 (2011)
19. Kirat, D., Nataraj, L., Vigna, G., Manjunath, BS.: Sigmal: a static signal processing based malware triage. In: Proceedings of the 29th Annual Computer Security Applications Conference, pp. 89–98 (2013)
20. Malwarebytes Labs. 2020 state of malware report, February 2020. https://resources.malwarebytes.com/files/2020/02/2020_State-of-Malware-Report.pdf
21. Leskovec, J., Rajaraman, A., Ullman, J.D.: Finding Similar Items, 2 edn., pp. 68–122. Cambridge University Press (2014)
22. Levy, O., Goldberg, Y.: Dependency-based word embeddings 2, 302–308 (2014)
23. Liu, Y., Jun, E., Li, Q., Heer, J.: Latent space cartography: visual analysis of vector space embeddings. Comput. Graph. Forum 38, 67–78 (2019)
24. Mikolov, T., Chen, K., Corrado, G., Dean, J.: Efficient estimation of word representations in vector space. In: Proceedings of Workshop at ICLR, 2013, January 2013
25. Mikolov, T., Sutskever, I., Chen, K., Corrado, G.s., Dean, J.: Distributed representations of words and phrases and their compositionality. In: Advances in Neural Information Processing Systems, 26, October 2013
26. Naili, M., Habacha, A., Ben Ghezala, H.: Comparative study of word embedding methods in topic segmentation. Procedia Comput. Sci. 112, 340–349 (2017)
27. O'Gorman, B.: Cryptojacking: A modern cash cow. Internet Security Threat Report, Symantec, září (2018). https://docs.broadcom.com/doc/istr-cryptojacking-modern-cash-cow-en
28. Saedi, C., Branco, A., Rodrigues, J., Silva, J.: Wordnet embeddings, August 2018. https://www.aclweb.org/anthology/W18-3016/
29. Salton, G., McGill, M.J.: Introduction to modern information retrieval (1986)
30. Sebastián, M., Rivera, R., Kotzias, P., Caballero, J.: AVclass: a tool for massive malware labeling. In: Monrose, F., Dacier, M., Blanc, G., Garcia-Alfaro, J. (eds.) RAID 2016. LNCS, vol. 9854, pp. 230–253. Springer, Cham (2016). https://doi.org/10.1007/978-3-319-45719-2_11
31. Stokes, J.W., Platt, J.C., Wang, H.J., Faulhaber, J., Keller, J., Marinescu, M., Thomas, A., Gheorghescu, M.: Scalable Telemetry Classification for Automated Malware Detection. In: Foresti, S., Yung, M., Martinelli, F. (eds.) ESORICS 2012. LNCS, vol. 7459, pp. 788–805. Springer, Heidelberg (2012). https://doi.org/10.1007/978-3-642-33167-1_45
32. Tamersoy, A., Roundy, K., Chau, D.H.: Guilt by association: large scale malware detection by mining file-relation graphs, August 2014
33. Wang, K., Parekh, J.J., Stolfo, S.J.: Anagram: A Content Anomaly Detector Resistant to Mimicry Attack. In: Zamboni, D., Kruegel, C. (eds.) RAID 2006. LNCS, vol. 4219, pp. 226–248. Springer, Heidelberg (2006). https://doi.org/10.1007/11856214_12
34. Xiong, H., Zhang, D., Martyniuk, C.J., Trudeau, V., Xia, X.: Using generalized procrustes analysis (gpa) for normalization of cdna microarray data. BMC Bioinform. 9, 25 (2008). https://doi.org/10.1186/1471-2105-9-25
35. Yin, Z., Shen, Y.: On the dimensionality of word embedding. In: Proceedings of the 32Nd International Conference on Neural Information Processing Systems, NIPS 2018, pp. 895–906, USA, 2018. Curran Associates Inc. (2018)

36. Zhang, Y., Jatowt, A., Bhowmick, S.S., Tanaka, K.: The past is not a foreign country: detecting semantically similar terms across time. IEEE Trans. Knowl. Data Eng. **28**(10), 2793–2807 (2016)
37. Zhang, Y., et al.: Familial clustering for weakly-labeled android malware using hybrid representation learning. IEEE Trans. Inf. Forensics Secur. **15**, 3401–3414 (2019)

Facilitating Parallel Fuzzing with Mutually-Exclusive Task Distribution

Yifan Wang[1], Yuchen Zhang[1], Chenbin Pang[2], Peng Li[3],
Nikolaos Triandopoulos[1], and Jun Xu[1(✉)]

[1] Stevens Institute of Technology, Hoboken, USA
jxu69@stevens.edu
[2] Nanjing University, Nanjing, China
[3] ByteDance, Beijing, China

Abstract. Fuzz testing, or fuzzing, has become one of the de facto standard techniques for bug finding in the software industry. In general, fuzzing provides various inputs to the target program with the goal of discovering un-handled exceptions and crashes. In business sectors where the time budget is limited, software vendors often launch many fuzzing instances in parallel as a common means of increasing code coverage. However, most of the popular fuzzing tools—in their parallel mode—naively run multiple instances concurrently, without elaborate distribution of workload. This can lead different instances to explore overlapped code regions, eventually reducing the benefits of concurrency. In this paper, we propose a general model to describe parallel fuzzing. This model distributes mutually-exclusive but similarly-weighted tasks to different instances, facilitating concurrency and also fairness across instances. Following this model, we develop a solution, called AFL-EDGE, to improve the parallel mode of AFL, considering *a round of mutations to a unique seed* as a task and adopting edge coverage to define the uniqueness of a seed. We have implemented AFL-EDGE on top of AFL and evaluated the implementation with AFL on 9 widely used benchmark programs. It shows that AFL-EDGE can benefit the edge coverage of AFL. In a 24-h test, the increase of edge coverage brought by AFL-EDGE to AFL ranges from 9.5% to 10.2%, depending on the number of instances. As a side benefit, we discovered 14 previously unknown bugs.

Keywords: Software testing · Parallel fuzzing · Performance

1 Introduction

Thanks to its direct and easy application to production-grade software without human aids, fuzzing is gaining tremendous popularity for security testing. In

---

Y. Wang and Y. Zhang—These authors contributed equally.
C. Pang—This work was done while Pang was a Visiting Scholar at Stevens Institute of Technology.

J. Garcia-Alfaro et al. (Eds.): SecureComm 2021, LNICST 399, pp. 185–206, 2021.
https://doi.org/10.1007/978-3-030-90022-9_10

today's business sectors, software systems are having shorter testing cycles [34], and therefore, the efficiency of code coverage becomes a critically desired property of fuzzing.

To escalate code coverage efficiency, there are two orthogonal strategies, one improving algorithms of fuzzing tools and one launching many fuzzing instances in parallel. The research community has intensively investigated the first strategy. Efforts along this line have revolutionized fuzzing from being program-structure-agnostic and black-box [2,5,28] to be program-structure-aware and grey-box/white-box [16,37,40,49,52], which significantly improved fuzzing efficiency by overcoming common barriers of code coverage.

However, the second strategy has been less studied and insufficiently developed. Existing fuzzing tools (*e.g.*, [8,37]) primarily follow American Fuzzy Lop (AFL) [52] to implement their parallel mode. Technically speaking, they run multiple identical instances in parallel. Depending on the implementation, different instances may either share the same group of seed inputs (or *seeds*) [8,37] or use separate groups of seed inputs but make periodical exchanges [52]. This type of parallel fuzzing, due to lack of synchronizations, leads different instances to run overlapped tasks, impeding the effectiveness of concurrency.

In this paper, we focus on unveiling the limitations of the parallel mode in existing fuzzing tools and presenting new solutions to overcome those limitations. We start with an empirical study of the parallel mode in AFL. By tracing the exploration of all instances across the fuzzing process, we discover that different instances are indeed running overlapped tasks despite many tasks remain unaccomplished (Sect. 2.2). We further demonstrate that this type of task overlapping can lead to reduced efficiency of code coverage.

Motivated and inspired by our empirical study, we propose a general model to describe parallel fuzzing. At the high level, the model enforces three desired properties. First, it distributes mutually-exclusive tasks to different instances, preventing the occurrence of overlaps. Second, it ensures every single task to be covered by at least one instance. This avoids the loss of fuzzing tasks and the code covered by those tasks. Finally, it assigns to each instance tasks with a similar amount of workload. Otherwise, some instances will be overloaded while the other instances are under-loaded, which can eventually degrade concurrency.

Guided by the model above, we develop a solution, called AFL-EDGE, towards facilitating the parallel mode in AFL. Our solution defines *a task* is to *run a round of mutations to a unique seed* and considers the control-flow edges (or *edges*) covered by a seed to determine its uniqueness. During the course of fuzzing, AFL-EDGE periodically distributes seeds that carry non-overlapped and similarly-weighted tasks to different instances, meeting the properties of our model. AFL-EDGE also enforces that all the unique seeds will cover the same set of edges as the original seeds. We envision that, in this way, AFL-EDGE can properly preserve the fuzzing capacity of AFL.

We have implemented AFL-EDGE on top of AFL, and we have evaluated AFL-EDGE with AFL using 9 widely adopted benchmark programs. Our evaluation shows that AFL-EDGE can significantly reduce the overlaps and hence, benefit the code coverage. Depending on the number of instances we launch, we can averagely reduce 57.1%–60.3% of the overlaps and bring a 9.5%–10.2% increase in code coverage with AFL. Our evaluation also demonstrates that, compared to the state-of-the-art solutions of improving parallel fuzzing [22,39], our solution not only brings higher improvement to efficiency of edge coverage but also better preserves the capacity of the fuzzing tools. As a side benefit, AFL-EDGE triggers over 6K unique crashes, corresponding to 14 new bugs.

Our main contributions are as follows.

- We present a general model to describe parallel fuzzing.
- We develop a solution to improve the parallel mode in AFL, following the guidance of our model.
- We have implemented our solution on top of AFL, which can seamlessly run with other fuzzing tools that also use AFL. Source code of our implementation will be made publicly available upon publication.
- We evaluated our solution with AFL on 9 widely used benchmark programs. It shows that our solution can effectively reduce the overlaps and increase the code coverage of AFL.

2   Background and Motivation

2.1   Grey-Box Fuzzing and Parallel Mode

In this research, we target grey-box fuzzing [25], the most popular category of fuzzing. Grey-box fuzzing generally follows the *feedback-scheduling-mutation* model presented in Fig. 1. This FSM model represents an iterative process, starting with a queue of seed inputs, or *seeds*, that are typically generated from certain known test cases. In a round of fuzzing, the *scheduling* picks a seed and feeds it to

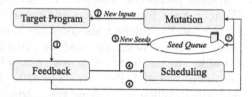

Fig. 1. A general model of grey-box fuzzing.

the *mutation* process for deriving new inputs to test the target program, expecting to trigger un-handled crashes or exceptions. Both the scheduling and mutation processes are based on *feedback* (e.g., crashes and code coverage) obtained from the program executions on the previously generated inputs. The fuzzer also collects feedback to decide whether an input under test should be added to the seed queue.

To improve the efficiency of code coverage, many grey-box fuzzing tools [8, 37,52] provide a parallel mode to run multiple instances concurrently. Their parallel mode mostly follows AFL. They start identically-configured instances and run them in parallel. Depending on the implementation, different instances may either share the same seed queue [37] or carry separate seed queues but periodically exchange seeds [52]. In the latter case, each instance borrows from other instances all the seeds that bring new code coverage. While intuition suggests that more fine-grained synchronizations can benefit the effectiveness of the above parallel fuzzing, none of the existing tools carry such synchronizations.

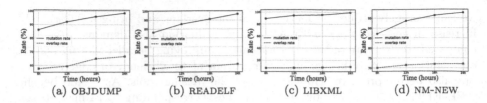

(a) OBJDUMP	(b) READELF	(c) LIBXML	(d) NM-NEW

Fig. 2. Results of measuring overlapped mutations: "mutation rate" - the portion of seeds mutated by at least one instance; "overlap rate" - the portion of seeds mutated by more than one instance.

2.2 Motivating Study

Sharing seeds across instances is an intentional design of AFL [51]. The goal is that "hard-to-hit but interesting test cases" can be used by all instances to guide their work. However, intuition suggests that such a design can lead different instances to mutate the same seeds, which may eventually reduce the effectiveness of concurrency. To validate this intuition and thus, motivate our research, we perform an empirical study based on AFL.

In our study, we run AFL on four popular benchmark programs (OBJDUMP, READELF, LIBXML, NM-NEW) with 2 parallel instances for 24 h. We trace the mutation process to understand which seeds are mutated by which instances. We repeat the tests five times and report the average results in Fig. 2. As shown by the results, different instances are indeed mutating overlapped seeds despite many seeds are never mutated, in particular when the fuzzing time is limited. Consider the results after 6 h as an example. On average, nearly 20% of the seeds are never mutated. However, over 42% of the seeds receive multiple rounds of mutations. When we increase the fuzzing time, we observe even higher rates of overlaps but still a group of non-mutated seeds.

Although we observe overlaps among mutated seeds and the overlaps indeed delay the mutations to all seeds, they may not necessarily impede the efficiency of code coverage. This is because AFL's mutation involves random operations. In this regard, running multiple rounds of mutations to the same seed—especially when the seed has higher potential—may produce code coverage comparable to applying the mutations to different seeds. To verify this possibility, we run another experiment. Specifically, we randomly collect 1,000 seeds produced in the above test of each program and equally split the seeds into group A and group B. First, we run AFL to mutate group A for multiple rounds and we calculate the increase of code coverage after each round of mutations, where we use control flow edges as the metric of code coverage and we consider the edges covered by the original 1,000 seeds as the baseline. Then, we repeat the experiment but replace the same $X\%$ of group A with un-mutated seeds from group B in each round. For example, when we set X to 10, we run the original group A in the first round but in every following round, we replace a fixed subset of 50 seeds with other non-muted ones from group B. Such an experiment enables us to simulate fuzzing scenarios where a different extent of overlapped mutations happen.

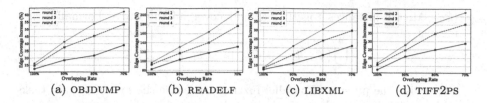

(a) OBJDUMP   (b) READELF   (c) LIBXML   (d) TIFF2PS

Fig. 3. Impacts of overlapped mutations to edge coverage. The baseline of "Edge Coverage Increase" is the edges covered by the original 1,000 seeds; "Overlapping Rate" indicates the portion of overlapped seeds between two consecutive rounds of mutations. Results from the first round are omitted since the first round is identical under different settings, i.e., mutating the initial 500 seeds. *Please note that the x-axis decreases from left to right.*

Figure 3 presents the results of the above experiment under different settings. With all the four programs, we observe a trend that fewer overlaps among the mutated seeds lead to a higher increase of code coverage. This empirically demonstrates that running AFL's mutations on different seeds can cover more edges than running the mutations on the same seeds. We believe such results align with AFL's design: AFL distributes mutation energies in a round according to the potential of a seed (based on metrics such as number of edges covered by the seed) and assigns more mutation cycles to seeds with higher potential, which eventually helps allocate sufficient mutations in a single round to exhaust the edges that can be derived from a seed.

To sum up, our empirical study shows that the parallel mode of AFL (and likely, many other fuzzing tools) can indeed bring overlaps, which further impedes the efficiency of code coverage. It is, therefore, necessary to investigate and develop better solutions of parallel fuzzing.

3   A General Model of Parallel Fuzzing

In this section, we propose a model to describe parallel fuzzing. The model is inclusive of the parallel mode in existing fuzzing tools and we envision it is general enough to apply to other solutions of parallel fuzzing.

Formally, a parallel fuzzing system consists of n instances $\{F_1, F_2, ..., F_n\}$. These instances together work on a set of m tasks $\{T_1, T_2, ..., T_m\}$, with the ith instance distributed to focus on a subset of tasks $\{T_{i1}, T_{i2}, ..., T_{im_i}\}$ $(m_i \leq m)$. Depending on the definition of tasks, $\{T_1, T_2, ..., T_m\}$ can require different amounts of workload to be completed, notated as $\{W_1, W_2, ..., W_m\}$. To improve the efficiency of parallel fuzzing, the system would desire to meet the following three properties.

- ($\mathbb{P}_1$) Different instances should work on disjoint subsets of tasks. This is to avoid overlaps and increase the extent of concurrency. Formally, given any two instances F_i and F_j $(i \neq j)$, the fuzzing system needs to ensure:

$$\{T_{i1}, T_{i2}, ..., T_{im_i}\} \cap \{T_{j1}, T_{j2}, ..., T_{jm_j}\} = \emptyset \tag{1}$$

- ($\mathbb{P}_2$) All the instances together should cover all the tasks. Formally, that means:

$$\bigcup_{i=1}^{n}\{T_{i1}, T_{i2}, ..., T_{im_i}\} = \{T_1, T_2, ..., T_m\} \tag{2}$$

Otherwise, the pursuit of parallel fuzzing can cause the loss of certain tasks and, essentially, miss the code that can be covered by those tasks.

- ($\mathbb{P}_3$) Different tasks should be assigned with a similar workload. Formally, the fuzzing system should maintain the following relation between any two instances F_i and F_j $(i \neq j)$:

$$\sum_{n=1}^{m_i} W_{in} \approx \sum_{n=1}^{m_j} W_{jn} \tag{3}$$

Otherwise, certain instances can receive under-loaded tasks and end with plenty of idle cycles, which in principle also harms concurrency.

While the above model is general, it overlooks the fact that different tasks can bring different benefits, in particular code coverage [9]. To this end, Eq. 1 should be amended to allow overlaps of tasks that carry higher returns such that these tasks have a higher chance to be picked and completed. To incorporate this consideration, we find that it is not mandatory to modify our model. Instead, we can replicate high-return tasks and consider their replicas as unique ones. This will achieve similar effects as allowing overlaps of those tasks.

4 Applications of Our Model

4.1 Existing Solutions

In the literature, two solutions of improving parallel fuzzing, P-FUZZ [39] and PAFL [22], fit into our model. Both P-FUZZ and PAFL consider *a fuzzing task is to run a round of mutations to a unique seed* and they distribute a similar amount of unique seeds to each instance. However, the two solutions take two opposite principles to define the uniqueness of a seed. P-FUZZ aims for conservativeness. It follows AFL and considers a seed that brings new code coverage at its birth to be unique. Such a principle preserves all seeds produced by AFL but can leave behind many overlaps. Consider Fig. 4, where `Seed-1` is born

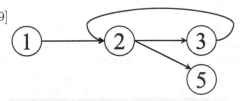

Seed-1: 1->2->5
Seed-2: 1->2->3->2->5

Fig. 4. An example of two seeds that cover overlapped sets of edges. The *upper* part presents the CFG; the *lower* part shows the two seeds.

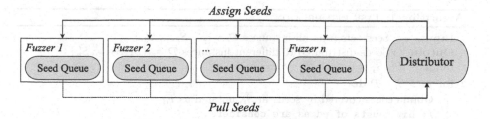

Fig. 5. Workflow of our solution to optimize parallel fuzzing.

before `Seed-2`, as an example. P-FUZZ will consider both seeds unique and mutate both seeds. However, `Seed-2` covers all the edges of `Seed-1` and thus, they actually overlap based on AFL's definition. Moreover, mutating `Seed-2` can likely produce the same code coverage as mutating both seeds, further illustrating the overlap.

In contrast, PAFL aims for effectiveness. It considers a seed unique only when the seed covers certain less-frequently visited edges. In this way, PAFL can massively reduce overlaps. However, it does not guarantee that the unique seeds can cover all the code covered by the original seeds. As such, it can skip certain code regions and lose the opportunities to cover code that can be derived from those code regions.

4.2 Our Solution

In this paper, we propose a new solution following our model. Similar to P-FUZZ and PAFL, we consider a fuzzing task is to run a round of mutations to a unique seed. However, as we will explain shortly, we adopt a strategy that achieves an effectiveness-and-conservativeness balance to define the uniqueness of a seed. Our solution follows the workflow in Fig. 5 to periodically distribute the tasks. In each round of task distribution, we pull seeds from all instances, partition them into un-overlapped while similarly-weighted sub-sets, and finally assign them back to each instance. In the rest of this section, we describe the design details and explain how they meet $\mathbb{P}_1$ - $\mathbb{P}_3$.

Defining Fuzzing Tasks. In our solution, we consider the entire set of tasks are to mutate seeds that cover all the (control flow) edges reached by the original seeds. In this way, we approximate the fuzzing goals of AFL and largely preserve the fuzzing space of AFL (i.e., produce similar effects as mutating every seed). To determine the uniqueness of a seed, we consider the edges and their hit counts[1] covered by the seed as criteria. But different from P-FUZZ, we consider *a seed is unique only if the seed covers one or more edges that other seeds do not cover.* This principle avoids the overlaps that P-FUZZ may incur. Referring back to the example in Fig. 4, when `Seed-1` and `Seed-2` both exist at the moment of

---

[1] A hit count in each of the following ranges is mapped to a unique value: [1], [2], [3], [4, 7], [8, 15], [16, 31], [32, 127], [128, ∞).

Algorithm 1: TASK DISTRIBUTION

    Input   : Seed sets from all instances $\mathcal{D} = \{\vec{S}_1, \vec{S}_2, ..., \vec{S}_n\}$
    Output : Seeds distributed to different instances $\mathcal{D}' = \{\vec{S}'_1, \vec{S}'_2, ..., \vec{S}'_n\}$
1 Initialize $\mathcal{D}'$: $\vec{S}'_1 = \emptyset$, $\vec{S}'_2 = \emptyset$,... $\vec{S}'_n = \emptyset$
2 for *each* $\vec{S}_i \in \mathcal{D}$ **do**
3 | Obtain edges covered by seeds in $\vec{S}_i$, notated as $\vec{E}_i$;
         | /* hit counts of edges are considered   */
4 end
5 $\vec{E} = \bigcap_{i=1}^{n} \vec{E}_i$;
6 Organize $\vec{E}$ into a control flow graph CFG;
    /* different hit counts of the same edge are represented as
       different edges   */
7 Copy CFG as CFG' and topologically sort CFG';
8 for *the deepest leaf node* L_i *in* CFG' **do**
9 | $k = random(1, n)$;
10 | Pick a seed s from $\vec{S}_k$ which covers L_i, maximizes $|edge(s) \bigcap edge(CFG')|$,
       | and has the minimal age;
11 | Add s to $\vec{S}'_k$;
12 | Remove $edge(s)$ from CFG';
13 end
14 for *each* $\vec{S}_i \in \mathcal{D}$ **do**
15 | **for** *each* $s \in \vec{S}_i$ **do**
16 | | **if** $edge(s) - edge(CFG) \neq \emptyset$ *and* $edge(s) - edge(\vec{S}'_i) \neq \emptyset$ **then**
17 | | | Add s to $\vec{S}'_i$;
18 | | **end**
19 | **end**
20 end
21 return $\mathcal{D}'$;

---

task distribution, we will consider Seed-1 non-unique since Seed-2 encapsulates all the edges of Seed-1. In the following, we describe how to pick unique seeds while running task distribution.

Distributing Fuzzing Tasks. In each round of task distribution, we pull all the seeds from each instance and re-run them with dynamic tracing. We gather the edges covered by each instance, notated as $\vec{E}_i$ for the ith instance. We then compute the intersections among the edges from all instances (i.e., $\bigcap_{i=1}^{n} \vec{E}_i$), and we notate the intersections as $\vec{E}$. By intuition, we can then randomly, evenly partition $\vec{E}$ into multiple sub-sets, assign each sub-set to a unique instance, and then pick seeds that visit those assigned edges for the instance to mutate. Such an idea, however, has a major problem. When we pick a seed to cover a particular edge, we will concurrently cover many other edges, which may essentially bring overlaps back. Consider the Fig. 6 as an example. By random distribution, we may sequentially pick Seed-2, Seed-3, and Seed-4, and distribute them to different instances.

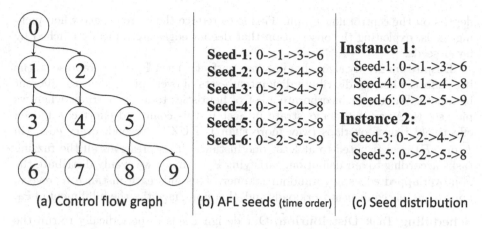

(a) Control flow graph   **(b) AFL seeds** (time order)   **(c) Seed distribution**

Fig. 6. An example of edge-coverage-based task distribution between 2 instances. The *left* part shows the CFG aggregated by the overlapped edges. The *middle* part show the seeds produced by AFL, sorted in time order. The *right* part presents the task distribution results.

According to our definition, this would create an edge-overlap between Seed-2 and Seed-3 + Seed-4, not satisfying our definition of uniqueness.

In this work, we design a greedy algorithm, shown in Algorithm 1, to provide *edge-coverage-based task distribution*. We aggregate the edges in $\vec{E}$ into a topologically sorted control flow graph, notated as CFG (line 1-6). We then recursively process the leaf edges on CFG (i.e., edges that end with leaf nodes on CFG). For the leaf edge with the largest depth, we randomly pick a fuzzing instance and elaborately pick a seed s from that instance to cover the leaf edge (line 9-10). To be specific, we select the seed that covers the maximal number of edges remaining on the CFG. If multiple seeds satisfy this condition, we pick the youngest one. We distribute s to the fuzzing instance where s comes from (line 11) and remove all edges covered by s from CFG (line 12). We repeat this process until all edges on the CFG are removed. After that, we preserve the seeds that visit edges in $\neg\vec{E}$ (line 14-20). To better illustrate our distribution algorithm, we present an example in Fig. 6, showing both the fuzzing progress and the distribution results. It is worth noting that when we pick a seed for leaf node 4→8, we favor Seed-4 over Seed-2 because Seed-4 is more recently derived. This prevents the pick of Seed-2 and avoids the overlap we mentioned before.

The above algorithm involves multiple heuristics, which strive for fewer overlaps and better efficiency. First, we prefer seeds that cover more non-distributed edges (line 10). The motivation is to quickly consume the distribution space and thus, minimize the number of required seeds and reduce the potential of overlaps. Second, we favor newer seeds. The rationale is that seeds newly generated have a higher chance to cover new edges than the older seeds. Thus, they have a lower chance of bringing in overlaps. Third, we prioritize edges that have larger depths on the control flow graph. This is to reduce the search space when picking seeds, exploiting the observation that deeper edges are typically reached by fewer seeds.

Despite our greedy algorithm may not perfectly meet $\mathbb{P}_1$ - $\mathbb{P}_3$, it represents the best effort. First, we distribute disjoint sub-sets of overlapped edges to different instances. We further incorporate a set of heuristics to avoid overlaps when we pick seeds. As we will demonstrate in Sect. 6, this combined effort can indeed effectively reduce overlaps (way more than P-FUZZ). Second, every edge (in $\vec{E}$ or $\neg\vec{E}$) is distributed to at least one instance. This preserves all the fuzzing tasks according to our definition, satisfying $\mathbb{P}_2$. Finally, we evenly distribute the non-overlapped edges in a random manner. This aids each instance to receive approximately equivalent workloads and, therefore, facilities the fulfillment of $\mathbb{P}_3$.

Scheduling Task Distribution. Our design needs to periodically re-run the task distribution. However, a low frequency of re-distribution may not timely avoid the accumulated overlaps while a high frequency can lead to a waste of computation cycles since fuzzing may not have produced many overlaps. In our design, we adjust the scheduling of task distribution based on the increase of edge coverage. We start the first round of distribution after the first hour, and we re-run it once the new edge coverage exceeds 10%.

5   Implementation

We have implemented our solution, called AFL-EDGE, on top of AFL (2.52b) and LLVM with around 100 lines of C code, 400 lines of C++ code, 300 lines of shell scrips, and 200 lines of Python code. All code will be released upon publication.

5.1   Collecting Edge Coverage

The task distribution of AFL-EDGE needs code coverage information of existing seeds. To support the need, we implement an LLVM pass to instrument the target program. Following a seed, the instrumented code will sequentially record each edge and output the final list at the end. To avoid collisions, we assign each basic block a unique 64-bit ID and concatenate the IDs of two connected basic blocks to represent the edge between them.

5.2   Distributing Fuzzing Tasks

AFL-EDGE requires to distribute seeds across fuzzing instances. To avoid intruding on the normal fuzzing process, we implement the task distributor as a standalone component. It follows the algorithm in Sect. 4.2 to determine the seeds that are assigned to each instance and saves the seeds in a file. Following the metadata organization of AFL, the seed file is added to the corresponding instance's working directory.

Table 1. Benchmark programs and evaluation settings. In the column of `Seeds`, `AFL` means we reuse the test-cases from AFL and `built-in` means that we reuse the test cases from the program.

Programs				Settings	
Name	Version	Driver	Source	Seeds	Options
LIBPCAP	1.10.0	TCPDUMP	[41]	AFL	-r @@
LIBTIFF	4.0.10	TIFF2PS	[19]	AFL	@@
LIBTIFF	4.0.10	TIFF2PDF	[19]	AFL	@@
BINUTILS	2.32	OBJDUMP	[15]	AFL	-d @@
BINUTILS	2.32	READELF	[15]	AFL	-a @@
BINUTILS	2.32	NM-NEW	[15]	AFL	-a @@
LIBXML2	2.9.7	XMLLINT	[26]	AFL	@@
NASM	2.14.2	NASM	[3]	built-in	-e @@
FFMPEG	4.1.1	FFMPEG	[6]	built-in	-i @@

5.3 Confining Fuzzing Tasks

Our design requires an instance to only mutate the sub-group of assigned seeds. Technically, we customize AFL to read the list of seeds assigned by the distributor and maintain them in a allow-list. When AFL schedules seeds for mutations, we only pick candidates on the allow-list. Such an implementation avoids introducing extra inconsistency to the fuzzing process. Considering that our distributor iteratively updates the seed list, the customized AFL periodically checks the seed file and updates the allow-list accordingly.

6 Evaluation

In this section, we evaluate AFL-EDGE, centering around three questions.

- $(\mathbb{Q}_1)$ Can AFL-EDGE reduce the overlaps among fuzzing instances?
- $(\mathbb{Q}_2)$ Can AFL-EDGE improve the efficiency of code coverage?
- $(\mathbb{Q}_3)$ Can AFL-EDGE preserve the fuzzing capacity of AFL?

6.1 Experimental Setup

Benchmarks. To answer the above questions, we prepare a group of 9 real-world benchmark programs. Details about the programs are presented in Table 1. All these programs have been intensively tested in both industry [43] and academia [32,40,49]. In addition, they carry diversities in both functionality and complexity.

Baselines. We run AFL as the baseline of our evaluation. To compare AFL-EDGE with the existing solutions, we also run P-FUZZ [39] and PAFL [22] on top of AFL. Because the implementations of P-FUZZ and PAFL are not publicly available, we re-implemented the two solutions following the algorithms presented in their publications [22,39].

Configurations. Specific configurations of the fuzzing process (e.g., seeds and program options) are listed in Table 1. To understand the impacts of the number of instances, we run each fuzzing setting respectively with 2, 4, and 8 AFL secondary instances. We do not run a primary instance because it involves deterministic mutations which bring disadvantages to vanilla AFL. For consistency, we conduct all the experiments on Amazon EC2 instances (Intel Xeon E5 Broadwell 96 cores, 186GB RAM, and Ubuntu 18.04 LTS), and we sequentially run all the tests to avoid interference. Each test is run for 24 h. To minimize the effect of randomness in fuzzing, we repeat each test 5 times and report the average results.

6.2   Analysis of Results

In Table 2, we present the results with AFL at the end of 24 h. We elaborate on the results as follows, seeking answers to Q_1 - Q_3.

Effectiveness of Overlap Reduction. The direct goal of AFL-EDGE is to reduce the overlaps among instances. To measure this goal, we consider the number of seeds that are disabled from each instance as the metric. As shown in Table 2 (the column for *overlap reduction rate*), AFL-EDGE can effectively reduce the potential overlaps in the parallel mode of AFL. To be specific, AFL-EDGE can prevent 60.0%, 60.3%, and 57.1% of the seeds from being repeatedly mutated when we respectively run 2, 4, and 8 parallel instances.

In comparison to existing solutions, AFL-EDGE reduces more overlaps than P-FUZZ but fewer than PAFL. Such results well comply with the designs of the three tools. P-FUZZ preserves all the seeds produced by AFL while PAFL aggressively skip seeds. In contrast, AFL-EDGE keeps seeds necessary to cover all the edges, pursuing a trade-off between conservativeness and effectiveness. As we will show later, while AFL-EDGE's strategy reduces fewer seeds in comparison to PAFL, it does not necessarily hurt code coverage and it can better preserve the fuzzing capacity (or more precisely, AFL-EDGE can cover more code that AFL covers).

Improvements to Code Coverage Efficiency. To understand whether the overlap reduction by AFL-EDGE can indeed benefit code coverage, we measure the number of edges covered in the tests. In Table 2 (the column of *edge coverage increase*), we present the increase of edge coverage brought by AFL-EDGE to AFL at the end of a 24-h test.

In summary, AFL-EDGE can consistently improve the efficiency of edge coverage of AFL, regardless of the benchmark and the number of instances. Specifically, AFL-EDGE increases the edge coverage by 10.0%, 10.2%, and 9.5%, respectively with 2, 4, and 8 instances. Another key observation is that the benefits brought by AFL-EDGE often decrease with the number of instances. We

Table 2. Statistical results of our evaluation with AFL in 24 h. In the table, "overlap reduction (%)" means the average percentage of seeds that the corresponding solution cuts from each instance; "edge-cov increase (%)" stands for the increase of code coverage that the corresponding solution brings to AFL; p-value demonstrates the statistical significance of the increase of code coverage (the smaller, the better); and "edge-cov overlap rate (%)" shows how much of the code covered by AFL is also covered by the corresponding solution.

Prog.	Tool	Statistical evaluation results with 2, 4, and 8 instances (AFL).											
		overlap reduction (%)			edge-cov increase (%)			p-value			edge-cov overlap (%)		
OBJDUMP	PAFL	60.6	80.8	89.5	1.9	0.0	0.3	0.32	0.72	0.10	95.5	94.9	95.8
	P-FUZZ	46.7	53.5	62.5	5.1	2.3	3.0	0.07	0.03	0.00	96.8	96.3	97.9
	AFL-EDGE	63.7	63.2	62.4	7.6	7.3	3.1	0.00	0.04	0.03	97.5	98.3	98.5
READELF	PAFL	81.2	86.8	88.4	5.6	-3.2	-3.6	0.03	0.19	0.12	92.5	92.1	93.0
	P-FUZZ	46.8	43.8	45.4	7.2	3.8	6.0	0.04	0.01	0.00	99.0	98.5	98.0
	AFL-EDGE	45.9	43.8	42.5	12.2	7.0	8.4	0.05	0.02	0.00	97.5	97.2	97.7
TIFF2PDF	PAFL	64.1	79.7	81.2	3.4	0.4	5.0	0.00	0.05	0.29	97.0	91.3	93.8
	P-FUZZ	42.2	60.1	64.1	5.5	6.3	8.5	0.01	0.04	0.04	98.5	97.0	97.9
	AFL-EDGE	62.4	59.5	58.5	9.0	5.6	11.2	0.00	0.02	0.00	98.5	95.9	99.1
NM-NEW	PAFL	46.2	52.6	55.9	4.0	4.8	0.2	0.10	0.07	0.19	96.6	96.2	97.5
	P-FUZZ	43.6	55.6	60.2	4.5	7.1	3.8	0.00	0.03	0.00	97.6	98.1	98.1
	AFL-EDGE	59.9	58.5	60.1	6.8	6.6	3.6	0.03	0.08	0.00	96.3	96.8	98.5
NASM	PAFL	64.2	82.7	54.7	5.5	14.6	2.4	0.05	0.01	0.06	99.8	99.3	99.8
	P-FUZZ	10.0	11.0	8.2	8.9	9.2	8.1	0.00	0.00	0.00	99.0	98.3	94.3
	AFL-EDGE	67.9	68.3	66.8	13.9	22.6	7.6	0.00	0.00	0.00	99.2	99.3	99.2
TIFF2PS	PAFL	57.1	81.9	89.2	7.8	15.0	8.7	0.03	0.02	0.02	82.3	89.9	96.6
	P-FUZZ	44.0	60.7	66.4	7.5	12.3	9.5	0.00	0.00	0.00	97.1	97.5	98.0
	AFL-EDGE	53.4	58.5	52.8	10.4	13.5	7.2	0.00	0.00	0.00	96.9	96.5	97.2
TCPDUMP	PAFL	66.4	80.3	84.4	8.2	10.6	7.7	0.19	0.03	0.06	84.7	86.6	88.5
	P-FUZZ	45.6	63.6	80.7	2.8	7.2	6.1	0.05	0.03	0.04	85.7	88.3	91.5
	AFL-EDGE	48.3	48.6	42.9	4.4	9.9	11.9	0.05	0.03	0.00	87.6	89.5	92.8
LIBXML2	PAFL	61.8	91.5	82.2	7.3	43.7	7.0	0.00	0.01	0.06	87.2	81.7	88.3
	P-FUZZ	41.0	48.5	51.8	5.1	11.7	21.3	0.00	0.01	0.00	97.9	89.3	97.6
	AFL-EDGE	68.9	69.2	65.6	7.5	7.6	29.1	0.00	0.04	0.00	98.6	93.3	98.2
FFMPEG	PAFL	94.5	90.7	91.4	17.9	23.4	4.1	0.04	0.01	0.38	86.8	85.2	87.0
	P-FUZZ	41.6	62.5	63.4	22.6	20.1	6.1	0.03	0.05	0.00	91.2	90.2	98.3
	AFL-EDGE	69.7	73.5	62.3	18.3	11.6	3.3	0.01	0.04	0.00	89.9	90.1	97.3
Ave.	PAFL	**66.2**	**80.8**	**79.7**	**6.9**	**12.1**	**3.5**	–	–	–	**91.4**	**90.8**	**93.4**
	P-FUZZ	**40.2**	**45.1**	**49.5**	**7.7**	**8.9**	**8.0**	–	–	–	**95.9**	**94.8**	**96.9**
	AFL-EDGE	**60.0**	**60.3**	**57.1**	**10.0**	**10.2**	**9.5**	–	–	–	**95.8**	**95.2**	**97.6**

believe the reason is that the fuzzers can get closer to saturation when more parallel instances are running. Therefore, the gap between AFL and AFL-EDGE shrinks at the end.

To further verify that the improvements by AFL-EDGE are statistically significant, we perform Mann Whitney U-test [27] on the five rounds of runs [18].

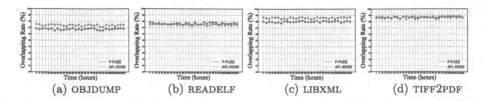

(a) OBJDUMP	(b) READELF	(c) LIBXML	(d) TIFF2PDF

Fig. 7. Overlap of code coverage between AFL-EDGE/P-FUZZ and AFL in the 120-h tests.

The p-values of the hypothesis test are presented in Table 2 (the column of *p-value*). In nearly all the cases, the p-values are smaller than 0.05, supporting that the improvements brought by AFL-EDGE are significant from a statistical perspective.

Finally, AFL-EDGE presents better overall performance than both P-FUZZ and PAFL. When applied to AFL, AFL-EDGE increases the edge coverage by 9.5% - 10.2%, outperforming P-FUZZ and PAFL in most of the cases. On the one hand, AFL-EDGE reduces more overlaps than P-FUZZ and thus, produces higher code coverage efficiency. On the other hand, PAFL in principle reduces more overlaps than AFL-EDGE, which indeed leads to higher edge coverage than AFL-EDGE in several cases (e.g., running AFL on TIFF2PS with 4 or 8 instances). However, in many other cases, PAFL can accidentally block valuable seeds and become unable to cover the related edges, eventually resulting in a lower edge coverage. This can be further supported by that PAFL even produces lower edge coverage than AFL in certain cases (e.g., running AFL on READELF with 4 or 8 instances).

Effectiveness of Preserving Fuzzing Capacity. As discussed in Sect. 4, AFL-EDGE can skip certain seeds produced by AFL. This may alter the fuzzing behaviors and, more concerningly, hurt the fuzzing capacity (i.e., missing edges that can be covered by vanilla AFL). To understand the impacts of AFL-EDGE to the fuzzing capacity, we perform another analysis where we examine whether AFL-EDGE and AFL are exploring different edges. Technically, we measure how many of the edges covered by AFL are also covered by AFL-EDGE. We show the results in Table 2 (the column of *edge overlap rate*). In summary, AFL-EDGE can prevalently cover more than 95% of the edges that are covered by AFL. Considering the existence of randomness, we believe such results strongly support that AFL-EDGE largely preserves the behaviors of the vanilla tools and does not significantly affect the fuzzing capacity.

In comparison to existing solutions (see Table 2), AFL-EDGE can preserve as much edge coverage as P-FUZZ. This further proves that AFL-EDGE well maintains the fuzzing space since P-FUZZ does not skip seeds and thus, its results represent the best efforts. Further, AFL-EDGE outperforms PAFL in covering the edges reached by AFL (96.2% v.s. 91.8%). This is because AFL-EDGE keeps seeds to cover all the original code to avoid losing fuzzing capacity while PAFL more aggressively skips seeds.

Table 3. Impacts of frequency of our task distribution.

Prog.	Setting	Number of edges covered in 24h			
		once/1h	*once/2h*	*once/4h*	*dynamic*
OBJDUMP	AFL-EDGE	33422	33828	33370	**34402**
READELF	AFL-EDGE	50932	53036	51927	**53839**

To validate the above observations in longer-term fuzzing, we extend the tests of AFL-EDGE to 120 h. We also run this test with P-FUZZ as a comparison. As shown in Fig. 7, AFL-EDGE consistently preserves the edges covered by AFL across the 120 h, producing results comparable to P-FUZZ. We note that in certain cases, AFL-EDGE even slightly outperforms P-FUZZ. This is mostly because AFL-EDGE has a higher efficiency of edge coverage than P-FUZZ and therefore, reaches more edges that AFL covers.

Impacts of Frequency of Task Distribution. Recall that AFL-EDGE needs to periodically distribute tasks (Sect. 4). Our hypothesis is that the frequency of distribution can affect the effectiveness of our solution and we dynamically adjust this frequency based on the growth of edges. To validate our hypothesis and demonstrate the utility of our dynamic approach, we perform another experiment where we run one round of distribution per 1 h, 2 h, and 4 h. In Table 3, we present the results. It shows that the frequency of distribution truly makes a difference and our dynamic adjustment indeed outperforms solutions with a fixed frequency.

Table 4. Comparison of seed distillation algorithms. The numbers show the amount of seeds picked by different algorithms.

Prog.	Number of seeds picked after distillation			
	Unweighted	Weight-Time	Weight-Size (cmin)	Ours
OBJDUMP	601	803	599	596
READELF	939	980	938	683
TCPDUMP	765	849	756	592
XML	689	862	686	434
NASM	490	724	492	452
NM	541	701	788	778
TIFF2PDF	785	920	778	778
TIFF2PS	822	916	817	802
FFMPEG	593	742	589	581

Effectiveness of Seed Distribution. In our algorithm of task distribution algorithm (Algorithm 1), the core idea is to pick a subset of seeds that cover the original edges, commonly known as *seed distillation*. Past efforts have developed several other seed distillation algorithms, including AFL-CMIN [50] (notated as *Size-Weighted*) and its variants (including [1], notated as *Unweighted*; [33,45], notated as *Time-Weighted*). Details of the algorithms are as follows.

- **Unweighted Algorithm.** This algorithm always picks a seed whose edges overlap with the non-covered edges the most. It repeats until all edges are covered.
- **Time-Weighted.** This algorithm iterates each non-covered edge and picks the seed with the shortest execution time to cover the edge, repeating this process until all edges are covered.

Table 5. Unique crashes/bugs discovered in our tests.

Prog.	AFL		PAFL		P-FUZZ		AFL-EDGE		Bug types
	Crash	Bug	Crash	Bug	Crash	Bug	Crash	Bug	---
FFMPEG	12	1	72	1	54	1	672	1	Heap overflow
TIFF2PDF	0	0	10	1	2	1	99	1	Failed allocation
TIFF2PS	0	0	0	0	126	1	260	3	Heap overflow
NASM	631	2	1872	6	1,430	6	5,765	9	Memory leaks stack overflow
Total	**643**	**3**	**1954**	**8**	**1612**	**9**	**6792**	**14**	—

- **Size-Weighted (AFL-CMIN).** This algorithm iterates each non-covered edge and picks the seed with the smallest size to cover the edge, repeating this process until all edges are covered.

We conduct an experiment to compare our algorithm with the existing algorithms: we run these algorithms on 1,000 random seeds from each of our benchmark programs and count the number of picked seeds. As shown in Table 4, our algorithm reduces more seeds than all the existing algorithms in every benchmark program, demonstrating better effectiveness. Note that we skipped some other algorithms (e.g., [17]) as they cannot ensure all original edges (or hit counts of edges) are preserved.

6.3   Evaluation of Bug Finding

In the course of evaluation, the fuzzing tools also trigger many crashes. We triage these crashes with AddressSanitizer [36] and then perform a manual analysis to understand the root causes. As shown in Table 5, AFL-EDGE triggers 6,792 unique crashes and 14 previously unknown bugs, outperforming both P-FUZZ and PAFL. Moreover, all the bugs detected by AFL and P-FUZZ are also detected by AFL-EDGE.

We also extended the evaluation of bug finding with the LAVA vulnerability benchmark [12]. However, we omitted the reporting of the results. Basically, our tests with AFL only trigger 1 LAVA bug, regardless of the parallel fuzzing solutions. The major reason is that all LAVA bugs require a four-byte unit in the input to match a random integer value, which is hard to be satisfied by AFL's mutations.

7 Related Works

7.1 Improvements to Algorithms of Grey-Box Fuzzing

Past research has brought three categories of algorithmic improvements to grey-box fuzzing. The first category explores new kinds of *feedback* to facilitate seed scheduling and mutation. AFL [52] considers code branches covered in a round of execution as feedback, which is further refined by Steelix [21], Col-lAFL [13], and PTrix [10] with more fine-grained, control-flow related information. TaintScope [44], Vuzzer [32], GREYONE [14], REDQUEEN [4], and Angora [8] use taint analysis to identify data flows that can affect code coverage.

The second category of research investigates how to use the above types of feedback to improve code coverage. FairFuzz [20], GREYONE [14], and Pro-Fuzzer [48] rely on the feedback to mutate the existing inputs and derive new ones that have a higher probability of reaching new code. AFLFast [7], Dig-Fuzz [53], and MOPT [23] consider the feedback as guidance to schedule inputs for mutation and prioritizes those with higher potentials of leading to new code.

The last category aims at improving *mutations* to remove common barriers that prevent fuzzers from reaching more code. Majundar et al. [24] introduce the idea of hybrid fuzzing, which runs concolic execution to solve complex conditions that are difficult for pure fuzzing to satisfy. The idea was followed and improved by many other works [30,40,49,53]. TFuzz transforms target programs to bypass complex conditions and forces the execution to reach new code. It then uses a validator to reproduce the inputs that meet the conditions in the original program. Angora [8] assumes a black-box function at each condition and uses gradient descent to find satisfying inputs, which is later improved by NEUZZ [38].

Differing from the above works, our research aims to improve the efficiency of the parallel mode of fuzzing, an orthogonal strategy to facilitate the efficiency of code coverage.

7.2 Improvements to Execution Speed of Fuzzing

Beyond algorithmic improvements, other research aims to improve the efficiency of fuzzing by accelerating the fuzzing execution. PTrix [10], Honggfuzz [42], and kAFL [35] use Intel PT [31] to efficiently collect control flow data from the target program. UnTracer [29], instead of tracing every round of execution, instruments the target programs such that the tracing only starts when new code is reached. RetroWrite [11] proposes static binary rewriting to trace code coverage in binary code without heavy dynamic instrumentation.

7.3 Improvements to Parallel Fuzzing

There are two lines of efforts towards better parallel fuzzing in the literature. Xu et al. [46] design new primitives to mitigate the contention in the file system and extend the scalability of the *fork* system call. These new primitives speed up the execution of the target programs when many instances are running in parallel. This line of efforts facilitates parallel fuzzing from a system perspective, which is orthogonal to our approach. Following the other line, P-FUZZ [39], PAFL [22] and Ye et al. [47] propose to distribute fuzzing tasks to different instances to avoid overlaps. We omit the details of P-FUZZ and PAFL since they have been discussed in Sect. 4 and evaluated in Sect. 6. The idea of [47] is to assign seeds that cover less-visited branches to different instances and further confine the mutations to focus on those branches. In comparison to AFL-EDGE, such an idea may skip the exploration of certain code regions and hurt the related fuzzing space. Further, this idea is essentially a variant of PAFL, and thus, we do not compare it with AFL-EDGE in our evaluation.

8 Discussion

In this section, we discuss some of the limitations in our work and the potential future directions.

8.1 Threats to Validity

The validity of our research faces three threats. First, our research is motivated by the intuition that overlapped mutations can reduce the efficiency of code coverage. Whether such an intuition is correct or not threatens the foundation of our research. To mitigate this threat, as presented in Sect. 2, we provide empirical evidence to support the fidelity of our intuition through empirical experiments with real-world programs. Second, AFL-EDGE skips seeds during task distribution, which by theory may reduce the fuzzing space. To validate this threat, we perform extensive experiments to show that AFL-EDGE largely preserves the edge coverage of AFL and thus, avoids hurting the fuzzing space (see Sect. 6.2). Finally, AFL-EDGE and AFL may detect different bugs and AFL-EDGE may miss the bugs detected by AFL. While we provide no theoretical proofs, our empirical evaluation with both real-world programs and standard benchmarks, as shown in Sect. 6.3, argues against such a threat.

8.2 More Fine-Grained Task Distributions Are Needed

AFL-EDGE considers a round of mutations to a seed as an individual task. This represents a coarse-grained definition of fuzzing tasks, which can still result in over-laps. For example, we cannot avoid overlapped mutations by different instances to different seeds. For further improvements, an example idea is to adopt more fine-grained definitions of tasks (e.g., defining fuzzing tasks based on mutations [47]).

8.3   Workloads Need to Be Considered

AFL-EDGE does not explicitly consider the workloads of different tasks. Instead, it relies on random distribution, expecting to achieve probabilistic equivalent workload assignment. This strategy can be further improved by estimating the workload attached to a seed. For instance, we can do such an estimation based on the size of the seed and the execution complexity of the seed (following the idea of AFL-CMIN [50] and QSYM [49]). We may also customize the estimation based on how the fuzzing tools determine the mutation cycles.

9   Conclusion

This paper focuses on the problem of parallel fuzzing. It presents a study to understand the limitations of the parallel mode in the existing grey-box fuzzing tools. Motivated by the study, we propose a general model to describe parallel fuzzing. This model distributes mutually-exclusive yet similarly-weighted tasks to different instances, facilitating concurrency and also fairness across instances. Guided by our model, we present a novel solution to improve the parallel mode in AFL. During fuzzing, our solution periodically distributes seeds that carry non-overlapped and similarly-weighted tasks to different instances, maximally meeting the requirements of our model. We have implemented our solution on top of AFL and we have evaluated our implementation with AFL on 9 widely used benchmark programs. Our evaluation shows that our solution can significantly reduce the overlaps and hence, accelerate the code coverage.

Acknowledgments. We would like to thank the anonymous reviewers for their feedback. This project was supported by NSF (Grant #: CNS-2031377). Any opinions, findings, and conclusions or recommendations expressed in this paper are those of the authors and do not necessarily reflect the views of the funding agency.

References

1. Abdelnur, H., State, R., Lucangeli, O.J., Festor, O.: Spectral fuzzing: Evaluation & feedback. [Research Report] RR-7193, NRIA (2010)
2. Aitel, D.: An introduction to spike, the fuzzer creation kit. Proceedings of the Black Hat USA (2002)
3. Anvin, H.P., Gorcunov, C., Chang Seok Bae, J.K., Kotler, F.B.: Nasm source code, July 1996. https://repo.or.cz/w/nasm.git
4. Aschermann, C., Schumilo, S., Blazytko, T., Gawlik, R., Holz, T.: Redqueen: Fuzzing with input-to-state correspondence. In: Proceedings of the 2019 Network and Distributed System Security Symposium, vol. 19, pp. 1–15. NDSS, Universitätsstraße 150, 44801 Bochum, Germany (2019)
5. Beizer, B.: Black-Box Testing: Techniques for Functional Testing of Software and Systems. Wiley, Hoboken (1995)
6. Bellard, F.: Ffmpeg source code. https://ffmpeg.org/releases/ffmpeg-4.1.tar.bz2
7. Böhme, M., Pham, V.T., Roychoudhury, A.: Coverage-based greybox fuzzing as markov chain. In: Proceedings of the 2016 ACM SIGSAC Conference on Computer and Communications Security, pp. 1032–1043. ACM, google (2016)

8. Chen, P., Chen, H.: Angora: efficient fuzzing by principled search. In: Proceedings of the 2018 IEEE Symposium on Security and Privacy, pp. 711–725. IEEE, Symposium on Security and Privacy, 1 Shields Ave, Davis, CA 95616 (2018)

9. Chen, Y., et al.: Savior: towards bug-driven hybrid testing. In: Proceedings of the 2020 IEEE Symposium on Security and Privacy, pp. 1–14. IEEE, Symposium on Security and Privacy, San Francisco, CA, USA (2020)

10. Chen, Y., et al.: Ptrix: efficient hardware-assisted fuzzing for cots binary. In: Proceedings of the 2019 ACM on Asia Conference on Computer and Communications Security, pp. 633–645. ACM, AsiaCCS, Auckland, New Zealand (2019)

11. Dinesh, S.: RetroWrite: Statically Instrumenting COTS Binaries for Fuzzing and Sanitization. Ph.D. thesis, figshare (2019)

12. Dolan-Gavitt, B., et al.: Lava: large-scale automated vulnerability addition. In: Proceedings of the 2016 IEEE Symposium on Security and Privacy, pp. 110–121. IEEE (2016)

13. Gan, S., et al.: Collafl: path sensitive fuzzing. In: Proceedings of the 2018 IEEE Symposium on Security and Privacy, pp. 660–677. No. 6, Symposium on Security and Privacy, San Francisco, CA, USA, May 2018

14. Gan, S., et al.: GREYONE: data flow sensitive fuzzing. In: Proceedings of the 29th USENIX Security Symposium, pp. 1–18. USENIX Association, Boston, MA, August 2020. https://www.usenix.org/conference/usenixsecurity20/presentation/gan

15. GNU: Index of /gnu/binutils, October 2019. https://ftp.gnu.org/gnu/binutils/

16. Godefroid, P., Levin, M.Y., Molnar, D.: Sage: whitebox fuzzing for security testing. Commun. ACM 55(3), 40–44 (2012)

17. Hayes, L., et al.: Moonlight: Effective fuzzing with near-optimal corpus distillation. arXiv:1905.13055v1 (2019)

18. Klees, G., Ruef, A., Cooper, B., Wei, S., Hicks, M.: Evaluating fuzz testing. In: Proceedings of the 2018 ACM SIGSAC Conference on Computer and Communications Security, pp. 2123–2138. ACM, CCS, Toronto, ON, Canada (2018)

19. Leffler, S.: Libtiff source code, November 2019. https://download.osgeo.org/libtiff/

20. Lemieux, C., Sen, K.: Fairfuzz: A targeted mutation strategy for increasing greybox fuzz testing coverage. In: Proceedings of the 33rd ACM/IEEE International Conference on Automated Software Engineering, pp. 475–485. ase, Montpellier, France (2018)

21. Li, Y., Chen, B., Chandramohan, M., Lin, S.W., Liu, Y., Tiu, A.: Steelix: program-state based binary fuzzing. In: Proceedings of the 2017 11th Joint Meeting on Foundations of Software Engineering, pp. 627–637. ACM, fse, PADERBORN, GERMANY (2017)

22. Liang, J., Jiang, Y., Chen, Y., Wang, M., Zhou, C., Sun, J.: Pafl: extend fuzzing optimizations of single mode to industrial parallel mode. In: Proceedings of the 2018 26th ACM Joint Meeting on European Software Engineering Conference and Symposium on the Foundations of Software Engineering, pp. 809–814 (2018)

23. Lyu, C., Ji, S., Zhang, C., Li, Y., Lee, W.H., Song, Y., Beyah, R.: Mopt: Optimized mutation scheduling for fuzzers. In: Proceedings of the 28th USENIX Security Symposium, pp. 1949–1966. USENIX, Santa Clara, CA, USA (2019)

24. Majumdar, R., Sen, K.: Hybrid concolic testing. In: Software Engineering, 2007. ICSE 2007. 29th International Conference on. pp. 416–426. IEEE, ICSE, Minneapolis, MN, USA (2007)

25. Manès, V.J.M., et al.: The art, science, and engineering of fuzzing: a survey. IEEE Trans. Softw. Eng. PP(21), 21 (2019)

26. Sergeant, M., Christian Glahn, P.P.: Libxml2 source code, September 1999. http://xmlsoft.org/libxml2/libxml2-git-snapshot.tar.gz
27. McKnight, P.E., Najab, J.: Mann-whitney u test. The Corsini encyclopedia of psychology **3**, 960–961 (2010)
28. Myers, G.J., Sandler, C., Badgett, T.: The Art of Software Testing. Wiley, Hoboken (2011)
29. Nagy, S., Hicks, M.: Full-speed fuzzing: reducing fuzzing overhead through coverage-guided tracing. In: Proceedings of the 2019 IEEE Symposium on Security and Privacy, pp. 787–802. IEEE, Symposium on Security and Privacy, SAN FRANCISCO, CA, USA (2019)
30. Pak, B.S.: Hybrid fuzz testing: Discovering software bugs via fuzzing and symbolic execution. School of Computer Science Carnegie Mellon University 0, 1–9 (2012)
31. R., J.: Intel processor trace (2013). https://software.intel.com/en-us/blogs/2013/09/18/processor-tracing
32. Rawat, S., Jain, V., Kumar, A., Cojocar, L., Giuffrida, C., Bos, H.: Vuzzer: application-aware evolutionary fuzzing. In: Proceedings of the Network and Distributed System Security Symposium, pp. 1–14. NDSS, San Diego, California, USA (2017)
33. Rebert, A., et al.: Optimizing seed selection for fuzzing. In: Proceedings of the 23rd USENIX Conference on Security Symposium, pp. 861–875. USENIX Association (2014)
34. Scale, F.: Top 10 software testing trends, February 2019. https://fullscale.io/top-10-software-testing-trends/
35. Schumilo, S., Aschermann, C., Gawlik, R., Schinzel, S., Holz, T.: kafl: hardware-assisted feedback fuzzing for OS kernels. In: Proceedings of the 26th USENIX Conference on Security Symposium, pp. 167–182. USENIX Association, Vancouver, BC, Canada (2017)
36. Serebryany, K., Bruening, D., Potapenko, A., Vyukov, D.: Addresssanitizer: a fast address sanity checker. In: Proceedings of the 2012 USENIX Conference on Annual Technical Conference. pp. 28–28. USENIX Association, Bellevue, WA, USA (2012)
37. Serebryany, K.: libfuzzer-a library for coverage-guided fuzz testing. LLVM project, p. 1 (2015)
38. She, D., Pei, K., Epstein, D., Yang, J., Ray, B., Jana, S.: Neuzz: efficient fuzzing with neural program smoothing. In: Proceedings of the 2019 IEEE Symposium on Security and Privacy, pp. 1–15. IEEE, Symposium on Security and Privacy, San Francisco, CA, USA (2018)
39. Song, C., Zhou, X., Yin, Q., He, X., Zhang, H., Lu, K.: P-fuzz: a parallel grey-box fuzzing framework. Appl. Sci. **9**(23), 5100 (2019)
40. Stephens, N., et al.: Driller: augmenting fuzzing through selective symbolic execution. In: In Proceedings of the 2016 Network and Distributed System Security Symposium, vol. 16, pp. 1–16. NDSS, San Diego, California, USA (2016)
41. McCanne, S., Craig Leres, V.J.: Tcpdump source code, October 2019. http://www.tcpdump.org/release/
42. Swiecki, R.: Honggfuzz (2015). http://honggfuzz.com
43. Teams, T.G.: Oss-fuzz - continuous fuzzing for open source software (2015). https://github.com/google/oss-fuzz
44. Wang, T., Wei, T., Gu, G., Zou, W.: Taintscope: a checksum-aware directed fuzzing tool for automatic software vulnerability detection. In: Proceedings of the 2010 IEEE Symposium on Security and Privacy, pp. 497–512. IEEE, Oakland, CA, United States (2010)

45. Woo, M., Cha, S.K., Gottlieb, S., Brumley, D.: Scheduling black-box mutational fuzzing. In: Proceedings of the Computer and Communications Security 2013. Association for Computing Machinery, New York, NY, USA (2013)

46. Xu, W., Kashyap, S., Min, C., Kim, T.: Designing new operating primitives to improve fuzzing performance. In: Proceedings of the 2017 ACM SIGSAC Conference on Computer and Communications Security, pp. 2313–2328. Association for Computing Machinery, New York, NY, United States (2017)

47. Ye, J., Zhang, B., Li, R., Feng, C., Tang, C.: Program state sensitive parallel fuzzing for real world software. IEEE Access **7**, 42557–42564 (2019)

48. You, W., et al.: Profuzzer: on-the-fly input type probing for better zero-day vulnerability discovery. In: Proceedings of the 2019 IEEE Symposium on Security and Privacy. IEEE, San Fransisco (2019)

49. Yun, I., Lee, S., Xu, M., Jang, Y., Kim, T.: QSYM: a practical concolic execution engine tailored for hybrid fuzzing. In: Proceedings of the 27th USENIX Conference on Security Symposium, pp. 745–761. USENIX Association, Baltimore, MD, USA (2018)

50. Zalewski, M.: afl-cmin, November 2013. https://github.com/mirrorer/afl/blob/master/afl-cmin

51. Zalewski, M., Google: Tips for parallel fuzzing, November 2013. https://github.com/mirrorer/afl/blob/master/docs/parallel_fuzzing.txt

52. Zalewski, M.: Afl technical details (2013). http://lcamtuf.coredump.cx/afl/technical_details.txt

53. Zhao, L., Duan, Y., Yin, H., Xuan, J.: Send hardest problems my way: Probabilistic path prioritization for hybrid fuzzing. In: Proceedings of the 2019 Network and Distributed System Security Symposium, p. 15. NDSS Symposium, San Diego, California (2019)

Flowrider: Fast On-Demand Key Provisioning for Cloud Networks

Nicolae Paladi[1,2（✉）], Marco Tiloca[2], Pegah Nikbakht Bideh[1], and Martin Hell[1]

[1] Lund University, Lund, Sweden
{nicolae.paladi,Pegah.nikbakht_bideh,martin.hell}@eit.lth.se
[2] RISE Research Institutes of Sweden - RISE Cybersecurity, Stockholm, Sweden
marco.tiloca@ri.se

Abstract. Increasingly fine-grained cloud billing creates incentives to review the software execution footprint in virtual environments. For example, virtual execution environments move towards lower overhead: from virtual machines to containers, unikernels, and serverless cloud computing. However, the execution footprint of security components in virtualized environments has either remained the same or even increased. We present Flowrider, a novel key provisioning mechanism for cloud networks that unlocks scalable use of symmetric keys and significantly reduces the related computational load on network endpoints. We describe the application of Flowrider to common transport security protocols, the results of its formal verification, and its prototype implementation. Our evaluation shows that Florwider uses up to an order of magnitude less CPU to establish a TLS session while preventing by construction some known attacks.

Keywords: Network security · Software defined networking · Secure communication · Key management · Cloud security

1 Introduction

Throughout the past decade, cloud computing has evolved to support a panoply of orchestration, deployment, and billing approaches. Notable trends are the use of resource description templates [11], emergence of serverless computing [24] and fine-grained resource billing [29,53]. Resource description templates allow to dynamically deploy workloads and provision them with cryptographic material or network and application configuration. Most major cloud providers offer serverless computing[1]. This defers the operation of the server platform to the cloud provider, while allowing developers to focus on the application code. Cloud users are billed for the number of function invocations and consumed computation resources, rather than for a pre-purchased unit of computation such as a

---

[1] See Amazon Lambda, Google Cloud Functions, Azure Functions, Salesforce Evergreen, etc.

© ICST Institute for Computer Sciences, Social Informatics and Telecommunications Engineering 2021
Published by Springer Nature Switzerland AG 2021. All Rights Reserved
J. Garcia-Alfaro et al. (Eds.): SecureComm 2021, LNICST 399, pp. 207–228, 2021.
https://doi.org/10.1007/978-3-030-90022-9_11

bare-metal server or a virtual machine. Finally, serverless plans are billed based on the CPU, memory, and I/O operations that functions consume. Fine-grained billing provides strong incentives to develop and deploy applications that utilize a minimum amount of computing resources. This calls for a rigorous review of software development and deployment approaches to reduce the use of computing resources.

Consider software-defined networking (SDN): separation of control and data planes helps network configuration and management; however, network operations security did not keep up with new capabilities enabled by SDN. So far, the distribution of cryptographic material to network endpoints leverage to a limited extent the logical centralization of network control [50]. As a result, public-key cryptography, rather than symmetric key cryptography, remains almost pervasively the tool of choice for enabling secure network traffic in virtualized deployments regardless of the network architecture. While public-key cryptography is robust and scalable, it introduces key management complexity and is relatively CPU-expensive; with fine-grained billing in place, this directly translates into additional financial costs. On virtualized hosts where tenants share a common entropy pool, generating asymmetric keys may slow down applications if sufficient entropy is not available [25]. Some network endpoints may even lack the computational capacity to generate cryptographic material without disrupting their own operations. Generating keys on a dedicated host with deep entropy pools can reduce the key creation overhead. On the other hand, while generating symmetric keys requires less computational power and has firmware support on many platforms, the use of symmetric keys leads to challenges such as secure key provisioning and key authentication. This introduces the research question: *can the SDN model be leveraged to conveniently provision symmetric keys and reduce computational resource consumption?*

We posit that the answer is *yes* and demonstrate this with Flowrider, a novel key provisioning mechanism for network endpoints in SDN deployments that considers the practicalities of cloud systems deployment. In particular, Flowrider takes a reactive, on-demand, and automatic approach that embeds key distribution into the network flow establishment. Furthermore, Flowrider makes key distribution agnostic of the network topology and communication patterns in the system, of which it does not require any early knowledge. Overall, Flowrider reduces the number of steps for providing symmetric key material to endpoints and the time required to set up secure communication.

By conveniently enabling the use of symmetric keys [46], Flowrider reduces by an order of magnitude the computation load of secure channel establishment on network endpoints and simplifies key management in SDN deployments [38], without compromising communication security properties. Minor modifications of network endpoints introduce another contribution - *flow-specific symmetric keys* - that enable per-flow cryptographic isolation of network traffic. Flowrider is compatible with common transport layer security protocol suites including (D)TLS v1.2 [12,40] and v1.3 [17,18]. Our contribution is three-fold:

- We describe a key provisioning mechanism that leverages the use of symmetric encryption keys in virtualized deployments within an administrative domain.
- We describe the mechanism and functioning of *flow-specific symmetric keys*, for establishing secure channels between network endpoints.
- We detail how the proposed mechanism works in the (D)TLS security suites v1.2 and v1.3, where it also prevents the "Selfie" attack [13] by construction.

Our Flowrider implementation shows reduced computation effort and fewer round-trips to generate authentication credentials and establish secure communication between endpoints. Note that Flowrider primarily targets controlled enterprise environments and does not focus on privacy for network endpoints.

The rest of this paper is organized as follows. We introduce the necessary background in Sect. 2 and describe the system model, threat model, and assumptions in Sect. 3. In Sect. 4, we introduce the Flowrider key provisioning mechanism. In Sect. 5, we describe the use of Flowrider with (D)TLS. In Sect. 6, we provide a formal security analysis of Flowrider with ProVerif, followed by an experimental evaluation in Sect. 7. We review the related work in Sect. 8 and conclude in Sect. 9.

2   Background

We first introduce the main concepts and context considered in the rest of the paper.

2.1   Deployment in Virtualized Environments

In modern distributed systems, workloads are commonly deployed using a resource orchestration system such as Kubernetes [14], Micado [28] or Rancher[2]. Workloads are deployed based on a resource description expressed in a template encoded in a domain-specific language such as TOSCA [49]. Based on the deployment template, an orchestrator creates and configures workload environments (virtual machine images, containers, or microservices), and deploys them on the underlying hardware. The orchestrator also deploys network components - such as the network controller and network functions - and implements a network configuration defining the communication topology between workload containers. Depending on operating considerations, the orchestrator may be co-located with the network controller. Orchestrators commonly maintain a control channel to patch and update the workloads, re-provision cryptographic material, and collect operation logs. Finally, deployments can be dynamically reconfigured depending on the availability of resources (such as memory, CPU, IO, and bandwidth).

---

[2] https://rancher.com/.

2.2 SDN and OpenFlow

SDN emerged in response to the increasing complexity of network deployments, facilitating operation and management of virtualized networks [1]. Its operational advantages lead to wide adoption in enterprise deployments [42]. We next introduce several relevant components of the SDN model.

The *data plane* contains hardware and software routing components and implements routing policies that satisfy network administrator goals. It is optimized for forwarding speed but may contain logic for in-network processing [39]. The *Southbound API* is a vendor-agnostic set of instructions implemented by the data plane, allowing two-way communication between the data and the control planes. In this paper, we consider the OpenFlow protocol [36]. The *control plane* is an abstraction layer transforming high-level network operator goals into discrete routing policies based on a global network view. *Network functions* are used by network administrators to express their network configuration goals using a set of high-level commands. Examples of such applications are firewalls, intrusion detection systems, traffic shapers, etc. In this paper, we use a custom network function to generate symmetric keys for establishing secure channels between network endpoints.

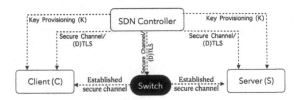

Fig. 1. High-level system architecture and components

2.3 Secure Channels

To establish a secure channel, two parties authenticate with each other and derive key material to protect their communication. To this end, two fundamental approaches exist.

The first approach uses a symmetric *pre-shared key* held by both parties. Advantages of this approach include the typically small size of keys, computationally efficient operations needed to use those keys, and resilience against cryptanalysis using quantum-based algorithms. On the other hand, pre-shared keys are typically more difficult to manage, requiring dedicated management procedures to provide, distribute, and revoke them. Management tasks become especially complicated in large and dynamic systems.

The second approach is based on public-key cryptography, where each party acquires the other's public share of a key pair. In practice, this is a bare *raw public key*, or a public *certificate* including the public key and signed by a trusted certification authority. This approach is widely used: since only public information is shared, management tasks are simpler compared to pre-shared keys and can be automated through dedicated Public Key Infrastructure. On the other hand, this approach results in much larger key material, heavier computation load when performing cryptographic operations, and higher entropy requirements on the communication parties.

3   Network Scenario

Consider the network scenario illustrated in Fig. 1: an orchestration node collocated on a network controller deploys two endpoints, i.e. C as Client and S as Server, as well as an OpenFlow Switch on the communication path between C and S. Also, it configures the network controller to establish and manage the network flows between the endpoints. For monitoring and patch management purposes, the orchestrator node establishes at deployment time and maintains a secure channel with the endpoints. Note that this approach is in-line with the industry best-practice recommendations [20].

We assume that the network controller established at deployment time three secure communication channels: with C, with S, and with the Switch. These can practically be enforced through (D)TLS sessions. The Switch is able to forward network traffic between C and S, according to the established flows.

For simplicity and with no loss of generality, we hereafter focus on the scenario in Fig. 1. Nevertheless, the solution presented in this paper seamlessly works also in more complex and scalable scenarios, where multiple switches, as well as multiple pairs of client and server peers, are deployed. We assume that the network deployment follows best practices in terms of capacity for network flows, flow establishment rate, and the number of peers engaged in acceptable traffic shapes. This includes proper allocation of bandwidth resources and a sufficient number of deployed switches to prevent bottleneck points and congestion.

With reference to Fig. 1, C intends to securely communicate with S. As discussed in Sect. 2.3, typical approaches to establish a secure communication channel rely on either: a symmetric key pre-shared between C and S; or asymmetric key material either pre-provisioned at orchestration time, exchanged during the secure channel establishment, or acquired out-of-band, such as through a custom PKI infrastructure. We argue that, currently, the above approaches display at least the following limitations.

First, if C and S use multiple network flows, communications on each network flow occur over secure channels created with the same pairwise set of key material. Thus, compromising the single set of key material leads to endangering the data security on all network flows between the two endpoints.

Second, asymmetric key material, e.g. raw public keys and public certificates require computationally- and resource-demanding operations on the endpoints. This becomes critical in virtualized environments and serverless model with fine-grained resource billing and limited entropy pools.

Third, while use of symmetric keys is computationally lightweight and faster than public-key approaches, they are rarely used to establish secure communication between endpoints due to constraints in key provisioning and management.

Symmetric keys are harder to distribute and revoke, especially in large-scale and dynamic distributed workload deployments.

Fourth, provisioning of symmetric key material must occur before communication between the endpoints can start. Moreover, it requires pre-knowledge of the network topology and of the communication patterns expected from the two endpoints, further complicating the management of symmetric key material. We describe an alternative solution allowing to: (i) provide per-flow key material, where a single key compromise does not affect the security of other flows; (ii) distribute symmetric key material in a way that is fast, dynamic, and automatic. This approach does not require a priori knowledge of the network topology and communication patterns among the involved endpoints; (iii) facilitate centralized maintenance of software and hardware for cryptographic operations and key generation.

Flowrider achieves this by provisioning the Client and Server with a *flow-specific* symmetric key used to establish a secure communication channel. Key provisioning is done *at flow installation time*, whenever the Client initiates a new communication session with the Server. This approach, further described in Sect. 4, can be used with various protocol suites for secure channel establishment. In Sect. 5, we additionally detail how it can be implemented in the (D)TLS suite without transcending the isolation between the transport and encryption layers of a communication session.

4   Key Provisioning Method

We next describe *Flowrider*, a novel key distribution method for cloud networks. In particular, Flowrider enables fast, automatic on-demand provisioning of symmetric pre-shared keys to peer endpoints. Pre-shared keys are distributed contextually with the establishment of a network flow between two endpoints and is associated with that respective network flow. Once received, the endpoints can use the pre-shared key to establish a secure channel for communicating over that network flow.

Flowrider builds on the following rationale: each time the Client initiates a session with the Server and triggers the establishment of a new network flow, the network controller generates a new symmetric pre-shared key associated to that flow, and provisions it to both endpoints. To convey the concept, in this paper we assume that the control plane operates in a reactive mode. However, this is not a hard requirement: packets can be matched on the switch while matching packets can be mirrored and upstreamed to the controller.

In the network scenario illustrated in Fig. 1, the network Controller provides the Client and the Server with symmetric per-flow keys. Key provisioning is done over the secure channel between the Controller and the Client (C) and Server (S), pre-established at deployment time. Key provisioning is contextual to establishment of a new network flow between C and S, involving the Switch and the Controller.

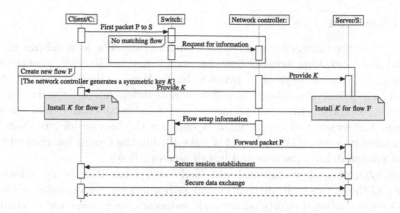

Fig. 2. Step-by-step general execution

We illustrate a run-through of Flowrider in Fig. 2, with the following steps:

1. C sends the first packet P addressed to S. The packet reaches the Switch.
2. The Switch does not find in its flow table a flow rule matching with packet P.
3. The Switch sends a control message to the network controller.
4. The network controller:
   (a) Generates a flow rule F to handle traffic between C and S matching packet P.
   (b) Generates a cryptographic symmetric key K associated to F, together with a related key identifier[3].
5. The network controller provisions the key K and the related key identifier to both C and S, through the respective pre-established secure channel. The network controller may additionally provide C with the IP address of S, echoing what is specified in the control message from the Switch.
6. C and S install the received key K and related key identifier. If the message from the controller includes also an IP address, C verifies that to be the destination address of its original request to S. This prevents possible internal adversaries from carrying out misbinding attacks based on IP-spoofing.
7. The network controller communicates to the Switch the new flow rule F.
8. The Switch forwards the packet P to S, according to the flow rule F.
9. C and S use the key K to establish a secure session, for example using the (D)TLS Handshake protocol (see Sect. 5).
10. C and S use the flow F to exchange packets over the established secure channel.

Note that steps 5 and 7 occur concurrently.

---

[3] As a possible optimization, the network controller may have generated in advance a number of symmetric keys, which would thus be immediately available to distribute.

4.1   Discussion

In Flowrider, the network controller distributes symmetric keys ad-hoc and on-demand when installing network flows between C and S. Flowrider generates and provisions symmetric keys on a per-flow basis. Hence, different flows between two peer endpoints are related to different and independent security domains. Therefore, compromising the symmetric key associated with a flow does not endanger the security of any other flow between the two endpoints. Note that provisioning symmetric key material is embedded in the OpenFlow control traffic to upstream matching packets and install network flows.

The symmetric key material provided with Flowrider is an alternative to state-of-the-art use of certificates and asymmetric cryptography. Flowrider reduces computational efforts on network endpoints, and hence lowers economic costs. It also reduces entropy requirements for the network endpoints, which is particularly important in virtualized networks.

Section 5 describes how Flowrider can be embodied in versions 1.2 and 1.3 of the security protocol suites TLS and DTLS, without transcending the isolation between the transport layer and (D)TLS. Flowrider is easily and effectively deployable in existing network scenarios that use (D)TLS. Further optimizations are possible, such as indirect provisioning of pre-shared keys to the Server endpoint, through local key derivation on the Server. Section 5.4 describes this optimization with (D)TLS.

The process in Fig. 2 refers to a common execution pattern, i.e. where the establishment of the network flow between C and S is triggered by C sending a first packet P. Flowrider supports alternative execution patterns, where the SDN deployment is not configured in reactive mode and establishing the network flow - and the consequent key provisioning to C and S - is triggered by the Switch or the network controller, forcing the installation or change of a flow rule. This can happen when enforcing management network policies at deployment time, or when dynamically addressing changes in the network topology and traffic load.

In case of a compromise, the Controller will revoke every flow key issued to a pair of peers. Determining if a peer was compromised can be achieved through intrusion- and anomaly-detection, which are out of the scope of this work. When the Controller determines that one peer P was compromised, the Controller promptly revokes each per-flow key K issued to P which is not yet expired, and notifies any other peer than P that has been provided with K, over the respective secure control channel. This requires the Controller to store at least the key identifier of each non-expired per-flow key.

5   Compatibility with (D)TLS

While Flowrider can be used with various common transport security protocols, we next discuss compatibility with the TLS and DTLS security suites. In Sects. 5.2 and 5.3, we describe the embodiment in version 1.2 and 1.3 of (D)TLS, allowing Flowrider to be immediately deployable without breaking existing security standards.

5.1 Transport Layer Security

Most of the network traffic exchanged today, especially on the Internet, is protected at the transport layer. That is, two communicating peers establish a secure channel, namely *session*, and use it to secure the entire application message. The protected message is then handed over to the transport layer, e.g. to the TCP or UDP protocol, for delivery to the other peer. Such secure communication is typically achieved using the protocol suites *Transport Layer Security* (TLS) and *Datagram Transport Layer Security* (DTLS).

The TLS 1.2 protocol suite [12] secures the exchange of application data over TCP among two peers, namely *Client* and *Server*, by preventing the eavesdropping, tampering, and forgery of exchanged messages. The two main protocols composing the TLS suite are the *Handshake* protocol and the encapsulation *Record* protocol. The Client initiates the Handshake execution with the Server, by sending a *ClientHello* Handshake message. Following the Handshake protocol, the two peers agree on a number of security parameters and establish key material to later secure their communications.

The Handshake execution is fundamentally based on two possible approaches, depending on the type of security material pre-installed on the two peers and used during the secure session establishment. In the first approach, the two peers own one or more symmetric pre-shared keys [19], and the Client can suggest to the Server which key it intends to use during the Handshake. In the second approach, the peers rely on asymmetric key pairs, and public keys are exchanged either as conveyed in public certificates [8] or as raw public keys [51] generated by manufacturers and installed on nodes before deployment. A node must use out-of-band means for validating raw public keys received from other peers, and usually retains a list of trusted peer identities. Upon successful Handshake completion, peers can exchange application data messages over the established secure session, using the Record protocol.

The DTLS 1.2 protocol suite [40] provides secure communication of application data over unreliable datagram protocols such as UDP. DTLS is based on TLS, provides equivalent security guarantees, and relies on analogous Handshake and Record protocols. The DTLS protocol suite has several differences from TLS, to deal with the unreliable underlying datagram transport protocols it runs on. In particular, it does not support stream ciphers, admits preserving secure sessions upon silently discarding invalid incoming messages, and includes an explicit fresh sequence number in every protected message. This allows to correctly distinguish and process incoming DTLS messages, also in case of out-of-sequence delivery due to the unreliable transport service.

Finally, DTLS introduces an optional additional exchange of a stateless *Cookie* between the Client and Server, as a first step of the Handshake. Upon receiving a first ClientHello message, the Server can reply with a *HelloVerifyRequest* message, including a locally generated value as Cookie. The Client must then reply by sending a second ClientHello, which includes the same Cookie. The Handshake further continues only if the Server successfully verifies the Cookie received in this second ClientHello. This forces the Client to prove its alleged source IP address, and, possibly in combination with additional means such as [33], complicates possible Denial of Service attacks against the Server performed by an active adversary able to spoof IP addresses.

TLS 1.3 was released to improve both performance and security assurances [18]. While fundamentally providing the same security guarantees as TLS 1.2, TLS 1.3: i) reduces the handshake by one round trip, while having more handshake messages also encrypted; ii) provides new functions for key material derivation, with improved key separation and facilitating cryptographic analysis; iii) always provides perfect forward secrecy if peers run the handshake through public-key based key establishment; iv) supports the latest key establishment, cipher, and signature algorithms, deprecating insecure or obsolete ones; and v) enables the exchange of early secure data at the beginning of the handshake, at the cost of sacrificing a subset of security properties for such data. While TLS 1.3 has been increasingly adopted since its release, TLS 1.2 is expected to continue being used for a long time, as (a dominant) protocol suite for secure communication.

5.2   Flowrider with (D)TLS 1.2

Assume the Client and Server intend to securely communicate using the TLS 1.2 [12] or DTLS 1.2 [40] protocol suite. With reference to the steps in Sect. 4 shown in Fig. 2, Flowrider can be embedded in the (D)TLS Handshake protocol as follows.

At Step (1), the first packet P from C addressed to S is either a TCP SYN (for a TLS handshake) or a *ClientHello* Handshake message (for a DTLS handshake). In either case, C performs the (D)TLS Handshake with S in pre-shared key mode [19].

Later on during the Handshake execution, i.e. at Step (9) of the Flowrider execution (see Sect. 4), C points S to key K to be used as a pre-shared key for mutual authentication and as input for deriving the (D)TLS session key material. C specifies the key identifier of the key K in the *PSK identity* field of the *ClientKeyExchange* Handshake message sent to S.

5.3   Flowrider with (D)TLS 1.3

Assume that the Client and Server intend to securely communicate using the TLS 1.3 [18] or DTLS 1.3 [17] protocol suite. Flowrider can be embedded in the (D)TLS Handshake protocol as follows (see Sect. 4, Fig. 2).

At Step (1), the first packet P from C addressed to S is either a TCP SYN (for a TLS handshake) or a *ClientHello* Handshake message (for a DTLS handshake). In either case, C performs the (D)TLS Handshake with S in pre-shared key mode. That is, as per (D)TLS 1.3 [17,18], C has to include in the *ClientHello* Handshake message:

1. A *psk_key_exchange_modes* ClientHello extension, which specifies the *psk_ke* or *psk_dhe_ke* key exchange mode.

2. A *pre_shared_key* ClientHello extension, present as the last extension and including a collection of offered pre-shared keys. This collection is structured as follows: (1) a list of key identifiers; (2) a list of *key binders*, one for each pre-shared key and in the same order as the key identifier list. Each key binder is an HMAC computed with a binder key derived from the corresponding pre-shared key. The key binder is computed over the *ClientHello* message up to and including the key identifier list of the *pre_shared_key* ClientHello extension.

S expects a valid hint of the pre-shared key already at the first (D)TLS *ClientHello* message. However, if DTLS is used, C does not have the key K and its key identifier from the network controller already at Step (1) of the Flowrider execution, where the first packet P addressed to S is already the *ClientHello* message. Thus, when starting a new communication flow in the DTLS case, the Client cannot produce a *ClientHello* message, as the per-flow symmetric key is not available yet. Intuitively, this is overcome by the network controller finalizing the original and incomplete *ClientHello* message, before the Switch eventually forwards it to the Server as per the newly established traffic flow. In particular, C stores a dummy pre-shared symmetric key and a related key identifier, which is not associated with any corresponding server. Then, the following adaptation of the Flowrider execution is performed, as also shown in Fig. 3.

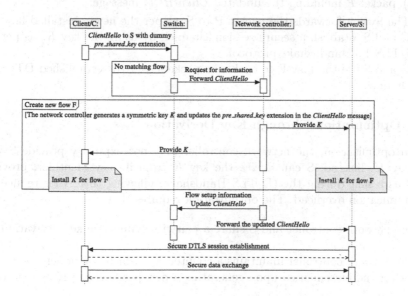

Fig. 3. Step-by-step execution for implementing Flowrider in DTLS 1.3

1. C sends the *ClientHello* message in the first packet P addressed to S. In particular, the *pre_shared_key* ClientHello extension offers only the dummy

pre-shared key used by C for this purpose. Then, the packet reaches the Switch.

2. The Switch fails to find in its flow table a flow rule matching with packet P.
3. The Switch sends a control message to the network controller, asking for information about setting up a new flow between C and S and also forwards the entire packet P, including *ClientHello*, to the network controller.
4. The network controller:
   (a) generates a new flow rule F to handle traffic between C and S akin to packet P;
   (b) generates a cryptographic symmetric key K associated to flow F, together with a related key identifier;
   (c) builds a new *pre_shared_key* ClientHello extension for the *ClientHello* message in the packet P. The new extension offers only the key K associated to flow F, and includes one consistently recomputed key binder. The recomputed extension replaces the one originally included in the *ClientHello* message in the packet P.
5. The network controller provisions the key K and the related key identifier to both C and S, through the respective pre-established secure channel.
6. Both C and S install key K and related key identifier.
7. The network controller replies to the Switch with:
   (a) information on handling packets in the new flow F;
   (b) packet P including the updated *ClientHello* message.
8. The Switch forwards the packet P to S, as per the newly installed flow F.
9. C and S establish a secure session/channel, by using the key K, as per the DTLS 1.3 Handhshake protocol.
10. C and S use the flow F to exchange packets over the established DTLS 1.3 channel.

5.4   Optimization Through Key Derivation

As an optimization, the network controller may not explicitly provide S with the key K. Instead, S can *derive* the key K from its key identifier, provided by C as a hint during the (D)TLS Handshake, allowing to further reduce the communication overhead. The optimization requires that:

- The network controller and S share a pairwise symmetric key-derivation key K^*.
- The network controller maintains a counter N_S, which is uniquely associated with S and incremented upon generating a new per-flow key K associated to S.
- The network controller generates the key K by means of a secure key derivation function $PRF(\cdot)$ that takes as input the key-derivation key K^* and a nonce N set as the current value of the counter N_S. $PRF(\cdot)$ can be based on a $HMAC$ function [30] and rely on the same data expansion scheme described in [12].

– Nonce N used to generate the key K is also used as the key identifier of that key.

In (D)TLS 1.2, the Client C simply specifies the nonce N as a key identifier for the key K in the *PSK identity* field of the *ClientKeyExchange* Handshake message. Upon receiving the *ClientKeyExchange* Handshake message, S derives the key K by means of $PRF(\cdot)$, using the retrieved nonce N and the key-derivation key K^*. This approach was discussed in [21].

In (D)TLS 1.3, the nonce N is used as the key identifier for the key K in the *pre_shared_key* ClientHello extension for the *ClientHello* message. In TLS 1.3, this is directly specified by C, after having received the key K from the network controller. In DTLS 1.3, this is specified by the network controller, when building the new *pre_shared_key* ClientHello extension for the *ClientHello* message in the packet P (see step (4c) in Sect. 5.3). In either case, upon receiving the *ClientHello* message, S derives the key K by means of $PRF(\cdot)$, using the retrieved nonce N and the key-derivation key K^*.

5.5   On Preventing the Selfie Attack

Flowrider prevents the reflection attack ("Selfie" [13]) against (D)TLS, which tricks a session peer into processing messages generated by itself, assuming they come from the other peer. This exploits the use of the same pre-shared key in two secure sessions, as (D)TLS client and (D)TLS server.

In an SDN deployment, a peer A (B) acting as (D)TLS client (server) results in one flow, as an exact combination of source address/port and destination address/port. Instead, peer A (B) acting as (D)TLS server (client) results in a different flow, with a flipped combination of source and destination address/port.

In Flowrider, the SDN Controller generates and provides two different pre-shared keys to peers A and B, one for each of the flows. A and B never use the same pre-shared key for both combinations of roles, as they always result in different flows, and distributed pre-shared keys are per-flow. Thus, a given peer gets one different pre-shared key for each role that such peer has with the other peer sharing the same key, and the Selfie attack is prevented by construction.

6   Formal Security Verification

We verified the security properties of Flowrider, using ProVerif [3]. ProVerif is based on the *applied pi calculus* modeling language and can represent processes, their interactions, and available security channels. ProVerif considers an active adversary (Dolev-Yao model [9]) that cannot decrypt encrypted messages without accessing the secret keys.

6.1   ProVerif Modeling

To model Flowrider with ProVerif, we started by declaring types, cryptographic functions, security assumptions, queries, and processes. Throughout the model, we maintain the assumption of a pre-established secure channel between the network controller and the endpoints (Client and Server), consistently with the network scenario presented in Sect. 3). The channels were securely established using key material assumed to be inaccessible and infeasible to derive for the adversary. The Client, the Server, the Switch, and the network controller are each modeled as independent, top-level processes.

We verified[4] the following security properties of Flowrider: i) the secure provisioning and resulting secrecy of key K, i.e. the key associated with the flow between the Client and Server (see Sect. 6.2); and ii) the mutual secure possession of key K by Client, Server, and controller (see Sect. 6.3). Note that we *do not* verify security properties that are assumed to be already satisfied, such as the security of the (pre-)established secure sessions and the security of session establishments themselves. In particular, the security of the TLS session establishment has been formally verified in [4].

6.2   Key Secrecy

In the protocol model we assume that, upon receiving from the controller the key K associated with the flow, C and S use it to derive the key material for the secure session. While this consists of executing a session establishment protocol, the model assumes that a cryptographically secure Key Derivation Function (KDF) is used to derive a single session key K_S as key material. The KDF takes as input the flow key K and context information related to the secure session. Once the Client-Server session is established, the Client sends a message M to the Server, encrypted using the session key K_S. We verified that the adversary cannot access the secret message, with the following query:

$$query(attacker(M)) \tag{1}$$

The model successfully verified the secrecy of message M. Since K was used as input to securely derive the session key K_S, in turn used to protect the message M, we conclude that the secrecy of key K is also preserved.

6.3   Mutual Secure Key Possession

In Flowrider, only the Client and Server with access to the flow key K can successfully establish a secure session with each other in a symmetric mode, over that flow. We verify that the parties that possess K can establish a secure session over the flow associated with K.

To this end, we verified that, if the Server receives an encrypted message M from the Client over a flow, then i) the Client has previously established a secure session with the Server over that flow; and ii) the Client has sent the message M to the Server, encrypted with the session key K_S derived from the flow key K associated to that flow.

---

[4] ProVerif scripts available at https://anonymous.4open.science/r/8e9da3de-6ccd-4f49-b925-389fbcc9bca6/.

ProVerif allows specifying send and receive operations, as well as to initiate and terminate communications between the Client and Server, by means of events such as Initclient(K_S), Termserver(K_S), Initserver(K_S, Ack) and Termclient(K_S, Ack), where K_S is the session key K_S derived from the flow key K. The session establishment is successfully completed by both parties when each of them received an acknowledgment from the other party, over that session. The formalized queries for the above events are:

$$inj - event(termclient(K_s, Ack))$$
$$==> inj - event(initserver(K_s, Ack)) \tag{2}$$

$$inj - event(termserver(K_s))$$
$$==> inj - event(initclient(K_s)) \tag{3}$$

Queries 2 and 3 verify that for all Initserver(K_S,Ack) and Initclient(K_S), events Termclient(K_S,Ack) and Termserver(K_S) were previously executed. ProVerif successfully verified both correspondence properties in queries 2 and 3. This implies that only the Client possessing the flow key K can connect to the Server over that flow, protecting messages with the session key K_S derived from K. This also implies that the Server accepts communications over that flow only from the Client corresponding to the flow key K, i.e. exchanging messages encrypted with the session key K_S derived from K.

The injective correspondence in query 2 and 3 verifies that the relation between correspondence events is one to one, implying that the Client with access to flow key K can successfully open a dedicated session with the Server. Injectivity holds and ProVerif verified the injective correspondence since the Server should complete the session establishment using the flow key only once for the session initiated by the Client.

6.4   Verifying the Optimization Through Key Derivation

Flowrider can be further optimized for certain (D)TLS protocol use cases (see Sect. 5.4). In this optimization, the controller does not send the flow key K to the Server. Instead, the Server locally derives the flow key K using a nonce generated by the controller and a long-term symmetric key shared with the controller. The nonce is used as a key identifier for the flow key K and is specified in the session establishment message addressed to the Server. We verified the optimized version of Flowrider and included the nonce in the first message sent out by the Client to the Switch.

$$event(termclient(K_s, Ack))$$
$$==> event(initserver(K_s, Ack)) \tag{4}$$

We verified the security properties discussed in Sects. 6.2 and 6.3. In this case, we verified only the correspondence, since we considered also multiple flows between the Client and the Server. For non-injective correspondence, the one to one relation between events is not required, but only the event after the arrow is executed prior to the event before the arrow. The formalized queries are:

$$event(termserver(K_s)) ==> event(initclient(K_s)) \qquad (5)$$

ProVerif verified the security properties of the optimized Flowrider version.

7   Experimental Evaluation

In order to understand the practical implementation aspects, trade-offs and performance of Flowrider, we implemented[5] it in a distributed virtualized environment. We ran the experiments on Google Compute Platform [44] in a `g1-small` virtual machine (VM) instance (1 vCPU, 1.7 GB memory).

The test bed is distributed between four Docker containers with the following roles (see Fig. 4): (a) Client, (b) Server, (c) Controller, (d) Open vSwitch (OvS). The endpoints (Client and Server) use TLS 1.3 [18] implemented with the GnuTLS library [34], version 3.6.5. Two distinct but closely related Client and Server implementations were created for using symmetric keys and certificates respectively. The controller container runs Ryu 3.12 and a custom Python

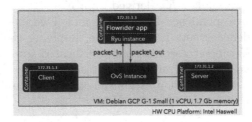

Fig. 4. System test bed

Table 1. Overview of the performance measurements data set

Type	PSK			PKI		
	Task clock, msec	CPU utilized	Time elapsed, msec	Task clock, msec	CPU utilized	Time elapsed, msec
Minimum	3.17	0.034	0.087	13.71	0.183	0.056
Maximum	4.43	0.049	0.097	16.06	0.269	0.080
Mean	3.37	0.037	0.089	14.31	0.24	0.058
Median	3.34	0.037	0.089	14.23	0.24	0.057
Stddev	0.096	0.001	0.0006	0.32	0.005	0.001
Variance	0.00923	0.000001	0.0000004	0.1081	0.00002	0.000002

---

[5] Implementation code available at https://anonymous.4open.science/r/8e9da3de-6ccd-4f49-b925-389fbcc9bca6/.

application, that defines packets to be matched and subsequently generates and delivers keys to the endpoints. The OvS container runs an instance of Open vSwitch that routes packets between endpoints and forwards predefined packet types to the controller.

We measured the performance of establishing a TLS session in two scenarios. We ran the TLS handshake in asymmetric mode using PKI certificates (vanilla scenario) and in pre-shared key (PSK) mode using symmetric keys (Flowrider scenario) consistently with the Flowrider embodiment for TLS 1.3 (see Sect. 5.3). The Client established a TLS session with the Server in the considered mode and terminated the session immediately afterward. We ran the experiment 10,000 times. In both cases, the OvS flow table did not contain any flows between the Client and the Server; as a result, the first Client message (TCP SYN) was forwarded to the controller in each scenario run.

We illustrate the results of our experimental evaluation in Fig. 5 and Table 1. Figure 5 shows that the 'PSK' scenario (representing Flowrider) performs better in terms of time spent on the task and CPU utilization. Time elapsed is longer for the 'PSK' scenario, partly due to the overhead introduced by the communication between the switch and the controller. However, the overhead is mostly offset by distributing the pre-shared keys after the first TCP packet, before the TLS session negotiation starts.

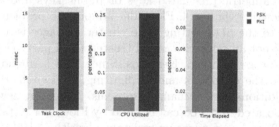

Fig. 5. Task Clock, CPU utilisation and Time elapsed for PSK/PKI scenarios

Table 1 presents a more detailed view. The mean task clock is lower in the Flowrider ('PSK') scenario (3.37 msec compared to 14.31 msec). The CPU utilization is *significantly* lower in the Flowrider ('PSK') scenario, with a mean of 0.037 versus 0.24 CPU. The time elapsed is about 30% higher in the case of the Flowrider ('PSK') scenario. However, considering that this delay occurs *once* at setup time and is not recurrent, we consider that this is an acceptable overhead.

The Flowrider scenario highlights an order of magnitude lower CPU consumption, due to the use of symmetric key material when establishing the TLS session. Note that the overall time to establish the secure channel does not change significantly. In fact, the very first step of the TCP session establishment triggers the distribution of the symmetric key, which is used to establish the TLS session in PSK mode.

8   Related Work

Protocols such as Kerberos [35] are widely used for symmetric key distribution. This involves a Key Distribution Center - a Trusted Third Party generating and distributing ephemeral keys to clients, without disclosing the secret shared key of the server. Internet applications often rely on an Authorization Server providing trusted assertions to servers about requesting clients [23].

Flowrider key distribution can be viewed as a three-party setting, with the switch acting as a relay and middleman. Three-party authenticated key exchange has received much attention. Its security was formalized by Bellare and Rogaway in [31] and much research has focused on the password-based variant, introduced in [41] and given for the three-party case in [32]. In the three-party password-based authenticated key exchange (3PAKE), low entropy secrets shared with the server are used to negotiate a session key between two parties. This protocol in [32] was shown to have weaknesses [6,52] and many variants have been proposed since then, some using a server public key [22,47], and some that do not [5,48]. More recent work on PAKE protocols include making them post-quantum secure, both in the two-party setting [26] and for three parties [7]. While authenticated key exchange protocols assume an unprotected channel and pre-shared keys, Flowrider uses TLS as the underlying protocol for distributing the key from the cluster manager to the involved parties. This can be accomplished either through symmetric pre-shared keys or public keys and is not predetermined by the Flowrider protocol. Flowrider adapts the problem of three-party key distribution to the SDN setting. The cluster manager is a natural part of the network, and not an otherwise added trusted third party (Key Distribution Center) as in the case with e.g., Kerberos. Since TLS is already used e.g., for deploying jobs to the endpoints and configuring the switch, there is no need to implement additional key exchange protocols. Moreover, new cryptographic primitives incorporated into TLS can be used by Flowrider to take advantage of improved ECC [2] and post-quantum resistant algorithms [15].

Key distribution for SDN deployments was explored in several contexts. Li *et al.* proposed a symmetric key generation and distribution for content delivery network interconnections using SDN and application-layer traffic optimization [45]. The mechanism relies on key generation on the endpoints and a central entity for matching and distributing key pairs. Similar to Flowrider, this relies on a central authority. However, it neither reduces the computational load on the endpoints nor improves the performance of the key exchange. Cloud frameworks commonly rely on a central authority to provision authentication material to virtual instances (either virtual machines or containers) before deployment [10,43]. Provisioning authentication credentials before instantiation reduces the computational load on the endpoints and reduces the entropy requirements. However, the use of public keys certificates for key establishment requires more round trips compared to protocols using symmetric keys.

Provisioning cryptographic material to network endpoints by storing it in trusted execution environments (TEEs) was explored in both academia and industry [27]. While this approach leverages hardware security guarantees to store the provisioned cryptographic material, it also introduces additional overhead on accessing the cryptographic material. This includes both provisioning the material to TEEs and retrieving it from TEEs. Finally, other less common approaches rely on information that may be public or not unique, such as the serial number of the device [16], or require manual steps that do not scale in production settings [37].

Flowrider builds on earlier work and leverages the OpenFlow protocol to enable symmetric key provisioning. In contrast to existing approaches, Flowrider drastically reduces the computational requirements for supporting end-to-end encryption; it reduces the number of steps for providing symmetric key material to two endpoints and hence for them to set up secure communication; finally, it allows granular cryptographic isolation of network flows. While Flowrider does not require TEE support on network endpoints, it is complementary to approaches provisioning credentials to TEEs.

9   Conclusion

We have presented Flowrider, a novel approach to distribute cryptographic symmetric keys to endpoints in software networks, contextually with network flow establishment. Flowrider efficiently provisions symmetric key material and significantly reduces the number of CPU cycles needed to establish a secure communication channel between two endpoints. Flowrider leverages the logical centralization of software-defined networks to enable efficient use of symmetric keys.

Furthermore, Flowrider makes key distribution agnostic of the network topology and communication patterns in the system, of which it does not require any early knowledge. Finally, Flowrider is compatible with the (D)TLS 1.2 and 1.3 security protocol suites, with only minor modifications to endpoint implementations. Our experimental performance evaluation shows that Flowrider requires up to an order of magnitude less CPU for a TLS session establishment. Future work will focus on the embodiment and evaluation of Flowrider in alternative protocols for secure channel establishment.

Acknowledgments. This work was financially supported in part by the Swedish Foundation for Strategic Research, with the grant RIT17-0035; by the H2020 project SIFIS-Home (Grant agreement 952652); VINNOVA and the CelticNext project CRITISEC and by the Wallenberg AI, Autonomous Systems and Software Program (WASP).

References

1. Greenberg, A., et al.: A clean slate 4D approach to network control and management. SIGCOMM Comput. Commun. Rev. **35**(5), 41–54 (2005). https://doi.org/10.1145/1096536.1096541
2. Langley, A., Hamburg, M., Turner, S.: Elliptic Curves for Security. RFC 7748, January 2016

3. Blanchet, B.: ProVerif: Cryptographic protocol verifier in the formal model (2020). https://prosecco.gforge.inria.fr/personal/bblanche/proverif/
4. Cremers, C., Horvat, M., Hoyland, J., Scott, S., van der Merwe, T.: A comprehensive symbolic analysis of TLS 1.3. In: Proceedings of the 2017 ACM SIGSAC Conference on Computer and Communications Security, pp. 1773–1788. Association for Computing Machinery, New York (2017)
5. Lin, C.-L., Sun, H.-M., Steiner, M., Hwang, T.: Three-party encrypted key exchange without server public-keys. IEEE Commun. Lett. **5**(12), 497–499 (2001)
6. Lin, C.-L., Sun, H.-M., Hwang, T.: Three-party encrypted key exchange: attacks and a solution. ACM SIGOPS Operat. Syst. Rev. **34**(4), 12–20 (2000)
7. Liu, C., Zheng, Z., Jia, K., You, Q.: Provably secure three-party password-based authenticated key exchange from RLWE. In: Heng, S.-H., Lopez, J. (eds.) ISPEC 2019. LNCS, vol. 11879, pp. 56–72. Springer, Cham (2019). https://doi.org/10.1007/978-3-030-34339-2_4
8. Cooper, D., Santesson, S., Farrell, S., Boeyen, S., Housley, R., Polk, W.: Internet X.509 Public Key Infrastructure Certificate and Certificate Revocation List (CRL) Profile. RFC 5280 (Proposed Standard), May 2008. https://doi.org/10.17487/RFC5280, https://www.rfc-editor.org/rfc/rfc5280.txt, updated by RFC 6818
9. Danny, D., Andrew, C.Y.: On the security of public key protocols. IEEE Trans. Inf. Theory **29**(2), 198–208 (1983)
10. Dodgson, D.S., Farina, R., Fontana, J.A., Johnson, R.A., Maw, D., Narisi, A.: Automated provisioning of virtual machines, January 2014, US Patent App. 13/547,148
11. Weerasiri, D., Barukh, M.C., Benatallah, B., Sheng, Q.Z., Ranjan, R.: A taxonomy and survey of cloud resource orchestration techniques. ACM Comput. Surv. 50(2) (May 2017). https://doi.org/10.1145/3054177
12. Dierks, T., Rescorla, E.: The Transport Layer Security (TLS) Protocol Version 1.2. RFC 5246 (Proposed Standard) (Aug 2008). https://doi.org/10.17487/RFC5246, https://www.rfc-editor.org/rfc/rfc5246.txt, updated by RFCs 5746, 5878, 6176, 7465, 7507, 7568, 7627, 7685, 7905, 7919
13. Drucker, N., Gueron, S.: Selfie: reflections on TLS 1.3 with PSK. J. Cryptol. **34**(3), 1–18 (2021). https://doi.org/10.1007/s00145-021-09387-y
14. Brewer, E.A.: Kubernetes and the path to cloud native. In: Proceedings of the Sixth ACM Symposium on Cloud Computing, SoCC 2015, p. 167. Association for Computing Machinery, New York (2015). https://doi.org/10.1145/2806777.2809955
15. Crockett, E., Paquin, C., Stebila, D.: Prototyping post-quantum and hybrid key exchange and authentication in TLS and SSH. In: NIST 2nd Post-Quantum Cryptography Standardization Conf. 2019, pp. 1–24. NIST, Gaithersburg (2019)
16. Moret, E., Hubbard, R., Watsen, K.A., Murthy, M., Beauchesne, N.: Systems and methods for provisioning network devices (April 2013), uS Patent 8,429,403
17. Rescorla, E., Tschofenig, H., Modadugu, N.: The Datagram Transport Layer Security (DTLS) Protocol Version 1.3, April 2021. https://tools.ietf.org/html/draft-ietf-tls-dtls13-43, work in Progress
18. Eric Rescorla: The Transport Layer Security (TLS) Protocol Version 1.3. RFC 8446 (Aug 2018). https://doi.org/10.17487/RFC8446
19. Eronen, P., Tschofenig, H.: Pre-shared key ciphersuites for transport layer security (TLS). RFC 4279 (Proposed Standard), December 2005. https://doi.org/10.17487/RFC4279. https://www.rfc-editor.org/rfc/rfc4279.txt
20. European Telecommunications Standards Institute: ETSI GS NFV-SEC 014 V3.1.1 (2018–04) - Network Functions Virtualisation (NFV) Release 3; NFV Security; Security Specification for MANO Components and Reference points (2018)

21. Selander, G.: WO/2015/002581 Key establishment for constrained resource devices (2015)
22. Yeh, H.-T., Sun, H.-M., Hwang, T.: Efficient three-party authentication and key agreement protocols resistant to password guessing attacks. J. Inf. Sci. Eng. **19**(6), 1059–1070 (2003)
23. Hardt, D.: The OAuth 2.0 Authorization Framework. RFC 6749 (Proposed Standard), October 2012. https://doi.org/10.17487/RFC6749. https://www.rfc-editor.org/rfc/rfc6749.txt, updated by RFC 8252
24. Baldini, I.: Serverless computing: current trends and open problems, pp. 1–20. Springer, Singapore (2017)
25. Damgård, I., Jakobsen, T.P., Nielsen, J.B., Pagter, J.I.: Secure key management in the cloud. In: Stam, M. (ed.) Cryptography and Coding, pp. 270–289. Springer, Heidelberg (2013)
26. Ding, J., Alsayigh, S., Lancrenon, J., Saraswathy, R.V., Snook, M.: Provably secure password authenticated key exchange based on RLWE for the post-quantum world. In: Cryptographers' Track at the RSA Conf. pp. 183–204. Springer, Cham (2017)
27. Sood, K., Shaw, J.B., Fastabend, J.R.: Technologies for secure inter-virtual network function communication, 2 August 2016, US Patent 9,407,612
28. Tamas, K., et al.: Micado, a microservice-based cloud application-level dynamic orchestrator. Future Gener. Comput. Syst. **94**, 937–946 (2019). https://doi.org/10.1016/j.future.2017.09.050
29. Thimmaraju, K., Schmid, S.: Towards Fine-Grained Billing For Cloud Networking (2020)
30. Krawczyk, H., Bellare, M., Canetti, R.: HMAC: Keyed-Hashing for Message Authentication. RFC 2104 (Informational), February 1997. https://doi.org/10.17487/RFC2104, https://www.rfc-editor.org/rfc/rfc2104.txt, updated by RFC 6151
31. Bellare, M., Rogaway, P.: Provably secure session key distribution: the three party case. In: Proceedings of the Twenty-Seventh Annual ACM Symposium on Theory of Computing, STOC 1995, pp. 57–66, Association for Computing Machinery, New York (1995)
32. Steiner, M., Tsudik, G., Waidner, M.: Refinement and extension of encrypted key exchange. ACM SIGOPS Operating Syst. Rev. **29**(3), 22–30 (1995)
33. Tiloca, M., Gehrmann, C., Seitz, L.: On improving resistance to denial of service and key provisioning scalability of the DTLS handshake. Int. J. Inf. Secur. **16**(2), 173–193 (2017)
34. Mavrogiannopoulos, N., et al.: GnuTLS Reference Manual. Samurai Media Ltd., London (2015)
35. Neuman, C., Yu, T., Hartman, S., Raeburn, K.: The Kerberos Network Authentication Service (V5). RFC 4120 (Proposed Standard), July 2005. https://doi.org/10.17487/RFC4120, https://www.rfc-editor.org/rfc/rfc4120.txt, updated by RFCs 4537, 5021, 5896, 6111, 6112, 6113, 6649, 6806, 7751, 8062, 8129
36. Open Networking Foundation: OpenFlow Switch Specification. Technical report ONF TS-025, Open Networking Foundation (March 2015), vol 1.5.1
37. Open vSwitch: Open vSwitch with SSL (2019). http://docs.openvswitch.org/en/latest/howto/ssl/
38. Paladi, N., Tiloca, M., Bideh, P.N., Hell, M.: On-demand key distribution for cloud networks. In: 2021 24th Conference on Innovation in Clouds, Internet and Networks and Workshops (ICIN), pp. 80–82 (2021). https://doi.org/10.1109/ICIN51074.2021.9385528

39. Bifulco, R., Boite, J., Bouet, M., Schneider, F.: Improving SDN with InSPired switches. In: Proceedings of the Symposium on SDN Research, SOSR 2016, pp. 11:1–11:12. ACM, New York (2016). https://doi.org/10.1145/2890955.2890962
40. Rescorla, E., Modadugu, N.: Datagram Transport Layer Security Version 1.2. RFC 6347 (Proposed Standard), January 2012. https://doi.org/10.17487/RFC6347, https://www.rfc-editor.org/rfc/rfc6347.txt, updated by RFCs 7507, 7905
41. Bellovin, S., Merritt, M.: Encrypted key exchange: password-based protocols secure against dictionary attacks. In: IEEE Symposium on Security and Privacy 0, 72, April 1992. https://doi.org/10.1109/RISP.1992.213269
42. Jain, S., et al.: B4: Experience with a globally-deployed software defined WAN. In: Proceedings of the ACM SIGCOMM 2013 Conference on SIGCOMM, SIGCOMM 2013, pp. 3–14. ACM, New York (2013). https://doi.org/10.1145/2486001.2486019
43. Martinelli, S., Nash, H., Topol, B.: Identity, Authentication, and Access Management in OpenStack: Implementing and Deploying Keystone. O'Reilly Media Inc, Sebastopol (2015)
44. Krishnan, S.P.T., Gonzalez, J.L.U.: Google Compute Engine, pp. 53–91. Apress, Berkeley (2015). https://doi.org/10.1007/978-1-4842-1004-8
45. Seedorf, J., Burger, E.: Application-Layer Traffic Optimization (ALTO) Problem Statement. RFC 5693 (Informational), October 2009. https://doi.org/10.17487/RFC5693, https://www.rfc-editor.org/rfc/rfc5693.txt
46. Selander, G., Paladi, N., Tiloca, M.: Security for distributed networking. World Intellectual Property Organization - PCT/EP2019/051456, July 2020
47. Lee, T.-F., Liu, J.-L., Sung, M.-J., Yang, S.-B., Chen, C.-M.: Communication-efficient three-party protocols for authentication and key agreement. Comput. Math. Appl. **58**(4), 641–648 (2009)
48. Chang, T.-Y., Hwang, M.S., Yang, W.-P.: A communication-efficient three-party password authenticated key exchange protocol. Inf. Sci. **181**(1), 217–226 (2011)
49. Binz, Ts., Breitenbücher, U., Kopp, O., Leymann, F.: TOSCA: portable automated deployment and management of cloud applications, pp. 527–549. Springer, New York (2014). https://doi.org/10.1007/978-1-4614-7535-4
50. Wang, H., Zhao, Y., Nag, A.: Quantum-key-distribution (qkd) networks enabled by software-defined networks (sdn). Appl. Sci. **9**(10), 2081 (2019)
51. Wouters, P., Tschofenig, H., Gilmore, J., Weiler, S., Kivinen, T.: Using Raw Public Keys in Transport Layer Security (TLS) and Datagram Transport Layer Security (DTLS). RFC 7250 (Proposed Standard), June 2014. https://doi.org/10.17487/RFC7250. https://www.rfc-editor.org/rfc/rfc7250.txt
52. Ding, Y., Horster, P.: Undetectable on-line password guessing attacks. ACM SIGOPS Operat. Syst. Rev. **29**(4), 77–86 (1995)
53. Zhu, Y., Ma, J., An, B., Cao, D.: Monitoring and billing of a lightweight cloud system based on linux container. In: 2017 IEEE 37th International Conference on Distributed Computing Systems Workshops (ICDCSW), pp. 325–329. IEEE, New York (2017)

Mobile Security and Privacy

Mobile Handset Privacy: Measuring the Data iOS and Android Send to Apple and Google

Douglas J. Leith(✉)

School of Computer Science and Statistics, Trinity College Dublin, Dublin, Ireland
doug.leith@tcd.ie

Abstract. We investigate what data iOS on an iPhone shares with Apple and what data Google Android on a Pixel phone shares with Google. We find that even when minimally configured and the handset is idle both iOS and Google Android share data with Apple/Google on average every 4.5 mins. The phone IMEI, hardware serial number, SIM serial number and IMSI, handset phone number etc. are shared with Apple and Google. Both iOS and Google Android transmit telemetry, despite the user explicitly opting out of this. When a SIM is inserted both iOS and Google Android send details to Apple/Google. iOS sends the MAC addresses of nearby devices, e.g. other handsets and the home gateway, to Apple together with their GPS location. Users have no opt out from this and currently there are few, if any, realistic options for preventing this data sharing.

Keywords: Privacy · iOS · iPhone · Google android · Google play services

1 Introduction

In this paper we investigate the data that mobile handset operating systems share with the mobile OS developer in particular what data iOS on an iPhone shares with Apple and what data Google Android on a Pixel phone shares with Google. While the privacy of mobile handsets has been much studied, most of this work has focussed on measurement of the app tracking/advertising ecosystem and much less attention has been paid to the data sharing by the handset operating system with the mobile OS developer. Handset operating systems do not operate in a standalone fashion but rather operate in conjunction with back-end infrastructure. For example, handset operating systems check for updates to protect users from exploits and malware, to facilitate running of field trials (e.g. to test new features before full rollout), to provide telemetry and so on. Hence, while people are using an iPhone the iOS operating system shares data with

This work was supported by SFI grant 16/IA/4610.

J. Garcia-Alfaro et al. (Eds.): SecureComm 2021, LNICST 399, pp. 231–251, 2021.
https://doi.org/10.1007/978-3-030-90022-9_12

Table 1. Summary of handset data shared with Apple and Google when user is not logged in.

	IMEI	Hardware serial number	SIM serial number	Phone number	Device IDs	Location	Tele-metry	Cookies	Local IP Address	Device Wifi MAC address	Nearby Wifi MAC addresses
Apple iOS	✓	✓	✓	✓	UDID, Ad ID	✓	✓	✓	✓	✗	✓
Google Android	✓	✓	✓	✓	Android ID, RDID/Ad ID, Droid-guard key	✗	✓	✓	✗	✓	✗

Apple and when using a Pixel the operating system shares data with Google, and this is part of normal operation.

We define experiments that can be applied uniformly to the handsets studied (so allowing direct comparisons) and that generate reproducible behaviour. Both Apple and Google provide services that can be, and almost always are, used in conjunction with their handsets, e.g. search (Siri, OkGoogle), cloud storage (iCloud, Google Drive), maps/location services (Apple Maps, Google Maps), photo storage/analytics (Apple Photo, Google Photos). Here we try to keep these two aspects separate and to focus on the handset operating system in itself, separate from optional services such as these. We assume a privacy-conscious but busy/non-technical user, who when asked does not select options that share data with Apple and Google but otherwise leaves handset settings at their default value.

In these tests we evaluate the data shared: (i) on first startup following a factory reset, (ii) when a SIM is inserted/removed, (iii) when a handset lies idle, (iv) when the settings screen is viewed, (v) when location is enabled/disabled, (vi) when the user logs in to the pre-installed app store. We note that these tests can be partly automated and used for handset operating system privacy bench-marking that tracks changes in behaviour over time as new software versions are released.

Table 1 summarises the main data that the handsets send to Apple and Google. This data is sent even when a user is not logged in (indeed even if they have never logged in). In addition to the data listed in this table, iOS shares with Apple the handset Bluetooth UniqueChipID, the Secure Element ID (associated with the Secure Element used for Apple Pay and contactless pay-ment) and the Wifi MAC addresses of nearby devices e.g. of other devices in a household of the home gateway. When the handset location setting is enabled these MAC addresses are also tagged with the GPS location.

Both iOS and Google Android transmit telemetry, despite the user explicitly opting out of this[1]. However, Google collects a notably larger volume of handset

---

[1] On iOS the Settings-Privacy-Analytics&Improvements option is set to off and on Google Android the Settings-Google-Usage&Diagnostics option is also set to off. We note that at the bottom of the Google text beside the "Usage&Diagnostics"

data than Apple. During the first 10 min of startup the Pixel handset sends around 1MB of data is sent to Google compared with the iPhone sending around 42 KB of data to Apple. When the handsets are sitting idle the Pixel sends roughly 1MB of data to Google every 12 h compared with the iPhone sending 52 KB to Apple i.e., Google collects around 20 times more handset data than Apple[2]. In 2020 it is estimated that in the US there are 113M iPhone users[3] and 129M Android users[4]. Assuming all of the Android users have Google Play Services enabled then scaling up our measurements suggests that in the US alone Apple collects around 5.8GB of handset data every 12 h while Google collects around 1.3TB of handset data. When the handset is idle the average time between iOS connections to Apple is 264 s, while Google Android connects to Google on average every 255 s i.e. both operating systems connect to their back-end servers on average every 4.5 min even when the handset is not being used.

With both iOS and Google Android inserting a SIM into the handset generates connections that share the SIM details with Apple/Google. Simply browsing the handset settings screen generates multiple network connections to Apple/-Google.

A number of the pre-installed apps/services are also observed to make network connections, despite never having been opened or used. In particular, on iOS these include Siri, Safari and iCloud and on Google Android these include the Youtube app, Chrome, Google Docs, Safetyhub, Google Messaging, the Clock and the Google Searchbar.

The collection of so much data by Apple and Google raises at least two major concerns. Firstly, this device data can be fairly readily linked to other data sources, e.g. once a user logs in (as they must to use the pre-installed app store) then this device data gets linked to their personal details (name, email, credit card etc.) and so potentially to other devices owned the user, shopping purchases,

---

option it says "Turning off this feature doesn't affect your device's ability to send the information needed for essential services such as system updates and security". Our data shows that the "essential" data collection is extensive, and likely at odds with reasonable user expectations.

[2] In response to initial publication of the measurements reported here Google's press response was "We identified flaws in the researcher's methodology for measuring data volume and disagree with the paper's claims that an Android device shares 20 times more data than an iPhone". We have since followed up with Google to clarify. In summary, the results presented here are correct and the methodology sound. In Google's own (unpublished) data volume measurements they include the bytes from TCP/IP headers and TCP ACKs, whereas the measurements reported here are of the data payload bytes sent, excluding these headers. While including such headers may make sense when the interest is in, for example, the impact of handset network traffic on a user's data plan usage they are largely irrelevant from a privacy perspective and in any case do not amount to a flaw in the methodology. .

[3] https://www.statista.com/statistics/236550/percentage-of-us-population-that-own-a-iphone-smartphone/.

[4] https://www.statista.com/statistics/232786/forecast-of-andrioid-users-in-the-us/.

web browsing history and so on. This is not a hypothetical concern since both Apple and Google operate payment services, supply popular web browsers and benefit commercially from advertising. Secondly, every time a handset connects with a back-end server it necessarily reveals the handset IP address, which is a rough proxy for location. The high frequency of network connections made by both iOS and Google Android (on average every 4.5 min) therefore potentially allow tracking by Apple and Google of device location over time.

With regard to mitigations, of course users also have the option of choosing to use handsets running mobile OSs other than iOS and Google Android, e.g. /e/OS Android[5]. But if they choose to use an iPhone then they appear to have no options to prevent the data sharing that we observe, i.e. they are not able to opt out. If they choose to use a Pixel phone then it is possible to startup the handset with the network connection disabled (so preventing data sharing), then to disable the various Google components (especially Google Play Services, Google Play store and the Youtube app) before enabling a network connection. In our tests this prevented the vast majority of the data sharing with Google, although of course it means that apps must be installed via an alternative store and cannot depend upon Google Play Services (we note that many popular apps are observed to complain if Google Play Services is disabled). However, further testing across a wider range of handsets and configurations is needed to confirm the viabillity of this potential mitigation. When Google Play Services and/or the Google Play store are used then this mitigation is not feasible and the data sharing with Google that we observe then appears to be unavoidable.

1.1   Ethical Disclosure

The mobile OS's studied here are deployed and in active use. Measurements of Google Play Services backend traffic were previously disclosed in [5], but the present study is broader in scope. We informed Apple and Google of our findings and delayed publication to allow them to respond. Google and Apple responded with a number of comments and clarifications, which we have incorporated into this paper. A key consideration is what mitigations are possible, and on what time scale can they be deployed. It seems likely that any changes to Apple iOS or Google Android, even if they were agreed upon, will take a considerable time to deploy and keeping handset users in the dark for along open-ended period seems incorrect.

2   Related Work

The privacy and security of mobile handsets has been the subject of a substantial literature, e.g. see [8,9] and references therein. However, there has been little work reporting on the traffic between handset operating systems and their associated backend servers. Probably closest to the present work is the recent

---

[5] https://e.foundation.

analysis of the data that web browsers share with their backend servers [4] and of the data shared by Google Play Services [5]. The latter is motivated by Covid contact tracing apps based on the Google-Apple Exposure Notification (GAEN) system, which on Android require that Google Play Services be enabled. The present work is broader in scope, but also motivated in part by this since the data shared by Apple iPhones running Covid contact tracing apps remains largely unknown. The measurements that we report here indicate that on an iPhone running a covid contact tracing app the data collection by Apple iOS is remarkably similar to that by Google Play Services on Android phones and users appear to have no option to disable this data collection by iOS.

To the best of our knowledge there has been no previous systematic work reporting measurements of the content of messages sent between iOS and its associated backend servers.

3 Threat Model: What Do We Mean by Privacy?

It is important to note that transmission of user data to backend servers is not intrinsically a privacy intrusion. For example, it can be useful to share details of the user device model/version and the locale/country of the device and this carries few privacy risks if this data is common to many users since the data itself cannot then be easily linked back to a specific user [6,11].

Issues arise, however, when data can be tied to a specific user, especially over extended durations and old/new device pairs. There are at least two main ways that this can occur. Firstly, when a user logs in, as they must to use the pre-installed app store, then this device data gets linked to their personal details (name, email, credit card etc.). Secondly, every time a handset connects with a back-end server it necessarily reveals the handset IP address which acts as a rough proxy for user location via existing geoIP services. Many studies have shown that location data linked over time can be used to de-anonymise, e.g. see [7,10] and later studies. This is unsurprising since, for example, knowledge of the work and home locations of a user can be inferred from such location data (based on where the user mostly spends time during the day and evening), and when combined with other data this information can quickly become quite revealing [10]. Pertinent factors here are (i) the presence of identifiers within transmitted messages that allow them to be linked together and (ii) the frequency with which messages are sent e.g. observing an IP address/proxy location once a day has much less potential to be revealing than observing one every few minutes.

Once device data is associated to a specific user it can then potentially be linked to other data held by Apple and Google, or by third parties. This might include other devices owned the user, shopping purchases, web browsing history and so on, and such data linkage can quickly lead to privacy breaches. This is not a hypothetical concern since both Apple and Google operate payment services and supply popular web browsers.

With these concerns in mind, two of the main questions that we try to answer in the present study are (i) What explicit identifying data does each operating system directly send to its backend servers and (ii) Does the data that each operating system transmits to backend servers potentially allow tracking of the IP address of the app instance over time.

4   Measurement Setup

4.1   Viewing Content of Encrypted Network Connections

All of the network connections we are interested in are encrypted. To inspect the content of a connection we route handset traffic via a WiFi access point (AP) that we control. We configure this AP to use mitmdump [3] as a proxy and adjust the firewall settings to redirect all WiFi HTTP/HTTPS traffic to mitmdump so that the proxying is transparent to the handset. In brief, when a process running on the handset starts a new network connection the mitmdump proxy pretends to be the destination server and presents a fake certificate for the target server. This allows mitmdump to decrypt the traffic. It then creates an onward connection to the actual target server and acts as an intermediary relaying requests and their replies between the app and the target server while logging the traffic. The setup is illustrated schematically in Fig. 1.

Fig. 1. Measurement setup. The mobile handset is configured to access the internet using a WiFi access point hosted on a laptop, use of cellular/mobile data is disabled. The laptop also has a wired internet connection. When an app on the handset starts a new network connection the laptop pretends to be the destination server so that it can decrypt the traffic. It then creates an onward connection to the actual target server and acts as an intermediary relaying requests and their replies between the handset app and the target server while logging the traffic.

The immediate difficulty encountered when using this setup is that handset system processes typically carry out checks on the authenticity of server certificates received when starting a new connection and abort the connection when these checks fail. To circumvent these checks we root/jailbreak each handset and configure it as follows:

Apple iOS. Cydia substrate is installed on a jailbroken iPhone and a custom substrate script is used to carry out bypass SSL certificate pinning within handset processes. On launch of a process this script is run and modifies the implementations of the SSL_se_custom_verify and SSL_get_psk_identity methods within the /usr/liblibboringssl.dylib library to bypass SSL certificate checks. This script is invoked on launch of all processes that make use of the com.apple.AuthKit, com.apple.UIKit and com.apple.aps.framework frameworks and also the following processes: com.apple.softwareupdated, com.apple.AssetCacheLocatorService, com.apple.imfoundation. IMRemoteURLConnectionAgent, com.apple.mobileactivationd, com. apple.itunescloudd, com.apple.identityservicesd, com.apple.akd, com.apple.itunesstored. The mitmproxy CA cert is also installed on the handset as a trusted certificate.

Google Android. On Android it is sufficient to install the mitmproxy CA cert as a trusted certificate in order to pass the SSL certificate checks carried out by Google Play Services and other system apps. However, unlike with iOS installing a trusted CA cert on Android requires rooting the phone. In Android 10 the system disk partition on which trusted certs are stored is read-only and security measures prevent it being mounted as read-write. Fortunately, folders within the system disk partition can be overriden by creating a new mount point corresponding to the folder, and in this way the mitmdump CA cert can be added to the /system/etc./security/cacerts folder.

4.2 Additional Material: Connection Data

The content of connections is summarised and annotated in the additional material available anonymously at https://www.dropbox.com/s/qaazwyaj2ihj4qa/apple_google_additional_material.pdf.

4.3 Hardware and Software Used

Mobile handsets: Google Pixel 2 running Android 10 (build QP1A.190711.019 with Google Play Services ver. 20.45.16 and Google Play ver. 23.0.11-21) rooted using Magisk v20.4 and Magisk Manager v7.5.1 and running Frida Server v12.5.2, Apple iPhone 8[6] running iOS 13.6.1 (17G80) and jailbroken using Checkra1n 0.10.2 and running Cydia 0.9. Laptop: Apple Macbook running Mojav 10.14.6 running Frida 12.8.20 and mitmproxy v5.0.1. Using a USB ethernet adapter the laptop is connected to a cable modem and so to the internet. The laptop

---

[6] We were constrained to use a pre-A12 iPhone as in later models a soft bootloader is used which Apple have patched to prevent jailbreaking. Similarly, we were prevented from using iOS 14 on the handset since no iOS 14 jailbreaks were available when we carried out our measurements. Recently, it has become possible to jailbreak iOS 14 on rather old hardware (iPhone 6's and earlier) but we leave collecting iOS14 to future work.

is configured using its built in Internet Sharing function to operate as a WiFi AP that routes wireless traffic over the wired connection. The laptop firewall is then configured to redirect received WiFi traffic to mitmproxy listening on port 8080 by adding the rule `rdr pass on bridge100 inet proto tcp to any port 80, 443 -> 127.0.0.1 port 8080`. Note that (i) at the firewall we blocked UDP traffic on port 443 so as to force any QUIC traffic to fall back to using TCP since we have no tools for decrypting QUIC, (ii) iOS uses port 5223 for Apple Push Notifications but we did not inspect this traffic, (iii) similarly Google Cloud Messaging uses port 5228 and (iv) both handsets use NTP and DNS. The handset is also connected to the laptop over USB and this is used as a control channel (no data traffic is routed over this connection). On iOS this is used to install the Cydia substrate script for bypassing SSL pinning within the system processes and on Android a root adb shell is used to install the mitmproxy CA cert on the handset as a trusted cert.

4.4   Device Settings

Apple iOS. Following a factory reset it is not possible to proceed with startup without first connecting the handset to a network, see Fig. 2(b) (there is no option to skip/continue). Connecting the handset to a WiFi network and proceeding, the user is presented with a number of option screens. Since our focus is on a privacy-conscious user we did not select any of the options that share data with Apple (we note that the opt-in options were always placed first and prominently highlighted while the opt-out option was de-emphasised, e.g. see Fig. 2(c) for a typical example). Specifically, (i) on the "Apps & Data" screen we selected the "Don't Transfer Apps & Data" option, (ii) on the "Keep Your iPhone Up to Date" screen we selected "Install Updates Manually", (iii) on the "Location Services" screen we selected "Disable Location Services", (iv) on the "Siri" and

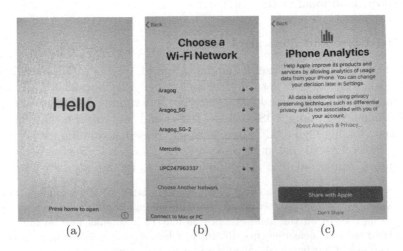

Fig. 2. Selected startup screens observed following iPhone factory reset.

"Screen Time" screens we selected "Set Up Later in Settings", (v) on the "iPhone Analytics" screen we selected "Don't Share" (see Fig. 2(c)). We did not log in to an Apple user account during the startup process, although the option was given to do this.

Google Android. Unlike with iOS, on Android following a factory reset it is possible to proceed with startup with and without a network connection. We collected data for both choices. Similarly to iOS, during startup the user is presented with a number of option screens and once again we did not select any of the options that share data with Google (we note that all of the option toggle switches default to the opt-in choice, and so it is necessary for the user to actively select to opt-out, e.g. see Fig. 3(c) for a typical example). Specifically, we deselected the (i) "Free up space" option, (ii) "Use location" option, (iii) "Allow scanning" option and (iv) the "Send usage and diagnostic data" option, see Fig. 3(c). Note that there is no option to deselect automatic updates, see the text shown at the bottom of the screen in Fig. 3(c). We did not log in to an Google user account during the startup process

4.5   Test Design

We seek to define simple experiments that can be applied uniformly to the handsets studied (so allowing direct comparisons) and that generate repoducible behaviour. Both Apple and Google provide services that can be used in conjunction with their handsets, e.g. search (Siri, OkGoogle), cloud storage (iCloud, Google Drive), maps/location services (Apple Maps, Google Maps), photo storage/analytics (Apple Photo, Google Photos). Here we try to keep these two aspects separate and to focus on the handset as a device in itself, separate

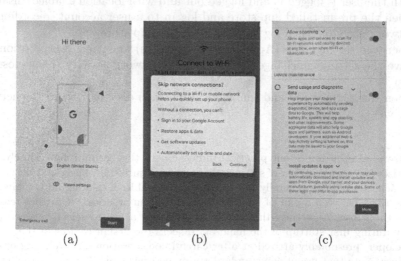

(a)   (b)   (c)

Fig. 3. Selected startup screens observed following Google Pixel 2 factory reset.

from optional services such as these. We also assume a privacy-conscious but busy/non-technical user, who when asked does not select options that share data with Apple and Google but otherwise leaves handset settings at their default values[7].

One important caveat is that while both Apple and Google provide an app store (Apple App Store, Google Play store), on iOS handsets the Apple App Store is the only way to install public apps whereas on Android handsets use of the Google Play store is optional, at least in principle, and other app stores can be used plus users have the option to directly install apps via the adb shell. Since confining users to pre-installed system apps is overly restrictive, the Apple App Store is not really an optional service on iPhones and we therefore include it in our tests. Note that use of the Apple App Store requires a user to log in to an Apple account, and so disclose their email address and other personal details. Because of this, for comparison we also consider the Google Play store (which also requires log in to a Google account and disclosure of a user's email address).

A second caveat is that on iPhones the pre-installed Apple Settings app must be used to configure device settings (e.g. to enable/disable location), and similarly on Android the Google Settings app must be used. Since these settings apps are not optional for handset users we also include them in our tests.

With these considerations in mind, for each handset we carry out the following experiments:

1. Start the handset following a factory reset (mimicking a user receiving a new phone), recording the network activity.
2. Remove and re-insert SIM, recording the network activity.
3. Following startup, leave the handset untouched for several days (with power cable connected) and record the network activity. This allows us to measure the connections made when the handset is sitting idle. This test is repeated with the user is logged in and logged out and with location enabled/disabled.
4. Open the pre-installed app store and log in to a user account, recording the network activity. Then log out and close the app store app.
5. Open the settings app (Apple/Google Settings) and view every option but leave the settings unchanged, recording the network activity. Then close the app.
6. Open the settings app and enable location, then disable. Record the network activity.

---

[7] There is also an important practical dimension to this assumption. Namely, each handset has a wide variety of settings that can be adjusted by a user and the settings on each handset are generally not directly comparable. Exploring all combinations of settings between a pair of handsets is therefore impractical. A further reason is that the subset of settings that a user is explicitly asked to select between (typically during first startup of the handset) reflects the design choices of the handset developer, presumably arrived at after careful consideration and weighing of alternatives. Note that use of non-standard option settings may also expose the handset to fingerprinting.

4.6   Finding Identifiers in Network Connections

Potential identifiers in network connections were extracted by manual inspection. Basically any value present in network messages that stays the same across messages is flagged as a potential identifier. Where possible we try to find more information on the nature of observed values from public documents, e.g. Apple and Google documentation, as well as by comparing them against known software and device identifiers e.g. the hardware serial number and IMEI of the handset. However, we note that there is little public documentation of the internal APIs between handset processes and their back-end servers and public privacy policy documents also tend to lack the necessary level of detail. We also contacted both Apple and Google for clarification of identifiers and data sent.

5   Startup Following Factory Reset of Handset

5.1   Apple iOS

Upon first startup, the iOS handset initially makes a series of connections to the sa.apple.com/grandslam endpoint. In the first connection the handset sends its Unique Device Identifier (UDID) via the X-Mme-Device-Id header value (this value persists across a factory reset). In the next connection the handset sends its hardware serial number together with the UDID, acting to link the two:

```
POST https://gsa.apple.com/grandslam/MidService/startMachineProvisioning
Headers
  X-Apple-Client-App-Name: Setup
  X-Apple-I-SRL-NO: C8PVCB1HJC67          //Handset hardware serial number
  X-MMe-Client-Info: <iPhone10,4> <iPhone OS;13.6.1;17G80> <com.apple.akd/1.0 (com
.apple.akd/1.0)>
  X-Mme-Device-Id: 7c2694081d97b...12dc5bc5    //UUID
  User-Agent: akd/1.0 CFNetwork/1128.0.1 Darwin/19.6.0
```

Later during the startup process the local IP address of the handset (i.e. not of the gateway, but of the handset itself) is sent in a POST request to /lcdn-locator.apple.com:

```
POST https://lcdn-locator.apple.com/lcdn/locate
Headers
  User-Agent: AssetCacheLocatorService/111 CFNetwork/1128.0.1 Darwin/19.6.0
POST body
{"locator-tag":"#eefc633e","local-addresses":["192.168.2.6"],"ranked-results":true
,"locator-software":[{"build":"17G80","type":"system","name":"iPhone OS","version
":"13.6.1"},{"id":"com.apple.AssetCacheLocatorService","executable":"
AssetCacheLocatorService",<...>
```

A connection to https://humb.apple.com/humbug/baa sends a base64 encoded payload that decodes to XML from com.apple.bluetoothd which contains the handset hardware serial number and a UniqueChipID value:

```
<...><key>AppID</key>
    <string>com.apple.bluetoothd</string>
<...><key>SerialNumber</key>
    <string>C8PVCB1HJC67</string> //Handset hardware serial number
    <key>UniqueChipID</key>
    <integer>2577607982549050</integer><...>
```

The `UniqueChipID` value is not the handset ECID (Exclusive Chip Identification) value[8], the unique serial number of the handset system-on-a-chip (SoC) hardware which is also sometimes referred to as the "Unique Chip ID".

A connection to `smp-device-content.apple.com/static/region/v2/config.json` shares the handset SEID (Secure Element ID) with Apple via header `x-apple-seid`:

```
GET https://smp-device-content.apple.com/static/region/v2/config.json
Headers
   X-Apple-I-MD-RINFO: 17106176
   X-Apple-I-MD-M: 5ekJNohUcJUP1EFYFrRt...myO+0J71jk6EljMp
   X-Apple-I-MD: AAAABQAAA...SjbTAAAAAw==
   User-Agent: Setup/1.0 CFNetwork/1128.0.1 Darwin/19.6.0
   x-apple-soc-type: t8015
   X-Apple-Web-Service-Session: 486081CF-EDD9-4B65-B5D3-0628E298C7D7
   x-apple-seid: 046E4BABBA4280017207172230942566E22AD196DF33D24C
```

The SEID identifies the secure element embedded in the NFC chip used by Apple Pay for contactless payment.

Despite selecting the 'Don't Share" option on the "iPhone Analytics" screen during the startup process, telemetry data is sent to `xp.apple.com/report/2/psr_ota`.

During the startup process 2.6GB of data is downloaded to the handset, a substantial quantity that appeared to consist mainly of software updates to the pre-installed apps. We observed roughly 42 KB of data sent to Apple servers (via URL parameters, headers and POST data).

5.2   Google Android

Upon startup the first connection that the Android handset makes that sends data is to Google Analytics endpoint `app-measurement.com`:

```
GET https://app-measurement.com/config/app/1%3A286455739530%3Aandroid%3
A4a942425ed36c2fa?app_instance_id=93a09622...1ee8f0e52&platform=android&
gmp_version=17786
```

The app instance id that is sent is linked to the device RDID (Resettable Device Identifier or so-called Ad ID, used for measurement and ads[9]) in a later call to `app-measurement.com`. The next connection is made by the Droid-Guard process (used for device attestation, part of Google's SafetyNet service), which send the device hardware serial number (which persists across a factory reset) to www.googleapis.com/androidantiabuse. The device RDID is now sent to www.gstatic.com and `app-measurement.com`. Early in the startup process a call is made to `youtubei.googleapis.com/deviceregistration` that sends a rawDeviceId value and in due course a call to the `android.clients.google.com/checkin` endpoint is made:

---

[8] By connecting the device to a macbook laptop then itunes reports the ECID as 9285220B9893A, which when converted to decimal is 2577607991855418. It can be seen that this is similar to the UniqueChipID, but not the same.

[9] See https://developers.google.com/ads-data-hub/guides/rdid-matching.

```
POST https://android.clients.google.com/checkin
POST body decoded as protobuf:
<...>
7: 85879...846810 // Google loggingId
9: "e60d...158" // Wifi Mac Address
10: "357...984248" // IMEI
11: ""
12: "Europe/Dublin"
14: 3
15: "bfMkwy...c2WT62otR8JkI=" //SHA-1 of OTA certs
16: "HT7A...4090" //Handset hardware serial number
<...>
24: "CgZmMZ-F5fTSEEAA...MFUwYaZqw" //Droidguard device key
<...>
```

This shares the handset Wifi MAC address, its hardware serial number and IMEI, effectively linking these three persistent device identifiers together. A subsequent call to android.clients.google.com/checkin further links these values to the Google AndroidId (a persistent device identifier that requires a factory reset to change) and a variety of security tokens[10]. The Droidguard device key is a large, opaque binary message: the contents are intentionally obfuscated by Google and it remains unclear whether it contains device/user identifiers[11].

Cookies are sent in a number of calls, starting with one to fonts.gstatic.com and then to play.googleapis.com (this call includes the AndroidId and so links that with the cookie).

Despite deselecting the "Send usage and diagnostic data" option during the startup process, a substantial quantity (approximately 1.2 MB) of telemetry/logging data is sent by the handset to play.googleapis.com/log/batch and play.googleapis.com/play/log. The handset also sends 1.1 MB of device data to www.googleapis.com/experimentsandconfigs and 181 KB to android.clients.google.com/checkin. In total, around 3.6 MB of data is sent to Google servers (via URL parameters, headers and POST data), see Fig. 4(a), and 952 MB of data are received. That is, almost two orders of magnitude more data is uploaded by Android (3.6 MB) than by iOS (42 KB) during startup, while Android downloads around a third (952 MB) of the data of iOS (2.6 GB).

6 Connections Made When Handset Is Idle

6.1 Apple iOS

When the iPhone is left idle, roughly every 2–3 days it sends data to gsas.apple.com/grandslam:

---

[10] There is a Google help page [1] for the /checkin endpoint with partial information on the data sent and the microG project [2] has also partially reverse-engineered the data format used by this endpoint (there is no documentation, but microG is open source). Our measurements are consistent with both of those.

[11] https://github.com/microg/GmsCore/issues/1139.

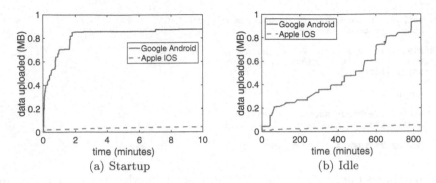

Fig. 4. Volume of data uploaded to Google and Apple servers (a) during first 10 min of startup after factory reset and (b) when handset lies idle.

```
POST https://gsas.apple.com/grandslam/GsService2/postdata
Headers
   User-Agent: akd/1.0 CFNetwork/1128.0.1 Darwin/19.6.0
   X-Apple-I-UrlSwitch-Info: MDAxMDI5LTA...GFOYQ== // x-apple-adsid base64 encoded
   X-Apple-HB-Token: MDAxMDI5LTA1LTk...5XN3dnPTO= // x-apple-adsid base64 encoded
   X-Mme-Device-Id: 7c2694081d...71412dc5bc5 //UDID
   X-Apple-I-MD-RINFO: 17106176
   X-Apple-I-SRL-NO: C8PVCB1HJC67 //Handset hardware serial number
   X-Apple-I-MD-M: 5ekJNohU...YjL2Z //Anisette machineID¹²
   X-Apple-I-MD: AAAABQAA...AAAAw==
POST body
<...>
          <key>iccid</key>
          <string>8935311180135555145</string> // SIM Integrated Circuit Card
Identifier
          <key>imei</key>
          <string>356765081821496</string> //Handset IMEI
<...>    <key>number</key>
                    <string>+35389...97590</string> // Handset phone number
<...>  <key>pn</key>
          <string>+35389...97590</string>
<...>  <key>ptkn</key>
          <string>7534B939D....6E2750CB0FD0</string>
<...>  <key>sn</key>
          <string>C8PVCB1HJC67</string> //Handset hardware serial number
<...>
```

It can be seen that this message sends (and links together) many handset identifiers including: the handset hardware serial number, the handset UDID, the IMEI, the SIM serial number, the handset phone number, the Apple advertising ID plus the X-Apple-I-MD-M security token/anisette machine identifier.

In addition, the handset makes a number of unexpected connections:

1. Although the user is not logged in to an Apple account (and so the Apple App Store cannot be used) periodic connections are made to init.itunes.apple.com and bag.itunes.apple.com that send a cookie that can act as a device identifier.
2. Similarly, since the user is logged out icloud is unused yet connections are made to icloud services that send device identifiers, including the handset UDID.

3. Although Siri is not enabled on the handset, connections are made to server smoot.apple.com by the parsecd process associated with Siri. When a URL is typed in Safari, corresponding telemetry logging the URL is sent to smoot.apple.com. Again, this occurs despite the fact that Apple telemetry is disabled in the device settings.

4. Although use of location is disabled, the locationd and geod processes associated with location services in the handset periodically make network connections. The locationd process downloads files that likely relate to GPS chipset settings, with no unique device identifiers sent. However, the geod process uploads binary messages to gsp85-ssl.ls.apple.com:

```
POST https://gsp57-ssl-locus.ls.apple.com/dispatcher.arpc
Headers
   User-Agent: geod/1 CFNetwork/1128.0.1 Darwin/19.6.0
POST body
\x00\x01\x00\x08en-IE_IE\x00\x0ecom.apple.geod\x00\x...ff8:4:2e:c:1c:28\x10\xa
...&\n\x0f8c:4:ff:13:2:9e\x10\xb...\x1170:4d:7b:95:14:c0\x10\...n\x11
70:4d:7b:95:14:c8\x10\xc0...\x10f2:18:98:92:17:5\x10...
```

It can be seen to contain the MAC addresses of nearby devices sharing the same WiFi network as the handset e.g. f2:18:98:92:17:5 is the WiFi MAC address of a nearby laptop, 70:4d:7b:95:14:c0 the MAC address of the WiFi access point. WiFi MAC addresses are known to be a sensitive device identifier, actively used for device tracking, and this has led to the introduction of MAC address dynamic randomisation in newer devices. However, the WiFi access point MAC address is typically static. While it is not clear what other information is contained in this binary message, Apple say that it does not contain any persistent device/user identifiers, only a single-use identifier used to manage duplicate messages. Note, however, that the message is necessarily tagged with the handset IP address and so can potentially be linked to other handset messages which do contain device/user identifiers, although there is no suggestion that Apple actually do this.

5. Despite selecting the 'Don't Share" option on the "iPhone Analytics" screen during the startup process, telemetry is sent to xp.apple.com. The message sent contains a cookie that links the telemetry to the user's Apple account DSID (a unique account identifier).

In addition, connections made by the adprivacyd process, which appears related to managing advertising settings, also send a cookie and transmit an opaque binary message.

The Safari browser makes periodic connections to the Google Safe Browsing anti-phishing service and connections are made to mesu.apple.com that appear to be checking for updates. However, no unique device identifiers appear to be sent in these connections [4].

When the handset is idle the average time between iOS connections to Apple servers is observed to be 264 s i.e. less than 5 min.

Inserting SIM into Handset. When a SIM is inserted the handset sends SIM identifiers to albert.apple.com:

```
POST https://albert.apple.com/deviceservices/activity/phoneNumberSimNotification
Headers
   User-Agent: CommCenter/7581 CFNetwork/1128.0.1 Darwin/19.6.0
POST body
<...>  <key>InternationalMobileEquipmentIdentity</key>
       <string>356765081821496</string> // IMEI
       <key>InternationalMobileSubscriberIdentity</key>
       <string>2721101</string>
       <key>PhoneNumber</key>
       <string>089...97590</string> // Phone number
       <key>SerialNumber</key>
       <string>C8PVCB1HJC67</string> // Handset hardware serial number
       <key>UniqueDeviceID</key>
       <string>7c2694081d97b76...2dc5bc5</string> //Handset UDID
<...>
```

Enabling Location. When location is enabled in the handset settings, additional handset network connections are made. In particular:

```
POST https://gsp10-ssl.apple.com/hcy/pbcwloc
Headers
   User-Agent: locationd/2394.0.33 CFNetwork/1128.0.1 Darwin/19.6.0
POST body decoded as protobuf:
<...>
 1: "f2:18:98:92:17:5" // Wifi MAC address of nearby device
 2: 11
 3: 18446744073709551584
 4 {
   1: 0x404aa..c4edd17953 // hex encoded handset latitude
   2: 0xc0193..5ed5618f3 // hex encoded handset longitude
<...>
```

The POST body not only contains a list of MAC addresses of devices sharing the same WiFi network as the handset but a pair of hex values that when converted to doubles give the latitude and longitude of the handset (accurate to within 10m of the true position). Similarly to the /dispatcher.arpc endpoint noted above, Apple say that this /pbcwloc message does not contain any persistent device/user identifiers, only a single-use identifier used to manage duplicate messages. The handset IP address is, however, still sent with the message and can potentially act as a device identifier. Note also that it takes only one device to tag a home gateway/WiFi hotspot MAC address with its GPS location and thereafter the location of all other messages reporting that MAC address is revealed, even if location is turned off on the handset.

In addition, connections to api-glb-dub.smoot.apple.com send a X-Apple-FuzzedLatLong header with the approximate device location (latitude and longitude) .

6.2 Google Android

When the Google Pixel 2 is left idle, roughly every 6 h it makes a connection to android.googleapis.com/checkin that sends many device identifiers:

```
POST https://android.googleapis.com/checkin
Headers
   Cookie: NID=204=sa8sIUm5eJ9...NabihZ3RNI
POST body decoded as protobuf:
```

```
 2: 3876027569814251330 //AndroidId
<...>
 6: "27205" //Mobile operator
 7: "27211" //SIM operator
 8: "WIFI::"
<...>
16 {
   1: "27211" //SIM operator
   2: "Tesco Mobile" //Mobile carrier
<...>
   6: "272110103800000" //SIM IMSI, uniquely identifies caller on cellular network
   7: "0AFFFFFFFFFFFFFFFFFFFFFFFFFFFFFFFFFFFFFF" //Mobile Group ID Level 1
   8: "\025\345" //SHA-256 hash of SIM IMSI
<...>
 9: "e60d4b46d158" //Wifi MAC address
10: "357537080984248" //IMEI
11: "" //When user is logged in this reports the user email address
12: "Europe/Dublin"
13: 0x41559e6d59911873  //Security token
14: 3
15: "bFMkwynjHzXGBPc2WT62otR8JkI="
16: "HT7AC1A04090" //Handset hardware serial number
<...>
24: "CgYqtj3OocES-2UKBoGpQIpsRtIQQA...Sy6P2voE9Sz" //Droidguard device key
<...>
```

In many ways this is akin to the iOS connection to gsas.apple.com/ grandslam/GsService2/postdata discussed above. The set of identifiers shared is slightly different, but the connection acts to link to together multiple long-lived device identifiers including the handset hardware serial number and IMEI, the SIM IMSI/serial number. In addition to these the android.googleapis.com/checkin connection shares the AndroidId (a persistent device identifier that requires a factory reset to change), the user email address (when the user is logged in). the handset Wifi MAC address, the opaque Droidguard binary device key and also tags these with a cookie.

The handset also connects regularly to Google's SafetyNet device attestation service at www.googleapis.com and to what seems to be Google's A/B testing infrastructure at www.googleapis.com/experimentsandconfigs. The SafetyNet connections send the hardware serial number, RDID device identifier (associated with advertising/measurement) and the Droidguard device key while the A/B testing connections send a cookie and authentication token together with device details.

Despite deselecting the "Send usage and diagnostic data" option during the startup process the handset sends a substantial volume of telemetry/logging data to Google servers, see Fig. 4(b). This occurs mainly to two endpoints, namely play.googleapis.com/log/batch and play.googleapis.com/play/log. The first is associated with Google Play Services and the second with the Google Play store app. Data is sent every 10–20 minutes, and sometimes more frequently. Logging/telemetry data sent to play.googleapis.com/log/batch is tagged with device AndroidId and an authentication token but the content is largely opaque (binary protobufs with complex structure). The messages sent to play.googleapis.com/log/batch appear to be aggregated from multiple logging sources, see Table 2 for a list of their names. The CARRIER_SERVICES and ANDROID_DIALER logging sources are observed to send details of mobile operator and phone number, amongst other things[12].

Table 2. Logging sources observed in play.googleapis.com/log/batch telemetry.

```
CARRIER_SERVICES, ANDROID_DIALER, ONEGOOGLE_MOBILE, GOOGLE_NOW_LAUNCHER, DRIVE,
COPRESENCE_NO_IDS, AUTOFILL_WITH_GOOGLE, SCOOBY_EVENTS, SCOOBY_EVENT_LOG, BEACON_
GCORE, NETREC, BRELLA, GOOGLE_HELP, PHOTOS, CALENDAR, CALENDAR_UNIFIED_SYNC, BUSINESS_
VOICE, IDENTITY_FRONTEND, GMS_CORE_PEOPLE, LATIN_IME, DL_FONTS, CAR, ICING, ACTIVITY_
RECOGNITION, ANDROID_CONTACTS, ANDROID_GROWTH, ANDROID_GSA, CLIENT_LOGGING_PROD,
GOOGLETTS, CAST_SENDER_SDK, ANDROID_VERIFY_APPS, ANDROID_DIALER, ANDROID_BACKUP,
ANDROID_MESSAGING, ANDROID_OTA, ANDROID_GMAIL, ANDROID_SNET_GCORE, GAL_PROVIDER,
GLAS, TACHYON_LOG_REQUEST, CLEARCUT_FUNNEL, CLEARCUT_LOG_LOSS, DIALER_ANDROID_PRIMES,
CARRIER_SERVICES_ANDROID_PRIMES, TURBO_ANDROID_PRIMES, PHOTOS_ANDROID_PRIMES,
ANDROID_MESSAGING_PRIMES, GOOGLETTS_ANDROID_PRIMES, SETTINGS_INTELLIGENCE_ANDROID_
PRIMES, ANDROID_GSA_ANDROID_PRIMES, SAFETYHUB_ANDROID_PRIMES, WIFI_ASSISTANT_PRIMES,
DRIVE_ANDROID_PRIMES, GMAIL_ANDROID_PRIMES, STREAMZ_ANDROID_GROWTH, STREAMZ_ANDROID_
GSA, STREAMZ_ONEGOOGLE_ANDROID, STREAMZ_HERREVAD, STREAMZ_CALENDAR, STREAMZ_PHOTOS_
ANDROID, STREAMZ_ANDROID_AUTH_ACCOUNT, STREAMZ_GELLER, STREAMZ_NGA, BUGLE_COUNTERS,
PSEUDONYMOUS_ID_COUNTERS, GMAIL_COUNTERS, WESTWORLD_COUNTERS, GOOGLE_KEYBOARD_
COUNTERS, ANDROID_CONTACTS_COUNTERS, WALLPAPER_PICKER_COUNTERS, PLATFORM_STATS_
COUNTERS
```

The messages sent to play.googleapis.com/play/log are tagged with the AndroidId and RDID persistent device identifiers.

Several pre-installed system apps make regular network connections that share device identifiers and details:

1. The Nexus launcher searchbar connects to www.google.com/complete/search using a cookie and events related to the app are logged by Google Analytics app-measurement.com.
2. The Clock app connects to Google Analytics ssl.google-analytics.com/batch.
3. The SafetyHub app periodically connects with Google's Firebase service at android.clients.google.com, sending the device AndroidId and the app FirebaseId
4. The Youtube app makes connections to youtubei.googleapis.com/youtubei/v1/account
   and youtubei.googleapis.com/youtubei/v1/log_event, both send a device identifier and an authentication token. The Youtube app (or a process on its behalf) also makes connections to www.googleadservices.com, sending the RDID device identifier used for advertsing. In addition, the Youtube app makes periodic probe connections to i.ytimg.com/generate_204 and youtubei.googleapis.com/generate_204.
5. The Chrome browser app makes periodic connections to the Google Safe Browsing anti-phishing service safebrowsing.googleapis.com and the Chrome update service pdate.googleapis.com. It also connects to accounts.google.com. No identifiers are sent.

---

[12] Google have since told us that on foot of our recent GAEN measurement study [5] version V52I and later of the CARRIER_SERVICES log source no longer transmit the handset phone number.

6. The Google Docs and Messaging apps (or a process on its behalf) connect to `growth-pa.googleapis.com/google.internal.identity.growth.` `v1.GrowthApiService/GetPromos`, sending device details but no unique identifiers.

7. Connections are made to `mobilenetworkscoring-pa.googleapis.` `com/v1/GetWifiQuality` that may include a device identifier (via the X-Client-Data header). The purpose of this connection is unclear.

When the handset is idle the average time between Android connections to Google servers is observed to be 255 s i.e. similar to the 264 s observed for iOS.

Inserting SIM into Handset. When a SIM is inserted into the handset a connection is made to `android.clients.google.com/fdfe/` `uploadDynamicConfig` that sends the SIM IMSI (which uniquely identifies a caller on the cellular network) and links this to the AndoidId:

```
POST https://android.clients.google.com/fdfe/uploadDynamicConfig
Headers
   user-agent: Android-Finsky/22.8.42-21<...>
   x-dfe-device-id: 35ca6a89e6662742 // hex-encoded AndroidId
   x-dfe-device-config-token: CisaKQoT...4MTQyMzM1
   x-dfe-device-checkin-consistency-token: ABFEt1VpT4...Cnef2U7bDsS2p
   x-dfe-phenotype: H4sIAAAAA...9cD-bQEAAA
   x-dfe-encoded-targets: CAESGLOVg...oE5ALQ+64G
POST body decoded as protobuf:
<...>
   1: 272110103800000 // SIM IMSI
   2: "Tesco Mobile" // Mobile carrier
   3: "0AFFFFFFFFFFFFFFFFFFFFFFFFFFFFFFFFFFFFFFFF" // Mobile Group ID Level 1
   4: "tescomobile.liffeytelecom.com" // Mobile carrier APN
<...>
   4: "dHVKO5LRPfOs71S8ynLFp9:..qXOTpK9e" '// Firebase id of Google Play store app
<...>
```

In addition, connections are made to `android.googleapis.com/` `checkin` and `/play.googleapis.com/log/batch`. The connection to `android.googleapis.com/checkin` shares the handset IMEI and SIM IMSI plus mobile carrier details with Google and links these to the AndroidId, handset hardware serial number, Wifi MAC address and a cookie. The connection to `/play.googleapis.com/log/batch`

```
POST https://play.googleapis.com/log/batch
Headers
   x-server-token: CAESKQDyi0h8ELN...KGowA
   user-agent: com.google.android.gms/204516037 <...>
   cookie: NID=204=VBQLUjKJOc3FW...X-1C0Ro // Cookie
POST body decoded as protobuf:
<...>
   1: 3876027569814251330 // AndroidId
  <...>
   5: "\324\020\010...(48.0.335972766-carrierservices\_V48E\_RC01
\032\'\010\340\203\273 \022 6.8.076 (Ent\_RC11.phone\_dynamic)2C\n
\003272\022\00211\032\014Tesco
Mobile\"(0AFFFFFFFFFFFFFFFFFFFFFFFFFFFFFFFFFFFFFFFF(\000\3...\n\r+35389...7590r
/\010..."\230\001\001"
   6: "CARRIER\_SERVICES"
   7: "204=VBQLUjKJOc3FWJoecvEe...X-1C0Ro" // Cookie
<other telemetry>
```

The +35389...7590 value is the handset phone number, the mobile carrier details are also sent.

Enabling Location. When the user is logged out and location is enabled no additional handset network connections are observed.

7   Connections When Interacting with Settings App

7.1   Apple iOS

When the Settings app is opened and the various options viewed (but not changed), this action generates multiple network connections:

1. A connection is made to idiagnostics.apple.com that sends the handset hardware serial number
2. Telemetry is sent to xp.apple.com.
3. The adprivacyd process makes connections to cf.iadsdk.apple.com/adserver/2.6/config, iadsdk.apple.com/adserver/2.6/optout/optout_optin and bag.itunes.apple.com. The connection to bag.itunes.apple.com sends a cookie.
4. The geod process makes connections to gspe35-ssl.ls.apple.com/geo_manifest/dynamic/config, gsp-ssl.ls.apple.com/ab.arpc and gsp64-ssl.ls.apple.com/hvr/v3/use. The latter two connections transmit binary messages which are largely opaque but which can be seen to contain SIM mobile carrier details, amongst other things.
5. The gamed process makes connections to init.gc.apple.com, static.gc.apple.com, profile.gc.apple.com. The latter two connections send authentication tokens that are linked to the device.
6. The Preferences agent makes connections to init.itunes.apple.com and play.itunes.apple.com which send authentication tokens that are linked to the device.

7.2   Google Android

When the Settings app is opened and a user navigates amongst the various options the following network connections are observed:

1. The helprtc process makes connections to firebaseinstallations.googleapis.com and android.clients.google.com. These send the Firebase Id and the device Android Id.
2. A connection is made to pagead2.googlesyndication.com that appears to send identifiers
3. Telemetry is sent to www.google.com. This is tagged with the device Android Id, the phone IMEI and includes mobile carrier details as well as information on the radio signal strength, battery level, volume settings, number of handset reboots, whether the phone is rooted.

8   Summary

We investigate what data iOS on an iPhone shares with Apple and what data Google Android on a Pixel phone shares with Google. We find that even when minimally configured and the handset is idle both iOS and Google Android share data with Apple/Google on average every 4.5 mins. The phone IMEI, hardware serial number, SIM serial number and IMSI, handset phone number etc. are shared with Apple and Google. Both iOS and Google Android transmit telemetry, despite the user explicitly opting out of this. When a SIM is inserted both iOS and Google Android send details to Apple/Google. iOS sends the MAC addresses of nearby devices, e.g. other handsets and the home gateway, to Apple together with their GPS location. Currently there are few, if any, realistic options for preventing this data sharing.

References

1. Learn about the Android Device Configuration Service, Google Help Pages. https://support.google.com/android/answer/9021432?hl=en. Accessed 5 Aug 2020
2. microG Project. https://microg.org/. Accessed 5 Aug 2020
3. Cortesi, A., Hils, M., Kriechbaumer, T., contributors: mitmproxy: A free and open source interactive HTTPS proxy (v5.01) (2020). https://mitmproxy.org/
4. Leith, D.J.: Web browser privacy: what do browsers say when they phone home? IEEE Access (2021). https://doi.org/10.1109/ACCESS.2021.3065243
5. Leith, D.J., Farrell, S.: Contact tracing app privacy: what data is shared By Europe's GAEN contact tracing apps. In: Proceedings of IEEE INFOCOM (2021)
6. Machanavajjhala, A., Kifer, D., Gehrke, J., Venkitasubramaniam, M.: l-diversity: Privacy beyond k-anonymity. ACM Trans. Knowl. Discovery Data (TKDD) 1(1), 3-es (2007)
7. Golle, P., Partridge, K.: On the anonymity of home/work location pairs. In: Pervasive Computing (2009)
8. Razaghpanah, A., Nithyanand, R., Vallina-Rodriguez, N., Sundaresan, S.: Apps, trackers, privacy, and regulators: a global study of the mobile tracking ecosystem. In: Proceedings of NDSS (2018). https://doi.org//10.14722/ndss.2018.23353
9. Reardon, J., Feal, Á., Wijesekera, P., On, A.E.B., Vallina-Rodriguez, N., Egelman, S.: 50 ways to leak your data: An exploration of apps' circumvention of the android permissions system. In: 28th USENIX Security Symposium (USENIX Security 19), pp. 603–620. USENIX Association, Santa Clara, CA, August 2019. https://www.usenix.org/conference/usenixsecurity19/presentation/reardon
10. Srivatsa, M., Hicks, M.: Deanonymizing mobility traces: using social network as a side-channel. In: Proceedings of the 2012 ACM Conference on Computer and Communications Security, pp. 628–637 (2012)
11. Sweeney, L.: k-anonymity: a model for protecting privacy. Internat. J. Uncertain. Fuzziness Knowl. Based Syst. 10(05), 557–570 (2002)

Who's Accessing My Data?
Application-Level Access Control
for Bluetooth Low Energy

Pallavi Sivakumaran[✉] and Jorge Blasco

Royal Holloway, University of London, Egham, UK
{pallavi.sivakumaran.2012,jorge.blascoalis}@rhul.ac.uk

Abstract. Bluetooth Low Energy (BLE) is a popular wireless technology deployed in billions of devices within the Internet-of-Things (IoT). The data on these devices is often related to user health or used to control safety-critical functionality, which makes it vital to protect the data from unauthorised access or manipulations. The only mechanism that is fully defined within the BLE specification for protecting sensitive data is *pairing*. This occurs at the device-level rather than at the application-level, and leaves BLE data vulnerable to unauthorised access at higher layers. When a BLE device interacts with a multi-application platform (i.e., a device that hosts more than one application, such as a mobile phone), when one application is able to access data from the BLE peer, all other applications on the same multi-application platform are also implicitly allowed the same access. The solutions suggested thus far for this vulnerability are either impractical for most users, not backward compatible with billions of existing devices, or do not suit normal BLE usage scenarios. In this paper, we conduct an analysis considering practical aspects regarding the BLE ecosystem, and thereafter propose a solution that will extend the available protection for BLE data to the application layer. Our solution ensures protection by default for BLE data, and is entirely backward compatible with existing BLE implementations, requiring no modification to resource-constrained BLE peripherals or companion applications. We also present an open-source proof-of-concept implemented on the Android-x86 platform. This, when tested against experimental and real-world devices and applications, demonstrates the viability and efficacy of our proposed solution.

Keywords: Bluetooth low energy · Application-level security · Multi-application platforms · GATT

This research has been partially sponsored by the Engineering and Physical Sciences Research Council (EPSRC) and the UK government as part of the Centre for Doctoral Training in Cyber Security at Royal Holloway, University of London (EP/P009301/1).

J. Garcia-Alfaro et al. (Eds.): SecureComm 2021, LNICST 399, pp. 252–272, 2021.
https://doi.org/10.1007/978-3-030-90022-9_13

1   Introduction

The Bluetooth Low Energy (BLE) technology enables compatible devices to exchange small amounts of discrete data over a wireless interface, in an energy-efficient manner. Typical usage scenarios, particularly in consumer applications, involve communications between a resource-constrained "peripheral", such as a fitness tracker or glucose monitor, with a more powerful "platform device", such as a mobile phone or personal computer (PC). More precisely, the communication will be between the BLE peripheral and an *application on* the phone or PC.

The Bluetooth specification, defined by the Bluetooth Special Interest Group (SIG), provides optional mechanisms for restricting access to BLE data on a per-device basis, via Bluetooth pairing. However, despite BLE being a full-stack protocol [28], the specification does not provide concrete, well-defined mechanisms for restricting access to BLE data on a per-*application* basis. This lack of application-level restrictions is problematic on devices such as mobile phones and computers, which normally host multiple applications. On such devices, when one application is able to access data from a BLE peripheral, all other applications are implicitly given access to the same data, even if the BLE data is protected by pairing [25]. This vulnerability makes it possible for unauthorised applications to access sensitive data from BLE peripherals. Depending on the BLE device, this could have serious consequences for user privacy (e.g., if user health data is leaked from fitness or medical devices) or safety (e.g., if a BLE door lock or eScooter is manipulated).

Previous suggested solutions include implementation of application layer security by developers or modification of the mobile platform [1, 18]. However, these do not enable protection by default across all possible implementations of the BLE technology. Platforms such as Android and iOS currently implement restrictions on applications by requiring the granting of some permissions by the user [1, 4]. However, these restrictions are not present on other multi-app platforms and, in any case, do not restrict access on a per-peripheral basis.

A solution that is proposed to mitigate this vulnerability must take into consideration not only technical limitations but also practical issues. That is, a highly secure solution is not particularly useful if it will not be implemented in the vast majority of BLE deployments. In this work, we define security and system requirements based on typical BLE configurations, usage mechanisms and user involvement. We also conduct a pragmatic multi-faceted stakeholder analysis. Based on these factors, we propose a specification-level solution, which meets the requirements that we have set out. Our solution achieves protection by default, minimal overhead for resource-constrained devices, and full backward compatibility with existing BLE systems.

To illustrate the viability and efficacy of our solution, we implement a Proof-of-Concept (POC) on the Android-x86 platform. Our POC demonstrates that, with practicable modifications to the multi-application platform, covert data access attempts are brought to the attention of users and are therefore defeated.

Key Contributions. In summary, our contributions are as follows:

- We set out requirements (Sect. 3) for a solution to the unauthorised data access vulnerability that is present in multi-application BLE platforms (Sect. 2).
- We perform a stakeholder analysis with practical considerations, and determine that an asymmetric specification-level modification ensures greatest coverage for a solution (Sect. 4).
- We describe (Sect. 5), evaluate (Sect. 6), and implement an open-source POC for (Sect. 8) a solution that involves minimal changes to the BLE stack.
- We detail benefits realised by our solution in addition to those implied by our set requirements (Sect. 7).

2   Background: Unauthorised Data Access in BLE

BLE is a full-stack protocol, which comprises three main subsystems: the Controller, the Host and Applications [28]. The functionality of the Controller and Host are defined within the core Bluetooth specification, while "applications" are defined in terms of *profiles* within individual specifications (e.g., Heart Rate Profile or Glucose Profile specification). Profile specifications in turn reference one or more *service* specifications. The core specification as well as profile and service specifications are defined and maintained by the Bluetooth SIG.

Each service referenced by a profile contains a number of *characteristics*, where a characteristic holds a single discrete piece of information. Services and characteristics are both types of BLE *attributes*, governed by the Attribute Protocol (ATT). The hierarchical structuring of attributes into characteristics and services is controlled by the Generic Attribute Profile (GATT).

Attributes can have different permissions applied to them: *access permissions* dictate whether an attribute can be read/written; *authentication/encryption permissions* indicate whether an authenticated/encrypted link (achieved via pairing) is required between the two devices before the attribute can be accessed; *authorisation permissions* indicate whether client authorisation is required.

SIG-defined service/profile specifications define security considerations in terms of the different permissions. For example, the Glucose Profile states "*All supported characteristics specified by the Glucose Service shall be set to Security Mode 1 and either Security Level 2 or 3*". The "*Security Mode 1... Level 2 or 3*" refers to encryption and authentication permissions. To satisfy the security requirements defined in the Glucose Profile, implementing devices (for example, a glucose meter and a mobile phone) must undergo pairing.[1]

Pairing takes place between the lower layers of the two devices, and does not extend to the application layer. If the mobile phone in this example hosted a single, trusted application, then the security requirements specified in the Glucose Profile might be sufficient to protect the glucose measurement data from unauthorised access.[2] However, mobile phones typically host numerous,

---

[1] The communicating devices will normally also *bond*, i.e., store long term keys.

[2] For the purpose of our discussion, we assume a secure pairing process.

potentially untrusted applications. Therefore, the fact that the Glucose Profile does not require restricting access at the application level means that, once one application on a mobile phone has triggered pairing (and bonding) with the glucose meter, any other application on the mobile phone will also be able to access the glucose measurement data. We have previously demonstrated that such access is possible in a covert manner on the Android platform [25].

We observe that authorisation permissions *can* restrict access at the application layer. However, implementing these permissions can reduce flexibility and interoperability by tying a BLE device to a single application (where the user may desire a choice). Also, these permissions are not required in any SIG-defined service specification except the Insulin Delivery Service. Further, the mechanism of *how* to accomplish client authorisation is left up to the developer. A large number of existing BLE devices either do *not* implement authorisation permissions or implement them in an insecure manner [25].

Note that the problem of unauthorised data access is present only when a platform hosts multiple applications, as with mobile devices. However, the vulnerable *data* tends to be that obtained from BLE peripherals, which typically host only a single application.

3 Environment

In this section, we outline our threat model (Sect. 3.1) and define a set of security and system requirements (Sects. 3.2, 3.3) that we believe should apply to any solution that addresses the problem of unauthorised BLE data access on multi-app platforms.

3.1 Threat Model

We make the assumption that any app on the multi-application platform issues BLE requests via a BLE stack implemented by the platform, i.e., the application cannot circumvent the stack that is implemented by the platform. We also assume that the application cannot directly access the components of the platform-implemented BLE stack or influence its operations by any means other than via robust platform APIs. In addition, we assume an honest and uncompromised platform and peripherals. However, *applications* are from multiple third-party developers and are assumed to be untrusted. These applications may abuse the unauthorised data access vulnerability to obtain and manipulate data being stored on a BLE peripheral without the user's knowledge and consent. This is the kind of behaviour our solution aims to protect against.

3.2 Security Requirements

To protect against unauthorised data access attacks at the application-layer, we define three main security requirements. These are based on typical multi-application platform configurations and usage, and the shortcomings that we have identified with existing restriction mechanisms.

SecRQ1: Prevention of Unauthorised Access to BLE Data. An application should not be able to access the data from a BLE peer device without the user's knowledge and explicit authorisation. Note that the term "authorised" in this context should not be confused with the "authorisation permissions" already defined within the Bluetooth specification.

SecRQ2: Per-Device Access Control. User authorisation should be granted to an application for every peer device *individually*. That is, if an application is granted permission to access one BLE peer device, it should not automatically be possible for that application to access any other BLE peer device.

SecRQ3: Access Revocation. The user must be able to revoke access that has previously been granted to an application for a BLE peer device. This limits the exposure of data in the event of late identification of malicious app behaviour.

3.3   System Requirements

There are billions of BLE-enabled devices in use today [6] and most are in consumer applications, where the end users are not necessarily highly technical. This results in a need for security solutions that do not require high levels of user involvement. In addition, most BLE peripherals are resource-constrained by design and will not be able to handle large amounts of processing. This makes complex cryptographic protocols less desirable. While these factors are not directly related to the security of a system, they need to be taken into consideration when proposing a security solution. We therefore define three key *system* requirements, bearing in mind user involvement, the number of BLE devices extant in the world today and the asymmetric nature of resources on communicating BLE devices.

SysRQ1: Protection by Default. All devices that implement (the modified version of) BLE should incorporate protection by default. Any specification-compliant BLE system should automatically protect against and be protected from unauthorised data access at the application layer, without the need for additional user intervention (beyond the explicit granting of permissions or authorisation).

SysRQ2: Backward Compatibility. Devices that incorporate the solution should function with existing devices. Given that billions of BLE-enabled devices exist today, a solution that obsoletes such a vast number of devices would not be acceptable.

SysRQ3: Minimal Overhead for Resource-Constrained Devices. The solution should not incur a significant processing overhead for the more resource-constrained device, as this would lead to greater power requirements and quicker battery drain, thereby defeating the purpose of BLE.

4 Devising a Solution Strategy

The requirements we have described in Sects. 3.2 and 3.3 are necessary for a secure and utilitarian solution to the unauthorised data access problem. However, the most secure solution is of no value if it will not be applied to a large proportion of the BLE ecosystem due to lack of technical capability or stakeholder involvement. In this section, we discuss the primary stakeholders in the BLE ecosystem and describe practical considerations that should be taken into account when proposing a solution. From this, we determine the most suitable solution strategy to ensure maximum coverage.

4.1 Stakeholders Within BLE

There are five primary stakeholders within the BLE ecosystem:

1. The *Bluetooth SIG* defines and maintains the Bluetooth specification, as well as BLE services and profiles (such as the Glucose Profile mentioned in Sect. 2).
2. *Chipset vendors* produce BLE-enabled chipsets, which are then used in platforms and peripherals. Chipset developers may also provide BLE stacks for their products, to enable developers to create BLE end products quickly and easily. Examples include Qualcomm, NXP, Nordic Semiconductor, Texas Instruments, STMicroelectronics, etc.
3. *Platform vendors* develop and maintain BLE-enabled platforms, typically supporting multiple applications. Prominent examples are Android, iOS/Mac OS, Windows and Linux.
4. *Developers* manufacture BLE-enabled end products (e.g., fitness trackers, medical monitoring devices, eScooters, smart locks). They normally also develop companion apps (that typically run on multi-app platforms) to interface with their products.
5. *Users* are the ultimate consumers for BLE-enabled products and services.

Users are only considered in terms of the impact of the vulnerability and the ease of applying a solution. Users are at most expected to update their devices' operating system or firmware and provide explicit authorisation to applications. We do not expect users to *implement* any part of a solution. We therefore confine the discussion on implementation to the first four entities.

4.2 Practical Considerations

When a BLE security solution is proposed, the likelihood of it being implemented depends on a number of factors. In this section, we analyse those factors in terms of the involved stakeholders.

Number of Entities. The likelihood of a solution being implemented depends in part on the number of entities that are required to implement it. The smaller the number, the easier it is to communicate the solution to them and the greater the reach of the solution. When considering BLE stakeholders in terms of numbers, the SIG is a single entity (albeit made up of a large number of members). This makes it a single point of communication, from which the solution will trickle down to implementing entities (platform vendors, chipset vendors and developers). There are a limited number of platform vendors, and the four most prominent platforms (Android, Windows, iOS, and Mac OS) account for over 95% of the worldwide OS market share [27]. BLE chipset vendors are more numerous than platform vendors, but not by a large margin (15–20 vendors [16]). Developers, on the other hand, are multitudinous (several hundreds [7]); it would therefore be very difficult to communicate a solution to all possible developers.

Stakeholder Participation. Not all stakeholders respond satisfactorily when they are made aware of a vulnerability. The security behaviour of a stakeholder tends to be associated with the prominence of the stakeholder (in terms of brand value, which may act as an incentive to adopt strong security practices), as well as the availability of organisational support, knowledge and resources [5,11,15]. The SIG and most platform/chipset vendors have clear, mature processes in place for vulnerability reporting, assessment and mitigation, whereas many developers may not even respond when informed of issues [20]. Further, in interdependent ecosystems such as BLE, where platforms and chipsets implement the specification, and developers create end-products on top of the platforms and chipsets, there is a certain degree of "responsibility relaying". That is, each stakeholder presumes that the responsibility for implementing the solution belongs to another stakeholder. This phenomenon of "passing the buck" is prevalent within IT security, with responsibility being transferred down the supply chain or to other stakeholders [21,24]. In the case of BLE, we postulate that only a specification-level change will induce most of the remaining stakeholders within the BLE ecosystem to incorporate a solution; the solution would have to be implemented in order to claim conformance with the specification.

Availability of Update Mechanism. Stakeholder participation, as described in preceding sections, is key to solution implementation, but equally so is the availability of an actual mechanism for performing the implementation. In the case of the Bluetooth specification, all updates are to a document, which can be updated in a straightforward manner. The solution must thereafter be implemented by the remaining stakeholders. Platform devices, such as mobile phones and computers, have fairly robust update mechanisms. Therefore, a solution implementation can be easily rolled out on these devices. Most modern BLE chipsets support over-the-air (OTA) firmware updates, enabling updates to applications and sometimes also to the BLE stack. However, many IoT devices do not incorporate such update mechanisms [30], which means that a large proportion of existing BLE *peripherals* cannot be modified.

4.3   Discussion

Based on the large number of BLE end-product developers, the lower likelihood of developer participation, and the lack of firmware update mechanisms in many BLE peripherals, we reach the conclusion that a security solution that does *not* require involvement from end-product developers is more likely to actually be implemented. We also observe that, because a single platform device normally communicates with multiple peripherals, an asymmetric solution involving changes to only the platforms (which are far fewer in number) will be an effort-efficient way to mitigate the unauthorised data access vulnerability for a larger proportion of the BLE ecosystem. Further, according to Sect. 4.2, a specification-level change is more likely to prompt changes to platform devices than individual communications with platform vendors. In addition, a specification-level change ensures security by default even if new BLE-enabled multi-app platforms are introduced in the future (without the need for communicating the solution to each new platform vendor individually).

5   Proposed Solution

In accordance with our analysis in Sect. 4, our proposed solution involves changes to the BLE stack and primarily involves modifications to multi-application platforms. Our solution also requires minor changes to the peripheral which, however, can be avoided while still retaining the expected outcome (see Sect. 7).

Our solution introduces three new BLE components/properties:

1. **ATT Access Database (AAD):** A database for storing application access permissions.
2. **ATT Access Manager (AAM):** A layer within the BLE stack, responsible for performing the main access control functions.
3. **Device/Platform Mode:** A property for a BLE system, which controls the behaviour of a BLE device with respect to the new functionality.

Sections 5.1 to 5.3 describe the purpose and, if relevant, the functionality of each of these elements in detail. Section 5.4 discusses concerns relating to user authorisation, while Sect. 5.5 describes access revocation.

5.1   The ATT Access Database (AAD)

The AAD stores per-device (i.e., BLE peer), per-application *access records*, as authorised by the user, for all applications that have made a GATT request for a BLE peer device, and for all such BLE peer devices connected to the platform. An access record has three components:

1. AppID: A unique identifier for the application that has made a GATT request to the platform. This must be assigned by the platform. It should not be possible for the application to manipulate its AppID.
2. DeviceID: A unique identifier for the BLE peer, e.g., the hardware address.
3. Permission: A value indicating whether access for an app (identified by AppID) to a BLE device (identified by DeviceID) is *Allowed* or *DenyListed*.

By default, records do not exist for an application until the application makes a GATT request. The first time a record is added to the AAD for an application-device pair, the associated permission will be as selected by the user. This is described in detail in Sect. 5.2.

Positioning of the AAD. Similar to the Security Database used within the existing design of BLE, the AAD does not feature within our modified BLE *stack*, but must be implemented by the platform in order for the BLE system to be operational. The AAD only communicates with the AAM. Therefore, the functionality of the AAD can also be subsumed into the AAM.

Access by Applications. The AAD must not be accessible to higher layer applications. It should not be possible for an application to query its AAD permissions or to add itself to the AAD, as that would defeat the access control mechanisms that are in place.

5.2   The ATT Access Manager (AAM)

We introduce the AAM as a new layer within the BLE Host sub-system. It serves as an access control mechanism for GATT requests. For this reason, it is logically positioned between GATT and the application layer. This position enables it to intercept and arbitrate all GATT requests while also not unduly interfering with applications or lower stack layers.

Basic Workflow. Figure 1 depicts the overall workflow when a GATT request is received from an application. When an application makes a GATT request, the platform passes the AAM a 3-tuple, consisting of the GATT request, the DeviceID corresponding to the BLE peer, and the AppID representing the requesting application. The DeviceID and AppID are assigned by the underlying platform (as described in Sect. 5.1).

The AAM separates out the three elements and queries the AAD for the DeviceID/AppID combination. The following outcomes are possible:

- **An entry exists** within the AAD for the AppID against the given DeviceID: The AAD forwards the corresponding permission value to the AAM.
  - **Stored permission is *DenyListed*:** This indicates that the user has expressly denied the application from accessing data on the specific BLE peer. The AAM indicates the deny-listed status to the platform, which should notify the requesting application that the request has failed and cannot succeed even after multiple tries.
  - **Stored permission is *Allowed*:** The AAM forwards the GATT request to ATT/GATT, receives the response, and forwards it to the platform.
- **No record exists** with the AAD for an AppID-DeviceID pair: This is signalled to the AAM, which in turn notifies the underlying platform that user authorisation is required. The user should be presented with options to allow or deny the application to access data from the BLE peer.

In this manner, only applications that are explicitly authorised by the user will be able to access data from the BLE peer, and because permissions are defined per-peer and per-application, the user has complete control over exactly which BLE devices each application can access.

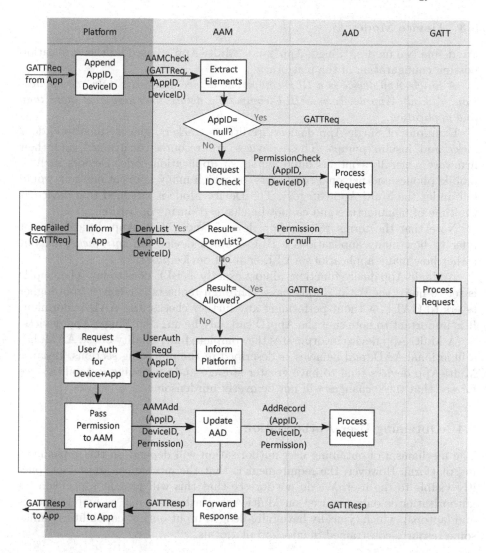

Fig. 1. Proposed workflow for GATT requests. Light grey areas are part of the BLE stack. Dark grey areas are platform/app components external to the stack.

Note also that, in this design, the functionality of GATT and other existing BLE stack components do not change. Therefore, changes to the stack are minimal. Further, the AAM only processes GATT *requests*; it forwards GATT responses as received to higher layers.

Null AppIDs. Upon receiving a null AppID, the AAM will forward the GATT request to ATT/GATT without any further checks. The AAM can only be sent null AppIDs if the underlying platform hosts a single application (see Sect. 5.3).

5.3   Device Mode

We define two modes, "Single-App" and "Multi-App", based on the application hosting configuration of the platform:

A Single-App device is a BLE-compatible device that hosts only one application. A Multi-App device is a BLE-compatible device that may host more than one application.

Examples of Single-App devices are fitness trackers, glucose monitors, door locks and insulin pumps. These devices are resource-constrained and their firmware generally contains only one set of application code. Devices such as mobile phones and personal computers, on which many applications run, would fall under the Multi-App category. The Device Mode is assigned to a device at the time of manufacture and cannot be changed during operation.

Note that the terms "Single-App device" and "Multi-App device" do not refer to how many applications a BLE-enabled device can *interface with*, but rather how many applications a BLE-enabled device *hosts*.

A Single-App device functions almost exactly as BLE does today. The AppID is set to null; the AAM simply passes through requests it receives from higher layers to GATT, without performing any further checks; the AAD is dormant. It is important to note that the AppID can only be null for Single-App devices.

A Multi-App device incorporates the complete functionality of the AAM, has a functional AAD, and behaves as described in the preceding sections. Because Multi-App devices tend to have greater storage and processing capabilities, we foresee that these changes will not be overly burdensome.

5.4   Obtaining User Authorisation

The mechanism of obtaining user authorisation will depend on the implementing platform. However, the requirement is that the mechanism must be explicitly visible to the user. We do not foresee that this will present a problem, as authorisation is only required on Multi-App platforms (such as mobile phones and laptops), which typically have fully-fledged input-output capabilities, unlike some resource-constrained Single-App platforms.

5.5   Access Revocation

It should always be possible for a user to revoke the access they have granted to an app, on a per-device basis. Similarly, it should be possible for a user to remove the *DenyListed* state for an application-device pair. This could be achieved in a similar manner to privacy controls on modern mobile and computer operating systems, where access to system resources are controlled on a per-application basis. Upon access revocation or state change, a command must be sent to the AAM, to notify the AAD to update the relevant record.

6   Requirements Analysis

In this section, we evaluate our proposed solution design against the requirements defined in Sect. 3.

SecRQ1: Prevention of Unauthorised Access to BLE Data. The AAM intercepts and processes all GATT requests from all applications on the platform. As long as the assumptions stated in Sect. 3.1 hold, no application will be able to circumvent the AAM checks and covertly access data from BLE peer devices.

SecRQ2: Per-Device Access Control. AAM checks are performed per-app, per-device. An app that has been authorised to access data from one BLE device will fail AAM checks if it has not been granted access to a different BLE device.

SecRQ3: Access Revocation. Explicit mechanisms exist within the AAM (as discussed in Sect. 5.5) to revoke access for any application that has previously been granted GATT access to a BLE device.

SysRQ1: Protection by Default. Because our solution involves the modification of the BLE specification itself (rather than of a single device, platform or application), every platform that is qualified against this design would incorporate the GATT access control mechanism, ensuring protection by default.

SysRQ2: Backward Compatibility. All new functionality in our design occurs locally, within a single device. The functionality of GATT and lower layers of the BLE stack operate as they have previously, and interface with BLE peers with no changes. Therefore, a device that implements this solution will be backward compatible with all existing BLE systems. We demonstrate this with our POC in Sect. 8, where a modified Android stack operates with an unmodified BLE peripheral. The changes also do not affect the existing Bluetooth services or profiles.

SysRQ3: Minimal Overhead for Resource-Constrained Devices. The processing described in Sect. 5.2 applies to Multi-App devices such as mobile phones, which are expected to have reasonably powerful operating systems and fewer restrictions in terms of battery usage. Most BLE peripherals have limited storage and do not support hosting multiple apps. Therefore, such devices will be defined as Single-App, and will be spared most of the processing overhead (Sect. 5.3).

7   Additional Benefits

In this section, we describe advantages of our proposed solution, in addition to those implied by the fulfilment of the requirements.

No Changes to Existing BLE Stack Layers. In our solution, a single new layer is added to the stack, and it is within this layer that the bulk of the access control behaviour is implemented. No modifications are required for any of the existing BLE stack layers, including the ATT/GATT layer, which is the only core layer that interfaces with the AAM (i.e., the requests received by GATT with the proposed new stack will be exactly as they are at present). This makes it easier for the Multi-App platform to implement the changes in a modular fashion (assuming the existing stack has also been developed in a similar manner).

No Changes to Applications. Our proposed solution requires no interaction between an application and the AAM. This means that applications that issue GATT requests will not require any changes, apart from possibly to handle a new error status. This is a significant advantage, as there are several thousand mobile applications with BLE capabilities in existence today [25,32], and making changes to all of them would be extremely challenging, as it would require cooperation from a large number of developers.

Equal Protection for All Services. A BLE device may implement services defined by the Bluetooth SIG, but may also implement its own custom services. As with the example provided in Sect. 2, most services and profiles defined by the SIG, including those that read user health data such as heart rate or glucose measurements, do not specify higher-layer protection as a security requirement. With our solution, protection is applied to both types of services, even if SIG-defined services do not specify authorisation permissions.

Protection Even in the Absence of Pairing. Many BLE peripherals tend not to have sufficient input-output capabilities, and therefore either implement weak pairing or no pairing at all [26]. Our solution is separate from and at a higher layer to possible link layer protection mechanisms such as pairing. Any GATT request from an application has to first pass through the AAM before it can be forwarded via the link layer to the BLE peer, which means that protection is applied at a much earlier step. This means that the proposed new stack will protect data on a BLE peer from access by an unauthorised application on a Multi-App platform even if the peripheral does not specify a requirement for pairing. Of course, if the peripheral does not require pairing, then its data can be eavesdropped over the wireless interface; it can also be accessed by a different unauthorised device. However, that is outside the scope of this work. Our work focuses on protecting data from unauthorised access *at the application layer*.

Most Changes Are to Mature Platforms. While a specification change would typically require a change to all devices that implement the BLE stack, the way in which the proposed change has been designed allows for the system to function even without any changes to existing peripherals. The only entities that will *require* changes are Multi-App platforms such as mobile or personal computer operating systems. These platforms tend to have a robust update mechanism in place already, which is familiar to users. This ensures greater likelihood of the changes actually being installed on end user devices.

Potential for Fine-Grained Access Control. Our current solution design enables an application to either access all data on a peripheral or none. This can be extended to enable fine-grained access control by access type (i.e., reads or writes) or even on a per-characteristic level (we note, however, that per-characteristic access control is inadvisable in most cases, as it would place too much decision burden on users who may not be aware of the purpose of each characteristic).

8 Proof of Concept

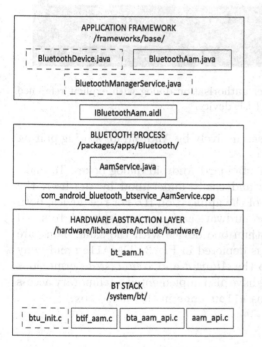

Fig. 2. Main changes made to Android architecture for POC. Utility functions not shown. Solid & dashed lines denote new & modified components, respectively.

In order to demonstrate the viability of our proposed solution, we have implemented a Proof-of-Concept on the Android-x86 platform.[3]

In this section, we discuss implementation details, describe the test setup, and evaluate the POC in terms of development effort, performance overheads and user experience.

8.1 Implementation Details

We selected the Android platform for our POC due to its open-source nature, large installation base and potential familiarity to readers. We used the Android-x86[4] code base, to be able to implement and test our solution on a virtual machine, without the need for expensive device installations.[5] The modified Android-x86 was built on a VM running Ubuntu 18.04.3 LTS with 128 GB RAM (8 GB for heap) and 8 cores.

---

[3] https://github.com/projectbtle/BLE-MultiApp-POC.

[4] Android-x86 is a port of Android for x86 platforms. It is based on the Android Open Source Project (AOSP) with some modifications.

[5] Android-x86 offers Bluetooth capabilities, which official Android emulators lack.

Figure 2 depicts the components within the Android-x86 framework that were modified or added for our proposed solution. Specifically, on Android, a GATT request (such as those for reading or writing characteristics) can only be issued after an app has called the `connectGatt` method. Because of this construct, and due to the nature of the Android architecture, we select `connectGatt` as the entry point for the AAM checks. We use the device's hardware address as the DeviceID and extract the Android app's application ID (which uniquely identifies an app on the Android platform [2]) to use as the AppID.

The actual AAM functionality is implemented within the BT stack. In keeping with Android's workflow for other BLE functionality, we implemented the AAM functionality along a path from the application framework to a custom AAM "layer" within the stack, as shown in Fig. 2. Within the AAM layer, the AAD is implemented as a linked-list of records,

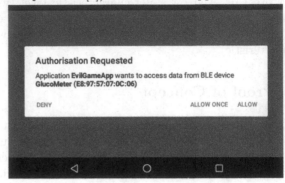

Fig. 3. User authorisation dialog with explicit reference to app and BLE device.

following the same structure that is used natively by Android for storing pairing credentials.

User authorisation is requested via standard Android dialog boxes. To make the contents of the dialog box clear and easily understood by the user, the application name is displayed instead of the application ID. For the device, both the device name (if available) and the hardware address are displayed, to avoid ambiguity in situations where more than one device with the same name are advertising in the vicinity. A sample is depicted in Fig. 3. The `Allow` and `Deny` options within the dialog box map to the *Allowed* and *DenyListed* permissions described in Sect. 5.1, respectively. We have also implemented a temporary access option *AuthReqd*, which is displayed as `Allow Once` in the dialog box.

8.2   POC Tests

To test our POC, we replicate the attack scenario described in [25]. The attack demonstrates covert access of data from a connected BLE device by an unauthorised app. We utilise four main components:

1. VMWare Workstation 14 Player on a Windows 10 laptop, with a CSR adapter, for running the original and modified Android-x86 builds.
2. Nordic nRF51 DK, in the role of a glucose meter ("GlucoMeter"). No pairing-protected characteristics.
3. Android app, in the role of a glucose monitoring app ("GlucoseApp").
4. Android app, in the role of a malicious app masquerading as a legitimate app, e.g., a game, which accesses BLE data covertly ("EvilGameApp").

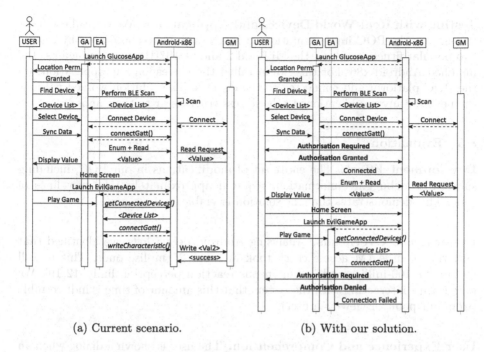

(a) Current scenario.   (b) With our solution.

Fig. 4. Interaction between User, GlucoseApp (GA), EvilGameApp (EA), Multi-App platform (Android-x86) and BLE GlucoMeter (GM). Items in *italics* are interactions between EA and Android-x86 that occur without user awareness. Items in **bold** are new user interaction elements.

We deploy a VM with the original Android-x86 build and perform the following functions in order: (i) Launch GlucoseApp. (ii) Scan for BLE devices. (iii) Connect to the GATT server on the "GlucoMeter" and read a characteristic. This will read a dummy value of 0x12345678. (iv) Launch EvilGameApp (which covertly identifies the existing connection to the GlucoMeter, calls `connectGatt` to it and writes the same characteristic). Figure 4a depicts the interactions between five main entities (the user, GlucoseApp, EvilGameApp, the Multi-App platform (i.e., Android-x86), and the BLE device) when going through the above test steps in the absence of any protection mechanism. We then repeat the tests using the modified Android-x86 build. Figure 4b illustrates the interaction between the five entities when our controls have been implemented. The two figures demonstrate that unauthorised data access is prevented with our solution because the covert data access attempt is brought to the attention of the user and defeated, i.e., protection is achieved due to explicit user awareness.

Testing with Pairing-Protected Data. We additionally modified the "GlucoMeter" to require pairing prior to data access. Re-running the tests again, we found that our controls worked in that scenario as well, as expected.

Testing with Real-World Devices and Applications. We verified the functionality of the POC implementation on real-world devices and apps by testing two popular fitness trackers, the Mi Band 2 and ID107HR/VeryFit, against the modified Android-x86. For this, we installed the corresponding applications on the POC platform and connected to the devices. The solution worked without the need for any modifications to the fitness trackers or to their apps.

8.3   Evaluation

Development Effort. The entire set of modifications in our POC, including substantial debugging information, required approximately 1500 new lines of code. This demonstrates that the solution is viable.

Performance Overheads. Analysing Android debug logs, we identified that performing an AAM access check took at most 25 milliseconds. This is well within the 100-millisecond instantaneous reaction perception limit [12,19]. We found while interacting with the system that this amount of time is indiscernible (from our point of view as a user).

User Experience and Comprehension. The user is shown a dialog when an application is first launched and attempts to access data from a BLE device. Once that dialog has been responded to, subsequent access attempts don't require user interaction. Therefore, it is the impact of the first dialog that needs to be analysed. Due to the prevailing Covid-19 situation, we were unable to conduct in-person tests. We therefore present here a theoretical analysis of the impact on user experience and comprehension.

If a malicious app professes to be benign but covertly accesses BLE data, then it may limit the number of permissions that it requests in order to trick the user into believing that it is harmless. In such a scenario, the presentation of a system dialog could serve to call the user's attention to the fact that covert data access is being attempted. Previous studies on user authorisation mechanisms [17], such as the ones used in the Android permission system, suggest that using a system dialog the first time a resource is accessed provides the optimal point for user decision making. Our proposal effectively achieves this by raising the authorisation dialog the first time a BLE resource is accessed. If the access to that resource (a BLE peripheral in our case) is malicious, the user won't see how the app functionality is related to the device access and will therefore deny it. Of course, if the malicious app portrays itself as a BLE accessory app, it is more likely for the user to allow access. Identifying malicious behaviour *after* access to the BLE peripheral has been granted (e.g., leakage of BLE data once it has been read from a device) is outside the current scope and is left as future work.

9   Limitations

Use of External Sources of Information. The proposed solution requires that the implementing platform supply unique application identifiers to a component within the BLE stack. This in effect removes the self-contained aspect of the stack by introducing an element external to the stack.

Reliance on Honesty of Platform. While the proposed solution enables the user to grant permissions on a per-device, per-app basis, the fact that the access control checks are entirely performed by the Multi-App platform implies that there is implicit reliance on the integrity and honesty of the platform. That is, there is an underlying assumption that the Multi-App platform will apply access control checks to all applications in an unbiased manner. However, it may be the case that a Multi-App platform which ships with its own set of apps may automatically authorise those apps to access any BLE peer, and only apply access control checks to third-party apps. This would then remove some of the visibility and control from the user. Circumventing such an issue would require a complex protocol between the platform and peripheral, and is outside the scope of this paper. For our work, we make the assumption of an honest and fair platform.

Complexities in Desktop/Laptop Environments. The solution we have proposed is straightforward to implement on mobile operating systems, where the level of user customisation, particularly regarding the BLE stack, is minimal. However, with operating systems such as Windows and Linux, there is a possibility that an application might use a BLE stack that is not provided by the OS. For example, it is possible on a Windows machine to utilise an external BLE adapter, instead of the system-provided Bluetooth capabilities. This is done manually, with additional hardware, and requires that the system Bluetooth be turned off. While such a setup is more likely to exist in testing scenarios than in normal user systems, it is still a consideration that should be factored in when implementing the solution.

10   Related Work

Various aspects regarding the security and privacy of Bluetooth Low Energy have been studied over the years. The BLE pairing process has come under specific scrutiny, with passive eavesdropping [10,23], authentication bypass [22], key entropy downgrade [3] and link encryption downgrade vulnerabilities [29,31] explored over time. Man-in-the-Middle/spoofing attacks have been described in [14,29]. Privacy concerns with BLE have also been widely studied [8,9,13].

The works most closely aligned with ours are [25] (which is our own work, where we first describe the unauthorised data access vulnerability for BLE) and [18]. In [18], the authors described unauthorised data access for Bluetooth BR/EDR (i.e., "Classic") devices by any Android app with Bluetooth permissions. They proposed an Android OS-level protection mechanism via bonding policies. Their solution assumes that the first app that pairs to a Bluetooth device is the authorised app and automatically creates a policy. Our solution makes no such assumption, particularly since, in the BLE case, the peripheral device may not require pairing at all. Further, the user may desire the use of a secondary application with additional features. Our solution instead explicitly informs the user of any application that makes a GATT request to a connected BLE device. This ensures that the user is aware of and can make decisions regarding whether or not to allow access. We also present our solution as a specification-level change, which then affords protection by default for the entire BLE ecosystem.

11   Conclusion

We have presented a modified Bluetooth Low Energy stack to solve the unauthorised data access vulnerability on multi-app platforms. Our solution fulfils stringent security and system requirements, and takes into account practical considerations in its design. It ensures protection by default, while maintaining backward compatibility with existing systems. No changes are required to apps or resource-constrained BLE peripherals, nor are changes required to existing stack layers. We have also implemented a proof-of-concept on the Android-x86 platform to illustrate our solution, and have demonstrated that the solution prevents unauthorised data access via explicit user awareness and authorisation.

References

1. Android: Bluetooth Low Energy overview (2020). https://developer.android.com/guide/topics/connectivity/bluetooth-le. Accessed 06 Feb 2021
2. Android: Set the application ID (2020). https://developer.android.com/studio/build/application-id. Accessed 20 Oct 2020
3. Antonioli, D., Tippenhauer, N.O., Rasmussen, K.: Low entropy key negotiation attacks on Bluetooth and Bluetooth Low Energy. IACR Cryptology ePrint Archive (2019)
4. Apple: If an app would like to use Bluetooth on your device (2019). https://support.apple.com/en-us/HT210578. Accessed 20 Oct 2020
5. Assal, H., Chiasson, S.: 'think secure from the beginning' a survey with software developers. In: Proceedings of the 2019 CHI Conference on Human Factors in Computing Systems, pp. 1–13 (2019)
6. Bluetooth Special Interest Group: 2020 Bluetooth market update (2020). https://www.bluetooth.com/bluetooth-resources/2020-bmu. Accessed 13 May 2020
7. Bluetooth Special Interest Group: LaunchStudio (2021). https://launchstudio.bluetooth.com/Listings/Search. Accessed 08 Feb 2021

8. Celosia, G., Cunche, M.: Fingerprinting Bluetooth-Low-Energy devices based on the Generic Attribute profile. In: Proceedings of the 2nd International ACM Workshop on Security and Privacy for the Internet-of-Things, pp. 24–31. ACM (2019)

9. Das, A.K., Pathak, P.H., Chuah, C.N., Mohapatra, P.: Uncovering privacy leakage in BLE network traffic of wearable fitness trackers. In: Proceedings of the 17th International Workshop on Mobile Computing Systems and Applications (2016)

10. Gomez, C., Oller, J., Paradells, J.: Overview and evaluation of Bluetooth Low Energy: An emerging low-power wireless technology. Sensors (2012)

11. Halderman, J.A.: To strengthen security, change developers' incentives. IEEE Security & Privacy (2010)

12. Hogan, L.C.: Performance is user experience (2014). https://designingforperformance.com/performance-is-ux. Accessed 15 Feb 2021

13. Issoufaly, T., Tournoux, P.U.: BLEB: Bluetooth Low Energy Botnet for large scale individual tracking. In: 2017 1st International Conference on Next Generation Computing Applications (NextComp), pp. 115–120. IEEE (2017)

14. Jasek, S.: Gattacking Bluetooth Smart devices. In: Black Hat USA (2016)

15. van der Linden, D., et al.: Schrödinger's security: opening the box on app developers' security rationale. In: 2020 IEEE/ACM 42nd International Conference on Software Engineering (2020)

16. Markets and Markets: IoT chip market (2021). https://www.marketsandmarkets.com/Market-Reports/iot-chip-market-236473142.html. Accessed 08 Feb 2021

17. Micinski, K., Votipka, D., Stevens, R., Kofinas, N., Mazurek, M.L., Foster, J.S.: User interactions and permission use on Android. In: Proceedings of the 2017 CHI Conference on Human Factors in Computing Systems, pp. 362–373 (2017)

18. Naveed, M., Zhou, X., Demetriou, S., Wang, X., Gunter, C.A.: Inside job: Understanding and mitigating the threat of external device mis-binding on Android. In: 21st Annual Network and Distributed System Security Symposium (2014)

19. Nielsen, J.: Response times: The 3 important limits (1993). https://www.nngroup.com/articles/response-times-3-important-limits. Accessed 15 Feb 2021

20. O'Donnell, L.: Consumers urged to junk insecure IoT devices. https://threatpost.com/consumers-urged-to-junk-insecure-iot-devices/145800. Accessed 12 Feb 2021

21. Ramachandran, R.: IoT connected healthcare devices: Challenges in cybersecurity and the way forward (2020)

22. Rosa, T.: Bypassing passkey authentication in Bluetooth Low Energy. IACR Cryptology ePrint Archive (2013)

23. Ryan, M.: Bluetooth: With low energy comes low security. In: 7th USENIX Workshop on Offensive Technologies (2013)

24. Schwartau, W.: Let's end pass-the-buck security (2004)

25. Sivakumaran, P., Blasco, J.: A study of the feasibility of co-located app attacks against BLE and a large-scale analysis of the current application-layer security landscape. In: 28th USENIX Security Symposium, pp. 1–18 (2019)

26. Sivakumaran, P., Blasco Alis, J.: A low energy profile: analysing characteristic security on BLE peripherals. In: Proceedings of the Eighth ACM Conference on Data and Application Security and Privacy, pp. 152–154. ACM (2018)

27. statcounter: Operating system market share worldwide. https://gs.statcounter.com/os-market-share. Accessed 06 Feb 2021

28. Woolley, M.: Bluetooth 5 (2019). https://www.bluetooth.com/wp-content/uploads/2019/03/Bluetooth_5-FINAL.pdf. Accessed 31 Aug 2020

29. Wu, J., et al.: BLESA: spoofing attacks against reconnections in Bluetooth Low Energy. In: 14th USENIX Workshop on Offensive Technologies (2020)

30. Zandberg, K., Schleiser, K., Acosta, F., Tschofenig, H., Baccelli, E.: Secure firmware updates for constrained IoT devices using open standards: a reality check. IEEE Access (2019)
31. Zhang, Y., Weng, J., Dey, R., Jin, Y., Lin, Z., Fu, X.: On the (in) security of Bluetooth Low Energy one-way Secure Connections Only mode (2019)
32. Zuo, C., Wen, H., Lin, Z., Zhang, Y.: Automatic fingerprinting of vulnerable BLE IoT devices with static UUIDs from mobile apps. In: Proceedings of the 2019 ACM SIGSAC Conference on Computer and Communications Security (2019)

HTPD: Secure and Flexible Message-Based Communication for Mobile Apps

Yin Liu[✉], Breno Dantas Cruz, and Eli Tilevich

Software Innovations Lab, Virginia Tech, Blacksburg, USA
{yinliu,bdantasc,tilevich}@cs.vt.edu

Abstract. In modern mobile message-based communication, malicious apps can illicitly access transferred messages via data leakage attacks. Existing defenses are overly restrictive, as they block all suspicious apps, malicious or not, from receiving messages. As a solution, we present a communication model that allows untrusted-but-not-malicious apps to receive messages. Our model—hidden transmission and polymorphic delivery (HTPD)—transmits sensitive messages in an encrypted envelope and delivers them polymorphically. Depending on the destination's trustworthiness, HTPD delivers either no data, raw data, or encrypted data. *Homomorphic* and *convergent* encryption allows untrusted destinations to securely operate on encrypted data deliveries. We realize HTPD as POLICC, a plug-in replacement of Android Inter-Component Communication middleware. POLICC mitigates three classic Android data leakage attacks, and allows untrusted apps to operate on delivered messages. Our evaluation shows that POLICC enables mobile apps to securely and flexibly exchange communication messages, with low performance and programming effort overheads.

Keywords: Mobile security · Message-based communication · Secure inter-component communication

1 Introduction

An essential part of modern mobile platforms is inter-app communication[1], which is typically message-based: apps send and receive various kinds of messages, some of which may contain sensitive data. When a malicious app accesses sensitive data, *data leakage* occurs. To prevent data leakage, modern mobile platforms (e.g., Android and iOS) customize their communication models to control how apps access message data. However, these models remain vulnerable to data leakage, commonly exploited by attacks that include interception, eavesdropping, and permission escalation. These attacks leak volumes of sensitive data,

---

[1] In Android, it is also called inter-component communication (ICC).

© ICST Institute for Computer Sciences, Social Informatics and Telecommunications Engineering 2021
Published by Springer Nature Switzerland AG 2021. All Rights Reserved
J. Garcia-Alfaro et al. (Eds.): SecureComm 2021, LNICST 399, pp. 273–294, 2021.
https://doi.org/10.1007/978-3-030-90022-9_14

as has been documented both in the research literature [11,13,21,34,40] and in vulnerability reporting repositories (e.g., CVE) [2,3,10].

To prevent data leakage, state-of-the-art approaches fall into two general categories: (1) taint message data to track and analyze its data flow [8,20], and (2) track call chains, as guided by a permission restriction policy for sending/receiving data [12,18,22]. Although these approaches[2] strengthen the security of message-based communication, their high false positive rates often render them impractical for realistic communication scenarios. Once any app in a call chain or data flow is identified as "malicious," even as a false positive, they can no longer receive any messages. Although "untrusted" may not be "malicious", these data flow monitoring approaches block all *untrusted-but-not-malicious* destinations. In addition, mobile users may change app permissions at any point, thus also causing false positives. With high false-positive rates, these prior approaches lack flexibility required to secure message-based communication, without blocking untrusted-but-not-malicious destinations from operating on delivered messages.

In this paper, we present HTPD, a novel model that improves the security of message-based communication. The model combines two key mechanisms: (1) hidden transmission of messages and (2) their polymorphic delivery.

Mechanism (1) serializes a message object with additional information (e.g., data integrity or routing information) as an encrypted binary stream, and then hides the resulting stream as the data field of another message used for transmission. Intercepting the transmitted message would not leak its hidden content to interceptors. In the meantime, it cannot be tampered with undetectably either: before delivering the message to a destination, the model retrieves the message's hidden content, using it to verify the message's integrity and destination.

Mechanism (2) steps away from the standard message delivery, in which the delivered message data is presented identically to all destinations, having so-called *monomorphic* semantic. Instead, depending on the destination's trustworthiness at runtime, the delivered message data is presented either in no form, raw form, or encrypted form, thus having *polymorphic* semantic. No data is presented for misrouted messages or when the message's integrity cannot be verified. Raw data is presented to destinations whose trustworthiness can be established. Encrypted data is presented to all other destinations. However, the received encrypted data can still be used in limited computational scenarios, due to homomorphic encryption (HE) and convergent encryption (CE), which preserve certain arithmetic and comparison properties of ciphertext, respectively.

To the best of our knowledge, our approach is the first to apply HE and CE to the design of message-based communication models. Homomorphic and convergent operations on sensitive data provide the middle ground between permitting access to raw data and denying access altogether. The primary barrier to widespread adoption of HE and CE has been their heavy performance overhead. The resulting escalation in execution time has rendered these encryption techniques a poor fit for intensive computational workloads of large statistical

---

[2] All of them target Android, due to its open-sourced codebase, which can be examined and modified.

analyses and machine learning. In contrast, our work demonstrates that HE and CE can effectively solve long-standing problems in the design of mobile message-based communication. Because mobile communication rarely involves large computational workloads, the inclusion of HE and CE provides the required security and flexibility benefits, without noticeable deterioration in user experience.

To reify our model, we developed POLICC, an Android middleware[3] that plug-in replaces Android inter-component communication (ICC). POLICC mitigates interception, eavesdropping, and permission escalation attacks, without preventing untrusted-but-not-malicious apps from operating on delivered message data. Although our design trades performance for security, our evaluation shows that, POLICC effectively mitigates these attacks while adding at most 40.4 ms and 2 mW overheads, as compared to the Android ICC counterpart.

This paper contributes:

(1) HTPD—a novel model that strengthens the security of message-based communication via hidden transmission and polymorphic delivery. This model retains the protection of prior models, but eliminates their unnecessary restrictions, so untrusted-but-not-malicious destinations can perform useful operations on the delivered message data.
(2) The first successful application of homomorphic and convergent encryption to the design of mobile message-based communication, offering operations on encrypted sensitive data as the middle ground between permitting access to raw data and denying access altogether.
(3) POLICC—a reification of HTPD that plug-in replaces Android ICC, mitigating interception, eavesdropping, and permission escalation attacks, without preventing untrusted-but-not-malicious apps from operating on delivered data. Through its plug-and-play integration with the Android system, POLICC requires only minimal changes to existing apps.
(4) An experimental evaluation that shows how POLICC prevents the aforementioned attacks carried out against benchmarks and real apps, while incurring low performance and programming effort overheads.

2 Threat Model

By following our model, message-based communication can prevent data leakage, so it would not be exploited by *interception, eavesdropping*, and *permission*

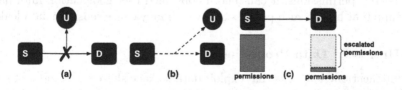

Fig. 1. Examples of attacks

---

[3] Similarly to prior works, we target Android as the dominant open-source platform.

escalation attacks. Our model can strengthen any message-based communication, but our reference implementation is Android-specific. We generally define each of the aforementioned attacks, and present examples of their real-world occurrences in Android apps.

2.1 Examples of Data Leakage Attacks

Interception: Figure 1-a demonstrates an interception attack: source S is transferring data to destination D, with U intercepting the transferred data. Another common name of this attack is *man-in-the-middle*.

In Android, apps can communicate with each other via inter-component communication (ICC). Using ICC, a source app sends an Intent[4] to user-permitted destination apps: with *explicit* Intents, only specific destinations can receive data; with *implicit* Intents, any destination that registers a certain Intent Filter[5] can receive data. As defined in Common Attack Pattern Enumeration and Classification (CAPEC) [1], an interception attack occurs when malicious apps inappropriately receive an implicit Intent by declaring a certain Intent Filter [5]. These attacks have been detected in many real-world Android apps [16], which even be used in some developer tools for benign purposes. For example, a developer tool, `Intent Intercept`, intercepts the transferred Intent to help developers in debugging ICC-based communication [4].

Eavesdropping: Figure 1-b demonstrates an eavesdropping attack: source S broadcasts data to destination D, but U (i.e., eavesdropper) can also receive the data. In Android, when an app broadcasts Intents, any app can receive them by declaring a certain Intent Filter. Consider a real eavesdropping attack reported in CVE, when WiFi is switched, the Android system broadcasts an Intent that contains detailed WiFi network information (e.g., network name, BSSID, IP, and DNS server). However, having declared the corresponding Intent Filter, any applications can receive this Intent and disclose the sensitive information[3].

Permission Escalation: Figure 1-c demonstrates a permission escalation attack: source S has been granted sufficient permissions to access sensitive data, but destination D has not. When S sends its sensitive data to D, D's permission is escalated. In Android, to access sensitive user data (e.g., GPS, contacts, and SMS), apps must secure the required permissions. As previously reported, attackers can force apps, with dissimilar permissions, to communicate sensitive data to other apps, thus leaking it to the destinations [10,36]. For example, if an app has GPS permissions, it can send its obtained user geolocation information to any app that has no such permissions, which may cause sensitive data leakage.

2.2 Untrusted Data Processing

The aforementioned attacks that exploit data leakage share the same root cause: a destination illicitly accesses and discloses or tampers with sensitive mes-

---

[4] In ICC, Intent objects serve as data delivery vehicles.

[5] Intent Filter declares expected Intent properties (action/category).

sage data. However, blocking all suspicious message transmissions may paralyze apps' legitimate operations. Consider the scenario from the eavesdropping attack above: if, having received a message containing the device's IP address, an untrusted app uses the received IP only for legitimate operations (e.g., host IP verification), is it reasonable to block all such message transmissions to strengthen security?

A more flexible solution could use homomorphic encryption (HE) and convergent encryption (CE), currently most commonly used for sending sensitive data to the cloud for processing by untrusted providers. Using HE/CE schemes, data owners encrypt and send their data to the cloud server. The cloud server operates on and returns the encrypted results to the data owner. Only the data owner, possessing the secret key, can decrypt the results. In the case above, an untrusted app can still receive the IP address's encrypted version to verify its host address, without accessing the raw IP address. By means of HE/CE, HTPD enables untrusted apps to operate on sensitive data without data leakage.

2.3 Assumptions and Scope

To counteract the threats, our design is subject to the following constraints:

(1) **Assumptions: Trustworthiness.** Since HTPD relies on apps' trustworthiness to determine whether to expose no data, raw data, or encrypted data, we assume that application trustworthiness can be reliably configured or calculated. Further, attackers cannot change the involved apps' trustworthiness. As an abstract metric of how to expose the data, the trustworthiness can be represented as many specific forms, such as permissions in the above example attacks (Sect. 3.1).

(2) **Scope: Message-based data leakage vulnerabilities.** HTPD's focus is message-based data leakage vulnerabilities. That is, the vulnerabilities should (a) cause data leakage, and (b) occur during message transmission. Hence, other attacks, such as denial of service (DoS)[6] that target data transmission (not data leakage), stealing data by breaking the system (not during message transmission), are out of scope. Also, since attacking key management to obtain decryption keys is an orthogonal issue, we consider it out of our scope. To mitigate this issue, HTPD should be used with proven key management schemes/systems.

3   The HTPD Model

We present the HTPD model and its application to Android ICC in turn next.

---

[6] Although DoS is not our focus, one of PoliCC's features mitigates them (see Sect. 6.4).

3.1   Definitions

(1) Source/Destination. In message-based communication, a *source* sends messages, and a *destination* receives messages. In mobile platforms, apps can be both source and destination.

(2) Sending and Receiving Points. We use the term *a sending point* to describe an API function, invoked by a *source* and passed message data, that starts transmitting messages. *A receiving point* is a callback API function, through which a *destination* retrieves the transferred message data.

(3) Trustworthiness. Trustworthiness measures the degree to which an app can be trusted. We use this metric to define how an app can access message data. An app whose trustworthiness is established can access raw message data; otherwise, encrypted data or no data. Trustworthiness can be measured in different ways: **(a)** data integrity (i.e., to detect data tampering) and destination examinations (i.e., to detect misrouting). For example, if the received message fails such examinations, the destination app should not access the raw data. **(b)** apps' permissions and the relationship between apps' permission sets. For example, if a source app's permission set is larger than that of a destination app, messages transmitted between them may become vulnerable to permission escalation attacks, causing data leakage (Sect. 2.1). **(c)** reputation score. For example, if an app's reputation score in app markets [26] is low, then allowing it to access raw data may cause data leakage. HTPD *can be parameterized with various measures of trustworthiness, as required for a given scenario of message-based communication. In particular, to determine an app's trustworthiness, our HTPD's reification uses both (a) and (b).*

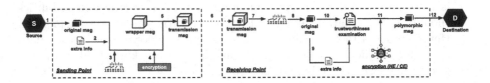

Fig. 2. HTPD transmission mechanisms

3.2   Transmission Mechanisms

Figure 2 depicts HTPD's hidden transmission and polymorphic delivery mechanisms. When a source starts transmitting a message (step 1), the message's data field is inserted with some extra information (e.g., custom routing) (step 2). After that, the message is serialized (step 3) and encrypted (step 4) to a binary stream, which becomes the data field of a newly created wrapper message. Hence, the original message is hidden within the wrapper message, which becomes *the transmission message* (step 5).

Next, the transmission message is dispatched via the system's standard communication channel (step 6). Once the transmission message arrives to its receiving point, its data field is extracted, decrypted, and deserialized into the original message (steps 7, 8). Then, the extracted extra information is used to examine the destination's trustworthiness (e.g., data integrity, app permissions), which determines in which form the message data can be accessed. In the cases of failed integrity checks or misrouted deliveries, HTPD would not disclose any data. If the destination's trustworthiness is established, HTPD reveals the raw form of the original message's data; otherwise, it encrypts the data into its homomorphically or convergently encrypted form (step 11). Due to its polymorphic delivery, the final received message is referred to as "polymorphic message" (step 12).

3.3 HTPD in Practice

To reify HTPD, we developed POLICC, a plug-in replacement of Android ICC. By mitigating Android ICC's data leakage vulnerabilities, POLICC prevents the aforementioned attacks (Sect. 2.1). Following the definitions above, apps serve as message source/destination, whose sending/receiving points are managed by POLICC (in Fig. 3). POLICC retains *Intent objects* as ICC transmission vehicles, but hides the original Intent object within a so-called *Host Intent* object, whose data field stores the original Intent object's encrypted serialized version.

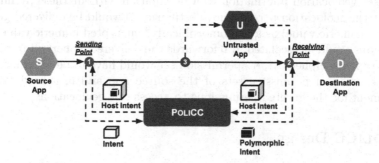

Fig. 3. POLICC solution overview

To guide its polymorphic delivery, POLICC computes the destination app's trustworthiness: (a) the delivered message's routing information[7], and (b) how the permission sets of the source and destination apps relate to each other. POLICC delivers no data from messages identified as tampered with or misrouted; it delivers raw data to destinations whose permission sets are equal to or exceed those of source apps; and it delivers homomorphically or convergently encrypted data to all other destinations.

---

[7] In Android ICC, routing information can be used for both data integrity and destination examinations (detailed in Sect. 5.2).

Consider how PoliCC prevents the attacks described in Sect. 2.1: **Preventing Interception Attacks.** As shown in Fig. 3, an interception attack can be carried out at the receiving point ❷: an untrusted app U becomes the final delivery destination by declaring a certain Intent Filter, or at point ❸ before the receiving point: with Android ICC, U intercepts the transferred data.

In the first case, having received the transferred Intent, U would be able to retrieve the contained raw data only if U's permission set equals to or exceeds that of the source app. Otherwise, the received data would be homomorphically or convergently encrypted, so it would not be leaked. In the second case, U would receive a Host Intent, containing only the encrypted and thus inaccessible original Intent. At this point, tampering with the Host Intent's routing information would be easily detected through data integrity and destination examinations at ❷.

Preventing Eavesdropping Attacks. As discussed in Sect. 2.1, an eavesdropping attack occurs when the Android system broadcasts an IP address (i.e., string value), received by both a trusted app D and an untrusted app U. Without sufficient permissions, U would receive the IP address as a convergently[8] encrypted string. Since convergent encryption makes it possible to compare encrypted values for equality, U can verify the host address by convergently encrypting the host address and comparing the result with the received data.

Preventing Permission Escalation Attacks. As discussed in Sect. 2.1, an escalation attack occurs when a source app with GPS permissions obtains and sends user geolocation information to a destination without these permissions. Without the geolocation permissions, destination D would be delivered geolocation (i.e., numeric value) as a homomorphically[9] encrypted numeric value, so no permissions would be escalated. If D forwards the delivered ciphertext to malware M to decrypt the ciphertext, M's permission set would have to be equal or greater than the union of permission sets of the source app and D, a hard-to-satisfy requirement for the granted permissions to access raw geolocations.

4 PoliCC Design

We next explain PoliCC's design and then describe its architecture and permission policies.

4.1 Design Choices

PoliCC follows several design choices that we made by consulting prior studies.

(1) **Why Intents?.** As its message delivery vehicle, PoliCC retains Intents to facilitate integration with existing apps, protecting their Intents from leakage. *Prior Finding: Apps commonly store data in Intent's extended data field* [38].

---

[8] Convergent encryption is applied to string data.
[9] Homomorphic encryption is applied to numeric data.

(2) **Why Focus on Integer and String?.** POLiCC supports operating on encrypted strings and integer values. *Prior Finding:Android API methods that manipulate Integer and String values (i.e., `putString` and `putInt`) are among the top 10 mostly used* [32].

(3) **Why Activity and Broadcast Communication?.** POLiCC supports `startActivity`. *Prior Finding: The `startActivity` ICC method is the most frequently used* [41]. Further, to demonstrate HTPD's applicability, POLiCC also supports `sendBroadcast`, whose data flow allows multiple destinations.

4.2   System Architecture

Figure 4 shows POLiCC's architecture. Via the Android ICC, a `Source App` sends a regular Intent object (step 1). The sending flow is redirected via an Xposed hook that forwards (step 2) the sent Intent object to POLiCC `Module`, which initiates a protection procedure (i.e., the sending point). The forwarded Intent is inserted with the source app's package name as another extended data field (i.e., its transmission history is recorded for permission examinations Sect. 5.2), and is then serialized and encrypted (via AES) into a byte array, with the result placed in a Host Intent object, thereby concealing the original Intent. It is the Host Intent object that continues its transmission through the Android ICC (step 3).

Right before delivering the Host Intent (i.e., the receiving point), POLiCC's another Xposed hook redirects (step 4) the Intent to POLiCC `Module`, which extracts the original Intent data and reconstructs the original Intent (Re-encapsulation). POLiCC then collects the routing information and the permission sets for both source and destination apps, passing them to the `Routing info & Permission Examination`. The routing information determines, via `Routing info Examination`, whether to return no data. The relationship between the permissions of the source and destination apps determines, via `Permission Examination`, whether to homomorphically or convergently encrypt the Intent's data. Finally, POLiCC delivers the `Polymorphic Intent` object to the `Destination App` (step 5). There is no separate `Polymorphic Intent` type. Rather, these entities are normal Intent objects, whose content has been protected.

User-configured (via `Configuration`) custom keys encrypt the decryption keys of homomorphic/convergent encryption, persisting them in Android private storage [27]. Note that, by relying on Android's private storage, we treat *key management* as orthogonal to our design, which can straightforwardly integrate more elaborate key management schemes as system services. In addition, by configuring PoliCC to notify of the transmission information (e.g., source/destination, permissions, data types, actions) (`Notify`), the user can stop the delivery of any PoliCC Intents.

With the design choices above, consider how our architecture secures the

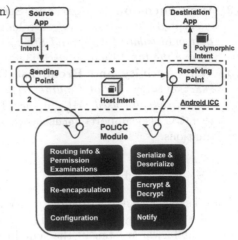

Fig. 4. PoliCC Architecture

Android ICC while enabling untrusted data processes. To transmit messages securely, PoliCC provides Host and Polymorphic Intents for ICC's data transmission flow of both Activity and Broadcast. The Host Intent acts as a transmission vehicle over the Android ICC; it hides the original Intent's data and routing information. The Polymorphic Intent delivers data polymorphically: only destination apps with sufficient permissions can access raw Intent data. To allow untrusted apps to operate on sensitive data securely, PoliCC provides arithmetic and comparison operations on ciphertext, enabled by homomorphic and convergent encryption: *Variant of Elgamal* encryption[10] [17] for `int`/`Integer`/`BigInteger` values and convergent encryption (combines SHA256 with AES) for `String` values. So `int`/`Integer`/`BigInteger` variables become `HEInteger` objects, and `String` ones become encrypted `String` objects.

4.3 Permission Policies

As discussed in Sect. 3.3, PoliCC uses Android app permissions and the relationship between the permission sets of the source/destination apps as the trustworthiness measure that determines whether to deliver raw data or encrypted data[11]. Hence, we design PoliCC as a policy-based middleware: an extensible set of policies governs data access and Intent routing. $\rightarrow$ indicates the *From-To* Intent transmission relationship within the device. E.g., $\{I \mid (S \rightarrow D)_t\}$ indicates that the source app S sends the Intent I to the destination app D at time t.

---

[10] As fully homomorphic encryption is slow, its partial variant achieves a practical performance security tradeoff.

[11] Because the "no data" delivery is caused by failed data integrity checks rather than permissions, we detail it in Sect. 5.2.

$P(S)_t$ denotes the permission set of app S at time t. If the user changes $P(S)$ at runtime, $P(S)_t \neq P(S)_{t+1}$. Hence, POLICC always dynamically analyzes permissions, reading the latest permissions for all apps. Further, I denotes the original Intent, and I_{EN} denotes that its data has been encrypted. We define the POLICC policies as follows:

(1) **Encryption & Decryption Policies.**
When D receives I (or I_{EN}) from S, if the permission set of S is a subset of or equal to that of D, I's (or I_{EN}'s) data remains unencrypted; encrypted otherwise:
If $\{I$ or $I_{EN} \mid (S \rightarrow D)_t\}$,

- iff $P(S)_t \subseteq P(D)_t$, return I
- otherwise, return I_{EN}

(2) **Permission Transitivity.** Whether a destination app receives I or I_{EN} is determined by the transitive closure of the permission relationships between the encountered apps in that Intent's transmission chain:
If $\{I \mid ((S \rightarrow D1)_t \rightarrow D2)_{t+1}\}$,

- iff $(P(S)_{t+1} \cup P(D1)_{t+1}) \subseteq P(D2)_{t+1}$, return I
- otherwise, return I_{EN}

5 Implementation

We describe POLICC's hidden transmission and polymorphic delivery.

5.1 Hidden Transmission

To seamlessly integrate hidden transmission into Android ICC, we had to determine: (1) where to place the sending/receiving points, and (2) how to pack message data into its delivery vehicle.

(1) **Hook Mechanism.** For POLICC to take control over the delivery of Intent objects, the hook mechanism taps into the Android ICC. ICC commences by invoking the standard Android APIs, `startActivity` to start an activity and `sendBroadcast` to send a broadcast, so we use them as "sending points." Similarly, ICC ends up the final delivery by invoking `performLaunchActivity` for the activity and `deliverToRegisteredReceiverLocked` for the broadcast, so we use them as "receiving points." POLICC intercepts the sending and receiving points by hooking into these API methods. Then, POLICC's custom code is injected to execute before or after the intercepted API methods, thus performing HTPD's transmission strategies.

(2) Host Intent. A Host Intent is derived from an original Intent by retaining the routing information (e.g., action, category) but removing the extended data (i.e., the data inserted via `putExtra`). Instead, the only pieces of extended data in Host Intent are serialized and encrypted representations of the original Intent. This implementation strategy is non-intrusive, thus requiring no changes to the source app's Intent API. Specifically, our implementation intercepts the built-in Intent transmission procedure at the points right before an Intent is dispatched (i.e., sending points) and delivered (i.e., receiving points). At the sending point, a Host Intent is constructed, replacing the original Intent; at the receiving point, the Host Intent's content is extracted, decrypted, and deserialized into the original Intent, which is then polymorphically delivered to the destination app (see Sect. 5.2). Notice that this strategy makes it possible to transmit Host Intents through the built-in Intent transmission channels. Because these two interception points cannot be bypassed, the Host Intents would always be constructed at the sending point, and the original Intent would always be reconstructed at the receiving point. In essence, POLICC can straightforwardly detect any tampering with the routing information of a Host Intent.

5.2 Polymorphic Delivery

To seamlessly integrate polymorphic delivery into Android ICC, we had to determine: (1) how to link trustworthiness (i.e., routing info and permission relationships) to delivery strategies (i.e., no data, raw data, or encrypted data), and (2) if it is possible to bypass our secure delivery mechanism and how to defend against it. We solve these problems as follows.

(1) Examining Routing Info and Permissions. As described above, in the sending point, POLICC re-encapsulates the original Intent object, retaining its routing information, and inserts the source app's information, which is checked as follows:

a) *to check the routing information*, having intercepted the Intent in the receiving point, POLICC extracts the routing information from both the Host and original Intents and compares them for equality (i.e., integrity check). Then, it checks whether the current destination is reachable through the original Intent's routing information (i.e., destination examination). If any of these checks fails, the Intent object may have been tampered with, causing POLICC to deliver no data to the destination app.

b) *to check the permission relationships between the source and destination apps*, from the original Intent, POLICC extracts the inserted source app information. Note that, before sending or forwarding an Intent (i.e., the sending point), POLICC appends the current source app's package name into the Intent's data field, thus keeping track of the Intent's transmission history. At the receiving point, POLICC computes the union of the permissions granted to all source apps, through which the Intent has passed in that transmission. Next, POLiCC obtains the destination app's permissions via the Android API. The results are compared based on the *permission transitivity policy* (see Sect. 4.3): if the destination app's permissions are not equal to or exceed the union of the source permissions set, POLiCC delivers the homomorphically/convergently encrypted data to the destination app.

(2) **Defense against *Encryption Bypassing* Attack.** When forwarding a polymorphic Intent with encrypted data to a sufficiently permitted destination app (see policies in Sect. 4.3), POLiCC decrypts the contained data. To that end, a special field, `isEncrypted`, reflects whether the extended data of a Polymorphic Intent has been encrypted, so as to prevent the encryption of ciphertext. However, malware can attempt to bypass the encryption process by maliciously setting the `isEncrypted` field of an unencrypted Intent to "true," an occurrence that we call an *encryption bypassing attack.*

To defend against this attack, POLiCC provides a simple but effective defense: when the `isEncrypted` field is set to "true", POLiCC first decrypts the data and then encrypts it again. However, decrypting unencrypted data produces an unusable value, out of which the original Intent data cannot be recovered[12]. Hence, this design effectively defends against the attacks that tamper with the `isEncrypted` field, albeit rendering the transferred data unusable as a result of invalid data attacks. Our design contends with the possibility of Intent data becoming damaged in such cases, as the main objective is to defend against data leakage attacks.

5.3   Computing with Encrypted Data

As discussed above, Intent's `String` data become convergently encrypted `String` objects, and `int/Integer/BigInteger` data become homomorphically encrypted `HEInteger` objects in order to allow untrusted-but-not-malicious apps to operate on ciphertext.

6   Evaluation

we seek to answer the following questions: **Q1. Effectiveness**: How effectively does POLiCC reduce the threats? **Q2. Cost**: What is the performance overhead of POLiCC on top of the Android ICC? **Q3. Effort**: How much additional programming effort is required to use POLiCC instead of Android ICC?

6.1   Environment Setup

Because POLiCC is implemented on top of the Xposed framework, our evaluation uses this framework's latest version (XposedBridge version-82 and Xposed

---

[12] With POLiCC's encryption implementation, decrypting unencpyted data destroys the original data, which may not be the case for other encryption implementations.

Installer-3.1.5). Besides, to make use of as many Android latest features as possible, while guaranteeing the compatibility of Android apps, we use the Android Nougat (7.x) and Lollipop (5.x), currently run by 28.2% (the first highest percentage among the 8 most popular Android versions [25]) and 17.9% (the fourth highest percentage) of Android devices. These Android releases as well as the latest one are vulnerable to all the aforementioned attacks. In all experiments, the devices are: Nexus 6 with Android 7.1.1, Moto X with Android 5.1, and Moto G2 with Android 5.1.1.

6.2   Evaluation Design

Q1. Effectiveness. As discussed in Sect. 2, PoLiCC plug-in replaces ICC to secure its message-based communication against interception, eavesdropping, and permission escalation attacks. To evaluate PoLiCC's security mechanisms, we simulated the attacks, discussed in Sect. 2.1, and conducted a case study with three real-world apps, discussed in turn next:

(1) Reproducing Attacks. To test how effectively PoLiCC defends apps against the attacks described in Sect. 2.1, we had to reproduce these attacks with real apps. Unfortunately, several of the apps, mentioned in the CVE entries describing the attacks, are not open-sourced, while the target attacks would be impossible to trigger in a black-box fashion. Hence, we had to recreate the described apps on our own.

   (a) To reproduce the interception attack on message-based communication at the receiving point, we created: source app S, destination app D, and interceptor app U. S invokes `startActivity(Intent)` to send an implicit Intent to D. However, by registering the same `Intent Filter`, the untrusted app U receives the same Intent object as well. *To reproduce the interception attack on message-based communication before the receiving point,* we implemented another interceptor app U2, which intercepts the sent Intent objects before they arrive at the receiving point, to misroute their delivery by tampering with their routing information. Without loss of generality, we assumed that the end-user had designated the destination apps as our untrusted apps U and U2.

   (b) To reproduce the eavesdropping attack, we created source and destination apps (i.e., S and D), with the same system-level permissions, and `IP Verification` app V with no such permissions. S invokes `sendBroadcast(Intent)` to broadcast an Intent to be received by D. The Intent object contains an IP address. However, by registering the same `Intent Filter`, V can receive the same Intent object as well.

   (c) To reproduce the permission escalation attack, we created GC, a `geolocation collecting` app, permitted to obtain geolocations from the GPS sensor, and DE, a `distance estimating` app, forbidden to read geolocations. To process the obtained geolocations, GC invokes `startActivity(Intent)` to directly send an explicit Intent to DE. DE receives the Intent, retrieves the contained geolocation, and estimates the distance of user movement.

We simulated the above attacks using Android ICC and PoLiCC, and then compared the respective outcomes. To determine whether PoLiCC's polymorphic delivery correctly responds to changes in app permissions, we carried out each attack scenario with sufficient and insufficient permissions. More importantly, to illustrate that apps with insufficient permissions can still execute useful operations, we reused the IP Verification V and distance estimater (DE) apps from the attack scenarios (b)(c) above to check if their original operations (i.e., verify host IP–V, estimate distance of movement–DE) can still be executed.

(2) *A case study with real-world apps.* We also evaluated how effective PoLiCC was at mitigating the aforementioned attacks in three open-source, real-world apps: Intent Intercept [4] (a debugging app), Mylocation [23] (a GPS app), and QKSMS [37] (a messaging app). By registering numerous Intent Filters, Intent Intercept intercepts implicit Intents and examines their data fields. Having the geolocation permissions (ACCESS_COARSE_LOCATION and ACCESS_FINE_LOCATION), Mylocation can obtain the user's geolocation and share it with other apps via an implicit Intent with the ACTION_SEND action. Using its Intent Filter for the ACTION_SEND action, QKSMS can receive the Intents containing this action. However, QKSMS has no geolocation permissions. In our case studies, we always used Mylocation as the source and QKSMS as the destination.

Q2. Cost. To determine whether PoLiCC's performance overhead is acceptable, we compare the respective execution time and energy consumption[13] taken to deliver Intent data from the source to the destination app by PoLiCC and the Android ICC. Our measurements (a) exclude prompting the user to approve the Intent transmission; (b) fix the length of intent data items (32 bytes for the String objects); (c) repeat all executions 20 times and then compute the average execution time; (d) trigger startActivity/startBroadcast 100 times in 5 minutes, measuring the amount of energy consumed by the participating apps and the system; and (e) fix the experimental device (i.e., Moto G2) to compare PoLiCC with the Android ICC. Besides, we isolate the time PoLiCC takes to deliver Intents to identify the performance bottlenecks.

Q3. Effort. To confirm PoLiCC's portability, we test it on combinations of devices that run the Lolipop and Nougat Android framework versions. To estimate PoLiCC's programming effort, we measure the uncommented lines of code (ULOC) required to modify the original source app's ICC code that sends an Intent to a destination app to (a) access the Intent data, and (b) retrieve and use homomorphically/convergently encrypted data.

---

[13] We measure energy consumption with PowerTutor 1.4 [35].

6.3   Results

Q1. Effectiveness.

Table 1. Effectiveness of POLiCC

Attacks	Permission	Data retrieved		Successful defense		Operations	
		ICC	PoliCC	ICC	PoliCC	ICC	PoliCC
Interception —at receiving point	insufficient	raw	encrypted	×	✓	-	-
	sufficient	raw	raw	×	×	-	-
Interception —before receiving point	-	raw	no data	×	✓	-	-
Eavesdropping	insufficient	raw	encrypted	×	✓	✓	✓
	sufficient	raw	raw	×	×	✓	✓
Permission Escalation	insufficient	raw	encrypted	×	✓	✓	✓
	sufficient	raw	raw	×	×	✓	✓

(1) Reproducing Attacks. Table 1 summarizes the outcomes of reproducing each of the attacks: *(a) For the interception attack on message-based communication at the receiving point* (i.e., row "Interception—at receiving point"), whether the interceptor app U's permissions are sufficient or not, Android ICC always delivers the Intent's raw data to U, thus leaking sensitive data to an untrusted party. In contrast, if U's permission set is smaller than that of the source app (i.e., insufficient permissions), POLiCC delivers encrypted Intent data, thus successfully preventing the attack. *For the interception attack on message-based communication before the receiving point* (i.e., row "Interception—before receiving point"), after U2 tampers with the Host Intent's routing information, its examination fails causing POLiCC to deliver no data to the destination app, thus repelling the attack.

(b) For the eavesdropping attack, whether the IP Verifi- cation V's permissions are sufficient or not, the Android ICC always delivers a raw IP address, thus leaking the data to V. In contrast, when V's permission set is smaller than that of the source app, POLiCC delivers convergently encrypted IP address. Although V cannot access the raw data, it can still validate the host IP using the received encrypted IP address (column "Operations").

(c) For the permission escalation attack, similar to the attacks above, the Android ICC always delivers an explicit Intent with a raw geolocation to the distance estimater (DE), so the attack succeeds in exfiltrating the sensitive geolocation. In contrast, POLiCC Intent data's encryption status is determined by the source/destination permission relationship. When DE has insufficient permissions, POLiCC delivers homomorphically encrypted longitude and latitude values, so their raw values are not leaked. More importantly, DE can still perform its distance estimation operation to approximate the distance by computing with the encrypted values.

In summary, the Android ICC leaves the data vulnerable to all three attacks, while POLiCC prevents these attacks and still preserves the ability of untrusted destination apps to operate on the received encrypted message data.

(2) Case study with real-world apps.

Case 1 (interception): (a) QKSMS acts as the malicious app that intercepts the implicit Intents sent by Mylocation. In the original setup, QKSMS always obtains the raw geolocation value. With POLICC, since QKSMS lacks the geolocation permissions, it obtains only a homomorphically encrypted geolocation. With the geolocation permissions added to QKSMS's manifest file, it is the end-user who determines the app's data access by granting or declining the geolocation permissions, so QKSMS obtains the raw or encrypted geolocation values, respectively.

(b) Intent Intercept acts as the malicious app that intercepts the implicit Intents. The app is configured to always obtain the implicit Intents sent by Mylocation. However, as it lacks GPS permissions, Intent Intercept can only access geolocation data that is homomorphically encrypted, so the raw geolocations are never leaked.

Case 2 (eavesdropping): To execute an eavesdropping attack, Mylocation sends the same Intent as in Case 1 via an added sendBroadcast. QKSMS receives this Intent via an added broadcast receiver, registered for the ACTION_SEND action. In the original setup, QKSMS always obtains the raw geolocation, irrespective of whether the end-user grants/declines the geolocation permissions. With POLICC, it is the end-user who determines the app's data access by granting or declining the geolocation permissions, so QKSMS obtains the raw or encrypted geolocation values, respectively.

Case 3 (permission escalation): To execute a permission escalation attack, Mylocation creates an explicit Intent containing a geolocation, sending it to an added Activity in QKSMS. In the original setup, this permission escalation attack always succeeds. With POLICC, the attack always fails, as long as QKSMS has no geolocation permissions.

Q2. Cost. Table 2 (at the top) shows POLICC's overheads. Specifically, POLICC's startActivity increases T by 28.3 ms, E_{app} by 0.8J, and ΔE_{sys} by 1mW; send- Broadcast increases T by 40.4 ms, E_{app} by 0.5J, ΔE_{sys} by 2 mW, as compared to the Android ICC counterparts. Table 2 (at the bottom) breaks down the execution time per each POLICC procedure. In both startActivity and sendBroadcast, the Sending/Receiving Points perform similarly: these procedures' hook and re-encapsulation mechanisms are fixed for all operations.

Since POLICC increases T by 40.4 ms (43.2 - 2.8 in sendBroadcast column) at most, its *execution time overheads* are in line with other related solutions (e.g., [29]'s performance overhead is ≈39 ms), with the total latency much lower than the Android response time limit (5000 ms [24]). Also, since POLICC increases E_{app} by 0.8J (8.7 - 7.9 in sendActivity column) and ΔE_{sys} by 2 mW (20 - 18) at most, its *energy consumption overheads* are negligible. It is POLICC's protection mechanisms (i.e., re-encapsulation, encryption/decryption) that incur these performance and energy overheads.

Table 2. PoliCC's Overheads (milliseconds–ms, Joules–J, milliwatt–mW)

ICCs	startActivity $(T \ / \ E_{app} \ / \ \Delta E_{sys})^*$	sendBroadcast $(T \ / \ E_{app} \ / \ \Delta E_{sys})^*$
Android ICC	57.0 ms / 7.9 J / 37 mW↑	2.8 ms / 5.3 J / 18 mW↑
PoliCC	85.3 ms / 8.7 J / 38 mW↑	43.2 ms / 5.8 J / 20 mW↑

Operations	Sending Point	Receiving Point
startActivity	28.2 ms	13.5 ms
sendBroadcast	28.8 ms	9.5 ms

* T: execution time (ms); E_{app}: energy consumed by source/destination apps
(J); ΔE_{sys}: additional system energy consumed by ICCs (mW).

Q3. Effort. We first confirm PoliCC's portability by testing its operations on three Android devices/versions: Nexus 6/Android 7.1.1, Moto X/Android 5.1, and Moto G2/Android 5.1.1 by running our subject apps on these devices in different combinations. This test has not revealed any deployment and operational issues. For source apps, the PoliCC API is indistinguishable from that of the Android ICC as well as for sufficiently permitted destination apps, as the delivered Polymorphic Intents return raw data. With insufficient permissions, additional code is required in destination apps to handle the delivered homomorphically/convergently encrypted data.

Nevertheless, the extra programming effort is small, as Table 3 demonstrates: in the source apps, PoliCC requires no deviation from the familiar Android ICC API (column "Send"). In the destination apps, the code for retrieving, using, and creating `int`/`Integer`/`BigInteger` and `String` objects require extra lines of code (columns "Retrieve", "Use", and "Create"): (a) For `BigInteger` and `String` objects (columns "BigInt." and "Str."), due to the inheritance hierarchies of their operations, the code for retrieving them is indistinguishable between the Android ICC and PoliCC (column "Retrieve"). To use the retrieved `String` object, 1 extra LOC is required to separate its convergently encrypted value. To use the retrieved `BigInteger` object, 1 extra LOC is required to check whether the data is homomorphically encrypted (column "Use"). (b) For `int`/`Integer` values (columns "int"/"Int."), their original receiving and operating methods are replaced with `HEInteger`'s methods (`add`, `subtract`, and `multiply`), taking 4 extra LOCs at most (columns "Retrieve" and "Use"). Finally, it takes 3 extra LOC to create homomorphically and convergently encrypted `int`/`Integer`/`BigInteger` and `String` values (column "Create").

Table 3. PoliCC's Extra Prog. Effort (ULOC)

Send	Retrieve		Use		Create	
	int/Int./BigInt	Str.	int/Int./BigInt	Str	int/Int./BigInt	Str.
0	1/1/0	0	4/4/1	1	3/3/3	3

6.4 Discussion

POLiCC's HTPD implementation may suffer from false positives/negatives if app permissions are granted incorrectly. This limitation can be mitigated by notifying users of potential security attacks. As an extra feature (Sect. 4.2), POLiCC's Notify module can be configured to report the transmission information (e.g., source/destination, permissions, data types, actions) to the user, who can then stop the delivery of any POLiCC Intents. Further, the Notify module can also mitigate the denial of service attacks: it can detect and block notifications floods from any source app. POLiCC performs Hook mechanism via Xposed. Note that we use Xposed to create a viable proof of concept to be able to evaluate POLiCC's security-enhancing properties. To commercially deploy HTPD, one can fully integrate it and its mechanisms with any Android release and other mobile platforms, despite the peculiarities of our reference implementation.

7 Related Work

Data Flow & ICC Calls Monitoring. Most of the existing solutions counteract data leakage attacks by monitoring the data flow or ICC calls. Taint-Droid [20] traces data flows by labeling sensitive data and transitively applying labels as the data propagates through program variables, files, and interprocess messages. If any tainted data is to leave the system via a sink (e.g., network interface), the system notifies the user about the coming data leakage. Flow-Droid [8] applies static taint analysis to check if any app lifecycle contains data leaks. XManDroid [12] tracks and analyzes the ICC data transferred in Intent objects at runtime to enforce the app's compliance with the defined permission policy. QUIRE [18] enables users to examine and terminate the chain of requests associated with an ICC call. ComDroid [16] statically analyzes *.dex binaries of Android apps to log potential component vulnerabilities. Besides, ComDroid tracks how an Intent object changes moving from its source to destination. Other state-of-the-art Intent vulnerabilities detectors (e.g., IccTa [31], DINA [6], DroidRA [33], SEALANT [30], IntentScope [28]) further improve the above methods for monitoring data flows & ICC calls. However, their reliance on overly restrictive policies prevents them from supporting Android application-specific data flows, also causing false-positives when data flows change unpredictably. In contrast, HTPD model systematically defends against data leakage attacks, requiring neither data flow nor call chain tracking.

Encryption. *Homomorphic encryption* enables computational operations on ciphertext, with some prior applications to mobile cloud computing. Carpov et al. [14] use homomorphic encryption to preserve the privacy of cloud-based health data. Drosatos et al. [19] use homomorphic encryption to preserve the privacy of crowd-sourced data accessed via the cloud. Besides, homomorphic encryption also can be used to compute the proximity of users in mobile social networks: Carter et al. [15] use homomorphic encryption to find common locations and friends via private set intersection operations that preserve user privacy. *Convergently encrypted* ciphertext can be compared, so this encryption can securely identify duplicated records. Bennett et al.'s convergent encryption-based encoding scheme allows boolean searches on ciphertext [9]. Anderson et al. apply convergent encryption to securely de-duplicate the number of backup files [7]. Wilcox-O'Hearn et al. apply convergent encryption to build a secure distributed storage [39]. PoLiCC brings homomorphic/convergent encryption to mobile computing to secure message-based communication while enabling untrusted apps to execute useful operations.

8   Conclusions

We have presented HTPD, hidden transmission and polymorphic delivery, a novel message-based communication model that secures message-based communication while allowing untrusted apps to operate on the received message data. As a reference implementation of HTPD, PoLiCC plug-in replaces and extends Android ICC to defend against common data leakage attacks, while also providing a uniform API for transmitting Intents. Our evaluation confirms that PoLiCC effectively prevents interception, eavesdropping, and permission escalation attacks, with low performance costs and programming effort overheads. In addition, we hope that our work would lead to HE and CE becoming widely accepted in the design space of mobile message-based communication.

Acknowledgements. The authors thank the anonymous reviewers, whose insightful comments helped improve this paper. NSF supported this research through the grant #1717065.

References

1. Common Attack Pattern Enumeration and Classification. capec.mitre.org/
2. CVE-2018-15752. cve.mitre.org/cgi-bin/cvename.cgi?name=CVE-2018-15752
3. CVE-2018-9489. cve.mitre.org/cgi-bin/cvename.cgi?name=CVE-2018-9489
4. Dev tool to view inter-app communication (2019). f-droid.org/en/packages/de. k3b.android.intentintercept/
5. Intent Intercept (2019). capec.mitre.org/data/definitions/499.html
6. Alhanahnah, M., et al.: Detecting vulnerable Android inter-app communication in dynamically loaded code. In: IEEE INFOCOM 2019, pp. 550–558. IEEE (2019)
7. Anderson, P., Zhang, L.: Fast and secure laptop backups with encrypted deduplication. In: LISA, vol. 10, p. 24th (2010)
8. Arzt, S., et al.: Flowdroid: Precise context, flow, field, object-sensitive and lifecycle-aware taint analysis for Android apps. Acm Sigplan Notices (2014)
9. Bennett, K., Grothoff, C., Horozov, T., Patrascu, I.: Efficient sharing of encrypted data. In: Batten, L., Seberry, J. (eds.) ACISP 2002. LNCS, vol. 2384, pp. 107–120. Springer, Heidelberg (2002). https://doi.org/10.1007/3-540-45450-0_8
10. Blasco, J., Chen, T.M., Muttik, I., Roggenbach, M.: Wild android collusions (2016)

11. Bosu, A., Liu, F., Yao, D.D., Wang, G.: Collusive data leak and more: large-scale threat analysis of inter-app communications. In: Asia Conference on Computer and Communications Security, pp. 71–85. ACM (2017)

12. Bugiel, S., Davi, L., Dmitrienko, A., Fischer, T., Sadeghi, A.R.: Xmandroid: A new Android evolution to mitigate privilege escalation attacks. Technische Universität Darmstadt, Technical Report TR-2011-04 (2011)

13. Bugiel, S., Davi, L., Dmitrienko, A., Fischer, T., Sadeghi, A.R., Shastry, B.: Towards taming privilege-escalation attacks on Android. In: NDSS (2012)

14. Carpov, S., Nguyen, T.H., Sirdey, R., Constantino, G., Martinelli, F.: Practical privacy-preserving medical diagnosis using homomorphic encryption. In: Cloud Computing, pp. 593–599. IEEE (2016)

15. Carter, H., Amrutkar, C., Dacosta, I., Traynor, P.: For your phone only: custom protocols for efficient secure function evaluation on mobile devices. Secur. Commun. Networks 7(7), 1165–1176 (2014)

16. Chin, E., Felt, A.P., Greenwood, K., Wagner, D.: Analyzing inter-application communication in Android. In: Proceedings of the 9th International Conference on Mobile Systems, Applications, and Services, pp. 239–252. ACM (2011)

17. Damgård, I., Groth, J., Salomonsen, G.: The theory and implementation of an electronic voting system. In: Secure Electronic Voting, pp. 77–99. Springer, Boston (2003). https://doi.org/10.1007/978-1-4615-0239-5_6

18. Dietz, M., Shekhar, S., Pisetsky, Y., Shu, A., Wallach, D.S.: Quire: lightweight provenance for smart phone operating systems. In: USENIX Security Symposium, vol. 31, p. 3 (2011)

19. Drosatos, G., Efraimidis, P.S., Athanasiadis, I.N., D'Hondt, E., Stevens, M.: A privacy-preserving cloud computing system for creating participatory noise maps. In: Computer Software and Applications Conference (COMPSAC), IEEE 36th Annual, pp. 581–586. IEEE (2012)

20. Enck, W., Gilbert, P., Han, S., Tendulkar, V., Chun, B.G., Cox, L.P., Jung, J., McDaniel, P., Sheth, A.N.: Taintdroid: an information-flow tracking system for realtime privacy monitoring on smartphones. ACM Trans. Comput. Syst. (TOCS) 32(2), 5 (2014)

21. Fang, Z., Han, W., Li, Y., Permission based Android security: Issues and countermeasures. Comput. Secur. 43, 205–218 (2014)

22. Felt, A.P., Wang, H.J., Moshchuk, A., Hanna, S., Chin, E.: Permission redelegation: attacks and defenses. In: USENIX Security Symposium (2011)

23. GDR!: My location (2019). https://tinyurl.com/yh9c8qok

24. Google: ANRs. developer.android.com/topic/performance/vitals/anr

25. Google: Distribution dashboard. developer.android.com/about/dashboards

26. Google: Google play (2018). play.google.com/store/apps?hl=en

27. Google: Data and file storage (2019). https://tinyurl.com/t6hr6t4

28. Jing, Y., Ahn, G.J., Doupé, A., Yi, J.H.: Checking intent-based communication in Android with intent space analysis. In: Proceedings of the 11th ACM on Asia Conference on Computer and Communications Security, pp. 735–746. ACM (2016)

29. Krohn, M., et al.: Information flow control for standard OS abstractions. In: ACM SIGOPS Operating Systems Review, vol. 41, pp. 321–334. ACM (2007)

30. Lee, Y.K., Yoodee, P., Shahbazian, A., Nam, D., Medvidovic, N.: SEALANT: a detection and visualization tool for inter-app security vulnerabilities in Android. In: Proceedings of the 32nd IEEE/ACM International Conference on Automated Software Engineering, pp. 883–888. IEEE Press (2017)

31. Li, L., et al.: Iccta: Detecting inter-component privacy leaks in Android apps. In: Proceedings of the 37th International Conference on Software Engineering-Volume 1, pp. 280–291. IEEE Press (2015)
32. Li, L., Bissyandé, T.F., Klein, J., Le Traon, Y.: Parameter values of android apis: a preliminary study on 100,000 apps. In: 2016 IEEE 23rd International Conference on Software Analysis, Evolution, and Reengineering, vol. 1, pp. 584–588 (2016)
33. Li, L., Bissyandé, T.F., Octeau, D., Klein, J.: Droidra: taming reflection to support whole-program analysis of Android apps. In: Proceedings of the 25th International Symposium on Software Testing and Analysis, pp. 318–329. ACM (2016)
34. Lu, L., Li, Z., Wu, Z., Lee, W., Jiang, G.: Chex: statically vetting android apps for component hijacking vulnerabilities. In: Proceedings of the 2012 ACM conference on Computer and communications Security, pp. 229–240. ACM (2012)
35. Mark Gordon, L.Z., Tiwana, B.: A power monitor (2019). ziyang.eecs.umich.edu/projects/powertutor/
36. Mimoso, M.: Mobile app collusion can bypass native android security (2016). https://tinyurl.com/jpndk7g
37. Moez BhattiCommunication: Qksms (2019). https://tinyurl.com/k8dd4u2
38. Octeau, D., et al.: Effective inter-component communication mapping in Android: An essential step towards holistic security analysis. In: USENIX Security (2013)
39. Wilcox-O'Hearn, Z., Warner, B.: Tahoe: the least-authority filesystem. In: 4th ACM international workshop on Storage security and survivability (2008)
40. Xu, K., Li, Y., Deng, R.H.: Iccdetector: Icc-based malware detection on Android. IEEE Trans. Inf. Forensics Secur. **11**(6), 1252–1264 (2016)
41. Zhou, Y., Jiang, X.: Dissecting Android malware: characterization and evolution. In: 2012 IEEE Symposium on Security and Privacy, pp. 95–109. IEEE (2012)

Smartphone Location Spoofing Attack in Wireless Networks

Chengbin Hu[1($\boxtimes$)], Yao Liu[1], Zhuo Lu[2], Shangqing Zhao[2], Xiao Han[1], and Junjie Xiong[1]

[1] Department of Computer Science and Engineering, University of South Florida,
Tampa, FL 33620, USA
{chengbin,yliu21,xiaoh,junjiexiong}@usf.edu
[2] Department of Electrical Engineering, University of South Florida,
Tampa, FL 33620, USA
{zhuolu,shangqing}@usf.edu

Abstract. GPS-free outdoor localization becomes popular because of the expanding scale of WiFi deployments in metropolitan areas. As a substitution or complement to the Global Positioning System (GPS), WiFi localization systems provide very accurate results in WiFi-rich area. However, the current WiFi localization systems are not robust to WiFi external signal attack. In this study, we implement a reverse engineering model to decode the Android WiFi localization system output. With the aid of reverse engineering mode, we implement both static and dynamic external signal attacks to make the smartphone believing it is located in another location or moving along the attacker's designed route using a portable programmed IoT device ESP8266. We also demonstrate that the WiFi based localization and navigation are vulnerable to external signal attacks by testing this attack on Android smartphone. Finally, we discuss the possible defense solutions and the future work. Our study indicates the smartphone is vulnerable to external signal attacks and there is an urgent need for defense solutions.

Keywords: Location security · Wireless signal · External signal attack

1 Introduction

Without a doubt, smartphones have become one of the most widely used technologies today. Billions of users in the world are relying on mobile positioning and navigation services on a daily basis [1]. Applications range from map navigation, service suggestion, to social media, all require accurate and authentic location data. In the meantime, the popularity of these location-based applications has become a honey pot for attackers. Those attackers aim to manipulate the location data, which is reported by smartphones, for criminal activities. In the past, the traditional positioning system relies on GPS signals. However, with the rapid development of WiFi technology, the WiFi-based positioning system has been widely used, which is not only as a complementary location-based service of GPS but also as a major positioning system [2].

© ICST Institute for Computer Sciences, Social Informatics and Telecommunications Engineering 2021
Published by Springer Nature Switzerland AG 2021. All Rights Reserved
J. Garcia-Alfaro et al. (Eds.): SecureComm 2021, LNICST 399, pp. 295–313, 2021.
https://doi.org/10.1007/978-3-030-90022-9_15

Because most positioning signals are not encrypted, the current positioning system is vulnerable to spoofing attacks where the attackers can send falsified wireless signals to change the smartphone location result. The previous research shows that a static attack that spoofs the smartphone location system to a false position is easy to achieve. But the dynamic attack that making the smartphone believe it is moving along the designed fake route of the attacker is limited [3]. In this paper, we exploit the current vulnerabilities of the Android wireless location system and design both static and dynamic attacks against it. We prove that it is feasible to attack the current smartphone location system and it is imperative to find a defense solution for this type of attack.

Numerous studies have attempted to explain the risks of location spoofing attack [4] and have created GPS, WiFi spoofers to alternate the positioning result of smartphones. Previous studies have shown that the positioning system is vulnerable to external signal attacks by broadcasting false GPS and WiFi positioning signals [5]. However, the current attacks still have a lot of limitations such as they require a specific shape of the route for a dynamic route or they can only spoof the device to a static position. Thus, it is important to study the possibility of the external signal attacks of current location systems and access the robustness of current location systems against these attacks.

In this paper, we first systematically study the current positioning system by designing a machine learning model using reverse-engineering to mimic the current Android positioning algorithm. Second, we design an external wireless signal spoofer using a portable IoT device. Third, we design the attacking algorithms on the device and evaluate the attack results using experiments. We also discuss defense solutions and future work. In summary, the key contributions of this paper include:

- We propose a machine learning model for building a reverse-engineering model of the Android WiFi positioning system. This proposed positioning model can mimic the positioning system and can help us to understand the attack and defense of the positioning system.
- We implement the external signal attack on a low-cost portable IoT device.
- We evaluate the attack in the real-world scenario. We prove the current smartphone is vulnerable to the external signal attack.

The rest of the paper is organized as follows. Section 2 introduces the background and threat model. Section 3 describes the WiFi positioning algorithm reverse-engineering. Section 4 shows the implementation of the attack. Section 5 demonstrates the result and evaluation of a real-world attack. Section 6 discusses the defense solutions and the future directions of our work. Finally, Sect. 7 concludes this paper.

2   Background and Threat Model

In this section, we start by providing the background of the smartphone positioning system, smartphone positioning system, positioning-based smartphone apps, and the external signal attacks. We then describe the unique challenges in attacking the smartphone positioning system.

Smartphone Positioning System. The current state-of-art smartphone positioning system uses multiple signal sources, including GPS, and WiFi as the input to determine the position of the device [6]. The Global Positioning System (GPS) is a traditional positioning system using satellite signals. Since the GPS positioning signal may not be available under certain conditions such as bad weather, dense buildings or intentionally blocking signal, the smartphone positioning system uses other Wireless signals such as the WiFi as a substitution or complement to the GPS. In this paper, we focus on Google geolocation API which is used for an Android-based WiFi localization system. In brief, the Android-based WiFi localization service relies on a central reference database as shown in Fig. 1 [7]. The central reference database is maintained by the location service company and stores most geolocation information of WiFi APs around the world. When a user device such as a smartphone initiates a request of location, the device starts to scan all the WiFi APs around it. Once the device gets all the BSSIDs/MAC/RSSI information of these APs, it starts to query the central reference database with these data. If the central reference database can find it, it will return a MAC: location pair for each MAC. Finally, the positioning algorithm computes the positioning result based on the data received from the central database. This positioning result can be reported alone or as a complement to increase the accuracy of GPS results.

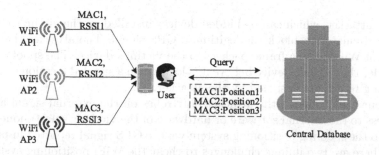

Fig. 1. WiFi localization service.

Positioning-Based Smartphone Apps. The use of location service represents one of the biggest advancements in smartphone technology. With the location service, the smartphone app can deliver online content to users based on their physical location. The popular location service-based smartphone apps include map navigation, service suggestion, social media, and game. These apps can provide users location-related content such as a positioning marker on the map and surrounding environment details. With the development of smartphone technology, the location service market grows rapidly. 55% of smartphone users use location-based services of the smartphone and the research study shows the young population more prefers to use the location services [8].

WiFi External Signal Attacks. The unencrypted civilian GPS signal is vulnerable to spoofing attacks. Many studies are showing that using a radio simulator or a satellite simulator to send false GPS data can successfully launch a location spoofing attack to GPS system [9,10]. In [9], The authors use a satellite simulator to attack a navigation system to create a dynamic route. However, their attack requires a new attack route that has the same shape as the real route drive, which is limited in many areas.

Some attacks are effective but not stealthy. In [11], the attack needs to inject malicious code into the smartphone application or modify the smartphone software system. This type of false GPS signal attack can be detected by the malware defense mechanism. Because the WiFi signal plays an important role in the positioning system, some studies use manipulated WiFi signals to spoof the positioning system. As reported in [12], the iPhone location can be relocated when attackers sending WiFi beacons to other locations. In addition, the Skylift project uses a low-cost ESP8266 WiFi chip to successfully manipulate the current location of an iPhone [13]. We notice that these WiFi signal-based attacks are limited to spoof the device to a single location in a static way. Therefore, it is urgent to test whether the attacker can spoof the device in a dynamic way that can let the device believe it is moving along a false route using WiFi signals.

2.1   Threat Model

In this paper, we design a novel attack against the smartphone positioning system.

The attacker, which can be hidden devices installed on the victim's car, uses a radio simulator to block the legitimate GPS signal. The attacker then sends the spoof WiFi beacon frame packets to the victim's device. The spoofing WiFi signals let the victim's device believe it is located on a spoofed location or moving according to a route designed by the attacker.

In our threat model, the attacker only relies on the external signal and has no access to the internal software or hardware of the victim's smartphone. Compared to the spoofing positioning system via the GPS signal reported in previous work, there are two unique challenges to cheat the WiFi positioning system.

Accuracy of Spoofing Result: First, to successfully attack the WiFi positioning system, an attacker needs to keep the error of the spoofing result to a minimum. This includes two parts, the final spoofing result should be close to the designed spoofing result. The positioning error should be minimal. In a common attack scenario, when a target device is moving on route A, the attacker wants to let the target device believe it is moving on route B by broadcasting the WiFi signals collected from route B. When there are a lot of legitimate WiFi access points, it is very hard to spoof the device without jamming these legitimate APs. To solve this challenge, Kumar, P., et al. [14] use an override method that mimics much more spoofing APs than legitimate APs (more than five times). These false AP signals can successfully attack the location-based apps on Android and iPhone devices. Therefore, the attacker can broadcast stronger WiFi signals and more SSIDs to increase the false input of the WiFi positioning algorithm, which can achieve a more accurate positioning result. Our study aims to solve how to increase the accuracy of the positioning result using the low power profile IoT device ESP8266.

Device Choice and Synchronization: Second, the attacker needs to find the best portable device that supports the 802.11 protocol. The attacker needs either a powerful device that is capable to broadcast all the required SSIDs or a more portable device that is easy to hidden. Although a common laptop can send the designed Wireless packets, it is too big for launching a secret attack. According to our attack scenario, the attacker prefers a small and quiet device that is easy to be overlooked. Therefore, a portable 802.11 g/n ESP8266 is used for sending WiFi beacon frames to simulate the WiFi APs [15]. The ESP8266 is a low-cost and small device that has the full function of sending 802.11 frames. According to our bandwidth test and the online test report, this device has a stable max transmission rate of 2.7 Mbps [16]. Since a legitimate AP beacon deliveries a beacon frame at about 0.018 Mbps, the theoretical capacity of the number of WiFi APs that one ESP8266 can send is around 150. However, during a WiFi external attack the ESP8266 needs more resources to execute our attack algorithm, this number drops to less than 60 in our experiment. Because in some WiFi density areas, there can be more than 60 WiFi APs in the environment. The attacker needs to find an optimal way to divide the dataset and synchronize the portable devices that are working together. The attacker can divide the total dataset D into several subsets for each portable device. Therefore, each subset contains a part of SSIDs in D. Then, these devices have to work coordinately to send the total dataset.

3   WiFi Positioning Algorithm Reverse-Engineering Model

As we know from the background, a WiFi positioning algorithm needs the data of WiFi APs and a central reference database as input. The output is GPS coordinates with longitude and latitude. There are four steps used in the reversing engineering of the current WiFi positioning algorithm: Data Capture, Preprocessing, Positioning Modeling, and Algorithm Evaluation shown as Fig. 2.

3.1   Data Capture

As we introduced, the WiFi positioning algorithm relies on the querying result of the central database. Therefore, the data capture includes a reconstruction of the central database. In addition, we also need to collect the training/testing data for geolocations that the attacker is using.

To reconstruct a central database, we need to provide the longitude and latitude for each WiFi AP. Therefore, the format of a record in the central database is shown as MAC: longitude, latitude. The Google geolocation API

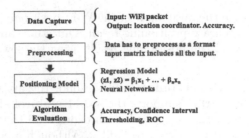

Fig. 2. Reverse-engineering model

can return a longitude and latitude pair based on the input GSM/WiFi data. Thus, we query the Google geolocation API for every WiFi AP for its associated longitude, latitude.

To collect the geolocation training/testing data, an Android phone Nexus 6 with WiFiManager API [17] is used for scanning WiFi SSIDs along a planned route. The WiFiManager API collects all the essential information about the SSIDs it discovers, such as RSSI, MAC, GPS positioning coordinates, timestamps, etc. We collect the WiFi SSIDs by driving through the route and record the SSIDs once per second. Among these data, RSSI and MACs are used as input data. The GPS positioning coordinates are used as the ground truth of the outcome data when observing certain SSIDs.

In this study, we collect three routes that represent 10 WiFi-rich areas, 10 WiFi-medium-rich areas, and 10 WiFi-poor areas. For each positioning (a certain longitude, latitude), the average number of WiFi APs is 26.8. We consider one position with its associated WiFi APs as a data record. There are 32142 data records in our total data set.

3.2 Preprocessing

As we discussed, the input data of training/testing includes a set of WiFi APs along with their RSSI. Each data record w is a set of WiFi APs shown as $\{mac_1, rssi_1, mac_2, rssi_2, \ldots, mac_n, rssi_n\}$. However, this format of the data record cannot be directly used as the input of the WiFi positioning algorithm. We need to first query the central database and transfer each MAC address information to longitude and latitude pair.

In addition, the longitude and latitude system is a global system which is very sensitive in a minor change. It is not good to build up a machine learning model using a sensitive input that has very little change. Therefore, we need to convert the longitude/latitude to (x,y) coordinates. The input records are therefore converted to the Cartesian coordinate system using this formula [18].

$$x = R \times cos(lat) \times cos(lon)$$

$$y = R \times cos(lat) \times sin(lon)$$

R is the radius of the Earth, we use the approximate value 6378137 m. The result (x, y) usually is very big for most longitude/latitude pairs. Therefore, we select an original point as (0, 0) and normalize all the points to this coordinate by subtracting the coordinate of this original point. Finally, the record of input data is shown as $\{x_1, y_1, rssi_1, x_2, y_2, rssi_2, \ldots, x_n, y_n, rssi_n\}$.

3.3   Positioning Modeling

Weighted Linear Regression Model. As we discussed before, the input data is a set of WiFi APs and their RSSI. After preprocessing, each record contains a set of coordinates and RSSI. The input data X therefore can be presented by a $n \times 3$ matrix where there are 3 columns of features of longitude, latitude, and RSSI.

$$X = \begin{bmatrix} r_1 \times x_1 & r_1 \times y_1 & r_1 \\ r_2 \times x_2 & r_2 \times y_2 & r_2 \\ \ldots & \ldots & \ldots \\ r_n \times x_n & r_n \times y_n & r_n \end{bmatrix}$$

The outcome data $y' = [x, y, z]$ is GPS coordinates with accuracy of the measurement. A weighted multivariate linear regression model can be represented as (1) here.

$$y' = [x, y, z] = [\beta_1\, \beta_2 \cdots \beta_n] \times \begin{bmatrix} r_1 \times x_1 & r_1 \times y_1 & r_1 \\ r_2 \times x_2 & r_2 \times y_2 & r_2 \\ \ldots & \ldots & \ldots \\ r_n \times x_n & r_n \times y_n & r_n \end{bmatrix} + [b1, b2, b3] \quad (1)$$

From the dimension of y' and X, we could know the parameter vector is a $1 \times n$ vector.

Neural Network Model. The Weighted Linear Regression Model (1) assumes a simple model that each input element will be multiplied by one parameter β_i. But this assumption may not help us get the most accurate model. Therefore, we implement a fully connected Neural Network Model for our dataset and set the number of parameters as flexible.

Here we define a $m \times 3n$ hidden layer weight matrix θ.

$$\theta = \begin{bmatrix} a_1 \\ a_2 \\ \ldots \\ a_m \end{bmatrix} = \begin{bmatrix} w_{11} & w_{12} & w_{13} & \cdots & w_{13n} \\ w_{21} & w_{22} & w_{23} & \cdots & w_{23n} \\ \ldots & \ldots & \ldots & \ldots & \ldots \\ w_{m1} & w_{m2} & w_{m3} & \cdots & w_{m3n} \end{bmatrix}$$

And we flat our input matrix as a $1 \times 3n$ vector. Thus, the output of first layer can be represented as (2).

$$
h(1) = g \left(\begin{bmatrix} w_{11} & w_{12} & w_{13} & \cdots & w_{13n} \\ w_{21} & w_{22} & w_{23} & \cdots & w_{23n} \\ \cdots & \cdots & \cdots & \cdots & \cdots \\ w_{m1} & w_{m2} & w_{m3} & \cdots & w_{m3n} \end{bmatrix} \times \begin{bmatrix} x_1 \\ y_1 \\ r_1 \\ x_2 \\ y_2 \\ r_2 \\ \cdots \\ \cdots \\ x_n \\ y_n \\ r_n \end{bmatrix} + \begin{bmatrix} b_1 \\ b_2 \\ \cdots \\ b_m \end{bmatrix} \right) \tag{2}
$$

Here g is an activation Relu function that we choose. The output of this layer $h(1)$ is a $1 \times m$ vector. We can therefore add the next layer after this layer using a $l \times m$ weight matrix to get a $1 \times l$ vector. And so on we can add more layers as (3) [19].

$$
h(n) = [g\left(\Sigma_m \theta_{nm} \left[\cdots [g\left(\Sigma_j \theta_{kj}[g(\Sigma_i \theta_{ji} \cdot x_i + b_i)] + b_k)\right] \cdots \right] + b_n)\right] \tag{3}
$$

4   Attack Overview

4.1   Goal of the Attacker

Here, we explore a novel attack against a smartphone positioning system by altering WiFi signals. The attack can be realized for two specific types. **Static Attack.** In a static attack, the attacker aims to spoof the smartphone positioning system to get a false position that is different from the real-world position. During this attack, the positioning result suggests a wrong location which is very far away from the user. **Dynamic Attack.** The attacker aims to send a false route data and the smartphone positioning system reports a false moving behavior of the current device. This may cause the malfunction of map applications and the user cannot go to the correct destination.

4.2   Attack Details

Data Collection: The static positioning data of other cities such as Paris, London are collected from the Wireless Geographic Logging Engine (WiGLE https://wigle.net/) website database through its public API. To collect the dynamic route data, an Android phone with WiFiManager API [17] is used for scanning WiFi SSIDs along a planned route B. The WiFiManager collects all the essential information about the SSIDs it discovers, such as RSSI, MAC, GPS positioning coordinates, timestamps, etc. The attacker collects the WiFi SSIDs by driving through the route B and record the SSIDs. Among these data, RSSI and MACs are mainly used for the attack. The GPS positioning coordinates are used as the ground truth of the current position when observing certain SSIDs. We collected four sets of static positioning data with each has 100 WiFi APs from WiGLE. For the dynamic attack data, we repeatedly collect the driving route 10 times using an Android phone while driving a car. This route contains both WiFi dense and sparse areas with an average number of 42.3 WiFi APs in each location of this route. The average driving time for this route is 3 min and 32 s. There are a total of 8967 WiFi APs in this dataset. Each WiFi AP record has corresponse RSSI, MAC, and GPS positioning information related to its SSID.

Beacon Frame Packet Design: We use specifically designed beacon frame packets as the attack signal to represent the spoofing WiFi APs. As shown in Fig. 3, the beacon frame packet we designed is a 51-bytes concise packet without any optional parameters (e.g. DS Parameter Set, CF Parameter Set, IBSS Parameter Set). We also use only a null byte for SSID information therefore the WiFi SSID is hidden and will not be reported by the smartphone if the user is searching for nearby available WiFi networks. Thus, timestamp, source address, and BSSID field are the only 3 fields that need to be changed. During the attack, the MAC information of each spoofing WiFi AP is written in the source address and the BSSID field of the beacon frame packet, and the timestamp is updated according to the system timer.

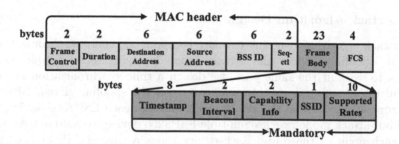

Fig. 3. The structure of spoofing beacon frame packet.

GPS Signal Jamming: Since GPS signal is primarily used for the positioning system, the legitimate GPS signal will affect the positioning system, which makes the system trust GPS location. The attacker first needs to block legitimate GPS signals. A GPS signal jammer is deployed for blocking legitimate GPS signals. The attacker uses a Universal Software Radio Peripheral (USRP) X300 for broadcasting the noise signal. The attacker uses a Gaussian noise signal to jam the GPS signal at 1575.42 MHz, which is the central frequency of Coarse/Acquisition (C/A) code of GPS information for civilian use.

Device Set Up: The attack is set up as shown in Fig. 4. The attacker first hides the GPS jammer (shown in Fig. 4 left part) in the car. Before launching the attack, the attacker places these portable ESP8266 devices around the victim and hides them (shown in Fig. 4 middle part). A typical attack scenario is to hide the device in the car as shown in Fig. 4 right part. A USB 5 V power is required for these devices, which can be easily set up by a portable USB charger. Firstly, the attacker uses his laptop to synchronize the timer of the attacker's devices using a synchronize algorithm as shown in Algorithm 1. After getting the same system timer, the attacker starts to broadcast the attack signals according to the location sequence as we mentioned above.

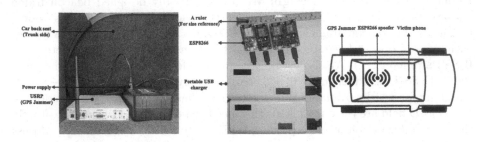

Fig. 4. The experiment setups for GPS jammer and ESP8266 spoofer

4.3   Attack Algorithm Design

The attack algorithm contains two key components: time synchronization for multiple spoofing devices and attack signal deploying. For multiple spoofing devices to work at the same pace, we design a time synchronization algorithm for multiple spoofing devices to send a part of the spoofing signal. After time synchronization, we send the attack signal through each ESP8266 device.

In our attack model, we use multiple ESP8266 devices to send out APs along with each point of the route. Each device sends a part of APs at each point. So every device will mimic a full route for the dynamic spoofing attack. To construct a dynamic route, we consider a WiFi AP set $\mathbb{W}$ is the total WiFi APs for the dynamic route. The full set $\mathbb{W}$ can be divided into a sequence of set $\mathbb{W}_1, \mathbb{W}_2, \ldots, \mathbb{W}_n$ according to the time sequence of WiFi APs. Thus, every subset is all the WiFi APs the device detect at one specific moment. In order to allocate all the WiFi APs to m available devices during an attack, we further divide each subset to m sets. Therefore, at time point 1, $\mathbb{W}_1$ will be divided into $\mathbb{W}_{11}, \mathbb{W}_{12}, \ldots, \mathbb{W}_{1m}$. Device 1 then sends WiFi beacon frames of $\mathbb{W}_{11}$; Device 2 sends WiFi beacon frames of $\mathbb{W}_{12}$ and so on. So at the next time point, Device 1 will send $\mathbb{W}_{21}$ and so on. To achieve this, every device needs to synchronize the time point to reconstruct the subsets $\mathbb{W}_1, \mathbb{W}_2, \ldots, \mathbb{W}_n$.

In order to synchronize the time for each device so that every device can send the data from the same point, we send the current epoch time number to ESP8266s from a laptop as described in Algorithm 1. At first, the device is marked as not received and not synchronized. The attacker first broadcasts the current time e to every ESP8266. If the status of the device is not received and not synchronized, the device will first record the e and then compute the base time b that the device is turned on by e minus the time elapsed since the device turned on. This is because the ESP8266 has a built-in time counter that can count how long has the device turned on. Therefore, the device can always use a base time to synchronize its step with other devices.

Algorithm 1. External signal attack algorithm

Input: e: Start epoch time from a laptop
      W: Attack data set
      n: Attack time length
Output: The current time of each device

 1: Broadcasting e to each attacker's device
 2: **For** each one of m devices **do**
 3:    $m \leftarrow$ device number
 4:    **If** Not received
 5:       Read e from laptop broadcasting
 6:       received = True
 7:    **End If**
 8:    **If** Not synchronized and received
 9:       $c \leftarrow$ time elapsed since the device turned on.
10:       $b \leftarrow e - c$
11:       synchronized = True.
12:    **End If**
13:    **While** synchronized is True
14:       $t \leftarrow b +$ time elapsed since the device turned on
15:       **If** $b > n$
16:          **Break While**
17:       **End If**
18:       send out W_{tm}
19:    **End While**
20: **End For**
21: **Return** $b +$ time elapsed since the device turned on

With the above synchronizing algorithm, the attacker may launch the attack by using several ESP8266s. As we mentioned, the attacker collects the spoofing dataset by real-world driving or directly from the WiGLE database. To successfully attack the smartphone, the attacker needs the verification from the reverse-engineering model to make sure the victim's device will get the desire positioning result. Therefore, for a list of attacking data A, we design an attack signal deploying algorithm to verify each part of the data and broadcast the verified data as shown in Algorithm 2. When the attacking data A is loaded, the attacker first checks each part of A and goes through the reverse-engineering model to verify the positioning result. If the positioning result is correct, the signal will be sent. Otherwise, that part of the data will be dropped. The attack can use this method to avoid some abnormal positioning results and being blocked by some defense mechanisms.

Algorithm 2. Attack Signal Deploying

Input: A, a sequence of collected WiFi APs
Output: Confirmed positioning location result

1: Pointer pt = start of A
2: **While** pt not meet the end of A
3:      location result lr = ReverseEng($pt-> aps$)
4:      **If** lr == collected gps position
5:          deploy $pt-> aps$ through ESP8266 according to the timestamp
6:      **else**
7:          drop current lr and aps
8:      **End If**
9:      pt = pt-¿next
10: **End While**

---

5   Attack Evaluation

Next, we evaluate the external signal attack on a smartphone-based setup on real-world data.

Attack Scenarios. We evaluate our attack by the following attack scenarios.

- *Static external signal attack.* This is the basic external signal attack. We want to spoof the positioning system of the smartphone to get another location that is different from the current position. In this case, we evaluate the relationship between the distance between the ground truth position and the spoofed location with the error of the positioning result.
- *Dynamic external signal attack.* This attack tries to spoof the smartphone and let it believe it is moving along a designed route while the smartphone is not following the route in the real world. In this attack scenario, we evaluate how well the smartphone following the designed route by the error of each designed point with the real positioning result.

Evaluation Metrics. The Wireless external signal attack aims to spoof the positioning system of the smartphone without raising an alert. The abnormal positioning result usually shows as a big error of positioning result and/or an impossible real-world location (e.g. A car is driving in the river). Therefore, how accurate the positioning result could be is an important metric to evaluate whether the attack can bypass the defense mechanism. We use the following metrics to evaluate the attack performance: (1) *Truth-designed distance.* This is the distance between the ground truth location and the designed attack location. This is shown as the red arrow in Fig. 5. The ground truth location is the real-world location of the smartphone. The designed attack location is the position that the attacker wants the smartphone to believe it is at. (2) *Designed-result distance.* This is the distance between the designed attack location and the positioning result. This is shown as the yellow arrow in Fig. 5. (3) *Positioning result standard error.* This is the standard error reported by the positioning system for each result.

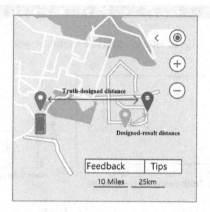

Fig. 5. Evaluation metrics: Truth-designed distance and Designed-result distance

Performance of the Static External Signal Attack: We conduct the static external signal attack using the spoofing signal collected from the WiGLE database. The attack is performed in a parking lot, the victim's smartphone is the author's phone and we place the attack devices in the author's car. As shown in Fig. 6, the smartphone positioning system is spoofed through our designed attack system and the user receives the false location results of other cities such as New York, Paris, London, and Berlin. The performance of the static external signal attack is shown in the left of Fig. 7. The y axis shows the designed-result distance and the error bar represents the positioning result standard error. As we can see the designed-result distance and positioning result standard error slightly increases when the truth-designed distance significantly increases (e.g. One country to another country). Compared to the control normal positioning error shown in the right of Fig. 6, both designed-result distance (mean 6.91 m) and positioning result standard error (mean 3.23 m) is within range of smartphone positioning result standard error control data (4.82 ± 5.93) m in 95% confidence interval which indicates the attack does not raise abnormal positioning result even when the attacker tries to spoof the smartphone to a very far location. Therefore, our study reveals the vulnerability that current smartphone apps will provide false location results to the user during the static external signal attack.

Fig. 6. Static external signal attack

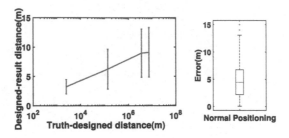

Fig. 7. Static external signal attack evaluation

Performance of the Dynamic External Signal Attack: In this attack, we collect the attack data as described in Sect. 3. The attack data contains all the WiFi APs in a 3 min 32 s length driving route as shown in Fig. 8 (A). Similar to the static attack environment, the attack is performed in the author's car. We choose a route with both WiFi dense and sparse areas. The average number of WiFi APs per location is 42.3 with a range from 6 to 100 as shown in the left of Fig. 9. We use four ESP8266s to synchronize this attack according to the algorithm 1. In this attack, an attacker is staying in the car at the start point without driving. The attacker blocks the GPS signal through GPS Jammer. He then uses the spoofing devices to broadcast the data of the route as shown in Fig. 8 (A).

During the attack, although the victim's smartphone is not moving, we can observe the positioning result shows the smartphone is moving according to the designed route of the attacker. In addition, to make sure the attack is successful, the spoofing WiFi signal RSSI is higher than the data we collected in the real world. This result can be observed from an RSSI histogram in Fig. 8 (B) and (C). We can observe a significant left shift of the RSSI peak, which indicates an increase of RSSI during the attack. Next, we want to evaluate the Designed-result distance, we notice that in the dynamic attack the number of WiFi spoofing signals is always changing and is highly related to the performance of the attack. We plot the number of WiFi APs with the Designed-result distance in the left of Fig. 9. Our result shows a Designed-result distance in (3.35 ± 1.16) m in the 95% confidence interval. To evaluate this metric, we choose the normal driving data without attack to compare with the result as shown in the middle and right of Fig. 9. Since normal driving data has no designed-result distance, we set the designed-result distance as 0 and compute the confidence interval from the positioning error. The normal driving data could be represented as (0 ± 15.23) m in the 95% confidence interval. The t-test of these two groups shows $t = 1.639, df = 414, p = 0.102$, which indicates the two groups are not statistically significant. This result indicates attackers successfully spoof the smartphone positioning system and the positioning result is close to the attacker's designed location.

Next, in order to evaluate the positioning result standard error during a dynamic attack, we check the relation between WiFi spoofing signals and the positioning error. As shown in the left of Fig. 10, the positioning result standard error is inversely correlated with the number of WiFi APs used in the attack. The positioning result standard error is (9.26 ± 8.53) in 95% confidence interval, which is not significantly different with the normal control driving data (8.74 ± 6.44) m $t = 1.074, df = 414, p = 0.2834$ in the middle of Fig. 9. In addition, the CDF of dynamic attack data in the middle of Fig. 10 is similar to the normal control driving data in the right of Fig. 9. More than 90% of errors are below 15 m. This indicates during the attack, most positioning error is considered normal and the smartphone defense system may not notice that there is an attack. If we plot the error with the number of WiFi APs, the pattern suggests a logarithmic regression as shown in the right of Fig. 10. This result suggests that the attacker needs more WiFi APs to reduce the standard error of positioning results and achieve an accurate attack result.

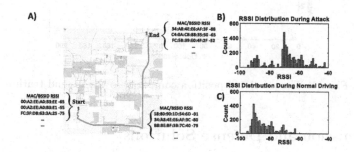

Fig. 8. Dynamic attack route and RSSI distribution

The current positioning system usually enables a position prediction model to predict the possible legit positioning result based on current position and speed. Therefore, we use a time-series long-short memory (LSTM) model to predict the legit position and compare it with the attacking result as described in [20]. The result is shown in Fig. 11. Here, the y-axis shows the distance travelled in prediction or the ground truth, which is based on the previous speed. The ground

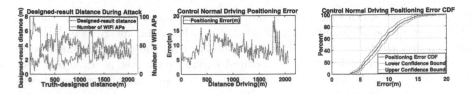

Fig. 9. Designed-result distance during attack and control normal driving positioning error

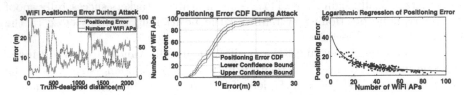

Fig. 10. Positioning result standard error during attack

truth matches the attack predicted with only an average error of 0.34 m. This error is much less than the threshold (5–10) m defined by GPS accuracy.

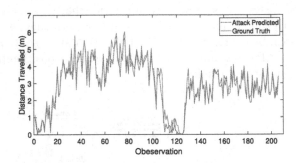

Fig. 11. The predicted position compared to the ground truth

6   Discussion and Defense Solutions

Our paper demonstrates the initial feasibility of manipulating the road navigation system through an external beacon frame spoofing attack. Based on our study, the threat becomes realistic as some users may not notice the navigation system when the user is not familiar with the current environment. Since the current smartphone navigation system is vulnerable to this external signal attack, it is important to explore the current smartphone system and find out an effective solution to this type of attack.

The main advantages of our proposed attack are the feasibility and the low-cost of the external dynamic signal attack. Our proposed attack requires only four ESP8266s as the WiFi signal source, which only cost $2 each. Since the Skylift project already performed this attack in a static way, we further extend this attack in a dynamic way that can attack victims on a moving vehicle [13]. Thus, the attack can mimic both static and dynamic scenarios. Our attack uses WiFi AP beacon frames as the attack signal which can be very similar to legitimate signals. The current defense mechanism can hardly detect our attack. Thus our attack is also highly efficient. The main limitation of our attack is that we need to block the legitimate GPS signals. The legitimate GPS signals can alert the victim's device that there is a positioning attack. Our current attack uses a separated USRP to block the GPS signals. Yet, there are some more portable ways to perform this job using other devices such as HackRF One Software Defined Radio (SDR) [10]. Thus, future studies should find a more convenient way to perform the attack and block the legitimate signals. Another limitation of this study is that we use much stronger WiFi signals from the ESP8266 to overwhelm other legitimate WiFi signals. This is a low-cost way to perform the attack and it assumes that sources of legitimate WiFi signals are much far away from the attacker's ESP8266s. This is correct under our attack thereat model because the attacker hides ESP8266s around the victim. In order to fully eliminate the effect of other WiFi beacons, we can block most WiFi channels and only use one channel to attack the victim's phone. But this method will significantly increase the cost of the attack.

Recently, the Decimeter-level localization techniques including the angle of arrival (AoA), angle of departure (AoD), and relative time of flight (rToF) begin to apply to WiFi localization system [21]. However, during our experiments, we find that the Android smartphone has not applied these techniques and uses the Google geolocation API that is mainly based on the RSSI. Although there are many technical difficulties to spoof these systems, it is still possible that the attacker can extend our attack to these designed systems by carefully positioned the ESP8266s in different directions around the victims. Thus, further research to prove the feasibility of this attack to the AoA/AoD/rToF WiFi localization systems is needed.

The traditional defense mechanism focus on abnormal result detection. However, the state-of-art defense solution now enables the signal checking such as WiFi-hotspot tags [22]. The straightforward defense solution is to verify each WiFi AP and make sure it is a legitimate signal. This requires a legitimate signal filter installed on the smartphone. A device signal fingerprint can be used for verification. The fingerprint can include the frequency pattern of the WiFi AP based on the manufacturer shown in the MAC address in the WiFi packet, the historical WiFi AP beacon frame packet recorded in the database, and/or other physical information of the WiFi signal. However, the attacker may collect the real-world signal and try to mimic the fingerprint information and bypass this approach. In addition, the smartphone system may cross-check the data of the inertial measurement unit (IMU) sensors to confirm the actual movement of the smartphone and compare it with the geolocation data of the smartphone positioning system [10]. This defense method in general suffers from accumulative IMU sensor errors and becomes ineffective as the time drifts. Also, [23] has demonstrated that IMU sensors are not sufficient to defend against location spoofing attacks under different scenarios.

7 Conclusions

In this paper, we explore the feasibility of external WiFi signal spoofing attacks the smartphone positioning systems. Real-world attack tests confirmed the attack effectiveness and vulnerability of the current smartphone system. We further discuss some possible defense solutions. We hope that our results can help in designing defense mechanisms for the current positioning system to the potential external WiFi signal spoofing attacks.

Acknowledgments. We appreciate constructive comments from anonymous reviewers. This work is supported by National Science Foundation (No 1553304).

References

1. Wahlström, J., Skog, I., Händel, P.: Smartphone-based vehicle telematics: a ten-year anniversary. IEEE Trans. Intell. Transp. Syst. **18**(10), 2802–2825 (2017)
2. Bell, S., Jung, W.R., Krishnakumar, V.: Wifi-based enhanced positioning systems: accuracy through mapping, calibration, and classification. In: Proceedings of the 2nd ACM SIGSPATIAL International Workshop on Indoor Spatial Awareness, pp. 3–9. ACM (2010)
3. Zeng, K.C., Shu, Y., Liu, S., Dou, Y., Yang, Y.: A practical gps location spoofing attack in road navigation scenario. In: Proceedings of the 18th International Workshop on Mobile Computing Systems and Applications, pp. 85–90 (2017)
4. Tippenhauer, N.O., Rasmussen, K.B., Pöpper, C., Čapkun, S.: Attacks on public wlan-based positioning systems. In: MobiSys. ACM, pp. 29–40 (2009)
5. Tippenhauer, N.O., Pöpper, C., Rasmussen, K.B., Capkun, S.: On the requirements for successful gps spoofing attacks. In: Proceedings of the 18th ACM Conference on Computer and Communications Security, pp. 75–86. ACM (2011)
6. Paek, J., Kim, J., Govindan, R.: Energy-efficient rate-adaptive gps-based positioning for smartphones. In: MobiSys, pp. 299–314 (2010)
7. Alizadeh-Shabdiz, F., Jones, R.K., Morgan, E.J., Shean, M.G.: Location-based services that choose location algorithms based on number of detected access points within range of user device, 4 December 2007, uS Patent 7,305,245
8. Schmitz Weiss, A.: Exploring news apps and location-based services on the smartphone. Journalism Mass Commun. Quarterly **90**(3), 435–456 (2013)
9. Zeng, K.C., Shu, Y., Liu, S., Dou, Y., Yang, Y.: A practical gps location spoofing attack in road navigation scenario. In: HotMobile. ACM, pp. 85–90 (2017)
10. Zeng, K.C., et al.: All your gps are belong to us: towards stealthy manipulation of road navigation systems. In: USENIX Security 2018 (2018)
11. Cao, Y., Luo, Q., Liu, J.: Road navigation system attacks: a case on gps navigation map. In: ICC 2019–2019 IEEE International Conference on Communications (ICC), pp. 1–5. IEEE (2019)

12. Tippenhauer, N.O., Rasmussen, K.B., Pöpper, C., Capkun, S.: iphone and ipod location spoofing: attacks on public wlan-based positioning systems," Technical report/ETH Zürich, Department of Computer Science, vol. 599 (2012)
13. Harvey, A.: Skylift (2017). https://github.com/adamhrv/skylift
14. Kumar, P., Duraimurugan, G., Kumar, G.M., Logesh, R., MyvizhiPraveen, L.: Prevention and localization of mac address spoofing attacks in wireless networks (2016)
15. Grokhotkov, I.: Esp8266 arduino core documentation. ESP8266 (2017)
16. Susiripala, A.: Load testing an esp8266 (2017). https://arunoda.me/blog/load-testing-an-esp8266
17. Larimer, J., Root, K.: Security and privacy in android apps. Google Developers (2012)
18. Russell, C.T.: Geophysical coordinate transformations. Cosmic Electrodynamics 2(2), 184–196 (1971)
19. Atanassov, K., Sotirov, S.: Index matrix interpretation of the multilayer perceptron. In: 2013 IEEE INISTA, pp. 1–3. IEEE (2013)
20. Rustamov, A., Gogoi, N., Minetto, A., Dovis, F.: Gnss anti-spoofing defense based on cooperative positioning. In: Proceedings of the 33rd International Technical Meeting of the Satellite Division of the Institute of Navigation (ION GNSS+ 2020), pp. 3326–3337 (2020)
21. Soltanaghaei, E., Kalyanaraman, A., Whitehouse, K.: Multipath triangulation: decimeter-level wifi localization and orientation with a single unaided receiver. In: MobiSys, pp. 376–388 (2018)
22. Ye, A., Li, Q., Zhang, Q., Cheng, B.: Detection of spoofing attacks in wlan-based positioning systems using wifi hotspot tags. IEEE Access 8, 39 768–39 780 (2020)
23. Narain, S., Ranganathan, A., Noubir, G.: Security of gps/ins based on-road location tracking systems. In: 2019 IEEE Symposium on Security and Privacy (SP), pp. 587–601. IEEE (2019)

IoT Security and Privacy

Compromised Through Compression
Privacy Implications of Smart Meter Traffic Analysis

Pol Van Aubel[(✉)] and Erik Poll

Digital Security group, Institute for Computing and Information Sciences,
Radboud University, Nijmegen, The Netherlands
{pol.vanaubel,erikpoll}@cs.ru.nl

Abstract. Smart metering comes with risks to privacy. One concern is
the possibility of an attacker seeing the traffic that reports the energy use
of a household and deriving private information from that. Encryption
helps to mask the actual energy measurements, but is not sufficient to
cover all risks. One aspect which has yet gone unexplored – and where
encryption does not help – is traffic analysis, i.e. whether the length of
messages communicating energy measurements can leak privacy-sensitive
information to an observer. In this paper we examine whether using
encodings or compression for smart metering data could potentially leak
information about household energy use. Our analysis is based on the
real-world energy use data of ±80 Dutch households.

We find that traffic analysis could reveal information about the energy
use of individual households if compression is used. As a result, when messages are sent daily, an attacker performing traffic analysis would be able
to determine when all the members of a household are away or not using
electricity for an entire day. We demonstrate this issue by recognizing
when households from our dataset were on holiday. If messages are sent
more often, more granular living patterns could likely be determined.

We propose a method of encoding the data that is nearly as effective
as compression at reducing message size, but does not leak the information that compression leaks. By not requiring compression to achieve the
best possible data savings, the risk of traffic analysis is eliminated.

Keywords: Privacy · Compression · Traffic analysis · Smart meter

1 Introduction

Privacy risks of smart metering have been analysed by looking at what information
can be deduced from energy measurements on household granularity [6,7,16,18].
This shows that smart metering measurements are privacy sensitive.

The smart meter can send, among other things, a daily report of meter values
to the system operator. For an individual meter this report in its plainest form
can grow to several kilobytes. For several reasons, amongst which is simply the
monetary cost of data, system operators want to limit the bandwidth used by
this communication. The standards used for this communication are IEC 62056,

© ICST Institute for Computer Sciences, Social Informatics and Telecommunications Engineering 2021
Published by Springer Nature Switzerland AG 2021. All Rights Reserved
J. Garcia-Alfaro et al. (Eds.): SecureComm 2021, LNICST 399, pp. 317–337, 2021.
https://doi.org/10.1007/978-3-030-90022-9_16

more commonly referred to as DLMS/COSEM. They allow for encoding and compression to be applied to the meter readings, before encrypting them and sending them to a central system [8–10].

Because these messages are encrypted, someone who can eavesdrop on the communication does not have access to the actual meter readings. However, traffic analysis may still be possible. In traffic analysis, we analyse the metadata of network communication: who communicates, when, how much, to whom, without regard to the contents of the communication. Encryption does not necessarily reduce the risk of traffic analysis, especially if, as is the case for DLMS/COSEM, the length of the messages is still known to the outside observer. The latest version of DLMS/COSEM, not yet standardized by the IEC, defines a new encoding method in addition to the existing encoding and compression options. This paper explores how these options can influence the length of typical messages and what information this may leak to an attacker.

In addition, we propose a method of encoding the data that is nearly as effective as compression at reducing message size, but is not vulnerable to traffic analysis by itself. This allows for data savings without introducing the risk of traffic analysis.

Attacker Model. The question we are concerned with in this paper is whether an attacker observing DLMS/COSEM traffic can learn privacy-sensitive information solely from the length of the messages when the encoding and compression options in DLMS/COSEM are used. We assume a passive attacker capable of capturing all DLMS/COSEM traffic, but not injecting or manipulating messages.

In the Dutch smart metering infrastructure, measurements are currently taken every 15 min, and sent in daily batches after midnight. We perform our analysis on the messages communicating these daily batches to the grid operator. The only source of information for the attacker is the length of these messages. For this research, we do not consider other types of messages like reports on power quality, because the link between them and potential privacy impact is unclear.

In Sect. 2 we relate this paper to existing research into the privacy of smart metering. In Sect. 3 we explain the relevant parts of the DLMS/COSEM communication standards: the encodings and compression. We also introduce our proposed alternative encoding that should prevent the problems we identify. In Sect. 4 we explain the setup for our analysis, and in Sect. 5 we show the results and discuss our findings. Finally, we suggest some avenues for future work in Sect. 6, and we discuss our findings and give some recommendations in Sect. 7.

2   Background

The encryption used in DLMS/COSEM does not hide the plaintext message length from the attacker, it only adds a constant overhead to every encrypted message. This means that an attacker may be able to derive privacy-sensitive information by analysing the length of messages, partially circumventing the protection that the encryption is supposed to provide.

We cover some related research on privacy aspects of smart metering and the situation in the Netherlands in Sect. 2.1. In Sect. 2.2 we explain why the length of encrypted messages may leak information about the data they contain. In Sect. 2.3 we relate this to existing work that analyses correlations between power use and compression, and explain our contribution.

2.1 Smart Metering Privacy

Privacy risks of smart metering have been analysed by looking at what information can be deduced from energy measurements of an entire household. Molina-Markham et al. show that with one measurement every second, very detailed household living patterns can be deduced [18]. Greveler et al. show that from similar data they can recognize household appliances like refrigerators, kettles, and coffee machines. Worryingly, they can even distinguish different television broadcasts being watched [6,7]. Liao, Stankovic, and Stankovic also show that detecting refrigerators, boilers, kettles, toasters, etc. is possible, and by doing so, can distinguish household activities [16].

All these focus on what can be learned from frequent unencrypted readings, on the order of a measurement per second. Such frequent measurements are not (currently) transmitted by Dutch smart meters – they send measurements taken every 15 min [20]. However, that does not mean that there are no privacy concerns for the data that *is* sent by the smart meters. The law introducing the smart meter in the Netherlands was initially blocked by the First Chamber of Parliament, because it did not adequately take consumer privacy into account. An important issue was that it mandated 15-min readings, and made the smart meter itself mandatory. The law was only passed after being rewritten to make the smart meter optional and the 15-min readings opt-in [1]. The Distribution System Operators (DSOs) themselves also consider some of the metering data – in particular the measurements of energy use – privacy-sensitive [4].

2.2 Traffic Analysis: Length as a Side-Channel

The research mentioned in Sect. 2.1 [6,7,16,18] uses the actual energy use data from the meter, which can be hidden by encryption. It may be possible, however, to use message size as a side-channel to gain information about the encrypted data, especially if encrypted messages directly leak the size of their plaintexts. E.g. consider the case where we have two batches of an equal number of meter readings: one containing a batch of 8-bit integers, and the other a batch of 32-bit integers. Even if we encrypt these before sending them to a client, an attacker can still trivially distinguish the two, just by seeing that the *size* of one message is much larger than the other.

Even when the messages being encrypted are the same length, using compression to save bandwidth may introduce possibilities for traffic analysis. E.g. now consider the case where we have two batches of meter readings, where one batch has measured "0" fifty times, and the other batch has fifty different measurements. These measurements take an equal amount of space in the message. If we only encrypt them and send them to a recipient, an attacker listening in would not be able to tell, based on size alone, which one we have sent. But if we compress them before encrypting, one message may compress down to say "50 times 0", whereas the other needs the space for all its individual measurements. The attacker looking at message length can deduce that one of these messages has a lot of repeating values, whereas the other does not.

Already in 2002 the existence of such a compression-induced length side-channel in encrypted messages was highlighted by Kelsey [12]. Langley hypothesized in 2011 that compression before encryption could be used in an attack to retrieve information being transmitted over the then-newly-developed SPDY protocol, without actually breaking the underlying cryptographic protocols [13]. This was put in practice within a year by Rizzo and Duong in the CRIME attack against HTTPS, SPDY, and TLS [19]. In 2013 Prado, Harris, and Gluck followed this with the BREACH attack against the compression in HTTP [5].

It is important to note that these attacks do not "break" the cryptography as such. Instead, the traffic analysis reveals the contents of parts of the communicated data, even though the messages remain encrypted.

2.3   Traffic Analysis to Learn Power Consumption

Encryption in the DLMS/COSEM standard primarily uses AES in Galois Counter Mode, which adds a constant overhead to each encrypted message and does not hide the plaintext message length from the attacker [8]. So from Sect. 2.2 we can conclude that an attacker who sees the message length may be able to learn information about the power consumption of a household by linking message length to the power consumption.

In the case of smart metering, all the messages containing energy measurements could in principle be the same size: they contain the same number of measurements encoded the same way, as we explain in Sect. 3. However, if compression is used, the messages can have different lengths.

Fehér et al. [2] show for a limited dataset that compression of smart metering data can result in correlation between message length and power consumption. They do not assess the practical implications of this correlation: the fact that one exists does not necessarily mean it can be used by observers to infer interesting information in real-life scenarios.

Our contribution is that we have analysed the effects that encoding and compression have on the energy use data of real Dutch households. We investigate whether an attacker performing traffic analysis could actually find a link between message length and power consumption and derive privacy-sensitive information from it. We confirm there exists such a correlation on a much larger dataset and show concrete risks to privacy stemming from these correlations. Furthermore, we propose an encoding that approaches the effectiveness of compression, but does not exhibit the same correlation as compression.

3 Encoding and Compression Options in DLMS/COSEM

As mentioned in Sect. 1, system operators want to limit the bandwidth used by the communication needed for smart metering. In this paper we deal with two orthogonal concepts: encoding and compression. Both of these accomplish a reduction in size. Encoding defines how individual data elements are represented in a message. It can transform individual data elements in the message to achieve a more efficient representation of the same information, e.g. by using smaller data types or by converting absolute to relative measurements. Compression, on the other hand, applies a compression algorithm to an entire message without regard to the data contained within. Importantly, compression and encoding can be applied *together*, first transforming the data into a smaller encoded version, then applying compression to it. We therefore consistently distinguish between encoding and compression.

In Sect. 3.1 we briefly introduce the DLMS/COSEM standards. In Sect. 3.2 we introduce the different encoding mechanisms used in our analysis, and in Sect. 3.3 we explain the compression mechanism used.

3.1 DLMS/COSEM

DLMS/COSEM (Device Language Message Specification / Companion Specification for Energy Metering) is a set of IEC standards that define

1. a COSEM object model that gives structure to the available information in the form of COSEM objects [9,10], and
2. a DLMS/COSEM communication stack that defines the messages and underlying communication layers [8] used to communicate the objects.

As part of 2, elements are encoded using ASN.1, with a tag length-value structure: every element is tagged with its type and, if the type does not have a predefined length, its length, followed by the encoded value of the element.

We can put all the 15-min energy consumption measurements of an entire day in a batched measurement object. The structure of such an object and a possible corresponding encoding as a message is given in Table 1. Each measurement is combined with a status code and timestamp stating when the measurement happened in a `Struct`, and all 96 `Structs` are wrapped in an `Array`. This example uses a straightforward encoding not designed to reduce the size, which we deduced from documentation and test cases available in DLMS/COSEM.

In this construction, every element is tagged with its type. The overhead of this can be significant: an object containing only 8-bit integers encoded this way would result in half of the message being spent on the type-tags of these integers.

Table 1. Structure of a batched measurement object (first two columns, based on DLMS/COSEM test cases), the encoding in the corresponding message (third column), and length of each encoded field. Most measurements have been omitted for brevity. The tags and lengths of the elements are included in the encoded values, and therefore accounted for in their length. E.g. the encoding of the measurement itself as a 4-byte integer needs 5 bytes due to the tag.

Object element	Value	Encoded value (hex)	Length (bytes)
Header		C4010000	4
Array (96 elements)		0160	2
Struct (3 elements)		0203	2
Date	2013-01-01 00:00:00	090C07DD0101 0500000000800000	14
Status	0	1100	2
Measurement	65530	060000FFFA	5
Struct (3)		0203	2
Date	2013-01-01 00:15:00	090C07DD0101 05000F0000800000	14
Status	0	1100	2
Measurement	65816	0600010118	5
⋮	⋮	⋮	⋮
Struct (3)		0203	2
Date	2013-01-01 18:30:00	090C07DD0101 05121E0000800000	14
Status	0	1100	2
Measurement	78286	06000131CE	5
⋮	⋮	⋮	⋮
Struct (3)		0203	2
Date	2013-01-01 23:45:00	090C07DD0101 05172D0000800000	14
Status	0	1100	2
Measurement	82362	06000141BA	5
Complete message		C401000001600203090C07DD01 01050000000080000011000600 00FFFA0203090C07DD01010500 0F00008000001100060001 0118 ⋮ 0203090C07DD010105121E0000 800000110006000131CE ⋮ 0203090C07DD010105172D0000 800000110006000141BA	2214

3.2   Possible Encodings in DLMS/COSEM

A new iteration of the DLMS/COSEM IEC standards is currently in development, currently forecast to be published in June 2022.

In the DLMS/COSEM standards there are two encoding options with the explicit purpose to save bandwidth:

1. NULL Coding (already standardized in [8–10])
2. Delta Coding (proposed as part of the next iteration of the standards)

In this section we explain both of these encodings and how they apply to our problem.

NULL Coding. In the current (2017) COSEM object model [9,10], a value may be replaced by a short NULL-value if it can be unambiguously derived from the previous instance of that object. For meter readings, this may happen when the meter reading is the same as the previous one. For timestamps, this may happen if an initial timestamp is transmitted and the periods between timestamps are known. We refer to this mechanism as NULL Coding.

It is important to note that NULL Coding can only work because the `Array` type is heterogeneous: looking at Table 1, not every `Struct` in the `Array` needs to have an identical layout, so the integer types they contain can change if the encoding allows for that. However, in DLMS/COSEM it is also possible to use a so-called `Compact-Array`. This is a homogeneous array type that specifies the type-tags of all its elements only once at the start, and requires every element to have an identical structure. This prevents use of NULL Coding for everything but timestamps in `Compact-Array`.

Delta Coding. A second option, which we refer to as Delta Coding, is proposed for the next (2022) version of the DLMS/COSEM IEC standards. Similar to NULL Coding, Delta Coding seeks to save bandwidth by only transmitting changes to the previous value. E.g. on a system where a meter reading is a 4-byte integer, but power is consumed in amounts that fit in a single byte, Delta Coding would save three bytes per message, or 75%.

Because DLMS/COSEM uses tag-length-value encoding, new integer types (delta types) are introduced so that a distinction can be made between Delta Coded values and absolute measurements. The proposed delta types are signed and unsigned integers of 8, 16, and 32 bits.

The proposed standard does not (yet) prescribe an exact way in which these delta types should be used. To still be able to perform a usable analysis, we have considered what we believe are the most straightforward ways to use delta types for our batched measurement messages, and have come up with several different encodings which are all included in our analysis.

Since messages are considered independent, the first measurement in a message will still need to be an absolute measurement regardless of which encoding is used. All following measurements in that message can be encoded as delta types. The ways in which this could be accomplished that we analysed are:

1. **Minimum-Length Delta Coding**: Since the encoded `Array` allows mixing of types, the most obvious way is to simply use the smallest possible encoding for each individual measurement. Since most Dutch household connections provide 3 x 25A @ 230V connections, the theoretical maximum consumption in 15 min is 4313Wh, a value that easily fits in a 16-bit delta type. However, we expect that a lot of interval measurements in periods with low energy use will fit in 8-bit deltas. This encoding will therefore result in a *variable* message length saving between 2 and 3 bytes per measurement when compared to the encoding shown in Table 1.
2. **N-bit Delta Coding**: Another option is to pick the smallest delta type in which all measurements of an entire batch fit, and encode all measurements except the first one using that type. This results in larger messages than option 1, but the message length would not depend (as much) on consumption. We explore this option for 8-bit, 16-bit, and 32-bit delta types, and we refer to these as N-bit Delta Coding.

Both options 1 and 2 are possible using the normal `Array` type, and we believe they are both possible interpretations of the proposed addition of delta types. However, choosing option 2 with a 16-bit delta type could result in more savings than the minimum-length Delta Coding, if a homogeneous `Compact-Array` is used. This does not appear to have been considered, so we propose this as an additional option and include it in our analysis:

3. **16-bit Compact Delta Coding**: We propose the structure laid out in Table 2: a `Compact-Array` using 16-bit delta types to encode all except the first value. For this to work, the first measurement must be encoded outside of the array, because it must have a non-delta type to base the deltas on. The overhead needed for this is dwarfed by the savings that a `Compact-Array` provides over an `Array`. We refer to this option as 16-bit Compact Delta Coding. As we have already explained, the theoretical maximum consumption of a Dutch household in 15 min is much smaller than 65535Wh, so we do not really need to consider this case with a 32-bit delta type. Conversely, it would not work with an 8-bit delta type because some measurements do exceed 255Wh, which would re-introduce the need for a variable length.

3.3 Compression Used in DLMS/COSEM

Both in the current and proposed versions of DLMS/COSEM, the packet compression mode of ITU-T V.44 [11] may be applied to messages. This mode uses a data compression method in the Lempel-Ziv (LZ) family of compression algorithms: Lempel-Ziv-Jeff-Heath (LZJH) compression [11, Annex B.1].

4 Experimental Setup

We want to determine whether applying the encoding and compression options of DLMS/COSEM could enable traffic analysis, and whether that traffic

Table 2. Structure of the batched measurement object from Table 1, encoded according to our proposed 16-bit Compact Delta Coding. Omitting most type tags allows for massive data savings.

Object element	Value	Encoded value (hex)	Length (bytes)
Header		C4010000	4
Struct (2 elements)		0202	2
Struct (3 elements)		0203	2
Date	2013-01-01 00:00:00	090C07DD0101 0500000000800000	14
Status	0	1100	2
Measurement	65530	060000FFFA	5
Compact Array		13	1
Type tags			
Struct (3)		0203	2
Date		09	1
Status		11	1
16-bit delta		20	1
Length (380 bytes)		8182017C	4
Entry			
Date	2013-01-01 00:15:00	00	1
Status	0	00	1
Measurement	65816	011E	2
⋮	⋮	⋮	⋮
Entry			
Date	2013-01-01 18:30:00	00	1
Status	0	00	1
Measurement	78286	0398	2
⋮	⋮	⋮	⋮
Entry			
Date	2013-01-01 23:45:00	00	1
Status	0	00	1
Measurement	82362	213	2
Complete message		C401000002020203090C07 DD01010500000000800000 1100060000FFFA13020309 11208182017C0000011E ⋮ 00000398 ⋮ 00000213	419

analysis could result in leaking private information. Our experiment consists of the following steps:

1. take publicly available real-world measurement data,
2. encode and compress them in the different possible combinations,
3. for each combination, attempt to find a relation between message length and energy consumption, and
4. use that relation to try to derive private information.

In Sect. 4.1 we introduce the dataset, and in Sect. 4.2 we explain how we generate messages from that dataset. In Sect. 5 we will cover steps 3 and 4.

4.1   The Zonnedael Dataset

For our analysis we use a publicly available dataset from the Dutch DSO Liander [15]. This dataset contains the real energy use data of 80 Dutch households, consensually collected for research purposes in 2013. Liander does not specify whether these households are within one neighbourhood. For our purposes this does not matter – all that matters is that these are real measurements from real households. Some filenames refer to this as the "Zonnedael" dataset, a fictitious name probably intended to better shield the data from deanonymization efforts. We therefore also refer to this data as the Zonnedael data.

The dataset contains relative energy measurements on a 15-min interval, at Watt-hour resolution. We use this dataset mainly because it is readily available, contains real-world data, and has the measurement frequency we need for our analysis.

4.2   Converting Metering Data to DLMS/COSEM Messages

We take the relative energy measurements from the Zonnedael dataset introduced in Sect. 4.1. Using Python, we transform the dataset into absolute measurements like they would be taken by a smart meter. We then generate batch messages covering 24-h periods starting at midnight, similar to how the Dutch infrastructure batches daily meter readings.

We construct messages:

1. without NULL Coding,
2. with NULL Coding applied only to dates, and
3. with NULL Coding applied to dates and Delta Coding applied to measurements.

For option 3, we implement the variants of Delta Coding mentioned in Sect. 3.2:

1. Minimum-Length Delta Coding,
2. fixed-length 32-bit, 16-bit, and 8-bit Delta Coding, and
3. our proposal of 16-bit Compact Delta Coding.

If a message cannot be encoded in a chosen encoding, that encoding is ignored for that message. This is e.g. the case when using 8-bit Delta Coding with measurements greater than 255Wh, or when particular measurements are missing from the dataset.

We compress each of these messages individually. Unfortunately, LZJH is a patented algorithm, with no open-source implementation available. Rather than attempt to write our own implementation, we decided to analyse the effects of compression using another member of the LZ family, Lempel-Ziv-Markov-chain (LZMA). Both algorithms are based on the concept of Lempel-Ziv complexity [14]. The basic operation of these algorithms is the same: repeated sequences of data in a stream are replaced by references to the earlier occurrences. Fehér et al. use the same rationale we do for their choice of using Lempel-Ziv-Welch as an approximation of the behaviour of LZJH in [2]. We therefore assume that our findings for LZMA will hold for LZJH as well, though it would be interesting to see our results reproduced by a meter manufacturer with access to an implementation of LZJH.

To actually perform the compression we use the routines available in Python's standard library [17].

We store the compressed and uncompressed version of each encoded message. We can then explore the relation between the length of the resulting messages and the energy measurements that they were generated from.

Note that we do *not* implement encryption. The AES-GCM encryption used in DLMS/COSEM only adds a constant amount of overhead to all messages, so the plaintext message length is known to the attacker. Since we do not look at the contents of the messages anyway, encrypting the messages would only add computational complexity without altering our findings. Even simulating encryption by adding a constant factor to the lengths is superfluous: our analysis would look the same regardless of whether we add a constant factor to all message lengths, because we are not interested in the absolute lengths, but in how they correlate with energy use.

5 Experimental Results

Our analysis using the real-world Zonnedael dataset introduced in Sect. 4.1 answers three questions:

1. Given the *un*compressed messages (for all encodings), can we find correlations between (daily) household energy use and message length?
2. Given the compressed messages (for all encodings), can we find correlations between (daily) household energy use and message length?
3. If this correlation exists, can we use message length to impact user privacy?

As a reminder, we can use all encodings with or without compression, which results in a total of 14 different options to analyse.

As we explain in Sect. 5.2, the answer to the first question is "no"—with one exception—whereas the answer to the second question is "yes". In Sect. 5.3

answer the third question by showing how we can use that correlation to impact user privacy, and we discuss the implications of our findings in Sect. 5.4. First, however, we look at how effective the encodings and compression actually are at saving data in Sect. 5.1.

5.1 Effectiveness of Encodings and Compression

The effectiveness of the encodings without compression applied is given in Table 3. NULL and Delta Codings are by themselves already very effective at reducing message length. NULL Coding shrinks the messages by a factor of 2.26, simply by eliminating the need to transmit every timestamp as a full 13-byte sequence. When Delta Coding is used, its effectiveness depends on the type of Delta Coding and the actual meter value, but it ranges from 2.26 up to 5.28.

An overview of compression effectiveness when applied to these encodings is given in Table 4. In addition to the tables, Figs. 1 and 2 give a visual indication of how effective the encodings and compression are at saving data.

Table 3. Message size & size reduction ratio for uncompressed messages. Sizes for the minimum-length Delta Coding are given as average. Size reduction ratio is given relative to the unencoded message.

Encoding	(Avg.) size	Reduction ratio
None	2214	—
NULL coding	979	2.26
Minimum-length delta coding	697	3.18
32-bit delta coding	979	2.26
16-bit delta coding	789	2.81
8-bit delta coding	694	3.19
16-bit compact delta coding	419	5.28

Table 4. Message size & size reduction ratio for compressed messages. Sizes are given as average. Size reduction ratio is given relative to the uncompressed, unencoded message from Table 3.

Encoding (compressed)	Avg. size	Reduction ratio
None	348	6.36
NULL coding	208	10.64
Minimum-length delta coding	196	11.30
32-bit delta coding	206	10.75
16-bit delta coding	181	12.23
8-bit delta coding	180	12.30
16-bit compact delta coding	179	12.37

The most important conclusions to draw from these results are:

- Uncompressed, our proposal of 16-bit Compact Delta Coding is overwhelmingly the best option, being much smaller than even the smallest messages of Minimum-length Delta Coding.
- Delta encoding using only 32-bit Deltas is equivalent to normal encoding with NULL Coding for dates, both achieving only a factor 2.26 improvement. Thus, using only 32-bit deltas is not an improvement on already existing options.
- 8-bit Delta Coding is 3.19 times better than no encoding. However, 8-bit Delta Coding is not very useful because it turns out that on average only 18.5% of messages can be encoded using *only* 8-bit Deltas. The per-household median for this is even lower, at 12%.
- Minimum-length Delta Coding is as effective as 8-bit Delta Coding for those messages that can be expressed in only 8-bit Deltas, and then shows a slight increase in space required as energy use increases. This is visible as a *very slight* upward slope in the green plot on the left-hand side of Fig. 1. However, this results in a correlation between energy used and message length, which is a problem, as we explain in Sect. 5.2.
- Compression is very effective in all cases. Something not apparent from Table 4, but which can be seen in Fig. 1, is that compression on the Delta Codings has a large spread in the lower ranges of energy use. This spread narrows as the total use increases.

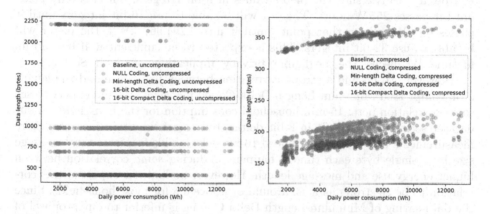

Fig. 1. Scatterplots of the relation between different encodings and data lengths of compressed & uncompressed messages of a single household. 8-bit Delta Coding removed because of its lack of usefulness and overlap with Minimum-length Delta Coding. Uncompressed encodings on the left, compressed encodings on the right.

5.2   Correlations of Encodings and Compression with Energy Use

We see strong correlations induced by compression on all encodings. Therefore, we first discuss the *uncompressed* versions of these encodings, and then discuss the effects of compression separately.

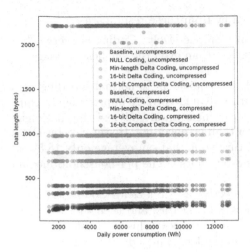

Fig. 2. Scatterplots from Fig. 1 combined into one graph. Notice that uncompressed 16-bit Compact Delta Coding is very close to the compressed baseline.

Uncompressed Messages. We can find no correlation between the size of the uncompressed versions of messages encoded with *most* encodings and the energy use of a household – which follows from these being flat lines in Fig. 1.

All the Delta Codings *except* the Minimum-Length Delta Coding are encodings where message size does not vary, so for them this is as expected.

Uncompressed versions of both NULL Coding and the baseline messages do show some variation, but this variation is not correlated with power use. This effect can be seen in the left graph of Fig. 1, in the form of minor outliers below the majority of message lengths. These messages are all one of three sizes. The reason for this is simple: at the start of its life, a smart meter will be able to transmit the meter values in 8-bit integers, but this only holds until it passes 255 W-hours. Then, it will be able to use 16-bit integers until it passes 65 kWh. From that point, until it hits 4,294,967 kWh, the meter will be able to use 32-bit integers. This is expected to be sufficient well beyond its lifetime. We discuss the (negligible) privacy implications of this in Sect. 5.3.

However, we *do* find a strong correlation between power use and the length of uncompressed Minimum-Length Delta-Coded messages. We did expect to see some correlation here: 15-min household consumption for the households in our dataset seems to mostly fit in 8-bit deltas, but as consumption increases more measurements in a message will need 16-bit deltas. This increases total message size by a single byte each time it happens, inducing *some* correlation between higher energy use and message length. However, we had not expected this correlation to be as strong as it is, around or above 0.8 for most households. Since the data-saving of Minimum-Length Delta Coding is inferior to our proposal of 16-bit Compact Delta Coding—which does not show any correlation—the safe option is to just use 16-bit Compact Delta Coding.

Compressed Messages. When compression is applied, results from our dataset show a strong correlation between the length of the messages and energy use, *regardless of the encoding used*. For the majority of customers, both the Pearson and Spearman correlations for all compressed messages with the power use are high, being at least 0.8 in most cases and 0.9 or higher in many. This is clearly visible in the upward slopes on the right-hand side of Fig. 1. The actual correlation looks to be more logarithmic than linear in nature, but that is not a problem for determining that the relation exists in the first place.

One possible explanation for this correlation is that the lowest energy use of each single household happens when the residents are away from home for extended periods of time, possibly entire days, and the load of a household in this situation is likely to be repetitive, allowing for more compression. To clarify, when the residents are away from home, only the "base load" of a household is being measured. The base load consists mostly of duty-cycling equipment such as freezers, or always-on equipment such as clocks. The base load will therefore be both fairly low and repetitive. As mentioned in Sect. 4.2, the LZMA compression algorithm we use is based on the concept of Lempel-Ziv complexity. Lempel-Ziv complexity is a measurement of how "repetitive" a sequence is, and the lower the Lempel-Ziv complexity of a sequence, the better it is compressed by an LZ algorithm. Because the lowest energy use of a household is that where only the base load is present, it makes sense that the best results of compression correlate with the lowest energy use, with the correlation being caused by the *repetitive nature* of the energy use. This explains why the correlation does not hold as well across households: the actual consumption of the most repetitive load may differ significantly from one household to the next.

This is only conjecture, however, which can be subject of future research.

5.3   Deriving Private Information from the Correlations

Using the insights from Sects. 5.1 and 5.2, we can now show the we can derive privacy-sensitive information using the link between power consumption and message length. We first discuss the issue where a *new* meter leaks that fact. Then we show that we can determine when a household went on holiday.

New Energy Meter. As mentioned in Sect. 5.2, uncompressed versions of both NULL Coding and the baseline messages do show some variation, because the meter starts counting from 0 and the initial messages can therefore use smaller integers to encode the measurements. However, the yearly use of an average Dutch household is between 1500 and 5000 kWh [21], depending on household composition and building type, so after only five days most households will already have passed the point where 32-bit integers are being used. The length of uncompressed messages therefore *does* leak that a new meter is installed, but the privacy impact of this data is questionable and the leak is only present for a few days at most. After this, the length is stable, and no further information can be recovered from these two *un*compressed encodings.

Determining Holidays and Other Absences. We now show that the compressed versions of all encodings definitely leak privacy-sensitive data in a real-world setting. The graphs in Fig. 3 show the power use over the course of the entire year for two different customers. They overlay the message lengths of compressed versions of a few different encodings, including our proposed 16-bit Compact Delta Coding.

We can assume that the lowest energy use indicates that the residents are absent from the house, and we know that message length strongly correlates with energy use. This does not allow us to make statements about these customers on an hour-to-hour basis, but it does allow us to recognize longer periods of absence because they break the somewhat irregular pattern of normal life.

As seen in Fig. 3, customer 17 has clearly gone on a longer vacation twice: once in June, and once in August. We also think there may have been a short period of absence in October, and we believe they went away for Christmas. On the other hand, customer 46 probably went on a short holiday in February, a long summer holiday in June and July, and a third holiday in October, but celebrated Christmas at home.

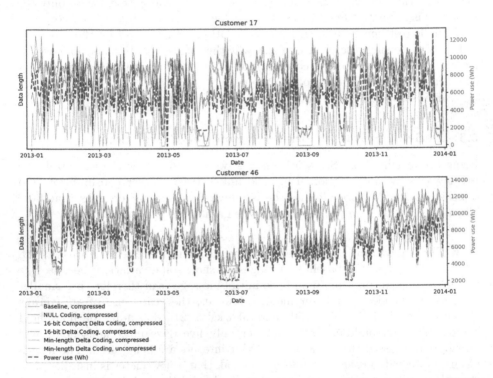

Fig. 3. The year in message lengths: household energy consumption of customer 17 (top) and 46 (bottom), plotted as actual power use (dashed blue) and the *normalized* message lengths (solid lines). The different message length plots in each graph are all the different encodings from which we can derive absences, all based on the same data for each customer. All except one are compressed: for Minimum-length Delta Coding the uncompressed version is also included. In all plots, it is very easy to recognize the valleys that indicate prolonged absence. The same plots for the other uncompressed encodings would just be horizontal lines across the year, providing no information, and are therefore omitted. The actual power use is only shown for validation; the effect is so striking it is clear we can derive the holiday periods from message length alone. (Color figure online)

5.4   Discussion

In Sect. 5.3 we showed that we can derive private information from the correlations we found. In this section we discuss the implications of these findings. We speculate on other patterns that could be uncovered using this kind of analysis, paying particular attention to the influence we expect frequency of transmission and measurement to have on the capabilities of an attacker. We also reflect on how big of a privacy risk our findings actually are.

Frequencies of Transmissions and Measurements. For the results we presented in Sect. 5.3 we specifically looked for absences on several consecutive days. However, this kind of analysis can also find patterns of single-day absences, e.g. somebody spending every Saturday away from home. In addition, if meters send smaller batches more frequently, we may be able to start distinguishing between work days and other days. This hypothesis is hard to verify using the Zonnedael dataset, because it does not include any information about what these patterns *actually* are for the households. However, our reasoning is fairly simple to explain. There are two key factors that play a role in this traffic analysis:

- Frequency of transmission
- Frequency of measurement

Changing the frequency of transmission has two effects – one that increases, and one that decreases our abilities:

- More frequent transmission leads to shorter time periods that information pertains to, which should make more detailed patterns emerge. E.g. if a batch of measurements is sent every 6 h, we may be able to recognize where in the day someone wakes up, whether they went to work, etc.
- More frequent transmission leads to fewer measurements per batch, lowering the correlation because compression has less of an impact. Initial results show that as we approach just a few hours in a period, so on the order of ten measurements in a message, correlation falls sharply.

The second point can then be counteracted by having more frequent measurements. As we approach the order of a message per minute, with measurement frequency of one second, we might in fact be able to approach the capabilities of the research mentioned in Sect. 2.1, and provide a very detailed view of household activity [6,7,16,18].

But there may also be a negative effect to increasing the measurement frequency. Since the individual measurements are hidden, we have no way of determining *why* a message has a certain length. Since the contents of the measurements actually influence the way compression behaves, it's likely there is a limit to how many measurements can be in a single message before adding more measurements make the analysis *less*, rather than more accurate. In addition, the number of different values for individual measurements may also start playing an important role. 15-min measurements on a Watt-hour resolution can be anything from 0 to a few thousand. When measured every second, however, they can only be between 0 and 5 for an average Dutch domestic connection.

With the Zonnedael dataset, we cannot really explore the influence of changing the frequency of measurements, because the measurements are fixed on a 15-min interval. However, in future work we may explore what patterns we are able to deduce from more frequent batches.

Real-World Situation. Although not really a question for our research, we should discuss the relationship between the *real world* and the kind of analysis that we show in this paper. The traffic analysis assumes that the attacker can eavesdrop on the communication of the meter. If the attacker needs to be physically close to the meter for this, then we should consider that the attacker can also simply observe the house to derive the same information we have shown to be derivable from energy use, and see that someone is away from home. But if the attacker can monitor all the traffic for an entire neighbourhood, or even city, or more, by e.g. examining GPRS traffic, the value of traffic analysis becomes apparent. This is clearly something to take into account in the smart metering infrastructure, even though there are a lot of other pressing privacy issues in this domain.

We do note that we have been assured that the potential problems we identified are not present in the existing Dutch DLMS/COSEM infrastructure. We have also made a lot of assumptions about the format of messages and the desired encodings, based on our interpretation of what the standards *allow*, not on what is actually used in practice. The industry should test whether these assumptions hold in existing DLMS/COSEM implementations.

6   Future Work

We have performed our analysis on the daily batches of 15-min interval measurements. We are aware of DSOs that are considering using shorter intervals, and reading them live. These scenarios should be explored in future work, as discussed in Sect. 5.4. The examined encodings and compression might end up influencing these message lengths in a totally different way. A real-world dataset with this granularity would be useful to perform this research, but we are currently unaware of the existence of such a dataset.

We have focused on the actual energy use by a household. The Dutch smart metering infrastructure also communicates other information, such as power quality. This information is treated as privacy-sensitive by Dutch DSOs [4], but the actual relation between power quality measurements and privacy remains largely unexplored. Both this relation and the subsequent impact of potential traffic analysis could be an avenue of future work.

We have suggested an alternative encoding scheme in Sect. 3.2 and Table 2 that already achieves very good data saving without being vulnerable to the kind of analysis we have done. Whether this solution is truly suitable for

DLMS/COSEM is an open question, and should be answered by the DLMS User Association.

If compression is still deemed necessary, a simple option is to determine an acceptable minimum length for energy use messages, and to pad any compressed messages to that length. This way they also become indistinguishable to an observer, and a good amount of compression can likely still be achieved without sacrificing privacy. The actual implementation and effectiveness of such a padding scheme should be considered by the DLMS User Association, or can be subject of future work.

The work presented by Fehér et al. proposes using the Generalized Deduplication [22] compression scheme, which should lead to lower correlations [2,3]. However, they do not show a complete absence of correlation in GD-compressed messages. So whether this scheme has the desired effect of making traffic analysis useless is an open question. It would be interesting to see if we can reproduce our results using the same dataset and this compression scheme.

7   Conclusions

Several options in the DLMS/COSEM specifications for communicating energy use measured by smart meters can result in variable-length messages and thereby may make traffic analysis possible. Since the AES-GCM encryption used in DLMS/COSEM does not hide the length of messages from an attacker, it has no effect on the possibility of traffic analysis. The options that result in variable length messages are:

1. NULL Coding, where a meter reading may be replaced by a shorter NULL value if it is identical to the previous reading;
2. Minimum-length Delta Coding, where a reading may be encoded in the *smallest* type in which it fits; and
3. compression.

An implementation may use both such an encoding and compression at the same time.

We have found that—in a real-world dataset, using our interpretation of possible DLMS/COSEM encodings—compressing batched energy measurement messages results in a strong correlation between message size and the daily energy use of households in all encodings that we have analysed. Using NULL Coding *without* compression does *not* show this correlation *in our dataset*, because very few measurements are ever identical to the previous one. But this does not rule out such a correlation existing in different datasets. Using Minimum-length Delta Coding without compression results in the same correlation as compression.

An attacker performing traffic analysis could therefore determine when all the members of a household are away. We have shown in Sect. 5.3 that we can actually use these correlations to identify periods in which households went on vacation, or whether they spent Christmas away from home. We conjecture that if these measurements were sent more often in smaller batches, e.g. four times per day, traffic analysis could reveal more detailed information and distinguish when people wake up, go to work, etc.

Whether this is actually an (un)acceptable privacy risk is up for debate. Our analysis assumed that meter readings are sent in a big batch, once per day, as is current practice in the Netherlands. However, neither compression nor variable-length encodings are currently in use in the Dutch metering infrastructure. So for now, the risk seems to be purely hypothetical. Also, how easy it is to eavesdrop on communication to then do traffic analysis will depend on the communication medium used and was outside the scope of our research.

Looking towards the future, the risk can easily be eliminated by ensuring there is no variation in the message length, sacrificing *some* data savings to eliminate this risk to user privacy. There are many ways to achieve this. We propose a construction that uses 16-bit Compact Delta Coding *without compression*, described in Sect. 3.2 and Table 2. This construction results in shorter uncompressed messages than even Minimum-length Delta Coding, and approaches the effectiveness of compression. However, because it does not result in messages that vary in length, it avoids the risk of traffic analysis.

References

1. Cuijpers, C., Koops, B-J.: Smart metering and privacy in Europe: lessons from the Dutch case. In: European Data Protection: Coming of Age, pp. 269–293. Springer, Heidelberg (2013). https://doi.org/10.1007/978-94-007-5170-5_12
2. Fehér, M., Yazdani, N., Aranha, D.F., Lucani Rötter, D.E., Hansen, M.T., Vester, F.E.: Side channel security of smart meter data compression techniques. In: IEEE International Conference on Communications, Control, and Computing Technologies for Smart Grids (SmartGridComm) (2020). https://doi.org/10.1109/SmartGridComm47815.2020.9302931
3. Fehér, M., Yazdani, N., Hansen, M.T., Vester, F.E., Lucani Rötter, D.E.: Smart meter data compression using generalized deduplication. In: IEEE Global Communications Conference (GLOBECOM) (2020). https://doi.org/10.1109/GLOBECOM42002.2020.9322393
4. Gedragscode slimme meters voor netbeheerders. Netbeheer NL (2017)
5. Gluck, Y., Harris, N., Prado, A.: BREACH: reviving the CRIME attack (2013). http://breachattack.com/
6. Greveler, U., Glösekötterz, P., Justus, B., Löhr, D.: Multimedia content identification through smart meter power usage profiles. In: Information and Knowledge Engineering, pp. 383–390. WorldComp (2012). https://worldcomp-proceedings.com/proc/p2012/IKE7720.pdf
7. Greveler, U., Justus, B., Löhr, D.: Identifikation von videoinhalten über granulare stromverbrauchsdaten. In: Sicherheit, Schutz und Zuverlässigkeit, pp. 35–45 (2012). http://subs.emis.de/LNI/Proceedings/Proceedings195/article6606.html
8. Electricity metering data exchange - the DLMS/COSEM suite - part 5-3: DLMS/COSEM application layer. IEC standard 62056-5-3:2017, International Electrotechnical Commission (2017). https://webstore.iec.ch/publication/27065

9. Electricity metering data exchange - the DLMS/COSEM suite - part 6–1: Object Identification System (OBIS). IEC standard 62056-6-1:2017, International Electrotechnical Commission (2017). https://webstore.iec.ch/publication/32782

10. Electricity metering data exchange - the DLMS/COSEM suite - part 6–2: COSEM interface classes. IEC standard 62056-6-2:2017, International Electrotechnical Commission (2017). https://webstore.iec.ch/publication/34317

11. International Telecommunication Union: Recommendation V.44 - Series V: Data Communication over the Telephone Network - Error Control - Data Compression Procedures (2000). https://www.itu.int/rec/T-REC-V.44-200011-I/en

12. Kelsey, J.: Compression and information leakage of plaintext. In: Daemen, J., Rijmen, V. (eds.) FSE 2002. LNCS, vol. 2365, pp. 263–276. Springer, Heidelberg (2002). https://doi.org/10.1007/3-540-45661-9_21

13. Langley, A.: Compression contexts and privacy considerations. spdy-dev mailing list (2011). https://groups.google.com/g/spdy-dev/c/B_ulCnBjSug/m/rcU-SIFtTKoJ

14. Lempel, A., Ziv, J.: On the complexity of finite sequences. IEEE Trans. Inf. Theory 22(1), 75–81 (1976). https://doi.org/10.1109/TIT.1976.1055501

15. Liander N.V.: Datasets slimme meter, "Zonnedael". https://www.liander.nl/partners/datadiensten/open-data/data, https://www.liander.nl/sites/default/files/Over-Liander-slimme-meter-dataset-2013-levering.zip

16. Liao, J., Stankovic, L., Stankovic, V.: Detecting household activity patterns from smart meter data. In: 2014 International Conference on Intelligent Environments, pp. 71–78 (2014). https://doi.org/10.1109/IE.2014.18

17. Python Software Foundation: lzma - compression using the LZMA algorithm. https://docs.python.org/3.9/library/lzma.html

18. Molina-Markham, A., Shenoy, P., Fu, K., Cecchet, E., Irwin, D.: Private memoirs of a smart meter. In: Workshop on Embedded Sensing Systems for Energy-Efficiency in Building, pp. 61–66. ACM (2010). https://doi.org/10.1145/1878431.1878446

19. Rizzo, J., Duong, T.: The CRIME attack. In: Ekoparty Security Conference (2012). https://docs.google.com/presentation/d/11eBmGiHbYcHR9gL5nDyZChu_-lCa2GizeuOfaLU2HOU/

20. Van Aubel, P., Poll, E.: Smart metering in the Netherlands: what, how, and why. Int. J. Electric. Power Energy Syst. 109, 719–725 (2019). https://doi.org/10.1016/j.ijepes.2019.01.001

21. Vereniging Nederlandse EnergieDataUitwisseling: Profielen elektriciteit (2016–2020). https://www.nedu.nl/documenten/verbruiksprofielen/

22. Vestergaard, R., Zhang, Q., Lucani Rötter, D.E.: Lossless compression of time series data with generalized deduplication. In: IEEE Global Communications Conference (GLOBECOM) (2019). https://doi.org/10.1109/GLOBECOM38437.2019.9013957

iDDAF: An Intelligent Deceptive Data Acquisition Framework for Secure Cyber-Physical Systems

Md Hasan Shahriar[1]([✉]), Mohammad Ashiqur Rahman[1], Nur Imtiazul Haque[1],
Badrul Chowdhury[2], and Steven G. Whisenant[3]

[1] Florida International University, Miami, USA
{mshah068,marahman,nhaqu004}@fiu.edu
[2] The University of North Carolina at Charlotte, Charlotte, USA
b.chowdhury@uncc.edu
[3] Duke Energy, Charlotte, USA
steven.whisenant@duke-energy.com

Abstract. Internet of Things (IoT) and Cyber-Physical Systems (CPSs) are creating hybrid platforms that are becoming ubiquitous in all modern infrastructure. As complex and heterogeneous systems are getting integrated, a malicious user can have tremendous opportunities to infiltrate networks, steal sensitive information, inject cleverly crafted false data into measurements, or overwhelm networks with fake packets. Such malicious activities can prevent legitimate requests or even mislead the control center to make erroneous decisions. Agility-based defense mechanisms are robust in deceiving adversaries by randomizing the sensor data at different communication hierarchy levels. While misleading the attackers, the control center must retrieve the actual data to operate the system correctly. Existing mechanisms consider sharing the exact remapping pattern with the control center. Such direct sharing raises the concern of further attacks on them and communication overheads. Hence, we propose iDDAF, an intelligent deception defense-based data acquisition framework that leverages system-agnostic prediction and remapping model at the controller level to ensure a comprehensive security solutions (CIA triad) for any hierarchical CPSs network. In this framework, the data reporting/relaying nodes randomize the associated sensor addresses/IDs and add decoy data, while the prediction mechanism at the control center reassigns the original IDs to the measurements and impute the missing data if necessary. Hence, any reconnaissance attempt fails, artfully altered measurements turn into random data injections, making it easy to remove them as outliers. Experimental results on the standard IEEE 14 bus system show that iDDAF can detect and completely mitigate different types of cyberattacks.

Keywords: Deception defense · Cyber-physical systems · Cyberattacks

© ICST Institute for Computer Sciences, Social Informatics and Telecommunications Engineering 2021
Published by Springer Nature Switzerland AG 2021. All Rights Reserved
J. Garcia-Alfaro et al. (Eds.): SecureComm 2021, LNICST 399, pp. 338–359, 2021.
https://doi.org/10.1007/978-3-030-90022-9_17

1 Introduction

Cyber-physical systems (CPSs) integrate sensing, communication, processing, and control from cyberspace and the physical world [13]. CPSs are everywhere - in transportation networks, smart grids, medicine, water management, and so on. A new dimension for CPSs has been opened up by the Internet of things (IoT), enabling real-time monitoring, data exchange, and optimum control. As a key element of the control system's control process, the state estimation (SE) plays a critical role in ensuring safety and proper control decisions [4,33]. In the era of heterogeneous sensor interaction, CPSs have become essential components of critical infrastructures while also creating a large attack surface for adversaries. Modern cyberattacks are so sophisticated that legacy defense techniques cannot stand up against them. By leveraging the targeted system's knowledge and state, adversaries can launch influential attacks, such as false data injection (FDI) attacks, covert attacks, zero dynamics attacks, replay attacks, and denial of service (DoS) attacks [14,32,40].

The CPSs' supervisory control and data acquisition (SCADA) devices typically lack the processing power to perform strong encryption on sensor data streams [5]. Data acquisition processes at critical infrastructures (such as power systems) are also constrained by maximum time delays. According to the IEC 61850 standard, GOOSE (generic object-oriented substation event) messages within power grid substations must be delivered with no more than a 4 ms delay [2]. Due to this limitation, high-end security may not be applied despite sufficient computational power at the substations networks.

Several studies have shown that sophisticated attackers can generate attack data, evading the existing defense mechanisms utilizing the information about the topology and states of the targeted systems [16,24,29,31]. A computer worm containing 500 kilobits of code, called Stuxnet, destroyed over a thousand Iranian uranium enrichment centrifuges in 2010 [19]. US smart grids could be breached by Stuxnet-like attacks causing an estimated $1 trillion loss to the government [9]. In Ukraine, a massive power outage has been caused by Black-Energy Malware, which targets the SCADA system with a DoS attack [17].

"All warfare is based on deception. Hence, when we are able to attack, we must seem unable; when using our forces, we must appear inactive; when we are near, we must make the enemy believe we are far away; when far away, we must make him believe we are near."—Sun tzu, the Art of War [37].

As the author said, in cyber war, deception also plays a vital role. To secure the data acquisition process in CPSs, we propose an intelligent **D**eception **D**efense-based **D**ata **A**cquisition **F**ramework (iDDAF) for any hierarchical SCADA network. The proposed framework secures the data acquisition steps by shuffling the reported sensors' addresses/IDs along with adding decoy data at each node in the hierarchy. The randomization patterns are changed periodically to obfuscate any reconnaissance attempt. Moreover, due to the deception, any attempt of coordinated stealthy cyberattack turns into a random data injection, which is easily detected and eliminated by the existing bad data detection techniques. As smart grid is a perfect example of modern CPSs, we consider a smart grid hierarchical communication network as our testbed.

As the sensor data are randomized at the network switches/nodes, the energy management system (EMS) needs to remap them to the original pattern. The existing works consider that the nodes share the randomization information with the EMS through a seed-based or a secure communication medium. In the seed-based approach, both the nodes and the EMS must be perfectly synchronized to share the remapping pattern. Failure of synchronization can lead to a different remapping pattern and direct the system to a hazardous scenario. On the other hand, sending remapping information through another dedicated communication channel further raises the question of security. Hence, we propose a novel secure and effective data-driven approach to overcome the existing concerns. In summary, the contributions of this paper are as follows:

- We implement deception as a defense in the networked control systems to defend against different cyberattacks. We design iDDAF, utilizing a prediction and a remapping model, for any CPSs hierarchical network that can misleads the stealthiest cyberattacks.
- We use a heuristic randomization algorithm to generate the deceptive IDs for the randomized sensors. An algorithm is designed to create a virtual subsystem at the nodes considering the underneath physical components to generate the decoy data supporting the ID randomization.
- We design and deploy a highly accurate model agnostic regression algorithm for estimating the state data based on previous states information. The prediction process enables the remapping algorithm to recover the original sensor measurements from the random data sequence. The remapping algorithm is defined as an optimization problem, which takes the reported (shuffled) and predicted data as inputs and finds the best possible set of recovered data, declining the malicious ones and imputing the missing measurements.
- We implement and evaluate the framework on a standard IEEE 14 bus system. The codes and data are publicly available at [1].

The rest of the paper is organized as follows: The models and objectives are explain in Sect. 2. We add sufficient background information in Sect. 3. Our proposed iDDAF is introduced in Sect. 4. In Sect. 5, we discuss the technical details of the framework. We also provide an example case study to demonstrate the data remapping process. The evaluation setup and result analysis are formulated in Sect. 6. The related works are discussed in Sect. 7. At last, we conclude the paper in Sect. 8.

2   Models and Design Objectives

In this section, we describe the system and threat models, along with the design objectives of iDDAF.

2.1   System Model

The future CPS network should have a hierarchical structure to minimize communication overhead and to ensure the system's stability, reliability, and efficiency [39]. Smart grids with hierarchy-based communication networks are becoming a more preferred choice as distributed generation, renewable energy, and electricity demand increase [20]. Figure 1 illustrates a hierarchical communication network in a smart grid – a model with two layers of substation switches.

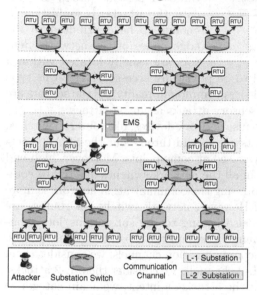

A sensor in a substation may be a remote terminal unit (RTU), an intelligent electronic device (IED), a phasor measurement unit (PMU), etc. A sensor is located within a substation and reports measurement data to its switch. Hence, the sensor are referred to as level-0 (L-0) elements of the network. A level-1 substation (L-1) receives measurement data from its own sensors only, whereas a level-2 substation (L-2) receives measurements from both its sensors and the L-1 substations underneath it. When a network has two levels, the L-2 switches report data directly to the EMS. In order to estimate the system states and make appropriate decisions after collecting remote sensor data, the EMS executes the SE-BDD

Fig. 1. Hierarchical communication network in a smart grid.

(Sect. 3.1) algorithm. The hierarchical structure can be considered like a tree, where the sensors are the leaf nodes, substation switches act as the internal nodes, and EMS is at the root. Additionally, we determine the communication channel based on the level of the incoming switch when sending data to the EMS. Therefore, a channel between L-1 and L-2 switches is defined as an L-1 channel, and a channel between the L-2 switch and EMS is an L-2 channel.

2.2   Attack Model

This subsection defines the attack model based on the attacker's abilities and goals. We consider the attack tree illustrated in Fig. 2 in this study. An adversary can exploit multiple vulnerable points of the data acquisition process.

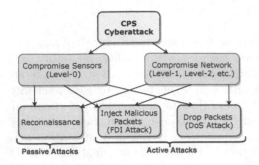

Fig. 2. Considered attack tree in CPSs.

The attacker's accessibility/ position into the network plays a very crucial role in the attack's success. In general, we classify an adversary's position into two groups. Firstly, the attacker can compromise the individual targeted sensors [6, 34]. In this case, the attacker is sophisticated enough to be distributed to the edge nodes of the network. Sensors are usually located within a substation, which are highly secured to be physically accessed. Since this type of attack comes with a great cost, it is less common in reality. As the sensors are the leaf nodes (L-0), we define such sensory attacks as an L-0 attack.

Secondly, the attacker can compromise network devices, like routers, switches, channels, and so on. As these elements are spread throughout the SCADA network, physical security can be compromised at some points. Moreover, high-end encryption may not be implemented in all the network switches due to low computational capabilities. Thus, compromising the communication network is more prevalent in the CPSs cyberattacks. However, network switches or routers are mostly in secured locations as they also belong to the substations/local control center. Thus, communication channels remain the most vulnerable points. When the attacker compromises L-1 communication channels, we consider them L-1 attacks; when they compromise L-2 channels, we consider them L-2 attacks.

On the other hand, depending on the attacker's intent, we again categorize the cyberattacks into two classes— active attacks, and passive attacks [35]. Passive attacks are the process of reconnaissance of the system states, where the attacker gets into the network, sniffs, and analyzes the packets without obstructing the normal operation of the system. The goal of such an attack is to study the parameters of the physical system and determine the optimal attack tactics without creating any attention of the defender. A passive attack is dangerous for the confidentiality of the system.

Active attacks are the injections of malicious data into the sensor measurements that help to achieve the attacker's goal. Active attacks exploit the integrity as well as the availability of sensor data. The effectiveness/stealthiness of the active attacks depends on the success of the passive attacks. We consider two influential cyberattacks, e.g., FDI attacks, and DoS attacks as the active attacks in the paper.

In the first case, the attacker injects malicious data into the network packets to mislead the system in a hazardous direction. In DoS attacks, the attacker drops the targeted packets, leaving the sensors from a critical part unavailable. As a result, the total system becomes unobservable and may collapse due to the delayed response. In this work, we evaluate the performance of iDDAF considering all the combination of cyberattacks as discussed.

2.3   Design Objectives

The key goals of our proposed framework is to provide a secure and robust data acquisition mechanism. Our design objectives are as follows:

- **Confidentiality**: To preserve the systems' privacy from the adversary, we hide the true information of the system and show the artfully crafted sensors data. Such move misleads the attacker and prevents reconnaissance attacks in the system states.
- **Integrity:** To maintain the unperturbed system operation, any malicious data injections need to be removed from the system control loop. Thus, we aim to mitigate the stealthy FDI injection attacks by identifying the compromised sensors and eliminate them from the SE procedure.
- **Availability:** To optimize the dynamic behaviour of the system in run-time, the system must be observable to EMS. However, in the case of DoS attacks, some parts of the system might go offline, making the whole system unobservable. We need to predict missing data and keep the system running around the optimal operating point
- To remap the randomized sensors data in agility-based defense, existing solutions consider explicit information sharing between the nodes of the network. However, our goal is to design an intelligent deceptive data acquisition framework, where the recovery process is totally independent and avoids such information sharing among the nodes.

3   Preliminaries

In this section, we discuss the terminologies that are used throughout the paper to facilitate readers' comprehension.

3.1   State Estimation and Bad Data Detector

SE is the process of determining the network's state based on redundant telemetry measurements. Let us assume that a CPS has n number of states variables, $\mathbf{x} = (x_1, x_2, \cdots, x_n)^T$, and m sensor measurements, $\mathbf{z} = (z_1, z_2, \cdots, z_m)^T$, with sufficient redundancy $(m >> n)$. The states vector $\mathbf{x}$ and the measurement set $\mathbf{z}$ are related as $\mathbf{z} = \mathbf{h}(\mathbf{x}) + \mathbf{e}$, where $\mathbf{h}(\mathbf{x})$ is the function relating the measurement set to the state data, and $\mathbf{e}$ is the set of noise/errors that follows a normal distribution [4]. The state variables in a power system, for instance, are the voltages on the buses (magnitude and phase). The sensor usually measures power flow data, bus power injections, and phasor measurement units (PMUs) data, etc.

DC power flow is a widely used technique in power industries for efficient and accurate real-time analysis due to its simplicity, robustness, and high computing speed [38]. Voltage magnitude is considered a unity in the DC system approximation. So the only state variables that are considered are bus phase angles. Besides, $\mathbf{h}(\mathbf{x})$ is the linear transformation using the Jacobian matrix, $\mathbf{H}$. For the linear measurement functions, $\mathbf{h(x)}$ the most probable system states vector $\hat{\mathbf{x}}$ can be estimated directly by solving:

$$\hat{\mathbf{x}} = (\mathbf{H}^T\mathbf{W}\mathbf{H})^{-1}\mathbf{H}^T\mathbf{W}\mathbf{z} \qquad (1)$$

$\mathbf{W}$ denotes diagonal weighting matrix. Thus, the best estimated measurement vector $\mathbf{z_{est}}$ can be calculated by $\mathbf{z_{est}} = \mathbf{h(\hat{x})}$ and the residuals set as $\mathbf{r} = ||\mathbf{z} - \mathbf{h(\hat{x})}||$. The Bad Data Detection (BDD) procedure is often coupled with SE to identify outliers. A measurement z_i is considered as a bad data and eliminated from the SE procedure if $||r_i|| > \tau$, where τ is error threshold. The estimation and removal process is repeated until no bad data is found in the considered measurement vector. At the end, an $SE-BDD.$ procedure returns the estimated states $\hat{\mathbf{x}}$, estimated measurements $\mathbf{z_{est}}$, residual vector $\mathbf{r}$, and the list of outliers.

3.2   Stealthy False Data Injection Attack

By injecting malicious data into the sensor reading, an attacker can alter the state estimation process. An attack vector consists of malicious data that is injected into a set of sensor measurements. So an anomaly occurs as a result of a random attacks; the compromised sensors become outliers at BDD, and the SE process is left unaffected. However, bypassing the BDD is possible if the attack vector is intelligently calculated based on the information of the targeted system [24,26]. Let us consider one scenario where the attacker wants to change the state variables set $\hat{\mathbf{x}}$ by the malicious amount $\mathbf{x^c}$. If (s)he injects false data $\mathbf{a}$ to the measurement set $\mathbf{z}$, the condition $\mathbf{a} = \mathbf{h(x^c)}$ ensures that such injection will bypass the BDD. Since $\mathbf{z}+\mathbf{a} = \mathbf{h(\hat{x}+x^c)}$, the residual $\mathbf{r} = ||(\mathbf{z}+\mathbf{a})-\mathbf{h(\hat{x}+x^c)}||$ $= ||\mathbf{z}-\mathbf{h(\hat{x})}+\mathbf{a}-\mathbf{h(x^c)}|| = ||\mathbf{z}-\mathbf{h(\hat{x})}||$. Data injection is thus rendered invisible to the residual vector, which allows the attack to remain stealthy. The attacker needs to know the topology, configuration, and measurements of the targeted system. For the rest of this paper, FDI is used to refer to stealthy FDI attacks.

4   iDDAF

The tasks of the iDDAF are categorized into two mechanisms: i) deception mechanism, and ii) remapping mechanism. The deception mechanism is implemented in the nodes of the network. As the first part of the deception, EMS assigns all the sensors into three groups: *fixed, randomized, decoyed*. The *fixed* sensors do not participate in the deception mechanism and are regarded as the regular sensors. On the other hand, *randomized* and *decoyed* sensors are considered in the deception process. EMS updates the groups periodically and lets the corresponding nodes know the sensors group information.

Later, during the data acquisition process, the nodes directly forward the packets of *fixed* sensors but craft the packets of others. They shuffle the IDs of the *randomized* sensors and add decoy data to *decoyed* sensors. The decoy data are calculated to support the SE on the *fixed* and *randomized* measurement data so that they remain topologically aligned and thus the randomization remains hidden to the attacker. This process continues until the packets reach EMS. As the nodes may need to analyze and modify the network packets, they need to be equipped with software-defined networking (SDN) controllers [8, 25]. An SDN controller has the ability to read, edit, and assemble packets in real-time. SDN is widely used in modern communication networks. In the absence of SDN switches, VMware and Nicira can also implement similar capabilities on conventional switches [7]. Once EMS receives the packets, it drops off the *decoy* data and restores the remaining data along with their original IDs before using them in the SE procedure. The remapping mechanism uses a regression-based prediction model that considers the historical time-series state data to predict the next state vector. However, as EMS receives a randomly shuffled sensor data, we define the ID remapping algorithm as a combinatorial optimization problem that provides the correct optimum sequence of reported measurement data. The remapping algorithm considers a reported measurement in the recovered data only if it is within a specific range of the prediction values. Hence, in the case of stealthy FDI attacks, any sudden change in any measurement reading takes it beyond the allowed threshold; and thus, is not considered in the recovered data. Such removal eliminates the compromised sensors and makes the system immune to the stealthy FDI attacks. However, due to the extensive reduction of compromised sensors or any DoS attack, the remapped measurement data might not be enough to make the system observable. In that case, the missing measurement readings are replaced with the predicted data, which ensures the system's observability.

5   Technical Details

This section elaborates on the working principle of iDDAF.

5.1   Deception Mechanism

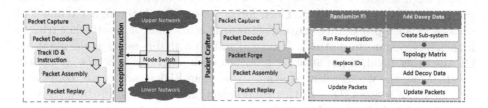

Fig. 3. Deception mechanism in the nodes of the hierarchical network

Figure 3 shows the tasks of the nodes for deception mechanism. Firstly, EMS sends the deception instructions to the sensors, and the nodes keep track of the instructions. The instruction contains a type flag where 0, 1, and 2 indicates *fixed*, *randomized*, and *decoyed*, respectively. Thus, each node constrains an m

dimensional array $\mathcal{T}$ to store the sensor-wise deception instructions, where m is the number of sensors. Later on, when the sensors report the measurement data, each node in the hierarchy crafts the packets for type 1 and 2 sensors as followings:

Algorithm 1: RanID($\mathcal{I}^{rec}, recIDs, randIDs, \mathcal{T}$)

---
1 initialize $\mathcal{I}^{rand} = \mathcal{I}^{rec}$;
2 **for** $i = 1$ to len($\mathcal{I}^{rec}$) **do**
3   **for** $j = 1$ to len(recID) **do**
4   **if** $\mathcal{I}^{rec}[i] = recID[j]$ and $\mathcal{T}[i] == 1$ **then**
5              $\mathcal{I}^{rand}[i] = randIDs[j]$;
6   break;
7   end
8 end

Randomizing IDs: The IDs of *randomized* sensors are shuffled among themselves. We propose a heuristic approach in the randomization. Algorithm 1 shows the *RandID* procedure, which replaces the *randomized* sensors' received IDs $\mathcal{I}^{rec}$ with $\mathcal{I}^{rand}$. The pair (*recIDs, randIDs*) contains the lists of IDs that defines randomization pattern for that node. The (*recIDs, randIDs*) pairs are generated heuristically and updated at a regular interval by the update instruction from EMS.

As the data packets contain randomized IDs, if the attacker is not aware of the deception, (s)he will be injecting the false data to the deceived locations. Let us assume that the $\mathcal{I}^{org} = \{o_1, o_2, ...o_{m-1}, o_m\}$ is the original sequence of m IDs for the measurement data at one layer, where the shuffled IDs $\mathcal{I}^{rand} = \{r_1, r_2, ...r_{m-1}, r_m\}$ are used with that measurement set. Thus, the probability that $\mathcal{I}^{org}$ and $\mathcal{I}^{rand}$ are exactly the same as $\frac{1}{k!}$, where k is the number of *randomized* sensors and $k \leq m$. For $k = 5$ the probability is 0.008 and $k = 10$ the probability is 2.75×10^{-7}. Thus, for a node with a little higher number of sensors m, such probability converges towards zero. Thus, if an attacker tries to launch a reconnaissance attack, (s)he will end up with different state estimation. On the other hand, if the attacker launches a targeted active attack, (s)he will be attacking the wrong set of sensors. Usually, an FDI attack vector contains a critical set of sensors. Due to this randomization, the attacker attacks sensors with the critical IDs, but they contain the measurement data of sensors coming from different parts of the system. Thus, removing those sensors does not create any issue for the observability of the system.

Algorithm 2: FindDecoy ($\mathbf{z}_{fix}$, $\mathbf{z}_{rand}$, $\mathbf{z}_{dec}$, H, α)

---

1 initialize the decoy data with the existing data, $\mathbf{z}_{decoy} \leftarrow \mathbf{z}_{dec}$;
2 $[\mathbf{r}_{fix}, \mathbf{r}_{rand}, \mathbf{r}_{decoy}] = \text{SE}([\mathbf{z}_{fix}, \mathbf{z}_{rand}, \mathbf{z}_{decoy}], H)$;
   /* run state estimation and amend decoy data   */
   /* repeat until the decoy data is harmonized   */
3 **while** $\|\mathbf{r}_{decoy}\| > \alpha$ **do**
4 | $[\mathbf{r}_{fix}, \mathbf{r}_{rand}, \mathbf{r}_{decoy}] = \text{SE}([\mathbf{z}_{fix}, \mathbf{z}_{rand}, \mathbf{z}_{decoy}], H)$;
5 | $\mathbf{z}_{decoy} \leftarrow \mathbf{z}_{decoy} - \mathbf{r}_{decoy}$;
6 **end**
7 **return** $\mathbf{z}_{decoy}$

Adding Decoy Data: ID randomization makes the deception more visible to the attacker as the random IDs do not follow the topological pattern. Thus, if the adversary runs the **SE-BDD** on the deceptive data that only contains both *randomized* and *fixed* IDs, the sensors with the *randomized* IDs will become outliers, and (s)he might end up with the actual state estimation. Thus, to support the ID randomization, we propose to add decoy data with the (*decoyed*) sensors, which supports the random IDs to be good data in the attacker's state estimation, making the actual (*fixed*) data outliers. Let's assume that $\mathbf{z}^i$ ($\in \mathbf{z}$) is the measurement vector consisting of only the sensors of i-th node. We define H_i as the topology matrix of the i-th sub-system, where the rows represent the sensors in $\mathbf{z}^i$, and the columns are for the substations where those sensors are located. Figure 4 shows a case of generating H_i from the system's full topology matrix H. Thus, we can define $\mathbf{z}^i$ as $[\mathbf{z}^i_{fix}, \mathbf{z}^i_{rand}, \mathbf{z}^i_{dec}]$, where $\mathbf{z}^i_{fix}$, $\mathbf{z}^i_{rand}$, and $\mathbf{z}^i_{dec}$ contains the fixed, randomized, and decoyed measurement data. Algorithm 2 shows the technique to calculate the decoy data $\mathbf{z}^i_{dec}$. The procedure takes the sub-system's randomized data, topology matrix H^i, and a threshold α.

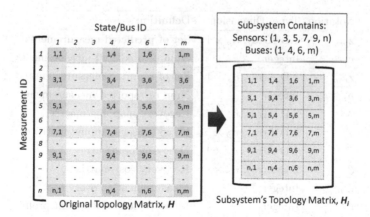

Fig. 4. Generation of sub-system topology matrix H_i

5.2 Remapping Mechanism

This section introduces the prediction-based remapping. Figure 5 shows the process of remapping using a second order polynomial regression model. In the following subsections, we explain different modules of the prediction-based remapping.

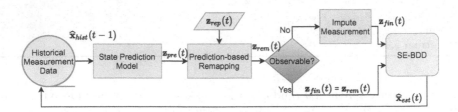

Fig. 5. Prediction-based remapping mechanism of iDDAF

Sensor Prediction: The first part of remapping is to train the regression model based on the past state estimation data, which estimates the current state vector. The estimated state vector is multiplied with a topology matrix H to generate the predicted measurement vector. The prediction model takes past k samples of the previous estimated state vector, $\hat{\mathbf{x}}^{hist}(t-1)$ and predict the next state $\mathbf{x}^{pre}(t)$, which generates the measurement sample, $\mathbf{z}^{pre}(t) = H\,\mathbf{x}_{pre}(t)$. Hence, in the regression algorithm, we provide an $n \times k$ dimensional historical state data $\hat{\mathbf{x}}_{hist}(t-1)$ and generate $n \times 1$ dimensional $\mathbf{x}^{pre}(t)$. Here, $\hat{\mathbf{x}}_{hist}(t-1) = [\hat{\mathbf{x}}(t-1),\ \hat{\mathbf{x}}(t-2),\ ....,\ \hat{\mathbf{x}}(t-k+1),\ \hat{\mathbf{x}}(t-k)]$.

Table 1. Modeling parameters of remapping algorithm.

Notation	Type, Dimension	Definition
$\mathbf{z}_{pre}$	1-D Array, $n_p \times 1$	Set of predicted measurements
n_p	Integer	Num of predicted measurements
$\mathbf{z}_{rep}$	1-D Array, $n_s \times 1$	Set of reported measurements
n_r	Integer	Num of reported measurements
$\mathcal{M}$	2-D Array, $n_p \times n_s$	Recovery mapping matrix
$\mathcal{F}$	2-D Array, $n_p \times n_s$	Fixed sensor mapping matrix
$\mathcal{D}$	1-D Array, $n_r \times 1$	Decoy mapping array
$\mathcal{C}$	2-D Array, $n_p \times n_s$	Recovery cost matrix
$\mathcal{O}^{Cost}_{Reco}$	Integer	Measurement recovery cost
$\mathcal{O}^{Prof}_{Assi}$	Integer	Measurement assignment profit
η	Integer	Recovery threshold

Sensor Remapping: Due to the deception, the sensor's measurement is crafted with randomized IDs, and the reported measurement vector, $\mathbf{z}_{rep}(t)$, needs to be reshuffled to get back to the original pattern. To do this remapping, we design an optimization algorithm to assign the best set of sensors IDs to $\mathbf{z}_{rem}(t)$ considering the predicted data $\mathbf{z}_{pre}(t)$.

Remapping Algorithm: This part explains the repairing algorithm. As we deal with different combinations of the data, we use mixed integer programming (MIP) to implement the combinatorial optimization problem. Table 1 shows the notations used in defining the constraints. Our goal is to find the ($n_p \times n_r$) dimensional binary matrix $\mathcal{M}$, where the positions of the ones represent the successful recovery of reported measurements. The rows and columns of the ones in $\mathcal{M}$ represent the IDs of predicted and reported measurement, respectively. For example, a one in the position (i, j) of $\mathcal{M}$ represents that the j-th reported reading in $\mathbf{z}_{rep}$ is the actual measurement of i-th sensor. Thus, the total number of ones in $\mathcal{M}$ indicates the number of recovered measurements.

fixed sensors do not participate in the randomization process during deception. Their IDs remain the same during the whole process and we explicitly define them during the repairing process. $\mathcal{F}$ is the 2-D binary mapping matrix, where the rows and columns represent the already known remapping of *fixed* sensors. On the other hand, $\mathcal{D}$ presents the 1-D binary mapping of the *decoyed* sensors. As shown in (2) and (3), each recovery of the randomized sensor comes with a cost, defines as the difference between the predicted and the reported value. In the case of a fixed ID, the cost is explicitly defined as zero. As shown in (4), the *decoyed* measurements are not assigned to any of the sensors.

$$\forall_{1,1\leq i,j \leq n_s, n_r} \quad \mathcal{F}_{i,j} == 0 \implies \mathcal{C}_{i,j} == |\mathbf{z}_{pre}^{i} - \mathbf{z}_{rep}^{j}| \tag{2}$$

$$\forall_{1,1\leq i,j \leq n_s, n_r} \quad \mathcal{F}_{i,j} == 1 \implies (\mathcal{M}_{i,j} == 1) \wedge (\mathcal{C}_{i,j} == 0) \tag{3}$$

$$\forall_{1\leq j \leq n_r} \quad \mathcal{D}_j == 1 \implies \sum_{i=1}^{n_s} \mathcal{M}_{i,j} == 0 \tag{4}$$

The recovery data must be within a specific range of the predicted data. Thus, as shown in (5), a recovery is valid only if the associated cost is within $\eta\%$ of the expected data. However, if there is no such reported value within that range, that sensor remains unassigned.

$$\forall_{1\leq i,j \leq n_s, n_r} \quad \mathcal{C}_{i,j} > |\mathbf{z}_{pre}^{i} \times \eta| \implies \mathcal{M}_{i,j} == 0 \tag{5}$$

The constraints in (6) mandate that any measurement can be assigned to almost one sensor and vice-versa.

$$\forall_{1\leq i \leq n_s} \sum_{j=1}^{n_r} \mathcal{M}_{i,j} \leq 1 \quad \text{and} \quad \forall_{1\leq j \leq n_r} \sum_{i=1}^{n_s} \mathcal{M}_{i,j} \leq 1 \tag{6}$$

As shown in (7), the ultimate goal is to assign as much measurements as possible (maximize assignment profit), while keeping the recovery cost to minimum.

This two objective functions are merged together in (8). Thus, the optimization maximizes the assignment profit by allocating as many sensors as possible and minimizes the recovery cost by assigning to the closest prediction. To ensure the maximum number of recovered sensors, we multiply the assignment profit by k and emphasize it than the recovery cost. Hence, there will always be a solution; however, no sensor will be recovered in the worst-case scenario. EMS will rely only on the fixed sensors to run the state estimation in such a rare case. Thus, it will be useful to select a set of fixed sensors that spans the system's critical parts and ensures observability.

$$\mathcal{O}_{Reco}^{Cost} = \sum_{i=1}^{n_s} \sum_{j=1}^{n_r} \mathcal{M}_{i,j} \times \mathcal{C}_{i,j} \quad and \quad \mathcal{O}_{Assi}^{Prof} = \sum_{i=1}^{n_s} \sum_{j=1}^{n_r} \mathcal{M}_{i,j} \quad (7)$$

$$\min \ (\mathcal{O}_{Reco}^{Cost} - k \times \mathcal{O}_{Assi}^{Prof}) \quad (8)$$

The successful execution of the program returns the matrix $\mathcal{M}$ from where we find the remapped pattern $z_{rem} = \mathcal{M} \times z_{rep}$, which is finally used by EMS in $SE - BDD$. If the system is observable, it finds the state vectors and takes the necessary control decision. However, if the system is unobservable, we use an imputation algorithm to fill up the missing data.

Data Imputation: If there is an L-1/L-2 FDI attack in the system, the recovery algorithm can remove the compromised measurement and may keep the system observable under sufficient randomization. However, in the case of L-0 attacks, dropping the compromised measurement during the repairing process may lead the system to unobservability. Besides, instead of an FDI attack, there can be a DoS attack, where the attacker's goal is to make some targeted critical measurement missing. In both cases, iDDAF replaces the missing data with the predicted measurements from $z_{pre}(t)$.

5.3   A 14 Bus Case Study

In this section, we provide a case study of prediction-based remapping in the IEEE 14 bus system [3] as shown Fig. 6. For the simplicity, we consider a case where 100% of sensors are reporting measurement data to EMS, and all of them are considered for randomization.

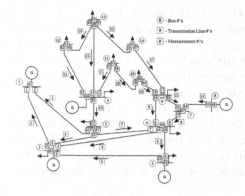

Fig. 6. IEEE 14-bus test system [28]

Remapping Under Normal Condition: Figure 7a shows the randomized reported measurement data, sensor-wise prediction, and the recovered data under normal operating conditions. The reported data contain random IDs; thus, the reported measurement vector's shape does not follow the predicted points. However, once the remapping algorithm assigns the random measurement values to the right IDs, the recovered data precisely follow the predicted data. However, sensors 8, 43, 44, 49, and 53 are not assigned to any measurement as the model cannot find any possible candidate for them. Those sensors may contain noises that deviate them from the predicted values. However, among 54 measurements, 49 of them are assigned to the right IDs, which is enough to make the system observable.

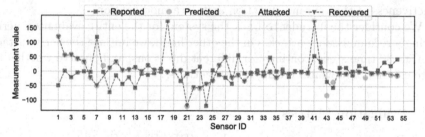

(a) Prediction-based remapping mechanism under normal condition

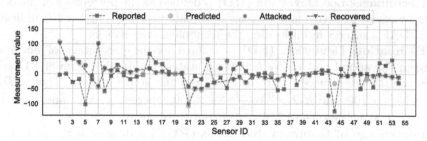

(b) Prediction-based remapping mechanism under FDI attack

Fig. 7. Prediction-based remapping under normal and attack conditions.

Remapping Under FDI Attack Condition: Figure 7b shows how prediction-based remapping eliminates the impact of the FDI attacks. In this case, we consider an FDI attack, where the targeted sensors are 8, 9, 15, 16, 17, 28, 29, 35, 36, 37, 44, 47, 50, and 54. However, due to the deception, these sensor IDs are used to send the data of 5, 6, 11, 15, 18, 24, 26, 27, 40, 41, 43, 46, 48, and 52, respectively. Hence, even though the attacker expects to be stealthy and bypass the BDD, the remapping mechanism mitigates the attack by declining the compromised sensors. Thus, among the attacked sensors 5, 6, 11, 26, 27, 40, 41, 43, and 52 are unassigned due to their suspicious values, which alleviates the impact of the FDI attack. Sensors 15, 18, 24, and 48 are not removed as their injection amounts are very small, within 5% of the predicted values. Further processing on this measurement data in the state estimation process removes the remaining outliers and make the system effectively immune to the attack.

6   Evaluation

We evaluate the robustness of iDDAF against three different types of attacks (e.g., Reconnaissance, FDI, and DoS) each in three different levels (e.g., L-0, L-1, and L-2). We run the evaluation on IEEE 14 bus system considering the attacker can compromise the maximum of five buses at a time. We use the 365 days of synthetic IEEE 14 bus system time-series data [1] to evaluate the effectiveness of the ID randomization and data modification.

We consider the intruder to be in the system for the entire evaluation period during a reconnaissance attack. On the other hand, we initiate the active attacks in every 30 time steps, continue for different durations, and observe whether the state estimation deviates during the executions.

6.1   Evaluation Metrics

The following metrics are used to evaluate iDDAF's performance:

Reconnaissance Deviation (RD) is defined as the percentage of the deviation between the actual and attacker's estimated states. A higher RD indicates the iDDAF's success in misleading the reconnaissance attacks.

Estimation Deviation (ED) is defined as the percentage of deviation between the actual and EMS's estimated states. Unlike RD, a lower ED indicates the iDDAF's success in recovering from the active attacks. Thus, $RD = \frac{||\hat{x}_{act} - \hat{x}_{dec}||}{||\hat{x}_{act}||} \times 100$, and $ED = \frac{||\hat{x}_{act} - \hat{x}_{ems}||}{||\hat{x}_{act}||} \times 100$, where $\hat{x}_{act}$, $\hat{x}_{dec}$, and $\hat{x}_{ems}$, are the actual, attacker's, and EMS's estimated state vector.

Percentage of Unobservable Cases (PUC) is defined as the percentage of attacks that create unobservability in the defender's estimation. The primary goal of DoS attacks is to increase the PUC as much as possible.

6.2   Reconnaissance Attack

This part shows how iDDAF ensures the system's privacy by randomizing the IDs and then adding decoy data. In this evaluation, we consider 60% of the sensors as *randomized*. With the remaining 40% sensors, we study the contribution of the decoy data and observe how the attacker's state estimation deviates from the actual ones. First, we consider the remaining 40% as fixed sensors (without adding any decoy data). In such a case, Fig. 8a shows an L-2 attacker is able to estimate the trend of the actual system states, even without 60% *randomized* sensors. As most of the measurements with the random IDs become bad data, the attacker is left with most of the fixed sensors as good data as they are topologically aligned. Later, we consider that 40% of the *fixed* sensors as *decoyed* sensors and added decoy data to validate the ID randomization. In this case, the random IDs get the support and become good data in the attacker's estimation and do not become the outliers. Figure 8b shows the attacker's estimation deviates from the actual ones and moves toward random directions whenever the nodes update the randomization patterns. On the other hand, Fig. 8c illustrates, EMS successfully remaps the IDs and estimates the state accurately. Even after 24 h of remapping, there is no deviation/overshooting from the actual values, which indicates the robustness of iDDAF.

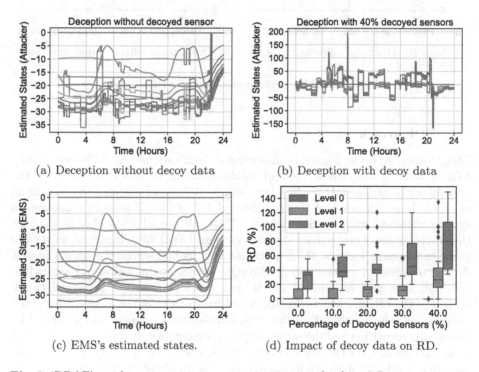

(a) Deception without decoy data

(b) Deception with decoy data

(c) EMS's estimated states.

(d) Impact of decoy data on RD.

Fig. 8. iDDAF's performance against reconnaissance attacks. (a–c: different colors indicate different states of different substations).

Figure 8d shows RD with 60% *randomized* sensors and different *decoyed* sensors for the passive attackers at different levels. As decoy data are added at the switch-levels (L-1/L-2), not at the sensors levels (L-0), RD is zero in case of

L-0 attacks. Such attacks are costly and infeasible as the attacker needs to be distributed and compromise the targeted sensors locally. A practical approach for reconnaissance is to compromise the network devices (L-1/L-2). In that case, adding more *decoyed* sensors supports the randomization, increases RD, and thus, misleads the attacker. Although iDDAF is ineffective against L-0 passive attacks, the following analysis shows, it can completely mitigate the L-0 active attacks, making such passive attacks futile.

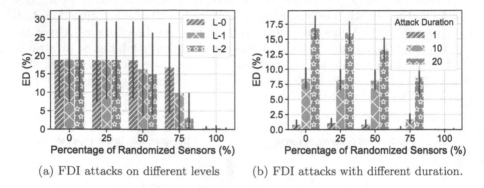

(a) FDI attacks on different levels   (b) FDI attacks with different duration.

Fig. 9. iDDAF's performance against FDI attacks.

6.3   FDI Attack

Single-step Attack: Figure 9a shows the system's robustness under single step FDI attacks in different levels and randomization. In this case, we vary the percentage of *randomized* sensors from 0% to 100% and consider the remaining as *fixed*. Here, the case of 0% *randomized* (100% *fixed*) sensors represents a system without any deception defense. Thus, all the FDI attacks compromise the correct sensors and remain stealthy with an ED of 20%. However, as we add more *randomized* sensors, the injections start to happen in the wrong places. As the *randomized* sensors also go through the remapping (filtering) algorithm, the malicious data are filtered out if they do not follow the predicted trend; and thus, the attack impacts are alleviated irrespective of the levels. With 100% *randomized* sensors, almost all the compromised measurements are removed by remapping algorithm and the attack impacts are completely mitigated. Although such filtering in L-0 FDI attacks may lead the system to unobservable situation, the critical missing data are imputed using the predicted values; and thus, the system retains the observability.

Multi-steps Attack: In this part, we analyze the impact of continuous FDI attacks on that state estimation. We consider the case of 1, 10, and 20 time-steps as the attack duration. In each case, a random L-2 FDI attack is initiated at every 30 time steps and continued for the considered duration. Figure 9b shows that ED for long-duration attack is higher due to the cascading effect. However, as more sensors are considered in randomization, the initial attack impact is perfectly handled by the remapping and estimation process so that no cascading effect is observed, making iDDAF robust against influential continuous attacks.

6.4   DoS Attack

This part evaluates iDDAF's defense against targeted DoS attacks. We consider the DoS attacks compromising the same sensors as we do in FDI attacks. However, instead of injecting false data, the attacker drops the packets of the targeted critical set of sensors to make the system unobservable.

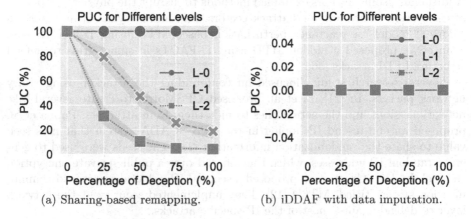

(a) Sharing-based remapping.   (b) iDDAF with data imputation.

Fig. 10. iDDAF's performance against DoS attacks.

Sharing-based Remapping: First, we show the performance of existing sharing-based remapping mechanisms, where the actual remapping pattern is already shared with the EMS. Figure 10a shows the PUC under DoS attacks at different levels. In the case of L-0 DoS attacks, sharing-based remapping completely fails to ensure the system's observability, as the attacker directly compromises the sensors. The randomization in the nodes after the L-0 DoS attack is not helpful anymore. However, in the case of L-1 or L-2 attacks, even though randomization deceives the attacker, in some cases, the system may still lose observability.

iDDAF's Predictive Remapping: On the other hand, Fig. 10b shows the same attack scenarios but with remapped with iDDAF. The figure shows iDDAF is entirely immune to any level of DoS attacks. Even in the worst-case scenario of L-0 DoS attacks, the missing critical measurements are replaced using the predicted values, and the system recovers from the DoS attacks.

7   Related Work

To deal with different cyber-attacks and mitigate sensory channels FDI attacks, several moving target defense (MTD) techniques are proposed. Several works introduced uncertainty/randomness into the CPS control loop. Griffith et al. proposed a method that includes stochastic and time-varying parameters in the control loops for CPSs [11]. To detect and minimize the impact of FDI attacks, Giraldo presented MTD by randomly varying the availability of telemetry sensor data [10]. Rahman et al. reduced the attack window by adding an uncertainty factor to the subset of sensors used to estimate the system's state [30]. Based on the skewness coefficients, Hu et al. proposed a stealthy attack detection strategy capable of identifying the forged residuals from the attack-free residuals [15]. Additionally, some authors examined methods to disrupt the physical properties of the system to invalidate its attack vectors. Lakshminarayana et al. proposed a formal model for reactance perturbation based MTD using D-FACTS [18]. Tian et al. proposed a hidden MTD using D-FACTs in smart grids to defend structured FDI attacks [36].

Several research studies focused on confounding the attacker using crafty network packets. In [21], Li et al. proposed CPSMorph to create several fake network sessions and the actual ones to hide them from attackers. Pappa et al. proposed an end-to-end IP hoping in the CPS SCADA system that uses seed value to share the randomization information [27]. The seeds were used to generate random IP addresses, which they shared over a public-private encryption channel. In [12], Groat et al. proposed a secured IPv6-based smart grid communication system titled, MT6D [12]. They implemented security at the network layer to defend against most of the IP-specific attacks.

In addition, some other research works are carried out on CPS for deceptive defense against stealthy attacks. Lin et al. proposed a randomized data acquisition into multiple rounds [22]. An SDN-enabled framework controls the flows in the network and collects measurements from randomly selected online sensors while spoofing data from the remainder. However, a clever attacker can inject false data into online devices since only a few sensors send original data at a given time. An attacker may also be able to identify the correct measurement by examining the pattern of sensor measurements. Additionally, they proposed virtualizing physical functions and crafting decoy data to disrupt reconnaissance attacks on power grids [23]. An attacker can still inject the FDI attack into a specific part of the system with no virtual nodes while ignoring the rest. Consequently, their proposed solution only secures the parts of the systems where virtual nodes are located, leaving other parts unsecured.

In the works mentioned above [22, 23], the data acquisition process is partially randomized, and only the mitigation of attacks is addressed. The existing solutions are attack-specific and thus, do not provide complete immunity. In contrast, our proposed iDDAF can be implemented on the entire system leaving no window for the attacker. Furthermore, iDDAF is the only framework that provides a complete security solution (CIA) against three different types of attacks.

8   Conclusion

CPSs are omnipresent in modern critical infrastructures. Moreover, the extensive integration of IoT technologies converts the CPSs into smart, efficient, and complex hybrid systems. However, such dependency creates a vast attack space that the attackers can exploit. Thus, to secure the CPSs hierarchical networks, we present iDDAF, an intelligent and secure data acquisition framework. iDDAF introduces deception while collecting measurement data by randomizing the sensor IDs and adding decoy data. The control center utilizes an a prediction model to predicts future measurement. Utilizing the expected data, an optimization algorithm recovers the original data sequence from the reported random/decoy data. The evaluation results on the standard IEEE 14 bus system demonstrate that iDDAF can successfully mitigate different influential cyberattacks through intelligent deception and remapping steps.

Acknowledgement. This research was partially supported by National Science Foundation (NSF) under award #1929183.

References

1. iddaf. https://sites.google.com/view/iddaf/home
2. Iec 61850-power utility automation. https://www.iec.ch/smartgrid/standards/
3. Ieee 14-bus system. https://www.icseg.iti.illinois.edu/ieee-14-bus-system/
4. Abur, A., Exposito, A.G.: Power System State Estimation: Theory and Implementation. CRC Press, Boca Raton (2004)
5. Ali, S., Qaisar, S.B., Saeed, H., Khan, M.F., Naeem, M., Anpalagan, A.: Network challenges for cyber physical systems with tiny wireless devices: a case study on reliable pipeline condition monitoring. Sensors **4**, 7172–7205 (2015)
6. Barua, A., Al Faruque, M.A.: Hall spoofing: a non-invasive dos attack on grid-tied solar inverter. In: 29th {USENIX} Security Symposium ({USENIX} Security 20) (2020)
7. Doherty, J.: SDN and NFV Simplified: A Visual Guide to Understanding Software Defined Networks and Network Function Virtualization. Addison-Wesley Professional, Boston (2016)
8. Dorsch, N., Kurtz, F., Georg, H., Hägerling, C., Wietfeld, C.: Software-defined networking for smart grid communications: applications, challenges and advantages. In: 2014 IEEE International Conference on Smart Grid Communications (2014)
9. Drinkwater, D.: Stuxnet-style attack. http://www.innotap.com/2015/07/stuxnet-style-attack-on-us-smart-grid-could-cost-government-1-trillion/
10. Giraldo, J., Cardenas, A., Sanfelice, R.G.: A moving target defense to detect stealthy attacks in cyber-physical systems. In: 2019 American Control Conference. IEEE (2019)
11. Griffioen, P., Weerakkody, S., Sinopoli, B.: A moving target defense for securing cyber-physical systems. IEEE Trans. Autom. Control **68**, 2016–2031 (2020)
12. Groat, S., Dunlop, M., Urbanksi, W., Marchany, R., Tront, J.: Using an ipv6 moving target defense to protect the smart grid. In: 2012 IEEE PES Innovative Smart Grid Technologies (ISGT), pp. 1–7. IEEE (2012)

13. Gunes, V., Peter, S., Givargis, T., Vahid, F.: A survey on concepts, applications, and challenges in cyber-physical systems. KSII Trans. Internet Inf. Syst. **8**(12), 4242–4268 (2014)
14. Haque, N.I., et al.: Machine learning in generation, detection, and mitigation of cyberattacks in smart grid: a survey (2020). arXiv preprint arXiv:2010.00661
15. Hu, Y., Li, H., Yang, H., Sun, Y., Sun, L., Wang, Z.: Detecting stealthy attacks against industrial control systems based on residual skewness analysis. EURASIP J. Wirel. Commun. Network. **2019**(1), 1–14 (2019). https://doi.org/10.1186/s13638-019-1389-1
16. Jafari, M., Shahriar, M.H., Rahman, M.A., Paudyal, S.: False relay operation attacks in power systems with high renewables (2021). arXiv preprint arXiv:2102.12041
17. Kovacs, E.: Blackenergy malware used in ukraine power grid attacks (2016)
18. Lakshminarayana, S., Yau, D.K.: Cost-benefit analysis of moving-target defense in power grids. In: 2018 48th Annual IEEE/IFIP International Conference on Dependable Systems and Networks (DSN), pp. 139–150. IEEE (2018)
19. Langner, R.: Stuxnet: dissecting a cyberwarfare weapon. IEEE Secur. Priv **9**, 49–51 (2011)
20. Li, B., Lu, R., Wang, W., Choo, K.K.R.: Ddoa: a dirichlet-based detection scheme for opportunistic attacks in smart grid cyber-physical system. IEEE Trans. Inf. For. Secur. **11**, 2415–2425 (2016)
21. Li, Y., Dai, R., Zhang, J.: Morphing communications of cyber-physical systems towards moving-target defense. In: 2014 IEEE International Conference on Communications (ICC), pp. 592–598. IEEE (2014)
22. Lin, H., Kalbarczyk, Z.T., Iyer, R.K.: Raincoat: randomization of network communication in power grid cyber infrastructure to mislead attackers. IEEE Trans. Smart Grid **5**, 4893–4906 (2018)
23. Lin, H., Zhuang, J., Hu, Y.C., Zhou, H.: Defrec: establishing physical function virtualization to disrupt reconnaissance of power grids' cyber-physical infrastructures. In: The Proceedings of 2020 Network and Distributed System Security Symposium (2020)
24. Liu, Y., Ning, P., Reiter, M.K.: False data injection attacks against state estimation in electric power grids. ACM Trans. Inf. Syst. Secur. **14**, 1–33 (2011)
25. Lu, Z., Sun, C., Cheng, J., Li, Y., Li, Y., Wen, X.: SDN-enabled communication network framework for energy internet. J. Comput. Netw. Commun. **2017** (2017)
26. Newaz, A., Sikder, A.K., Rahman, M.A., Uluagac, A.S.: A survey on security and privacy issues in modern healthcare systems: attacks and defenses (2020)
27. Pappa, A.C., Ashok, A., Govindarasu, M.: Moving target defense for securing smart grid communications: architecture, implementation & evaluation. In: 2017 IEEE Power & Energy Society Innovative Smart Grid Technologies Conference (ISGT) (2017)
28. Rahman, M.A., Al-Shaer, E., Kavasseri, R.: Impact analysis of topology poisoning attacks on economic operation of the smart power grid. In: International Conference on Distributed Computing Systems (ICDCS) (2014)
29. Rahman, M.A., Shahriar, M.H., Masum, R.: False data injection attacks against contingency analysis in power grids: poster. In: Proceedings of the 12th Conference on Security and Privacy in Wireless and Mobile Networks, pp. 343–344 (2019)
30. Rahman, M.A., Al-Shaer, E., Bobba, R.B.: Moving target defense for hardening the security of the power system state estimation. In: Proceedings of the First ACM Workshop on Moving Target Defense, pp. 59–68 (2014)

31. Rahman, M.A., Shahriar, M.H., Jafari, M., Masum, R.: Novel attacks against contingency analysis in power grids (2019). arXiv preprint arXiv:1911.00928
32. Shahriar, M.H., Haque, N.I., Rahman, M.A., Alonso, M.: G-ids: generative adversarial networks assisted intrusion detection system. In: IEEE 44th Annual Computers, Software, and Applications Conference (COMPSAC). IEEE (2020)
33. Shahriar, M.H., Sadiq, M.J., Uddin, M.F.: Stability analysis of grid connected PV array under maximum power point tracking. In: 2016 9th International Conference on Electrical and Computer Engineering (ICECE), pp. 499–502. IEEE (2016)
34. Sikder, A.K., Petracca, G., Aksu, H., Jaeger, T., Uluagac, A.S.: A survey on sensor-based threats and attacks to smart devices and applications. IEEE Commun. Surv. Tutor. **23**, 1125–1159 (2021)
35. Simmonds, A., Sandilands, P., van Ekert, L.: An ontology for network security attacks. In: Manandhar, S., Austin, J., Desai, U., Oyanagi, Y., Talukder, A.K. (eds.) AACC 2004. LNCS, vol. 3285, pp. 317–323. Springer, Heidelberg (2004). https://doi.org/10.1007/978-3-540-30176-9_41
36. Tian, J., Tan, R., Guan, X., Liu, T.: Enhanced hidden moving target defense in smart grids. IEEE Trans. Smart Grid **2**, 2208–2223 (2018)
37. Tzu, S., Tzu, S., Sun, W., Vu, S.C., et al.: The Art of War, vol. 361. Oxford University Press, Oxford (1971)
38. Van Hertem, D., Verboomen, J., Purchala, K., Belmans, R., Kling, W.L.: Usefulness of dc power flow for active power flow analysis with flow controlling devices. In: The 8th IEE International Conference on AC and DC Power Transmission, pp. 58–62 (2006). https://doi.org/10.1049/cp:20060013
39. Wang, S., Zhang, Y., Yang, Z., Chen, Y.: A graphical hierarchical cps architecture. In: 2016 International Symposium on System and Software Reliability. IEEE (2016)
40. Yampolskiy, M., Horvath, P., Koutsoukos, X.D., Xue, Y., Sztipanovits, J.: Systematic analysis of cyber-attacks on cps-evaluating applicability of dfd-based approach. In: 2012 5th International Symposium on Resilient Control Systems. IEEE (2012)

PhD and Poster Track

Encouraging the Adoption
of Post-Quantum Hybrid Key Exchange
in Network Security

Alexandre Augusto Giron[1,2]([⊠]) [ID]

[1] Graduate Program in Computer Science, Information and Statistics Department
(INE), Federal University of Santa Catarina (UFSC), Florianópolis, SC, Brazil
[2] Federal University of Technology - Parana (UTFPR), Toledo-PR, Brazil
`alexandregiron@utfpr.edu.br`

Abstract. Post-Quantum Cryptography (PQC) is under standardization, and a transition from "classic" cryptography to PQC is likely to
occur. Combining classic cryptography with PQC in a Hybrid form can
ease such transition. In this context, this research aims at the challenges
of designing a Post-Quantum Hybrid Key Exchange (KEX). The focus
here is on the hybrid forms and in their adoption in widely-used network
protocols. The methodology of this research includes: (1) a systematic
review of the challenges of the design of Hybrid KEX; (2) to evaluate proposals in network protocols (such as TLS 1.3); and (3) to provide security
analysis for the proposals. It is believed that these hybrids will contribute
to the evolution of network security: by giving protection against attackers with or without quantum capabilities but also minimizing possible
compatibility issues.

Keywords: Post-quantum cryptography · Hybrid key exchange ·
Network security

1 Research Problem

1.1 Contextualization

Several popular network protocols for security have a **Key Exchange** (KEX) in
its specification, namely the TLS [31], SSH [35], and IKE [21], all of them including the Diffie-Hellman-Merkle (DH, for short) [20] or, at least, a DH variant
such as the Elliptical Curve DH [16]. KEX and Key-Establishment Methods [27]
have the same meaning and they are used when two parties want to communicate securely with symmetric cryptography. They solve efficiently a distribution
problem: how to share symmetric keys in advance.

Generally, Key-Establishment methods are built with Public-Key Cryptog-
raphy and have two distinct types [3]: one is the *Key-Agreement*, with the DH
KEX as an example; and the second type is called *Key-Transport*, where a Key-
Encapsulation Mechanism (KEM) is used. A KEM encrypts a cryptographic key

© ICST Institute for Computer Sciences, Social Informatics and Telecommunications Engineering 2021
Published by Springer Nature Switzerland AG 2021. All Rights Reserved
J. Garcia-Alfaro et al. (Eds.): SecureComm 2021, LNICST 399, pp. 363–371, 2021.
https://doi.org/10.1007/978-3-030-90022-9_18

using the public key of the corresponding recipient. The main difference is that KEMs have, in general, one party controlling the secret information generation (i.e., the key) that both parties will share. On the other hand, key-agreement have the parties negotiating and actively participating in the shared secret generation. Both KEX types end producing the *shared secret* [3], which is used to derive a symmetric cryptographic key for the parties.

During a key-establishment, a Key-Derivation Method may be required to obtain the keying material used to encrypt the communication. An important property is the *key freshness*: a new key can be derived avoiding a new KEX for this purpose. Therefore, key-derivation can reduce the amount of new KEX messages exchanged through the communication channel [27]. Besides, key-derivation methods assist the Forward Secrecy (FS) feature of KEX [7]. In this case, every session is unique and protected by a key derived from ephemeral and long-term secrets. FS keeps the security of past communications in the case of a compromise of long-term keys of the participants [2]. Additionally, the key-derivation can be used to expand keying material to the desired size of an encryption algorithm.

However, due to the major security threat imposed by quantum computing on public-key cryptography, KEX as used today will become broken when quantum computers are available. Consequently, network protocols such as TLS, SSH, and others become vulnerable [33]. On the other hand, in preparation to early response to this threat, researchers started the development of new schemes of cryptography, called by **Post-Quantum Cryptography** (PQC). Currently, international agencies have ongoing standardization processes for PQC [11,25]. The main objective is to give users protection against attackers with quantum capabilities. PQC is built upon classes of mathematical problems that do not have efficient and (known) solutions, both by quantum and traditional (non-quantum) computers. Consequently, different schemes for Post-Quantum KEX are under research [34].

On the other hand, it is not recommended to drop the "classical" (or traditional) cryptography in use today for PQC. First, it is unknown when a quantum computer will be available in practice, but, hypothetically, there is the possibility of the "record-now-decrypt-later" attacker. This possibility requires an earlier response to this quantum threat [8], meaning that the need for PQC in key-establishment methods is more urgent than the need for PQC authentication. In this context, Schank et al. [32] defined the *transitional security* property: when it provides both pre-quantum authentication and post-quantum confidentiality. Secondly, its security is under heavy research effort to provide confidence in the security of PQC and fundament its standardization. The quantum threat is not the only one to cryptography, in addition to some characteristics of PQC, such as greater size of public keys and/or signatures, that may turn the adoption infeasible in some contexts. For example, deploying a KEX implementation of the Classic McEliece algorithm in TLS and SSH protocols was unsuccessful [10].

1.2   Motivation

The recommended solution for some of those challenges is to use a hybrid construction, such as a **Post-Quantum Hybrid KEX**. Hybrid KEXs are being studied to support to the Post-Quantum Cryptography (PQC) while maintaining compatibility with the "traditional" methods. The term traditional here corresponds to the KEXs based on Integer Factorization or Discrete Logarithm (and the elliptical-curve variant) [3]. In practice, a Hybrid KEX is composed of (at least) two algorithms, requiring at least one to be based on traditional cryptography and another based on PQC. The most important feature of such a hybrid is to maintain the security of the scheme in case of a break in the traditional algorithm [4].

The term Hybrid in this context should not be confused with Hybrid Encryption (HE) [23], where HE is a conjunction of symmetric and asymmetric cryptography. In addition, a hybrid could include Quantum-Key Distribution (QKD) [30], in the context of quantum cryptography. However, QKD is not considered in this work because the focus here is to protect those who do not have access to quantum computers, but want to be protected against quantum attackers. More specifically, Hybrid modes for KEX have the goal of negotiating two or more algorithms (PQC and traditional ones) and use them combined. In this way, users can still have compatibility in network protocols whenever possible and expect (or hope for) earlier protection against quantum attackers. For an easier transition to a "post-quantum world", the Hybrid approaches are recommended.

However, the design of a Hybrid KEX have additional challenges, summarized below:

- The core of the Hybrid KEX involves a *cryptographic combiner* [4]. It keeps the security of the whole KEX as long as one of the two (or more) components remains secure, i.e., that was not broken yet.
- A design decision involves how many algorithms will be combined in the Hybrid approach. In practice, it seems that two algorithms is the common choice [14,33,34], but there is not much research regarding this decision [10].
- A consequence of a Hybrid KEX is the need to convey more cryptographic data (e.g., public keys/shares of each algorithm). They are required, but some approaches could reduce network communication costs (detailed in Sect. 3.1). On the other hand, suppose that there is a secure way of *linking public keys*, where pk_i of the i-th KEX could be efficiently computed from pk_{i+1}. This means that the conveying method can optimize by half the amount of cryptographic data required for transmission. If such an approach is possible, the hybrid construction could bring less impact on the network protocols. Following the recommendation in the work of Crockett et al. [10], wasting or duplicating bytes should be avoided whenever possible.
- The impact in the Key-Derivation Method. Originally, a key-derivation receives as input a shared secret information to derive keying material, but with Hybrid KEX the shared secret is different. For example, the openssl fork of the OQS project [34] concatenates two shared secrets (from Elliptical Curve DH and a PQC KEM), relying on the key-derivation to complete the

combining operation and derive symmetric keys. On the other hand, there are some combiners designed in conjunction to the derivation of keys, but not evaluated in practice yet [4,9,15].

Additionally, limitations present in network protocols should be considered in the design of Hybrid KEX. Specific packet sizes, performance constraints, latency, handshake messages and negotiations of cryptographic "suites" are some examples [10]. Solving these constraints would avoid compatibility issues between users.

The overall challenges should not discourage the adoption of Hybrid KEXs. Instead, such challenges can motivate the research for improvements that would directly benefit users and designers of network protocols. Hybrid constructions can be a first step towards the adoption of post-quantum cryptography.

1.3   Text Organization

The remaining text is organized as follows. Section 2 summarizes the objectives of this research and Sect. 3 presents Hybrid approaches available in the literature. Section 4 shows the activities planned to accomplish the goals of this research, and Sect. 5 discuss the expected results. Section 6 summarizes the current stage of the research, followed by acknowledgements and the references.

2   Outline of the Objectives

The main objective of this research is to devise improvements and evaluate Post-Quantum Hybrid KEXs to encourage its adoption. The evaluations shall address the constraints of the development of Hybrid KEXs. In addition, a set of specific goals of this research are described below:

- Provide a systematic study of the state-of-the-art Hybrid KEX, allowing to comprehend the available methods and identify possible open problems.
- Contribute to this research topic with improvements for Hybrid KEXs methods, addressing constraints and challenges for its adoption. Examples include the evaluation of different cryptographic combiners, present in Hybrid KEXs.
- Provide a security analysis for the evaluations of Hybrid KEX in network protocols. Automated tools such as Tamarin [24] can be used.

Evidently, the KEX method is just a part of all of the security mechanisms employed in network protocols. There are indeed challenges in Hybrid construction that have not been well studied yet compared to non-hybrid KEXs. Focusing on the hybrid constructions, the next section introduces these challenges.

3   State of the Art

The state-of-the-art approaches are classified here according to the challenges related to the Hybrid KEX design. Three types are highlighted: (i) conveying approaches; (ii) combining approaches; and (iii) key-derivation methods.

3.1   Conveying in Hybrid KEX

The initial steps of Hybrid KEX require transmission of cryptographic data by the corresponding parties. In KEMs, a public key is sent to the receiver, which responds with a ciphertext encapsulating the secret key. Key-agreement parties transmit public *keyshares*, analogous to public keys but used to compute the shared secret information. Therefore, the conveying payload in Hybrids is a sum of the payloads of each KEX ingredient.

Some conveying approaches found in the literature are generic but could be applied to hybrid designs. First, the **concatenation approach** is the most simpler to implement. For example, the public keys are concatenated prior to be sent to the other party. Concatenation is the conveying approach in the OQS project. The second approach is to **compress** data. Compression can be performed in different ways, such as compression through rounding, which is performed in Kyber [6]; and packing public matrices in Frodo KEX [1,5]. In addition, RFC 8879 [13] describes how to compress digital certificates for TLS, not specifically to the PQC context but it could reduce the amount of data transmitted between the parties. One last approach for conveying is called by **Hash-and-URL** [19,21], in which the hash of the data and the location where the complete data can be fetched is sent. It is a solution that focuses more on compatibility than actually solving the problem, since the conveying is delegated to a secondary protocol.

It seems that there is not much research attention to the conveying challenge [10]. Indeed, the most challenging part of conveying in Hybrid KEX is the increased size, directly proportional to the number of KEX ingredients. In addition, the computational cost and security of any operation (e.g., compression) must be considered. Generally, the size is most affected by the PQC algorithm. It is worth mentioning that this issue can be mitigated by selecting a PQC algorithm with smaller keys/ciphertexts.

3.2   Cryptographic Combiners

Research in cryptographic combiners is older than in PQC Hybrids [12,17]. A combiner is a construction that takes as input N cryptographic schemes and combines them into one scheme. In Post-Quantum Hybrid KEXs, they are used to combine shared secrets of each KEX ingredient [4]. Again, there is the **concatenation** approach, used in several evaluations [9,18,19,28,33,34], simpler to implement but requires a key-derivation method to hold the security of the Hybrid KEX. More elaborated approaches for combining are built using XOR and/or PRFs as the core operation to combine shared secret information [4,9,15].

All of the XOR-based and PRF-based works of combiners provide security proofs of their proposals, endorsing its adoption in Hybrid KEX. These security proofs are of utmost importance because the combiner is the core operation of the Hybrid construction. On the other hand, there is a lack of practical experiments (with implementations) using these combiners. These experiments would contribute to this research topic, allowing to compare computational costs, design decisions, security properties, among others.

3.3 Key-Derivation in Hybrid Designs

Briefly, the Key-Derivation aspect in Hybrid KEX is addressed in two ways. First, some works do not focus in Key-derivation and therefore they rely on known derivation methods, such as HKDF, HMAC or SHA-based derivation [10, 28,33]. In this way, Hybrid designs can fit in network protocols, such as TLS and SSH, and avoid some compatibility issues. Secondly, the XOR-based and PRF-based combiners (Sect. 3.2) are designed to derive keying material by themselves. Literature states that the key-derivation aspect in Hybrid KEX requires more attention, as well as the combiner, in order to answer its impact on the security of the hybrid scheme [26].

4 Methodology

This Ph.D. research is based on the following activities:

A1: A systematic study of Key-derivation methods in the context of Hybrid KEXs. More specifically, a Systematic Mapping Study (SMS) [22,29] allows a better understanding of a research topic and its nomenclatures. Besides, SMS allows bringing forward new classifications for the state-of-the-art approaches and the remaining open problems.

A2: Literature review about KEXs and key-derivation methods of well-known network protocols. It is necessary to understand in detail how the KEX is designed in such protocols, in order to propose improvements that fit in their KEX methods.

A3: An in-depth study about security analysis and formal proofs. The aim of this activity is to provide the assurance that the eventual modifications proposed maintain its security. Security experiments and formal proofs are planned in this work, for example, by using the Tamarin prover or other methods.

A4: Design and development Hybrid KEXs in network protocols using different combiners [4]. The Open Quantum Safe project (OQS) [34] will be used as a basis for the development.

A5: Design proposals and evaluations that address different conveying methods are also planned. For instance, compression techniques and a method for "linking" of public keys. The objective is to reduce the amount of data being exchanged. The tradeoff of the computing overhead versus impact in the network protocol shall be considered in the analysis. In addition, an evaluation of the impacts of more than two algorithms in hybrids settings is also planned.

A6: Establish metrics for the evaluations, depending on the focus of the experiment. It may include handshake completion times, throughput (connections/second), and other metrics, such as the execution times of cryptographic primitives. The purpose is to build a methodology to simulate and test the proposals under real-world network conditions.

A7: Provide a security analysis of the protocols modified in this work.

In summary, the proposal of this work is to design, experiment, and give security proofs to address the main constraints in Hybrid KEX: different methods for (i) conveying data; (ii) combining data; and (iii) deriving the keying material. The focus is in the context of Post-Quantum Hybrid KEXs and network protocols such as TLS 1.3.

5   Expected Outcome

The expected outcome of this research can be summarized in three perspectives:

- Supporting the transition to PQC.
- Propose improvements and practical experiments with Post-Quantum Hybrid KEXs, encouraging its adoption in today's world.
- Contribute to the evolution and analysis of widely-used network protocols (such as TLS 1.3).

Supporting the transition to Post-Quantum Cryptography is important, giving users that do not have quantum computing capabilities an expected protection against quantum attackers. Understanding the design challenges of hybrid constructions is fundamental for their adoption. In this context, evaluations and security analysis of Hybrid KEX would help developers and engineers to design it and adopt it in their protocols. However, a careful analysis is needed, because one security flaw would impact every user of such protocols. In addition, it is expected that this research and future experiments would help to understand the performance and security of a protocol while changing its ciphersuites. Firstly, by evaluating the experiments in scenarios as realistic as possible, and secondly, by using state-of-the-art formal security analysis methods and tools.

The popularization of Hybrid KEX is also an aspect that this work is aiming to contribute. Although that these post-quantum hybrids may compose a temporary approach, they combine the advantages of both classical cryptography and PQC, which is important for several reasons. When the quantum computer will be commercially available is not yet known, and quantum computing is not the only threat to cryptography. Hypothetically, if a quantum computer becomes available today, hybrid approaches will still be needed until the confidence in PQC security is well established. In addition, by further researching these hybrids, other benefits and applications could be discovered, highlighting the relevance of this area for the near future of computer security.

6   Stage of the Research

Currently, this PhD research is prior to the qualifying stage. Regarding the activities detailed in Sect. 4, A1 and A2 are considered completed; A3 and A4 are ongoing work. Regarding activity A1, a Systematization-of-Knowledge (SoK) paper is in preparation. Besides, the experiments described in A3 and A4 are being researched and under development.

Acknowledgements. I would like to say thanks to my Ph.D. Supervisor Ricardo Custódio, and also for the additional support of the UTFPR in this research.

References

1. Alkim, E., et al.: Frodokem learning with errors key encapsulation (2020)
2. Barker, E., Chen, L., Keller, S., Roginsky, A., Vassilev, A., Davis, R.: Recommendation for pair-wise key-establishment schemes using discrete logarithm cryptography. Technical report, National Institute of Standards and Technology (2017)
3. Barker, E., Chen, L., Roginsky, A., Vassilev, A., Davis, R., Simon, S.: Recommendation for pair-wise key-establishment schemes using integer factorization cryptography. Technical report, National Institute of Standards and Technology (2019)
4. Bindel, N., Brendel, J., Fischlin, M., Goncalves, B., Stebila, D.: Hybrid key encapsulation mechanisms and authenticated key exchange. In: Ding, J., Steinwandt, R. (eds.) PQCrypto 2019. LNCS, vol. 11505, pp. 206–226. Springer, Cham (2019). https://doi.org/10.1007/978-3-030-25510-7_12
5. Bos, J., et al.: Frodo: take off the ring! practical, quantum-secure key exchange from lwe. In: Proceedings of the 2016 ACM SIGSAC Conference on Computer and Communications Security, CCS '16, pp. 1006–1018. Association for Computing Machinery, New York (2016). https://doi.org/10.1145/2976749.2978425
6. Bos, J., et al.: Crystals-kyber: a cca-secure module-lattice-based kem. In: 2018 IEEE European Symposium on Security and Privacy (EuroS&P), pp. 353–367. IEEE, London (2018)
7. Boyd, C., Nieto, J.G.: On forward secrecy in one-round key exchange. In: Chen, L. (ed.) IMACC 2011. LNCS, vol. 7089, pp. 451–468. Springer, Heidelberg (2011). https://doi.org/10.1007/978-3-642-25516-8_27
8. Brendel, J., Fischlin, M., Günther, F.: Breakdown resilience of key exchange protocols and the cases of newhope and tls 1.3. IACR Cryptol. ePrint Arch. **2017**, 1252 (2017)
9. Campagna, M., Petcher, A.: Security of hybrid key encapsulation. Cryptology ePrint Archive, Report 2020/1364 (2020). https://eprint.iacr.org/2020/1364
10. Crockett, E., Paquin, C., Stebila, D.: Prototyping post-quantum and hybrid key exchange and authentication in tls and ssh. Cryptology ePrint Archive, Report 2019/858 (2019)
11. ETSI: White paper no. 8, quantum safe cryptography and security; an introduction, benefits, enablers and challenges (2015). https://www.etsi.org/images/files/ETSIWhitePapers/QuantumSafeWhitepaper.pdf
12. Even, S., Goldreich, O.: On the power of cascade ciphers. ACM Trans. Comput. Syst. (TOCS) **3**(2), 108–116 (1985)
13. Ghedini, A., Vasiliev, V.: Tls certificate compression. RFC 8879, RFC Editor (2020)
14. Ghosh, S., Kate, A.: Post-quantum forward-secure onion routing. In: Malkin, T., Kolesnikov, V., Lewko, A.B., Polychronakis, M. (eds.) ACNS 2015. LNCS, vol. 9092, pp. 263–286. Springer, Cham (2015). https://doi.org/10.1007/978-3-319-28166-7_13
15. Giacon, F., Heuer, F., Poettering, B.: KEM combiners. In: Abdalla, M., Dahab, R. (eds.) PKC 2018. LNCS, vol. 10769, pp. 190–218. Springer, Cham (2018). https://doi.org/10.1007/978-3-319-76578-5_7
16. Hankerson, D., Menezes, A.J., Vanstone, S.: Guide to Elliptic Curve Cryptography. Springer-Verlag, New York (2006). https://doi.org/10.1007/b97644
17. Harnik, D., Kilian, J., Naor, M., Reingold, O., Rosen, A.: On robust combiners for oblivious transfer and other primitives. In: Cramer, R. (ed.) EUROCRYPT 2005. LNCS, vol. 3494, pp. 96–113. Springer, Heidelberg (2005). https://doi.org/10.1007/11426639_6

18. van Heesch, M., van Adrichem, N.L., Attema, T., Veugen, T.: Towards quantum-safe vpns and internet. Cryptology ePrint Archive, Report 2019/1277 (2019)
19. Heider, T.: Towards a Verifiably Secure Quantum-Resistant Key Exchange in IKEv2. Master's thesis, Ludwig Maximilian University of Munich (2019)
20. Hellman, M.E.: An overview of public key cryptography. IEEE Commun. Mag. **40**(5), 42–49 (2002)
21. Kaufman, C., Hoffman, P., Nir, Y., Eronen, P., Kivinen, T.: Internet key exchange protocol version 2 (ikev2). STD 79, RFC Editor (2014). http://www.rfc-editor. org/rfc/rfc7296.txt
22. Kitchenham, B.A., Budgen, D., Brereton, O.P.: Using mapping studies as the basis for further research-a participant-observer case study. Inf. Softw. Technol **53**(6), 638–651 (2011)
23. Kurosawa, K., Desmedt, Y.: A new paradigm of hybrid encryption scheme. In: Franklin, M. (ed.) CRYPTO 2004. LNCS, vol. 3152, pp. 426–442. Springer, Heidelberg (2004). https://doi.org/10.1007/978-3-540-28628-8_26
24. Meier, S., Schmidt, B., Cremers, C., Basin, D.: The TAMARIN prover for the symbolic analysis of security protocols. In: Sharygina, N., Veith, H. (eds.) CAV 2013. LNCS, vol. 8044, pp. 696–701. Springer, Heidelberg (2013). https://doi.org/ 10.1007/978-3-642-39799-8_48
25. NIST: Post-quantum cryptography (2016). https://csrc.nist.gov/Projects/Post-Quantum-Cryptography, Accessed 36 June 2020
26. Ott, D., Peikert, C., et al.: Identifying research challenges in post quantum cryptography migration and cryptographic agility (2019)
27. Paar, C., Pelzl, J.: Understanding Cryptography: A Textbook for Students and Practitioners. Springer, Heidelberg (2010). https://doi.org/10.1007/978-3-642-04101-3
28. Paquin, C., Stebila, D., Tamvada, G.: Benchmarking post-quantum cryptography in TLS. In: Ding, J., Tillich, J.-P. (eds.) PQCrypto 2020. LNCS, vol. 12100, pp. 72–91. Springer, Cham (2020). https://doi.org/10.1007/978-3-030-44223-1_5
29. Petersen, K., Vakkalanka, S., Kuzniarz, L.: Guidelines for conducting systematic mapping studies in software engineering: an update. Inf. Softw. Technol. **64**, 1–18 (2015)
30. Pirandola, S., et al.: Advances in quantum cryptography. Adv. Opt. Photon. **12**(4), 1012–1236 (2020). https://doi.org/10.1364/AOP.361502, http://aop.osa. org/abstract.cfm?URI=aop-12-4-1012
31. Rescorla, E.: The transport layer security (tls) protocol version 1.3. RFC 8446, RFC Editor (2018)
32. Schanck, J.M., Whyte, W., Zhang, Z.: Circuit-extension handshakes for tor achieving forward secrecy in a quantum world. Proc. Priv. Enhancing Technol. **2016**(4), 219 – 236 (2016). https://doi.org/10.1515/popets-2016-0037, https:// content.sciendo.com/view/journals/popets/2016/4/article-p219.xml
33. Sikeridis, D., Kampanakis, P., Devetsikiotis, M.: Assessing the overhead of post-quantum cryptography in tls 1.3 and ssh. In: Proceedings of the 16th International Conference on emerging Networking EXperiments and Technologies, pp. 149–156. Association for Computing Machinery, New York (2020)
34. Stebila, D., Mosca, M.: Post-quantum key exchange for the internet and the open quantum safe project. In: Avanzi, R., Heys, H. (eds.) SAC 2016. LNCS, vol. 10532, pp. 14–37. Springer, Cham (2017). https://doi.org/10.1007/978-3-319-69453-5_2
35. Ylonen, T., Lonvick, C.: The secure shell (ssh) protocol architecture. RFC 4251, RFC Editor (2006). http://www.rfc-editor.org/rfc/rfc4251.txt

Quantitative and Qualitative Investigations into Trusted Execution Environments

Ryan Karl[✉]

University of Notre Dame, Notre Dame, IN 46556, USA
rkarl@nd.edu

Abstract. I propose to develop a quantitative and qualitative framework to integrate a Trusted Execution Environment (TEE) into the pipeline of secure computation by combining it with other cryptographic primitives. Such a hybrid framework will utilize mathematical and statistical modeling techniques to decide how to combine TEE and cryptographic primitives and evaluate the potential for performance improvement by moving secure computation processes into or out of a TEE. Ideally, I will be able to determine when to combine TEEs with pure-cryptography techniques to improve performance for a task, instead of simply using either method alone and only achieving suboptimal performance. The final goal is to design and develop an actionable decision-making framework, and utilize it to optimize the secure computation process.

Keywords: Trusted Execution Environment · Hybrid secure computation · Performance optimization and modeling

1 Introduction

Background: Third-party analysis on private records is becoming more important due to widespread data collection for various analysis purposes in business, government, academia, etc. This can be observed in many real life applications, such as the Smart Grid, Social Network Services, Location Based Services, etc.[8]. While existing service providers support large scale high performance computation over unencrypted data, data in its plaintext form often contains private information about individuals, and the publication of such data may violate legal agreements such as HIPPA, GDPR, etc. Current best practices for secure, privacy preserving computation over this data (i.e., Secure Multiparty Computation (MPC), Fully Homomorphic Encryption (FHE), etc.) generally incur huge computation and/or communication overheads when compared to computing over plaintext data. A promising approach towards secure computation, that can be significantly faster than expensive cryptographic approaches, is to utilize a Trusted Execution Environment (TEE), a secure area of the main processor

© ICST Institute for Computer Sciences, Social Informatics and Telecommunications Engineering 2021
Published by Springer Nature Switzerland AG 2021. All Rights Reserved
J. Garcia-Alfaro et al. (Eds.): SecureComm 2021, LNICST 399, pp. 372–383, 2021.
https://doi.org/10.1007/978-3-030-90022-9_19

that leverages hardware and software components to guarantee code and data loaded inside the TEE will be protected from malicious tampering or eavesdropping by software operating at a higher privilege level.

Research Goal: While TEEs are a promising technology that have seen major adoption in industry, their performance has not been rigorously studied in comparison to pure cryptography techniques. Currently there is no comprehensive, up-to-date study that provides qualitative and quantitative information to prospective users on whether a TEE is a useful addition to their system. The general assumption is that TEE is always superior to cryptographic primitives, however there exist lightweight primitives that have high efficiency and/or throughput. In order to better understand the benefits of deploying TEEs in the wild, I propose to design a framework that can quantify the potential for performance improvement or degradation by migrating all or part of a system into or out of a TEE.

The proposed framework will ensure that users have a deep understanding of what segments of code are the best candidates for a migration to a TEE to improve performance. Note that my framework will not ignore existing data protection mechanisms (e.g., pure cryptography solutions). Rather, it tries to complement the competing privacy-preserving computation methods, to better understand the advantages and drawbacks of TEEs when compared to more traditional techniques. Ideally, it will identify situations where using both techniques together will offer superior performance to using one of the techniques in isolation. The contribution of the proposed framework is noteworthy: it assists security specialists in analyzing their projects and determining if a TEE is right for them based on both performance and resource availability. It will contribute to the adoption and growth of the intelligent use of TEEs in the data privacy ecosystem and protect potential users from naively using TEEs incorrectly and slowing down their system performance.

Research Challenges and Intellectual Merit: Many challenges exist in the framework design. TEEs come with their own set of constraints, including computational overhead due to expensive encrypted context switching operations, a lack of access to reliable and sophisticated parallel computing technologies, and code size constraints. Therefore, it is challenging to know which tasks are best suited for migration into a TEE, and which are better suited for other pure cryptography techniques. A rigorous analysis would be of great value to system designers during the early stages of planning their system designs, so they could avoid investing too much time in a technology that is not well suited to their application. No one has yet attempted a quantitative study to model which types of computing paradigms or operations are best suited for either domain, which adds difficulty to this task.

Preliminary Work: My own prior work suggests that there are several scenarios where combining TEEs and pure cryptographic approaches together can provide superior performance to simply using one technique on its own. Many protocols are complex enough that the logic of certain components are better suited for TEEs, while other components are more ideal for utilizing pure cryptography techniques, and this is discussed in more detail in Sect. 3. No one has yet attempted a quantitative study to model which types of computing paradigms or operations are best suited for either domain or how to develop a hybrid computing approach that combines pure cryptography with TEEs to obtain optimal performance. These challenges add intellectual merit to this task.

Broader Impacts: In the long term, the proposed project has the potential to assist security specialists in analyzing their projects and quantifying how a TEE can improve their system's performance based on their resources. This project's broader impact will contribute to the adoption and growth of the use of TEEs in the data privacy ecosystem, and protect potential users from incorrectly using TEEs in a way that introduces unacceptable vulnerabilities or slows down their systems. I propose to utilize theoretic techniques to model runtime, and also run empirical tests to determine the real world runtime of computational tasks. This will determine which tasks are better suited for TEEs and which are more appropriate to pure cryptography techniques. I plan to leverage the framework to inform the system design process when investigating whether to migrate part of a real world secure polynomial aggregation protocol into or out of a TEE. Each of the methodologies and TEEs discussed in this framework will be evaluated thoroughly to determine the pros and cons of using a TEE to solve this research problem.

2   Privacy-Preserving Computation Today

Although there is also a growing need for technology that supports privacy-preserving time-series data analysis, there are relatively few techniques that offer practical levels of performance and accuracy. Fully Homomorphic Encryption (FHE), Differential Privacy (DP), Secure Multiparty Computation (MPC), or Oblivious Polynomial Evaluation (OPE) might be used individually as black boxes to solve this problem, but each have significant constraints that negatively impact their practical deployment in the real world [9]. FHE's high computational overhead leads to significant slowdown that makes it impractical in large-scale settings. DP adds noise to the final output of the function, and the resulting accuracy loss can greatly harm the predictive power of any analysis. MPC requires participants to send multiple messages during protocol execution, which can seriously degrade overall runtime. OPE also requires multiple messages to be sent, and is primarily focused on the two party setting, which limits its applicability in large scale data analysis.

Private Stream Aggregation (PSA): PSA is a form of distributed secure computing that is promising for achieving this functionality. With this technique, users independently encrypt their input data and send it to an aggregator in a way that allows the aggregator to efficiently learn the aggregation results of time-series data without being able to infer individual data. PSA is generally superior to other types of secure computation paradigms (e.g., MPC, FHE) in large-scale applications involving time-series data because of its extremely low overhead and the ease of key management [11]. Notably, PSA is non-interactive (i.e., users send their time-series data in a "stream" and only one message is sent per time interval) and asynchronous (i.e., users can leave after submitting their inputs), making it more efficient in communication than most existing alternative techniques [14]. Although PSA is a mature field of study, prior work in this field is mostly limited to simple aggregation (sum, average, etc.). Due to these limitations, it is challenging for even the most advanced PSA protocols to be deployed in real-world applications.

Trusted Execution Environments (TEEs): One of the most prevalent TEEs in modern computing is Intel SGX. I review Intel SGX below, as most modern TEEs support a majority of the services it provides. Intel SGX is a set of new CPU instructions that can be used by applications to set aside private regions of code and data. It allows developers to (among other things) protect sensitive data from unauthorized access or modification by malicious software that may be running at superior privilege levels. To do this, the CPU protects an isolated region of memory called Processor Reserved Memory (PRM) against other non-enclave memory accesses, including the kernel, hypervisor, etc. Sensitive code and data is encrypted and stored as 4KB pages in the Enclave Page Cache (EPC), a region inside the PRM. Even though EPC pages are allocated and mapped to frames by the OS kernel, page-level encryption guarantees confidentiality and integrity. In addition, to provide access protection to the EPC pages, the CPU maintains an Enclave Page Cache Map (EPCM) that stores security attributes and metadata associated with EPC pages. This allows for strong privacy and integrity guarantees if applications can be written in a two part model [4].

Applications must be split into a secure part and a non-secure part. The application can then launch an enclave, which is placed in protected memory, that allows user-level code to define private segments of memory, whose contents are protected and unable to be read or saved by any process outside the enclave. Enclave entry points are defined during compilation. The secure execution environment is part of the host process, and the application contains its own code, data, and the enclave, but the enclave contains its own code and data too. An enclave can access its application's memory, but not vice versa, due to a combination of software and hardware cryptographic primitives. Only the code within the enclave can access its data, and external accesses are always denied. When it returns, enclave data stays in the protected memory. In some operating systems, enclaves must be less than 128 MB, which presents a constraint on the size of SGX dependent programs. The enclave is decrypted "on the fly" only within the CPU itself, and only for code and data running from within the enclave itself. This is supported by an autonomous piece of hardware called the Memory Encryption Engine (MEE) that protects the confidentiality and integrity of the CPU-DRAM traffic over a specified memory range. The code running within the enclave is therefore protected from being "spied on" by other code. Although the enclave is trusted, no process outside it needs to be trusted (including the operating system itself) [4]. Before performing computation on a remote platform, a user can verify the authenticity of the trusted environment. By using the attestation mechanism, a third party can establish that software is running on an Intel SGX enabled device and within an enclave.

3   Open Questions to Answer

Although a large variety of techniques for secure computation exist, currently two of the most practical (in terms of performance) are lattice-based Private Stream Aggregation and Trusted Execution Environments. However, although it is known these techniques can be utilized to efficiently process different types of tasks, there is still a great deal of uncertainty regarding which techniques are best suited for different types of computation. I seek to answer the following research questions: "How much speedup, if any, can I expect to gain if I migrate sections of code into a TEE? Also, can I meaningfully quantify any potential speedup while taking resource costs into account? Furthermore, can I organize computational tasks in a meaningful way that will assist potential TEE users in designing their computation pipeline?"

Advantages of TEEs. A significant advantage of TEEs over PSA is support for branching computer logic (i.e., if else statements). Modern TEEs allow users to simply utilize basic C++ syntax to support such statements. However, due to the underlying mathematics, PSA does not have any built in techniques for achieving this functionality, since conditional statements on ciphertexts cannot be evaluated (practically), because the encrypted values cannot be seen to determine which branch to take. There is some work that leverages Lagrange Interpolation [12] to formulate a polynomial function that allows for homomorphic thresholding, but this techniques requires an expensive preprocessing step that makes it far more impractical for computing conditional statements than utilizing a TEE. In addition, TEEs do not suffer from noise when performing addition or multiplication over encrypted values. This means we can perform as many computations over encrypted data as we would like without encountering any slow down. With lattice-based PSA, every operation adds some noise to the result of the computation, such that in practice there is a limit to the amount of computation that can be performed before the result is not recoverable. Note that it is possible to utilize a technique known as bootstrapping to remove this noise periodically, in order to allow for an unlimited number of operations to be computed over ciphertexts, but this technique adds significant overhead to the overall runtime of a program, and in practice it is usually not used.

Advantages of PSA. TEEs do have several drawbacks that raise questions regarding when they are superior to or inferior to PSA. By their nature, TEEs require that users have specialized trusted hardware and firmware in order to utilize the technology, and this raises some compatibility issues in certain environments that can prevent TEE code from being as portable as PSA based techniques. Also, current TEEs are limited to a finite amount of space that can be set aside in a system to store encrypted data. This space is typically known as an enclave, and is generally limited to 128 or 256 MB on state of the art TEEs. In practice, TEEs can encounter significant overhead when paging is triggered, due to overflowing the space constraints of an enclave, and this makes computing over large quantities of data impractical when compared to PSA. However, Intel recently announced that it plans to dramatically increase the maximum size of enclaves in future releases to be approximately 1 TB, so it is unclear if

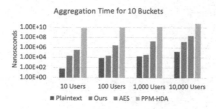

Fig. 1. Histogram aggregation experimental results

this issue will remain significant in the long term [1]. In addition, current TEEs have difficulties utilizing parallel computing techniques, such as multi-threading [13] due to the lack of common synchronization primitive support often found on traditional operating systems. Also, leveraging threading within the Intel SGX can introduce security vulnerabilities [15]. Although efforts are underway to provide additional support for parallel computing, in order to mitigate against side-channel attacks (particularly timing attacks) it seems that for the immediate future parallelism inside a TEE will be inferior to standard techniques available from an OS.

4   Current Stage of Research

During previous projects, I did some exploratory work investigating the usefulness of combining TEEs with PSA to improve performance. The results suggest that for different problems, each method may sometimes be superior if used on its own, but there are circumstances when combining the two approaches may ultimately yield better performance. For instance, when I investigated methods to improve the speed of private histogram calculations, I found that utilizing standard encryption algorithms, such as AES, to simply pass data into an enclave to be computed over, or pure cryptography based solutions (such as the PPM-HDA [7]), that does not utilize a TEE, does not always offer the best performance overall. Instead, our novel approach of leveraging a TEE combined with shuffling algorithms outperformed these baseline techniques, and our approach was within one order of magnitude of plaintext computations in some scenarios, as seen in Fig. 1. This suggests that intelligently combining PSA with a TEE may at times offer the best overall performance potential.

I also observed this when investigating techniques to provide non-interactive fault tolerance to PSA schemes by leveraging a TEE. In the original design, I incurred significant additional computational overhead, since the aggregation step was done inside the TEE. In an effort to improve efficiency, I outsourced some aggregation computation to the untrusted aggregator to improve performance and avoid the MEE's overhead. Current literature suggests most TEEs run common functionalities over an order of magnitude slower than what can be achieved on comparable untrusted hardware, due to the overhead of computing within the enclave [10]. This protocol modification allowed for the somewhat expensive aggregation step to be done on more powerful, albeit untrusted

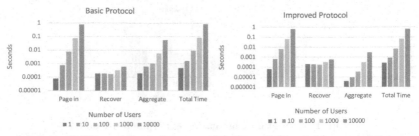

(a) Overall Time of Basic Scheme   (b) Overall Time of Improved Scheme

Fig. 2. Cryptonite (PSA) experimental results

hardware, that has better access to parallel computing resources, without compromising security. This effect can be observed in Fig. 2, where the aggregation time can be dramatically improved if this is performed outside the TEE. This suggests that combining TEEs with pure cryptography can lead to performance improvement over simply leveraging TEEs on their own.

Based on these observations, I conjectured that their may be instances where a hybrid approach, that combines TEEs with pure cryptography techniques, such as PSA, may offer ideal performance that avoids the trade offs of using either technique in isolation. With this in mind, I designed a framework to support privacy-preserving polynomial aggregation, by combining any preexisting PSA scheme with a TEE. Note that PSA based on pure cryptography only supports either addition or multiplication, but I need to leverage both to compute a polynomial function. This seems to suggest that traditional PSA alone cannot support polynomial calculations, but integrating a TEE allows additional secure functionality that supports computing more complex functions. This technique essentially performs the multiplicative components of polynomial evaluation using PSA, but then decrypts the intermediate data inside the enclave, so that privacy is still preserved, while computing the additions needed to recover the final output. During a case study when I simulated computing a regression task over several public datasets from the UCI database, I compared the performance of this method of combining a TEE with PSA with an approach that only utilizes pure cryptography (PDA [8]). I found that this method is at least an order of magnitude faster, as shown in Fig. 1. This result is encouraging, and I feel that a deeper investigation of which components should be done in a TEE and which should be outsourced is needed to obtain optimal overall performance. This problem may be ideal to use as a case study for validating our framework.

5   Proposed Methodology

5.1   Framework Design

I plan to quantitatively examine TEE performance when compared to existing secure computation techniques (i.e., PSA) to determine which types of program

Table 1. Cryptonomial performance on UCI dataset

Datasets	Records	Features	Our time	PDA time	Speedup
Census	48,842	14	2.85 s	355 s	125×
Bank	45,211	17	2.75 s	341 s	124×
Insurance	9,822	14	0.64 s	74 s	115×
White wine	4,898	11	0.35 s	33 s	94×
Red wine	1,599	11	0.17 s	12 s	71×

logic are better suited for TEEs, and which might be faster outside a TEE using advanced parallel computing over encrypted data. Through the course of this investigation, I plan to develop a mathematical/statistical model that can be used to investigate program logic that computes over plaintexts, and determine which approach will offer better performance, or if there might be merit in constructing a hybrid approach that uses both techniques. Although I may change the modeling techniques I use during the investigation based on our results, currently regression analysis [5] seems to be the most promising technique for this study. Regression analysis is frequently used successfully for prediction and forecasting after training a model using numerical data [5]. Also, it is known that regression analysis can be used to infer causal relationships between independent and dependent numerical data [2]. As a result, it seems to be a strong candidate method for developing a general model to better understand how to estimate overall runtime based on experimental data. However, regression analysis is known to have several weaknesses that may require us to utilize different techniques [5]. I plan to develop benchmarks that evaluate the runtime and algorithmic complexity for the following operations, to determine which are faster for each approach (Table 1):

1. Integer add/subtract/multiply/divide
2. Float add/subtract/multiply/divide
3. Trigonometric Functions (sine, cosine, ..)
4. Variable Declaration
5. Assignment Operation
6. Logical Operations (i.e., $\geq$, $\leq$, etc.)
7. 1D array allocation
8. Vector addition/subtraction/product (i.e. dot, cross. etc.)
9. Matrix addition/subtraction/product (i.e. dot, cross. etc.)
10. Other Relevant Operations

In addition, I will need to investigate the impact of parallel computing when performing this profiling, since although TEEs are limited to CPUs at this time, purely cryptographic techniques can take advantage of advanced hardware resources such as GPUs, etc., that will impact the overall performance potential. With enough empirical data, I should be able to apply a number of techniques, such as regression analysis, to fit the data and learn in detail what trends occur

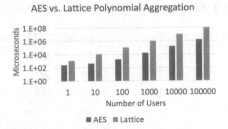

Fig. 3. Lattice aggregation vs. TEE aggregation

as I increase the amount of data and operations performed. While this may seem simple, there are a number of complicating factors that often make it unclear which technique offers faster performance/speed.

If I perform most computation in the TEE, I seem to gain processing time improvement over PSA based approaches, since AES encryption and decryption are significantly faster than their lattice based counterparts, due to a variety of factors, including hardware optimization. Also, it is known that computing basic operations over homomorphically encrypted data is considerably slower than performing the same operations over their associated plaintexts. However, the context switch involved in passing data between trusted and untrusted space is known to be a significant bottleneck in many applications, and if I exceed the size of the enclave, this will induce severe paging overheads that have the potential to significantly decrease performance. Also, it is known that some TEEs (e.g., Intel SGX) have difficulties exploiting multi-threading [13] due to the lack of common synchronization primitives often found on traditional operating systems, and leveraging threading within TEEs can introduce security vulnerabilities [15] which compromise data privacy.

On the other hand, although AES encryption is faster than FHE based techniques, recently there have been a number of significant optimizations proposed for lattice-based PSA that significantly improve its performance for certain scenarios. Besides increasing the overall runtime, these optimizations allow us to use the SIMD paradigm when using lattice based PSA, that can dramatically improve runtime for many common applications. This combined with advanced parallel computing techniques on high performance hardware, such as GPUs, could provide better performance in certain specific scenarios. Due to this large variety of complicating factors, it is critical to obtain foundational data to learn which approach offers better performance in specific scenarios. After gathering the data, I will be able to build a theoretical model to understand which logic is impacted by bottlenecks in either approach, build analytical tools to help guide development processes.

Our preliminary data, shown in Fig. 3 suggests that without utilizing lattice-based optimizations such as SIMD, and without utilizing side-channel attack resistant logic inside the TEE, utilizing trusted hardware can be significantly faster than a pure cryptography approach. To have a more nuanced understanding of the differences in performance between the two approaches, I must first develop program logic for inside the TEE that utilizes mitigation strategies to protect against side channel attacks [6]. Then, I must develop program logic using lattice-based cryptography with optimizations (i.e., RNS, SIMD, etc.) and parallel computing techniques. Note that because I can encode multiple plaintext values into a single ciphertext using SIMD optimization, it is nontrivial to adapt some algorithms to take full advantage of the SIMD's potential to improve performance.

5.2   Case Study

The final remaining problem that I plan to address is determining if there are ways to improve the performance of existing protocols for privately computing a polynomial function over a group of users' inputs. More specifically, I seek to answer the question "Is it possible to improve the current performance of privacy preserving polynomial stream aggregation algorithms by intelligently migrating subsections of the algorithms' implementation into or out of a TEE?" Specifically, I considered the problem of allowing a set of users in S to privately compute a polynomial function over their collected time-series data, such that an untrusted aggregator only learns the final result, and no individual honest user's data is revealed. More formally, I aim at supporting polynomial evaluation over users' time-series input data in the following format of a *general multivariate polynomial*: $f(\{x_{i,j}\}_{i \in S, j=1,...,z}) = \sum_{j=1}^{z} c_j(\prod_{i \in S} \mathbf{m}_{i,j,ts}^{e_{i,j}})$, where z is the number of product terms in the polynomial, c_j and $e_{i,j}$ are public parameters, and $\mathbf{m}_{i,j,ts}$ are secret data from the i-th user at time stamp ts.

Previously, I developed a framework, which can convert any PSA scheme amenable to a complex canonical embedding [3] into a privacy-preserving stream polynomial evaluation scheme, that supports general stream polynomial evaluation. Currently, The framework performs the majority of computation outside of the TEE, and only a small amount inside the TEE. However, during the design and implementation of the protocol, I speculated that our framework was flexible enough that it might be possible to modify it to either perform additional computation inside of the TEE, to potentially improve performance, or move more computation outside of the TEE , to lessen the reliance on trusted hardware and improve performance.

The first path forward would be to potentially pass everything into the enclave to speed up computation, by cutting down on the amount of comparatively expensive homomorphic operations. Instead, I might have all parties agree on a polynomial function to compute, encrypt all of their data with a traditional cryptographic primitive, such as AES, and send it into the enclave to be decrypted and aggregated. Alternatively, to compute the polynomial, I might be able to add in multiplicative and/or additive secret shares, that I could perhaps use to mask the final output until the sum of all of the products are combined.

The approach to do most computation in the TEE seems promising, since AES encryption and decryption are significantly faster than their lattice based counterparts, due to a variety of factors. In addition, there is the potential that I might have a much smaller amount of data to pass into the enclave, and the context switch involved in passing data between trusted and untrusted space is known to be a significant bottleneck in many applications. Note that the AES ciphertexts for each user would likely be only roughly 16 bytes in size, whereas their lattice-based counterparts can be roughly 10 KB in size.

However, there are cons involved too that also make the pure cryptography approach promising as well. It is known that some TEEs (e.g., Intel SGX) have difficulties exploiting multi-threading [13] due to the lack of common synchronization primitives often found on traditional operating systems, and leveraging threading within TEEs can introduce security vulnerabilities [15] which compromise data privacy. Further, the MEE adds additional overhead into computing over data inside the TEE, and there are also space constraints. Nevertheless, computing this result without a TEE might have better performance, as I would have access to the full amenities of modern parallel computing, including special high performance hardware, such as GPUs, etc. My hope is that by performing a deeper quantitative and qualitative investigation into TEEs, it will become apparent which pipeline offers the best performance for this research problem.

References

1. Bradley, T.: Intel takes confidential computing to another level with 'ice lake' security capabilities. Forbes (2020)
2. Chatterjee, S., Hadi, A.S.: Regression Analysis by Example. John Wiley & Sons, Hoboken (2015)
3. Cheon, J.H., Kim, A., Kim, M., Song, Y.S.: Floating-point homomorphic encryption. IACR Cryptol. ePrint Arch. **2016**, 421 (2016)
4. Costan, V., Devadas, S.: Intel SGX explained. IACR Cryptol. ePrint Arch. **2016**, 86 (2016)
5. Draper, N.R., Smith, H.: Applied Regression Analysis, vol. 326. John Wiley & Sons, Hoboken (1998)
6. Götzfried, J., Eckert, M., Schinzel, S., Müller, T.: Cache attacks on intel SGX. In: Proceedings of the 10th European Workshop on Systems Security, pp. 1–6 (2017)
7. Han, S., Zhao, S., Li, Q., Ju, C.H., Zhou, W.: PPM-HDA: privacy-preserving and multifunctional health data aggregation with fault tolerance. TIFS **11**(9), 1940–1955 (2015)
8. Jung, T., Han, J., Li, X.Y.: PDA: semantically secure time-series data analytics with dynamic user groups. TDSC **15**(2), 260–274 (2018)
9. Liu, D., Yan, Z., Ding, W., Atiquzzaman, M.: A survey on secure data analytics in edge computing. IEEE Internet Things J. **6**(3), 4946–4967 (2019)
10. Mofrad, S., Zhang, F., Lu, S., Shi, W.: A comparison study of intel SGX and AMD memory encryption technology. In: ACM HASP, pp. 1–8 (2018)
11. Shi, E., Chan, H., Rieffel, E., Chow, R., Song, D.: Privacy-preserving aggregation of time-series data. In: NDSS. Internet Society (2011)
12. Tan, B.H.M., et al.: Efficient private comparison queries over encrypted databases using fully homomorphic encryption with finite fields. In: IEEE TDSC (2020)
13. Tramer, F., Boneh, D.: Slalom: Fast, verifiable and private execution of neural networks in trusted hardware. In: ICLR (2018)

14. Valovich, F., Aldà, F.: Computational differential privacy from lattice-based cryptography. In: Kaczorowski, J., Pieprzyk, J., Pomykała, J. (eds.) NuTMiC 2017. LNCS, vol. 10737, pp. 121–141. Springer, Cham (2018). https://doi.org/10.1007/978-3-319-76620-1_8
15. Weichbrodt, N., Kurmus, A., Pietzuch, P., Kapitza, R.: AsyncShock: exploiting synchronisation bugs in intel SGX enclaves. In: Askoxylakis, I., Ioannidis, S., Katsikas, S., Meadows, C. (eds.) ESORICS 2016. LNCS, vol. 9878, pp. 440–457. Springer, Cham (2016). https://doi.org/10.1007/978-3-319-45744-4_22

Phishing Web Page Detection with Semi-Supervised Deep Anomaly Detection

Linshu Ouyang[1,2]([⊠]) and Yongzheng Zhang[1,2]

[1] Institute of Information Engineering, Chinese Academy of Sciences, Beijing, China
{ouyanglinshu,zhangyongzheng}@iie.ac.cn
[2] School of Cyber Security, University of Chinese Academy of Sciences,
Beijing, China

Abstract. Phishing web page is one of the most serious threats to the users of the Internet. Recently, deep learning-based phishing detection methods have achieved significant improvement. However, these supervised deep neural networks require a large number of training samples. They also have difficulties in detecting novel phishing web pages. Using anomaly detection approaches is a possible way out yet is currently less explored, possibly due to two reasons. First, HTML codes lie in high dimensional discrete space which is difficult to handle for existing anomaly detection methods. Second, existing anomaly detection methods may find other types of anomalies that are beyond the scope of phishing.

In this paper, we propose a novel semi-supervised deep anomaly detection-based phishing webpage detection method. We first utilize a multi-head self-attention network to learn feature representation that is suitable for anomaly detection from HTML codes. Then we build a semi-supervised learner with Gaussian prior and contrastive loss to fulfill an end-to-end anomaly detector that is specifically optimized for detecting phishing webpages. Extensive experiments on a real-world dataset demonstrate that the accuracy of our method outperforms other state-of-the-art methods by a large margin.

Keywords: Phishing · Semi-supervised learning · Anomaly detection

1 Introduction

Phishing is a kind of social engineering attack that tricks the victims to perform specific actions by imitating trusted web pages [17]. It's one of the most prevalent attacks due to its effectiveness and low cost [1].

Many phishing detection methods have been proposed in the last decades. Traditional detection methods typically focus on designing informative features and utilize sophisticated classifiers such as SVM [5] or Random Forest [4]. In recent years, several deep learning-based phishing detection methods achieved

© ICST Institute for Computer Sciences, Social Informatics and Telecommunications Engineering 2021
Published by Springer Nature Switzerland AG 2021. All Rights Reserved
J. Garcia-Alfaro et al. (Eds.): SecureComm 2021, LNICST 399, pp. 384–393, 2021.
https://doi.org/10.1007/978-3-030-90022-9_20

significant performance improvement [6,10,16]. These methods typically use URL or HTML as input and utilize CNN or RNN to perform classification.

However, these supervised deep learning-based methods require plenty of training samples to learn accurate decision boundaries. This limits the model's ability to detect unknown phishing webpages. On the contrary, anomaly detection approaches have stronger abilities to detect novel phishing webpages, but applying anomaly detection to phishing webpage detection faces several challenges. Traditional anomaly detection methods require manually designed features, which is less effective compared to deep learning-based methods. Also, there exist several types of anomalies in web pages. Existing anomaly detection methods may detect other types of anomalies beyond phishing webpages.

In this paper, we propose a novel semi-supervised deep anomaly detection-based phishing detection method to address these problems. With HTML codes as inputs, we first employ a multi-head self-attention network [7] to perform feature learning and output the anomaly scores. Then we use a prior distribution of anomaly scores to guide the model to learn a representation of normality. Finally, we utilize a novel contrastive loss function to fulfill end-to-end semi-supervised training to finetune the anomaly scoring network towards phishing webpage detection.

Our method combined the strength of deep learning on automatic feature learning and the ability of anomaly detection in detecting novel anomalies. The adoption of the semi-supervised learning paradigm further reduces the false positive rate of the anomaly detection model. Compared with the existing deep learning-based methods, our method achieves higher detection accuracy with fewer training samples, and better performance in detecting novel unknown phishing web pages. Compared with traditional anomaly detection-based methods, we can automatically extract more comprehensive features, thus achieve higher detection accuracy, and can better adapt to the evolution of phishing attacks (Fig. 1).

2   Methods

In this section, we describe our method in detail. With the raw HTML codes as inputs, our anomaly scoring network directly learns and outputs the anomaly scores. We also use a prior distribution of the normal samples to generate reference labels to guide the learning of the network. Finally, the output of the network and the reference labels are fed into the contrastive loss to fulfill end-to-end semi-supervised learning.

2.1   Anomaly Scoring Network

Consider a raw HTML code x, we first split it into a sequence of tokens by spaces and punctuations: $(w_1, w_2, \cdots, w_m)$. Then we embed these tokens with an embedding layer E that maps each token w_m to a k-dimensional learnable vector $E(c) \in R^k$:

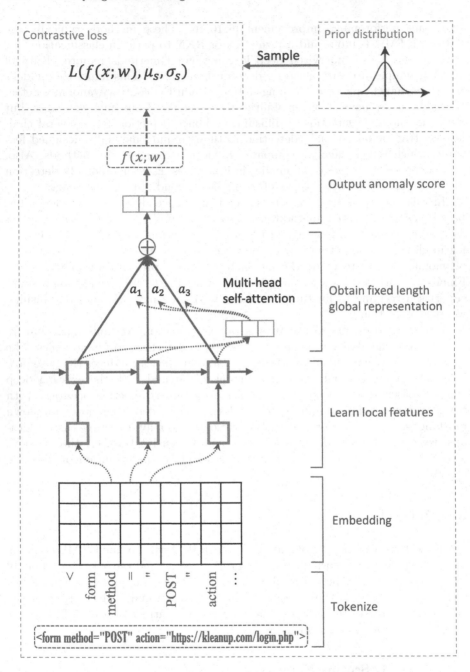

Fig. 1. The architecture of our proposed semi-supervised deep anomaly detection-based phishing detection model. There are three main components: 1) Anomaly scoring network that learns the feature and outputs the anomaly scores. 2) Gaussian prior that generate pseudo labels to guide the learning of the network. 3) Contrastive loss function that fulfill end-to-end semi-supervised training of the network.

$$(\mathbf{e_1}, \mathbf{e_2}, \cdots, \mathbf{e_m}) = (E(w_1), E(w_2), \cdots, E(w_m)) \qquad (1)$$

Next, we fed the above sequence of embedded vectors into an RNN to extract their local context features:

$$Q = (\mathbf{q_1}, \mathbf{q_2}, \cdots, \mathbf{q_m}) = \mathrm{RNN}(\mathbf{e_1}, \mathbf{e_2}, \cdots, \mathbf{e_m}) \qquad (2)$$

The output of the above RNN is a sequence of vectors. Since the lengths of the HTML codes are variable, the lengths of the outputs are also variable. To obtain a fixed-length vector representation for each HTML code, a common method is using the attention mechanism. However, vanilla attention only focuses on one type of information. This is insufficient for phishing detection since it is crucial to synthesize multiple types of information from different locations of the HTML codes to accurately understand the anomalous behavior of the webpage. Therefore, we adopt the multi-head self-attention mechanism on the output of the RNN.

We first use a two-layer fully connect layer to obtain a set of attention weights:

$$A = \mathrm{softmax}(W_2 \tanh(W_1 Q^T)) \qquad (3)$$

Then we use these attention weights to sum the output of the RNN to obtain the fixed-length sample representation:

$$\mathbf{m} = \mathrm{flatten}(AQ) \qquad (4)$$

This vector is then passed through a fully connected layer and an activation function, outputting the anomaly score:

$$f(x; \phi) = \mathrm{sigmoid}(\mathbf{w_f}\mathbf{m} + \mathbf{b}) \qquad (5)$$

where ϕ represents all of the learnable parameters of the network.

2.2   Prior Distribution

To guide the training of the above anomaly scoring network to find good representations of normal HTML codes, a crucial task is to define appropriate learning targets. A naive solution is to use 0 as the learning target for all of the normal HTML codes. However, this may lead the network to converge to a degenerate solution where all the data points are transformed to a single point. To avoid this problem, we employ a Gaussian distribution as the prior distribution of the anomaly scores of the normal samples to generate pseudo labels. Using these pseudo labels as the learning targets of the anomaly scoring network provides a normalization effect and makes the model more robust to unclean training datasets. Specifically, we sample a small set of scores from the standard Gaussian distribution for each batch of samples in the training phase:

$$S = \{s_1, s_2, \cdots, s_n\} \sim \mathcal{N}(0, 1^2) = \frac{1}{\sqrt{2\pi}} e^{-x^2/2} \qquad (6)$$

We call this set a reference set. Then we calculate the mean μ_s and variance σ_s of this reference set.

2.3 Contrastive Loss

The output of the anomaly scoring network and the μ_s, σ_s of the reference set are fed into the contrastive loss to fulfill end-to-end learning. We first calculate the distance between the output of the anomaly scoring network and the center of the reference set:

$$D = \frac{f(x; \phi) - \mu_s}{\sigma_s} \tag{7}$$

D represents the probability that the sample x is anomalous.

Then, we define the constrastive loss:

$$\mathbf{L}(f(x; \phi), \mu_s, \sigma_s) = (1 - Y)\frac{1}{2}D^2 + (Y)\frac{1}{2}\max(0, m - D)^2 \tag{8}$$

Minimizing this loss will push the anomaly scoring network to learn a meaningful representation of HTML codes and assign small scores for normal samples. In this way, we achieve end-to-end semi-supervised anomaly scoring training. Starting from the loss function, the gradient is first passed back to the attention layer, then to the RNN layer, finally to the embedding layer.

3 Experiments

In this section, we conduct extensive experiments to evaluate the proposed method. First, we introduce the settings of the experiments. Then we compare the performance of our proposed method with other state-of-the-art methods.

3.1 Dataset

To reliably evaluate the performance of the methods, we collect a large set of real web pages.

Data Collection. The phishing webpages are collected from PhishTank and OpenPhish, which are widely used as data sources in previous phishing webpage detection researches. For normal web pages, we build a crawler that treats TrancoTop1M as the start point. Our crawler pays special attention to the login pages in normal web pages since these pages are the common impersonate target.

Dataset Construction. Most existing phishing detection researches use balanced datasets, in which the number of phishing and normal samples are nearly equal. However, these datasets can't reliably evaluate the phishing detection methods in the real world where the number of phishing web pages is significantly less than normal web pages. In this work, we build a highly unbalanced dataset to simulate the real scenario. We divide the dataset into three parts: training set, validation set, and test set. To evaluate the ability of our proposed method to detect unknown phishing web pages, we adopt the group split method that divides the dataset according to the domain of each sample to ensure that samples of the same domain will not appear in the training set and test set at the same time. Table 1 shows the statistics of the final dataset.

Table 1. The statistics of the dataset.

Class	Train	Validation	Test	All
Phishing	132	38	137	307
Benign	7306	1822	5953	15081
All	7438	1860	6090	15388

Table 2. Phishing web page detection performance comparison.

Type	Method	AUC-ROC	AUC-PR	F1	Precision	Recall	Accuracy
Classification	SVM	0.8104	0.2472	0.3260	0.3237	0.3284	0.9694
	RNN	0.8170	0.2835	0.4014	0.3877	0.4160	0.9720
Anomaly detection	OC-SVM	0.8657	0.1980	0.1189	0.064	**0.8102**	0.7298
	PCA	0.7291	0.0625	0.1203	0.070	0.4233	0.8607
	IsolationForest	0.8337	0.1950	0.1883	0.1120	0.5912	0.8853
	Our method	**0.8788**	**0.4745**	**0.5044**	**0.6404**	0.4160	**0.9816**

3.2 Performance Metric

Due to the highly imbalanced nature of the dataset, it's not appropriate to use accuracy alone as the metric. Instead, we report multiple metrics, including AUC-ROC, AUC-PR, F1, Precision, Recall, and Accuracy. F1 and accuracy require a previously specified classification threshold. AUC-ROC and AUC-PR are thresholds-invariant metrics that aggregate the performance of the model across all possible thresholds. Among them, AUC-PR is considered the most important metric in our experiments since it focuses on the anomaly class.

3.3 Compared Methods

The competing methods can be grouped into two categories: supervised classification-based methods and anomaly detection-based methods.

The first group of methods is supervised classification-based methods.

- **Manual features+SVM**: Das et al. [4] extracts several features for phishing web page detection and utilizes the support vector machine (SVM) to perform classification.
- **HTMLPhish**: HTMLPhish [10] is the state-of-the-art supervised deep learning-based phishing HTML detection method that combines a character-level CNN and a word-level CNN into an end-to-end classifier.

The second group of methods is anomaly detection-based methods. We extract features as Das et al. [4] and utilize these anomaly detection methods to perform phishing web page detection.

- **One-Class SVM (OC-SVM)**: OC-SVM [13] is a classic anomaly detection method.

- **IsolationForest**: IsolationForest [8] is the state-of-the-art anomaly detection method before the decade of deep learning.
- **Deep Support Vector Data Description (Deep SVDD)**: Deep SVDD [12] is the state-of-the-art deep learning-based anomaly detection method.

3.4 Implementation Details

We implement the proposed method with PyTorch and run the experiments on a GPU with 11GB memory. The hyperparameters of our model include the embedding dimension, the hidden layer dimension, and the size of the reference set. We adjust these hyperparameters based on the performance of the model on the validation set. Both the embedding dimension and the hidden layer dimension are set to 64, the size of the reference set is set to 5. We use Adam as the optimizer with a learning rate of 0.01. When the loss stops decreasing for 3 consecutive epochs, we reduce the learning rate to 0.001 and then learn until the loss stops falling for another 3 consecutive rounds.

3.5 Performance Comparison

In this section, we compare our proposed method with other state-of-the-art phishing webpage detection methods. There are two major questions we aim to address:

- Is our method more accurate than the unsupervised anomaly detection-based methods?
- Is our method more accurate than the supervised deep learning-based method?

The performance of our proposed method and five competing methods are shown in Table 2. Our method outperforms other methods by a large margin in terms of all metrics except recall. Although IsolationForest achieves better recall than our method, its precision is significantly lower. The better performance of our method comparing with the supervised classification-based methods demonstrates that our semi-supervised anomaly detection approach can utilize the labeled training data more effectively. Also notice that the unsupervised anomaly detection-based methods have significantly worse detection accuracy than supervised classification-based methods, but our method achieves better performance than supervised methods.

4 Related Work

The method we proposed is conceptually related to previous phishing web page detection methods, and anomaly detection methods.

4.1 Traditional Phishing Web Page Detection

Traditional phishing web page detection methods can be broadly divided into three categories.

The first group is rule-based approaches. The blacklist/whitelist methods rely on a constantly maintained list of known phishing web pages [2]. The heuristic-based approaches [11] rely on experts designed rules to detect phishing web pages. These approaches are simple, precise, and fast, but have low recall and cannot detect zero-day phishing attacks[14].

The second group is visual similarity-based approaches [3,9], which detect phishing web pages by examining the visual similarity between phishing web pages and well-known non-phishing web pages. These methods can detect zero-day phishing web pages, but at cost of high computation. Besides, they can only detect the phishing web pages that impersonate well-known targets.

The final group is machine learning-based approaches [15,18,19] . These methods typically rely on features designed by experts [1,4,5] and classification algorithms such as SVM. This group of methods can detect zero-day phishing attacks, but the performance is limited by the expressive power of manually designed features.

4.2 Deep Learning Based Phishing Web Page Detection

Recently, with the advancement of deep learning, several phishing web page detection methods based on deep text classification models have been proposed.

Wang et al. [16] proposed PDRCNN, an improved deep learning phishing web page detection method that uses URL as input only. Their method treats URL as sequences of characters and utilize a fused neural network architecture that combines recurrent neural network and convolutional neural network.

Huang et al. [6] proposed to use attention-based hierarchical RNN to improve the phishing detection accuracy. Their method also uses URL as input only, but their hierarchical RNN structure learns the features from both character level and word level. The Attention mechanism was adopted to let the neural network focus on the important area of the URL.

Recently, Opara et al. [10] made the first attempt to apply the deep learning method to HTML input. They combined the character-level CNN and word-level CNN to improve the detection accuracy. They achieved significant improvement compared to traditional machine learning-based approaches. However, they ignore the inherent structure information of HTML, and CNN has difficulties in capturing long-range semantics in HTML.

4.3 Anomaly Detection

OC-SVM [13] conduct anomaly detection by learning an optimal hyper-plane that separates the normal samples from the origin. IsolationForest [8] utilizes the random forest to conduct anomaly detection. Anomalies tend to have a short path in the partitioning tree. Deep SVDD [12] is one of the first works in deep anomaly detection. It utilizes neural networks to learn the feature representation that transforms the normal samples into a small hypersphere.

5   Conclusions

We have presented our semi-supervised deep anomaly detection approach for phishing web detection. Our method combined the strength of feature learning from deep learning with the ability to detect novel phishing samples from anomaly detection. The experimental results demonstrate that our approach achieves better performance than existing deep learning-based and anomaly detection-based phishing webpage detection methods.

References

1. AlEroud, A., Zhou, L.: Phishing environments, techniques, and countermeasures: a survey. Comput. Secur. **68**, 160–196 (2017)
2. Cao, Y., Han, W., Le, Y.: Anti-phishing based on automated individual white-list. In: Proceedings of the 4th Workshop on Digital Identity Management, pp. 51–60. ACM (2008)
3. Chiew, K., Fatt, J.C.S., Sze, S., Yong, K.S.C.: Leverage website favicon to detect phishing websites. Secur. Commun. Netw **2018**, 7251750:1-7251750:11 (2018)
4. Das, A., Baki, S., Aassal, A.E., Verma, R.M., Dunbar, A.: Sok: a comprehensive reexamination of phishing research from the security perspective. IEEE Commun. Surv. Tutor. **22**(1), 671–708 (2020)
5. Dou, Z., Khalil, I., Khreishah, A., Al-Fuqaha, A.I., Guizani, M.: Systematization of knowledge (sok): a systematic review of software-based web phishing detection. IEEE Commun. Surv. Tutor. **19**(4), 2797–2819 (2017)
6. Huang, Y., Yang, Q., Qin, J., Wen, W.: Phishing URL detection via CNN and attention-based hierarchical RNN. In: 18th IEEE International Conference On Trust, Security And Privacy In Computing And Communications/13th IEEE International Conference On Big Data Science And Engineering, TrustCom/BigDataSE, pp. 112–119. IEEE (2019)
7. Lin, Z., et al.: A structured self-attentive sentence embedding. In: 5th International Conference on Learning Representations, ICLR 2017, Toulon, France, 24–26 April 2017, Conference Track Proceedings. OpenReview.net (2017)
8. Liu, F.T., Ting, K.M., Zhou, Z.: Isolation forest. In: Proceedings of the 8th IEEE International Conference on Data Mining (ICDM 2008), Pisa, Italy, 15–19 December 2008, pp. 413–422. IEEE Computer Society (2008). https://doi.org/10.1109/ICDM.2008.17
9. Mao, J., Li, P., Li, K., Wei, T., Liang, Z.: Baitalarm: detecting phishing sites using similarity in fundamental visual features. In: 2013 5th International Conference on Intelligent Networking and Collaborative Systems, pp. 790–795. IEEE (2013)
10. Opara, C., Wei, B., Chen, Y.: Htmlphish: enabling phishing web page detection by applying deep learning techniques on HTML analysis. In: 2020 International Joint Conference on Neural Networks, pp. 1–8. IEEE (2020)
11. Ramesh, G., Krishnamurthi, I., Kumar, K.S.S.: An efficacious method for detecting phishing webpages through target domain identification. Decis. Supp. Syst. **61**, 12–22 (2014)

12. Ruff, L., et al.: Deep one-class classification. In: Dy, J.G., Krause, A. (eds.) Proceedings of the 35th International Conference on Machine Learning, ICML 2018, Stockholmsmässan, Stockholm, Sweden, 10–15 July 2018, vol. 80, pp. 4390–4399. Proceedings of Machine Learning Research, PMLR (2018). http://proceedings.mlr.press/v80/ruff18a.html

13. Schölkopf, B., Platt, J.C., Shawe-Taylor, J., Smola, A.J., Williamson, R.C.: Estimating the support of a high-dimensional distribution. Neural Comput. **13**(7), 1443–1471 (2001). https://doi.org/10.1162/089976601750264965

14. Sheng, S., Wardman, B., Warner, G., Cranor, L., Hong, J., Zhang, C.: An empirical analysis of phishing blacklists. In: CEAS 2009 (2009)

15. Stobbs, J., Issac, B., Jacob, S.M.: Phishing web page detection using optimised machine learning. In: 2020 IEEE 19th International Conference on Trust, Security and Privacy in Computing and Communications (TrustCom), pp. 483–490 (2020)

16. Wang, W., Zhang, F., Luo, X., Zhang, S.: PDRCNN: precise phishing detection with recurrent convolutional neural networks. Secur. Commun. Netw **2019**, 2595794:1-2595794:15 (2019)

17. Whittaker, C., Ryner, B., Nazif, M.: Large-scale automatic classification of phishing pages. In: Proceedings of the Network and Distributed System Security Symposium, NDSS 2010. The Internet Society (2010)

18. Xiang, G., Hong, J.I., Rosé, C.P., Cranor, L.F.: CANTINA+: a feature-rich machine learning framework for detecting phishing web sites. ACM Trans. Inf. Syst. Secur. **14**(2), 21:1-21:28 (2011)

19. Zhao, P., Hoi, S.C.H.: Cost-sensitive online active learning with application to malicious URL detection. In: Proceedings of the 19th ACM SIGKDD International Conference on Knowledge Discovery and Data Mining, pp. 919–927. ACM (2013)

Poisoning Attack for Inter-agent Transfer Learning

Zelei Cheng$^{(\boxtimes)}$ (ID) and Zuotian Li (ID)

Purdue University, West Lafayette, IN 47906, USA
cheng473@purdue.edu

Abstract. In reinforcement learning, high sample complexity is a big challenge to deal with. Inter-agent transfer learning is one solution to this challenge that can leverage the experience of other more competent agents. In this paradigm, a student can make a query to the teacher and the teacher will give some action advice given the current state. However, most previous works ignored the instruction reliability problem. In this work, we investigate the instruction reliability issue based on the one-to-one teaching framework and formulate the poisoning attack as an optimization problem. By solving the optimization problem, the attacker can significantly influence the performance of the student in three different query models. Evaluation highlights that we need to consider the instruction reliability when using teacher-student frameworks in reinforcement learning.

Keywords: Poisoning attack · Inter-agent transfer learning · Reinforcement learning

1 Introduction

Reinforcement Learning is learning how to map states to actions such that the expected return can be maximized [27]. The agent learns a policy through the interaction with the environment and the environment will give the feedback in the form of numerical reward. The reinforcement learning framework has gained great popularity in recent years and the related learning methods have been developed to handle increasingly complicated problems [30]. However, as the task is more and more complex, reinforcement learning can suffer from the high sample complexity challenge [18], where the reinforcement learning agents cannot sample all the state space and action space due to various concerns, e.g., limited time, security issue [11]. Therefore, how to address the high sample complexity is an urgent need for solving complex tasks.

Transfer learning leverages the previous knowledge in one or more source tasks to assist the current target task [9]. Recently, it has been combined with reinforcement learning. Clouse et al. [7] proposed a teaching method for reinforcement learning where a human expert teaches the reinforcement learning

© ICST Institute for Computer Sciences, Social Informatics and Telecommunications Engineering 2021
Published by Springer Nature Switzerland AG 2021. All Rights Reserved
J. Garcia-Alfaro et al. (Eds.): SecureComm 2021, LNICST 399, pp. 394–404, 2021.
https://doi.org/10.1007/978-3-030-90022-9_21

agent to accelerate the learning rate. Then multiple teacher-student frameworks are proposed to transfer the knowledge from the teacher to the student. Samples of previous interactions with the environment will then be mapped to the student's policy space. Moreover, the teacher is not limited to human experts, but also well-trained reinforcement learning agents [29] and reinforcement learning agents learning in progress [22]. Typically, it is a one-teacher-one-student pairwise relationship.

Although most previous work assumes that the student should take the teacher's action advice without any condition, the instruction reliability should be considered in practice. Here are some reasons: first, the student's query or the teacher's advice might be corrupted or lost, e.g., due to unreliable communication channel; second, teachers can be compromised or malicious to pollute the student's policy; even if we assume that all teachers are honest, teachers might have worse policies than the student's in some cases. Therefore, it is meaningful to investigate the performance of the teacher-student framework considering the instruction reliability issue. Felipe Leno Da Silva et al. [11] pointed out that how to perform instruction reliability determination effectively is still an open problem.

In this work, we investigate the instruction reliability issue of the teacher-student framework under a one-to-one scenario, where one teacher teaches one student. Especially, we construct poisoning attacks for this scenario and formulate the attacks as an optimization problem. Through experiments, we can see the damage caused by our proposed attacks. Future work will be investigating the more complicated teacher-student frameworks.

2 Related Work

2.1 Transfer Learning for Reinforcement Learning

In reinforcement learning [28], an agent learns an optimal policy to finish a task through trial and error approaches. The policy learning process is enabled by the interaction between the agent and the environment. Typically, reinforcement learning can be modeled as a Markov Decision Process. When the agent observe its current state s_t, it will take some action a_t from its policy π_t. Then the environment will give the feedback, i.e., the agent's new state s_{t+1} and numeric reward r_t. The reinforcement learning agent uses $< s_t, a_t, r_t >$ to update its policy π_t in order to maximize its cumulative reward in the long run. The interaction will occur repeatedly until the end of the learning process. However, sometimes the state-action space is too large to sample, it might be expensive for agents to explore all possible state-action pairs [18,19]. To this end, transfer learning is applied to solve this issue where the agents can leverage the knowledge of multiple source tasks to accelerate the accomplishment of target tasks.

Typically, transfer learning for reinforcement learning can be divided into two categories, i.e., single-agent transfer and inter-agent transfer [11]. Single-agent transfer includes value function transfer [31], policy reuse [15], and multi-task learning [33]. Learning from feedback [16], action advising [10], and learning from demonstration [5] are examples of inter-agent transfer. Especially, in this paper, we focus on inter-agent transfer learning where a student leverages the experience of another, more competent agent. Torrey and Taylor [32] introduced a teacher-student framework for reinforcement learning where a student will execute the action his teacher advises and proposed a budget model for teaching where the teacher may only give such advice a limited number of times. Based on the budget model, Zimmer et al. [35] modeled when to teach as a reinforcement learning problem and provided an efficient technique to choose the right moment to give advice. However, most work assumes that the teacher is an expert that has domain knowledge. Recently, Omidshafiei et al. [22] suggested that every agent can be another's teacher and proposed a two-level learning framework for cooperative multi-agent reinforcement learning, i.e., task-level learning and advising-level learning.

Nevertheless, previous work mostly does not take instruction reliability into account. They simply assumed that all instructions are reliable, and proceeds immediately to the knowledge merging step [11].

2.2   Poisoning Attack

Poisoning attacks usually occur in the training phase of the machine learning system with the target to compromise the integrity [3], for example, injecting some malicious data into the training dataset. The training phase involves training dataset collection and the learning process. Most poisoning attacks happen during the collection of the training datasets as known as data poisoning attacks [4,14,17]. For example, Cao et al. [6] proposed data poisoning attacks to local differential privacy protocols that can inject fake users into the protocols such that the local perturbed data will be carefully crafted before submitted to the data collector. A few works investigate the poisoning attack occurring in the learning process. Fang et al. [13] proposed local model poisoning attacks to federated learning. The attackers upload the adversarial local update by calculating how to deviate the global model to the inverse direction of the correct weight update. Our work falls in the second category, i.e., poisoning attack in the learning process.

For the objective of the poisoning attacks, generally, there are two types: untargeted poisoning attack [20,25,34] which aims to cause a higher testing error for testing examples, and targeted poisoning attack [24,26], where the machine learning model produces unexpected predictions. The poisoning attack we'll discuss here will fall into the first category.

3   System Model

3.1   Reinforcement Learning Setting

Here we consider a multi-agent reinforcement learning setting, where two agents are involved as Fig. 1 shows. One reinforcement learning agent is the teacher and another is the student.

The teacher and the student interact with the same environment and they have the same task. Therefore, there is no need to measure the similarity between the teacher's task and the student's task as [2]. Typically, the teacher should have more experience than the student. For example, the teacher has already interacted with the environment several times before the student starts interacting with the environment.

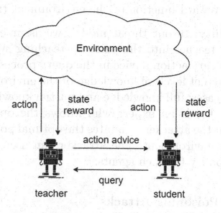

Fig. 1. One-to-one teaching relationship

We assume that the teacher and the student share the same state space S^+ and action space A, i.e., a homogeneous setting. Thus, the teacher's advice can be directly adopted without the need for action space mapping.

3.2 Student Query Model

The query budget model as [32] will be considered in this paper to simulate the actual limit of communication condition. Here we consider three query models:

1. Random query: The student makes a query with probability p;
2. Ask important [1]: If $I(s) = \max_a Q(s,a) - \min_a Q(s,a) > threshold$, the student will make an query;
3. Ask uncertain [8]: If $I(s) = \max_a Q(s,a) - \min_a Q(s,a) < threshold$, the student will make an query.

4 Attacking Inter-agent Transfer Learning

4.1 Threat Model

We characterize our threat model with respect to an attacker's goal and capability.

Attacker's Goal: Given a one-to-one teaching framework, the attacker's goal is to pollute the student's policy and minimize the student's long-term accumulated reward. Note that such attacks are categorized as untargeted poisoning attacks, which make the student's reinforcement learning system unusable. This attack is well-motivated in real-world reinforcement learning applications. For instance, an attacker may be interested in providing misleading or life-threatening information to reinforcement learning agents such that he can cause damage to the competitor's reinforcement learning systems. Previous work regarding adversarial attacks to reinforcement learning systems such as [12,21,23] achieves this goal by manipulating the reward function or the environment transition dynamics.

Attacker's Capability: In our threat model, we assume the attacker is able to inject a malicious teacher into the pairwise teaching system. The malicious teacher can send arbitrary action advice in the query process to the student. The attacker can have different levels of knowledge of the environment. In particular, here we consider two cases: full knowledge and partial knowledge. Full knowledge means that the attacker is an expert who knows the optimal policy. Partial knowledge means that the attacker estimates the optimal policy through previous interactions with the environment. The attacker can use either a deterministic policy or stochastic policy to teach agents.

4.2   Formulating Poisoning Attacks

We formulate the poisoning attacks for inter-agent transfer learning as an optimization problem, which should minimize the accumulated reward of the student. No matter whether the attacker is an expert, the attacker knows or has an estimate of the optimal policy $\pi^*(\mathcal{S}^+)$. What the attacker needs to do is make the student's policy deviate from the optimal policy as much as possible. More specifically, in each iteration when the student inquires the attacker, the attacker should choose the action advice sampled from the non-optimal policy. However, to make the attack nontrivial to be detected, the short-term observation of the student should not be changed too much.

Given the current state s_t, the attacker uses the (estimated) optimal policy $\pi^*(s_t)$. Suppose the advising policy of the attacker is denoted as $\pi'(s_t)$. The attacker's goal is to find the optimal policy to make $\pi'(s_t)$ deviate from $\pi^*(s_t)$ as much as possible without letting the student know. It requires to ensure that the short-term observation should not be changed too much. Mathematically,

$$\max D_{\mathrm{KL}}(\pi'(s_t)\|\pi^*(s_t))$$
$$\text{s.t. } \|r'_t - r^*_t\| < \epsilon \tag{1}$$

where r'_t denotes the reward after executing the teacher's action advice and r^*_t denotes the reward after executing the action sampled from the optimal policy. The Kullback-Leibler divergence $D_{\mathrm{KL}}(.,.)$ is defined as

$$D_{\mathrm{KL}}(P\|Q) = \sum_{x \in \mathcal{X}} P(x) \log\left(\frac{P(x)}{Q(x)}\right) \tag{2}$$

where P and Q are two discrete probability distribution defined on the same probability space. Note that KL divergence also applies to continues probability distribution where summation can be replaced with integral.

4.3   Solving the Optimization Problem

The proposed attack is based on solving the aforementioned optimization problem in Eq. (1). However, the optimal solution depends on the concrete applications.

For example, when it comes to Hallway Game which we will use for evaluation later, the reward will always be 0 until the agent reaches the opposite state. Therefore, as long as the agent not reaching the opposite state, the reward will be 0 regardless of what action to be chosen. Thus, the optimization problem has been simplified as solving the optimal advising policy $\pi'(s_t)$ such that the KL divergence is maximized. Since in Hallway Game, if the agent is initiated on the left side, the optimal policy should be always going right, i.e., $\pi^*(s_t) = [0, 1]$. To make the KL divergence maximized, $\pi'(s_t) = [1, 0]$ should be the optimal solution. The analysis is similar for initiating the agent on the right side.

Therefore, in a target-oriented reward mechanism, i.e., that the reward only occurs if the agent reaches the target, we can relax our optimization problem without the constraint. The new optimization problem should be

$$\max D_{KL}(\pi'(s_t) \| \pi^*(s_t)) \tag{3}$$

For simplicity, let's consider the action space to be a discrete space. Assume that there are n actions can be chosen. Then the two distributions in Eq. (3) can be written as

$$\pi'(s_t) = [p_1', p_2', \ldots, p_n'] \tag{4}$$

with the constraint $\sum_{i=1}^{n} p_i' = 1$.

$$\pi^*(s_t) = [p_1^*, p_2^*, \ldots, p_n^*] \tag{5}$$

with the constraint $\sum_{i=1}^{n} p_i^* = 1$.

Then the KL divergence can be interpreted as

$$D_{KL}(\pi'(s_t) \| \pi^*(s_t)) = \sum_{i=1}^{n} p_i' \log(\frac{p_i'}{p_i^*}) \tag{6}$$

If $\exists j$ such that $p_j^* = 0$, obviously, one optimal solution is that $p_j' = 1$ with other elements in $\pi'(s_t)$ equals to zero.

Otherwise, if $\forall j, p_j^* \neq 0$, w.l.g., we assume that $p_1^* \leq p_2^* \leq \cdots \leq p_n^*$. To maximize the KL divergence, the optimal solution should be $p_1' = 1$ with other elements in $\pi'(s_t)$ equals to zero.

5   Evaluation

5.1   Experiment Setup

Environment: Hallway Game. In Hallway Game [22], an agent receives $+1$ reward by navigating to opposite states in a 17-grid hallway.

The game will terminate if the agent has reached the terminal state or the number of iterations reaches the threshold.

Compared Cases: We will consider four different assumptions for the teacher: 1) Honest teacher who will teach the optimal policy; 2) No teacher; 3) Malicious teacher (fixed policy) who knows the optimal policy but will teach the worst policy; 4) Malicious teacher (grid search) who estimates the optimal policy through previous interactions with the environment but will teach the worst policy (which is solved by the aforementioned optimization problem).

The performance of the student under three query models will be tested in the experiments, i.e., random query, ask important, ask uncertain.

Reinforcement Learning Setting: There are two agents involved in this reinforcement learning task. One is the teacher and the other is the student.

The student uses a Q-learning algorithm to finish the reinforcement learning task. Once the query condition satisfies, the student will ask the teacher for advice. Then the teacher gives action advice, and the student will directly adopt this advice and reach a new state. The detailed algorithm we use in the experiments is in Algorithm 1.

Algorithm 1: Q-learning with query

---

    parameter : step size α, discount rate γ, small $\epsilon > 0$

1 Initialize $Q(s,a)$, for all $s \in \mathcal{S}^+, a \in \mathcal{A}(s)$, arbitrarily except that $Q(\text{terminal}, \cdot) = 0$;

2 **foreach** *episode* **do**

3   Initialize S;

4   **foreach** *step of episode* **do**

5   **if** *the query condition satisfies* **then**

6   Query the teacher

7   Get the teacher's action advice A

8   **end if**

9   **else**

10   Use $\epsilon - greedy$ method to choose action

11   A for S according to the policy π derived from Q table

12   **end if**

13   Take action A, observe R, S';

14         $Q(S, A) \leftarrow Q(S, A) + \alpha[R + \gamma \max_a Q(S', a) - Q(S, A)]$;

15         $S \leftarrow S'$;

16   **end foreach**

17 **end foreach**

5.2   Results

We perform experiments corresponding to the aforementioned settings. We test the performance of four cases under three query models. Figure 2 shows the performance of the student under the random query model with different teacher assumptions. Figure 3 shows the performance of the student under the ask important model with different teacher assumptions. Figure 4 shows the performance of the student under the ask uncertain model with different teacher assumptions.

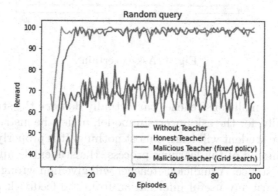

Fig. 2. Random query

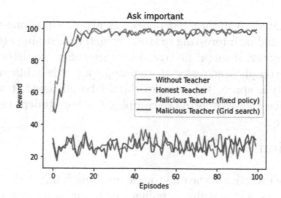

Fig. 3. Ask important

Generally, an honest teacher can accelerate the learning process of the student. Compared with the case that no teacher is involved, the student can gain higher rewards with an honest teacher (an expert).

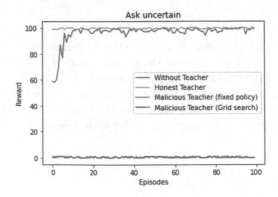

Fig. 4. Ask uncertain

Nevertheless, a malicious teacher can actually damage the student's learning process. Especially, for the ask uncertain model, under the instruction of a malicious teacher, the student will learn almost nothing. It is properly due to the fact that at the beginning of the learning process, the student is unclear and needs the teacher's assistance. A malicious teacher will give him wrong instruction and make him not learn any useful information from the feedback provided by the environment.

6   Future Work

Our work is limited to untargeted poisoning attacks in a one-to-one teaching framework. It would be interesting to study targeted poisoning attacks under this framework. Moreover, it might be trivial for the student to detect the attacks in an easy task. In complicated tasks where a single agent has difficulty in exploring all the state-action space, the attacks should be efficient. It should be more interesting to investigate other more complex teacher-student relationships.

7   Conclusion

In this paper, we investigate the one-to-one teaching framework. We demonstrate that inter-agent transfer learning is vulnerable to our poisoning attacks that give poisonous action advice to the student during the learning process. In particular, to minimize the accumulated reward of the student, an attacker can craft the action advice such that the advising policy deviates the most from the optimal policy. Moreover, finding such crafted action advice can be formulated as an optimization problem. Through evaluation, our results highlight that we need to consider the instruction reliability when using teacher-student frameworks in reinforcement learning.

References

1. Amir, O., Kamar, E., Kolobov, A., Grosz, B.J.: Interactive teaching strategies for agent training. In: Proceedings of the Twenty-Fifth International Joint Conference on Artificial Intelligence, pp. 804–811 (2016)
2. Barekatain, M., Yonetani, R., Hamaya, M.: Multipolar: multi-source policy aggregation for transfer reinforcement learning between diverse environmental dynamics. arXiv preprint arXiv:1909.13111 (2019)
3. Barreno, M., Nelson, B., Sears, R., Joseph, A.D., Tygar, J.D.: Can machine learning be secure? In: Proceedings of the 2006 ACM Symposium on Information, Computer and Communications Security, pp. 16–25 (2006)
4. Biggio, B., Nelson, B., Laskov, P.: Poisoning attacks against support vector machines. In: Proceedings of the 29th International Conference on International Conference on Machine Learning, pp. 1467–1474 (2012)
5. Brys, T., Harutyunyan, A., Suay, H.B., Chernova, S., Taylor, M.E., Nowé, A.: Reinforcement learning from demonstration through shaping. In: Twenty-fourth International Joint Conference on Artificial Intelligence (2015)
6. Cao, X., Jia, J., Gong, N.Z.: Data poisoning attacks to local differential privacy protocols. In: 30th USENIX Security Symposium (USENIX Security 2021) (2021)
7. Clouse, J.A., Utgoff, P.E.: A teaching method for reinforcement learning. In: Machine Learning Proceedings 1992, pp. 92–101. Elsevier (1992)
8. Clouse, J.A.: On integrating apprentice learning and reinforcement learning. University of Massachusetts Amherst (1996)
9. Da Silva, F.L., Costa, A.H.R.: A survey on transfer learning for multiagent reinforcement learning systems. J. Artif. Intell. Res. **64**, 645–703 (2019)
10. Da Silva, F.L., Hernandez-Leal, P., Kartal, B., Taylor, M.E.: Uncertainty-aware action advising for deep reinforcement learning agents. In: Proceedings of the AAAI Conference on Artificial Intelligence, vol. 34, pp. 5792–5799 (2020)
11. Da Silva, F.L., Warnell, G., Costa, A.H.R., Stone, P.: Agents teaching agents: a survey on inter-agent transfer learning. Auton. Agent. Multi-Agent Syst. **34**(1), 1–17 (2020)
12. Everitt, T., Krakovna, V., Orseau, L., Legg, S.: Reinforcement learning with a corrupted reward channel. In: Proceedings of the 26th International Joint Conference on Artificial Intelligence, pp. 4705–4713 (2017)
13. Fang, M., Cao, X., Jia, J., Gong, N.: Local model poisoning attacks to byzantine-robust federated learning. In: 29th USENIX Security Symposium (USENIX Security 2020), pp. 1605–1622 (2020)
14. Fang, M., Yang, G., Gong, N.Z., Liu, J.: Poisoning attacks to graph-based recommender systems. In: Proceedings of the 34th Annual Computer Security Applications Conference, pp. 381–392 (2018)
15. Fernández, F., Veloso, M.: Probabilistic policy reuse in a reinforcement learning agent. In: Proceedings of the fifth International Joint Conference on Autonomous Agents and Multiagent Systems, pp. 720–727 (2006)
16. Griffith, S., Subramanian, K., Scholz, J., Isbell, C.L., Thomaz, A.L.: Policy shaping: Integrating human feedback with reinforcement learning. Georgia Institute of Technology (2013)
17. Jagielski, M., Oprea, A., Biggio, B., Liu, C., Nita-Rotaru, C., Li, B.: Manipulating machine learning: poisoning attacks and countermeasures for regression learning. In: 2018 IEEE Symposium on Security and Privacy (SP), pp. 19–35. IEEE (2018)

18. Kakade, S.M.: On the sample complexity of reinforcement learning. Ph.D. thesis, UCL (University College London) (2003)
19. Lattimore, T., Hutter, M., Sunehag, P.: The sample-complexity of general reinforcement learning. In: International Conference on Machine Learning, pp. 28–36. PMLR (2013)
20. Li, B., Wang, Y., Singh, A., Vorobeychik, Y.: Data poisoning attacks on factorization-based collaborative filtering. In: Proceedings of the 30th International Conference on Neural Information Processing Systems, pp. 1893–1901 (2016)
21. Ma, Y., Zhang, X., Sun, W., Zhu, X.: Policy poisoning in batch reinforcement learning and control. In: Advances in Neural Information Processing Systems (2019)
22. Omidshafiei, S., et al.: Learning to teach in cooperative multiagent reinforcement learning. In: Proceedings of the AAAI Conference on Artificial Intelligence, vol. 33, pp. 6128–6136 (2019)
23. Rakhsha, A., Radanovic, G., Devidze, R., Zhu, X., Singla, A.: Policy teaching via environment poisoning: training-time adversarial attacks against reinforcement learning. In: International Conference on Machine Learning, pp. 7974–7984. PMLR (2020)
24. Shafahi, A., et al.: Poison frogs! Targeted clean-label poisoning attacks on neural networks. In: Proceedings of the 32nd International Conference on Neural Information Processing Systems, pp. 6106–6116 (2018)
25. Sharif, M., Bhagavatula, S., Bauer, L., Reiter, M.K.: Accessorize to a crime: real and stealthy attacks on state-of-the-art face recognition. In: Proceedings of the 2016 ACM SIGSAC Conference on Computer and Communications Security, pp. 1528–1540 (2016)
26. Suciu, O., Marginean, R., Kaya, Y., Daume III, H., Dumitras, T.: When does machine learning *fail*? Generalized transferability for evasion and poisoning attacks. In: 27th USENIX Security Symposium (USENIX Security 2018), pp. 1299–1316 (2018)
27. Sutton, R.S., Barto, A.G.: Reinforcement Learning: An Introduction. MIT Press, Cambridge (2018)
28. Sutton, R.S., Barto, A.G., et al.: Introduction to Reinforcement Learning, vol. 135. MIT Press, Cambridge (1998)
29. Taylor, A., Duparic, I., Galván-López, E., Clarke, S., Cahill, V.: Transfer learning in multi-agent systems through parallel transfer (2013)
30. Taylor, M.E., Stone, P.: Transfer learning for reinforcement learning domains: a survey. J. Mach. Learn. Res. **10**(7), 1633–1685 (2009)
31. Taylor, M.E., Stone, P., Liu, Y.: Transfer learning via inter-task mappings for temporal difference learning. J. Mach. Learn. Res. **8**(9), 2125–2167 (2007)
32. Torrey, L., Taylor, M.: Teaching on a budget: agents advising agents in reinforcement learning. In: Proceedings of the 2013 International Conference on Autonomous Agents and Multi-agent Systems, pp. 1053–1060 (2013)
33. Wilson, A., Fern, A., Ray, S., Tadepalli, P.: Multi-task reinforcement learning: a hierarchical Bayesian approach. In: Proceedings of the 24th International Conference on Machine Learning, pp. 1015–1022 (2007)
34. Yang, G., Gong, N.Z., Cai, Y.: Fake co-visitation injection attacks to recommender systems. In: NDSS (2017)
35. Zimmer, M., Viappiani, P., Weng, P.: Teacher-student framework: a reinforcement learning approach. In: AAMAS Workshop Autonomous Robots and Multirobot Systems (2014)

PQC-SC Workshop

An Efficient Post-Quantum PKE from RLWR with Simple Security Proof

Parhat Abla[1,2]([✉]) and Mingsheng Wang[1]

[1] State Key Laboratory of Information Security,
Institute of Information Engineering, CAS, Beijing, China
parhat@iie.ac.cn
[2] School of Cyber Security, University of Chinese Academy of Sciences,
Beijing, China

Abstract. In this paper, we propose a public-key encryption scheme based on the Ring Learning With Rounding (RLWR) problem. Our scheme is seen as RLWR based variant of Saber (NIST PQC standardization round 3 candidate scheme). The design motivation is to overcome the very involved security proofs of LWR based public-key encryption schemes. To simplify the previous very involved security proofs, we introduce an intermediate problem which is at least as hard as RLWE problem. In contradiction to the previous LWR based schemes, our construction shares simple and intuitive security proof. We first present an IND-CPA public-key encryption scheme, and then apply a variant of the Fujisaki–Okamoto transforms to create a CCA- secure KEM. Our parameterization of the final KEM and the reference implementation shows that the performance of our scheme is comparable with the NIST PQC standardization round 3 candidates.

Keywords: RLWR · Lattice · Post-quantum · Encryption

1 Introduction

Since the ground breaking work of Shor [27], there has been a rising interest in post-quantum cryptography. Recently the interest of constructing post-quantum cryptographic primitives going up another level by the announcement of National Institute of Standards and Technology (NIST) that looking towards the standardization of post-quantum cryptography [1]. Among the submissions to the NIST, most of the constructions are based on the lattice problems. Furthermore, three [6,17,29] of the four round 3 finalists (public-key encryption and key-encapsulation algorithms) are lattice based primitives.

Since the work of Ajtai [2] showed the worst-case to average-case reduction on lattice problems, lattice based cryptography obtains much of interest. Yet the cryptographic schemes are inefficient until Regev [26] introduced the Learning With Errors (LWE) problem. Although the work of [26] presented a reduction

© ICST Institute for Computer Sciences, Social Informatics and Telecommunications Engineering 2021
Published by Springer Nature Switzerland AG 2021. All Rights Reserved
J. Garcia-Alfaro et al. (Eds.): SecureComm 2021, LNICST 399, pp. 407–423, 2021.
https://doi.org/10.1007/978-3-030-90022-9_22

from LWE to the shortest vectors problem on lattice, yet the reduction involves quantum algorithms. The later works [12,22] improved the reduction and consider the LWE problems over rings (RLWE) [21,24]. Let $R := \mathbb{Z}[x]/(x^n + 1)$ for some n of power of 2, and R_q be the quotient ring R/qR, then given the pair $(a, b) \in R_q \times R_q$ where a is uniform over R_q, the RLWE problem asks to distinguish if the ring element b is from a uniform distribution over R_q or $b = a \cdot s + e$ for some $s \in R_q$ and e sampled from some distribution over R_q. There are many constructions of public key encryption schemes based on the LWE problem or the RLWE problem [3,6,11,17,19,23,28].

The work of [9] considered a deterministic variant of LWE problem, called Learning With Rounding (LWR), in which the error term e is fixed by the ring elements a and s, namely $e := a \cdot s - \frac{q}{p}\lceil\frac{p}{q}a \cdot s\rfloor$[1]. One obvious intuitive advantage of LWR over LWE is that there is no need to sample the error term. The work [9] showed that if the ring modulus q is exponentially larger than the rounding modulus p, then the LWR problem can be reduced to the underlying LWE problem, and thus reduced to the hard problems on lattices. However the reduction remains valid for polynomially sized modulus q if there is a restriction on the number of LWR samples [4,5,10,20].

Contributions. Intuitively, the current RLWR based public key encryption schemes [7,17] use two-fold rounding operation in the encryption procedure. In other words, the public keys of [7,17] are generated by proceeding a rounding operation from R_q to R_p. Then the encryption algorithm proceeds a further rounding operation to the public keys (say from R_p to R_t) to disguise the message. From the hardness assumption of LWR problems, the outputs from the rounding operation should be uniformly distributed over the corresponding rings (R_p or R_t). Yet the security proof is more involved [17] or obscure [7]. Another disadvantage is that the modulus q could be much larger if the modulus t (corresponding to the second rounding) is not small, and this heavily affects the efficiency of the scheme.

In this work, we construct a public key encryption scheme based on the RLWR problem. The main design motivation of the scheme is that our scheme shares more simple security proof. As mentioned above, previous public key encryption schemes based on LWR problems use two-fold rounding. Yet in this paper, we overcome this by introducing an intermediate problem called LWR with auxiliary error. This intermediate problem is different from the RLWE problem, yet it is at least as hard as RLWE problem. We show that one rounding operation (R_q to R_p) is sufficient for the security proof of our construction, and the security proof is really simple. We also provide the IND-CCA secure key encapsulation and reference implementation of our scheme. We use the latest techniques [13] to accelerate the polynomial multiplications. The performance shows that our scheme has some advantages over the 3rd round NIST postquantum cryptography standardization candidates.

---

[1] For a real $x \in \mathbb{R}$, $\lceil x \rfloor$ denotes the nearest integer to x. q and p are ring modulus such that $p < q$, mostly we require $p|q$.

Organization. In Sect. 2, we introduce preliminaries; we present our IND-CPA public key encryption scheme in Sect. 3, and provide asymptotic correctness as well as the security proof of our IND-CPA scheme. In Sect. 4, we present an IND-CCA secure key encapsulation scheme, and provide correctness and security results in the classic random oracle model and quantum oracle model, respectively. We present parameterizations and performances of our scheme in the last section.

2 Preliminaries

Notations. Let $\mathbb{R}$ be the set of real numbers, $\mathbb{Z}$ be the set of integers. For a real number $x \in \mathbb{R}$, use $\lfloor x \rfloor$ to denote the largest integer that $\leq x$, use $\lceil x \rceil$ to denote the integer $\lfloor x + 1/2 \rfloor$, and use $\lceil x \rceil$ to denote the smallest integer that $\geq x$. We use upper-case bold letters to denote matrices (e.g., $\vec{A}$). For a probability distribution χ, we use $x \leftarrow \chi$ to denote that x is sampled from distribution χ. For a set S, we use $x \xleftarrow{\$} S$ to denote that x is sampled from uniform distribution over the set S. For a polynomial ring R, we use $\|a\|_p$ to denote the p-norm of corresponding coefficient vector of $a \in R$, we omit the subscript p if $p = 2$. The function $\mathsf{negl}(\cdot)$ denotes the negligible function, that is $\mathsf{negl}(\lambda) < \frac{1}{\lambda^c}$ for the parameter λ and any constant c. We say an event happens overwhelmingly if the probability that the event not happens is negligible.

2.1 Cryptographic Definitions

Here we recall some definitions of public key encryption scheme that we will use in the following sections.

Public Key Encryption.

Definition 2.1. *A public key encryption scheme Π_{PKE} consist of algorithms* $(\mathsf{KeyGen}, \mathsf{Enc}, \mathsf{Dec})$ *as follows:*

$\mathsf{KeyGen}(1^\lambda) \rightarrow (\mathsf{pk}, \mathsf{sk})$: *On input the security parameter, it outputs the public key pk and secret key sk.*

$\mathsf{Enc}(m, \mathsf{pk}) \rightarrow \mathsf{ct}$: *On input the public key pk and the message m, it outputs the ciphertext ct corresponding to the message m.*

$\mathsf{Dec}(\mathsf{sk}, \mathsf{ct}) \rightarrow m$: *On input the secret key sk and ciphertext ct, it outputs the decrypting message m corresponding to the ciphertext ct.*

Correctness. For a PKE scheme Π_{PKE}, we say it is δ−correct if the following holds for the parameter $\delta \geq 0$:

$$\mathbf{E}\left[\max_{m \in \mathcal{M}} \Pr\left[m' \neq m \,\middle|\, \begin{array}{l} \mathsf{ct} \leftarrow \mathsf{Enc}(\mathsf{pk}, m); \\ m' \leftarrow \mathsf{Dec}(\mathsf{sk}, \mathsf{ct}) \end{array}\right]\right] \leq \delta,$$

where $\mathcal{M}$ is the message space, and the expectation is taken over the $(\mathsf{pk}, \mathsf{sk}) \leftarrow \mathsf{KeyGen}(1^\lambda)$.

Security. For any PPT adversary $\mathcal{A}$, the advantage of $\mathcal{A}$ against a PKE scheme in the indistinguishability under chosen-plaintext attacks (IND-CPA) security game, denoted $\mathsf{Adv}_{\mathsf{PKE}}^{\mathsf{IND\text{-}CPA}}(\mathcal{A})$, is defined as

$$\Pr\left[b' = b \,\middle|\, \begin{array}{l} (\mathsf{pk}, \mathsf{sk}) \leftarrow \mathsf{KeyGen}(1^\lambda); \\ (m_0, m_1) \leftarrow \mathcal{A}(pk); \\ b \leftarrow \{0,1\}; c^* = \mathsf{Enc}(\mathsf{pk}, m_b); \\ b' \leftarrow \mathcal{A}(c^*, pk) \end{array}\right] < \mathsf{negl}(\lambda).$$

Since the adversary can encrypt any message by itself using the public key, the IND-CPA security is a passive security notion that the adversary doesn't interact with the party who owns the secret key. A natural security model extension is the indistinguishability under chosen-ciphertext attacks (IND-CCA) security, in which the adversary is allowed to query the decryption algorithm except on the challenge ciphertext c^*. Note that there are many works on transforming a IND-CPA secure PKE to IND-CCA secure one by using classic random oracles [15] or quantum accessible oracles [16,18].

2.2   Lattices and Distributions

Lattices. An n-dimensional lattice is a discrete subgroup in the space $\mathbb{R}^n$. For a matrix $\vec{B} = [b_1, \cdots, b_n]$ of column vectors are linearly independent, a lattice generated by the matrix $\vec{B}$ is the integer combinations of the column vectors of $\vec{B}$.

Gaussians. For a real $s > 0$, we define the n-dimensional gaussian function with parameter s as $\rho_s(x) := \exp(-\pi \frac{\|\vec{x}\|^2}{s^2})$. For any n-dimensional vector $\vec{c}$, define the shifted gaussian by $\rho_{s,\vec{c}} := \exp(-\pi \frac{\|\vec{x}-\vec{c}\|^2}{s^2})$. The distribution function of the spherical continuous gaussian D_s over $\mathbb{R}^n$ is proportional to ρ_s. For $\delta > 0$, we call a random variable X over $\mathbb{R}$ is δ-subgaussian with parameter $s > 0$, if for all $t \in \mathbb{R}$, the (scaled) moment-generating function satisfies: $E[e^{2\pi t X}] \leq e^\delta \cdot e^{\pi s^2 t^2}$. B-bounded symmetric random variable X(i.e., $|X| \leq B$) is 0-subgaussian with parameter $B\sqrt{2\pi}$, and thus the centered binomial distribution is also subgaussian. Therefore in this paper we focus on binomial distribution as it is close to small gaussian distributions [8].

Rings. Let the ring $R := \mathbb{Z}[x]/\Phi(x)$ for some cyclotomic polynomial $\Phi(x)$, and let R_q be the quotient ring R/qR for some modulus q, we say a is sampled from R (or R_q) by binomial distribution with parameter η, we mean by that the corresponding coefficient vector of a is sampled from the n-dimensional binomial distribution over integers, simply write $a \leftarrow \mathsf{Bin}_\eta$. In this paper, we set $\Phi(x) := (x^n + 1)$ for some n of a power of 2. For a set $S \in \mathbb{Z}$, we use R_S to denote the set of ring elements such that each coefficients are in the set S, and we let $x \leftarrow \mathcal{U}(S)$ to denote the uniform distribution over the set of ring elements R_S. We use $\|a\|_p$ to denote the p-norm of the coefficient vector the ring element $a \in R$. Similarly, $\|a\|_\infty$ denotes the largest coefficient of the ring element a.

2.3 LWR Problem

Here in this section, we recall the ring version of the RLWR problem. Let $\lceil * \rfloor_{q \to p}$ be the rounding function that for an integer $x \in \mathbb{Z}$ $\lceil x \rfloor_{q \to p} = \lceil \frac{q}{p} x \rfloor$, and it applies over the ring elements coefficient-wise. We recall the RLWE distribution over the ring R_q as follow.

Definition 2.2. *The R-LWR$_{n,p,q,\chi}$ distribution is the distribution of the pair $(a, b) \in R_q \times R_p$, where a is uniform over R_q and $b = \lceil a \cdot s \rfloor_{q \to p}$ for some $s \leftarrow \chi$.*

We recall the R-LWR$_{n,p,q,\chi}$ problem as follows.

Definition 2.3. *Given a pair $(a, b) \in R_q \times R_p$ for the random $a \leftarrow R_q$, the R-LWR$_{n,p,q,\chi}$ problem asks to distinguish if the pair is from the R-LWR$_{n,p,q,\chi}$ distribution or the uniform distribution over $R_q \times R_p$.*

The LWR (RLWR) problem was introduced in [9]. However, the work of [9] showed the hardness of RLWR problem for the sub-exponential modulus q. Note that the work of [9] considered the statistical property in the reduction, thus the hardness of LWR is regardless of the number of the LWR samples. Later works [4,5,10,20] showed that polynomial modulus is enough to show the hardness of LWR problem if we consider the polynomial number of samples. Note that polynomial number of LWR samples are sufficient for the encryption schemes and other cryptographic protocols, thus a polynomially modulus is sufficient for this work.

3 The Basic Encryption Scheme

In this section, we present detailed description of our basic encryption scheme. In addition, we further provide the asymptotic correctness and the IND-CPA security of the scheme.

3.1 The Scheme Description

The description of our encryption scheme is shown as in the Algorithm 1, 2, and 3. The set param contains all the scheme related parameters such as dimension of the ring, modulus p, q, message space, security parameter λ, and others. On input a λ-bit length seed, the deterministic algorithm $\mathsf{Gen}_a(\cdot)$ outputs a random ring element $a \in R_q$. On input a random seed, the algorithm Bin_η outputs a ring element whose each coefficients are sampled from binomial distribution of parameter η. On input an integer $x \in \mathbb{Z}_q$, the rounding function $\lceil x \rfloor_{q \to p}$ is defined as $\lceil x \rfloor_{q \to p} := \lceil \frac{p}{q} x \rfloor \mod p$. If the input is a ring element, the rounding function applies coefficient-wise. Note that we want the modulus p and q satisfies $2p|q$, thus the quantity $\frac{q}{2p}$ is an integer.

Algorithm 1: IND-CPA.KeyGen(param)

1: $(seeds) \xleftarrow{\$} \{0,1\}^\lambda$
2: $a \leftarrow R_q$
3: $s \leftarrow \text{Bin}_\eta(seeds)$
4: $b := \lceil a \cdot s \rfloor_{q \to p}$
5: **Return:** pk $:= (a,b)$, sk $:= s$

Algorithm 2: IND-CPA.Enc(pk $= (a,b), \mu \in R_2$)

1: $seedr \xleftarrow{\$} \{0,1\}^\lambda$
2: $r \leftarrow \text{Bin}_\eta(seedr)$
3: $u \xleftarrow{\$} \mathcal{U}\left(\left[\frac{-q}{2p}, \frac{q}{2p}\right) \cap \mathbb{Z}\right)$
4: $c_0 := \lceil a \cdot r \rfloor_{q \to p}$
5: $c_1' := \frac{q}{p} b + (u \mod q/p) \mod q.$
6: $c_1 := \lceil c_1' \cdot r \rfloor_{q \to p} + \lceil \frac{p}{2} \rceil \mu$
7: **Return:** ct $:= (c_0, c_1)$

Algorithm 3: IND-CPA.Dec(ct $= (c_0, c_1)$, sk $= s$)

1: $\mu' := c_1 - c_0 \cdot s$
2: $\mu'' := \lceil \mu' \rfloor_{p \to 2}$
3: **Return:** μ''

For simplicity we didn't explicit the param in the input of the encryption and the decryption algorithms, yet they implicitly contain it.

Remark 3.1. *Note that the message space in the encryption algorithm is R_2, However it can be enlarged to R_t for some small t by the cost of increasing the decryption failure probability. Compressing the ciphertexts also applicable to above encryption scheme, however it increases the failure probability as well.*

3.2 Correctness and Security

Correctness. The correctness of above scheme described in the Algorithm 1 to Algorithm 3 is given by the following theorem. In Sect. 5, we will show the correctness of the scheme in the concrete parameter settings.

Theorem 3.2. *Let the rounding modulus $p \geq 10$ Let s, r, u be the random variables as in the Algorithm 1 and Algorithm 2, u is uniform over $R_{[\frac{-q}{2p}, \frac{q}{2p})}$, and $err_b \leftarrow \chi_s$, $err_{c_0} \leftarrow \chi_r$, $err_{c_1} \leftarrow \chi_{s,r,u}$, where the distributions are defined below. Let δ be the probability that*

$$\delta := \Pr[\|(err_b + u) \cdot r + err_{c_1} - err_{c_0} \cdot s\|_\infty \geq \frac{q}{5}], \tag{1}$$

then the scheme described in the Algorithm 1 to Algorithm 3 is $(1 - \delta)$-correct. For a random ring element $a \in R_q$, the distribution χ_x indexed by $x \in R$ is the distribution of $\left(a \cdot x - \frac{q}{p}\lceil a \cdot x \rfloor_{q \to p}\right)$, and $\chi_{x,y,z}$ indexed by $x, y \in R$ is the distribution of $\left((\frac{q}{p}\lceil a \cdot x \rfloor_{q \to p} + z)y - \frac{q}{p}\lceil(\frac{q}{p}\lceil a \cdot x \rfloor_{q \to p} + z)y\rfloor\right)$.

Proof. From the description of the Algorithm 3, it's not hard to see that the scheme is $(1-\delta)$-correct if $\Pr[\||\mu'' - \mu\||_\infty > 0] \leq \delta$. Thus showing $\Pr[\||\mu'' - \mu\||_\infty \leq 0] \leq 1 - \delta$ is sufficient to the theorem.

The description of Algorithm 1 and Algorithm 2 tell that:

$$\frac{q}{p}b = a \cdot s + err_b, \quad c_0 = \frac{p}{q}(a \cdot r + err_{c_0}), \quad c_1 = \frac{p}{q}(c_1' \cdot r + err_{c_1}) + \lceil\frac{p}{2}\rceil\mu,$$

for some $err_b, err_{c_0}, err_{c_1} \in R_q$, and are distributed accordingly to the distribution χ_s, χ_r and $\chi_{s,r}$ as the theorem assumption. From the decryption procedure, we have following

$$\mu' \quad = \frac{p}{q}\left(c_1' \cdot r + err_{c_1}\right) + \lceil\frac{p}{2}\rceil\mu - \frac{p}{q}(a \cdot r + err_{c_0}) \cdot s \tag{2}$$

$$= \frac{p}{q}\left((\frac{q}{p}b + u) \cdot r + err_{c_1}\right) - \frac{p}{q}(a \cdot r \cdot s + err_{c_0} \cdot s) + \lceil\frac{p}{2}\rceil\mu \tag{3}$$

$$= \frac{p}{q}\left((err_b + u) \cdot r + err_{c_1} - err_{c_0} \cdot s\right) + \lceil\frac{p}{2}\rceil\mu, \tag{4}$$

where the first equality is by the decryption algorithm that $\mu' = c_1 - c_0 \cdot s$; the second equality is by the definition of $c' = \frac{q}{p}b + u$ in Algorithm 2; the last equality is by $\frac{q}{p}b = a \cdot s + err_b$ and rearranging them. We further have that

$$\mu'' = \lceil\mu'\rfloor_{p \to 2} = \lceil\frac{2}{q}\left((err_b + u) \cdot r + err_{c_1} - err_{c_0} \cdot s\right) + \frac{2}{p}\lceil\frac{p}{2}\rceil\mu\rfloor. \tag{5}$$

Since $\||(err_b + u) \cdot r + err_{c_1} - err_{c_0} \cdot s\||_\infty \geq \frac{q}{5}$ holds with probability δ and $p \geq 10$, hence $\||\mu'' - \mu\||_\infty \leq \lceil\frac{2}{5} + \frac{1}{p}\rfloor = 0$ holds with probability $1 - \delta$. This completes the proof. $\qquad\square$

Security. The security of the encryption scheme given in Algorithm 1 to Algorithm 3 can be reduced to the hardness of RLWR problem. To show the security of the scheme, we introduce an intermediate problem RLWR with auxiliary error (RLWE-AE) problem. The definition of RLWE-AE problem is as follow.

Definition 3.3. *For integers p, q such that $2p|q$ and a distribution Bin over R_q, the R-LWR-AE$_{n,p,q,\chi}$ problem gives as challenge $(a, b) \in R_p \times R_p$, where $a \xleftarrow{\$} R_p$, and asks to decide if $b = \lceil(\frac{q}{p}a + u) \cdot s\rfloor_{q \to p}$ for some $s \leftarrow \mathsf{Bin}$ and $u \xleftarrow{\$} \mathcal{U}([\frac{-q}{2p}, \frac{q}{2p}) \cap \mathbb{Z})$, or b is from uniform distribution over R_p.*

One obvious difference between this problem and the RLWE problem is that the errors here are uniformly distributed while the errors in the RLWE problems are from the gaussian distribution. In practice sampling a uniform element is easier than sample a gaussian element. The following lemma shows the hardness of R-LWR-AE problem. The proof of above lemma given in the Appendix A.1

Lemma 3.4. *Let p, q be the integers such that $2p|q$, and χ be some distribution, then the RLWR with auxiliary error problem R-LWR-AE$_{n,p,q,\chi}$ is no easier than the RLWR problem R-LWR$_{n,p,q,\chi}$.*

The security of our encryption scheme, described in the Algorithm 1, 2 and 3, is given by the following theorem.

Theorem 3.5. *The encryption scheme given in the Algorithm 1, 2 and 3 is IND-CPA secure if the underlying R-LWR$_{2n,p,q,\text{Bin}_\beta}$ problem is hard.*

Proof. We show the theorem by showing that if the underlying LWR problem is hard, then the ciphertexts (c_0, c_1) are computationally indistinguishable from the uniform elements in $R_p \times R_p$ regardless of the message encrypted, and thus the IND-CPA security is follows. To show this, we introduce following hybrid games.

Game$_1$	Game$_2$	Game$_3$
1: $seeds, seedr \xleftarrow{\$} \{0,1\}^{256}$	1: $seeds, seedr \xleftarrow{\$} \{0,1\}^{256}$	1: $seeds, seedr \xleftarrow{\$} \{0,1\}^{256}$
2: $a \xleftarrow{\$} R_q$	2: $a \xleftarrow{\$} R_q$	2: $a \xleftarrow{\$} R_q$
3: $s \leftarrow \text{Bin}_\eta(seeds)$	3: $s \leftarrow \text{Bin}_\eta(seeds)$	3: $s \leftarrow \text{Bin}_\eta(seeds)$
4: $b = \lceil a \cdot s \rfloor_{q \to p}$	4: $\boxed{b \xleftarrow{\$} R_p}$	4: $b \xleftarrow{\$} R_p$
5: $r \leftarrow \text{Bin}_\eta(seedr)$	5: $r \leftarrow \text{Bin}_\eta(seedr)$	5: $r \leftarrow \text{Bin}_\eta(seedr)$
6: $c_0 = \lceil a \cdot r \rfloor_{q \to p}$	6: $c_0 = \lceil a \cdot r \rfloor_{q \to p}$	6: $\boxed{c_0 \xleftarrow{\$} R_p}$
7: $u \leftarrow \mathcal{U}\left[\frac{-q}{2p}, \frac{q}{2p}\right]$	7: $u \leftarrow \mathcal{U}\left[\frac{-q}{2p}, \frac{q}{2p}\right]$	7: $u \leftarrow \mathcal{U}\left[\frac{-q}{2p}, \frac{q}{2p}\right]$
8: $c_1' := \frac{q}{p}b + (u \bmod \frac{q}{p})$	8: $c_1' := \frac{q}{p}b + (u \bmod \frac{q}{p})$	8: $c_1' := \frac{q}{p}b + (u \bmod \frac{q}{p})$
9: $c_1 := \lceil c_1' \cdot r \rfloor_{q \to p} + \lceil \frac{p}{2} \rceil \mu$	9: $c_1 := \lceil c_1' \cdot r \rfloor_{q \to p} + \lceil \frac{p}{2} \rceil \mu$	9: $\boxed{c_1 \xleftarrow{\$} R_p}$
10: $\beta \leftarrow \{0,1\}$	10: $\beta \leftarrow \{0,1\}$	10: $\beta \leftarrow \{0,1\}$
11: **if** $\beta = 1$ **then**	11: **if** $\beta = 1$ **then**	11: **if** $\beta = 1$ **then**
12: return (a, b, c_0, c_1)	12: return (a, b, c_0, c_1)	12: return (a, b, c_0, c_1)
13: **else** $\beta = 0$	13: **else** $\beta = 0$	13: **else** $\beta = 0$
14: return $(a, b, \mathcal{U}(R_p \times R_p))$	14: return $(a, b, \mathcal{U}(R_p \times R_p))$	14: return $(a, b, \mathcal{U}(R_p \times R_p))$

Note that the Game$_1$ is subtle different from the original IND-CPA game that here in Game$_1$, the adversary $\mathcal{A}$ is given the public keys (a, b) and the challenge pair (c_0, c_1), and $\mathcal{A}$'s goal is to guess the random number β. We call $\mathcal{A}$ wins in Game$_i$ if it correctly guesses the random bit β. The IND-CPA security of the scheme is obvious if $\mathcal{A}$'s advantage in Game$_1$ is negligible. Let $\text{Adv}_\mathcal{A}^{\text{Game}_i}$ to denote the advantage of $\mathcal{A}$ in the Game$_i$ for $i \in \{1, 2, 3\}$, namely $\text{Adv}_\mathcal{A}^{\text{Game}_i} = |\Pr[\mathcal{A} \text{ win Game}_i] - \frac{1}{2}|$. We also use Game$_i \stackrel{c}{\approx}$ Game$_j$ to denote the indistinguishability of two games. To show the theorem, we have following lemmas and proofs are defer to Appendix A.3 and Appendix A.2.

Lemma 3.6. *If the R-LWR$_{n,p,q,\text{Bin}_\beta}$ problem is hard, then Game$_1 \stackrel{c}{\approx}$ Game$_2$.*

Lemma 3.7. *If the R-LWR$_{2n,p,q,\text{Bin}_\beta}$ problem is hard, then Game$_2 \stackrel{c}{\approx}$ Game$_3$.*

Above two lemmas show that

$$\text{Adv}_\mathcal{A}^{\text{Game}_1} \leq \text{Adv}_\mathcal{A}^{\text{Game}_2} + \text{negl}(n) \leq \text{Adv}_\mathcal{A}^{\text{Game}_3} + \text{negl}(n) \leq \text{negl}(n),$$

where the first and second inequalities are from Lemma 3.6 and Lemma 3.7; the last inequality is from the fact that $\mathsf{Adv}_{\mathcal{A}}^{\mathsf{Game}_3} = 0$, this is because the 4-tuples (a, b, c_0, c_2) are uniform over $R_q \times R_p^3$ and independent of the random bit β. This completes the proof. □

4   The CCA Secure Scheme

In this section, we present our IND-CCA secure KEM construction, and we show its correctness and security results.

Scheme Description. Let $G : \{0, 1\}^* \to \{0, 1\}^{256 \times 2}$ and $H : \{0, 1\}^* \to \{0, 1\}^{256}$ be the two hash functions, our KEM construction consists of 3 algorithms (KeyGen, Encaps, Decaps) presented in the following Algorithm 4, 5 and 6. The key generation algorithm is the same as the Algorithm 1 except that here the secret key contains an extra 256 bit random string. The encapsulation and decapsulation algorithms are obtained by using a KEM variant of F-O transform [15,16] to our basic IND-CPA scheme given in the previous section.

Algorithm 4: IND-CCA.KeyGen(1^λ)

1: $(seeds, z) \xleftarrow{\$} \{0, 1\}^{256}$
2: $a \xleftarrow{\$} R_q$
3: $s \leftarrow \mathsf{Bin}_\eta(seeds)$
4: $b := \lceil a \cdot s \rfloor_{q \to p}$
5: **Return:** $\mathsf{pk} := (a, b), \mathsf{sk} := (s, z)$

Algorithm 5: IND-CCA.Encaps ($\mathsf{pk} = (a, b),$)

1: $\mu \xleftarrow{\$} \{0, 1\}^{256}$
2: $(\hat{K}, rand) := G(\mathsf{pk}|\mu)$
3: $(c_0, c_1) := \mathsf{IND\text{-}CPA.Enc}(\mathsf{pk}, \mathsf{Encode}(\mu); rand)$
4: $\mathsf{ct} := (c_0, c_1)$
5: $K := H(\hat{K}|\mathsf{ct})$
6: **Return:** (ct, K)

Algorithm 6: IND-CCA.Decaps ($\mathsf{ct} = (c_0, c_1), \mathsf{pk} = (a, b), \mathsf{sk} = (s, z)$)

1: $\mu' := \mathsf{Decode}(\mathsf{IND\text{-}CPA.Dec}(\mathsf{ct}, s))$
2: $(\hat{K}', rand') := G(\mathsf{pk}|\mu')$
3: $(c_0', c_1') := \mathsf{IND\text{-}CPA.Enc}(\mathsf{pk}, \mathsf{Encode}(\mu'); rand')$
4: $\mathsf{ct}' := (c_0', c_1')$
5: **if** $\mathsf{ct} = \mathsf{ct}'$ **then**
6:     **Return:** $K := H(\hat{K}'|\mathsf{ct})$
7: **else**
8:     **Return:** $K := H(z|\mathsf{ct})$

Correctness. Note that the randomness in the encryption procedure in Algorithm 5 is determined by the message to be encrypted, and thus the decryption failure probability is affected by the number of queries, denoted q_G, to the RO G. If the underlying IND-CPA encryption scheme is δ-correct, then the resulting scheme in the Algorithm 4, 5, and 6 is $q_G\delta$-correct [16].

Security. Note that using the variant of F-O transform [16], the final scheme can be proven IND-CCA secure in the random oracle model. The IND-CCA security of the encryption scheme described in the Algorithm 4, 5, and 6 is given by the following results.

Theorem 4.1 (ROM, [16]). *If the encryption scheme* PKE *described in the Algorithm 1, 2, and 3 is δ-correct, for any* IND-CCA *adversary $\mathcal{A}$ against the encryption scheme given in Algorithm 4, 5, and 6, and let q_G, q_H be the number of (might be quantum) queries made by $\mathcal{A}$ to the random oracles G and H, then there is an adversary $\mathcal{B}$ against the* PKE *such that*

$$\mathsf{Adv}_{\mathcal{A}}^{\mathsf{IND\text{-}CCA}} \leq \frac{2q_G + q_H + 1}{\sqrt{|\mathcal{M}|}} q_G \sqrt{\delta} + 3\mathsf{Adv}_{\mathsf{PKE}}^{\mathsf{IND\text{-}CPA}}(\mathcal{B}), \tag{6}$$

where $\mathcal{M}$ is the message space.

Note that the above theorem is illustrates the IND-CCA security of the scheme assuming the adversary enables to query the RO's as much as it's desire. Yet the RO's are publicly available, consider the case where the adversaries may capable of quantum computers, we want the encryption scheme provides security in this scenario. Fortunately, the scheme in the Algorithm 4, 5, and 6 is designed by applying the paradigm of variants of F-O transform [15,16,18], and thus provide the IND-CCA security in the presence of quantum accessible ROs. The following theorem and the corollary describe this kind of security.

Theorem 4.2 (QROM, [18]). *If the encryption scheme* PKE *described in the Algorithm 1, 2, and 3 is δ-correct, for any* IND-CCA *adversary $\mathcal{A}$ against the encryption scheme given in Algorithm 4, 5, and 6, able to query the random oracles with quantum states, let q_G, q_H be the number of (might be quantum) queries made by $\mathcal{A}$ to the random oracles G and H, then there is an adversary $\mathcal{B}$ against the* PKE *such that*

$$\mathsf{Adv}_{\mathcal{A}}^{\mathsf{IND\text{-}CCA}} \leq 2q_H \frac{1}{\sqrt{|\mathcal{M}|}} + 4q_G \sqrt{\delta} + 2(q_G + q_H)\sqrt{\mathsf{Adv}_{\mathsf{PKE}}^{\mathsf{IND\text{-}CPA}}(\mathcal{B})}, \tag{7}$$

where $\mathcal{M}$ is the message space.

Note that the message space of our scheme is exponentially in security parameter and the basic encryption scheme described in the Algorithm 1, 2, and 3 is IND-CPA secure by Theorem 3.5, then the first and third term in the right hand side of the above inequation is negligible. Thus the encryption scheme described in Algorithm 4, 5, and 6 is IND-CCA secure if the encryption scheme PKE described in the Algorithm 1, 2, and 3 is overwhelmingly correct.

5 Parameter Settings and Implementation

In this section, we provide concrete parameters for our encryption scheme and performance of C reference implementation.

5.1 Parameter Settings

To instantiate the encryption scheme, we select the concrete parameters such that the resulted scheme has low decryption failure and provides desired bit security. However, setting the parameters according to the theoretical results definitely affects the performance of the scheme. Thus in practice we pay more attention to the concrete security of the scheme.

Decryption Failure. The asymptotic correctness result for the scheme is presented in the Theorem 3.2, yet in practice we need more precise estimation of the failure probability as the encryption scheme is instantiated with concrete parameters. For our encryption scheme in the concrete parameters, we first compute the distribution function of each error terms involved in the Theorem 3.2. Intuitively, the larger the error terms the harder to solve the corresponding LWR problem. However, increasing the errors result in increasing the decryption failure probability. Note that each coefficient of the error polynomial is discrete and upper bounded by small positive, thus we can compute the probability distribution of each coefficients of error terms. then we compute the overall distribution of the final error. Note that this procedure is independent of the running time of the scheme, and thus any tools can be used to compute this failure probability. Here we use a python script similar as [6,17] to estimate the failure probability of our encryption scheme in the concrete settings, and results are shown in Table 1.

Concrete Security. As we showed in the previous sections, our scheme is based on the ring LWR problem. However the best way to solve RLWR problem now is to treat it as a LWE problem with deterministic errors, and further estimate the security of corresponding LWE problem with same dimension and modulus. There are two types of attacks to estimate the concrete security of LWE based crypto-systems: primal attack and dual attack [25]. Apply this two types of attacks to estimate the concrete bit security of a crypto-system is the main stream in the lattice based literatures [6,17,25]. Recently, Dachman-Soled et al. [14] formalized the primal attack and found a novel improvement to attack a few NIST second round post-quantum cryptography standardization candidate schemes [7,29]. Thus we use both the folklore estimation method and the recent method to estimate the concrete bit security of our scheme. The bit security of our scheme in the concrete parameter settings is shown in the Table 1.

Parameterization. As we showed in the security proof of our scheme, we need the ring modulus q and rounding modulus p to satisfy $2p|q$. Thus we set the ring modulus q be a multiple of $2p$, e.g., $q = 2^k \cdot p$ for some integer $k \in \mathbb{Z}^+$. Here we choose them a power of 2, yet any other settings are possible. Concrete parameterization of our scheme is shown in the following Table 1, where the

$\log(q)$ or $\log(p)$ mean that logarithmic function of the modulus q or p. The η denotes the binomial parameter. If the classic computer used to solve the corresponding SVP problem respect to the LWR problem, we call it the classic security of the LWR problem (as showed in the Table 1), otherwise the quantum algorithms are used, then we call it the quantum security of the LWR problem as we split the security column into two sub-columns). The space complexity of the public keys and ciphertexts are computed in bytes (B). As shown in the Table 1, the Scheme1 reaches 128-bit classic security, and the Scheme2 reaches 256-bit classic security.

Table 1. Parameter settings of our schemes.

	n	$\log(q)$	$\log(p)$	η	Failure	Security	
						Classical	Quantum
Scheme1	512	11	8	2	2^{-115}	134	121
Scheme2	1024	13	10	4	2^{-128}	274	250

The following Table 2 shows the space complexity of our Schemes and NIST PQC standardization 3-rd round lattice based PKE finalist schemes. We compare them in 128-bit security settings and 256-bit security settings.

Table 2. Space complexity comparison with NIST PQC standardization lattice based PKE finalists.

	pk(B)	sk(B)	ct(B)	Failure	Classic
Scheme1	608	768	1024	2^{-115}	134
LightSaber [17]	672	832	736	2^{-120}	118
Kyber512 [6]	800	1632	768	2^{-139}	118
ntruhps2048509 [29]	699	903	699	$2^{-214.3}$	118
Scheme2	1312	1888	2560	2^{-128}	274
FireSaber [6]	1312	1760	1472	2^{-168}	260
Kyber1024 [6]	1184	2400	1084	2^{-174}	256
ntruhrss701 [29]	1138	1418	1138	$2^{-213.9}$	118
ntruhps4096821 [29]	1230	1588	1230	2^{-769}	118

5.2   Implementation

Sampling. Our encryption scheme need two type of sampling: sampling from binomial distribution with small parameter, and sampling from uniform distribution over a small centered symmetric range. The binomial sampling procedure can be accomplished by sampling uniform bit strings. Namely, a sample from binomial distribution Bin_η is sampled as follow: first sample a bit string $(str1_i, str2_i)_{i=1}^\eta \in \{0,1\}^\eta$, then output $\sum_{i\in[\eta]}(str1_i - str2_i)$. Since the modulus q and p are power of 2, the uniform sample procedure in the Algorithm 2 is by simply sample a $\log(\frac{q}{p})$ bit string, then subtract $\frac{q}{2p}$ form the integer representation of the bit string and output the result. Thus the whole sampling procedure is as quick as generating random strings. To sample a random ring element $a \in R_q$, we first feed *Output eXtendable Function* (OXF) a random seed to obtain large random bits, and then generate the random element a with these bits. Note that this method reduces randomness of a to the security of OXF, yet the public key size of our scheme is improved significantly.

Rounding. Since the scheme modulus q and p are set to be the power of 2, thus the rounding procedure as simple as bit shift operation.

Multiplication. As the settings of the modulus p and q be some power of 2 ease the sampling and rounding procedure, yet the multiplication operation is important as the those operation, and might even have more impact on the performance of the scheme. However, as our parameter settings, the polynomial multiplication can't be accelerated by the NTT. Yet we use Karatsuba algorithm to implement the polynomial multiplication, and the Table 3 shows the performance of our schemes.

Performance. All the cycle counts in Table 3 were obtained on Macbook pro equipped with Quad-Core Intel(R) Core(TM) i5-8257U CPU@3.9 Ghz (turbo boost on) processor. We use g++11 with optimization falgs *-march=native -O3 -fomit-frame-pointer -fwrapv -Qunused-arguments*. For the random oracles we use SHA3 functions (implemented in fips202). The performance is shown in the following Table 3.

Table 3. Performance comparison with NIST PQC standardization lattice based PKE finalists (in cycles).

	KeyGen	Enc	Dec
LightSaber [17]	39561	40154	32064
Kyber512 [6]	54189	57557	61409
ntruhps2048509 [29]	5695661	397765	576719
Scheme1	27741	54586	64617
FireSaber [6]	81327	84558	85517
Kyber512 [6]	123693	125461	137841
ntruhps4096821 [29]	15263307	770705	1434187
Scheme2	87092	180290	253419

The above table shows that the performance of our scheme is comparable with LightSaber and Kyber512. Note that the recent work of [13] showed that the Saber encapsulation can be improved about 22%, thus our schemes also can be improved significantly by using the same techniques from [13]. We only provide reference C implementation, thus further optimizations are possible. Furthermore, we didn't consider the ciphertext compression, and thus a carefully designed integration of ciphertext compression with efficient implementation will result in more efficient scheme than ours. Note that the plain LWR version of our encryption scheme is similar to ours, thus we only consider the ring LWR version here.

Acknowledgement. Mingsheng Wang is supported by the Shandong Provincial Key Research and Development Program under Grant Number 2019JZZY020127.

A   Appendix

A.1   Proof of Lemma 3.4

Proof. We show the lemma by contradiction. Namely, we show that if there is an algorithm $\mathcal{A}$ that can solve the problem $R\text{-LWR-AE}_{n,p,q,\chi}$, then we can construct a simulator Sim which solves the RLWR challenge with the same advantage. Our construction of Sim is as follows:

Sim(a, b)
    On input the pair $(a, b) \in R_q \times R_p$ of RLWR challenge, it gives the pair $(\lceil a \rfloor_{q \to p}, b)$ to the algorithm $\mathcal{A}$. If $\mathcal{A}$ outputs 1 (mean that the input pair $(\lceil a \rfloor_{q \to p}, b)$ is from the $R\text{-LWR-AE}_{n,p,q,\chi}$ distribution), then Sim also outputs 1 to mean that (a, b) is from the $R\text{-LWR}_{n,p,q,\chi}$ distribution. Otherwise, if the $\mathcal{A}$ outputs 0 (mean that the input pair is from a uniform distribution over $R_p \times R_p$), then Sim also outputs 0 to mean that the pair (a, b) is from uniform distribution over $R_q \times R_p$.

Note that showing the following two statements suffices for the lemma: (1) if the input pair (a, b) is from uniform distribution over $R_q \times R_p$, then from $\mathcal{A}$'s view the pair $(\lceil a \rfloor_{q \to p}, b)$ is from the uniform distribution over $R_p \times R_p$, (2) if the input pair (a, b) is from $R\text{-LWR}_{n,p,q,\chi}$ distribution, then from $\mathcal{A}$'s view the pair $(\lceil a \rfloor_{q \to p}, b)$ is a sample from the distribution $R\text{-LWR-AE}_{n,p,q,\chi}$.

    The statement (1) is straight from the fact the $2p|q$ and the definition of the rounding function $\lceil * \rfloor_{q \to p}$, namely the rounding procedure maps a uniform element in R_q to a uniform element in R_p.

    Next we show (2), if $b = \lceil a \cdot s \rfloor_{q \to p}$ for the $a \xleftarrow{\$} R_q$ and an element $s \in R_q$, then we prove that $b = \lceil (\frac{q}{p} a' + u) \cdot s \rfloor_{q \to p}$ for a uniform $a' := \lceil a \rfloor_{q \to p}$, and a uniform ring element $u = a - \frac{q}{p} a'$ whose coefficients are in $[\frac{q}{2p}, \frac{q}{2p})$, where the uniformity is taken over the uniformity of $a \in R_q$. Note that the uniformity of a' is by a same argument as the argument of the statement (1), and it's easy to see that the coefficients of u in $[\frac{q}{2p}, \frac{q}{2p})$. Therefore, we now show uniformity of u. In other words, for any $u_0 \in [\frac{q}{2p}, \frac{q}{2p})$, we show that $\Pr_a[u = u_0] = \left(\frac{p}{q}\right)^n$, that is

$$\Pr_a[u = u_0] = \Pr_a[a = \frac{q}{p}a' + u_0]$$

$$= \sum_{a_p \in R_p} \Pr_a[a = \frac{q}{p}a' + u_0 \wedge a' = a_p]$$

$$= \sum_{a_p \in R_p} \frac{1}{q^n} = \left(\frac{p}{q}\right)^n,$$

where the second equality is by the union bound; the third equality is by the uniformity of a over R_q. This completes the proof. $\square$

A.2   Proof of Lemma 3.7

Proof. We show the lemma by two steps: (1) we show that the advantage of $\mathcal{A}$ in Game_2 is no larger than that of an intermediate game Game_3' we introduced, and (2) from the view of $\mathcal{A}$ the two games Game_3' and Game_3 is indistinguishable if the $R\text{-LWR}_{2n,p,q,\mathsf{Bin}_\beta}$ problem is hard. The difference between the Game_2 and the intermediate game Game_3' is the way they generate b and c_1 as follow

$$b \overset{\$}{\leftarrow} R_p, c_1 = \lceil (\frac{q}{p}b + u) \cdot r \rfloor_{q \to p}, \text{ and } b \overset{\$}{\leftarrow} R_q, c_1 = \lceil b \cdot r \rfloor_{q \to p}$$

Note that (1) is follows from the Lemma 3.4 that the advantage of $\mathcal{A}$ in Game_2 is no larger than that of Game_3'. Furthermore, an analogue reduction as in the proof of Lemma 3.6 shows (2). This completes the proof.

$\square$

A.3   Proof of Lemma 3.6

Proof. The Game_2 is different from the Game_1 by the way the pk generated, that b is generated by computing the rounding function $\lceil a \cdot s \rfloor_{q \to p}$ for some secret $s \in R_q$, but it is sampled uniformly over the ring R_p in the Game_2. The lemma follows if from the view of $\mathcal{A}$ the two games are indifferent. We show this by contradiction. Assume that $\mathcal{A}$ can distinguish these two games, then we construct an algorithm Sim as follows that can solve the $R\text{-LWR}_{n,p,q,\mathsf{Bin}_\beta}$.

$\mathsf{Sim}(a,b)$

On input the pair $(a,b) \in R_q \times R_p$ of $R\text{-LWR}_{n,p,q,\mathsf{Bin}_\beta}$ challenge, it simulate every step in $\mathsf{Game}_1($ or $\mathsf{Game}_2)$ for $\mathcal{A}$ except the step2 and step 4 that it uses (a,b) instead of sampling or computing them.

Note that if the pair (a,b) is from $R\text{-LWR}_{n,p,q,\mathsf{Bin}_\beta}$, then Sim exactly simulated the Game_1 for $\mathcal{A}$, if the pair (a,b) is from uniform distribution over $R_q \times R_p$, then Sim exactly simulated the Game_2 for $\mathcal{A}$. Therefore, if $\mathcal{A}$ can distinguishes the two games with noticeable probability, then Sim can solve $R\text{-LWR}_{n,p,q,\mathsf{Bin}_\beta}$ problem with same probability. This is contradicts the lemma assumption that $R\text{-LWR}_{n,p,q,\mathsf{Bin}_\beta}$ problem is hard. Thus from the view of $\mathcal{A}$ the two games are indifferent, and the lemma follows. $\square$

References

1. NIST (2020). https://csrc.nist.gov/projects/post-quantum-cryptography
2. Ajtai, M.: Generating hard instances of lattice problems (extended abstract). In: 28th ACM STOC, pp. 99–108. ACM Press (May 1996)
3. Alkim, E., Ducas, L., Pöppelmann, T., Schwabe, P.: Post-quantum key exchange - a new hope. In: Holz, T., Savage, S. (eds.) USENIX Security 2016, pp. 327–343. USENIX Association (August 2016)
4. Alperin-Sheriff, J., Apon, D.: Dimension-preserving reductions from LWE to LWR. IACR Cryptol. ePrint Arch. **2016**, 589 (2016)
5. Alwen, J., Krenn, S., Pietrzak, K., Wichs, D.: Learning with rounding, revisited. In: Canetti, R., Garay, J.A. (eds.) CRYPTO 2013. LNCS, vol. 8042, pp. 57–74. Springer, Heidelberg (2013). https://doi.org/10.1007/978-3-642-40041-4_4
6. Avanzi, R., et al.: CRYSTALS-kyber. submission to the NIST post-quantum cryptography standardization project. NIST National Institute of Standards and Technology (2020)
7. Baan, H., et al.: Round5: compact and fast post-quantum public-key encryption. In: Ding, J., Steinwandt, R. (eds.) PQCrypto 2019. LNCS, vol. 11505, pp. 83–102. Springer, Cham (2019). https://doi.org/10.1007/978-3-030-25510-7_5
8. Bai, S., Langlois, A., Lepoint, T., Stehlé, D., Steinfeld, R.: Improved security proofs in lattice-based cryptography: using the Rényi divergence rather than the statistical distance. In: Iwata, T., Cheon, J.H. (eds.) ASIACRYPT 2015. LNCS, vol. 9452, pp. 3–24. Springer, Heidelberg (2015). https://doi.org/10.1007/978-3-662-48797-6_1
9. Banerjee, A., Peikert, C., Rosen, A.: Pseudorandom functions and lattices. In: Pointcheval, D., Johansson, T. (eds.) EUROCRYPT 2012. LNCS, vol. 7237, pp. 719–737. Springer, Heidelberg (2012). https://doi.org/10.1007/978-3-642-29011-4_42
10. Bogdanov, A., Guo, S., Masny, D., Richelson, S., Rosen, A.: On the hardness of learning with rounding over small modulus. In: Kushilevitz, E., Malkin, T. (eds.) TCC 2016. LNCS, vol. 9562, pp. 209–224. Springer, Heidelberg (2016). https://doi.org/10.1007/978-3-662-49096-9_9
11. Bos, J.W., et al.: Frodo: take off the ring! practical, quantum-secure key exchange from LWE. In: Weippl, E.R., Katzenbeisser, S., Kruegel, C., Myers, A.C., Halevi, S. (eds.) Proceedings of the 2016 ACM SIGSAC Conference on Computer and Communications Security, Vienna, Austria, 24–28 October 2016, pp. 1006–1018. ACM (2016)
12. Brakerski, Z., Langlois, A., Peikert, C., Regev, O., Stehlé, D.: Classical hardness of learning with errors. In: Boneh, D., Roughgarden, T., Feigenbaum, J. (eds.) 45th ACM STOC, pp. 575–584. ACM Press (June 2013)
13. Chung, C.M., Hwang, V., Kannwischer, M.J., Seiler, G., Shih, C., Yang, B.: NTT multiplication for NTT-unfriendly rings new speed records for saber and NTRU on cortex-m4 and AVX2. IACR Trans. Cryptogr. Hardw. Embed. Syst. **2021**(2), 159–188 (2021)
14. Dachman-Soled, D., Ducas, L., Gong, H., Rossi, M.: LWE with side information: attacks and concrete security estimation. In: Micciancio, D., Ristenpart, T. (eds.) CRYPTO 2020. LNCS, vol. 12171, pp. 329–358. Springer, Cham (2020). https://doi.org/10.1007/978-3-030-56880-1_12
15. Fujisaki, E., Okamoto, T.: Secure integration of asymmetric and symmetric encryption schemes. In: Wiener, M. (ed.) CRYPTO 1999. LNCS, vol. 1666, pp. 537–554. Springer, Heidelberg (1999). https://doi.org/10.1007/3-540-48405-1_34

16. Hofheinz, D., Hövelmanns, K., Kiltz, E.: A modular analysis of the Fujisaki-Okamoto transformation. In: Kalai, Y., Reyzin, L. (eds.) TCC 2017. LNCS, vol. 10677, pp. 341–371. Springer, Cham (2017). https://doi.org/10.1007/978-3-319-70500-2_12

17. Jan-Pieter D'Anvers, S.S.R., Karmakar, A., Vercauteren, F.: SABER: Submission to the NIST post-quantum cryptography standardization project. NIST National Institute of Standards and Technology (2020)

18. Jiang, H., Zhang, Z., Chen, L., Wang, H., Ma, Z.: IND-CCA-secure key encapsulation mechanism in the Quantum Random Oracle Model, revisited. In: Shacham, H., Boldyreva, A. (eds.) CRYPTO 2018. LNCS, vol. 10993, pp. 96–125. Springer, Cham (2018). https://doi.org/10.1007/978-3-319-96878-0_4

19. Jin, Z., Zhao, Y.: Optimal key consensus in presence of noise. Cryptology ePrint Archive, Report 2017/1058 (2017). http://eprint.iacr.org/2017/1058

20. Liu, F.-H., Wang, Z.: Rounding in the rings. In: Micciancio, D., Ristenpart, T. (eds.) CRYPTO 2020. LNCS, vol. 12171, pp. 296–326. Springer, Cham (2020). https://doi.org/10.1007/978-3-030-56880-1_11

21. Lyubashevsky, V., Peikert, C., Regev, O.: On ideal lattices and learning with errors over rings. In: Gilbert, H. (ed.) EUROCRYPT 2010. LNCS, vol. 6110, pp. 1–23. Springer, Heidelberg (2010). https://doi.org/10.1007/978-3-642-13190-5_1

22. Peikert, C.: Public-key cryptosystems from the worst-case shortest vector problem: extended abstract. In: Mitzenmacher, M. (ed.) 41st ACM STOC, pp. 333–342. ACM Press (May/June 2009)

23. Peikert, C.: Lattice cryptography for the internet. In: Mosca, M. (ed.) PQCrypto 2014. LNCS, vol. 8772, pp. 197–219. Springer, Cham (2014). https://doi.org/10.1007/978-3-319-11659-4_12

24. Peikert, C., Regev, O., Stephens-Davidowitz, N.: Pseudorandomness of ring-LWE for any ring and modulus. In: Hatami, H., McKenzie, P., King, V. (eds.) 49th ACM STOC, pp. 461–473. ACM Press (June 2017)

25. Poppelmann, T., et al.: NewHope - submission to the NIST post-quantum cryptography standardization project. NIST National Institute of Standards and Technology (2019)

26. Regev, O.: On lattices, learning with errors, random linear codes, and cryptography. In: Gabow, H.N., Fagin, R. (eds.) 37th ACM STOC, pp. 84–93. ACM Press (May 2005)

27. Shor, P.W.: Algorithms for quantum computation: Discrete logarithms and factoring. In: 35th FOCS, pp. 124–134. IEEE Computer Society Press (November 1994)

28. Zhang, J., Zhang, Z., Ding, J., Snook, M., Dagdelen, Ö.: Authenticated key exchange from ideal lattices. In: Oswald, E., Fischlin, M. (eds.) EUROCRYPT 2015. LNCS, vol. 9057, pp. 719–751. Springer, Heidelberg (2015). https://doi.org/10.1007/978-3-662-46803-6_24

29. Zhang, Z., et al.: NTRU - technical report, national institute of standards and technology. NIST National Institute of Standards and Technology (2020)

Kyber on ARM64: Compact Implementations of Kyber on 64-Bit ARM Cortex-A Processors

Pakize Sanal[1]([✉]), Emrah Karagoz[1], Hwajeong Seo[2], Reza Azarderakhsh[1,4], and Mehran Mozaffari-Kermani[3]

[1] Florida Atlantic University, Boca Raton, USA
{psanal2018,ekaragoz2017,razarderakhsh}@fau.edu
[2] Hansung University, Seoul, South Korea
hwajeong84@gmail.com
[3] University of South Florida, Tampa, USA
mehran2@usf.edu
[4] PQSecure Technologies, LLC, Boca Raton, FL, USA

Abstract. Public-key cryptography based on the lattice problem is efficient and believed to be secure in a post-quantum era. In this paper, we introduce carefully-optimized implementations of Kyber encryption schemes for 64-bit ARM Cortex-A processors. Our research contribution includes optimizations for Number Theoretic Transform (NTT), noise sampling, and AES accelerator based symmetric function implementations. The proposed Kyber512 implementation on ARM64 improved previous works by 1.79×, 1.96×, and 2.44× for key generation, encapsulation, and decapsulation, respectively. Moreover, by using AES accelerator in the proposed Kyber512-90s implementation, it is improved by 8.57×, 6.94×, and 8.26× for key generation, encapsulation, and decapsulation, respectively.

Keywords: Post-quantum cryptography · Kyber · ARM64 · Vectorized implementation

1 Introduction

The integer factorization and discrete logarithm problems, where RSA and Elliptic Curve Cryptography (ECC) are based on, can be easily solved by using Shor's algorithm [21] on a quantum computer. For this reason, the Post-Quantum Cryptography (PQC) standardization process is initiated by NIST in 2016 to choose quantum-resistant algorithms for the upcoming quantum era. In this process, Crystals-Kyber (shortly *Kyber*) [5] is one of the promising candidates among the third round finalists announced in 2020. It is an IND-CCA2-secure lattice-based key-encapsulation mechanism (KEM), and its security is based on the hardness of solving the learning-with-errors problem in module lattices (MLWE problem). In addition, it is comparably fast due to the small parameter size. It is easier to

J. Garcia-Alfaro et al. (Eds.): SecureComm 2021, LNICST 399, pp. 424–440, 2021.
https://doi.org/10.1007/978-3-030-90022-9_23

implement because the main primitives are modular reductions, small polynomial multiplications, and Number Theoretic Transformation (NTT) operations.

Several works devoted to improve the performance of a primitive of Kyber or of the scheme itself in several platforms. NTT operations are optimized on Advanced Vector Extensions 2 (AVX2) (see [16,20]) and on Cortex-M4 (see [1,7]). It is also accelerated by using GPU (see [11,18]) and hardware accelerators (see [2,4,8,10,12,14,22,23]). However, an efficient implementation of Kyber on high-end ARM processor (i.e. ARMv8 Cortex-A) was not conducted. Since the high-end ARM is widely used in smartphone, smartwatch, and laptop computer, the efficient implementation should be highly considered.

Our Contribution. We propose an optimized implementation of Kyber on 64-bit ARMv8 processors. Primitive operations of Kyber are fully vectorized in ASIMD instructions. The reduction and NTT operations are improved by 3.0–5.0× and 4.0–6.0×, respectively, compared to its optimized C implementation. Moreover, we implement full parameters for Kyber schemes. For example, Kyber512 implementation outperforms by 1.79×, 1.96×, and 2.44×, for key generation, encapsulation, and decapsulation, respectively. Lastly, we use acceleration of symmetric functions through cryptography extension of 64-bit ARMv8 processors. Results show that Kyber512-90s w/accelerator is faster than w/o accelerator by 8.57×, 6.94×, and 8.26×, for key generation, encapsulation, and decapsulation, respectively.

Our code is available at https://github.com/psanal2018/kyber-arm64.

Outline. The paper is organized as follows. Section 2 presents an overview of the Kyber algorithm. In Sect. 3, we introduce the ARMv8-A architecture. In Sect. 4, proposed implementations of Kyber on 64-bit ARM Cortex-A processors are presented. In Sect. 5, the performance evaluation of proposed implementations is described. Finally, the conclusion is given in Sect. 6.

2 Kyber

In this section, we give a brief description of the functions included in Kyber. The details of the algorithm is given in its specification document [19].

2.1 Mathematical Background

The basic elements in Kyber are the polynomials in the ring $\mathbb{Z}_q[X]/(X^n + 1)$, denoted by R_q, with $n = 256$ and $q = 3329$ in all variants of Kyber. The polynomials can be represented as a vector of linear polynomials by using Number-Theoretic Transform (NTT): for a polynomial $f = \sum_{i=0}^{255} f_i X^i$ in R_q,

$$\mathsf{NTT}(f) = (\hat{f}_0 + \hat{f}_1 X, \hat{f}_2 + \hat{f}_3 X, \ldots, \hat{f}_{254} + \hat{f}_{255} X)$$

where

$$\hat{f}_{2i} = \sum_{j=0}^{127} f_{2j} \zeta^{(2i+1)j} \quad \text{and} \quad \hat{f}_{2i+1} = \sum_{j=0}^{127} f_{2j+1} \zeta^{(2i+1)j}$$

with $\zeta = 17$ being the 256-th primitive root of unity. Two polynomials f and g in R_q can be efficiently multiplied by using NTT:

$$\mathsf{NTT}(f) \circ \mathsf{NTT}(g) = \hat{f} \circ \hat{g} = \hat{h}$$

where $\circ$ is the component-wise multiplication of linear polynomials, that is,

$$\hat{h}_{2i} + \hat{h}_{2i+1}X = (\hat{f}_{2i} + \hat{f}_{2i+1}X)(\hat{g}_{2i} + \hat{g}_{2i+1}X) \mod (X^2 - \zeta^{2i+1})$$

for $i = 0, 1, \ldots, 127$. Then, the product of f and g is

$$fg = \mathsf{NTT}^{-1}(\hat{h}) = \mathsf{NTT}^{-1}(\mathsf{NTT}(f) \circ \mathsf{NTT}(g)).$$

2.2 Compression and Encoding

An element $x \in \mathbb{Z}_q$ is converted to an d-bit integer by $\mathsf{Compress}_q(x, d)$. An d-bit integer x is converted to a $\mathbb{Z}_q$ element by $\mathsf{Decompress}_q(x, d)$. They are defined as follows:

$$\mathsf{Compress}_q(x, d) = \lceil (2^d/q) \cdot x \rfloor \mod 2^d \text{ and } \mathsf{Decompress}_q(x, d) = \lceil (q/2^d) \cdot x \rfloor$$

where $\lceil a \rfloor$ is the closest integer to a. When each function is applied to a polynomial (or a vector/matrix of polynomials), it is applied to each coefficient individually. In addition, a polynomial (or a vector/matrix of polynomials) is serialized to byte arrays by using $\mathsf{Encode}_\ell()$ function, where ℓ is the bit-length of each coefficient. On the other hand, $\mathsf{Decode}_\ell()$ is the inverse of $\mathsf{Encode}_\ell()$, and it deserializes the byte arrays to polynomials. Lastly, $\mathsf{Parse}()$ converts a byte stream to the NTT representation of a polynomial in R_q.

2.3 Sampling

The noise is sampled from a centered binomial distribution (CBD), denoted by B_η, for $\eta = 2$ or $\eta = 3$. For a sample $(a_1, \ldots, a_\eta, b_1, \ldots, b_\eta) \leftarrow \{0, 1\}^{2\eta}$, the output is computed as $\sum_{i=1}^{\eta}(a_i - b_i)$. Using B_η, a polynomial $f = \sum_{i=0}^{255} f_i X^i$ in R_q can be sampled by sampling each coefficient f_i deterministically from 512η-bit output $(\beta_0, \ldots, \beta_{512\eta-1})$ of a pseudo-random function:

$$f_i = \sum_{j=0}^{\eta-1}(\beta_{2i\eta+j} - \beta_{2i\eta+j+\eta})   i = 0, 1, \ldots, 255.$$

For this purpose, Kyber uses a function namely CBD_η, which takes 512η-bit input and outputs the corresponding polynomial.

2.4 Parameters

The fixed parameters are $n = 256$ and $q = 3329$. The parameter k represents the dimension of the matrix of polynomials in R_q. The parameter pair (η_1, η_2) are used in CBD_η function for sampling. The parameter pair (d_u, d_v) is used in $\mathsf{Compress}$ and $\mathsf{Decompress}$ functions. The list of parameters are given in Table 1.

Table 1. Kyber parameters.

Algorithm	NIST-Level	n	q	k	(η_1, η_2)	(d_u, d_v)
KYBER512	1 (AES-128)	256	3329	2	(3,2)	(10,3)
KYBER768	3 (AES-192)	256	3329	3	(2,2)	(10,4)
KYBER1024	5 (AES-256)	256	3329	4	(2,2)	(11,5)

2.5 Symmetric Functions

Kyber makes a use of a pseudo-random function (PRF), an extendable output function (XOF), two hash functions H, and G, and a key-derivation function (KDF). These functions are specified in Table 2. At this point, Kyber has an alternative version Kyber-90s which uses SHA-2 hash functions and AES, while Kyber uses SHA-3 hash functions.

Table 2. Symmetric primitives in Kyber.

Symmetric primitive	Kyber	Kyber-90s
XOF	SHAKE-128	AES-256 in CTR mode
H and G	SHA3-256 and SHA3-512	SHA-256 and SHA-512
PRF (s, b)	SHAKE-256$(s\|\|b)$	AES-256 in CTR mode (key $= s$ and nonce $= b$)
KDF	SHAKE-256	SHAKE-256

2.6 Kyber-PKE and Kyber-KEM

Kyber-PKE is an IND-CPA-secure public-key encryption scheme. It encrypts messages of a fixed length of 32 bytes. It contains three algorithms: Key Generation, Encryption, and Decryption.

In Kyber-PKE Key Generation, the polynomial matrix $\mathbf{A}$ is randomly generated, and the polynomial vectors $\mathbf{s}$ and $\mathbf{e}$ are sampled according to B_{η_1}. Then, normally, the secret key is $\mathbf{s}$ and the public key is $\mathbf{As} + \mathbf{e}$. However, for efficient implementation purposes, the multiplication $\mathbf{As}$ is performed in NTT domain by generating $\mathbf{A}$ in NTT domain (i.e. $\hat{\mathbf{A}}$) and transforming $\mathbf{s}$ to $\hat{\mathbf{s}} = \mathsf{NTT}(s)$. To avoid NTT^{-1} operation, $\mathbf{e}$ is also transformed to $\hat{\mathbf{e}}$ and added to $\hat{\mathbf{A}} \circ \hat{\mathbf{s}}$. Therefore, the values of secret and public keys are left in NTT domain and encoded to sk and pk, respectively. In addition, the seed for randomness is appended to the public key for letting the recipient generate the matrix $\mathbf{A}$.

In Kyber-PKE Encryption, the message m is encrypted to the ciphertext $c = (c_1, c_2)$ by using the public key pk and random coins r. The polynomial vector $\mathbf{t}$ and the matrix $\mathbf{A}$ are obtained using the public key. The polynomial vector $\mathbf{r}$ is sampled according to B_{η_1} using r. The polynomial vector $\mathbf{e}_1$ and the polynomial e_2 are sampled according to B_{η_2} using r. Then, normally, the ciphertext $c = (c_1, c_2)$ is $(\mathbf{A}^T \mathbf{r} + \mathbf{e}_1, \mathbf{t}^T r + e_2 + m)$. However, multiplications are performed in NTT domain and then transformed to the normal domain by using NTT^{-1}. Moreover, the ciphertext is compressed and encoded.

In Kyber-PKE Decryption, the polynomial vector $\mathbf{u}$ and the polynomial v are obtained from the ciphertext by decoding and decompressing. The vector $\mathbf{s}$ is obtained from the secret key. Then, the message m is $v - \mathbf{s}^T \mathbf{u}$. Again, the multiplications are performed in NTT domain and then transformed to the normal domain by using NTT^{-1}.

Nonce values (which are 0 in the beginning of the algorithms) are incremental in each computation. Algorithms are given in Algorithm 1, 2, and 3.

Algorithm 1: Kyber-PKE Key Generation

Output : secret key and public key pair (pk, sk)

1: $d \xleftarrow{\$} \{0,1\}^{256}$
2: $\rho, \sigma \leftarrow G(d)$
3: $\hat{\mathbf{A}} \leftarrow \mathsf{Parse}(\mathsf{XOF}(\rho, \mathsf{nonce}\texttt{++}))$ $\triangleright$ Generate matrix $\mathbf{A} \in R_q^{k \times k}$ (in NTT domain)
4: $\mathbf{s} \leftarrow \mathsf{CBD}_{\eta_1}(\mathsf{PRF}(\sigma, \mathsf{nonce}\texttt{++}))$ $\triangleright$ Sample $\mathbf{s} \in R_q^k$
5: $\mathbf{e} \leftarrow \mathsf{CBD}_{\eta_1}(\mathsf{PRF}(\sigma, \mathsf{nonce}\texttt{++}))$ $\triangleright$ Sample $\mathbf{e} \in R_q^k$
6: $\hat{\mathbf{s}} \leftarrow \mathsf{NTT}(\mathbf{s})$
7: $\hat{\mathbf{e}} \leftarrow \mathsf{NTT}(\mathbf{e})$
8: $\hat{\mathbf{t}} \leftarrow \hat{\mathbf{A}} \circ \hat{\mathbf{s}} + \hat{\mathbf{e}}$ $\triangleright$ $\mathbf{t} := \mathbf{As} + \mathbf{e}$ (in NTT domain)
9: $pk \leftarrow \mathsf{Encode}_{12}(\hat{\mathbf{t}}) \| \rho$
10: $sk \leftarrow \mathsf{Encode}_{12}(\hat{\mathbf{s}})$
11: **return** (pk, sk)

Algorithm 2: Kyber-PKE Encryption

Input   : public key pk, message m, random coins $r \in \{0,1\}^{256}$
Output : ciphertext $c = (c_1, c_2)$

1: $\hat{\mathbf{t}} \leftarrow \mathsf{Decode}_{12}(pk)$
2: $\rho \leftarrow pk$
3: $\hat{\mathbf{A}} \leftarrow \mathsf{Parse}(\mathsf{XOF}(\rho, \mathsf{nonce}\texttt{++}))$ $\triangleright$ Generate matrix $\hat{\mathbf{A}} \in R_q^{k \times k}$ in NTT domain
4: $\mathbf{r} \leftarrow \mathsf{CBD}_{\eta_1}(\mathsf{PRF}(r, \mathsf{nonce}\texttt{++}))$ $\triangleright$ Sample $\mathbf{r} \in R_q^k$
5: $\mathbf{e}_1 \leftarrow \mathsf{CBD}_{\eta_2}(\mathsf{PRF}(r, \mathsf{nonce}\texttt{++}))$ $\triangleright$ Sample $\mathbf{e}_1 \in R_q^k$
6: $e_2 \leftarrow \mathsf{CBD}_{\eta_2}(\mathsf{PRF}(r, \mathsf{nonce}\texttt{++}))$ $\triangleright$ Sample $e_2 \in R_q$
7: $\hat{\mathbf{r}} \leftarrow \mathsf{NTT}(\mathbf{r})$
8: $\mathbf{u} \leftarrow \mathsf{NTT}^{-1}(\hat{\mathbf{A}}^T \circ \hat{\mathbf{r}}) + \mathbf{e}_1$ $\triangleright$ $\mathbf{u} := \mathbf{A}^T \mathbf{r} + \mathbf{e}_1$
9: $v \leftarrow \mathsf{NTT}^{-1}(\hat{\mathbf{t}}^T \circ \hat{\mathbf{r}}) + e_2 + \mathsf{Decompress}_q(\mathsf{Decode}_1(m), 1)$ $\triangleright$ $v := \mathbf{t}^T \mathbf{r} + e_2 + m$
10: $c_1 \leftarrow \mathsf{Encode}_{d_u}(\mathsf{Compress}_q(\mathbf{u}, d_u))$
11: $c_2 \leftarrow \mathsf{Encode}_{d_v}(\mathsf{Compress}_q(v, d_v))$
12: **return** $c = (c_1, c_2)$

Algorithm 3: Kyber-PKE Decryption

Input   : secret key sk, ciphertext $c = (c_1, c_2)$
Output : message m

1: $\mathbf{u} \leftarrow \mathsf{Decompress}_q(\mathsf{Decode}_{d_u}(c_1), d_u)$
2: $v \leftarrow \mathsf{Decompress}_q(\mathsf{Decode}_{d_v}(c_2), d_v)$
3: $\hat{\mathbf{s}} \leftarrow \mathsf{Decode}_{12}(sk)$
4: $m \leftarrow \mathsf{Encode}_1(\mathsf{Compress}_q(v - \mathsf{NTT}^{-1}(\hat{\mathbf{s}}^T \circ \mathsf{NTT}(\mathbf{u})), 1)$
5: **return** m

On the other hand, Kyber-KEM is an IND-CCA2-secure KEM and it is constructed from Kyber-PKE using (a slightly tweaked) Fujisaki-Okamoto transform. It contains three steps: Key Generation, Encapsulation, and Decapsulation. In the first step, Alice generates the public and secret keys by using Kyber-PKE Key Generation algorithm, and shares her public key with Bob. In the second step, Bob encrypts the message to the ciphertext by using Kyber-PKE Encryption algorithm, and sends the ciphertext to Alice. He also computes the shared secret by using the message, Alice's public key, and the ciphertext. In the last step, Alice decrypts the ciphertext to the message by using Kyber-PKE Decryption algorithm, and then verifies whether it can be encrypted to the same ciphertext (sent by Bob) by following similar steps as Bob did by using Kyber-PKE Encryption algorithm. If ciphertexts match, Alice computes the shared secret by using the message, her public key, and the ciphertext. Otherwise, she computes the shared secret by using a random value and the ciphertext. Details of Kyber-KEM are illustrated in Fig. 1.

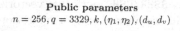

Public parameters
$n = 256, q = 3329, k, (\eta_1, \eta_2), (d_u, d_v)$

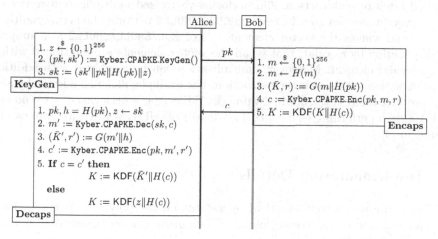

Fig. 1. Kyber-CCA-KEM.

3   ARMv8-A Architecture

ARMv8-A is a 64-bit architecture. It provides 31 general purpose registers which can hold 32-bit values in registers w0-w30 or 64-bit values in registers x0-x30. It provides SIMD (Single Instruction Multiple Data) instruction set, which can process 128 bit data per instruction on average. The SIMD vectorization is possible for same data per vector registers and it does not allow carry handling. There are 32 128-bit registers (v0-v31), which can be divided into lanes which are 8, 16, 32, or 64 bits wide. They are defined via operand suffix b, indicated byte, h indicates half-word, s indicates word, d indicated double-word. For instance, v0.8h create a vector with eight 16-bit elements. Single element of a vector can be accessed via square brackets (e.g. v0.4s[0] is the first 32-bit element of the vector v0, and v1.8h[2] is the third 16-bit element of the vector v1).

The ARMv8-A has a various SIMD instructions. Load and store operations are performed by using LD and ST operations. Each has 4 types according to the degree of interleaving: LD1/ST1, LD2/ST2, LD3/ST3 and LD4/ST4. For example, LD1 fills the vector va first, and continues to fill the vector vb later. However, LD2 fills the vectors va and vb simultaneously, that is, one element for va and the next element for vb, another element for va again and so on. LD3 follows a similar order for the vectors va, vb and vc. ZIP1/ZIP2 zip two vectors into a single vector according to even/odd indices. UZP1/UZP2 concatenate even or odd elements from two vectors. The SXTL/SXTL2 instructions widens the lower/upper halfs of the source register (e.g. widens 8-bit elements to 16-bit elements). TBL is an instruction used for permutation according the indices given in a look-up table. SSHR/USHR performs vectorized signed/unsigned right shift operations. AND/ORR are bitwise and/or operations. ADD/SUB performs vectorized addition/subtraction. MUL performs vectorized multiplication restricted to the vector element size, however, SMULL/SMULL2 perform the actual multiplication and widens the vector element. All of MUL/SMULL/SMULL2 also support multiplication by a scalar, that is, all the vector elements are multiplied with a single scalar element. Moreover, multiplication can be combined with addition or subtraction within a single instruction. For example, MLA/MLS adds/subtracts the product to/from the original value (i.e. MLS c, a, b performs $c \leftarrow c + ab$ and MLA c, a, b performs $c \leftarrow c - ab$). The details of ARMv8-A architecture can be found in [3].

4   Implementation Details

Kyber performs the mathematical operations on the polynomials in R_q. Each polynomial, and its representation in NTT-domain, can be serialized as a vector of length 256 as follows:

$$f = \sum_{i=0}^{255} f_i X^i \rightarrow (f_0, f_1, \ldots, f_{255})$$

and

$$\hat{f} = \mathsf{NTT}(f) = (\hat{f}_0 + \hat{f}_1 X, \dots, \hat{f}_{254} + \hat{f}_{255} X) \rightarrow (\hat{f}_0, \dots, \hat{f}_{255}).$$

The addition and subtraction of two polynomials f and g can be performed component-wise on their serialized forms: $f_i \pm g_i$ or $\hat{f}_i \pm \hat{g}_i$. However, the multiplication is only performed in NTT domain (for efficiency) by multiplying component-wise pairs: $(\hat{f}_{2i}, \hat{f}_{2i+1}) \circ (\hat{g}_{2i}, \hat{g}_{2i+1})$. Modular reductions can also be performed component-wise: $f_i \bmod q$, or $\hat{f}_i \bmod q$.

In our implementation, the basic goal is to vectorize the input and take the advantage of SIMD operations on ARM. As $q = 3329$ is a 12-bit integer, the input values can be stored in 16-bit (or multiples of 16-bit). Later, 16-bit values are vectorized in vx.8h registers. In addition, 32-bit values are vectorized in vx.4s registers, if needed. Here, x is the vector index in $\{0, 1, \dots, 31\}$.

4.1 Reduction

For a given 16-bit integer a, Barrett reduction computes the centered representative congruent to $a \bmod q$, that is, the unique integer x in the interval $\left[-\frac{q-1}{2}, \dots, \frac{q-1}{2}\right]$ such that $x = a \bmod q$. It uses a special constant value $r = \lfloor (2^{26} + \lfloor q/2 \rfloor)/q \rfloor)$, which is 20159 as $q = 3329$. On the other hand, for a given 32-bit integer a, Montgomery reduction computes 16-bit integer congruent to $aR^{-1} \bmod q$, where $R = 2^{16}$, in the interval $[-q+1, \dots, q-1]$.

We use the vectorized form of Barrett reduction as given in Listing 1. We use the vectorized form of Montgomery reduction inplaced in tomont (see Listing 2) and fqmul (see Listing 3) functions. The tomont function performs the conversion of polynomial coefficients from normal domain to Montgomery domain by multiplying them with $t = 2^{32} \bmod q$ first and by applying the Montgomery reduction later. As $q = 3329$, the constant values in tomont are $q' = 62209 = q^{-1} \bmod 2^{16}$ and $t = 1353$. Moreover, the fqmul function performs the multiplication of two $\mathbb{Z}_q$-elements and then apply the Montgomery reduction. It uses the constant value q' as defined before. In the comments of the listings, $(x)_{hi}$ and $(x)_{lo}$ refer to the most significant and the least significant 16-bit of a 32-bit integer x, respectively.

Listing 1: BARR: Vectorized Barrett Reduction
$(r = \lfloor (2^{26} + \lfloor q/2 \rfloor)/q \rfloor)$

Input	: va.8h $= [a_0, a_1, \dots, a_7]$ and vq.8h $= [q, r, \dots]$	
	(vx is an intermediate vector)	
Output	: va.8h $= [a_0, a_1, \dots, a_7]$	$(a_0, a_1, \dots, a_7)$

1: SQDMULH	vx.8h, va.8h, vq.h[1]	$\triangleright\ x \leftarrow (2 \cdot a \cdot r)_{hi}$
2: SSHR	vx.8h, vx.8h, 11	$\triangleright\ x \leftarrow x \gg 11$
3: MLS	va.8h, vx.8h, vq.h[0]	$\triangleright\ a \leftarrow a - q \cdot x$

Listing 2: TOMONT: Vectorized conversion of polynomial coefficients from normal domain to Montgomery domain ($q' = q^{-1} \bmod 2^{16}$ and $t = 2^{32} \bmod q$)

Input : va.8h = $[a_0, a_1, ..., a_7]$ and vq.8h = $[q, q', t, ...]$
            (vx, vy, vz, vt are intermediate vectors)
Output : va.8h = $[a_0, a_1, ..., a_7]$

```
1: MUL       vx.8h, va.8h, vq.h[2]                  ▷ x ← (t · a)_lo
2: SQDMULH   vy.8h, va.8h, vq.h[2]                  ▷ y ← (2 · a · t)_hi
3: MUL       vz.8h, vx.8h, vq.h[1]                  ▷ z ← (q^{-1} · x)_lo
4: SQDMULH   vt.8h, vz.8h, vq.h[0]                  ▷ t ← (2 · q · z)_hi
5: SHSUB     va.8h, vy.8h, vt.8h                    ▷ a ← (y − t)/2
```

Listing 3: FQMUL: Vectorized Multiplication followed by Montgomery Reduction

Input : Vectors va.8h = $[a_0, ..., a_7]$, vb.8h = $[b_0, ..., b_7]$ and vq.8h = $[q, q', ...]$
            (vx, vy, vz, vt are intermediate vectors)
Output : vc.8h = $[c_0, c_1, ..., c_7]$

```
1: MUL       vx.8h, va.8h, vb.8h                    ▷ x ← (a · b)_lo
2: SQDMULH   vy.8h, va.8h, vb.8h                    ▷ y ← (2 · a · b)_hi
3: MUL       vz.8h, vx.8h, vq.h[1]                  ▷ z ← (q^{-1} · x)_lo
4: SQDMULH   vt.8h, vz.8h, vq.h[0]                  ▷ t ← (2 · q · z)_hi
5: SHSUB     vc.8h, vy.8h, vt.8h                    ▷ c ← (y − t)/2
```

4.2 NTT Operations

In NTT, the state-of-art computation is performed using Butterfly operations. As $n = 256 = 2^8$ in Kyber, the Butterfly operations are performed in 7 levels. In each level, the serialized representation $(f_0, f_1, \ldots, f_{255})$ are filled into the 8×16-bit vectors, and each two vectors (according to some distance in each level) are updated using Butterfly operation in NTT (see Listing 4). In the end, the its NTT representation (i.e. $(\hat{f}_0, \hat{f}_1, \ldots, \hat{f}_{255})$) is obtained. Vice versa, a vector in NTT domain can also be transformed to the normal domain by using the Butterfly operation in NTT^{-1} (see Listing 5).

4.3 Polynomial Operations

Polynomials stored in the vectors are simply added or subtracted using ADD or SUB instructions as many times as needed. For the multiplication, two linear polynomials $a_0 + a_1 X$ and $b_0 + b_1 X$ are multiplied to compute their product $c_0 + c_1 X$ in modulo $X^2 - \zeta_k$ as mentioned in Sect. 2.1. For this purpose, we use the BASEMUL function (see Listing 6) as the vectorized multiplication of two linear polynomials.

Listing 4: Butterfly operation in NTT

Input	: va.8h $= [a_0, a_1, ..., a_7]$	$(a_0, a_1, ..., a_7)$
	vb.8h $= [b_0, b_1, ..., b_7]$	$(b_0, b_1, ..., b_7)$
	vz.8h $= [z_0, z_1, ..., z_7]$	$(\zeta_0, \zeta_1, ..., \zeta_7)$
	(vc is an intermediate vector)	
Output	: va.8h $= [a_0, a_1, ..., a_7]$	$(a_0, a_1, ..., a_7)$
	vb.8h $= [b_0, b_1, ..., b_7]$	$(b_0, b_1, ..., b_7)$

1: FQMUL   vc.8h, vz.8h, vb.8h
2: SUB   vb.8h, va.8h, vc.8h $\triangleright b \leftarrow a - b \cdot \zeta$
3: ADD   va.8h, va.8h, vc.8h $\triangleright a \leftarrow a + b \cdot \zeta$

Listing 5: Butterfly operation in NTT^{-1}

Input	: va.8h $= [a_0, a_1, ..., a_7]$	$(a_0, a_1, ..., a_7)$
	vb.8h $= [b_0, b_1, ..., b_7]$	$(b_0, b_1, ..., b_7)$
	vz.8h $= [z_0, z_1, ..., z_7]$	$(\zeta_0, \zeta_1, ..., \zeta_7)$
	(vc is an intermediate vector)	
Output	: va.8h $= [a_0, a_1, ..., a_7]$	$(a_0, a_1, ..., a_7)$
	vb.8h $= [b_0, b_1, ..., b_7]$	$(b_0, b_1, ..., b_7)$

1: MOV   vc.16b, va.16b $\triangleright c \leftarrow a$
2: ADD   va.8h, vc.8h, vb.8h $\triangleright a \leftarrow b + c$
3: BARR   va.8h $\triangleright a \leftarrow \text{BarrettRed}(a)$
4: SUB   vb.8h, vc.8h, vb.8h $\triangleright b \leftarrow b - c$
5: FQMUL   vb.8h, vz.8h, vb.8h $\triangleright b \leftarrow b \cdot \zeta$

4.4 Noise Sampling

Vectors are sampled according to B_2 or B_3 since $\eta \in \{2, 3\}$. We use CBD2 (see Listing 7) and CBD3 (see Listing 8) when $\eta = 2$ and $\eta = 3$, respectively. We initialize some vector registers (as many as needed) in the beginning: the vectors vmi are used for masking and the vector vs is used for shuffling. As mentioned in Sect. 2.3, every 4 bits (resp. 6 bits) produce an output when $\eta = 2$ (resp. $\eta = 3$). Therefore, CBD2 takes a 128-bit input and produces 32 output values (which are stored in vc0.8h, vc1.8h, vc2.8h and vc3.8h). Similarly, CBD3 takes a 96-bit input and produces 16 output values (which are stored in vc0.8h and vc1.8h). For these functions, we mainly followed the steps in Kyber's AVX implementation given in [6].

4.5 Symmetric Functions

As described in Table 2, Kyber requires SHAKE-128/256, SHA-256/512, SHA3-256/512, and AES-256 for XOF, H, G, PRF, and KDF. For hash functions, we utilized the implementation provided by PQClean [13]. For the AES implementation, we utilized the AES accelerator in the target board. If the board does not support the AES accelerator, we utilized PQClean AES implementations.

Listing 6: BASEMUL: Vectorized multiplication of two linear polynomials

Input   : va0.8h = [a0_0, ..., a0_7] and va1.8h = [a1_0, ..., a1_7] as $a_0 + a_1 X$
          vb0.8h = [b0_0, ..., b0_7] and vb1.8h = [b1_0, ..., b1_7] as $b_0 + b_1 X$
          vz.8h = [z$_0$, −z$_0$, ..., z$_3$, −z$_3$] as ζ values
          (vd is an intermediate vector)

Output : vc0.8h = [c0_0, ..., c0_7] and vc1.8h = [c1_0, ..., c1_7] as $c_0 + c_1 X$

```
1: FQMUL    vc0.8h, va1.8h, vb1.8h
2: FQMUL    vc0.8h, vc0.8h, vz.8h                    ▷ c₀ ← a₁ · b₁ · ζ
3: FQMUL    vd.8h, va0.8h, vb0.8h
4: ADD      vc0.8h, vc0.8h, vd.8h                    ▷ c₀ ← c₀ + a₀b₀
5: FQMUL    vc1.8h, va0.8h, vb1.8h
6: FQMUL    vd.8h, va1.8h, vb0.8h
7: ADD      vc1.8h, vc1.8h, vd.8h                    ▷ c₁ ← a₀ · b₁ + a₁ · b₀
```

Lines 2, 4, 7 annotations: $\triangleright\ c_0 \leftarrow a_1 \cdot b_1 \cdot \zeta$; $\triangleright\ c_0 \leftarrow c_0 + a_0 b_0$; $\triangleright\ c_1 \leftarrow a_0 \cdot b_1 + a_1 \cdot b_0$

Listing 7: CBD2: Vectorized noise sampling for $\eta = 2$

Input   : va.16b = [a$_0$, a$_1$, ..., a$_{15}$],   (input values)
          vm0.16b = [0x55, ..., 0x55], vm1.16b = [0x33, ..., 0x33],
          vm2.16b = [0x03, ..., 0x03], vm3.16b = [0x0F, ..., 0x0F]   (masking)
          (vd, ve, vf are intermediate vectors)

Output : vc0.8h = [c0_0, c0_1, ..., c0_7] vc1.8h = [c1_0, c1_1, ..., c1_7]
          vc2.8h = [c2_0, c2_1, ..., c2_7] vc3.8h = [c3_0, c3_1, ..., c3_7]

```
 1: USHR    vd.8h, va.8h, 1
 2: AND     va.16b, va.16b, vm0.16b
 3: AND     vd.16b, vd.16b, vm0.16b
 4: ADD     va.16b, va.16b, vd.16b
 5: USHR    vd.8h, va.8h, 2
 6: AND     va.16b, va.16b, vm1.16b
 7: AND     vd.16b, vd.16b, vm1.16b
 8: ADD     va.16b, va.16b, vm1.16b
 9: SUB     va.16b, va.16b, vd.16b
10: USHR    vd.8h, va.8h, 4
11: AND     va.16b, va.16b, vm3.16b
12: AND     vd.16b, vd.16b, vm3.16b
13: SUB     va.16b, va.16b, vm2.16b
14: SUB     vd.16b, vd.16b, vm2.16b
15: ZIP1    ve.16b, va.16b, vd.16b
16: ZIP2    vf.16b, va.16b, vd.16b
17: SXTL    vc0.8h, ve.8b
18: SXTL2   vc1.8h, ve.16b
19: SXTL    vc2.8h, vf.8b
20: SXTL2   vc3.8h, vf.16b
```

Listing 8: CBD3: Vectorized noise sampling for $\eta = 3$

Input   : va.16b $= [a_0, a_1, ..., a_7]$
vs.16b $= [-1, 11, 10, 9, -1, 8, 7, 6, -1, 5, 4, 3, -1, 2, 1, 0]$,   (shuffle)
vm0.4s $= [0x00249249, ...]$, vm1.4s $= [0x006DB6DB, ...]$
vm2.4s $= [0x00000007, ...]$, vm3.4s $= [0x00070000, ...]$,
vm4.4s $= [0x00030003, ...]$,   (masking)
(vd is an intermediate vectors)

Output : vc0.4s $= [c0_0, c0_1, c0_2, c0_3]$ and vc1.4s $= [c1_0, c1_1, c1_2, c1_3]$

```
 1: TBL     va.16b, va.16b, vs.16b
 2: USHR    vd.4s, va.4s, 1
 3: USHR    vc0.4s, va.4s, 2
 4: AND     va.16b, va.16b, vm0.16b
 5: AND     vd.16b, vd.16b, vm0.16b
 6: AND     vc0.16b, vc0.16b, vm0.16b
 7: ADD     va.4s, va.4s, vd.4s
 8: ADD     va.4s, va.4s, vc0.4s
 9: USHR    vd.4s, va.4s, 3
10: ADD     va.4s, va.4s, vm1.4s
11: SUB     va.4s, va.4s, vd.4s
12: SHL     vd.4s, va.4s, 10
13: USHR    vc0.4s, va.4s, 12
14: USHR    vc1.4s, va.4s, 2
15: AND     va.16b, va.16b, vm2.16b
16: AND     vd.16b, vd.16b, vm3.16b
17: AND     vc0.16b, vc0.16b, vm2.16b
18: AND     vc1.16b, vc1.16b, vm3.16b
19: ADD     va.8h, va.8h, vd.8h
20: ADD     vd.8h, vc0.8h, vc1.8h
21: SUB     va.8h, va.8h, vm4.8h
22: SUB     vd.8h, vd.8h, vm4.8h
23: ZIP1    vc0.4s, va.4s, vd.4s
24: ZIP2    vc1.4s, va.4s, vd.4s
```

---

5   Performance Results

Benchmark results were measured both ARM and Apple chips. The ARM board is on Google Pixel 3 Android smartphone. The processor (Snapdragon 845) on it has 8 cores including 4 of ARM Cortex-A53 (@1.77 GHz) and 4 of ARM Cortex-A75 (@2.8 GHz) based. Performance results are taken by using Cortex-A75 processor. The executable is aarch64 cross-compiled on Linux operating system (Ubuntu 20.04) with gcc-9.

The Apple board is on iPad mini 5-th generation. The processor (A12 Bionic) on it has 6 cores including 2 of Vortex (@2.49 GHz) and 4 of Tempest (@1.54 GHz) based. Performance results are taken by using Vortex processor on Apple operating system (iPadOS 14.3).

The reference C code is originally obtained from [13] as the clean format of Kyber Round 3 submission [6]. Then, cycle count function is changed as how is written in Microsoft's SIDH code [17]. The clock is set as CLOCK_MONOTONIC which gives more accurate results than CLOCK_REALTIME.

Results shown in the Tables 3 and 4 are median values for 1,000 tests. The Table 3 shows reference and optimized implementation performance results for the arithmetic functions in Kyber. Notice that these results are same for all Kyber variants, because each Kyber variant has the same number of polynomial coefficients (e.g. $n = 256$). The overall performance results of key generation (K), encapsulation (E) and decapsulation (D) for all Kyber variants (including Kyber-90s) are presented in Tables 4. They show that the optimized implementation is $\sim 2\times$ faster than reference implementation even though the arithmetic functions are optimized $\sim 5\times$ faster. The main reason here is that the hashing operations mainly in the matrix generation part and in other various sums up to a big portion of the timing results as it is also indicated in the paper [1]. Detailed percentages of these functions are illustrated in the Fig. 2.

Table 3. Comparison of clock cycles for functions of Kyber schemes on 64-bit ARM Cortex-A75@2.8 GHz. (Ref-C: Reference C implementation [13]. Opt: Our optimized implementation.)

| Functions | Timing [cc] | | Ref-C [13]/Opt |
	Ref-C [13]	Opt	
Reduction			
poly_tomont (Montgomery Red)	1,896	437	4.34
poly_reduce (Barrett Red)	2,187	294	7.44
NTT			
poly_ntt (NTT+Barrett Red)	11,228	1750	6.42
poly_invntt_tomont (InvNTT)	17,500	2624	6.67
poly_basemul_montgomery	5,396	1168	4.62

5.1   Cryptography Extension for Kyber-90s

64-bit ARMv8 Cortex-A processor supports cryptography extension, which accelerates AES encryption, SHA-1, SHA-224, and SHA-256[1]. In CT-RSA'15, compact implementations of AES-GCM were presented [9]. They utilized new cryptography instructions including 64-bit polynomial multiplication (e.g. PMULL and PMULL2) and AES operations (e.g. AESE (AddRoundKey, SubBytes, and ShiftRows) and AESMC (MixColumns)) for high-performance. In PQCrypto'18, SPHINCS with different cryptographic hash functions on ARMv8-A platform

---

[1] Recent ARM architecture even supports SHA-3, SHA-512, SM3, and SM4 functions.

was presented [15]. The implementation of SHA256 is optimized with cryptography extension (SHA256H, SHA256H2, SHA256SU0, and SHA256SU1). HARAKA implementation is optimized with AES extension. These dedicated instruction sets are also beneficial for a variant of Kyber, namely Kyber-90s, suggested by Kyber team. This new scheme utilizes AES-256 in counter mode and SHA2 instead of SHAKE. Kyber512-90s can be further optimized with AES-256 accelerator. We evaluated Kyber512-90s on 64-bit Apple A12 processors@2.49 GHz. Reference implementations require 279,751, 292,742, and 305,511 clock cycles for key generation, encryption, and decryption while optimized implementations with ARM64 assembly and AES-256 accelerator require 32,640, 42,158, and 36,982 clock cycles for key generation, encryption, and decryption, respectively. The implementation with accelerator shows 8.57×, 6.94×, and 8.26× faster than the implementation without the AES accelerator.

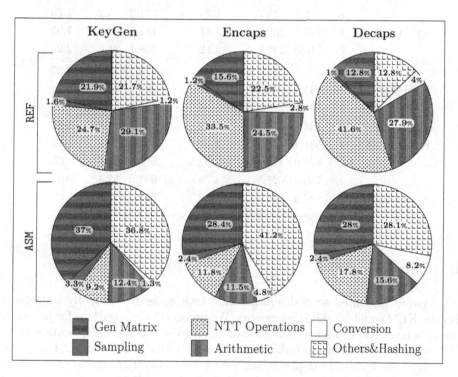

Fig. 2. Percentages of used functions in Keygen, Encapsulation and Decapsulation

Table 4. Comparison of clock cycles for Kyber schemes. (Ref-C: Reference C implementation [13]. Opt: Our optimized implementation.)

Schemes		ARM Cortex-A75 @2.8 GHz			Apple A12 @2.49 GHz w/AES accelerator		
		Timing [cc] Ref-C	Opt	Ref-C/Opt	Timing [cc] Ref-C	Opt	Ref-C/Opt
Kyber512	K	145.8	81.7	1.79	60.4	34.9	1.78
	E	205.2	104.9	1.96	77.7	37.7	2.06
	D	248.5	101.9	2.44	94.6	37.2	2.53
Kyber768	K	247.5	138.0	1.79	106.0	62.2	1.70
	E	327.8	173.4	1.89	131.9	60.8	2.16
	D	383.0	168.6	2.27	146.7	60.0	2.44
Kyber1024	K	385.1	222.7	1.73	171.2	95.2	1.79
	E	476.7	262.8	1.81	182.2	93.0	1.95
	D	546.0	257.7	2.12	209.1	91.0	2.29
Kyber512-90s	K	270.5	205.6	1.32	279.7	32.6	8.57
	E	334.5	236.7	1.41	292.7	42.1	6.94
	D	375.1	230.7	1.63	305.5	37.0	8.26
Kyber768-90s	K	491.7	379.2	1.30	554.2	56.4	9.82
	E	581.4	426.1	1.36	576.0	64.5	8.92
	D	632.9	417.1	1.52	590.7	57.0	10.35
Kyber1024-90s	K	790.3	625.8	1.26	941.9	87.1	10.80
	E	897.3	680.5	1.32	964.8	93.8	10.28
	D	959.6	669.4	1.43	983.0	83.5	11.76

6   Conclusion

This paper presented several optimization techniques to efficiently implement Kyber-KEM on 64-bit ARM processors. We proposed optimizations for primitive operations of Kyber and symmetric functions to accelerate the execution time. A combination of these optimizations achieved 1.79×, 1.96×, and 2.44× faster than previous Kyber512 implementations for key generation, encapsulation, and decapsulation, which set new speed records for Kyber-KEM on an 64-bit ARM processor.

Acknowledgment. The authors would like to thank the reviewers for their comments. This work is supported in parts by a grant from NSF-2101085.

References

1. Alkim, E., Alper Bilgin, Y., Cenk, M., Gérard, F.: Cortex-M4 optimizations for $\{R, M\}$ LWE schemes. IACR Trans. Crypt. Hardware Embed. Syst. **2020**(3), 336–357 (2020). https://doi.org/10.13154/tches.v2020.i3.336-357, https://tches.iacr.org/index.php/TCHES/article/view/8593
2. Alkim, E., Evkan, H., Lahr, N., Niederhagen, R., Petri, R.: ISA extensions for finite field arithmetic: accelerating Kyber and NewHope on RISC-V. IACR Trans. Crypt. Hardware Embed. Syst. **2020**(3), 219–242 (2020). https://doi.org/10.13154/tches.v2020.i3.219-242, https://tches.iacr.org/index.php/TCHES/article/view/8589
3. ARM: ARM architecture reference manual ARMv8, for ARMv8-A architecture profile. https://developer.arm.com/documentation/ddi0487/fc/. Accessed 15 Jan 2021
4. Bisheh-Niasar, M., Azarderakhsh, R., Mozaffari-Kermani, M.: High-speed NTT-based polynomial multiplication accelerator for CRYSTALS-kyber post-quantum cryptography. Cryptology ePrint Archive, Report 2021/563 (2021). https://eprint.iacr.org/2021/563
5. Bos, J., et al.: CRYSTALS - Kyber: a CCA-secure module-lattice-based KEM. In: 2018 IEEE European Symposium on Security and Privacy (EuroS&P), pp. 353–367. IEEE (2018). https://doi.org/10.1109/EuroSP.2018.00032
6. Bos, J., et al.: Kyber project. https://github.com/pq-crystals/kyber. Accessed 12 Dec 2020
7. Botros, L., Kannwischer, M.J., Schwabe, P.: Memory-efficient high-speed implementation of Kyber on Cortex-M4. In: Buchmann, J., Nitaj, A., Rachidi, T. (eds.) AFRICACRYPT 2019. LNCS, vol. 11627, pp. 209–228. Springer, Cham (2019). https://doi.org/10.1007/978-3-030-23696-0_11
8. Chen, Z., Ma, Y., Chen, T., Lin, J., Jing, J.: Towards efficient Kyber on FPGAs: a processor for vector of polynomials. In: 2020 25th Asia and South Pacific Design Automation Conference (ASP-DAC), pp. 247–252 (2020). https://doi.org/10.1109/ASP-DAC47756.2020.9045459
9. Gouvêa, C.P.L., López, J.: Implementing GCM on ARMv8. In: Nyberg, K. (ed.) Topics in Cryptology — CT-RSA 2015. LNCS, vol. 9048, pp. 167–180. Springer, Cham (2015). https://doi.org/10.1007/978-3-319-16715-2_9
10. Greconici, D.: Kyber on RISC-V. Master's Thesis (2020). https://www.ru.nl/publish/pages/769526/denisa_greconici.pdf
11. Gupta, N., Jati, A., Chauhan, A.K., Chattopadhyay, A.: PQC acceleration using GPUs: FrodoKEM, NewHope, and Kyber. IEEE Trans. Parallel Distrib. Syst. **32**(3), 575–586 (2021). https://doi.org/10.1109/TPDS.2020.3025691
12. Huang, Y., Huang, M., Lei, Z., Wu, J.: A pure hardware implementation of CRYSTALS-KYBER PQC algorithm through resource reuse. IEICE Electron. Exp. **17**(17), 20200234 (2020). https://doi.org/10.1587/elex.17.20200234
13. Kannwischer, M., Rijneveld, J., Schwabe, P., Stebila, D., Wiggers, T.: The PQClean project. https://github.com/PQClean/PQClean. Accessed 10 Dec 2020
14. Karabulut, E., Aysu, A.: RANTT: a RISC-V architecture extension for the number theoretic transform. In: 2020 30th International Conference on Field-Programmable Logic and Applications (FPL), pp. 26–32 (2020). https://doi.org/10.1109/FPL50879.2020.00016
15. Kölbl, S.: Putting wings on SPHINCS. In: Lange, T., Steinwandt, R. (eds.) PQCrypto 2018. LNCS, vol. 10786, pp. 205–226. Springer, Cham (2018). https://doi.org/10.1007/978-3-319-79063-3_10

16. Longa, P., Naehrig, M.: Speeding up the number theoretic transform for faster ideal lattice-based cryptography. In: Foresti, S., Persiano, G. (eds.) CANS 2016. LNCS, vol. 10052, pp. 124–139. Springer, Cham (2016). https://doi.org/10.1007/978-3-319-48965-0_8
17. Microsoft: PQCrypto-SIDH project. https://github.com/microsoft/PQCrypto-SIDH. Accessed 13 Dec 2020
18. Ono, T., Bian, S., Sato, T.: Automatic parallelism tuning for module learning with errors based post-quantum key exchanges on GPUs. In: 2021 IEEE International Symposium on Circuits and Systems (ISCAS), pp. 1–5 (2021). https://doi.org/10.1109/ISCAS51556.2021.9401575
19. Schwabe, P., et al.: CRYSTALS-KYBER algorithm specifications and supporting documentation. Technical report, National Institute of Standards and Technology (2020). https://csrc.nist.gov/projects/post-quantum-cryptography/round-3-submissions
20. Seiler, G.: Faster AVX2 optimized NTT multiplication for ring-LWE lattice cryptography. Cryptology ePrint Archive, Report 2018/039 (2018). https://eprint.iacr.org/2018/039
21. Shor, P.: Algorithms for quantum computation: discrete logarithms and factoring. In: Proceedings 35th Annual Symposium on Foundations of Computer Science, pp. 124–134. IEEE (1994). https://doi.org/10.1109/SFCS.1994.365700
22. Xing, Y., Li, S.: A compact hardware implementation of CCA-secure key exchange mechanism CRYSTALS-KYBER on FPGA. IACR Trans. Cryptogr. Hardware Embed. Syst. **2021**(2), 328–356 (2021). https://doi.org/10.46586/tches.v2021.i2.328-356, https://tches.iacr.org/index.php/TCHES/article/view/8797
23. Yaman, F., Mert, A.C., Ö-ztürk, E., Savaş, E.: A hardware accelerator for polynomial multiplication operation of CRYSTALS-KYBER. PQC scheme. Cryptology ePrint Archive, Report 2021/485 (2021). https://eprint.iacr.org/2021/485

Compressed SIKE Round 3 on ARM Cortex-M4

Mila Anastasova[1(✉)], Mojtaba Bisheh-Niasar[1], Reza Azarderakhsh[1,2], and Mehran Mozaffari Kermani[3]

[1] Computer and Electrical Engineering and Computer Science Department and I-SENSE, Florida Atlantic University, Boca Raton, FL, USA
{manastasova2017,mbishehniasa2019,razarderakhsh}@fau.edu
[2] PQSecure Technologies, LLC, Boca Raton, FL, USA
[3] Computer Engineering and Science Department, University of South Florida, Tampa, FL, USA
mehran2@usf.edu

Abstract. In 2016, the National Institute of Standards and Technology (NIST) initiated a standardization process among the post-quantum secure algorithms. Forming part of the alternate group of candidates after Round 2 of the process is the Supersingular Isogeny Key Encapsulation (SIKE) mechanism which attracts with the smallest key sizes offering post-quantum security in scenarios of limited bandwidth and memory resources. Even further reduction of the exchanged information is offered by the compression mechanism, proposed by *Azarderakhsh et al.*, which, however, introduces a significant time overhead and increases the memory requirements of the protocol, making it challenging to integrate it into an embedded system. In this paper, we propose the first compressed SIKE implementation for a resource-constrained device, where we targeted the NIST recommended platform STM32F407VG featuring ARM Cortex-M4 processor. We integrate the isogeny-based implementation strategies described previously in the literature into the compressed version of SIKE. Additionally, we propose a new assembly design for the finite field operations particular for the compressed SIKE, and observe a speedup of up to 16% and up to 25% compared to the last best-reported assembly implementations for p434, p503, and p610.

Keywords: Compressed Supersingular Isogeny Key Encapsulation (SIKE) · Post-Quantum Cryptography (PQC) · ARM Cortex-M4

1 Introduction

Public key cryptography is essential for the confidentiality and integrity of data transmitted through an insecure channel. The classical schemes used nowadays such as RSA and the ECC family, however, are going to be broken when a large-scale quantum computer is developed. Driven by the technology progress

© ICST Institute for Computer Sciences, Social Informatics and Telecommunications Engineering 2021
Published by Springer Nature Switzerland AG 2021. All Rights Reserved
J. Garcia-Alfaro et al. (Eds.): SecureComm 2021, LNICST 399, pp. 441–457, 2021.
https://doi.org/10.1007/978-3-030-90022-9_24

the National Institute of Standards and Technology (NIST) [1] initialized a standardization process aiming at optimizing and evaluating the post-quantum candidates. In 2020, Round 3 of the competition has started, where the post-quantum secure Key Encapsulation Mechanisms are divided into two subgroups – finalists and alternate candidates. Forming part of the alternate candidates is the only isogeny-based cryptosystem – Supersingular Isogeny Key Encapsulation (SIKE) mechanism, which, based on the Supersingular Isogeny Diffie-Hellman (SIDH) algorithm [2], attracts with the smallest public key and ciphertext sizes (i.e., 330 and 346 bytes for the NIST security level 1 implementation). Thus, it ensures negligible communication latency of the algorithm and comes into use in a bandwidth-limited environment.

In 2016, *Azarderakhsh et al.* proposed even further reduction of the transmitted information in [3] where the team reduced the size of the data by a factor of 2 by applying a novel idea for compression mechanism. The significant timing overhead introduced when using the compression incited optimizations in the computational cost of the scheme presented in [4–6]. The compression mechanism, however, still introduces a non-negligible timing overhead and requires more available memory, making the protocol execution difficult on low-end devices which offer limited resources.

The compressed SIKE is the algorithm with the closest communication latency to today's cryptosystems. The extremely compact key sizes offered by the Elliptic Curve Cryptography (ECC) family lead to multiple optimizations of the algorithm targeting software and hardware [7–10] reporting indisputable time and energy efficiency. Nevertheless, despite the inexpensive computational cost and the extremely low key sizes, this classical crypto scheme will not ensure secure data transmission in the scenario of large quantum computers which leads to the NIST post-quantum standardization effort, where the complexity of some algorithms, such as SIKE, introduces higher computational cost. Thus, several researchers have centered their work on improving the efficiency of the PQ scheme on software [11–15], targeting ARMv7-M, ARMv7-A and ARMv8 ARM-based architectures, and hardware [16–19] targeting the Xilinx Virtex 7 FPGA family hardware platform.

Contribution. In this work, we propose the first implementation of compressed SIKE, targeting the resource-restricted processor ARM Cortex-M4. We integrate the finite field strategies proposed in [12] and [11] into the compressed SIKE implementation, we hand-code additional subroutines and report the achieved results. Our contributions are itemized as follows:

- We propose optimal usage of the memory, increasing the size of the stack to 128 KB and creating a memory region in the Core Coupled Memory (CCM RAM) increasing the RAM from 112 KB as proposed in PQM4 [20] to 192 KB. For the correct execution of compressed SIKEp610, we split large structures residing in the memory into parts and allocate them in the stack and the CCM RAM ensuring that the program does not overwrite illegal memory regions exceeding the size of the stack.

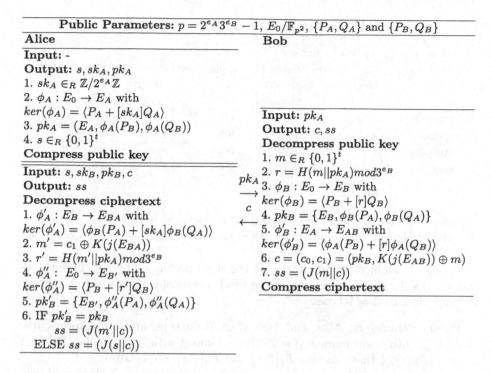

Public Parameters: $p = 2^{e_A}3^{e_B} - 1$, $E_0/\mathbb{F}_{p^2}$, $\{P_A, Q_A\}$ and $\{P_B, Q_B\}$

Alice

Input: -
Output: s, sk_A, pk_A
1. $sk_A \in_R \mathbb{Z}/2^{e_A}\mathbb{Z}$
2. $\phi_A : E_0 \to E_A$ with
$ker(\phi_A) = \langle P_A + [sk_A]Q_A \rangle$
3. $pk_A = (E_A, \phi_A(P_B), \phi_A(Q_B))$
4. $s \in_R \{0,1\}^t$
Compress public key

Input: s, sk_B, pk_B, c
Output: ss
Decompress ciphertext
1. $\phi'_A : E_B \to E_{BA}$ with
$ker(\phi'_A) = \langle \phi_B(P_A) + [sk_A]\phi_B(Q_A) \rangle$
2. $m' = c_1 \oplus K(j(E_{BA}))$
3. $r' = H(m'||pk_A)mod3^{e_B}$
4. $\phi''_A : E_0 \to E_{B'}$ with
$ker(\phi''_A) = \langle P_B + [r']Q_B \rangle$
5. $pk'_B = \{E_{B'}, \phi''_A(P_A), \phi''_A(Q_A)\}$
6. IF $pk'_B = pk_B$
  $ss = (J(m'||c))$
  ELSE $ss = (J(s||c))$

Bob

Input: pk_A
Output: c, ss
Decompress public key
1. $m \in_R \{0,1\}^t$
2. $r = H(m||pk_A)mod3^{e_B}$
3. $\phi_B : E_0 \to E_B$ with
$ker(\phi_B) = \langle P_B + [r]Q_B \rangle$
4. $pk_B = \{E_B, \phi_B(P_A), \phi_B(Q_A)\}$
5. $\phi'_B : E_A \to E_{AB}$ with
$ker(\phi'_B) = \langle \phi_A(P_B) + [r]\phi_A(Q_B) \rangle$
6. $c = (c_0, c_1) = (pk_B, K(j(E_{AB})) \oplus m)$
7. $ss = (J(m||c))$
Compress ciphertext

Fig. 1. SIKE algorithm [23]. H, K and J denote hash functions.

- We implement additional subroutines particular for compressed SIKE in an efficient assembly language - multi-precision subtraction with correction $2p$ and $4p$ and multi-precision multiplication of 256×256- and 320×320-bit length, where we apply the strategies described in the isogeny-based works [12] and [11].
- We integrate the previous best-reported arithmetic operations optimizations proposed in [12] and [11] and report a speedup of up to 25% and up to 16%, respectively, after integrating the new subroutine implementation for p434, p503, and p610 compressed SIKE primes.

2 Preliminaries

This section presents a detailed description of the (un)compressed SIKE protocol and a description of the target platform. For a more comprehensive description of the algorithms refer to [21] and [22].

2.1 SIKE

The Supersingular Isogeny Key Encapsulation mechanism forms part of the alternate candidates after NIST Round 2, thus it is still going through significant

Table 1. Round 2 SIKE public parameters [23].

Curve: $E_0/\mathbb{F}_{p^2}$: $y^2 = x^3 + 6x^2 + x$					
Parameter set	NIST Security Level	Public Key Size (B) Standard	Cipher Text Size (B)	Public Key Size (B) Compressed	Cipher Text Size (B)
SIKEp434	1	330	346	197	236
SIKEp503	2	378	402	225	280
SIKEp610	3	462	486	274	336
SIKEp751	5	564	596	335	410

improvements for the high- and low-end target devices. In this work, we present the first design of the compressed SIKE protocol targeting ARM Cortex-M4 processor.

Detailed graphical representation of the steps performed by the communication parties during the execution of the SIKE protocol is shown in Fig. 1 where they are described as follows:

- Public Parameters: Alice and Bob start from supersingular elliptic curve $E_0/\mathbb{F}_{p^2}$ with prime number $p = 2^{e_A}3^{e_B} - 1$ along with basis points $\{P_A, Q_A\}$ and $\{P_B, Q_B\}$ that generate $E_0[2^{e_A}]$ and $E_0[3^{e_B}]$, respectively.
- Key Generation: Alice computes a random integer $sk_A \in_R \mathbb{Z}/2^{e_A}\mathbb{Z}$ and uses it to compute a secret isogeny ϕ_A, where she uses the image curve E_A and the image points $\phi_A(P_B), \phi_A(Q_B)$ to form her public key pk_A.
- Encapsulation: Bob computes his secret key r based on Alice's public key and a random message m, which he uses to compute the kernel of his secret isogeny and to form his public key as $pk_B = \{E_B, \phi_B(P_A), \phi_B(Q_A)\}$. He computes a second isogeny, which leads him to the final image curve E_{AB}. He generates a ciphertext appending the message m masked by $j(E_{AB})$ of the curve to his public key.
- Decapsulation: Alice uses her secret key and Bob's public key projection points to reach curve E_{BA}, which since it is isomorphic to E_{AB} features the same j-invariant. She uses the unmasked value m to obtain Bob's secret key and uses it to re-compute his public key, where by comparing the result with c_0, she computes the shared secret or uses random value, preventing further communication.

2.2 Compression Mechanism

The insignificant bandwidth required for the execution of SIKE motivated several research teams to work and further optimize the size of the exchanged data. As shown in Table 1, there is a considerable difference between the key sizes of the standard and the compressed version of SIKE, which features the smallest key sizes among the post-quantum candidates even before the compression mechanism is applied.

The key compression mechanism has been proposed in 2016 and, due to the applications of compressed SIKE into the IoT world where the resources are strictly limited, it has gone through several modifications aiming at improving the main drawback of the protocol – the performance. In Fig. 2, the compression and decompression of the public information are shown, where the actual content of the communicated information has been modified with the improvements introduced by several research groups. Nevertheless, the compression mechanism requires the execution of three main steps: basis generation, pairing and discrete logarithms computations, where these phases introduce a non-negligible overhead to the execution of the algorithm.

The compression mechanism, proposed by *Azarderakhsh et al.* [3], reduces the size of the Supersingular Isogeny Diffie-Hellman, base of SIKE, public information by a factor of 2 – from $8log_2p$ to $4log_2p$. The improvement is achieved by replacing the previous public key tuple $\{E_A, \phi_A(P_B), \phi_A(Q_B)\}$ by new representation $\{j(E_A) \in \mathbb{F}_{p^2}, a_1, a_2, b_1, b_2 \in \mathbb{Z}_{3^{e_3}}\}$ with the j-invariant of the curve and four integers such that $\phi_A(P_B) = a_1 R_1 + a_2 R_2$ and $\phi_A(Q_B) = b_1 R_1 + b_2 R_2$ for canonical basis $\{R_1, R_2\}$ for $E_A[3^{e_3}]$. However, the additional computation of new points of order 3^{e_3}, the pairing algorithm revealing that the points actually form basis for $E_A[3^{e_3}]$ and discrete logarithms allowing the representation of the two image points with 4 coordinates in $\mathbb{F}_{p^2}$ using only 4 values in $\mathbb{Z}_{3^{e_3}}$, introduces and overhead of more than $10\times$ the execution time of the uncompressed algorithm.

Costello et al. have proposed several computational optimizations of the compression algorithm in [4], where they additionally achieve further key size reduction to $\frac{7}{2}log_2p$ by sending $\{j(E_A) \in \mathbb{F}_{p^2}, \alpha, \beta, \gamma \in \mathbb{Z}_{3^{e_3}}\}$ when normalizing three of the elements with a deterministically chosen invertible element. Their computation improvements are based on efficient torsion basis generation, fast Tate pairing [24,25] (replacing the Weil pairing), SIDH specific inversion-free pairing formulas, and highly optimized formulas for solving discrete logarithms. The improvements made by the authors decrease the performance overhead of the compression mechanism which leads to the integration of the proposed key size optimizations into the NIST standardization process SIDH protocol proposal.

In [26], *Zanon et al.* have proposed the use of entangled basis generation, which has further application in the isogeny-based hash functions and is proved to be more than $15\times$ more efficient than the usual basis generation. They achieve further performance improvement of the decompression by using shared elligator technique and reverse basis decomposition. The authors continue with the optimizations by applying an *optimal* strategy for the discrete logarithms and by exploiting particular characteristics of the entangled basis that speed up the Tate pairing computation.

Later, *Naehrig et al.* [5] have reduced the compression overhead by integrating dual isogenies to pull back the deterministically generated basis points to the original elliptic curve E. The use of dual isogeny $\hat{\phi}$ is applied in the basis generation and the pairing step, where the Tate pairings evaluate $\tau_{3^{e_3}}(P_B, \hat{\phi}_A(R_1))$, $\tau_{3^{e_3}}(P_B, \hat{\phi}_A(R_2))$, $\tau_{3^{e_3}}(Q_B, \hat{\phi}_A(R_1))$ and $\tau_{3^{e_3}}(Q_B, \hat{\phi}_A(R_2))$

instead of $\tau_{3^{e_3}}(\phi_A(P_B), R_1)$, $\tau_{3^{e_3}}(\phi_A(P_B), R_2)$, $\tau_{3^{e_3}}(\phi_A(Q_B), R_1)$ and $\tau_{3^{e_3}}(\phi_A(Q_B), R_2)$, leading to significant speedup since the computations are pulled back to the fixed starting curve and no changes throughout different executions of the protocol occur.

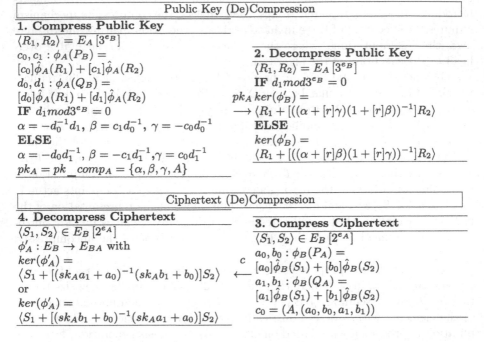

Fig. 2. Public key/ciphertext (de)compression. For more details refer to [22].

This work has been continued by *Pereira et al.* in [6] where they improve further the shared elligator technique, which allows to deterministically find a point on an elliptic curve, by integrating another two bits of information into the public key, showing the correct ternary basis generators. The implementation is performed by sharing two counter variables, generated during the compression phase, which allow the decompression step to be straightforward executed finding the correct basis points of the curve by accessing specific entry of precomputed tables. The authors also propose the use of x-only point addition formula which results in a much more efficient decompression step. The paper also proposed an increase of the ciphertext size (eliminating the previous reduction proposed in [4]), showing a trade-off between transmitted data size and computational overhead, which makes the comparison between the transmitted key and the re-computed one easier and results in a speedup of the decapsulation phase.

Finally, *Hutchinson et al.* [27] propose techniques for reducing the pairing and discrete logarithm tables by a factor of 4 by signed digit representation of exponents and torus-based representation of cyclotomic subgroup elements. These techniques introduce a slight overhead, however, are crucial for the integration of compressed SIKE into low-end devices with limited resources.

A detailed description of the compression and decompression steps taken by Alice and Bob are presented in Fig. 2 which are described as follows:

- Public key compression: Alice computes the unique dual isogeny $\hat{\phi}_A$ of her secret isogeny map which she uses to pull back the canonical basis points R_1, R_2, generating $E_A[3^{e_B}]$, to the elliptic curve with Mongtomery coeffiecient equal to 0 such that $\hat{\phi}_A(R_1), \hat{\phi}_A(R_2) \in E_{A'=0}$. She then computes 4 discrete logarithms, using optimal Pohlig-Hellman [28] strategy, c_0, c_1, d_0, d_1 and finally obtains the value of $\alpha, \beta, \gamma \in (\mathbb{Z}_{3^{e_3}})^3$, that form part of the compressed public key replacing $\phi_A(P_B)$ and $\phi_A(Q_B)$.
- Public key decompression: Bob recovers the value of the canonical basis points R_1, R_2 and uses them along with the triplet from Alice's public key to compute the kernel of his second isogeny.
- Ciphertext compression: Bob computes canonical basis points S_1, S_2 to compress his public key, which forms part of the ciphertext. For efficiency reasons [6] the triplet is not computed but rather a linear combination of the four values of a_0, a_1, b_0, b_1 are sent to Alice, introducing a tradeoff between ciphertext length and decompression (thus decapsulation) execution time.
- Ciphertext decompression: Alice computes the canonical basis S_1, S_2 and uses the four values sent by Bob to compute her second isogeny and to reach the elliptic curve $\phi'_A : E_B \to E_{BA}$, featuring the same j-invariant as E_{AB} which helps her to recover the value of the masked message m.

2.3   ARMv7-M Architecture

The fast development of the Internet of Things world results in extremely high demand for low-end devices, which can be integrated into any real-time embedded system. Thus, NIST has announced the Reduced Instruction Set Computer (RISC) ARM Cortex-M4-based microcontroller STM32F407VG as the target microcontroller for the implementation and benchmarking of the post-quantum secure schemes on resource-constraint devices. The standardization effort has incited the implementation of the PQM4 library [20], which integrates test and benchmark framework used in this work to perform the measurements.

The STM32F407VG microcontroller features 1 MB of flash memory and 192 KB of RAM. However, the memory map of the device Fig. 3 shows the division of the RAM into 3 different memory blocks – 2 consecutive SRAM blocks of 112 KB and 16 KB, and 1 Cored Coupled Memory (CCM RAM) block of 64 KB in a separate memory region. In PQM4, for efficiency reasons, only the first SRAM memory region is used for the execution of SIKE, thus the resources of the device are brought down to only 112 KB, which results to be insufficient for the execution of the compressed SIKE protocol.

The 3-stage pipeline of the ARMv7-M architecture allows the fast execution of the instruction set, where most of the instructions require a single clock cycle. However, the load/store design requires another extra cycle for the completion

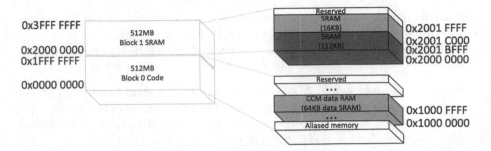

Fig. 3. Memory map of STM32F407VG device. The memory region used in PQM4 library [20] for the execution of SIKE is marked in red. (Color figure online)

of memory access instructions. In some particular cases, the instructions can be scheduled, thus the additional cycle is absorbed by the following instruction, however, depending on the nature of the implemented crypto scheme, this scheduling technique may be or may not be feasible to apply.

The platform, based on ARMv7-M architecture, features 16 32-bit General Purpose Registers (GPRs) and another 32 32-bit Floating-Point Registers (FPRs). Two of the GPRs are reserved for the Stack Pointer and the Program Counter, therefore, cannot be modified by the programmer, whereas the use of all FPRs is allowed, providing another 1024 bits of register space. Furthermore, the access cost for the information stored in the FPRs consists of a single clock cycle. The VMOV instruction ensures instant data transfer between the two register sets, where it can be used to replace memory accesses, reducing the cost of LDR and STR instructions.

The use of Multiply ACcumulate (MAC) instructions has been the focus of several researchers in the last years due to the execution of up to 3 operations in a single clock cycle, thus we have integrated the use of UMULL and UMAAL into our work.

The procedure call standard for ARM architecture [29] states that the core registers R4–R11 and floating-point registers S16–S31 are not callee-saved, thus their value should be preserved among function calls by (v)pushing them in the stack at the beginning of a subroutine and (v)popping them at the end of a function call.

3   Compressed SIKE on STM32F407VG

The resource-constrained target platform and the PQM4 library settings did not allow the execution of the compressed SIKE for security levels 3 and 5. We applied some changes to the architecture of the linker file to make possible the execution of compressed SIKEp610 on the STM32F407VG platform. Furthermore, we implemented finite-field and multi-precision arithmetic particular for compressed SIKE in assembly language to speed up further the execution time of the protocol.

3.1 Configuration Modifications

The PQM4 library, base of our benchmarking, provides an implementation of the uncompressed SIKE, however, does not integrate the compressed SIKE due to the resource limitations of the target platform. The library configurations for SIKE are designed to fit the needs of the crypto scheme eliminating slow SRAM regions overhead. Specifically, for the execution of SIKE, the authors of the library integrate the use of only the first 112 KB of SRAM, where the following 16 KB are not in use due to efficiency reasons.

The execution of the compressed SIKE, however, requires large data structures, needed for the dual isogeny computation, which sizes increase with the number of isogeny maps needed thus with the security level of the algorithm. For the primes p610 and p751 the 112 KB of SRAM were not enough to store the allocated local tables and resulted in stack overflow, causing the program to break due to overwriting illegal memory regions.

To allow the correct execution of compressed SIKEp610, we increased the size of the stack including the extra 16 KB of SRAM by modifying the linker file. However, a total of 128 KB of SRAM was still not enough for the compressed SIKEp610 execution. Therefore, we created a new memory region, which we placed inside the CCM RAM memory. We had to split the large dynamically allocated data structures into parts and place them separately into the SRAM (the stack) or the CCM RAM region. The CCM RAM memory is primarily designed for running code fast (with zero wait states) thus, placing some variables in this region may result in a speedup of the execution without any modification on the algorithm design. However, for precise measurement results, the PQM4 [20] benchmark framework suggests running the code @24 MHz which eliminates all wait states and ensures an accurate number of clock cycles. Thus, the performance improvements discussed in this work are solely a result of the hand-coded assembly subroutines described in the following sections. The memory increase allowed us to execute the compressed SIKEp610 algorithm, where we had to perform some slight changes to the code, splitting the data structures and addressing them accordingly during the execution. The compressed SIKEp751 requires more memory than the entire 192 KB of RAM, thus, it is not the focus of this work.

3.2 Field Subtraction and Multi-Precision Multiplication

In this work, we integrated the arithmetic operations underlying SIKE described in [12] and [11] into the implementation of compressed SIKE. The compressed crypto scheme, however, requires other functions, specific to the compression mechanism of SIKE. We implemented them in assembly language, integrating the strategies described in the literature, in particular, in [12] and [11], where, due to the performance optimizations and the invocation rate of the subroutines, we end up with a significant speedup.

Field Subtraction. The importance of long integer modular addition and subtraction for cryptography is undeniable and its high invocation rates incite continuous improvement of these arithmetic operations [11,12,30]. The implementation of long integer addition/subtraction requires proper management of the carry/borrow propagation among the different limbs of the operands. The integration of correction step in the subtraction subroutine, bringing the integer back into the finite field specified by the security level implementation of the protocol, implies the execution of one extra long-integer addition, where in the scope of the compressed SIKE there are two different functions – subtract with correction $2p$ and $4p$, performing $a - b + 2p$ and $a - b + 4p$, respectively. We implement these functions in an efficient assembly code using the implementation strategies described in [11].

First, we apply the blocking strategy, where we split the long integer into several parts as shown in Fig. 4. We perform the subtraction and addition steps to each block managing the carry/borrow propagation with the help of carry/borrow catcher/activator, using the reduced instruction set SBC and RSBC. This strategy allows to reduce the number of registers used for the carry/borrow management and to increase the block size from 4 words per block to 5. Thus, the memory access latency is reduced along with the number of multiple load/store instructions which ensures scheduled code and minimal overhead.

Second, we integrate the block operation alternation, where we flip the applied add/sub instructions as shown in Fig. 4 among consecutive blocks allowing to manage the carry/borrow propagation using simply the ADCS/SBCS instructions. Therefore, we reduce the number of carry/borrow catchers/activators and use fewer instructions per modular subtraction.

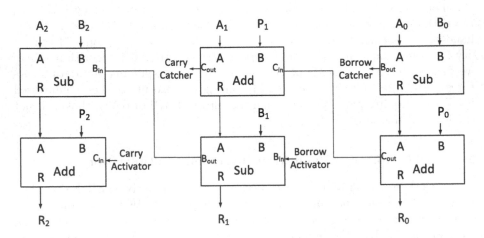

Fig. 4. Subtraction with correction P, where P represents $2p$ or $4p$.

Multi-precision Multiplication. Due to the extremely high invocation rate of the multi-precision multiplication in the scope of SIKE and compressed SIKE, its fast implementation becomes crucial for the crypto scheme's performance. Several research groups have been working on optimizing the multi-precision multiplication function by applying the Karatsuba method [30], [31], focusing on the powerful MAC instruction set [32,33] and reducing the memory accesses by reusing the loaded values in the register set as long as possible [12,34].

The implementation of compressed SIKE integrates multiplication subroutines of smaller sizes than the length of the primes, due to the new values contained into the public key and the ciphertext messages. In particular, the compressed SIKE uses multi-precision multiplication of two operands consisting of 8 32-bit words for p434 and p503 and 10 32-bit words for p610. The multiplication results are not reduced, therefore, the outputs are two times longer than the operand sizes. In Fig. 5, we describe the implementations of both lengths of multi-precision multiplications using the visual rhombus representation where every diagonal line denotes a limb from the operand. The white dots show a 32×32-bit multiplication of the words from the operands corresponding to the crossing diagonals. The stroked white fields represent the consecutive accumulative multiplications and are referred to as rows in the literature. Finally, the red numbers denote the floating-point registers storing the partial results, where they are used in a consecutive order increasing from right to left. To reduce the execution timing of the multi-precision multiplication and thus to increase the efficiency of the entire protocol, we implemented the functions using assembly code as proposed in [12] and [11]. We used the Multiply ACcumulate instructions UMULL and UMAAL, implementing the Refined-Operand Caching design proposed in [12] with a maximum row size equal to 4. We implemented 256×256- and 320×320-bit multiplications, where we use the FP register set as a cache memory, storing the partial result values resulting from the different row calculations as shown in Fig. 5, using the low-cost VMOV instruction.

Table 2. Compressed SIKE arithmetic performance cost @24 MHz.

Implementation	Timing [cc×10⁶]								
	sub_2p	sub_4p	mul	sub_2p	sub_4p	mul	sub_2p	sub_4p	mul
	SIKEp434 compressed			SIKEp503 compressed			SIKEp610 compressed		
SIDH v3.3[1]	577	579	4,940	656	656	4,940	813	813	8,034
This work	135	135	202	147	147	202	180	180	296

[1] [35]

The implementation of all the finite field operations is performed in constant time, including the work in [12] and [11], which has been adapted to the compressed SIKE algorithm in the scope of this work. We have performed our measurements, as described in Sect. 4, running the algorithm @24 MHz and

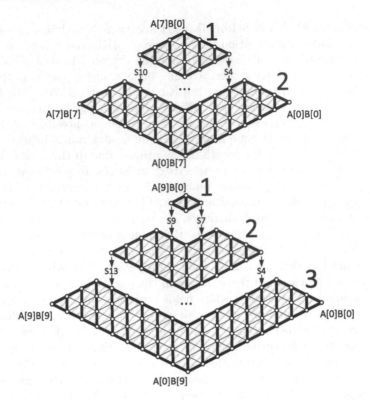

Fig. 5. 256 × 256- and 320 × 320-bit multiplication, using the FPRs as cache level 1 storing partial result values.

@168 MHz, for achieving a precise number of clock cycles and for reporting the minimal timing that the protocol can be executed, respectively. The underlying arithmetic operations are the reason for the performance speedup of the entire protocol due to the pyramid-like structure of the isogeny-based post-quantum scheme. In Table 2, we report the obtained performance after we have implemented the subtraction and the multiplication functions in assembly language. We compare our performance with the previous best (and only) implementation of the given subroutines which we have obtained from [35] implemented in portable C language. The comparison table shows that the target-specific implementation of the subtraction and multiplication is improved by 76.60% and 95.91%, respectively, for p434, 77,59% and 95.91% for p503, and 77.86% and 96.32% for p610. The global performance of compressed SIKE is improved significantly by the implementation optimizations of the functions but also due to the high invocation ratio of these arithmetic operations.

4   Performance Evaluation

In this section, we present the results that we obtained after applying the optimization strategies (the changes described in Sect. 3.1 apply for compressed SIKEp610 only). We performed our experiments and report the results in Table 3, targeting the processor Cortex-M4 using the board STM32F407VG and the benchmark framework PQM4 [20], running it @24 MHz which sets the processor to zero wait state, and @168 MHz, providing the performance cost for systems, running at the maximum controller speed, showing the protocol execution time in seconds. We have placed our code segment in the ROM memory while the data segment is placed in the RAM region, where the use of the CCM RAM is dedicated to the storage of large local data structures that exceed the size of the stack. The obtained performance improvements are a result of the integration of the target-specific subroutine implementation since the slow frequency used for the precise measurements ensures zero wait states thus the use of the CCM RAM has no impact on the overall execution time. The reported results show the performance of compressed SIKE Round 3, where the work presented in [5] and [6] is adapted to the implementation design.

Table 3. Compressed SIKE Round 3 performance cost and speedup @24 MHz aiming precision of the reported clock cycles and @168 MHz reporting timing results for real world scenario.

| Implementation | Timing [$cc \times 10^6$] | | | | Speedup | Timing Total | |
| | @24MHz | | | | | @168MHz | |
	KeyGen	Encaps	Decaps	Total	[%]	[$cc \times 10^6$]	[sec]
SIKEp434 compressed							
SIDH v3.3[1]	1,088	1,715	1,272	2,987	94.1	3,017	18.00
Seo et al.[2]	79	133	98	232	24.9	240	1.43
Anastasova et al.[3]	76	119	89	209	16.7	246	1.46
This work	68	99	74	174	-	212	1.26
SIKEp503 compressed							
SIDH v3.3[1]	1,638	2,601	1,920	4,521	94.5	4,519	27.00
Seo et al.[2]	111	181	137	319	21.8	333	1.98
Anastasova et al.[3]	99	164	125	289	13.9	359	2.14
This work	89	143	106	249	-	318	1.89
SIKEp610 compressed							
SIDH v3.3[1]	3,244	4,909	3,889	8,798	94.5	8,775	52.00
Seo et al.[2]	220	333	278	611	20.4	627	3.73
Anastasova et al.[3]	191	306	255	561	13.2	635	3.78
This work	187	267	219	487	-	564	3.36

We compare the results with the previous best-reported implementation strategies of the finite field arithmetic needed for the long integer operations in

Table 4. PQC Round 3 finalists and alternate candidates timing results, memory usage and transmitted data on STM32F407VG using PQM4 [20].

Implementation	Timing [cc×10⁶]			Memory [B]			Data [B]
	KeyGen	Encaps	Decaps	KeyGen	Encaps	Decaps	pk+ct
Security Level I							
Kyber512	0.46	0.57	0.53	2,396	2,484	2,500	1,568
ntruhps2048509	79.66	0.56	0.54	21,392	14,068	14,800	1,398
lightsaber	0.36	0.49	0.46	5,332	5,292	5,308	1,408
BIKE L1	25.06	3.40	54.79	44,108	32,156	91,400	3,113
FrodoKEM640aes	48.35	47.13	46.59	31,992	62,488	83,104	19,336
FrodoKEM640shake	79.33	79.70	79.15	26,600	51,976	72,592	19,336
SIKEp434compressed	68.26	99.50	74.86	68,636	41,380	7,940	433
	65.4%	47.6%	3.9%				56.1%
SIKEp434	41.28	67.40	72.02	6,108	6,468	6,748	676
Security Level II							
SIKEp503compressed	89.76	143.17	106.26	88,192	53,696	9,008	505
	54.4%	49.9%	4.5%				54.5%
SIKEp503	58.12	95.53	101.73	7,360	7,736	8,112	780
Security Level III							
Kyber768	0.76	0.92	0.86	3,276	2,968	2,988	2,272
ntruhps2048677	143.73	0.82	0.82	28,504	9,036	19,728	1,862
saber	0.66	0.84	0.79	6,364	6,316	6,332	2,080
ntruhrss701	153.10	0.38	0.87	27,560	7,400	20,552	2,276
ntrulpr761	0.74	1.29	1.39	13,168	20,000	24,032	2,206
sntrup761	10.83	0.70	0.57	61,508	13,320	16,952	2,197
SIKEp610compressed	187.67	267.35	219.80	85,740	78,532	11,524	616
	76.9%	37.2%	12.1%				53.9%
SIKEp610	106.07	194.90	196.12	10,490	10,908	11,372	948

SIKE after integrating them into the compressed SIKE protocol. Even though we propose the first integration of compressed SIKE on low-end Cortex-M4, we integrate the code presented in [12] and [11] to provide comparison results. Table 3 reports performance optimizations of 25%, 21% and 20% for SIKEp434, SIKEp503 and SIKEp610, respectively, comparing our work with [12] and 16%, 14% and 13%, compared to the design in [11]. The measurements when running the board @24 MHz represent a precise number of clock cycles, however, for real-time applications, where the execution speed is of great importance, we increase the frequency to 168 MHz, offered by the STM32F407-Discovery board, and report the performance in terms of clock cycles and seconds. We observe that the execution of the compressed SIKE mechanism is significantly improved, where it still represents its main drawback, while offering the smallest key sizes, and reducing the communication latency to minimal in comparison to the rest of the post-quantum candidates.

In Table 4, we present the compressed SIKE algorithm comparing it with the rest of the post-quantum candidates in the NIST standardization effort to offer a better understanding of the advantages and disadvantages of each one of the protocols and to stress again on the main benefit of compressed SIKE – the key sizes. Even though SIKE forms part of the alternate candidates in the NIST PQ process, we believe that it is applicable in multiple scenarios, especially in low-end real-time and IoT systems, where the data transmission latency should be minimal and the resource capabilities of the devices are constrained. In Table 4, we describe the timing of the post-quantum safe candidates, the memory requirements of each scheme, and the size of the public data. We denote the Round 3 finalists in bold, where the rest of the schemes are alternate candidates. We report the timing overhead introduced by the compression mechanism of SIKE in red color and the public information overhead when running uncompressed SIKE in green.

5   Conclusions

In this work, we presented the first implementation of compressed SIKE targeting the low-end device STM32F407VG, which is the NIST recommended platform for benchmarking the post-quantum secure protocols. We increased the stack and added a new memory region placed in the CCM RAM memory, which allowed to execute compressed SIKEp610 without corrupting the memory. Further, we implement subtraction and multiplication compressed-specific subroutines in assembly code to maximize the speedup.

We hope to push SIKE and compressed SIKE further in the PQC NIST competition by continuing our optimization effort since they offer the smallest key sizes, therefore, ensure insignificant communication cost.

Acknowledgments. The authors would like to thank the reviewers for their detailed comments. This work is supported in parts by an award from NSF 2101085.

References

1. T.N.I. of Standards and T. (NIST): Post-quantum cryptography standardization, 2017–2018. https://csrc.nist.gov/projects/post-quantum-cryptography/post-quantum-cryptography-standardization. Accessed 6 Jun 2021
2. Jao, D., De Feo, L.: Towards quantum-resistant cryptosystems from supersingular elliptic curve isogenies. In: Yang, B.-Y. (ed.) PQCrypto 2011. LNCS, vol. 7071, pp. 19–34. Springer, Heidelberg (2011). https://doi.org/10.1007/978-3-642-25405-5_2
3. Azarderakhsh, R., Jao, D., Kalach, K., Koziel, B., Leonardi, C.: Key compression for isogeny-based cryptosystems. In: Proceedings of the 3rd ACM International Workshop on ASIA Public-Key Cryptography, pp. 1–10 (2016)
4. Costello, C., Jao, D., Longa, P., Naehrig, M., Renes, J., Urbanik, D.: Efficient compression of SIDH public keys. In: Coron, J.-S., Nielsen, J.B. (eds.) EUROCRYPT 2017. LNCS, vol. 10210, pp. 679–706. Springer, Cham (2017). https://doi.org/10.1007/978-3-319-56620-7_24
5. Naehrig, M., Renes, J.: Dual isogenies and their application to public-key compression for isogeny-based cryptography. In: Galbraith, S.D., Moriai, S. (eds.) ASIACRYPT 2019. LNCS, vol. 11922, pp. 243–272. Springer, Cham (2019). https://doi.org/10.1007/978-3-030-34621-8_9

6. Pereira, G., Doliskani, J., Jao, D.: x-only point addition formula and faster compressed SIKE. J. Cryptogr. Eng. **11**(1), 57–69 (2021). https://doi.org/10.1007/s13389-020-00245-4
7. Fujii, H., Aranha, D.F.: Curve25519 for the Cortex-M4 and beyond. In: Lange, T., Dunkelman, O. (eds.) LATINCRYPT 2017. LNCS, vol. 11368, pp. 109–127. Springer, Cham (2019). https://doi.org/10.1007/978-3-030-25283-0_6
8. Seo, H.: Memory efficient implementation of modular multiplication for 32-bit ARM Cortex-M4. Appl. Sci. **10**(4), 1539 (2020)
9. Niasar, M.B., El Khatib, R., Azarderakhsh, R., Mozaffari-Kermani, M.: Fast, small, and area-time efficient architectures for key-exchange on curve25519. In: IEEE 27th Symposium on Computer Arithmetic (ARITH), vol. 2020, pp. 72–79. IEEE (2020)
10. Bisheh Niasar, M., Azarderakhsh, R., Kermani, M.M.: Efficient hardware implementations for elliptic curve cryptography over Curve448. In: Bhargavan, K., Oswald, E., Prabhakaran, M. (eds.) INDOCRYPT 2020. LNCS, vol. 12578, pp. 228–247. Springer, Cham (2020). https://doi.org/10.1007/978-3-030-65277-7_10
11. Anastasova, M., Azarderakhsh, R., Kermani, M.M.: Fast strategies for the implementation of SIKE round 3 on ARM Cortex-M4. IEEE Trans. Circ. Syst. I Reg. Pap. **68**(10), 4129–4141 (2021)
12. Seo, H., Anastasova, M., Jalali, A., Azarderakhsh, R.: Supersingular isogeny key encapsulation (SIKE) round 2 on ARM Cortex-M4. IEEE Trans. Comput. **70**, 1705–1718 (2020)
13. Seo, H., Liu, Z., Longa, P., Hu, Z.: SIDH on ARM: faster modular multiplications for faster post-quantum supersingular isogeny key exchange. IACR Trans. Cryptogr. Hardware Embed. Syst. **2018**, 1–20 (2018)
14. Koziel, B., Jalali, A., Azarderakhsh, R., Jao, D., Mozaffari-Kermani, M.: NEON-SIDH: efficient implementation of supersingular Isogeny Diffie-Hellman key exchange protocol on ARM. In: Foresti, S., Persiano, G. (eds.) CANS 2016. LNCS, vol. 10052, pp. 88–103. Springer, Cham (2016). https://doi.org/10.1007/978-3-319-48965-0_6
15. Seo, H., Sanal, P., Jalali, A., Azarderakhsh, R.: Optimized implementation of SIKE round 2 on 64-bit ARM Cortex-A processors. IEEE Trans. Circ. Syst. I Regul. Pap. **67**, 2659-2671 (2020)
16. Elkhatib, R., Azarderakhsh, R., Mozaffari-Kermani, M.: Efficient and Fast Hardware Architectures for SIKE Round 2 on FPGA. Cryptology ePrint Archive 2020/611, Technical report (2020)
17. Koziel, B., Ackie, A.-B., El Khatib, R., Azarderakhsh, R., Kermani, M.M.: SIKE'd up: fast hardware architectures for supersingular isogeny key encapsulation. IEEE Trans. Circ. Syst. I Regul. Pap. **67**, 4842–4854 (2020)
18. Elkhatib, R., Azarderakhsh, R., Mozaffari-Kermani, M.: Highly optimized montgomery multiplier for SIKE primes on FPGA. In: IEEE 27th Symposium on Computer Arithmetic (ARITH). IEEE, vol. 2020, pp. 64–71 (2020)
19. Phoon, J.-H., Lee, W.-K., Wong, D.C.-K., Yap, W.-S., Goi, B.-M.: Area-time-efficient code-based postquantum key encapsulation mechanism on FPGA. IEEE Trans. Very Large Scale Integr. (VLSI) Syst. **28**(12), 2672–2684 (2020)
20. Kannwischer, M.J., Rijneveld, J., Schwabe, P., Stoffelen, K.: pqm4: testing and benchmarking NIST PQC on ARM Cortex-M4 (2019)
21. Jao, D., De Feo, L.: Towards quantum-resistant cryptosystems from supersingular elliptic curve isogenies. In: 4th International Workshop on Post-Quantum Cryptography, PQCrypto 2011, pp. 19–34 (2011). https://doi.org/10.1007/978-3-642-25405-5_2

22. SIKE: Sike website. https://sike.org/. Accessed 6 Jun 2021
23. Jao, D., et al.: Supersingular Isogeny Key Encapsulation. Submission to the NIST Post-Quantum Standardization Project (2017). https://sike.org/
24. Barreto, P.S.L.M., Kim, H.Y., Lynn, B., Scott, M.: Efficient algorithms for pairing-based cryptosystems. In: Yung, M. (ed.) CRYPTO 2002. LNCS, vol. 2442, pp. 354–369. Springer, Heidelberg (2002). https://doi.org/10.1007/3-540-45708-9_23
25. Galbraith, S.D., Harrison, K., Soldera, D.: Implementing the tate pairing. In: Fieker, C., Kohel, D.R. (eds.) ANTS 2002. LNCS, vol. 2369, pp. 324–337. Springer, Heidelberg (2002). https://doi.org/10.1007/3-540-45455-1_26
26. Zanon, G.H., Simplicio, M.A., Pereira, G.C., Doliskani, J., Barreto, P.S.: Faster key compression for isogeny-based cryptosystems. IEEE Trans. Comput. **68**(5), 688–701 (2018)
27. Hutchinson, A., Karabina, K., Pereira, G.: Memory optimization techniques for computing discrete logarithms in compressed SIKE (2021)
28. Pohlig, S., Hellman, M.: An improved algorithm for computing logarithms overGF(p) and its cryptographic significance (corresp.). IEEE Trans. Inf. Theor. **24**(1), 106–110 (1978)
29. Earnshaw, R.: Procedure call standard for the ARM architecture. ARM Limited (October 2003)
30. Koppermann, P., Pop, E., Heyszl, J., Sigl, G.: 18 seconds to key exchange: limitations of supersingular isogeny Diffie-Hellman on embedded devices. IACR Cryptol. ePrint Arch. **2018**, 932 (2018)
31. De Santis, F., Sigl, G.: Towards side-channel protected X25519 on ARM Cortex-M4 processors. In: Proceedings of Software Performance Enhancement for Encryption and Decryption, and Benchmarking, Utrecht, The Netherlands, pp. 19–21 (2016)
32. Hutter, M., Wenger, E.: Fast multi-precision multiplication for public-key cryptography on embedded microprocessors. In: Preneel, B., Takagi, T. (eds.) CHES 2011. LNCS, vol. 6917, pp. 459–474. Springer, Heidelberg (2011). https://doi.org/10.1007/978-3-642-23951-9_30
33. Seo, H., Kim, H.: Multi-precision multiplication for public-key cryptography on embedded microprocessors. In: Lee, D.H., Yung, M. (eds.) WISA 2012. LNCS, vol. 7690, pp. 55–67. Springer, Heidelberg (2012). https://doi.org/10.1007/978-3-642-35416-8_5
34. Seo, H., Kim, H.: Consecutive operand-caching method for multiprecision multiplication. J. inf. Commun. Convergence Eng. **13**(1), 27–35 (2015)
35. PQCryptov3.3: Sidh library. https://github.com/Microsoft/PQCrypto-SIDH

A Quantum Circuit to Speed-Up the Cryptanalysis of Code-Based Cryptosystems

Simone Perriello$^{(\boxtimes)}$ ⓘ, Alessandro Barenghi$^{(\boxtimes)}$ ⓘ, and Gerardo Pelosi ⓘ

Department of Electronics, Information and Bioengineering,
DEIB Politecnico di Milano, 20133 Milan, Italy
{simone.perriello,alessandro.barenghi,gerardo.pelosi}@polimi.it

Abstract. The significant interest in cryptographic primitives providing sound security margins when facing attacks with quantum computers is witnessed by the ongoing USA National Institute of Standards and Technology Post-quantum Cryptography Standardization process. Sound and precise evaluation of the amount of computation required to break such cryptographic primitives by means of quantum computers is required to be able to choose the cryptosystem parameters.

We present a full description of a quantum circuit to accelerate the computation of the solution of the Information Set Decoding problem , which is currently the best known non-structural attack against code-based cryptosystems. We validate our design running it on small instances of error correction codes, which allowed a complete validation on the AtoS QLM quantum computer simulator. We detail the circuit accelerating the exponential complexity search phase in the Lee and Brickell variant of the ISD solver, and provide its computational complexity for cryptographically relevant parameters taken from the third round candidates in the USA post-quantum standardization process.

Keywords: Post-quantum cryptography · Code based cryptography · Information set decoding

1 Introduction

The overwhelming majority of widely employed asymmetric cryptographic primitives rely on the assumption that factoring large integers or solving discrete logarithms in cyclic groups with large prime order are infeasible tasks. The most efficient algorithms for integer factoring and the computation of discrete logarithms in numerical cyclic groups with prime order, the *general number field sieve* and the *index calculus*, run in sub-exponential computation time. However, in a pioneering work in 1994, Peter Shor formulated an algorithm running on a quantum computer that computes integer factorization in polynomial time [25]. The same algorithm can be adapted to solve the discrete logarithm problem on any cyclic group [24].

© ICST Institute for Computer Sciences, Social Informatics and Telecommunications Engineering 2021
Published by Springer Nature Switzerland AG 2021. All Rights Reserved
J. Garcia-Alfaro et al. (Eds.): SecureComm 2021, LNICST 399, pp. 458–474, 2021.
https://doi.org/10.1007/978-3-030-90022-9_25

Given the significant efforts put in the construction of large scale quantum computers, designing quantum-computing resistant asymmetric primitives has become a pressing need. This need is also witnessed by the USA National Institute of Standards and Technology (NIST) standardization effort which has begun in November 2017 and has recently entered its third round phase [19], selecting a portfolio of (post-quantum) cryptosystems withstanding cryptanalysis with quantum computers.

Among the mathematical trapdoors available to build a post-quantum cryptographic primitive, cryptosystems based on linear codes represent a prime candidate, with three candidates present in the third round of the NIST standardization effort. The hard problem underlying code-based cryptosystems is either decoding an error affected codeword of a random linear code, or finding an error vector corresponding to a syndrome of a random linear code. Such problems were shown to be NP-hard in [6], and were employed to build two families of cryptosystems, namely McEliece's [13] and Niederreiter's [20]. Both of them build the trapdoor function out of a non-random, efficiently decodable code, constituting the private key of the cryptosystem, and out of an obfuscated representation of the same code, made indistinguishable from a completely random one, which acts as the public key.

The most effective cryptanalytic tool, agnostic to the choice of the non-random efficiently decodable code, is the Information Set Decoding (ISD) technique, proposed by Prange [23]. The original proposal was refined with improvements on the computation complexity, albeit with diminishing rewards over time [3]. The cumulative impact of all the improvements has indeed a small repercussion in the choice of the key size [8]. A crucial point in designing cryptosystem parameters to provide a predetermined computational security margin is to evaluate the computational complexity of the ISD algorithms considering the potential speedups that can be provided by a quantum computer. Currently, only studies providing asymptotic costs as a function of the cryptosystem parameters (e.g., key sizes) are present for quantum accelerated ISDs [7, 14]. While asymptotic bounds help to understand the complexity trend, providing finite-regime estimates of the computation demands of cryptanalysis of code-based cryptosystems would allow to derive a more precise estimate of their parameters (e.g., key sizes). In this work, we describe a quantum circuit to accelerate the Lee and Brickell approach to ISD [16], which improves over [23]. The choice of the Lee-Brickell variant allows us to proceed with a quantum circuit that does not need any quantum RAM element, but only standard quantum gates. In a related work [22], the authors propose a complete circuit to implement a quantum version of [23].

Contribution. The aim of this paper is to provide first concrete measures to be used in the evaluation of the complexity parameters required by the NIST post-quantum cryptography program. To the best of our knowledge, this is the first detailed implementation of a quantum circuit that aims to speed up an ISD algorithm. We design the quantum circuit to speed up the exponential time search-phase of the Lee and Brickell (LB) algorithm, while leaving the polynomial time input preparation to a classical controller. We analyze the circuit complexity of our solution, and validate the soundness of the approach by simulating the circuits with the Atos Quantum Learning Machine (QLM) [2]. We report results on the cryptographically relevant parameters proposed for two code-based cryptosystems included in the third round of the NIST post-quantum standardization initiative, showing gains between $2^{10} \times$ and $2^{20} \times$ with respect to a purely classic ISD implementation.

2   Background

In this section, we recall the basic notions underlying code-based asymmetric cryptography, the ISD strategy and provide background information on quantum computing and Grover's algorithm.

2.1   Code Based Cryptosystems

An $[n, k]$ binary linear error correcting code $\mathcal{C}$ is a k-dimensional vector subspace of $\mathbb{F}_2^n$, whose n-length (column) vectors are called codewords. Codes are designed in such a way that the minimum Hamming distance between any two codewords is at least d, a value known as *code distance*. Starting from a k-bit long input message, $m \in \mathbb{F}_2^k$, the objective of the code is to transform m into a codeword $c \in \mathcal{C}$ by adding to it $r=n-k$ redundant bits, a process known as *encoding*.

$\mathcal{C}$ can be completely characterized by a generator matrix $G \in \mathbb{F}_2^{k \times n}$ such that $\mathcal{C} = \{c \in \mathbb{F}_2^n : c = G^T m\}$. In other words, a codeword $c \in \mathcal{C}$ is obtained through a linear combination of the rows of G. As an alternative to G, a linear code can be described using the so-called parity-check matrix $H \in \mathbb{F}_2^{r \times n}$ as $\mathcal{C} = \{c \in \mathbb{F}_2^n : Hc=0\}$, with $HG^T = 0_{r \times k}$.

The process of removing the r redundant bits of information from a (possibly erroneous) codeword is called *decoding*. Specifically, the *codeword decoding* problem consists in retrieving the original message m starting from a corrupted codeword $y = c + e$, where $c \in \mathcal{C}$ and e is an $n \times 1$ binary (column) vector with Hamming weight $\mathrm{WT}(e) = t$, $0 < t < \lfloor \frac{d}{2} \rfloor$. To this end, we can equivalently recover either c or e. To recover the error e, many algorithms use the so-called *syndrome*, i.e. the $r \times 1$ (column) vector s defined as $s = Hy = H(c+e) = He$. This problem is known as *syndrome decoding*.

If H is randomly chosen among the ones in $\mathbb{F}_2^{r \times n}$ with rank k, both the codeword decoding problem and the syndrome decoding problem are NP-hard [6]. To build a sound cryptosystems, we can therefore start from a non-random and efficiently decodable code with parity-check matrix H', and then conceal it through a multiplication with a random non-singular matrix S, yielding $H = SH'$. The random-looking matrix H can then be used by anyone to send a message over a public channel: it suffices to encode the message as an error vector e of weight t, compute its syndrome and send it. An attacker trying to recover the original message e is then forced to find the solution to the syndrome decoding problem for an apparently random parity-check matrix H.

2.2   Information Set Decoding (ISD)

The state-of-the-art method to efficiently solve the *syndrome decoding* problem is based on ISD techniques. The underlying intuition, due to Prange in [23], is to see the syndrome s as obtained by the sum of the t columns of H indexed by the bit-positions in the error vector e containing a term equal to one. To find out the bit-positions in e corresponding to an asserted bit, Prange's idea is to guess k bit-positions in e corresponding to a zero-bit. After that, by using a permutation matrix $P_{n \times n}$, Prange's algorithm continues by packing all the columns of H indexed by the said k positions to the leftmost part of H, obtaining a new matrix $\hat{H} = HP$. The next step brings $\hat{H}$ in reduced row echelon form, simultaneously finding a linear transformation represented by an $r \times r$ non-singular matrix U, such that $U\hat{H} = [V_{r \times k} \mid I_r]$. The leftmost matrix $V_{r \times k}$ is a random-looking matrix, while I_r is an identity matrix with size r. The procedure fails if the reduced row echelon form cannot be obtained, i.e., whenever the rightmost $U\hat{H}$ has a singular $r \times r$ submatrix on its right instead of an identity matrix. In this case, we guess another permutation matrix $P_{n \times n}$ and we recompute the reduced row echelon form.

Observing that $s = He = (HP)P^{-1}e = \hat{H}(P^{-1}e)$, we have that $\bar{s} = Us = U\hat{H}P^{-1}e = [V_{r \times k} \mid I_r]P^{-1}e$. The permutation is expected to pack in the r rightmost columns of H all its columns indexed by the bit-positions of e corresponding to an asserted bit. As a consequence, also the vector $P^{-1}e$ will have its t asserted bits in its r trailing elements, i.e.: $P^{-1}e = [0_{k \times 1} | e'_{r \times 1}]$. For this reason, $\bar{s}$ can be seen as the syndrome of the permuted error $P^{-1}e$ through the permuted and row echelon reduced parity-check matrix $U\hat{H} = [V_{r \times k} \mid I_r]$, i.e.: $\bar{s} = [V_{r \times k} \mid I_r][0_{k \times 1} | e'_{r \times 1}] = e'_{r \times 1}$. Indeed, in the case that the chosen permutation packs k positions of e corresponding to unasserted bits on its top part, then the multiplication between the syndrome and U produces the non-zero part of the permuted error vector itself. To test if the permutation P actually packed k-zero positions of the error in the first k rows, Prange's algorithm checks if the Hamming weight of $\bar{s}$ is equal to the one of the error vector, t. In this case, the error vector can be retrieved by calculating $P[0_{k \times 1} | \bar{s}] = P[0_{k \times 1} | e'_{r \times 1}] = e$. If the test for the permutation correctness fails, the algorithm restarts, picking another random permutation and repeating the reduced-row-echelon form computation and the test on $\bar{s}$. The complexity of Prange's algorithm can be derived by observing that it is a Las Vegas algorithm, that is, a randomized algorithm which always produce a correct result (i.e., the value of e or it notifies about a *failure*) in a finite running time. The expected runtime of the algorithm depends on the expected number of times, $\mathcal{N}$, it must guess the permutation matrix before succeeding, as well as on the dimensions of H, n and r, and the weight t of the error vector e, i.e.: $C_{\text{Prange-ISD}}(n, r, t) = \mathcal{N} \cdot C_{\text{Prange-iter}}(n, r)$. Since each matrix guess is independent of the others, $\mathcal{N}$ is computed as $\mathcal{N} = \frac{1}{\text{Pr}_{succ}}$, with Pr_{succ} being the probability that a single computation succeeds. In Prange's algorithm, Pr_{succ} is computed by dividing the number of permuted error vector admissible by the hypotheses, i.e. all the vector configurations having all the t error-affected bits in the last r positions, by the total number of possible error vector configurations, i.e., $\text{Pr}_{succ} = \binom{r}{t}/\binom{n}{t}$. An additional factor that makes a single iteration of the algorithm fail is the probability that the procedure computing the reduced row echelon form of $\hat{H}$ does not succeed. However, the probability that a random $r \times r$ binary matrix is non-singular is $\prod_{i=1}^{r}(1-\frac{1}{2^i})$ [3], a factor quickly converging to ≈ 0.2887 for increasing values of r. This contribution adds a constant factor of about 4 to the number of repetitions $\mathcal{N}$ be done by Prange's ISD. As a consequence, the prevailing cost in a single repetition of Prange's algorithm is the computation of the row-echelon form reduction of $\hat{H}$, which takes $C_{\text{RREF}} = \frac{3nr^2}{4} + \frac{nr}{4} - \frac{n}{2} + \frac{3r^2}{4} - \frac{r}{2}$ bit operations via a simple Gaussian elimination. Finally, to compute Us and to check the weight of $\bar{s}$, the algorithm requires $\mathcal{O}(r^2)$ and $7r + \log_2(r)$ bit operations.

Lee and Brickell's ISD. The exponential contribution to the algorithmic complexity of Prange's ISD comes from the number of iterations that have to be computed, which is exponential in n and t. The ISD algorithm proposed by Lee and Brickell [16] reduces the average number of iterations, at the cost of adding a computation with exponential complexity for each iteration.

The main idea of this optimization is to tolerate the presence of $p \geq 1$ asserted bits of the permuted error, $P^{-1}e$, in its leftmost k bit-positions adding all the possible $\binom{k}{p}$ choices of columns from the V matrix before performing the check on the weight of Us. To do so, consider $P^{-1}e = [e'_{k \times 1} | e''_{r \times 1}]$, with $\text{WT}(e') = p$ and $\text{WT}(e'') = t - p$. Denoting as $v_j, 0 \leq j < k$, the j-th column of the submatrix V of $\hat{H}$, $U\hat{H} = [V_{r \times k} | I_r]$, we can now rewrite $\bar{s} = Us$ as $\bar{s} = [V | I_r][e'_{k \times 1} | e''_{r \times 1}] = Ve'_{k \times 1} + e'' = e'' + \sum_{j \in \text{supp}(e')} v_j$, where $\text{supp}(w)$ denotes the set of indexes of the asserted components/bits in w. Rearranging the terms, we obtain $\bar{s} - \sum_{j \in \text{supp}(e')} v_j = e''$, which states that, if p asserted components were present in the portion of the permuted binary error vector multiplied by V, the weight $\text{WT}\left(\bar{s} - \sum_{j \in \text{supp}(e')} v_j\right) = \text{WT}\left(\left(\bigoplus_{j \in \text{supp}(e')} v_j\right) \oplus \bar{s}\right)$ corresponds to the number of asserted components of the permuted error portion multiplied by I, that is $t - p$.

Given a parity-check matrix H and a syndrome s, the Lee and Brickell's variant of the ISD thus requires each iteration of the algorithm to compute the reduced row echelon form of the permuted parity-check matrix $\hat{H}$ deriving U such that $U\hat{H} = [V|I_r]$, compute $\bar{s} = Us$ and then test, for all the $\binom{k}{p}$ possible sums of p columns of V, if adding them to $\bar{s}$ yields a vector with Hamming weight equal to $t - p$. If the check is successful, then the positions of the asserted bits in the permuted error vector portion e'' are derived from the positions of the asserted bits in vector resulting from the sum of $\bar{s}$ and the p columns of V that have been selected, while the positions of the asserted bits in e' are derived from the indexes of the columns of V that have been added to the syndrome $\bar{s}$.

The computational cost of a single iteration of the Lee and Brickell algorithm is $C_{\text{Lee-Brickell-iter}}(n, r, p) = C_{\text{RREF}} + \mathcal{O}(r^2) + O\left((rp + 7r + \log_2(r))\binom{k}{p}\right)$ bit operations. The last term considers the cost of performing $p - 1$ additions of r-bit long vectors for each weight test, plus the linear cost of the weight test itself. Such an increase in the computation cost of a single iteration is traded off for a significant increase in the probability of success of a single iteration (i.e., the

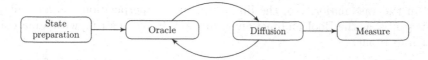

Fig. 1. High level overview of Grover's algorithm to speed up the computation of the zeroes of a generic Boolean function.

guessing of a matrix $\boldsymbol{P}$), which becomes $\mathrm{Pr}_{\mathrm{LB}-succ} = \frac{\binom{k}{p} \cdot \binom{r}{t-p}}{\binom{n}{t}}$. We note that, while p is a free parameter in the Lee-Brickell ISD variant, its asymptotically optimal value was found to be 2 with classic computing, and tested by exhaustive search in [3].

The exponential-time exhaustive search with complexity $\mathcal{O}\left(rp\binom{k}{p}\right)$ for the position of the p remaining errors in the permuted error vector is the main candidate to be sped up by a quantum computer. Indeed, the reduced row echelon form computations and the matrix-vector multiplications, required in the remainder of the algorithm, are polynomial-time procedures, which have a negligible impact on the iteration time for cryptographically relevant parameters [9].

2.3 Grover's Algorithm

In this work we will rely on the algorithmic framework proposed by Grover [12], in short known as Grover's algorithm. The algorithm finds the value of the input $x^* \in \{0,1\}^n$ such that the Boolean function $f : \mathbb{F}_{2^n} \mapsto \mathbb{F}_2$ evaluates to 1, under the assumption that only a single value x^* exists, in $\mathcal{O}(\sqrt{2^n})$ function computations. The classical algorithm, on the other hand, needs $\mathcal{O}2^n$ function computation to obtain the result.

Grover's framework, summarized in Fig. 1, relies on four steps, of which the second and the third are repeated $\mathcal{O}(\sqrt{2^n})$ times: the preparation of a quantum computer input state, the computation of the so-called oracle function, the computation of a diffusion function, and a final measurement stage. The end goal of the algorithm is to obtain x^* with a high probability upon measurement, using as few iterations as possible of the oracle and diffusion steps. We will now detail the description of the first three stages of the Grover framework.

State Preparation. The framework proposed by Grover begins by constructing a uniform superposition of all the possible basis states, $|\psi_0\rangle$. Each basis state can be thought as labeled with binary strings corresponding to the elements of the Boolean function f, all with equal amplitudes. Denoting with $\mathbb{D} \subseteq \{0,1\}^n$ the domain of function f, with $|\mathbb{D}| = d$, we want to have an input quantum state described as

$$|\psi_0\rangle = \frac{1}{\sqrt{d}} \sum_{x \in \mathbb{D}} |x\rangle = \alpha_r^* |x^*\rangle + \alpha_r \sum_{x \neq x^*} |x\rangle \tag{1}$$

where α_r and α_r^* are the amplitudes associated to states $x \neq x^*$ and x^* respectively. At this point we have $\alpha_r = \alpha_r^* = \frac{1}{\sqrt{d}}$. In the original article by Grover, and in the vast majority of the literature, such superposition contains all the basis states, as the Boolean function admits any Boolean string with a matching length as input.

Oracle Function Computation. The computation of the oracle function in Grover's framework aims at identify the basis state corresponding to x^*, the value we are looking for. One computation doing so acts on $n + 1$ qubits, where the first n encode the input to f and the last one is initialized to 0 and maps $|x, 0\rangle \mapsto |x, f(x)\rangle$, in which the comma is used to stress the action of the oracle on the last qubit. Concretely, this computation can be performed with a set of quantum gates corresponding to the classical gates required to compute f applied to the first n qubits, adding the result to the last qubit. The computation employed in Grover's algorithm starts from the previous approach and considers what happens if, instead of setting the last qubit to $|0\rangle$, it is set to $|-\rangle = \frac{1}{\sqrt{2}}(|0\rangle - |1\rangle)$.

It can be shown that the computation maps $|x, -\rangle \mapsto (-1)^{f(x)} |x, -\rangle$, effectively storing the information on whether the basis vector is the one corresponding to x^* in the sign of the amplitude of the basis vector itself. The use of the additional result qubit, although convenient for explanation purposes, is not required in practical implementation, and the computation performed is then represented as $|x\rangle \mapsto (-1)^{f(x)} |x\rangle$. Applying this computation to the initial state prepared during the state preparation step $|\psi_0\rangle$ yields the following mapping:

$$\alpha_r^* |x^*\rangle + \alpha_r \sum_{x \neq x^*} |x\rangle \;\mapsto\; -\alpha_r^* |x^*\rangle + \alpha_r \sum_{x \neq x^*} |x\rangle$$

effectively singling out the basis vector representing x^* by changing the sign of its amplitude α_r^*.

Diffusion. The task of the diffusion stage is to build on the output of the oracle stage to produce a superposition in which α_r^*—the amplitude of the vector representing x^*—increases its modulus. To do so, Grover observed that the state after the oracle can be rewritten as

$$|\xi\rangle = -\alpha_r^* |x^*\rangle + \alpha_r \sum_{x \neq x^*} |x\rangle = |\psi_0\rangle - 2\alpha_r^* |x^*\rangle \tag{2}$$

From this, Grover observed that applying the linear transform $S = 2 |\psi_0\rangle\langle\psi_0| - I$ to $|\xi\rangle$, and recalling that we indicate with d the size of the domain of the function f, we obtain:

$$|\psi_1\rangle = S |\xi\rangle = \frac{d-4}{d} |\psi_0\rangle + \frac{2}{\sqrt{d}} |x^*\rangle$$

Therefore, the state $|\psi_1\rangle$ is a non-uniform superposition of all the possible basis states, where the one representing the value x^* has twice the amplitude with respect to a uniform superposition. Concretely, the S transform is computed as PS_0P^{-1}, where S_0 is a transform inverting the sign of the amplitude of the all-0 quantum state, while P is the transform which maps the $|0^n\rangle$ state onto $|\psi_0\rangle$.

Number of Iterations. Grover observes that applying again the oracle computation and diffusion procedure to $|\psi_1\rangle$ will keep increasing the amplitude of the desired basis state, while reducing the others. The computation is repeated for a number of times sufficient to make the probability amplitude of the searched state $|x^*\rangle$ grow to a point where measuring the superposition will yield it with high probability. Care must be taken in choosing the right number of iterations since the probability of success does not increase monotonically with the number of iterations. It can be shown indeed that the optimal number of iterations to have a close to 1 chance of observing $|x^*\rangle$ upon measurement is $\approx \mathcal{O}(\sqrt{d})$. As shown in [10] we can also use half the number of iterations to have a probability close to 50% to observe $|x^*\rangle$.

Amplitude Sign Flip Subcircuit. The goal of this subcircuit, used in both the oracle and the diffusion stage, is to invert the sign of the amplitude associated to a specific quantum state, and it can be implemented as a multi-controlled Z (MCZ). This gate indeed inverts the sign of the all-1's state, while leaving all other states unchanged. If the MCZ involves m qubits, $m-1$ qubits act as control qubits, while one acts as target. Our goal is therefore to express the state for which we want to change the sign of the amplitude as an all 1-state right before performing the sign flip. For the oracle, this goal requires to translate the $|x^*\rangle$ into an all-1 state on the qubits expressing the result of the function evaluation. On the other hand, in the diffusion stage, S_0 requires a sign inversion of the all-0 state. As a consequence, to be able to use the MCZ, we need to apply an X gate before and after the MCZ in order to have a transform equivalent to S_0.

Another relevant difference between the oracle and diffusion phase is in the involved qubits. While in the oracle the circuit acts on all the qubits storing the result of the oracle computation, in the diffusion the involved qubits are the ones storing the input quantum state superposition. In the plain version of Grover's algorithm those qubits are identical, but it is not necessarily the case.

3   A Quantum Circuit to Speed-Up ISD Iterations

In this section, we describe our approach to the acceleration of the exponential-time exhaustive search for the sum of the p columns of V which, added to the transformed syndrome $\bar{s}$, yields a weight $t - p$ vector, as required in the Lee-Brickell ISD. To employ the algorithmic framework proposed by Grover, we recast the problem of finding the correct sum of p columns of V into a Boolean function with a mono-dimensional output. We consider the Boolean function f, $f : \mathbb{D} \to \{0,1\}$, where $\mathbb{D} \subseteq \{0,1\}^k$ is the set of all the weight-p, length-k Boolean vectors. Let $x \in \mathbb{D}, x = (x_0, \ldots, x_{k-1})$; we define f as:

$$f(x_0, \ldots, x_{k-1}) = \begin{cases} 1 & \text{if } \mathrm{W_T}\left(\left(\bigoplus_{j \in \mathrm{supp}(e')} v_j\right) \oplus \bar{s}\right) \\ 0 & \text{otherwise} \end{cases} \tag{3}$$

The goal of the algorithm is to find the unique input x^* for which f returns 1. As explained in Sect. 2.3 we need to create a quantum circuit, the oracle, that inverts the sign of the amplitude of $|x^*\rangle$, leaving all other quantum states untouched. To exploit the power of quantum computing we additionally want to prepare an equal-weight superposition of all the possible inputs at once.

3.1 Preparing a Superposition of All Column Selections

As per Eq. (3), our algorithm expects as input a state which is the superposition of states representing length-k, weight-p Boolean strings. This state, called Dicke state and represented as $|D_p^k\rangle$, is defined as $|D_p^k\rangle = \binom{k}{p}^{-\frac{1}{2}} \sum_{\mathrm{W_T}(x)=p} |x\rangle$, $\quad x \in$ $\{0,1\}^k$. To the best of our knowledge, the most efficient quantum circuit to prepare a Dicke state for a generic value of p is the one presented in [18], which is an improvement over the previous best algorithm presented in [5]. The solution proposed in [5] is quite efficient, as it only requires p X gates, and $\mathcal{O}(k + kp)$ CNOT gates and RY gates, with an overall depth equal to $\mathcal{O}(k)$. The work of [18] improves the previous solution in its cost in CNOT and RY gates to $\mathcal{O}(k + p^2)$, while keeping the same circuit depth: we report the detailed cost of generating $|D_p^k\rangle$ in Table 1.

We recall that the qubits involved in the input preparation will be used in the diffusion stage. As explained in Sect. 2.3, in the amplitude sign flip stage we have to apply an X gate on the involved qubits before and after the flip. In our algorithm the involved qubits are the ones belonging to the sel register.

3.2 Designing Grover's Oracle Function

We now describe the quantum circuit to compute Grover's oracle function for the Boolean function f. This quantum circuit is split in five stages: i) the selection of a set of columns of V corresponding to the set entries of the Boolean input vector $|x\rangle$, ii) the computation of the actual Boolean sum (xor) of the columns themselves and the syndrome $\bar{s}$, iii) the computation of the Hamming weight of the result of ii), iv) the comparison of the Hamming weight with the integer value $t - p$ and v) the amplitude sign flip if the previous comparison is successful.

In order to leave the input states $|x\rangle \neq |x^*\rangle$ unaltered, as demanded by the oracle model, we have to perform an uncomputation of the oracle circuit before the flip phase, along the lines of the common compute-uncompute paradigm of quantum computing. Since the uncomputation is simply the application of the same gates in reverse order, we do not detail this portion of the circuit.

For the sake of clarity, we will assume that r is a power of two in the description. We will employ a running example where V is a 4×4 binary matrix and the transformed syndrome $\bar{s}$ vector is 4 elements long, with the following values:

$$V = \underbrace{\left.\begin{bmatrix} 1 & 1 & 0 & 0 \\ 1 & 0 & 1 & 1 \\ 1 & 1 & 1 & 0 \\ 0 & 1 & 0 & 1 \end{bmatrix}\right\}}_{k} r \qquad \bar{s} = \begin{bmatrix} 0 \\ 1 \\ 1 \\ 0 \end{bmatrix}$$

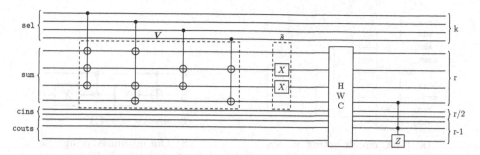

Fig. 2. High level overview of the circuit employed as the Grover oracle.

Figure 2 depicts the instance of the proposed circuit corresponding to the running example. The circuit acts on four quantum registers: sel (k qubit wide), containing the input superposition; sum (r qubit wide), containing the superposition of the addition of the columns of V after stage ii); cin ($\frac{r}{2}$ qubit wide) and cout ($r - 1$ qubit wide), used by the Hamming weight computation and check (stage iii) and iv)) to store carries.

Columns and Syndrome Addition. We compute in superposition all the possible Boolean sums (xor) of p columns out of k from the matrix V, storing them in the sum register. We note that the matrix V is known to the classical controller circuit driving the quantum computer at each repetition of the ISD procedure, and can therefore be considered as fixed from the quantum computer standpoint.

To compute the sum we employ each i-th qubit of the sel register, set to the $|D_p^k\rangle$ state, to drive a group of CNOT gates, one for each set term in the i-th column of V. Considering our running example, the first (topmost in Fig. 2) qubit of sel controls three CNOT gates acting on the first three bits of sum, since v_0, the first column of V, is equal to $[1110]^T$. Performing the addition of the columns of V in this fashion requires an amount of CNOT gates equal to the number of set terms in the matrix V. Since V is the result of a reduced row echelon form computation on a random matrix, we expect that, on average, half of its elements will be equal to 1, giving therefore an average of $\frac{rk}{2}$ CNOT (and a worst case of rk CNOTs). From a circuit depth standpoint, we note that, if $k \geq r$ (as it is extremely common in code-based cryptography) it is possible to schedule the action of the rk CNOTs of the worst case in a circuit with depth at most k. Indeed, such a scheduling is possible as there are k controlling lines which pilot r CNOTs each. It is thus possible, at each gate layer, to run CNOTs with both the controlling and controlled bits different from each other.

Finally, the circuit needs to add (xor) the transformed syndrome $\bar{s}$ to the contents of the sum register, regardless of the choice of added columns from V. This is done via a set of X gates, applied to the qubits in sum corresponding to set terms in the $\bar{s}$ vector. In our running example, the X gates are applied to the second and third qubits of sum, as the transformed syndrome value $\bar{s}$ is [0110].

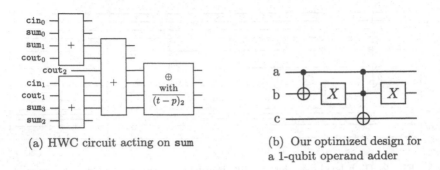

(a) HWC circuit acting on sum

(b) Our optimized design for a 1-qubit operand adder

Fig. 3. (a)) shows the two subcircuits used for Hamming weight compute and check on the sum register for the running example. The computation result is stored on $cout_2$, $cout_1$ and sum_3. Afterward, it is compared against the one's complement of the Boolean representation of the constant value $(t - p)_2$. (b)) shows our construction of an adder working with two 1-qubit register. The sum of the input value a and b is put in c and b, where c is the most significant bit.

We observe that the syndrome addition will require at most r X gates, and $\frac{r}{2}$ gates on average, that can be interleaved with the previous column additions.

Computing the Hamming Weight. After completing the sum of the columns of V and the transformed syndrome $\bar{s}$, the oracle circuit computes the Hamming weight of the result (stage iii)). This is depicted in Fig. 2 as the Hamming Weight Check gate, (HWC for short), acting on sum, cin and cout, while Fig. 3a reports the full HWC circuit for our running example. Our approach to computing the Hamming weight stems from the classical one employing a logarithmic depth adder tree. We compute the superposition of the values of the Hamming weights of the r-sized sum register using an adder tree of depth $\log_2(r)$. The first layer of the adder tree has only 1 qubit operand adders that store their carry-out on a qubit from cout. Later layers of the adder tree use the output of early layers to calculate the sum, until we obtain a single sum as output of the last layer. To be able to use quantum adders in our circuit, we used Cuccaro proposal of [11], a reversible variant of the classical ripply carry adder. The Cuccaro adder performs a partially in-place addition by storing the sum of its two input registers x and y, containing the binary representation of values a and b respectively, on y. It also uses an additional qubit for the carry-in and one more to store the carry-out. The carry-in qubit is always restored to its initial state at the end of the adder circuit and can thus be reused by all adders. However, to run all the adders at the same layer in parallel, we employ a total number of carry-in qubits exactly equal to the number of adders at the first layer.

To compute the number of gates required by the HWC subcircuit, we observe that a Cuccaro adder acting on two n-qubit input registers requires $2n-1$ CCNOT gates, $5n+1$ CNOT gates and $2n$ X gates, with a depth of $2n+6$. For $n=1$, we enhanced Cuccaro proposal by implementing an adder (Fig. 3b) requiring only 1 CCNOT, 1 CNOT and 2 X gates with depth 4. The adder tree

Table 1. Number of quantum gates and depth as a function of Lee-Brickell ISD parameters for the different subcircuits. We need an additional MCZ($\log_2(r)$) gate for the Oracle stage and an MCZ($k-1$) gate for the Diffusion stage.

State preparation		Diffusion	
Cost metric	Dicke state i)	Cost metric	v)
X	p	X	$k + 2p$
CNOT	$5kp - 5p^2 - 2k$	CNOT	$10kp - 10p^2 - 4k$
RY	$4kp - 4p^2 - 2k + 1$	RY	$8kp - 8p^2 - 4k + 2$
Depth	$\mathcal{O}(k)$	Depth	$\mathcal{O}(k)$

	Oracle	
Cost metric	Column addition ii)	Hamming weight compute iii), check iv)
X	r	$8r - 2\log_2(r) - 2\log_2(t-p) - 6$
CNOT	rk	$9r - 10\log_2(r) - 22$
CCNOT	0	$6r - 4\log_2(r) - 6$
Depth	$\mathcal{O}(k)$	$2\log_2^2 r + 14\log_2(r) - 8$

circuit requires $\log_2(r)$ layers. The i-th layer employs $r/(2^i)$ adders, for a total of $\sum_{i=1}^{\log_2(r)} \frac{r}{2^i} = r-1$ adders. Consequently, $\frac{r}{2}$ carry-in and $r-1$ carry-out ancillary qubits are required. Each adder belonging to the i-th layer accepts as input two i-qubit strings. We can therefore compute the overall number of gates required as $\sum_{i=1}^{\log_2(r)} \frac{r}{2^i} \text{ADD\_COST}(i)$, with $\text{ADD\_COST}(i)$ denoting the gate cost of a single adder accepting as inputs two i-qubit strings. The summation expansion gives the gate-count shown in Table 1. The global depth can be computed by summing together the depth of just a single adder per level, since at the same level all the adders act on distinct qubits and therefore be run in parallel.

Since Cuccaro's adder reuses one of the input registers to store part of the sum, at stage i the result is stored on $i+1$ qubits. Therefore, in the final stage, the overall sum is stored on $\log_2(r) + 1$ qubits, that we will denote as **hw**.

Checking the Hamming Weight Value and Flipping Stage. The final stage of the oracle function for Grover's algorithm compares the obtained Hamming weight values in superposition with the target weight of $t - p$ (stage iv)) and flips the amplitude of the states where a match occurs (stage v)). For this reason, we perform a xor operation between the **hw** register, containing the superposition of Hamming weight computed in phase iii), and the one's complement of the Boolean representation of the constant value $(t - p)_2$. In this way, if a certain state is such that $\text{WT}(\mathbf{hw}) = t - p$, all the qubits belonging to **hw** will be in state $|1\rangle$. As a result, we can apply the multi-controlled Z (MCZ) to invert the sign of the amplitude of $|x^*\rangle$. This process requires only X gates. Indeed, in the worst case, $p = t$ and the value of the addend is the all-ones string represented on $\log_2(r) + 1$ qubits, a quantity smaller than r. As a result, we need $\log_2(r) + 1 - \log_2(t - p)$ X gates to carry out the xor operation. If the output of stage iii) is a state containing the binary representation of $t - p$, the said basis state will have, inside the hw register, an all-ones bitstring. We finally employ hw in a multicontrolled Z gate to perform the amplitude sign flip, as described in Sect. 2.

A noteworthy point to analyze is how the n-controlled Z gate is translated into a sequence of elementary gates. The approach used in [4] requires $2^n - 2$ CNOT gates, $2^n - 1$ gates $\in SU(2)$. Therefore, the number of gates increases exponentially with the number of control qubits, producing a huge impact on the resource consumption, without however impacting adversely the number of qubits required. On the other hand, in [21], a simpler approach was presented, requiring n additional qubits and an equal number of CCNOT, plus 1 CZ. The total depth of this decomposition is $\mathcal{O}(n)$.

4   Experimental Evaluation

To validate the functionality of the proposed circuit for the Grover oracle function and the entire resulting Grover we employed codes smaller than the ones employed in cryptographic systems, to allow their simulation on classic hardware. We chose the original Hamming code $(n, k, d) = (7, 4, 3)$, which is able to correct $t = 1$ error bit, and random codes up to $n = 23$ and $k = 12$ able to correct more than one error bit.

The validation of our Grover-accelerated Lee-Brickell search was done precomputing a pair $(V, \bar{s})$ matching Lee-Brickell requirements on the weights of the two portions of the permuted error $P^{-1}e$. We employed this pair $(V, \bar{s})$ to simulate the execution of the corresponding quantum circuit on the Atos Quantum Learning Machine [2] simulator. After successfully validating the soundness of our circuit, we simulated the execution of the entire ISD procedure, including the classical random guessing of the required permutation.

To evaluate the computational complexity advantage of our solution with cryptographically relevant parameters, we consider the parameter sets for each of the NIST security levels for both the Classic McEliece [8] cryptosystem, the finalist in the NIST Post quantum standardization effort among code based cryptosystems, and Bike [1], one of the alternate candidates. We left out the HQC [17] cryptoscheme from our analysis since its specification consider a raw asymptotic limit, independent from the ISD technique used. The NIST security levels are defined as the computational effort of breaking one of the three AES variants, and therefore correspond to a computational effort of about 2^{128} (level 1), 2^{192} (level 3) or 2^{256} (level 5) AES encryptions. Table 2 reports the number of gates, split by kind, and the number of qubits needed to build the Grover oracle according to our design. Table 2 also reports the optimal value of p for the Lee-Brickell ISD with our technique. The first noteworthy point is that the optimal value of p, obtained through an exhaustive design space exploration, is higher than the one for the classic counterpart, i.e. $p = 2$. This is a result of speeding up the exponential search of the Lee and Brickell ISD, therefore comparatively reducing the amount of computation to be done for a given choice of the p parameter.

Table 2. Number of gates, qubits and depth required to build the proposed quantum circuit. Figures are relative to the value of p minimizing the total number of gates required.

Scheme	NIST level	p	Grover Iter.s	Grover Depth	Grover Qubits	X	CNOT	CCNOT	RY	CZ	Tot.
BIKE	1	3	2^{18}	2^{34}	2^{15}	2^{36}	2^{45}	2^{35}	2^{36}	2^{19}	2^{45}
	3	3	2^{20}	2^{37}	2^{16}	2^{38}	2^{49}	2^{37}	2^{39}	2^{21}	2^{49}
	5	3	2^{21}	2^{38}	2^{17}	2^{40}	2^{51}	2^{40}	2^{40}	2^{22}	2^{51}
McEliece	1	13	2^{57}	2^{71}	2^{12}	2^{71}	2^{78}	2^{70}	2^{75}	2^{58}	2^{78}
	3	15	2^{67}	2^{81}	2^{12}	2^{81}	2^{89}	2^{81}	2^{85}	2^{68}	2^{89}
	5	27	2^{124}	2^{139}	2^{13}	2^{139}	2^{147}	2^{138}	2^{144}	2^{125}	2^{147}

Table 3. Comparison between our hybrid Lee-Brickell algorithm, the classical Lee-Brickell algorithm and the full-quantum Prange algorithm proposed in [7].

Scheme NIST Level		Proposed hybrid ISD (total)				Classic ISD		Quantum [7]	
	p	Quant. gates	Class. gates	Depth	Qubits	p	Asymp. Time	Asymp. Gates	Asymp. Qubits
BIKE 1	3	2^{161}	2^{159}	2^{159}	2^{15}	2	2^{165}	2^{111}	2^{29}
3	3	2^{228}	2^{225}	2^{225}	2^{16}	2	2^{232}	2^{147}	2^{31}
5	3	2^{295}	2^{291}	2^{291}	2^{17}	2	2^{299}	2^{182}	2^{32}
McEliece 1	13	2^{152}	2^{106}	2^{145}	2^{12}	2	2^{162}	2^{107}	2^{23}
3	15	2^{194}	2^{139}	2^{186}	2^{12}	2	2^{206}	2^{129}	2^{24}
5	27	2^{300}	2^{188}	2^{291}	2^{13}	2	2^{321}	2^{189}	2^{26}

The second point is that our design requires a relatively small amount of qubits, at most 2^{17}, making our design plausible even in the scenario where quantum computers with millions of qubits are not available. We notice also that the circuit depths obtained for the optimal p of the BIKE cryptosystem are below the 2^{40} mark reported by NIST as the most stringent bound for the plausibility of a sequential computation [19].

We note that the depth of our quantum circuit does not depend on the value of p, while the number of gates involved depends on $\mathcal{O}(p^2)$. However, the largest contribution of p to the total computational cost of the quantum part of our algorithm, $\mathcal{O}\left(\sqrt{\binom{k}{p}}\right)$, is given to the number iterations. Therefore, hardware realizations of quantum computers will only tolerate depths lower than the one required by the optimal choice of p, our algorithm can be re-tuned to adapt.

Furthermore, our approach can be parallelized over multiple separate quantum computers, thanks to the probabilistic nature of the ISD. Indeed, all the iterations of the ISD algorithm can be run in parallel: separate controllers can prepare independent pairs of $(\boldsymbol{V}, \bar{\boldsymbol{s}})$ to be fed to the quantum computers, simply taking care of exploring separate portions of the column permutation space.

Table 3 reports the overall computational cost of our quantum accelerated Lee-Brickell algorithm, compared to the estimated gate counts for its classic counterpart. In order to estimate the number of repetitions of the oracle-diffusion computations, we consider a number of repetitions which allows us to reach a probability as close as possible to 1 to observe $|x^*\rangle$ upon measurement. It is possible to halve the number of Grover iterations accepting a success probability close to 50%; however, given the total computational effort, a factor of 2 does not have a significant impact.

Table 3 also reports the results of the asymptotic estimates for the number of quantum gates and qubits required by the high level description of a Prange's ISD algorithm provided in [7]. The approach of [7] employs a full-quantum strategy, in which the guess of the information set and the reduced row echelon form computation are also performed by the quantum device. The proposal reports a number of qubits equals to $n^{\mathcal{O}(1)}$. Given that we must represent the whole generator matrix $G \in \mathbb{F}_2^{k \times n}$ and the codeword $c \in \mathbb{F}_2^n$, it is reasonable to assume that the cost will be in the order of $\mathcal{O}(n^2)$. The estimate for the number of gates provided in [7] is $\mathcal{O}(n^3)$ for a single Grover iteration, with a number of iterations equal to $\sqrt{\binom{n}{k}/0.29\binom{n-t}{k}}$. It is worth noting that [7] leaves the input preparation and diffusion stage out of the gate counts, while they require additional quantum gates, and considers only asymptotic gate costs. Further research is therefore needed in order to have closed-form figures for the proposed quantum circuit.

We highlight that a promising direction for future work is the realization of quantum ISD circuits concretizing the approaches of [14,15]. Indeed, the works evaluate only the expected asymptotic computation costs of two ISD approaches, highlighting that they have the potential to improve on the ones of Prange and Lee-Brickell.

5   Concluding Remarks

We presented a quantum circuit to speed up the execution of the exponential-time portion of the Lee and Brickell's ISD algorithm. Our proposal allows to implement a quantum accelerator for the Lee-Brickell variant of the ISD, keeping the circuit depth within the most stringent bounds pointed out by the USA NIST [19], and a qubit count varying from 2^{13} to 2^{17} for all set of parameters of two finalists of the NIST competition. Our solution gains a factor between $2^{10} \times$ and $2^{20} \times$ in speed with respect to the purely classic implementation, providing a concrete quantification of the number of gates of the quantum circuit. The proposed solution also allows to pipeline the classic and quantum computations hiding the classic controller latency and allows to parallelize the operations on multiple quantum accelerators.

Acknowledgment. The research activity was partially funded by Atos Italia S.p.A. with a research grant on quantum computing.

References

1. Aragon, N., Barreto, P.S.L.M., Bettaieb, S., Bidoux, L., Blazy, O., et al.: BIKE: bit flipping key encapsulation. https://bikesuite.org
2. Atos: Quantum Learning Machine. https://atos.net/en/solutions/quantum-learning-machine
3. Baldi, M., Barenghi, A., Chiaraluce, F., Pelosi, G., Santini, P.: A finite regime analysis of information set decoding algorithms. Algorithms **12**(10), 209 (2019). https://doi.org/10.3390/a12100209
4. Barenco, A., et al.: Elementary gates for quantum computation. Phys. Rev. A **52**(5), 3457 (1995)
5. Bärtschi, A., Eidenbenz, S.: Deterministic preparation of dicke states. In: Gąsieniec, L.A., Jansson, J., Levcopoulos, C. (eds.) FCT 2019. LNCS, vol. 11651, pp. 126–139. Springer, Cham (2019). https://doi.org/10.1007/978-3-030-25027-0_9
6. Berlekamp, E.R., McEliece, R.J., van Tilborg, H.C.A.: On the inherent intractability of certain coding problems (Corresp.). IEEE Trans. Inf. Theory **24**(3), 384–386 (1978). https://doi.org/10.1109/TIT.1978.1055873
7. Bernstein, D.J.: Grover vs. McEliece. In: Sendrier, N. (ed.) PQCrypto 2010. LNCS, vol. 6061, pp. 73–80. Springer, Heidelberg (2010). https://doi.org/10.1007/978-3-642-12929-2_6
8. Bernstein, D.J., et al.: Classic mceliece: conservative code-based cryptography (2020). https://classic.mceliece.org/nist/mceliece-20201010.pdf
9. Bernstein, D.J., Lange, T., Peters, C.: Smaller decoding exponents: ball-collision decoding. In: Rogaway, P. (ed.) CRYPTO 2011. LNCS, vol. 6841, pp. 743–760. Springer, Heidelberg (2011). https://doi.org/10.1007/978-3-642-22792-9_42
10. Boyer, M., Brassard, G., Høyer, P., Tapp, A.: Tight bounds on quantum searching. Fortschritte der Physik: Progr. Phys. **46**(4–5), 493–505 (1998)
11. Cuccaro, S.A., Draper, T.G., Kutin, S.A., Moulton, D.P.: A new quantum ripple-carry addition circuit. arXiv quant-ph/0410184 (2004)
12. Grover, L.K.: A fast quantum mechanical algorithm for database search. In: Miller, G.L. (ed.) Twenty-Eighth Annual ACM Symposium on the Theory of Computing, Philadelphia, Pennsylvania, USA, 22–24 May 1996, pp. 212–219. ACM (1996). https://doi.org/10.1145/237814.237866
13. J. Mceliece, R.: A Public-Key Cryptosystem Based on Algebraic Coding Theory. JPL DSN Progress Report 44 (1978)
14. Kachigar, G., Tillich, J.-P.: Quantum information set decoding algorithms. In: Lange, T., Takagi, T. (eds.) PQCrypto 2017. LNCS, vol. 10346, pp. 69–89. Springer, Cham (2017). https://doi.org/10.1007/978-3-319-59879-6_5
15. Kirshanova, E.: Improved quantum information set decoding. In: Lange, T., Steinwandt, R. (eds.) PQCrypto 2018. LNCS, vol. 10786, pp. 507–527. Springer, Cham (2018). https://doi.org/10.1007/978-3-319-79063-3_24
16. Lee, P.J., Brickell, E.F.: An observation on the security of McEliece's public-key cryptosystem. In: Barstow, D., Brauer, W., Brinch Hansen, P., Gries, D., Luckham, D., Moler, C., Pnueli, A., Seegmüller, G., Stoer, J., Wirth, N., Günther, C.G. (eds.) EUROCRYPT 1988. LNCS, vol. 330, pp. 275–280. Springer, Heidelberg (1988). https://doi.org/10.1007/3-540-45961-8_25
17. Melchor, C.A., et al.: Hamming quasi-cyclic (hqc). NIST PQC Round **2**, 4–13 (2018). https://pqc-hqc.org/documentation.html
18. Mukherjee, C.S., Maitra, S., Gaurav, V., Roy, D.: Preparing dicke states on a quantum computer. IEEE Trans. Quant. Eng. **1**(1), 1–17 (2020). https://doi.org/10.1109/TQE.2020.3041479

19. National Institute of Standards and Technology: Post-Quantum Cryptography Standardization process (2017). https://nist.gov/pqcrypto
20. Niederreiter, H.: A public-key cryptosystem based on shift register sequences. In: Pichler, F. (ed.) EUROCRYPT 1985. LNCS, vol. 219, pp. 35–39. Springer, Heidelberg (1986). https://doi.org/10.1007/3-540-39805-8_4, http://dl.acm.org/citation.cfm?id=20110.20114
21. Nielsen, M.A., Chuang, I.L.: Quantum Computation and Quantum Information: 10th Anniversary Ed. Cambridge University Press, Cambridge (2010). https://doi.org/10.1017/CBO9780511976667
22. Perriello, S., Barenghi, A., Pelosi, G.: A complete quantum circuit to solve the information set decoding problem. In: Proceedings of the IEEE International Conference on Quantum Computing and Engineering, QCE 2021, Broomfield, CO, USA, 18–22 October 2021 (Fully virtual event). IEEE (2021)
23. Prange, E.: The use of information sets in decoding cyclic codes. IRE Trans. Inf. Theory 8(5), 5–9 (1962). https://doi.org/10.1109/TIT.1962.1057777
24. Roetteler, M., Naehrig, M., Svore, K.M., Lauter, K.: Quantum resource estimates for computing elliptic curve discrete logarithms. In: Takagi, T., Peyrin, T. (eds.) ASIACRYPT 2017. LNCS, vol. 10625, pp. 241–270. Springer, Cham (2017). https://doi.org/10.1007/978-3-319-70697-9_9
25. Shor, P.W.: Polynomial-time algorithms for prime factorization and discrete logarithms on a quantum computer. SIAM Rev. 41(2), 303–332 (1999). https://doi.org/10.1137/S0036144598347011

Hardware Deployment of Hybrid PQC: SIKE+ECDH

Reza Azarderakhsh[✉], Rami Elkhatib, Brian Koziel, and Brandon Langenberg

PQSecure Technologies LLC, Boca Raton, FL, USA
{razarder,rami.elkhatib,brian.koziel,brandon.langenberg}@pqsecurity.com

Abstract. In this work, we present a small architecture for quantum-safe hybrid key exchange targeting ECDH and SIKE. This is the first known hardware implementation of ECDH/SIKE-based hybrid key exchange in the literature. We propose new ECDH and EdDSA parameter sets defined over the SIKE primes. As a proof-of-concept, we evaluate SIKEX434, a hybrid PQC scheme composed of SIKEp434 and our proposed ECDH scheme X434 over a new, low-footprint architecture. Both schemes utilize the same 434-bit prime to save area. With only 1663 slices on a small Artix-7 device, our SIKE architecture can compute an entire hybrid key exchange in 320 ms. This is the smallest SIKE architecture in the literature. The hybrid SIKEX434 adds approximately 16% communication overhead and 10% latency overhead over SIKEp434. The additional overhead to support multiple primes indicates the need for new standardized ECC parameters for area-efficient designs in the future.

Keywords: Hybrid cryptosystem · Isogeny-based cryptography · Elliptic curve cryptography · Field-programmable gate array

1 Introduction

Quantum computers will bring about a new paradigm in computing technology, producing huge advances in various technological, medical, and financial sectors. While seen as a great boon for society, the major downside is that quantum computers can also be used maliciously to break the foundational security in the internet and various digital applications. Within hours, a large-scale quantum computer can break cryptosystems such as RSA and elliptic curve cryptography through Shor's algorithm [41]. Other cryptosystems such as AES can be weakened through Grover's algorithm [22], but not fully broken.

Given the uncertainty of when a large-scale quantum computer will emerge and the threats it poses, the National Institute of Standards and Technology (NIST) has solicited and evaluated classical and quantum-safe (post-quantum) candidates in its post-quantum cryptography (PQC) standardization project [8]. Now in its third round of review, there are still no clear winners, as a variety

© ICST Institute for Computer Sciences, Social Informatics and Telecommunications Engineering 2021
Published by Springer Nature Switzerland AG 2021. All Rights Reserved
J. Garcia-Alfaro et al. (Eds.): SecureComm 2021, LNICST 399, pp. 475–491, 2021.
https://doi.org/10.1007/978-3-030-90022-9_26

of tradeoffs in performance, communication overhead, security foundation, side-channel resistance, and so on continue to be evaluated. Although this standardization process was initiated in 2017, the winner has not been announced and no standards have been created. Historically, adoption of new cryptosystems is slow as standards must be created, new cryptosystems must be deployed, and an entire infrastructure slowly upgrades, perhaps even taking decades.

With the impending emergence of a large-scale quantum computer, hybrid key exchanges are seen as a solution to ease the transition to a quantum-safe infrastructure. A hybrid key exchange is a cryptosystem that uses multiple key exchange algorithms to reach a shared secret. The benefit here is that now an attacker must break each key exchange algorithm rather than simply one, greatly strengthening the key exchange. For instance, one hybrid key exchange could be pairing an extensively studied classically-safe key exchange with a quantum-safe alternative. Another example could be pairing two or more quantum-safe schemes. There are several classes of known quantum-safe key exchanges and signature schemes, but, unfortunately, there are still many gaps in quantifying their resistance to attacks and more research is still needed. Hybrid key exchanges allow us to hedge our risks and confidence in quantum-safe schemes.

Here, we investigate a hybrid key exchange composed of the classically-safe elliptic curve Diffie-Hellman (ECDH) and the quantum-safe supersingular isogeny key encapsulation (SIKE) [24] mechanism. ECDH and other elliptic curve schemes have been the de facto standard for public-key cryptography because of their small key sizes and competitive performance. Among quantum-safe key exchanges, there are many tradeoffs in terms of security confidence, performance, and communication overhead. However, SIKE is a NIST PQC Round 3 Alternative candidate based on isogenies of elliptic curves that features the smallest public key sizes but suffers from slow performance. By addressing shared computational similarities between ECDH and SIKE, we present a low-area hardware implementation of hybrid ECDH+SIKE.

Contributions:

- We propose new RFC 7748-style ECDH parameter sets over SIKE primes, including X434, X503, and X610.
- We propose new RFC 8032-style EdDSA parameter sets over SIKE primes, including Ed434, Ed503, Ed610, and Ed751.
- We propose, implement, and evaluate a small hybrid PQC architecture that performs SIKEX434, a hybrid PQC composed of SIKEp434 and X434. This is the smallest NIST Security Level 1 SIKE implementation in the literature.

2   Elliptic and Isogeny-Based Cryptography

Elliptic curve cryptography centers on the cryptographic applications of elliptic curves defined over finite fields. The primary applications in our digital society have been key establishment through the elliptic curve Diffie-Hellman (ECDH) key exchange and authentication through the elliptic curve digital signature algorithm (ECDSA). We define an elliptic curve over a finite field as the set of all points (x, y) over the algebraic closure of $\mathbb{F}_q$ which statisfy the short Weierstrass curve equation below. This set, together with the point at infinity, is a group, while pairs in $\mathbb{F}_q \times \mathbb{F}_q$ form a subgroup. The short Weierstrass equation is:

$$E/\mathbb{F}_q \; : \; y^2 = x^3 + ax + b$$

where $a, b, x, y \in \mathbb{F}_q$. This set forms an abelian group over addition for which point addition and doubling can be defined. A series of point addition and doublings can compute an elliptic curve point multiplication, $Q = kP$ where $k \in \mathbb{Z}$ and $P, Q \in E$. ECDH and ECDSA are protected by the elliptic curve discrete logarithm problem (ECDLP), where given P, Q it is infeasible to find k as the size of the abelian group becomes large. We note that we have defined an elliptic curve here using the "traditional" short Weierstrass curve. New constructions of elliptic curves have shown additional benefits when used in an implementation. In the following sections, we choose to use Montgomery [39] curves for ECDH and twisted Edwards [3,16] curves for EdDSA (an ECDSA alternative) for better performance, implementation simplicity, and conformity to existing RFC standards. Elliptic curve cryptosystems defined over these elliptic curves are still protected by the ECDLP. However, the ECDLP is only hard for classical computers, whereas quantum computers can take advantage of Shor's algorithm [41] to efficiently factor the point multiplication and find k.

Isogeny-based cryptography has become a hot topic in the cryptographic community. In particular, we are focused on isogenies between elliptic curves. An isogeny can be thought of as a mapping between elliptic curves that preserves the point at infinity. Given elliptic curves E and E', it is difficult to find the isogeny ϕ such that $\phi : E \to E'$. This problem is still considered to be difficult for quantum computers.

Isogenies of elliptic curves were first proposed as a key-exchange over ordinary elliptic curves in 2006 in independent works by Couveignes [14] and Rostovtsev and Stolbunov [40]. Isogenies of supersingular elliptic curves were also proposed as a hash function in 2006 by Charles, Lauter, and Goren [7]. In 2010, Childs, Jao, and Soukharev [9] investigated the quantum resistance of isogenies over ordinary elliptic curves and found a new quantum subexponential time algorithm to compute isogenies. To counteract this quantum attack, Jao, De Feo, and Plût [15] proposed a new quantum-safe isogeny-based key exchange based on the difficulty to compute isogenies between *supersingular* elliptic curves, known as the supersingular isogeny Diffie-Hellman (SIDH) key exchange. Of known quantum-safe key exchange schemes, SIDH provided the smallest public key size at the cost of slower performance. Since the discovery of SIDH, the research of isogenies of elliptic curves in cryptography has continued to gain momentum, with new applications [20,25,44], security analyses [1,13,19,21,28,29,43], bandwidth reductions [2,11,12], and performance boosts [10,17,27,30–34,36].

Within the NIST PQC standardization project, the Supersingular Isogeny Key Encapsulation (SIKE) scheme was the only submitted isogeny-based cryptosystem. SIKE can be thought of as an upgrade to the SIDH key exchange, with

Table 1. Proposed ECDH parameter sets over SIKE primes

SIKE scheme	SIKE Security level	Public Key (Bytes)	Ciphertext (Bytes)	ECDH a coef	base x-coord	Pollard Rho attack (ops)	Public Key (Bytes)
$p434$	1	330	346	439,322	4	$2^{215.4}$	55
$p503$	2	378	402	308,290	2	$2^{249.8}$	63
$p610$	3	462	486	1,135,802	2	$2^{303.5}$	77
$p751$	5	564	596	624,450	3	$2^{374.2}$	94

better defense against active attacks and IND-CCA security. At this time, SIKE is currently in the third round of NIST PQC standardization as an alternative candidate. Among NIST PQC candidates, SIKE features by far the smallest public key sizes. The primary downsides are that its security problem is among the newest and that it is slow. Since SIKE's submission, the confidence in SIKE's hard problem has improved (with new and smaller parameter sets) and new implementations and optimizations continue to improve performance. SIKE is protected by the difficulty to compute isogenies between elliptic curves. Specifically, SIKE uses a slight variation of this problem over supersingular elliptic curves where a kernel defines the isogeny. Because of the breadth of theory in elliptic curve and isogeny-based cryptography, we point the reader to [18] for a more in-depth review of isogeny fundamentals.

3 Proposed Hybrid Key Exchange Based on Elliptic Curves

ECDH+SIKE. Our proposed hybrid key exchange is based on ECDH and SIKE which both relate to different hard problems based on elliptic curves defined over finite fields. Here, we define a Montgomery [39] curve over a finite field $\mathbb{F}_q$ as the collection of all points (x, y) and point at infinity that satisfy the Montgomery [39] form:

$$E/\mathbb{F}_q \ : \ by^2 = x^3 + ax^2 + x$$

SIKEp434. In the SIKE submission to the NIST PQC standardization project, there are 4 different parameter sets based on varying levels of security ranging from NIST Level 1 which is believed to be as hard as brute-forcing AES128 to NIST Level 5 which is believed to be as hard as brute-forcing AES256. For a low-area implementation, the NIST Level 1 parameters are the obvious pick. SIKEp434 is the parameter set, where all arithmetic is defined over a finite field $\mathbb{F}_q = \mathbb{F}_{p^2}$ with the 434-bit prime $p_{434} = 2^{216}3^{137} - 1$. The primary computations in SIKE include a double-point multiplication, large-degree isogeny, and the SHAKE256 hash. As a key encapsulation mechanism, SIKE includes three different phases: key generation, key encapsulation, and key decapsulation. Lastly, the starting elliptic curve is

$$E_0/\mathbb{F}_{p^2} \; : \; y^2 = x^3 + 6x^2 + x$$

New ECDH Schemes for SIKE Primes. In order to further reduce a hybrid PQC implementation's area footprint, we propose new parameter sets for ECDH, which we call X434, X503, and X610 that share the SIKE prime. The SIKE elliptic curves are specially crafted to be supersingular elliptic curves. These are necessary for supersingular isogeny-based cryptography, but are weak for classical elliptic curve schemes such as ECDH. To find appropriate curves for X434, X503, and X610, we searched for an elliptic curve with the smallest value $a_{24} = (a+2)/4$ such that the curve and its quadratic twist both have an order of the form four multiplied by a large prime (4·prime), similar to how Ed448 was found [23]. This a_{24} value is important for elliptic curve scalar multiplication over Montgomery curves. Our chosen curve over the $p434$ SIKE prime, called X434, has $a = 439322$ and $b = 1$, thus:

$$E/\mathbb{F}_p \; : \; y^2 = x^3 + 439322x^2 + x$$

The base point is at $x = 4$. This elliptic curve satisfies the Safecurves criteria, described on safecurves.cr.yp.to. For instance, the Pollard Rho attack would take approximately $2^{215.4}$ operations, which is close to the security strength of AES256. Since this curve was to be paired with the quantum-safe SIKE Level 1, we opted for a high-strength ECDH parameter set. We summarize each SIKE scheme and corresponding RFC 7748-style curve [35] in Table 1. Note that each curve has a Montgomery b coefficient of 1. We do not claim X751 as a contribution as it was originally found in [12].

Our proposed and implemented X434 key exchange scheme was adapted from the X25519 and X448 key exchanges described in RFC 7748 [35]. Specifically, a private scalar is created by choosing a random 55 byte value, setting bit 433, and clearing bits 0, 1, 434, 435, 436, 437, 438, and 439. These bits are set and cleared to ensure that a proper public key is generated. The key exchange is composed of 2 different phases: the key generation and the key agreement phases, each requiring an elliptic curve scalar point multiplication. Upon receiving a public key from another party for the key agreement phase, bits 434 through 439 are cleared. Lastly, public and shared keys are 55 bytes long.

SIKEX434 Operation. From here on, we call the hybrid key exchange with SIKEp434 and X434 as "SIKEX434". Since SIKEp434 is a key encapsulation mechanism and X434 is a Diffie-Hellman key exchange, we combine the two into a key encapsulation mechanism. In Fig. 1, we illustrate an example of a hybrid key exchange with SIKEX434. In this example, a client wants to establish a secure channel with a server using X434. First, the client generates a public key for X434 and SIKEp434. Then, in the Client Hello message, the client concatenates the two public keys. X434 and SIKEp434 public keys are 55 and 330 bytes, respectively, so a combined public key is 385 bytes, which is about 17% larger than simply a SIKEp434 public key. Upon receiving the Client Hello message, the server continues the key exchange by performing a public key generation

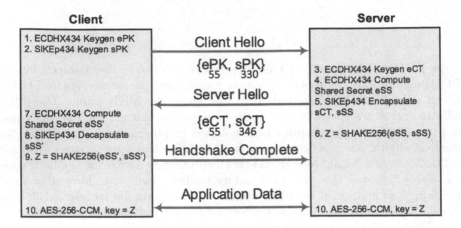

Fig. 1. Proposed SIKEX434 hybrid key exchange. 385 bytes are sent in Client Hello and 401 bytes are sent in Server Hello.

for X434, computing the X434 shared secret, and SIKEp434 encapsulating the SIKEp434 public key. For ease of notation, the output of X434 key generation on the server side is considered a ciphertext. The Server Hello is composed of the 55 byte X434 ciphertext and 346 byte SIKEp434 ciphertext, for a total 401 bytes. The Server can then use SHAKE256 (which is already included as part of SIKE) as a key derivation function by hashing the 55 byte X434 shared secret and 16 byte SIKEp434 shared secret. Upon receiving the Server Hello, the Client can proceed by computing the X434 shared secret and decapsulating the SIKEp434 ciphertext. Upon completion, the Client can similarly use the key derivation function to find the final shared key. If the hybrid key exchange was successful, both parties can use the shared key in AES to send and receive messages.

Key Derivation Methods. Since we are using two different public-key cryptosystems for SIKEX434, we must create a shared secret from the SIKEp434 shared key and X434 shared key. For this, we adapt the methods from [6] which combine the shared keys by concatenating or cascading the shared secrets before applying a pseudo-random function. For simplicity, we perform the concatenation key derivation function (CtKDF) combiner by concatenating the X434 shared key and SIKEp434 shared key and hashing them using the SHAKE256 function (which is already a part of SIKE). Further, if necessary, the concatenation KDF could include generated public keys, a context, and the length of the output as additional inputs in the SHAKE256 hash function. See [6] for further security analysis on generic hybrid key encapsulation methods.

The Case Against X25519 and X448. Here, we made the choice to go against Curve25519 and Curve448, two well-known curves for ECDH and EdDSA, to save area. X25519 uses a much smaller prime size and would have drastically sped up the classical cryptosystem used in a hybrid key exchange. Meanwhile, X448 uses a slightly larger, but better-shaped prime than X434, most likely resulting

Table 2. Proposed EdDSA parameter sets over SIKE primes

SIKE scheme	SIKE/EdDSA prime	SIKE			EdDSA		
		Security level (Bytes)	Public Key (Bytes)	Ciphertext (Bytes)	d coef	Public Key (Bytes)	Signature (Bytes)
$p434$	$2^{216}3^{137} - 1$	1	330	346	109,831	55	110
$p503$	$2^{250}3^{159} - 1$	2	378	402	77,073	63	126
$p610$	$2^{305}3^{192} - 1$	3	462	486	283,951	77	144
$p751$	$2^{372}3^{239} - 1$	5	564	596	156,113	94	188

in a similar timing profile. However, because SIKE is limited (for reasonable performance) to only smooth isogeny-friendly primes such as SIKEp434 we cannot use these standardized ECDH primes. Although we do not have results (at this time), pairing X25519 or X448 would mean that our modular multiplier as we describe in Sect. 5 would be much larger. For instance, consider taking X25519 with the Montgomery multiplier we describe in the following section. X25519's prime was specifically chosen for its pseudo-Mersenne prime shape that cannot be taken advantage of by SIKE primes. For Montgomery multiplication, this would result in more arithmetic logic (small multipliers) to compute the Montgomery q constant each computation. Furthermore, additional registers and control logic would be needed to switch between the X25519 multiplication reduction and the SIKEp434 multiplication reduction. Lastly, the latency of SIKE is significantly longer than ECDH, so including X25519 would only have a tiny improvement in total latency of a hybrid key exchange.

4 Proposed EdDSA Schemes over SIKE Parameters

In addition to ECDH for a hybrid key establishment, digital signatures are another strong use case for elliptic curves. Although elliptic curve-based digital signatures would also be broken by a sufficiently large quantum computer, the use cases and security longevity between key establishment and authentication are different. For instance, quantum-safe key establishment must be implemented and deployed well in advance of large-scale quantum computers as retroactive decryptions could break past secure communications. The concern here is that highly confidential communications including top-secret classified information that is encrypted with classical cryptosystems could be broken well before it was supposed to be declassified. One primary application of digital signatures is authentication. Retroactive authentication is not so much an issue in our digital infrastructure as authenticating a session is typically short-term. When large quantum computers are available, implementations using classical-safe digital signature schemes can make the switch to quantum-safe digital signature schemes and carry on business as usual.

Here, we see elliptic curve-base digital signatures as an important complement to hybrid PQC schemes. Similar to our parameter selection for RFC 7748-style [35] ECDH parameter sets, we can also create new parameter sets for RFC 8032-style [26] Edwards Digital Signature Algorithm (EdDSA). We chose to go with EdDSA over ECDSA as EdDSA features improved performance, implementation simplicity, and no need to generate a nonce for each signature. Up until now, Ed25519 [4] and Ed448 [23] were the primary EdDSA curves. Although it uses a curve defined over a smaller prime, Ed25519 is less ideal for a small footprint implementation with SIKE as it uses SHA-512 whereas Ed448 uses SHAKE256. SHAKE256, used in all SIKE parameter sets, is based on the Keccak [5] sponge family of hashes and is standardized in SHA-3.

New EdDSA Schemes for SIKE Primes. Here, we propose new parameter sets for EdDSA, which we call Ed434, Ed503, Ed610, and Ed751 that share the primes used of the corresponding SIKE versions SIKEp434, SIKEp503, SIKEp610, and SIKEp751, respectively. All EdDSA schemes are defined over twisted Edwards curves of the following form:

$$E/\mathbb{F}_q \ : \ ax^2 + y^2 = 1 + dx^2y^2$$

To find appropriate curves for Ed434, Ed503, Ed610, and Ed751, we fixed $a = 1$ and searched for the smallest positive d value such that both the curve and its quadratic twist have 4·prime order and d was not a square in $\mathbb{F}_q$. If d is not a square, then the Edwards curve arithmetic is complete. We summarize our found curves in Table 2.

Another method to search for the Edward curve parameters could have been to apply an isomorphism from the Montgomery curves, similar to how Ed25519 was created as an isomorphism from X25519. For instance, applying a similar isomorphism from X434 to Ed434 would have created the curve, $E/\mathbb{F}_p \ : \ x^2 + y^2 = 1 + (109830/109831)x^2y^2$. Furthermore, the birational equivalence is further that $x_{Ed} = \sqrt{439324}x_{Mont}y_{Mont}$ and $y_{Ed} = (x_{Mont} - 1)(x_{Mont} + 1)$. The isomorphic base point is then $(x, \frac{3}{5})$, for which x is positive. We opted to find smaller twisted Edwards curves to save space when storing the curve and base point. Also, interestingly enough, the Edwards d coefficients of the EdYYY schemes are equal to the Montgomery a_{24} for each of the XYYYschemes. For instance, Ed434 uses a d coefficient of 109,831, which is equal to X434's $a_{24} = (439322 + 2)/4 = 109831$.

Ed434. Here, we describe the operation for Ed434, an RFC 8032-style [26] EdDSA scheme over the SIKE prime $p434$. This is depicted in Fig. 2. The EdDSA schemes over other SIKE primes are extremely similar. Ed434 is the collection of all points (x, y) that satisfy the twisted Edwards elliptic curve form (note that $a = 1$) over the finite field $p434 = 2^{216}3^{137} - 1$:

$$E/\mathbb{F}_p \ : \ x^2 + y^2 = 1 + 109831x^2y^2$$

Ed434 Key Generation. The Ed434 public key is generated by first collecting 55 bytes of random data. These 55 bytes are hashed using SHAKE256 and the output digest is the first 110 bytes. The lower 55 bytes of this output digest are pruned to an output s by setting bit 433, and clearing bits 0, 1, 434, 435, 436, 437, 438, and 439. This result is interpreted as a scalar and used to perform a scalar point multiplication over the base point $A = [s]B$. Finally, this point

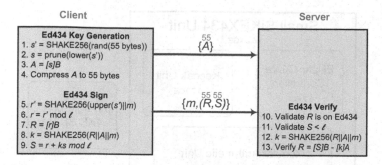

Fig. 2. Proposed Ed434 digital signature scheme.

result is compressed by encoding the first 55 bytes with the y-coordinate and the least significant bit of the x-coordinate is copied to the most significant bit of the final byte, resulting in a 55 byte public key.

Ed434 Sign. A message is signed by first SHAKE256 hashing the upper 55 bytes of the secret key hash with the message to a 110-byte r. r is reduced modulo the large prime order of the curve, ℓ, and interpreted as a scalar to perform a scalar point multiplication over the base point $R = [r]B$. Point R is represented in the compressed Edwards form as was done with the public key A. SHAKE256 is once again used to hash R, A, and the message to a 110-byte digest k. Lastly, the signature component S is computed by performing $S = r + k \cdot s \bmod \ell$. The final signature is the compressed Edwards point R and the scalar S, totaling to 110 bytes.

Ed434 Verify. A message and signature is verifed by first validating the point R and scalar S are of the correct form. This entails checking that R decodes to a valid Ed434 point and that the scalar S is less than the large prime order of Ed434. Note that decoding an Ed434 Edwards point involves a few exponentiations in a similar manner to Ed448, but no square roots are needed (see Sect. 5.2.3 of RFC 8032 [26]). Upon validating signature components R and S, SHAKE256 is once again used to hash R, A, and the message to a 110-byte digest k. Lastly, this k value is used to verify the group equation $[S]B = R + [k]A$. If the left and right side are equal, then the signature is valid. Note that similar to [4], one can instead check that the encodings of the left and right hand side of $R = [S]B - [k]A$ match to avoid decoding point R.

5   ECC/SIKE for Small Devices

Here, we present some details and results of our small footprint architecture to accelerate SIKE and ECDH over the 434-bit prime. Our core components and area numbers are shown in Fig. 3.

Field Addition. At the lowest level, ECDH and SIKE are composed of modular addition and multiplication over p_{434}. One primary reason to create the parameter set for X434 was so that the field arithmetic unit could be reused between

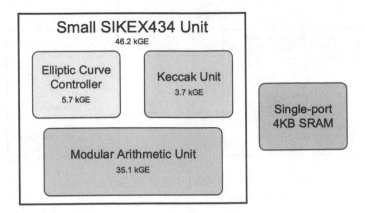

Fig. 3. High-level components of the small SIKEX434 unit. The numbers below the component indicate its size in Gate Equivalents (GE).

the two key exchanges. To keep interface and arithmetic overhead low, all data in our architecture is stored by 32-bit word in a single-port 4KB SRAM. Each intermediate $\mathbb{F}_p$ value requires 55 bytes or 14 words. For a given cycle we can only perform one read or write operation of 32-bit data. $\mathbb{F}_p$ addition performs $c = a + b$ where $a, b, c \in \mathbb{F}_p$. Thus, if $a + b > p$, then we perform a reduction and the result is $c = a + b - p$. $\mathbb{F}_p$ subtraction is similar, but a reduction is performed by adding p if the result is negative. For addition and subtraction, we first load one full operand, perform the addition or subtraction, perform a reduction, and store the result. Our architecture can internally store two full $p434$ registers, so we store the addition/subtraction result in register 1 and store the conditional reduction result in register 2. We choose the correct register to store back in our SRAM by checking the negative bit of operand 2 for $\mathbb{F}_p$ addition and the negative bit of operand 1 for $\mathbb{F}_p$ subtraction. An $\mathbb{F}_p$ addition/subtraction requires 48 cycles.

Field Multiplication. The modular multiplier is the largest piece of this architecture. It is an intense computation which is used extensively for both SIKEp434 and X434. Since the multiplication of two similarly sized values produces a result double the size, an expensive reduction is also needed. Unfortunately, efficient modular multiplication with $p434$ is limited to Barrett or Montgomery multiplication algorithms. Our modular multiplier is adapted from the carry-save adder Montgomery multiplier from [42] with a digit size of 4-bits. Montgomery multiplication [38] converts expensive division operations into shift operations, which are extremely cheap in hardware. In each cycle, this systolic modular multiplier computes 4 bits of a modular multiplication result. Since the final result is in two different buffers, one for sum and one for carry, we finish the computation by adding these two buffers with our field addition unit. By limiting this modular multiplier to only support $p434$, we can optimize away many gates in this multiplier architecture, such as any AND gate connected to the modulus registers. For $p434$, this is 434 AND gates. If multiple primes were to be supported, then there would have to be some storage to swap between primes, these AND gates would have been included, and there would be a larger critical path. An $\mathbb{F}_p$ multiplication requires 158 cycles.

Controller. The controller handles all sequencing necessary for ECDH point multiplications and SIKE isogenies. The controller reads from a program ROM that contains all elliptic curve-related subroutines. Each subroutine is composed of a sequence of $\mathbb{F}_p$ addition, subtraction, and multiplication, and $\mathbb{F}_{p^2}$ addition, subtraction, multiplication, and squaring. There are 1058 instructions total in our program ROM, for which the Fermat's Little Theorem-based $\mathbb{F}_p$ inversion required almost 600. ECDH used the classical Montgomery ladder. The isogeny and point arithmetic required for SIKE are the fastest known formulas in the literature that can be found in [24]. The large-degree isogeny requires a number of pivot points for efficient computation and our architecture can store up to 6 pivot points.

Keccak Unit. SIKE utilizes SHAKE256 as a hash function throughout its operation. However, the latency of SIKE's isogeny arithmetic dominates the computations, so we opted for an extremely small SHAKE256 module. SHAKE256 is based on the Keccak sponge family of hashes. Most fast implementations utilize 1600 registers to represent the full Keccak internal state. Our implementation simply reuses the single-port 4KB SRAM to hold the 1600-bit state. Our implementation utilizes various shifts and arithmetic functions as part of the Keccak sponge family, but performed over a single word at a time. Depending on the size of a SHAKE256 hash, generally each permutation operation takes slightly over 220,000 cycles, which is still significantly less than a SIKE operation.

Verification. SIKE and ECDH were tested separately and then put together for hybrid key exchange. SIKE was tested against the SIKE submission's Known Answer Tests and ECDH was tested against python-generated key generation and key agreement test vectors. Our hybrid key exchange generated a shared secret by using the concatenation key derivation function method from [6]. Essentially, a shared secret was produced by hashing a concatenation of the SIKEp434 and X434 shared secrets with SHAKE256 and using the first 256 bits of the result.

6   Hybrid Architecture Results

Here, we describe our small SIKEX434 hardware implementation results. For FPGA results, we used the NIST PQC recommended Artix-7 FPGA. We synthesized the SIKEX434 core with Xilinx Vivado 2019.2 to a Xilinx Artix-7 xc7a200tffbg676-2 device. On the ASIC side, we synthesized using Synopsis Design Compiler Q-2019.12 with the TSMC 65nm library tcbn65lptc. All results were obtained after place-and-route.

Table 3. FPGA results of small SIKEX434 accelerator on a Xilinx Artix-7.

Frequency	Area				
MHz	# FFs	#LUTs	# Slices	# DSPs	#BRAMs
195	1,942	5,841	1,663	0	1

Table 4. ASIC results of small SIKEX434 accelerator on 65nm tcbn65lptc. Note that this excludes the single-port 4KB SRAM.

Frequency	Critical path	Area	
MHz	ns	um^2	GE
278	6.41	66,578	46,235

Area. We present our FPGA results in Table 3 and ASIC results in Table 4. On the FPGA side, we used a total of 1663 slices for our entire design and one 36k BRAM. This equated to 1942 flip-flops and 5841 look-up tables. The maximum frequency for this configuration was 195 MHz. For the ASIC, we synthesized at 100 MHz, which the Synopsys Compiler easily beat, giving a slack of 6.41 ns. The critical path is thus 3.59 ns, which corresponds to a frequency of 278 MHz. The total area of the design was 66,578 um^2 which we converted to gate equivalents (GE) by dividing by 1.44, which was the size of a NAND gate in um^2. Note that this excludes the single-port 4KB SRAM. We further break down the size of the 46.2 kGE in Fig. 3. The finite field accelerator took the majority of the design at 35.1 kGE. This area could continue to go down notably by reducing the digit size of the systolic multiplier from 4 down to 1 or 2 at the expense of almost quadrupling or doubling the resulting time, respectively.

Timing. The latencies between operations are identical between the two device targets, which are presented in Table 5. The "E + D" column includes the key encapsulation and decapsulation time as was done in the SIKE submission. Since key generation only needs to be performed a single time by a party, it is expected that the encapsulation and decapsulation timings are the customer-felt latency. As the timings show, the SIKEX434 E + D time for ASIC is 175.2 ms and the time for an entire SIKEX434 hybrid key exchange is 224.1 ms. Note that given more aggressive timing for the synthesis that these numbers can continue to improve at the cost of increased area. However, higher frequencies greatly impact the resulting power and energy consumption.

SIKEX434 Overhead. Comparing SIKEp434 to SIKEX434 shows a 9.5% increase of latency for the additional hybrid computations. These hybrid computations include four additional X434 operations as well as two additional SHAKE256 KDF operations. On the communication side, SIKEX434 requires 16.3% additional overhead. A timing breakdown of each cryptosystem's primitives are presented in Fig. 4.

Table 5. Latency of operations on our SIKEX434 accelerator. Note that the latency is identical for Artix-7 and ASIC.

Scheme	Latency	Time (ms)	
	$(cc \times 10^6)$	Artix-7	ASIC
		@195 MHz	@278 MHz
X434 Keygen	1.2	6.2	4.3
X434 KeyAgree	1.2	6.2	4.3
SIKEp434 Keygen	12.4	63.6	44.6
SIKEp434 Encap	21.4	109.8	77.0
SIKEp434 Decap	23.1	118.5	83.1
SIKEp434 E + D	44.5	228.2	160.1
SIKEp434 Total	56.9	291.8	204.7
SIKEX434 Keygen	13.6	69.7	48.9
SIKEX434 Encap	24.1	123.6	86.7
SIKEX434 Decap	24.6	126.2	88.5
SIKEX434 E + D	48.7	249.7	175.2
SIKEX434 Total	62.3	319.5	224.1

Table 6. Area comparison of isogeny architectures on a Artix-7 at approximately NIST security level 1 (SIKEp434).

Work	# FFs	# LUTs	# Slices	# DSPs	#BRAMs
Massolino et al. [37] (128)[1,2]	7,202	11,943	3,491	57	21
Massolino et al. [37] (256)[1,2]	11,661	22,673	7,329	162	37
Koziel et al. [27]	24,328	21,946	8,006	240	26.5
This work	**1,942**	**5,841**	**1,663**	**0**	**1**

1. Implementation also includes SIKEp503, SIKEp610, and SIKEp751
2. (128) and (256) refer to 128-bit and 256-bit multipliers, respectively

Comparison. A fair comparison with other implementations is difficult as their focus has generally been on performance. Since our focus is on NIST Security Level 1, we summarize Artix-7 area and timing comparison results in Tables 6 and 7, respectively. The SIKE submission's hardware implementation is based on the high performance implementation from [27]. For SIKEp434, this implementation requires 8006 slices, 240 DSPs, and 26.5 BRAMs to compute SIKEp434 in 14.4 ms on the Artix-7. This is 16 times faster than our implementation for 5 times as many slices and significantly more BRAMs and DSPs. The more area-efficient implementation from [37] supports all four SIKE parameter sets using a hardware software co-design methodology. Their smaller implementation implements SIKEp434 in just over 50 ms with 3415 slices, 57 DSPs, and 21 BRAMs. This is over 4 times faster at the cost of 2 times as many slices and again significantly more BRAMs and DSPs. Unfortunately, this disparity in BRAMs and

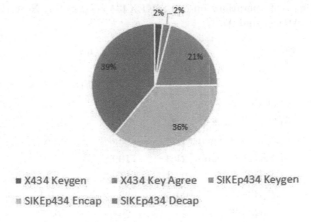

Fig. 4. Timing breakdown of SIKEp434 and X434 primitives. Note that X434 operations are performed twice in a full SIKEX434 operation.

Table 7. Timing comparison of isogeny architectures on a Artix-7 at approximately NIST security level 1 (SIKEp434). Note that SIKE total time includes key encapsulation and decapsulation.

Work	Freq. (MHz)	Cycles ($cc \times 10^6$)	Total time (ms)
Massolino *et al.* [37] (128)	145.1	27.3	52.8
Massolino *et al.* [37] (256)	109.1	8.6	31.7
Koziel *et al.* [27]	132.2	1.91	14.4
This work	**163.1**	**44.5**	**228.2**

DSPs make a fair area-time comparison difficult. Hopefully there will be more ASIC area results for SIKE implementations in the future for more accurate comparisons of resource cost. Nonetheless, this implementation shows a lower area bound for SIKEp434 and SIKEX434 hardware implementations.

7   Conclusion

In this work, we proposed the hybrid key exchange SIKEX434 composed of SIKEp434 and X434 as well as new ECDH and EdDSA schemes over SIKE parameters SIKEp434, SIKEp503, SIKEp610, and SIKEp751. We presented the smallest SIKE architecture in the literature for this design that is 1663 slices in FPGA and 46 kGE and 4KB SRAM in ASIC. This design can accomplish the entire SIKEX434 on ASIC in less than 250 ms. An expected segment of a key exchange will also take less than a tenth of a second. SIKEX434 adds approximately 16% communication overhead and 10% latency overhead. With a 385 byte public key and 401 byte ciphertext, this hybrid key exchange is still 50% smaller than the next smallest key in the NIST PQC contest. As research continues into quantum computer attacks on cryptosystems, adapting and innovating hybrid key exchange schemes will be necessary as we transition to a fully quantum-safe infrastructure.

Acknowledgment. This work has been funded by a DoD contract W911NF2010328 granted to PQSecure Technologies.

Intellectual Property Disclosure. Some of these techniques may be covered by US and/or international patents.

References

1. Adj, G., Cervantes-Vázquez, D., Chi-Domínguez, J.J., Menezes, A., Rodríguez-Henríquez, F.: On the cost of computing isogenies between supersingular elliptic curves. In: Cid, C., Jacobson Jr., M.J. (eds.) Selected Areas in Cryptography - SAC 2018–25th International Conference, Calgary, AB, Canada, August 15–17, 2018, Revised Selected Papers, Lecture Notes in Computer Science, vol. 11349, pp. 322–343. Springer, Heidelberg (2018). https://doi.org/10.1007/978-3-030-10970-7_15

2. Azarderakhsh, R., Jao, D., Kalach, K., Koziel, B., Leonardi, C.: Key compression for isogeny-based cryptosystems. In: Proceedings of the 3rd ACM International Workshop on ASIA Public-Key Cryptography, pp. 1–10 (2016)

3. Bernstein, D.J., Birkner, P., Joye, M., Lange, T., Peters, C.: Twisted edwards curves. In: Vaudenay, S. (ed.) AFRICACRYPT 2008. LNCS, vol. 5023, pp. 389–405. Springer, Heidelberg (2008). https://doi.org/10.1007/978-3-540-68164-9_26

4. Bernstein, D.J., Duif, N., Lange, T., Schwabe, P., Yang, B.-Y.: High-speed high-security signatures. J. Cryptogr. Eng. **2**(2), 77–89 (2012)

5. Bertoni, G., Daemen, J., Peeters, M., Van Assche, G., Van Keer, R.: Keccak Implementation Overview (2012)

6. Campagna, M., Petcher, A.: Security of hybrid key encapsulation. Cryptology ePrint Archive, Report 2020/1364 (2020). https://eprint.iacr.org/2020/1364

7. Charles, D.X., Lauter, K.E., Goren, E.Z.: Cryptographic hash functions from expander graphs. J. Cryptol. **22**(1), 93–113 (2007). https://doi.org/10.1007/s00145-007-9002-x

8. Chen, L., et al.: Report on Post-Quantum Cryptography. NIST IR 8105 (2016)

9. Childs, A.M., Jao, D., Soukharev, V.: Constructing elliptic curve isogenies in quantum subexponential time. J. Math. Cryptol. **8**(1), 1–29 (2014)

10. Costello, C., Hisil, H.: A simple and compact algorithm for SIDH with arbitrary degree isogenies. In: Takagi, T., Peyrin, T. (eds.) ASIACRYPT 2017. LNCS, vol. 10625, pp. 303–329. Springer, Cham (2017). https://doi.org/10.1007/978-3-319-70697-9_11

11. Costello, C., Jao, D., Longa, P., Naehrig, M., Renes, J., Urbanik, D.: Efficient compression of SIDH public keys. In: Coron, J.-S., Nielsen, J.B. (eds.) EUROCRYPT 2017. LNCS, vol. 10210, pp. 679–706. Springer, Cham (2017). https://doi.org/10.1007/978-3-319-56620-7_24

12. Costello, C., Longa, P., Naehrig, M.: Efficient algorithms for supersingular isogeny diffie-hellman. In: Robshaw, M., Katz, J. (eds.) CRYPTO 2016. LNCS, vol. 9814, pp. 572–601. Springer, Heidelberg (2016). https://doi.org/10.1007/978-3-662-53018-4_21

13. Costello, C., Longa, P., Naehrig, M., Renes, J., Virdia, F.: Improved classical crypt-analysis of SIKE in practice. In: Kiayias, A., Kohlweiss, M., Wallden, P., Zikas, V. (eds.) PKC 2020. LNCS, vol. 12111, pp. 505–534. Springer, Cham (2020). https://doi.org/10.1007/978-3-030-45388-6_18
14. Couveignes, J.M.: Hard Homogeneous Spaces. Cryptology ePrint Archive, Report 2006/291 (2006)
15. De Feo, L., Jao, D., Plût, J.: Towards quantum-resistant cryptosystems from super-singular elliptic curve isogenies. J. Math. Cryptol. **8**(3), 209–247 (2014)
16. Edwards, H.M.: A normal form for elliptic curves. Bull. Am. Math. Soc. **44**, 393–422 (2007)
17. Faz-Hernández, A., López, J., Ochoa-Jiménez, E., Rodríguez-Henríquez, F.: A faster software implementation of the supersingular isogeny diffie-hellman key exchange protocol. IEEE Trans. Comput. **67**(11), 1622–1636 (2018)
18. Feo, L.D.: Mathematics of Isogeny Based Cryptography. CoRR, abs/1711.04062 (2017)
19. Galbraith, S.D., Petit, C., Shani, B., Ti, Y.B.: On the security of supersingu-lar isogeny cryptosystems. In: Cheon, J.H., Takagi, T. (eds.) ASIACRYPT 2016. LNCS, vol. 10031, pp. 63–91. Springer, Heidelberg (2016). https://doi.org/10.1007/978-3-662-53887-6_3
20. Galbraith, S.D., Petit, C., Silva, J.: Identification protocols and signature schemes based on supersingular isogeny problems. In: Takagi, T., Peyrin, T. (eds.) ASI-ACRYPT 2017. LNCS, vol. 10624, pp. 3–33. Springer, Cham (2017). https://doi.org/10.1007/978-3-319-70694-8_1
21. Gélin, A., Wesolowski, B.: Loop-abort faults on supersingular isogeny cryptosys-tems. In: Lange, T., Takagi, T. (eds.) PQCrypto 2017. LNCS, vol. 10346, pp. 93–106. Springer, Cham (2017). https://doi.org/10.1007/978-3-319-59879-6_6
22. Grover, L.K.: A fast quantum mechanical algorithm for database search. In: Pro-ceedings of the Twenty-Eighth Annual ACM Symposium on Theory of Comput-ing, STOC 1996, pages 212–219, New York, NY, USA. Association for Computing Machinery (1996)
23. Hamburg, M.: Ed448-goldilocks, a new elliptic curve. Cryptology ePrint Archive, Report 2015/625 (2015). https://eprint.iacr.org/2015/625
24. Jao, D., et al.: Supersingular isogeny key encapsulation. Submission to the NIST Post-Quantum Standardization Project (2017)
25. Jao, D., Soukharev, V.: Isogeny-based quantum-resistant undeniable signatures. In: Mosca, M. (ed.) PQCrypto 2014. LNCS, vol. 8772, pp. 160–179. Springer, Cham (2014). https://doi.org/10.1007/978-3-319-11659-4_10
26. Josefsson, S., Liusvaara, I.: Edwards-curve digital signature algorithm (eddsa). RFC **8032**, 1–60 (2017)
27. Koziel, B., Ackie, A.B., Khatib, R.E., Azarderakhsh, R., Kermani, M.M.: Sike'd up: fast hardware architectures for supersingular isogeny key encapsulation. IEEE Trans. Circ. Syst. I Reg. Papers **67**(12), 4842–4854 (2020)
28. Koziel, B., Azarderakhsh, R., Jao, D.: An exposure model for supersingular isogeny diffie-hellman key exchange. In: Smart, N.P. (ed.) CT-RSA 2018. LNCS, vol. 10808, pp. 452–469. Springer, Cham (2018). https://doi.org/10.1007/978-3-319-76953-0_24
29. Koziel, B., Azarderakhsh, R., Jao, D.: Side-channel attacks on quantum-resistant supersingular isogeny Diffie-Hellman. In: Adams, C., Camenisch, J. (eds.) SAC 2017. LNCS, vol. 10719, pp. 64–81. Springer, Cham (2018). https://doi.org/10.1007/978-3-319-72565-9_4

30. Koziel, B., Azarderakhsh, R., Jao, D., Mozaffari-Kermani, M.: On fast calculation of addition chains for isogeny-based cryptography. In: Chen, K., Lin, D., Yung, M. (eds.) Inscrypt 2016. LNCS, vol. 10143, pp. 323–342. Springer, Cham (2017). https://doi.org/10.1007/978-3-319-54705-3_20

31. Koziel, B., Azarderakhsh, R., Mozaffari-Kermani, M.: Fast hardware architectures for supersingular isogeny diffie-hellman key exchange on FPGA. In: Dunkelman, O., Sanadhya, S.K. (eds.) INDOCRYPT 2016. LNCS, vol. 10095, pp. 191–206. Springer, Cham (2016). https://doi.org/10.1007/978-3-319-49890-4_11

32. Koziel, B., Azarderakhsh, R., Mozaffari-Kermani, M.: A high-performance and scalable hardware architecture for isogeny-based cryptography. IEEE Trans. Comput. **67**(11), 1594–1609 (2018)

33. Koziel, B., Azarderakhsh, R., Mozaffari-Kermani, M., Jao, D.: Post-quantum cryptography on FPGA based on isogenies on elliptic curves. IEEE Trans. Circ. Syst. I Reg. Papers **64**(1), 86–99 (2017)

34. Koziel, B., Jalali, A., Azarderakhsh, R., Jao, D., Mozaffari-Kermani, M.: NEON-SIDH: efficient implementation of supersingular isogeny diffie-hellman key exchange protocol on ARM. In: Foresti, S., Persiano, G. (eds.) CANS 2016. LNCS, vol. 10052, pp. 88–103. Springer, Cham (2016). https://doi.org/10.1007/978-3-319-48965-0_6

35. Langley, A., Hamburg, M., Turner, S.: Elliptic curves for security. RFC **7748**, 1–22 (2016)

36. Liu, W., Ni, J., Liu, Z., Liu, C., O'Neill, M.: Optimized modular multiplication for supersingular isogeny diffie-hellman. IEEE Trans. Comput. **68**(8), 1249–1255 (2019)

37. Massolino, P.M.C., Longa, P., Renes, J., Batina, L.: A compact and scalable hardware/software co-design of SIKE. Cryptology ePrint Archive, Report 2020/040 (2020). https://eprint.iacr.org/2020/040

38. Montgomery, P.L.: Modular multiplication without trial division. Math. Comput. **44**(170), 519–521 (1985)

39. Montgomery, P.L.: Speeding the pollard and elliptic curve methods of factorization. In: Mathematics of Computation, pp. 243–264 (1987)

40. Rostovtsev, A., Stolbunov, A.: Public-key cryptosystem based on isogenies. Cryptology ePrint Archive, Report 2006/145 (2006)

41. Shor, P.W.: Algorithms for quantum computation: discrete logarithms and factoring. In: 35th Annual Symposium on Foundations of Computer Science (FOCS 1994), pp. 124–134 (1994)

42. Sutter, G., Deschamps, J.P., Imaña, J.L.: Modular multiplication and exponentiation architectures for fast RSA cryptosystem based on digit serial computation. IEEE Trans. Ind. Electroni. **58**(7), 3101–3109 (2011)

43. Ti, Y.B.: Fault attack on supersingular isogeny cryptosystems. In: Lange, T., Takagi, T. (eds.) PQCrypto 2017. LNCS, vol. 10346, pp. 107–122. Springer, Cham (2017). https://doi.org/10.1007/978-3-319-59879-6_7

44. Yoo, Y., Azarderakhsh, R., Jalali, A., Jao, D., Soukharev, V.: A post-quantum digital signature scheme based on supersingular isogenies. In: Kiayias, A. (ed.) FC 2017. LNCS, vol. 10322, pp. 163–181. Springer, Cham (2017). https://doi.org/10.1007/978-3-319-70972-7_9

CPS-STS Workshop

Towards Stealing Deep Neural Networks on Mobile Devices

Shashank Reddy Danda[✉] 🆔, Xiaoyong Yuan 🆔, and Bo Chen 🆔

Michigan Technological University, Houghton, MI 49931, USA
{sdanda,xyyuan,bchen}@mtu.edu

Abstract. Recently, deep neural networks (DNN) are increasingly deployed on mobile computing devices. Compared to the traditional cloud-based DNN services, the on-device DNN provides immediate responses without relying on network availability or bandwidth and can boost security and privacy by preventing users' data from transferring over the untrusted communication channels or cloud servers. However, deploying DNN models on the mobile devices introduces new attack vectors on the models. Previous studies have shown that the DNN models are prone to model stealing attacks in the cloud setting, by which the attackers can steal the DNN models accurately. In this work, for the first time, we study the model stealing attacks on the deep neural networks running in the mobile devices, by interacting with mobile applications. Our experimental results on various datasets confirm the feasibility of stealing DNN models in mobile devices with high accuracy and small overhead.

Keywords: Deep neural network · Model stealing · Privacy · Mobile devices

1 Introduction

Deep neural networks (DNNs) have been pervasively used in various computer vision tasks, such as objects detection, image classification, and face recognition. Due to the high business value of DNNs, model stealing attacks have been conducted in recent years, in which an attacker attempts to duplicate a victim machine learning/neural network model by querying the victim model and training a surrogate model to replicate the victim model's functionality. Such a novel attack has become a serious security threat to many machine learning services today, as the machine learning models represent the business advantages of service providers and training a model from scratch is costly and time-consuming.

Tramèr et al. [9] successfully stole machine learning models, including decision tree, support vector machine, and regression models, with an accuracy of around 100%. A line of recent works has shown the feasibility of stealing more complex yet powerful machine learning models like DNNs [3, 8, 10, 13–15]. However, most existing model stealing attacks are conducted on public cloud services, where the DNN models are run on the cloud servers [2, 11].

© ICST Institute for Computer Sciences, Social Informatics and Telecommunications Engineering 2021
Published by Springer Nature Switzerland AG 2021. All Rights Reserved
J. Garcia-Alfaro et al. (Eds.): SecureComm 2021, LNICST 399, pp. 495–508, 2021.
https://doi.org/10.1007/978-3-030-90022-9_27

Nowadays, with the increasing computing power and the recent advance of light-weighted neural networks, DNNs have been increasingly deployed on mobile computing devices. By leveraging open-source deep learning frameworks (e.g., TensorFlow Lite and PyTorch Mobile), the developers can smoothly integrate well-trained DNN models with mobile applications under minimal effort. Compared with the cloud-based DNN services, this type of on-device DNN can provide immediate responses without relying on network availability or bandwidth, and boost security and privacy as users' data do not need to be transferred over untrusted communication channels or cloud servers. The question is, are the model stealing attacks feasible on the on-device DNN? Mobile devices today suffer from malware attacks. By performing various attacks like phishing or social engineering, the malware may get installed in a victim's mobile device. Thanks to the built-in isolation of the mobile applications (e.g., the Android application sandbox), the malware cannot directly have access to the DNN model of a victim mobile application (even if the malware can obtain a higher system privilege, gaining access to the DNN model, the model may have been stored encrypted). However, by interacting with the mobile application, the malware may conduct a model stealing attack similar to that in a cloud setting.

In this work, we aim to confirm the feasibility of the model stealing attacks on mobile devices. This task is non-trivial as the mobile devices are equipped with much less memory and computational power compared to the cloud servers and the malware which performs the model stealing attacks should minimize its consumption of computation and memory to avoid being noticed by the device's owner. We have proposed a model stealing approach for mobile devices by performing interactions with the victim's mobile applications running DNN models (i.e., *the victim models*). We have conducted the model stealing experiments based on several popular machine learning applications and datasets under one of the following two practical assumptions: 1) the attackers have access to the training data, and 2) the attackers do not have access to the training data but can use some public datasets. Our experimental results confirm that the model stealing attacks are feasible on mobile devices with high accuracy (i.e., the accuracy obtained by the attackers is close to that of their victim models) and high efficiency (i.e., the computational cost on the mobile devices is small). Our major contributions are summarized below:

- We have proposed a model stealing approach on mobile devices by interacting with a victim's mobile device.
- We have successfully extracted a stolen model with an accuracy similar to that of the victim model.
- We have investigated several system metrics of mobile devices during conducting the model stealing attacks to verify the feasibility of model stealing in mobile devices.
- We have conducted a rigorous evaluation of model stealing attacks on several machine learning applications and datasets under two practical assumptions.

2   Related Work

CNN networks can be easily stolen or replicated using several different factors which include creating a synthetic dataset and training a model with this synthetic dataset which gives an almost equal performance with the victim model as stated in [1]. They can obtain good accuracy using cloud-based APIs and performing evaluation using facial expression, object, and crosswalk classification datasets. The experiments conducted by them show that model stealing can be performed using cloud-based APIs by querying a target network. Several other methods such as ES attacks were proposed for model stealing the models without any data hurdles as shown in [10]. These attacks train the models using several iterations and obtain a copy of the victim model. Several image datasets were used and the models built were stolen with some less accuracy rate compared to the victim models' accuracy. Tramèr et al. [9] showed an extraction of some of the models like logistic regression, decision trees, and other models. These models are demonstrated against online services as BigML and Amazon machine learning. Their results show how the machine learning models should be deployed securely and the countermeasures of new model extraction.

Cloud-based model stealing was performed in [15] using DNN models by reducing the number of queries required to steal the target model. The accuracy achieved in their work was also good enough to prove that model stealing is successfully performed. A data-free model stealing attack which is called MAZE was proposed in [4] which does not require any type of data for model stealing. It uses some generative models and creates some synthetic data which helps for stealing the models. Their method depends on zeroth-order gradient estimation to perform optimization and finally gives a stolen model with a high accuracy. The proposed method was able to give better accuracy which provides a normalized clone accuracy. Hyperparameters which are very crucial in building a machine learning model can also be stolen as stated in [12]. Those hyperparameters store confidential information of the model and they were able to successfully extract the hyperparameters for different machine models which include ridge regression, support vector machine, logistic regression and neural network models. Orekondy in [13] stated that a lot of machine learning models were deployed on several platforms. They proposed a model stealing functionality of black box model which is known as Knockoff Nets. They validated the model stealing using several datasets with the help of image analysis APIs which provided some good model stealing results. Exploratory based machine learning attack was proposed in [7] on several deep learning models to infer them as a black box and the results obtained after extraction are quite similar to that of the victim model.

Kariyappa in [5] proposed a methodology called "adaptive misinformation" to avoid model stealing. They have conducted experiments by performing several queries on the target model and generated a dataset that can be used for training the stolen model. A good defense mechanism was shown by comparing several other existing defenses in terms of security and accuracy of the models. Matthew Jagielski in [14] proposed some extraction attacks which can steal some remotely

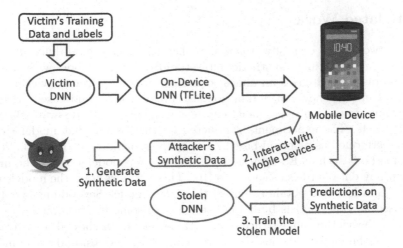

Fig. 1. The workflow of the proposed model stealing approach on mobile devices.

deployed models where they used billions of images to perform model stealing and the performance of the stolen model is evaluated in terms of accuracy and fidelity.

3   A Model Stealing Approach on Mobile Devices

In this section, we propose a model stealing approach for mobile devices, by which the mobile malware can steal the DNN model deployed on a victim mobile application. We prepare for a well-trained DNN model as a victim model, convert it to tflite format, and deploy it on a mobile device. The proposed model stealing attack consists of three main steps: (1) generating synthetic data, (2) interacting with the victim mobile device and getting predictions on the synthetic from the victim model, and (3) transferring the knowledge to the stolen DNN model by training it on the synthetic data and obtained predictions. The workflow of our model stealing is illustrated in Fig. 1. We then train a stolen DNN model based on the synthetic data and obtained predictions using CopyCat [1].

3.1   Generating Synthetic Datasets

We have considered two threat models in generating synthetic datasets. In the first threat model, we assume that the attack has access to the victim model's training data or its data distribution, namely problem domain (PD). Therefore, the attacker can extract the synthetic data from the original dataset on which the victim model is trained. In the second threat model, we consider a more practical scenario, where the attacker has no knowledge of the victim model's training data and only has access to public datasets, namely non-problem domain (NPD). There is no overlap between PD and NPD. Moreover, the data generated in the NPD dataset belong to different categories from the problem domain. We will discuss the details of NPD datasets in Sect. 4. Note that we store the synthetic data in the mobile device and generate labels in a separate file by running interactions using the data records from the dataset.

3.2 Interacting with Mobile Devices

Second, the attacker interacts with mobile devices by querying the synthetic data and aims to get the predictions on synthetic data from the victim model. Given the constrained computational capabilities on the mobile device, the attacker controls the number of interactions using different numbers of samples from the dataset rather than the entire dataset. By interacting with the DNN model deployed on the mobile device, the attacker obtains the corresponding predictions and stores them in a different folder from the synthetic data.

3.3 Training the Stolen Model

The attacker uses the synthetic data and predictions from the mobile device to train a stolen model. We follow the models stealing approach proposed in CopyCat CNN [1] We assume that the attacker does not know about the target model's neural network architecture, but the different neural networks do not affect the effectiveness in transferring the knowledge to a different model, which has been shown in many recent works. Therefore, the attacker can set up a widely used model and train it on the synthetic data and obtained predictions. Moreover, previous works have shown that using pre-trained models would be a very good start for performing model stealing, which saves the attacker much time in training the DNN models. In addition, a large number of pre-trained models are publicly available nowadays, which can be well utilized by the attacker. Specifically, the attacker can first update the output layer to match the required machine learning tasks (e.g., in the image classification task, the output dimension is changed to the number of classes). Then the attacker can freeze some parameters of the pre-trained models and train the rest of them on the synthetic data to fit the problem domain.

4 Experimental Methodology

This section shows the creation of copycat models from the target network models and a proper comparison is made with the victim model's performance which is evaluated using the test data. In this work, we have worked on several different models on different types of datasets which include MNIST, CIFAR-10 and ImageNet. All the copycat models which include the model created using the PD dataset, NPD are evaluated using the different datasets e.g., MNIST, CIFAR-10, and ImageNet. These are the most widely used datasets for image classification and the copycat models are evaluated in three real-world problems. The models that we have used include LeNet-5, ResNet-18, and MobileNetV2 models. All these models were able to give good accuracies after generating the copycat models. The reason why we have chosen these datasets where the sizes of the images were different and this made us to justify that the interactions can be performed using Android applications for different sizes of images.

4.1   Test Dataset and Standard Methods

In all the experiments, we used the same test dataset for evaluating all the standard and copycat models' performance. The standard methods include finding the performance of the victim model, i.e., the model trained on the original dataset and evaluated on the remaining amount of the data. There is also an alternate standard method where we can also take some less amount of data from the same problem domain with the original labels and perform evaluations using the test data. So, here we have only chosen the victim model accuracy for performing comparisons. The test data and the standard method are described below:

Test Dataset. For all the copycat and the victim models, some part of the dataset which does not belongs to the training dataset is divided as the test data set. All these stolen models were also evaluated using this test dataset and the performance is compared between all the models. Attackers have no access to this data.

Model Trained with Original Domain. This model acts as the victim model trained on the original dataset and is not accessible by anyone. In our experiments, we have evaluated whether this model can be stolen from mobile devices by performing interactions across the devices. Here we have considered three trained models. The LeNet-5 model is trained on the MNIST dataset, ResNet-18 trained on the CIFAR-10 dataset, and the MobileNetV2 model trained on the ImageNet dataset. All these models are trained and evaluated on the testing data and finally converted to TensorFlow lite format which can be easily deployed on mobile devices. The model cannot be accessed by everyone and the attacker can only generate the output labels using these models.

4.2   Copycat Attacks

We have conducted the attacks one of the following: 1) the model trained with the images from the same problem domain but stolen predictions, and 2) the model with non-problem domain images which are completely different from that of the original images and the labels are generated using the target model.

Model Trained From the Same Problem Domain and Stolen Predictions. In this case, the images are from the same problem domain and labels are stolen using the victim model. The images are completely different from that of the images used for training the victim model. We have considered training the model on three different datasets. At first, the MNIST handwritten images were used and here we have considered a total of 10,000 images. Several queries were performed with different sizes starting from 250 to 5,000 and evaluated the performance of the stolen model with these different sizes. Finally, the number of interactions which gave better performance is selected and performed these interactions using the mobile application. Using this we can test the performance of the Android application and can state whether the attacker can perform these interactions and steal the model. Similarly, we have also conducted experiments using the CIFAR-10 dataset by considering 10,000 images and passing several queries. Finally, for the ImageNet dataset since the dataset is very huge, we are able to collect 100,000 images and performed up to 100,000 queries. We finally evaluated the performance using 10,000 samples and like that of MNIST, we deployed the model on a mobile application and evaluated the performance of the application.

Model Trained from Non-problem Domain and Stolen Predictions. Compared to PD, this NPD possess images which are completely different from the problem domain. These images possess some labels which are not considered, and the new labels are generated using the victim model which are called stolen predictions. We have considered training the model on three different datasets. At first, the MNIST Fashion and KMNIST images were used and here we have considered a total of 50,000 images. Several queries were performed with different sizes starting from 250 to 50,000 and evaluated the performance of the stolen model with these different sizes. Finally, the number of interactions which gave better performance is selected and performed these interactions using the mobile application. Using this we can test the performance of the Android application and can state whether the attacker can perform these interactions and steal the model. Similarly, we have also conducted experiments using the CIFAR-100 dataset by considering 50,000 images and passing several queries. Finally, for the ImageNet dataset since the dataset is very huge, we have chosen Stanford car dataset and ISIC skin cancer images. We are able to collect 100,000 images and performed queries up to 100,000. We finally evaluated the performance using 10,000 samples and like that of MNIST, we deployed the model on mobile application and evaluated the performance of the application. Here the stolen predictions are different from the originals, which shows some different distributions of classes for each type.

5   Experimental Results

We have performed model stealing attacks in mobile devices, by stealing copycat CNN models using a few different datasets. Using the adversarial robustness toolbox, we generate a class for the random data and use this dataset for training the duplicate model [1,6]. For each dataset we have performed several experiments and the copycat models are evaluated under PD and NPD conditions.

Here in all these cases, the stolen predictions are used. The labels are obtained by running interactions on mobile devices where we have deployed our victim models. The data stolen using the victim model deployed in our mobile device is used as the final data for performing stealing. The models are evaluated, and the performance of each model is compared with the victim model's performance for each dataset.

5.1   General Setup

The MNIST and CIFAR-10 datasets were directly loaded from TensorFlow and pre-processed. We obtained the ImageNet from its official website. We trained the LeNet-5 and ResNet-18 model but we used MobileNetV2 pretrained model for the ImageNet dataset. Some image augmentation techniques were also used. All the models which we trained use SGD as the optimizer. For each model we have used different epoch numbers, i.e., 5 for MNIST, 50 for CIFAR-10, and ImageNet datasets. We have built an Android application using Android studio and we ran the application successfully on Samsung S10 plus device with the latest Android 11 OS, 8 GB memory, and 128 GB internal storage. The application has TensorFlow lite models deployed in it. Interactions with the Android application were performed on the mobile device and, we accessed the CPU and memory usage when running the interactions. To train the copycat model, we used an Intel(R) Core(TM) i7-3770 3.40 GHz with 32GiB of RAM and NVIDIA GeForce GTX 1070 with 8GiB of memory, managed with Ubuntu 18.04.5 LTS (GNU/Linux 4.15.0-118-generic x86-64) with NVIDIA CUDA Framework 11.0 and cuDNN 10.2.

Table 1. Accuracy for the stolen models vs. victim model

Dataset	Model architecture	Accuracy		
		Victim model	PD	NPD
MNIST	LeNet-5	97–98%	95%	93–94%
CIFAR-10	ResNet-18	92%	90–91%	80–81%
ImageNet	MobileNetV2	71.3%	81.2%	73.5%

5.2   Attacks on the MNIST Dataset

The MNIST handwritten image dataset is widely used for image classification and the images here are of 28×28 pixels. The total classes here are 10 and the dataset comprises of 60000 images. The model which we have used here is the LeNet-5 CNN model and is trained on 50,000 samples. The victim model is evaluated using the remaining 10,000 samples. For performing model stealing, under PD we have used these 10,000 test images for performing training and evaluation. Coming to NPD, we have used MNIST fashion and KMNIST images for generating synthetic dataset,s and the labels are stolen using the victim model. The final evaluation is done using the above-mentioned 10,000 images from the original test dataset. The results obtained are shown below: Here PD stands for the images collected from the same dataset. NPD stands for non-problem domain data collected from different sources (MNIST fashion images and KMNIST images). These duplicate images and the original dataset images were collected using the original trained model by running interactions on mobile devices. In all the cases except PD a total of 50,000 images were collected and used for training the model. Different numbers of queries were performed which are of different lengths. These range from 250–50,000 for the NPD case and 250–5000 for PD case were submitted to the victim classifier which is deployed on a mobile device to steal it. In all cases, the more the number of queries, the more accuracy is. For PD we do not need more samples since the dataset is from the original domain itself but with stolen predictions.

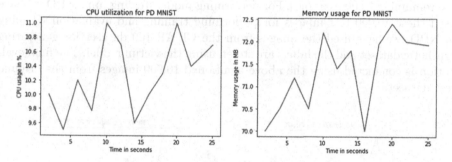

Fig. 2. CPU and memory usage after performing interactions in PD (MNIST).

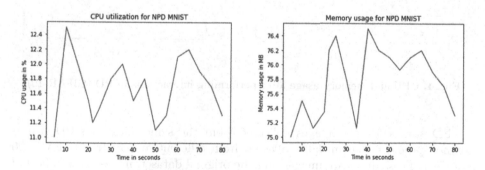

Fig. 3. CPU and memory usage after performing interactions in NPD (MNIST).

Finally, the copycat model's accuracy for PD dataset is about 95% which is very close to that of the victim models' accuracy which is 97–98% (Table 1). The accuracy of NPD model is between 93–94% which is somewhat low compared to the victim model (Table 1).

Figure 2 and 3 show the performance of the mobile device after running interactions. For the problem domain, running 5000 interactions took a short time to
generate the labels. The CPU utilization rate was around 10–11% and the memory occupied was around 72–73 MB. Similarly, the best number of interactions
for NPD was 50000 which took around 80 s to run interactions. The CPU utilization rate was around 12–13% and the memory occupied was around 76–77 MB.
The CPU utilization rate and memory consumed show that model stealing is
feasible using the MNIST dataset.

5.3   Attacks on the CIFAR-10 Dataset

The CIFAR-10 dataset is also used for image classification and the images here
are of 32×32 pixels. The total classes here are 10 and the entire dataset comprises of 60,000 images. The model which we have used here is ResNet-18 CNN
model and is trained on 50,000 samples. The victim model is evaluated using
the remaining 10,000 samples. For performing model stealing, under PD we have
used these 10,000 test images for performing training and evaluation. Coming
to NPD, we have used the images from the CIFAR-100 dataset for generating
synthetic dataset and the labels are stolen using the victim model. The final evaluation is conducted using the above-mentioned 10,000 images from the original
test dataset.

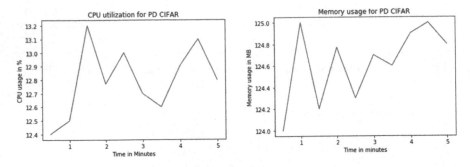

Fig. 4. CPU and memory usage after performing interactions in PD (CIFAR-10).

PD stands for the images collected from the same dataset. NPD stands
for non-problem domain data collected from different sources (the CIFAR-100
dataset). These duplicate images and the original dataset images were collected
using the original trained model by running interactions on mobile devices. In
all the cases except PD, a total of 50,000 images were collected and used for
training the model. Different numbers of queries were performed which are of
different lengths. These range from 250–50,000 for the NPD and 250–5000 for
PD case were submitted to the victim classifier on mobile device to steal it. For
PD we do not need more samples since the dataset is from the original domain
itself but with stolen predictions. Finally, Table 1 shows the copycat model's

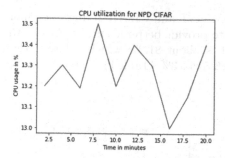
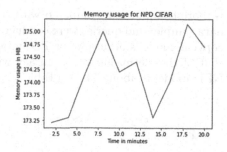

Fig. 5. CPU and memory usage after performing interactions in NPD (CIFAR-10).

accuracy for the PD dataset is about 90–91% which is very close to that of the victim models' accuracy which is 92%. The accuracy of the NPD model is very low which is 80–81% (Table 1).

Figure 4 and 5 show the performance of the mobile devices after running the interactions. For the problem domain, running 5,000 interactions took very less time i.e., 5 min to generate the labels compared to NPD. The CPU utilization rate was around 13–14% and the memory occupied was around 124–125 MB. Similarly, the best number of interactions for NPD was 50,000 which took around 20 min to run interactions. The CPU utilization rate was around 14% and the memory occupied was around 176 MB. The CPU utilization rate and memory consumed show that model stealing is feasible on the CIFAR dataset.

5.4 Attacks on the ImageNet Dataset

The ImageNet dataset is the most popularly used image dataset and several pretrained models are present which are trained on this dataset. This dataset is very huge and comprises of 1.2 million training samples and evaluated using 100,000 test samples. The pretrained models on this dataset are widely used in several other image classification problems by performing transfer learning. In our experiment, we have chosen a pretrained MobileNetV2 model for image classification and the images here are of 224×224 pixels. The total number of classes here are 1,000 which consists of several different categories. The model which we have used here is the MobileNetV2 model and is trained on 1.2 million samples. The victim model is evaluated using 100,000 samples. For performing model stealing, under PD we have used 100,000 test images for performing training and evaluation. Coming to NPD, we have used Stanford car dataset and ISIC skin cancer images for generating synthetic dataset,s and the predictions are stolen using the victim model. The final evaluation is done using 10,000 images from the original test dataset which are not used for training the copycat model.

In all the cases a total of 100,000 images were collected and used for training the model. Different numbers of queries were performed which are of different lengths. These range from 250–100,000 for the PD and NPD case were submitted to the victim model on a mobile device to steal it. Since the ImageNet dataset is more complicated, compared with the MNIST and CIFAR-10 datasets, more data samples and queries were conducted to provide better accuracy. Finally, the copycat model's accuracy for PD dataset is about 81.2% which is higher than that of the victim models' accuracy which is 71.3% (Table 1). The accuracy of NPD model is about 73.5% (Table 1).

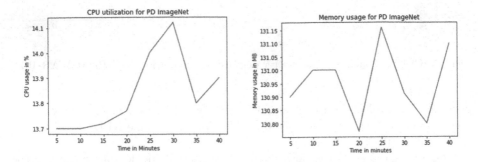

Fig. 6. CPU and memory usage after performing interactions in PD (ImageNet).

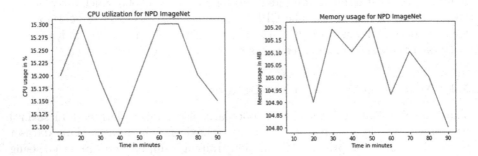

Fig. 7. CPU and memory usage after performing interactions in NPD (ImageNet).

Figure 6 and 7 show the performance of the mobile device after running the interactions. For the problem domain, running 100,000 interactions took 35–40 to generate the labels. The CPU utilization rate was around 14–15% and the memory occupied was around 131–132 MB. Similarly, the best number of interactions for NPD was also the same i.e., 100,000 which took around 80–90 to run interactions. The CPU utilization rate was around 15–16% and the memory occupied was around 100–105 MB. The CPU utilization rate and memory consumed show that model stealing is feasible using the ImageNet dataset.

6   Discussion

Conducting the Model Stealing Attacks in Practice. To conduct a model stealing attack, the malware can contact a remote server (e.g., a command-and-control server) to generate a synthetic dataset. The synthetic dataset can then be downloaded locally in the victim's mobile device for the interactions later. The final synthetic dataset (after labels are generated by interacting with the victim model, they will be incorporated into the synthetic dataset) will be sent to the remote server to train the copycat model. Therefore, the major computation in the victim device is interacting with the model to generate the labels, which is not very expensive as shown in our experiments.

Automating the Interactions with Any Mobile Applications. To make the model stealing attacks more practical, the malware should be able to interact with any victim mobile applications. Automating this process itself is a challenging problem considering the heterogeneity of interactions in different mobile applications. In our experiments, the interaction was specific for a self-built application (with a self-crafted DNN model). We will investigate this problem in our future work.

7   Conclusion

Nowadays, deep neural networks have been increasingly deployed on mobile computing devices. In this paper, we have identified the privacy risks of deep neural network models on mobile devices by performing model stealing attacks. We demonstrated the feasibility of model stealing attacks on mobile devices in terms of stolen models' prediction performance and model stealing efficiency. We have conducted experiments on several popular machine learning applications and datasets. Our experimental results have shown that the accuracies of stolen models are very close to that of the victim models. Moreover, we have shown that although interactions are required in model devices for model stealing, the computational cost of stealing models on mobile computing devices is small. We hope our work could shed light on future research on protecting on-device deep neural networks.

Acknowledgment. Bo Chen was supported by US National Science Foundation under grant number 1938130-CNS, 1928349-CNS, and 2043022-DGE. The work of Xiaoyong Yuan was supported in part by US National Science Foundation under SHF-2106754.

References

1. Correia-Silva, J.R., Berriel, R.F., Badue, C., de Souza, A.F., Oliveira-Santos, T.: Copycat CNN: model stealing knowledge by persuading confession with random non-labeled data. In: 2018 International Joint Conference on Neural Networks (IJCNN) (2018)

2. Goodfellow, I.J., Shlens, J., Szegedy, C.: Explaining and Harnessing Adversarial Examples (2015). arXiv:1412.6572 [stat.ML]
3. Guo, S., Zhao, J., Li, X., Duan, J., Mu, D., Xiao, J.: A black-box attack method against machine-learning-based anomaly network flow detection models. Secur. Commun. Netw. **2021** (2021)
4. Kariyappa, S., Prakash, A., Qureshi, M.: MAZE: data-free model model stealing attack using zeroth-order gradient estimation (2020). arXiv:2005.03161
5. Kariyappa, S., Qureshi, M.K.: Defending against model stealing attacks with adaptive misinformation (2019). arXiv:1911.07100
6. Nicolae, M.I., et al.: Adversarial Robustness Toolbox v0.2.2. CoRRabs/1807.01069 (2018)
7. Shi, Y., Sagduyu, Y., Grushin, A.: How to steal a machine learning classifier with deep learning. In: 2017 IEEE International symposium on technologies for homeland security (HST). IEEE (2017)
8. Szegedy, C., et al.: Intriguing properties of neural networks (2014). arXiv:1312.6199
9. Tramèr, F., Zhang, F., Juels, A., Reiter, M.K., Ristenpart, T.: Model stealing machine learning models via prediction APIs. In: 25th USENIX Security Symposium (USENIX Security), pp. 601–618. USENIX Association, Austin (2016)
10. Yuan, X., Ding, L., Zhang, L., Li, X., Wu, D.: ESAttack: model stealing against deep neural networks without data hurdles (2020). arXiv:2009.09560
11. Model Stealing. Accessed 15 May 2021, https://www.mlsecurity.ai/post/what-is-model-modelstealing-and-why-it-matters
12. Wang, B., Gong, N.Z.: Stealing hyperparameters in machine learning. In: IEEE Symposium on Security and Privacy (SP) (2018)
13. Orekondy, T., Schiele, B., Fritz, M.: Knockoff nets: stealing functionality of black-box models. In: Proceedings of the IEEE/CVF Conference on Computer Vision and Pattern Recognition (2019)
14. Jagielski, M., Carlini, N., Berthelot, D., Kurakin, A., Papernot, N.: High accuracy and high fidelity extraction of neural networks, PP. 1345–1362 (2020)
15. Yu, H., Yang, K., Zhang, T., Tsai, Y.Y., Ho, T.Y., Jin, Y.: CloudLeak: large-scale deep learning models stealing through adversarial examples. In: Network and Distributed System Security Symposium (2020)

Phishing Website Detection from URLs Using Classical Machine Learning ANN Model

Said Salloum[1,2](✉) ⓘ, Tarek Gaber[1,3] ⓘ, Sunil Vadera[1] ⓘ, and Khaled Shaalan[4] ⓘ

[1] School of Science, Engineering, and Environment, University of Salford, Salford, UK
S.A.S.Salloum@edu.salford.ac.uk
[2] Machine Learning and NLP Research Group, University of Sharjah, Sharjah, UAE
[3] Faculty of Computers and Informatics, Suez Canal University, Ismailia 41522, Egypt
[4] Faculty of Engineering and IT, The British University in Dubai, Dubai, UAE

Abstract. Phishing is a serious form of online fraud made up of spoofed websites that attempt to gain users' sensitive information by tricking them into believing that they are visiting a legitimate site. Phishing attacks can be detected many ways, including a user's awareness of fraud protection, blacklisting websites, analyzing the suspected characteristics, or comparing them to recent attempts that followed similar patterns. The purpose of this paper is to create classification models using features extracted from websites to study and classify phishing websites. In order to train the system, we use two datasets consisting of 58,645 and 88,647 URLs labeled as "Phishing" or "Legitimate". A diverse range of machine learning models such as "XGBOOST, Support Vector Machine (SVM), Random Forest (RF), k-nearest neighbor (KNN), Artificial neural network (ANN), Logistic Regression (LR), Decision tree (DT), and Gaussian naïve Bayes (NB)" classifiers are evaluated. ANN provided the best performance with 97.63% accuracy for detecting phishing URLs in experiments. Such a study would be valuable to the scientific community, especially to researchers who work on phishing attack detection and prevention.

Keywords: Fraud protection · Cybersecurity · Machine learning · Phishing Detection · URL

1 Introduction

As the magnitude and sophistication of cybersecurity assaults grows, social engineering is regarded one of the most effective and simple strategies for obtaining inside and private data [1]. Phishing, as defined by the Anti-Phishing Working Group (APWG) [2] is a crime that involves the theft of financial account records and identity through the use of technical deception and social engineering. Additionally, delusive email messages and email addresses are utilized in the plan of social engineering where they hunt individuals who are heedless of this fraud and make them accept that they are connected to a legitimate and trusted group. They are created in such a way that guide users towards fake websites and eventually misleading them to disclose their username and password

J. Garcia-Alfaro et al. (Eds.): SecureComm 2021, LNICST 399, pp. 509–523, 2021.
https://doi.org/10.1007/978-3-030-90022-9_28

which is essential financial information. Whereas, technical subterfuge plans place hostile software in a computer system with the aim of documents theft by usually utilizing techniques that misleads users to fake websites or capturing their account username and password [3]. Moreover, a software like HTTrack is easily accessible to consumers allowing them to make an identical match of any website and use them for any reason. At the same time, in order to shield users from above mentioned attacks, the organizations must make people aware of the different ways to identify phishing emails or links. Therefore, this is the reason that qualified consumers fall into this trap by accessing hostile website supposing it to be a legitimate one, eventually disclosing their personal and sensitive information. Hence, it is seen that user awareness is essential together with computer-based solutions in order to gain a protection from phishing strike. Allowing a computer to have potentiality recognizing malicious websites, this solution would help users from staying away from them. A URL presents a universal address of a document in the World Wide Web and can be utilized to identify original sites in the event of fake sites made by pretenders. Hence, a common way to identify illicit phishing websites depends on their Uniform Resource Locators (URLs).

A blacklist of malicious URLs that are created by the anti-virus class can be one problem-solving perspective; however, this perspective is not considered as all-inclusive because of recent malicious URLs coming up frequently. Therefore, a perspective that can classify a recent, unknown URL into a phishing or legitimate website immediately is required. Usually, this perspective uses machine-learning, where a model created by the training groups of familiar attacks helps in classifying recent phishing sites.

Although the correct technology combined with security knowledge can protect a person from phishing attacks, implementing these in one's daily life might be difficult. Not to mention the ever-evolving new phishing attack patterns against which internet users and even existing email security solutions are powerless. Therefore, there seems to be an urgent need for new and improved methods of detecting phishing websites despite the availability of existing ones. Machine learning classifiers come into play here. Machine learning which is part of artificial intelligence (AI), employs a data mining approach to extract both known and unknown features from a data set, which are then combined with a classification algorithm to detect cyber-attacks and classify them as phishing. The objective of this paper is to develop a method to identify phishing attacks on a website. The study presents a phishing detection system to detect phishing attacks and harmful websites to accomplish this. To identify the attacks, the study described in this paper leverages features from website URLs and a Machine Learning technique. The potentials of generally utilized machine-learning algorithms on a similar phishing data set have been contrasted as the main aim in this study. To categorize URLs, we tried out general machine learning algorithms for instance "XGBOOST, Support Vector Machine (SVM), Random Forest (RF), k-nearest neighbor (KNN), Artificial neural network (ANN), Logistic Regression (LR), Decision tree (DT), and Gaussian naïve Bayes (NB)" classifiers. However, training data sets that include phishing URLs that exist in the public domain are very few. Therefore, it is an issue while creating a machine-learning-based perspective for the above-mentioned problem. Hence, the machine learning approaches, which depend on the available datasets, are required to be assessed for their efficacy. Furthermore, utilization of these datasets is performed in this paper with components from the data URLs been pulled out and the availability of class labels.

This paper is organized as follows: the related work in classifying phishing URLs is described in Sect. 2, the specific aspects of data set and methodology is presented in Sect. 3, the test results along with discussion is presented in Sect. 4, and the limitations of the recent work and the future work is outlined in Sect. 5.

2 Literature Review

This section focuses on the relevant research work done by predecessors on phishing attacks as a whole and summarises the classification techniques which were used for the detection of web phishing.

2.1 Phishing Attack Approaches

One of the types of phishing is spoofing emails, where a phisher emails users a fake email address to deceive people so that they end up opening the email [4–8]. This allows the phisher to influence the user in gaining access to their private information [9]. Typically, a simple mail transfer protocol (SMTP) is used for email spoofing [10]. The phisher does these kinds of attacks using a spoofed email address that looks like a legal identity. To steal the data of well-known organizations is the purpose of such attacks [11]. The phisher makes fake accounts on known social media sites like Facebook, YouTube, Twitter, WhatsApp, Gmail, Instagram, and LinkedIn, where people share their profile of private information with complete disregard of privacy issues that may arise, this allows the phishers to send out requests to people while claiming to be a legitimate identity [9, 12]. The provision of a set of features that allow the correct URL classification is paramount because a URL plays a huge role on a website. The financial assets of an organization are under threat of a phisher's attack as well. Detection of phishing URLs and blacklisting are a few ways that can be used to reduce this problem [13]. A threat to system privacy is a Trojan horse that implements an action when the user clicks on a file. Most of the sites require people to enter their personal information, including job advertisements and illegal banking sites, which gain the interest of the users. Once a person enters his/her information on the Trojan horse, they became a fall prey to phishing [5, 14].

2.2 Classification of web Phishing detection Schemes

To this day, there have been many techniques developed to stop phishing attacks and guarantee the safety of users online. The detection of fake URLs and spoofed email is very difficult, and they are irrepressible. Blocking harmful emails and fake URLs are the best ways to stop phishing. An approach to detect and classify harmful URLs was proposed by [15], where the detection of malicious URLs is done by using a proactive approach in which the lexical analysis is used; also the proposal of a feature set is made for categorizing harmful URLs; additionally, the obfuscation technique is analyzed for the mitigation of these URLs [15]. PLIFER is a method based on ML technique introduced by [16], which uses ten features that are extracted, the application of Random Forest (RF), and the age of domains of the URLs in the detection of a phishing website. This method's success is that it can classify phishing emails 96% of the time. Labelled data sets are used in classification techniques to detect phishing.URL and textual based features are used by various classification techniques. Features such as IP address, domain name, geographic properties as input in the classification of phishing are URL-based features.

The classification of such features is done through ML algorithms [17]. The use of hyperlinks in the pages of a website was proposed by [18]. Hyperlink features set as well as multiple ML approaches are used in tandem. Or the detection of phishing website's hyperlink features is one such approach. This approach is able to detect phishing with up to 98% preciseness as wee as being language-independent [19]. A model based on the ML algorithms which are used for the detection of phishing websites was proposed by [20] and is called the feature selection model hybrid ensemble feature selection (HEFS). A cumulative distribution gradient algorithm is applied for the extraction of the primary set. To get the second feature set a function called the data perturbation ensemble is used. An ensemble learner RF is used for detecting phishing websites. HEFS was able to detect phishing attributes with an accuracy of 94.6% as shown in the results [20]. A twofold technique that used the ensemble ML model for the classification of phishing websites was proposed by [21]. In the first step, RF classifier was applied and the results were integrated with feedforward NN. For the validation of the performance of the ensemble, K-fold cross-validation was used. For a publicly available data set [21] the results showed 93.41% accuracy with the use of the RF_NN model.

Li et al. [22] proposed a stacking model which uses URL features and HTML for the detection of phishing websites. The stacking model consists of the combination of Gradient boosted decision tree, light boosting machine (LightGBM), and XGradient-Boost. This approach is able to show 97.3% accuracy when applied to publicly available data sets [22]. A real-time anti-phishing system that can detect phishing URLs is given by [23]. This method used 7 classification algorithms [decision tree, K-star, AdaBoost, kNN (n = 3), SMO, RF, and Naïve Bayes] and various natural language processing-based features. NLP-based features have also been used in combination with RF. A data set made by the authors comprising of 73,575 URLs was used for the validation of this technique, and it showed 97.98% accuracy better than all previous models [23].

Dogukan et al. [24] suggested an anti-phishing system based on URL features named PHISH-SAFE to evaluate the performance of the proposed solution. This approach, which has its roots in machine learning, is adapted utilizing over 33,000 phishing and legitimate URLs, as well as SVM and Naive Bayes classifiers. Furthermore, the system uses 14 different URL elements to determine whether a website is phishing or legitimate. The use of an SVM classifier resulted in a 90% accuracy rate in detecting phishing websites.

Sahingoz et al. [23] suggested a real-time anti-phishing system with language independence, use of a large amount of phishing and legitimate data, real-time execution, detection of new websites, independence from third-party services, and use of feature-rich classifiers among its unique features. This system employs seven different categorization methods and features based on natural language processing (NLP). According to the experimental and comparison findings of the developed classification methods, the Random Forest approach with solely NLP-based characteristics performs best, with a 97.98% accuracy rate for phishing URL detection.

Chriwstou et al. [25] attempted to construct a machine learning model that detects fraudulent URLs by training the SVM and Random Forests algorithms on malicious and benign datasets. This model was built to be used in conjunction with the Splunk platform and was influenced by previous approaches in the literature. They assessed the algorithms' performance in terms of precision and recall, with Random Forests achieving up to 85% precision and 87% recall and SVM achieving up to 90% precision and 88% recall using only descriptive features.

Gupta et al. [26] built a model for phishing detection with the maximum accuracy of 99.57% using the Random Forest algorithm. The experimental model employed the ISCXURL-2016 dataset and 11964 examples of legitimate and phishing URLs to detect phishing attempts with only 9 lexical features. This model performed well when tested against a variety of machine learning classifiers, however, it did have certain drawbacks. This model, for example, lacked advanced deep learning algorithms to evaluate its approach. Furthermore, 9 lexical features are insufficient for a model to be classified as successful.

In terms of the detection rate, the results of this review indicate that there is a need for up-to-date learning software such as machine learning as well as extra features to improve the accuracy of phishing detection systems. Machine learning models allow datasets to be used in the development of knowledge bases, requiring more time for training. Consequently, some parallel processing approaches will be extremely beneficial to these systems.

This research is very useful and focuses on the supervised ML approach, which can be used to detect phishing websites that use publicly available resources. There have been various approaches that show success in phish detection with high accuracy in blocking the attempts of malicious websites in luring people, with the affirmation of reports that the algorithm used in these approaches can detect and filter the phishing scams. However, the threat is still not over because the previous approaches ignored the text inside websites, which led to people being deceived. To fix this, a robust model based on machine learning algorithms has been proposed that can detect and block phishing schemes in websites.

2.3 URLs and Attackers' Techniques

A variety of techniques are used by attackers in order to avoid being detected by system admins or security systems. Figure 1 represents a general design of a URL. Moreover, the components of URLs should be noted in order to understand the attitude of attackers. To approach the web page, a URL begins with its protocol name in a typical form. Subsequently, situated is the subdomain and the Second Level Domain (SLD) name that usually represents the organization name in the server hosting. In the last, the Top-Level Domain (TLD) name that displays the domains in the DNS root zone of the Internet occurs.

The path of the page in the server represents the inside address whereas, the domain name (hostname) of the web page is found in the earlier parts and in the HTML structure

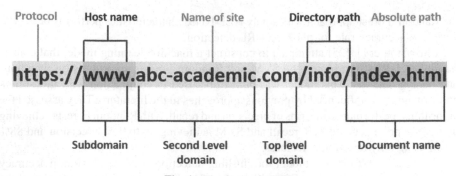

Fig. 1.   The Parts of a URL

the page name is seen. Furthermore, the names utilized for phishing purposes, a considerable attempt is made by companies of cybersecurity to find out illicit domain via the name. This is because the constitution of SLD and TLD makes the distinctive and important part of a URL, called a domain name. However, the blocking of IP addresses can simply be done in order to halt access to web pages found in the domain name if it is recognized as phishing. Moreover, only at the initial time, the SLD name can be created, it is also seen that the attacker can locate or purchase it with ease for phishing purpose even though usually the company name and kind of activity is displayed on the SLD name. In addition, due to the reason that inside address structure relies on the attacker directly, by expanding the SLD via path and file names attackers can create limitless URLs. The detection system should consider the techniques of attack used by the attackers because there are certain essential ways adopted to weaken the users for instance cybersquatting, typosquatting, variable characters, and joint use of words. They do this to expand their attacking performance to steal additional sensitive information.

3   Methodology

This section details the proposed framework of phishing detection using URL features based on website properties. Feature selection techniques, selected data sets, ML algorithms, and performance evaluation measures are applied in experimenting with this proposal. The experimental setup for this suggested model is depicted in Fig. 2; there are multiple steps in the process. First, a dataset of phishing websites is selected; then a feature selection algorithm is used to analyze the top attributes. The features are fed into the ML classifiers after being normalized. The training of the features will be done using classical machine learning models, such as "XGBOOST, SVM, RF, KNN, ANN, LR, DT, and NB". Detection of phishing websites will be achieved by using best-performing algorithms (i.e., separating legitimate from phishing websites).

3.1   Dataset

Additional illustration and apprehension of phishing and legal actions can be obtained from the dataset. Hence, collecting a dataset is an important initial step. Sustaining the

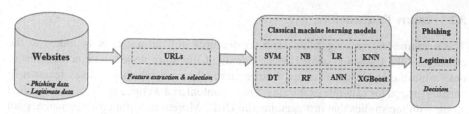

Fig. 2. The proposed approach

outcome validity, the dataset step is essential. For additional evaluation and to predict and anticipate the subsequent occurrence of phishing, the outcome obtained from the examined dataset is utilized. The entire features were gathered from [27]. Furthermore, Fig. 3 demonstrates the four group's value relies on the specific sub-strings; whereas, the first group is based on values of the features on the entire URL string [27]. The external services for instance Google search index and the URL resolve metrics are on which the last group attributes are based. After eliminating the target phishing attribute, there are 111 attributes in the dataset that indicate if the specific case is phishing (value 1) or legitimate (value 0). A total of 58,645 instances make up the dataset, of which 27,998 instances have been categorized as legitimate, whereas 30,647 instances have been categorized as phishing websites. [27]. The reason for these is to imitate the actuality of the original circumstances with the presence of additional legitimate websites. Since the 88,647 instances are present in the second variant of the dataset, where 58,000 instances are labeled as legitimate, and 30,647 instances labeled as phishing. Utilizing the website of Phishtank [28], at first, we gathered a list of 30,647 established phishing URLs for this preparing procedure. Secondly, 58,000 legitimate website URLs were collected from the list of legitimate URLs, attained from the Alexa ranking website [29]. Furthermore, a list of 27,998 community labeled along with organized URLs was attained as well [30], as these URLs are signifying impartially reported news they are legitimate in that aspect too. Moreover, the variants of the datasets mentioned above, we made those utilizing the URL lists of phishing and legitimate websites. All the instances from the *dataset_small* and more instances of extracted features by Alexa top sites list of URLs are found in the bigger and additional unstable dataset. While, the lesser, additional stable dataset *dataset_small* consists instances of features taken out from Phishtank URLs along with instances of extracted features via community labeled and organized URLs which are presented as to be legitimate [27].

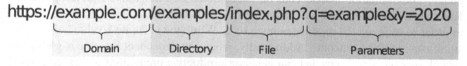

Fig. 3. URL components [27].

3.2 Feature Extraction

The machine-learning algorithms and the features utilized are directly linked to the efficacy of the trained system. Hence, a detailed literature review is done in order to determine the important features. Furthermore, the research that utilizes features in various groups for example examining e-mail content and website analysis were studied along with the studies that just examine the URL. Moreover, within the hostname, path sections, and domain the attributes of the URL were individually assessed. The 111 various features found in our study were attained with Python programming language inscribed scripts.

Figure 4 shows the list of features utilized in our study as the top 85 features were selected following their classification from the RF Classifier, to attain a considerable accuracy rate.

URL	Domain	Directory	File name	Parameters	Format
qty_dot_url	qty_dot_domain	qty_dot_directory	qty_dot_file	qty_dot_params	Number of "." signs
qty_hyphen_url	qty_hyphen_domain	qty_hyphen_directory	qty_hyphen_file	qty_hyphen_params	Number of "-" signs
qty_underline_url	qty_underline_domain	qty_underline_directory	qty_underline_file	qty_underline_params	Number of "_" signs
qty_slash_url	qty_slash_domain	qty_slash_directory	qty_slash_file	qty_slash_params	Number of "/" signs
qty_questionmark_url	qty_questionmark_domain	qty_questionmark_directory	qty_questionmark_file	qty_questionmark_params	Number of "?" signs
qty_equal_url	qty_equal_domain	qty_equal_directory	qty_equal_file	qty_equal_params	Number of "=" sings
qty_at_url	qty_at_domain	qty_at_directory	qty_at_file	qty_at_params	Number of "@" signs
qty_and_url	qty_and_domain	qty_and_directory	qty_and_file	qty_and_params	Number of "&" signs
qty_exclamation_url	qty_exclamation_domain	qty_exclamation_directory	qty_exclamation_file	qty_exclamation_params	Number of "!" signs
qty_space_url	qty_space_domain	qty_space_directory	qty_space_file	qty_space_params	Number of " " signs
qty_comma_url	qty_comma_domain	qty_comma_directory	qty_comma_file	qty_comma_params	Number of "," signs
qty_plus_url	qty_plus_domain	qty_plus_directory	qty_plus_file	qty_plus_params	Number of "+" signs
qty_asterisk_url	qty_asterisk_domain	qty_asterisk_directory	qty_asterisk_file	qty_asterisk_params	Number of "*" signs
qty_hashtag_url	qty_hashtag_domain	qty_hashtag_directory	qty_hashtag_file	qty_hashtag_params	Number of "#" signs
qty_dollar_url	qty_dollar_domain	qty_dollar_directory	qty_dollar_file	qty_dollar_params	Number of "$" signs
qty_percent_url	qty_percent_domain	qty_percent_directory	qty_percent_file	qty_percent_params	Number of "%" signs
length_url	length_domain	length_directory	length_file	length_params	Number of characters

Fig. 4. Dataset attributes are based on URL, domain, file name, and URL parameters [27].

3.3 System Implementation and Performance Evaluation

Amongst the machine learning algorithms utilized in the experiment include: XGBOOST, SVM, RF, KNN, ANN, LR, DT, and NB. The models made with these algorithms trained via utilizing the Sklearn library within the Python programming language. The evaluation that depends on the distance of k neighbors is developed by the KNN algorithm which is quick and effective. Although, extensive memory is required in order to estimate the distance in huge data. While the accurate k value holds a great significance for the outcome. Additionally, when the dependent variable is gathered in two classes the algorithms that can generate productive predictions are called Logistic Regression. However, the adverse impact on prediction is seen by the factors for instance repeating of features, outlier values, and features inconsistency. Moreover, an algorithm that can operate with a huge group of independent variables and is simply executed is known as SVM. The drawbacks of this algorithm are that it does not work properly in considerable noise and it is not appropriate for huge databases, although within non-linear issues it can provide efficient results by utilizing the basic trick. Furthermore, an algorithm that performs by splitting the dataset into sub-sections in order to set up a tree is known as a Decision Tree. Every node in this tree is allocated to a feature while every leaf is allocated to a class. Even though being simply illustrated is the plus point of this algorithm also contains less hyperparameter, but within smaller data sets and multi-class it does not work efficiently, and it is simply overfitted. An algorithm that places its pace and production at the forefront is known as XGBoost. It depends on gradient boosted decision trees. Although the plus point of this algorithm is its focus to lessen the errors present in the old tree, this is done by creating another tree. Yet, this procedure is time-consuming. Just like the earlier mentioned decision tree algorithm, this one can also be overfitted effortlessly. Additionally, a classification algorithm that performs as per Bayes' theorem and it depends on conditional probability is known as Gaussian Naive Bayes. The advantage of this algorithm is that it requires a shorter training time, and it has a simple application, but what makes it undesirable is the assumption that features are independent to all and its lesser estimation with low data. By producing the great number of trees in the dataset Random Forest is an algorithm that performs with the method of Ensemble Learning. The advantages of this algorithm are that it is slightly influenced by noise, does not need feature scaling, splits into subtrees, is strong, and resistant to detachment (overfit). Yet, it requires memory and processor power as it has been training for quite some time. Lastly, an algorithm having a formation such as biological neural networks and it performs with at the minimum of three layers is known as Artificial Neural Network (ANN), it has the ability to determine the link amongst the features and observe it properly as it utilizes less stat when training the model. However, it needs more processor power and memory which usually relies on the dimensions of the model along with its susceptibility to overfitting. In addition, a computer with Core™ i7-10750H 2.6 GHz processor having a memory of 16 GB Ram was utilized for the experiments. However, 10-Fold Cross-Validation was executed to attain the experimental outcome, in order to get the stats validated.

4   Experimental and Evaluation

For data splitting - training 70%, testing 30% - and algorithm evaluation, we have used the scikit learn library 12. The evaluation process for all the techniques includes a split of training 70%, test 30%, and 10-folds cross-validation. Furthermore, the entire experiments were performed on a Lenovo (LEGION 5 15IMH05H GAMING Core™ i7-10750H 2.6 GHz 1TB + 512 GB SSD 16GB 15.6" (1920x1080) 144 Hz BT WIN10). The loading of the entire dataset to Jupyter Notebook in the Anaconda environment is the initial step, afterward utilizing all URL features it is then classified using each of the 8 techniques. Subsequently, 8 of the methods having the highest accuracy were chosen and were assessed for their performance on Huddersfield phishing datasets, and the performance of every technique was evaluated with criteria of precision, accuracy, F-measure, and recall. The measurement of classifiers with respect to quality comprises employing Precision, Accuracy, Recall, and F1-measures. The confusion matrix given in Table 1 can be examined to understand these measures.

Table 1. Confusion matrix.

Confusion matrix	Predicted positive	Predicted negative
Actual positive	TP	FN
Actual negative	FP	TN

To evaluate the performance of our model, a confusion matrix is employed. A confusion matrix represents a table that presents an overview of the classification and segmentation performance. A two-class confusion matrix is used frequently to put forward the positive and negative classes for a few of the binary classification problems. It can be seen in Table 1 that the four cells of the matrix in this research are true positives (*TP*), false positives (*FP*), true negatives (*TN*), and false negatives (*FN*) [31]. *TP* refers to the total correct predictions which are positive, *FN* signifies the total incorrect predictions which are negative, *FP* refers to the total incorrect predictions which are positive, and *TN* signifies the total correct predictions which are negative. These four results can be used to obtain the four measures of classification performance.

$$\text{Precision} = \frac{\text{TP}}{\text{TP} + \text{FP}} \quad (1)$$

$$\text{Recall} = \frac{\text{TP}}{\text{TP} + \text{FN}} \quad (2)$$

$$\text{F1-measure} = 2 \times \frac{\text{Precision} \times \text{Recall}}{\text{Precision} + \text{Recall}} \quad (3)$$

$$\text{Accuracy} = \frac{(\text{TP} + \text{TN})}{(\text{TP} + \text{FP} + \text{TN} + \text{FN})} \quad (4)$$

The traditional models used for comparison include "XGBOOST, SVM, RF, KNN, ANN, LR, DT, and NB". A succession of experiments has been performed using traditional machine learning methods to present equal parallel contrast between models. Models were selected based on their comparable and competitive outputs. The results have been recorded correctly without any bias in choosing models. The outcomes for the entire dataset utilized were attained in 8 various algorithms. The training time and precision, accuracy, F-measure, and recall rate are shown in Table 2. As per these data, the brief training time was seen with the NB algorithm whereas, utilizing the ANN classifier having a 97.63% of accuracy rate, the excessive test classification outcome was attained in the model.

Figure 5 illustrated the attained values of all the learning algorithms also the suitable execution time amongst the models tested are of "XGBOOST, SVM, RF, KNN, ANN, LR, DT, and NB" where the most suitable time was of the algorithm NB. The detection time of a web page by its URL is crucial in terms of utilizing the suggested system in runtime. Additionally, intending to avoid the third-party services available on the internet the execution time could be reduced. Moreover, the execution time of 100 URLs and 1 URL address does not have substantial variance because of the trained system formation. When detecting Phishing URLs, the computers utilizing the algorithm NB or DT requires a shorter time as compared to using some others. However, with the addition of test time, only the algorithm SVM and RF show a difference in time as compared to the other algorithms. Furthermore, for the examination of 1 URL, it is desirable to utilize the higher accuracy rate algorithm at the time of modeling the system. Therefore, the NB algorithm will be suitable to utilize in the scenario. Also, the ANN algorithm can be utilized since the train time and high accuracy rate is seen when choosing an algorithm.

Table 2. Test results of classifiers on Dataset

Algorithm	Precision	Recall	F-Measure	Accuracy	Time (sec.)
ANN	0.969	0.975	0.971	**0.976**	43.1
DT	0.933	0.954	0.943	0.955	23.3
KNN	0.894	0.876	0.888	0.884	328.6
LR	0.882	0.896	0.890	0.892	39.4
NB	0.969	0.973	0.978	0.970	**10.2**
RF	0.934	0.962	0.962	0.968	658.2
SVM	0.925	0.925	0.962	0.855	989.7
XGBOOST	0.948	0.963	0.965	0.941	549.9

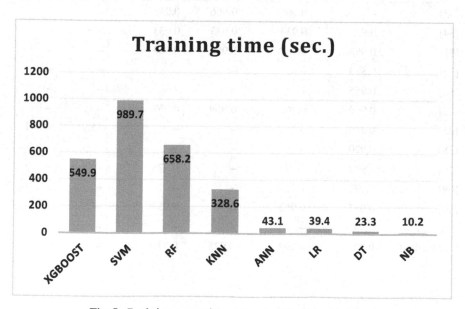

Fig. 5. Real-time execution of the classification algorithms

5   Comparison with Previous Work

The artificial neural networks' performance was highly encouraging, given that the modeled ANN was able to deliver a good conclusion despite the problem's great complexity. In the test phase, the ANN had a 97.6% accuracy rate. Table 3 shows a comparison of the ANN's accuracy with that of studies that used the ANN approach to detect phishing. Despite the good results obtained generally, Table 3 reveals that ANN's accuracy was among the best of the research analyzed. It is worth noting that an MLP was employed. In other words, in some circumstances, only a single strategy was used instead of two related procedures, indicating that the ANN-MLP is a good alternative for solving the problem [32]. It is also worth emphasizing that the comparison was done based on phishing detection accuracy, i.e., in the application of the problem rather than in the database because the bases employed in the two studies were different. In future experiments, the order of the qualities should be changed in order to find better groups for the ANNs to analyze. In future researches, the order of the qualities should be changed in order to find better groups for the ANNs to analyze. Its goal is to greatly expand the training and testing database in order to improve the ANN's generalization capability and, as a result, its performance in solving the classification issue.

Table 3. Comparative table

Study	Accuracy	Precision	Recall	F-Measure	FPR	TPR
[33]	–	0.966	0.966	0.966	–	–
[34]	0.933	0.933	0.933	0.933	7.0	–
[9]	0.958	0.967	0.958	0.960	–	–
[35]	0.889	–	–		–	–
[36]	0.955	–	–	–	–	–
[37]	0.969	0.969	0.969	0.969	–	–
[35]	0.849	–	–	–	15.91	85.61
[38]	0.920	–	–	–	–	–
[19]	0.972	0.974	–	0.975	–	–
[39]	0.972	–	–	–	–	–
[40]	0.955	0.952	0.961	0.957	–	
[32]	0.982	–	–	–	–	–
Our method	**0.976**	0.969	0.975	0.971	–	–

6   Conclusions and Future Works

The use of denounced phishers, lessons for beginners, and the development of methods of visualizing and integrating toolbars with the web browser have all been set in motion to decrease phishing attacks. Even though the training of users on phishing costs a lot as well as the hopeful outcome of these procedures, yet phishing detection rates are low. Furthermore, machine-learning techniques have proved to be quite effective in defeating phishing. A strategy, employing ML and based on certain features, utilizes models in order to identify whether a website is legitimate or phishing. In this work, we execute a phishing detection system using certain machine learning algorithms. Further, the current datasets in the literature are used to evaluate the proposed system, and the results obtained are compared to the results of the most recent study. Our goal is to shortlist the best machine learning algorithm and detect phishing URLs, which is done by comparing the false negative, wrong positive, and accuracy rate of each algorithm.

As a result of this study, we investigated the strength of machine learning in spite of adverse learning techniques in terms of phishing detection. In addition, the study also looks at analyzing numerous features of both legitimate and phishing URLs through the technique of machine learning to detect phishing URLs. Machine learning is an auspicious method to differentiate between the websites that are legitimate or phishing. As seen that the purpose of phishing websites is to seize all the sensitive information of an individual for instance their credit card details, username and password and all various private data. All of this is accomplished by deceiving them into believing that these websites are legitimate. Although, machine learning can set out to downgrade the accuracy of a trained classifier model, as this method is liable to an adverse learning technique. In order to detect phishing websites, the following algorithms are utilized for instance; XGBOOST, Support Vector Machine (SVM), Random Forest (RF), k-nearest neighbor (KNN), Artificial neural network (ANN), Logistic Regression (LR), Decision tree (DT), and Gaussian naïve Bayes (NB)" algorithms. When evaluating our model by utilizing eight different machine learning algorithms, the ANN was found to produce the highest accuracy rate at 97.63%. In addition, for phishing website detection, experiments were repeatedly carried out using various (orthogonal and oblique) random forest classifiers. According to the contrasted outcome, it was found that the proposed system had high accuracy rates and increased phishing detection efficacy.

As a result, as far as future work is concerned, we should first develop a large and current dataset of Phishing Detection System-dependent URLs. Also utilizing certain hybrid algorithms along with NLP based features models stated in [23] we must utilize this dataset and aim to strengthen our system. The next step involves combining SVM with a web browser and employing large numbers of beginners in the pilot study. At last, we combine the proposed technique with different feature extraction models to evaluate its use in a real-world setting.

References

1. Salloum, S., Gaber, T., Vadera, S., Shaalan, K.: Phishing email detection using natural language processing techniques: a literature survey. Procedia Comput. Sci. **189**, 19–28 (2021)
2. Anti-Phishing Working Group. Phishing Activity Trends Report 1st Quarter 2020. https://docs.apwg.org/reports/apwg_trends_report_q3_2020.pdf.
3. Anti-Phishing Working Group. Phishing Activity Trends Report 3rd Quarter 2020 (2020). https://docs.apwg.org/reports/apwg_trends_report_q3_2020.pdf.

4. Gunawardena, S., Kulkarni, D., Gnanasekaraiyer, B.: A steganography-based framework to prevent active attacks during user authentication. In: 2013 8th International Conference on Computer Science & Education, pp. 383–388 (2013)

5. Gupta, S., Singhal, A., Kapoor, A.: A literature survey on social engineering attacks: phishing attack. In: 2016 international conference on computing, communication and automation (ICCCA), pp. 537–540 (2016)

6. Mujtaba, G., Shuib, L., Raj, R.G., Majeed, N., Al-Garadi, M.A.: Email classification research trends: review and open issues. IEEE Access **5**, 9044–9064 (2017)

7. Gualberto, E.S., De Sousa, R.T., Thiago, P.D.B., Da Costa, J.P.C.L., Duque, C.G.: From feature engineering and topics models to enhanced prediction rates in phishing detection. IEEE Access **8**, 76368–76385 (2020)

8. Sonowal, G., Kuppusamy, K.S.: PhiDMA–a phishing detection model with multi-filter approach. J. King Saud Univ. Inf. Sci. **32**(1), 99–112 (2020)

9. Zamir, A., et al.: Phishing web site detection using diverse machine learning algorithms. Electron. Libr. **38**, 65–80 (2020)

10. Salloum, S.A., Alshurideh, M., Elnagar, A., Shaalan, K.: Machine learning and deep learning techniques for cybersecurity: a review. In: Hassanien, A.-E., Azar, A.T., Gaber, T., Oliva, D., Tolba, F.M. (eds.) AICV 2020. AISC, vol. 1153, pp. 50–57. Springer, Cham (2020). https://doi.org/10.1007/978-3-030-44289-7_5

11. Caputo, D.D., Pfleeger, S.L., Freeman, J.D., Johnson, M.E.: Going spear phishing: Exploring embedded training and awareness. IEEE Secur. Priv. **12**(1), 28–38 (2013)

12. Allen, J., Gomez, L., Green, M., Ricciardi, P., Sanabria, C., Kim, S.: Social network security issues: social engineering and phishing attacks. In: Proceedings Student-Faculty Research Day, CSIS, Pace University (2012)

13. Xiang, G., Hong, J., Rose, C.P., Cranor, L.: Cantina+ a feature-rich machine learning framework for detecting phishing web sites. ACM Trans. Inf. Syst. Secur. **14**(2), 1–28 (2011)

14. Wadhwa, A., Arora, N.: A review on cyber crime: major threats and solutions. Int. J. Adv. Res. Comput. Sci. **8**(5) (2017)

15. Mamun, M., Rathore, M., Lashkari, A., Stakhanova, N., Ghorbani, A.: Detecting malicious urls using lexical analysis. In: Chen, J., Piuri, V., Chunhua, S., Yung, M. (eds.) NSS 2016. LNCS, vol. 9955, pp. 467–482. Springer, Cham (2016). https://doi.org/10.1007/978-3-319-46298-1_30

16. Fette, I., Sadeh, N., Tomasic, A.: Learning to detect phishing emails. In: Proceedings of the 16th International Conference on World Wide Web, pp. 649–656 (2007)

17. Das Bhattacharjee, S., Talukder, A., Al-Shaer, E., Doshi, P.: Prioritized active learning for malicious url detection using weighted text-based features. In: 2017 IEEE International Conference on Intelligence and Security Informatics (ISI), pp. 107–112 (2017)

18. Kumar, N., Chaudhary, P.: Mobile phishing detection using naive Bayesian algorithm. Int. J. Comput. Sci. Netw. Secur. **17**(7), 142–147 (2017)

19. Jain, A.K., Gupta, B.B.: A machine learning based approach for phishing detection using hyperlinks information. J. Ambient. Intell. Humaniz. Comput. **10**(5), 2015–2028 (2018). https://doi.org/10.1007/s12652-018-0798-z

20. Chiew, K.L., Tan, C.L., Wong, K., Yong, K.S.C., Tiong, W.K.: A new hybrid ensemble feature selection framework for machine learning-based phishing detection system. Inf. Sci. (Ny) **484**, 153–166 (2019)

21. Nagaraj, K., Bhattacharjee, B., Sridhar, A., Sharvani, G.: Detection of phishing websites using a novel twofold ensemble model. J. Syst. Inf. Technol. **20**, 321–357 (2018)

22. Li, Y., Yang, Z., Chen, X., Yuan, H., Liu, W.: A stacking model using URL and HTML features for phishing webpage detection. Futur. Gener. Comput. Syst. **94**, 27–39 (2019)

23. Sahingoz, O.K., Buber, E., Demir, O., Diri, B.: Machine learning based phishing detection from URLs. Expert Syst. Appl. **117**, 345–357 (2019)

24. Jain, A., Gupta, B.B.: PHISH-SAFE: URL features-based phishing detection system using machine learning. In: Bokhari, M., Agrawal, N., Saini, D. (eds.) Cyber Security. AISC, vol. 729, pp. 467–474. Springer, Singapore (2018). https://doi.org/10.1007/978-981-10-8536-9_44

25. Christou, O., Pitropakis, N., Papadopoulos, P., McKeown, S., Buchanan, W.J.: Phishing url detection through top-level domain analysis: a descriptive approach (2020). arXiv Prepr. arXiv2005.06599

26. Gupta, B.B., Yadav, K., Razzak, I., Psannis, K., Castiglione, A., Chang, X.: A novel approach for phishing URLs detection using lexical based machine learning in a real-time environment. Comput. Commun. **175**, 47–57 (2021)

27. Vrbančič, G., Fister, I., Jr., Podgorelec, V.: Datasets for phishing websites detection. Data Br. **33**, 10643 (2020)

28. http://www.phishtank.com

29. https://www.alexa.com

30. Lab, O.C.: Url testing lists intended for discovering website. In: Censorship (2014)

31. Sammut, Claude, Webb, Geoffrey I. (eds.): Encyclopedia of Machine Learning and Data Mining. Springer, Boston (2017). https://doi.org/10.1007/978-1-4899-7687-1

32. Ferreira, R.P., et al.: Artificial neural network for websites classification with phishing characteristics. Soc. Netw. **7**(02), 97 (2018)

33. Sameen, M., Han, K., Hwang, S.O.: PhishHaven—an efficient real-time ai phishing URLs detection system. IEEE Access **8**, 83425–83443 (2020)

34. Zaini, N.S., et al.: Phishing detection system using machine learning classifiers. Indones. J. Electr. Eng. Comput. Sci **17**(3), 1165–1171 (2019)

35. Korkmaz, M., Sahingoz, O.K., Diri, B.: Detection of phishing websites by using machine learning-based URL analysis. In: 2020 11th International Conference on Computing, Communication and Networking Technologies (ICCCNT), pp. 1–7 (2020)

36. Pradeepthi, K.V., Kannan, A..: Performance study of classification techniques for phishing URL detection. In: 2014 Sixth International Conference on Advanced Computing (ICoAC), pp. 135–139 (2014)

37. Osho, O., Oluyomi, A., Misra, S., Ahuja, R., Damasevicius, R., Maskeliunas, R.: Comparative evaluation of techniques for detection of phishing URLs. In: Florez, H., Leon, M., Diaz-Nafria, J.M., Belli, S. (eds.) ICAI 2019. CCIS, vol. 1051, pp. 385–394. Springer, Cham (2019). https://doi.org/10.1007/978-3-030-32475-9_28

38. Sahingoz, O.K., Baykal, S.I., Bulut, D.: Phishing detection from urls by using neural networks. Comput. Sci. Inf. Technol. **8**(17), 41–54 (2018)

39. Sindhu, S., Patil, S.P., Srcevalsan, A., Rahman, F., An, M.S.: Phishing detection using random forest, SVM and neural network with backpropagation. In: 2020 International Conference on Smart Technologies in Computing, Electrical and Electronics (ICSTCEE), pp. 391–394 (2020)

40. Zhang, N., Yuan, Y.: Phishing detection using neural network. In: CS229 Lect. notes (2012)

Author Index